THE BIG PICTURE

CHRISTOPHER HALL

Mayo Publishing, Inc.
4454 SW Wyndham Lane
Portland, OR 97221

www.bigpicture2012.com

Cover Design and Formatting by Launchpad Press, Cody, WY
www.launchpad-press.com

ISBN-13: 978-0-9848-007-0-4

First Edition, January 2012
Printed in the United States of America

Dedication

This book is dedicated to Niki and Fritz Hall for all of their love, patience and support. Also, special thanks to anyone in Oregon whose last name is Opsahl.

Contents

INTRODUCTION

N orman Thomas, the six-time Socialist Party candidate for president, reportedly said, "The American people will never knowingly adopt socialism, but under the name of liberalism they will adopt every fragment of the socialist program until one day America will be a socialist nation without ever knowing how it happened." He was only half right. Fortunately, America is waking up.

Barack Obama's full-throttled, pedal-to-the-metal acceleration toward centralized Big Government is alarming the passengers. More and more health care decisions are being made in Washington instead of doctors' offices. Food, toilets, light bulbs, garage sales, etc—every aspect of daily life is under the microscope of government bureaucrats deciding what we can and cannot do. As the economy teeters on the cliff, President Obama seems determined to push it off. Privacy rights are eroding as federal agents secretly track citizens' bank accounts, credit card transactions and e-mails; worse, they want to extend their tentacles further. Much further.

President Obama's lack of leadership is unmatched by any other president in U.S. history. He brings to mind Hans Christian Andersen's fairy tale, *The Emperor's Clothes*. In this case, however, it's not that the Emperor hasn't any clothes, it's that the clothes have no Emperor. Barack Obama simply does not possess the gravitas that the presidency requires.

The president's mishandling of the Gulf Oil Spill irrefutably proves his managerial incompetence. "The Spill" turned into "The Disaster" precisely because he is incapable of handling a critical challenge. There was no leadership. There was no initiative. He was passive. As a result, the fiasco degenerated into a morass of petty bureaucrats squabbling and overruling each other in an arena that lacked adult supervision. The man who was supposed to be at the center of it all, who should have been leading an organized effort to resolve the crisis, wasn't there. Habitually, he is the last person to show up for any crisis. Voting "present" just doesn't cut it for the President of the United States.

We shouldn't be surprised by the president's limitations. As Mayor Rudy Giuliani summed up, "He's had so little experience in practical matters. Here's a man who got to the presidency without ever balancing a business budget, a government budget (still hasn't passed a government budget), never had any leadership positions, never had to take responsibility, never had to see the practical consequences of a darn thing in his life. And now we put him in the most difficult executive job in the country with no executive experience."

Although Obama came to the Oval Office with no experience, he doesn't appear to have learned much from his on-the-job training, either. His dithering and procrastinating has produced a climate of uncertainty where the whole world hangs in limbo while he twiddles his thumbs and figures out what his next move will be (after changing his mind several times). Will Obama deploy National Guard troops to the Mexican border, or won't he? Will he pass a budget, or won't he? Will he impose "sanctions that will bite" on Iran, or won't he? Will he "cut the deficit in half before the end of my first term," or won't he? Will he try Bush administration officials for drafting interrogation protocols, or won't he? Will he close Gitmo, or won't he? Will he decide to try Khalid Sheikh Mohammed in Manhattan this week, only to change his mind next week? And change it again? How many Obamacare exemptions will he grant? How many days, weeks or months does he need to decide whether to send troops to

Afghanistan while American soldiers are dying? What will the EPA seize next? Will there be another stimulus? And another? And another? How many lines in the sand will he draw for Israel, Iran or North Korea?

As destructive as his policies are, the economy is stagnant chiefly because of fiscal and regulatory uncertainty. Every time President Obama frivolously changes his policies, it weakens his authority and impairs the entire world's faith in his leadership. People will not follow a president who lacks confidence in his own decisions.

America has elected a president who routinely insults and abuses our allies while coddling and rewarding our enemies. World leaders generally regard him as weak, timid and ill-informed. He is a lightweight and a pushover in matters of diplomacy. As one Asian leader stated, "We in Asia are convinced that Obama is not strong enough to confront his opponents, but we fear he is not strong enough to support his friends."

Perhaps the most important reason for writing *The Big Picture* is to challenge voter amnesia. A president's first two years in office are more relevant than the third and fourth years; since he's not campaigning it is a more accurate snapshot of what his second term would look like.

Americans forgot about Bill Clinton's first two years. In 1994 his prospect for reelection was bleak. That's when he called in political consultant extraordinaire Dick Morris to resuscitate his presidency. According to Morris, "When I helped Bill Clinton move to the center, the key thing we did was to get the country to forget how he screwed up in '93 and '94. Nobody focused on Hillarycare or gays in the military, the gas tax or the income tax increase. In '96 the election was all about welfare reform, budget balancing and all that stuff."

In the 2012 election, Barack Obama will champion populist causes.

He will triangulate issues and posture himself as above the fray. If it still works for him, he will continue to blame George Bush. He will *not* run on his record. With political memories being short-lived, he will try to sweep most of his first two years under the rug. *The Big Picture* seeks to hold President Obama accountable for the hundreds of items that have now been largely forgotten. The president should explain why his administration cooperated with British officials in releasing the Lockerbie bomber. Voters should ask about his multiple promises to slash the budget deficit in half by the end of his first term. Why did the president tell voters that Obamacare was not a tax, and then, once it passed, turn around and argue in federal court that it is a tax?

"Part III" of *The Big Picture* is a timeline of daily summaries of President Obama's first two years in office (*with my italicized commentary*). The objective is to show how all of the affairs surrounding the Obama presidency developed and unraveled simultaneously. There are many books that do an excellent job of discussing isolated issues in a vacuum, disconnected from the commotion of Obama's day-to-day governing. I think it is important to see how these issues evolved in relation to everything else. One cannot truly appreciate the scope of Obama's executive inadequacy until he/she beholds his White House bungling several issues at once. For instance, on February 18, 2010:

> President Obama met with the Dalai Lama. Not only did the president treat the Dalai Lama like trash, but after their meeting he had the Dalai Lama literally taken out with the trash!

> Congressman Joe Sestak (D-PA) announced that the Obama administration tried to bribe him with a cushy job if he would not

contest Senator Arlen Specter's senate seat in a primary election.

After stonewalling for three months, Attorney General Eric Holder admits that he has hired "at least nine" Justice Department attorneys who previously worked for terrorist detainees.

Five Muslim solders were arrested for conspiring to poison the food supply at Fort Jackson, South Carolina.

All of this happened on just one day. It is one of hundreds of examples of the daily barrage of incompetence, radicalism, dithering, shoving allies, being shoved by adversaries, snubs, lack of transparency, trouncing privacy rights and...well, you get the idea.

After skimming through a few weeks of the timeline, you will notice patterns in the White House's decision-making process. Once "the big picture" starts coming into focus, the Obama administration's actions become predictable and it is possible to anticipate the trajectory of events. For instance, the Obama administration was caught flat-footed when the U.S. lost its AAA bond rating in August 2011. No one else was impressed by the wisdom of Obama's stimulus package, bailouts or Obamacare. Other nations adopted budgetary austerity measures and cautioned against Obama's profligate spending. Market analysts and bond traders forecast America would lose its credit rating. The credit agencies Moody's and S&P warned multiple times that America's bond rating was in peril. In fact, China's Dagong Global Credit Rating Co. had already demoted the creditworthiness of U.S. debt. Characteristically, the administration ignored what was obvious to the rest of the planet and chirped that the U.S. will never lose its AAA credit rating, despite projections of $trillion-plus deficits year after year after year.

Based on the record, it is a likely scenario that America will lose its reserve currency status if Barack Obama is reelected. Owning the reserve currency has enormous economic and political benefits for the United States. As the president squanders American diplomatic prestige on the world's stage, he is committed to a course that will wreck the dollar's position as the world's reserve currency. While Obama continues to debase the value and stability of our currency, countries around the globe are thunderously condemning the dollar's hegemony. Instead of trying to preserve and maintain America's economic advantage, the administration publicly declared it is "quite open" to scrapping the dollar in favor of a global reserve currency managed by the International Monetary Fund (IMF). As usual, President Obama is always eager to surrender American power, advantage and sovereignty to unelected foreign institutions that are unaccountable to the American people.

Another pattern that emerges in "Part III" is Obama's partiality to totalitarianism. In June 2009, Iranians rioted for days over their rigged election results. As the regime's police state cracked down hard, President Obama played dead. He said he did not want the U.S. to be seen as "meddling" in the affairs of other countries.

Just a few weeks later, the people of Honduras overthrew and ousted their Marxist president, Manuel Zelaya. President Obama didn't mind "meddling" then. He sided with socialists, communists and Marxists in condemning the coup. Using the full might of his office, Obama "meddled," hampered, intervened and punished Honduras while trying to reinstate the socialist Zelaya.

In either case, Obama's action or inaction favors regimes with the heaviest government control. The next time there is an uprising in Wherever-stan, we can be reasonably certain what Obama's stance will be.

A single drop of paint on a canvass is just a single drop of paint on a canvas. Several more drops and some brushstrokes are needed to create a painting. Likewise, one scrap of news is not enough to represent the Obama presidency. Several thousand data points, however, are sufficient to produce *The Big Picture*—it is an alarming portrait of America's 44th President.

The inescapable conclusion is that Barack Obama does not have the character, capacity, aptitude or judgment to be president. Read this book however you like – you can go straight through or skip around. Mark it up with your pen, underline passages, make notes and share your thoughts with your friends. It is up to you to wake up, America.

PART I

The following is a list of 50 reasons <u>NOT</u> to reelect President Obama, listed in no particular order of importance:

1. The Supreme Court
2. The Gulf Oil Disaster
3. Stimulus
4. China
5. You May Know Him by the Company He Keeps
6. Bush Bashing
7. Obamacare
8. Taxes
9. Muslim Outreach Reaches Too Far
10. The 6 I's
11. Net Neutrality
12. Eric Holder's Department of "Justice"
13. Czars
14. Great Britain
15. The End Justifies the Means
16. The Declining Dollar
17. Christianity
18. The Birther Issue
19. Russia
20. Budget/Deficit/Debt
21. Mortgage Programs
22. Generalities Without Specifics or "The Man Without a Plan"
23. The San Joaquin Valley

PART II

The following are *very brief* descriptions of the Top 50 reasons <u>NOT</u> to reelect Barack Obama.

1. SUPREME COURT

With his two radical Supreme Court appointments, President Obama has carried on the liberals' time-honored tradition of changing America through the judiciary. The Supreme Court currently has four justices in their 70s; it is quite likely that there will be at least one new appointment in the next term. Supreme Court justices are appointed for life. Can America afford to be saddled with an Obama Court for twenty, thirty or forty years?

2. GULF OIL DISASTER

History may treat Obama's bungling of the Gulf oil disaster as the biggest blight of his presidency (there are so many to choose from). A squabbling mosh pit of bureaucrats and technocrats, who were more focused on their own in-fighting than actually solving the problem, quickly filled the president's vacuum of leadership. The EPA overruled the Army Corps of Engineers, who overruled the Fish and Wildlife Service, who overruled the Coast Guard, who was at odds with the Department of Interior, etc. The president was weak; his dithering ineffectiveness and lack of initiative allowed a bad situation to become an out-of-control situation.

Executive management is a skill set just like hitting a baseball, appraising real estate or flying a jet. President Obama has proven that he has neither the management skills nor leadership ability to cope with another crisis, should one arise.

3. STIMULUS

"As president, I expect to be judged—and should be judged— by the results of this program."

In promoting the stimulus, Obama warned and scared Americans that unemployment could reach as high as 8.5%. Despite the stimulus, unemployment climbed considerably higher and jobs were lost in forty-nine out of fifty states.

In order to boast about the achievements of the stimulus plan, the administration had to invent the heretofore-unknown metric of "saved or created" jobs. The "most transparent administration" has still not disclosed how it is possible to calculate whether a job was "saved."

What did the stimulus accomplish? It gave us a mismanaged spoils system with whopping deficits of wasted dollars paid to cronies, dead people, and prisoners. The average cost of a job "saved or created" was between $228,000 and $250,000.

4. CHINA

Before Obama took office, it was unthinkable that a U.S. Treasury secretary would be openly mocked while visiting a foreign country—but such is the level of respect our forty-fourth Commander in Chief receives around the world. Nero benignly played his fiddle while Rome burned; Obama goes several steps further by throwing gasoline onto the fire. While China and other countries are expanding their economies through freer markets, Obama is punishing the American economy with more laws, more taxes, and more regulations.

The bewildering debt the United States owes China is an actual national security risk. And the president wants to borrow even more! Now that China is rising economically, they are beefing up their military, too.

President Obama is willing to grant our economic advantage, military superiority, and national sovereignty to the rest of the world. Now he is willing to cede moral authority as well. Instead of condemning China's human rights record, he invokes Arizona to proclaim to China (and the rest of the world) that the U.S. is a human rights violator. President Obama's feebleness was most dramatically displayed when he meekly submitted to China's demands not to meet with the Dalai Lama (and then eventually publicly humiliated him).

5. YOU MAY KNOW HIM BY THE COMPANY HE KEEPS

President Obama associates himself with Marxists, radicals and people with a very different agenda for America's future. Every ideology, person or stance Obama has embraced has been in opposition to capitalism. Presumably, his presidential appointees reflect his views and where he wants to take the country.

- He launched his political career in the living room of communist terrorists **Bill Ayers** and **Bernadine Dohrne** (who also supported the Manson Family).
- Green Jobs Czar **Van Jones** was openly communist.
- Climate Change Czar **Carol Browner** served as a commissioner for the Socialist International.
- Manufacturing Czar **Ron Bloom**, said, "We kind of agree with Mao, that political power comes largely from the barrel of a gun" and that

"the free market is nonsense."

- White House Communications Director **Anita Dunn** proudly declares that the communist mass murderer Mao Tse Tung is one of her favorite political philosophers.

- His spiritual adviser is the openly Marxist preacher **Jim Wallis**.

- He regularly meets with union radicals like **Richard Trumka** and **Andy Stern**, who said, "Workers of the world unite: it's not just a slogan anymore, it's the way we're going to have to do our work."

- FCC Diversity Czar **Mark Lloyd** praises Hugo Chavez's Marxist revolution in Venezuela.

- Safe Schools Czar **Kevin Jennings** provided high school students with "fisting kits" and an education in "fisting."

- Science Czar **John Holdren** believes in the "de-development" of the West and a global re-distribution of wealth.

- Administrator of Medicare/Medicaid **Donald Berwick** believes, "Excellent health care is, by definition, redistributional."

- His Secretary of State, **Hillary Clinton**, goes around the world championing the cause of taxing "the rich" and bragging that in the U.S., "We tax everything that moves and doesn't move."

- His Transportation Secretary, **Ray LaHood**, believes it is the proper role of government to "coerce" people out of their cars" and "change people's behavior."

- Secretary of Energy **Steven Chu** openly admits that gasoline should be more unaffordable rather than more affordable.

- Department of Homeland Security Secretary **Janet Napolitano** roughly believes that anyone critical of centralized power is a potential enemy of the state.

- Secretary of Health and Human Services **Kathleen Sebelius** threatens to gag and silence opposition.

- Labor Secretary **Hilda Solis** actively promotes using the might of the federal government to represent workers who are here illegally.

- Interior Secretary **Ken Salazar** believes the proper role of government isn't to cooperate with corporations to solve problems, but rather to "keep the boot on the neck" of corporations.

6. BUSH BASHING

Barack Obama handles most problems with his two-step managerial style:

1. Dithering until he has to wing it, making haphazard, seat-of-the-pants decisions (this step is often accompanied by one, two, five or ten frivolous adjustments, reversals or changes of mind), and

2. After the fact, haphazard, seat-of-the-pants excuse making.

His most frequent excuse is blaming George W. Bush for anything and everything that is wrong. Several times a week, administration officials bemoan the current state of affairs that was "inherited" from Bush. President Obama did not "inherit" anything from Bush. It is the job he signed up for. He spent more than a year canvassing all fifty states (fifty-seven by his count) asking people to vote for him, convincing them that he knew how to solve America's problems.

Whether it is the Gulf oil disaster, Afghanistan, ballooning deficits, his failed stimulus— all problems foreign and domestic—Obama's instinct is to shift the focus and use President Bush as a scapegoat. In the rare instances that blaming Bush doesn't succeed, he moves on to blame Glenn

Beck, the twenty-four–hour news cycle, or some other imagined cause of his own failures.

7. OBAMACARE

On February 25, 2010, President Obama held his one and only sham of a health care summit with Republicans present. Representative Eric Cantor (R-VA) sat next to his copy of the three-foot-high, 2,400-page bill that the President dismissed as a cheap prop. It's pretty ironic that he would sign the very bill that he considers to be a "cheap prop."

Despite the fact that no one, including President Obama, read the bill, he was determined to sign it into law. The Patient Protection and Affordable Care Act (a.k.a. "Obamacare") was so awful on its merits that Congress had to be bribed with special favors and extraordinary pork-barrel projects in order to get it passed. Normal process was trampled through the sleaziest of all "reconciliation" procedures. The White House basically admitted that the end justified the means.

The law was slapped together so haphazardly that, even though it imposed an insurance mandate, by January 1, 2011, the administration still had no clue as to what coverage should be required. In less than a year after its passage, hundreds of waivers were given to companies, cronies, and assorted Obama supporters who did not want to be encumbered by the monstrosity.

8. TAXES

Barack Obama loves your money! If you wish to keep your own earnings he will accuse you of greed while he tries to filch it. Perhaps Hillary

Clinton said it best when she told a group of Pakistanis, "We tax everything that moves and doesn't move."

The Obama administration will grub for every penny in every citizen's pocket. It is not beyond them to freeze accounts of online gamblers, tax health insurance plans, and to go on an international scalp-hunting mission by intimidating foreign banks and threatening foreign countries. In fact, President Obama is willing to stoop as low as taxing the BP compensation payments to out-of-work Gulf Coast victims.

9. MUSLIM OUTREACH REACHES TOO FAR

Parts of the Muslim world are at war with everything that is not Muslim. No other religions are in such bloody conflict with one another. In the U.S., Europe, Australia, Lebanon and the Phillipines, it is Muslims versus Christians; in India, Muslims versus Hindus; in Thailand, Muslims versus Buddhists; in Israel, Muslims versus Jews.

President Obama's disingenuous cautions against "jumping to conclusions" when a fanatical Muslim shouts "*Allahu Akbar*" and opens fire on a military base does nothing to assess and address the problem. Instead, the president wishes to appease the Muslim world with scholarships, multicultural Ramadan programs, championing the Ground Zero Mosque, and training 1,500 Palestinian soldiers. And, of course, he has made multiple speeches flattering Islam. None of this has had any effect on mollifying the lunatic fringe that wishes to destroy, not only the U.S., but civilization as well. The mindset that Obama is trying to appeal to does not understand, nor does it want, win-win negotiations. Moderate Muslims must be flabbergasted by President Obama's overarching attempts to satisfy the extremist elements of their faith.

10. THE 6 I's

Quite simply, why does Obama do the things he does? Ignorance? Ideology? Indifference? Indolence? Incompetence? Insanity?

Take a look at deficit spending. On February 1, 2010, President Obama scolded and lectured Americans that the government "cannot continue to spend as if deficits don't have consequences." On the same day he proposed a $3.83 trillion budget with a $1.6 trillion deficit. Ignorance? Ideology? Insanity? Take your pick.

Perhaps the worst environmental catastrophe to hit the U.S. was the Gulf oil disaster. President Obama had the opportunity to polish his suit of armor, seize the reins and show America what true leadership is all about. Instead, he dallied while executive departments overruled each other. No one, especially President Obama, appeared to be in control. Why? Was he too indolent to get off the golf course and do his job effectively? Was he too incompetent to know how to do his job? Or was he merely indifferent about the fates of red-state citizens who probably wouldn't vote for him anyway?

11. NET NEUTRALITY

"Net neutrality" is the government's foothold for taking over the Internet and, probably, other forms of media, too. Its origins begin with Marxist professor Robert McChesney, who said, "At the moment, the battle over network neutrality is not to completely eliminate the telephone and cable companies. We are not at that point yet. But the ultimate goal is to get rid of the media capitalists in the phone and cable companies and to divest them from control." McChesney also believes, "Any serious effort to reform the media system would have to necessarily be part of a revolutionary program to overthrow the capitalist system itself."

Despite a U.S. Court of Appeals ruling against the FCC's enforcement of net neutrality, the administration says the President is "committed" to it. Undeterred by the checks and balances of the judicial branch of government, the FCC redrafted its regulations and asserted that it has jurisdiction over the Internet.

12. ERIC HOLDER'S DEPARTMENT OF "JUSTICE" (DOJ)

Part of the radical's agenda requires going against whatever "the system" is for. Hiring Maoist advisers and slapping long-standing allies are good ways to fight "the system." Putting Eric Holder in charge of the DOJ is another is another way to fulfill the radical's creed.

From dropping voter fraud investigations against the Association of Community Organizations for Reform Now (ACORN) to dropping the New Black Panther voter intimidation case, Attorney General Holder sends a clear message that election tampering is permissible if it favors President Obama.

Obama's DOJ is preoccupied with fighting Overseas Contingency Operations (previously known as the "War on Terror") against the Bush administration. Eric Holder contrives that declassifying CIA interrogation memos will make Americans safer. Investigating Bush officials for drafting interrogation protocols and threatening to release forty-four photos is also supposed to ensure America's safety. Justifications are manufactured under the rubric of transparency; however, Eric Holder is not forthcoming about the hiring of Justice Department attorneys who previously worked for terrorist detainees.

The attorney general has still not made a convincing argument for having Khalid Sheikh Mohammed's trial in lower Manhattan, the scene of the 9/11 attacks. Even worse, he put the country through eighteen months of turmoil changing his mind over and over. This is part of the Obama administration's overall pattern of announcing definite plans that they really aren't all that definite about.

States' rights are anathema to liberals. So, it's not surprising that Obama's Department of Justice would sue the State of Arizona for attempting to do what the president refuses to do.

13. CZARS

It took the Romanov Dynasty 304 years to produce 18 Czars. It took Barack Obama just six months to produce thirty-two. Amassing more and more power for the executive branch is part of his all-out assault on the legislative and judicial branches. Obama believes in centralized power and centralized planning. The rule of law is an obstacle to be hurdled, not obeyed. The will of the people, as voiced by their elected representatives in Congress, is a mere inconvenience to be shrugged off. His belief in the supremacy of bureaucracy is stifling. The only way he could have made the Gulf oil disaster worse would have been to appoint a Gulf Oil Czar.

14. GREAT BRITAIN

No other country's history, culture, and national interests are so intertwined with our own. Americans and Britons have traditionally cherished this "special relationship." So, it comes as no surprise that Obama never misses a chance to treat our strongest ally with shocking indignity.

Many of his administration's insults to the British can be found in Parts III and IV, but there are three events that never received the publicity they deserved.

1. In March 2009, a British newspaper called the State Department to inquire about the shabby treatment Prime Minister Gordon Brown received during his visit to Washington. A State Department official said, "There's nothing special about Britain. You're just the same as the other 190 countries in the world. You shouldn't expect special treatment."

2. In June 2009, the U.S. shipped four Guantanamo detainees to Bermuda (a British territory) without notifying the British authorities. An incensed British official commented, "The Americans were fully aware of the foreign policy understanding we have with Bermuda, and they deliberately chose to ignore it. This is not the kind of behavior one expects from an ally."

3. In August 2009, Abdelbaset al-Megrahi, the Lockerbie bomber, was returned to Libya on compassionate grounds. The Obama administration fervently condemned Megrahi's release. Obama himself claimed that he contacted the victims' families to express his disapproval. The British maintained, "The U.S. was kept fully in touch about everything that was going on with regard to Britain's discussions with Libya." News eventually surfaced that U.S. had participated in discussions about Megrahi's release and Obama was just milking the controversy to preserve his image.

15. THE END JUSTIFIES THE MEANS

Obamacare is a good example of the president using any means necessary to get what he wants. He campaigned on openness, transparency and
process. Instead, America got secrecy, confusion, and procedural dishon-
esty. Senior Adviser David Axelrod perfectly summed up Obama's end-
justifies-the-means philosophy when discussing health care: "Ultimately,
this is not about a process, it's about results."

Time and again President Obama has circumvented Congress to advance his progressive agenda. For instance, he waited until Congress was
out of session before appointing radicals like Dr. Donald Berwick and
Craig Becker to the Centers for Medicare/Medicaid and the National Labor Relations Board. Why wouldn't he want America's elected representatives to decide on these appointees? Because in ObamaWorld, the end
justifies the means.

16. THE DECLINING DOLLAR

The U.S. dollar is the world's reserve currency. Other countries hold
U.S. currency because of their faith in the dollar as a reliable store of value
to ensure financial stability.

American money is as close as the world has come to an international
currency. Many countries trade with each other using dollars.

Because the dollar is so widely used, the U.S. enjoys many advantages.
For instance, Americans do not have to pay to exchange currency when
conducting business. Reserve currency status also makes it cheaper for
the U.S. government to borrow money.

As President Obama cedes U.S. sovereignty to foreign bodies, and surrenders America's prestige around the world, he also seems determined to squander the dollar's dominance as the reserve currency. Obama's debt explosion and the Fed's "quantitative easing" are causing much of the world to lose confidence in the dollar. Washington's reckless policies threaten to destroy the value of the dollar and any other currency that is tied to it. As a matter of fact, countries are already agreeing that they will not trade in U.S. currency. Instead of shoring up America's financial stability and maintaining our economic advantage, the Obama administration has said it is "quite open" to having the world replace the dollar with a global currency managed by the International Monetary Fund (IMF).

The administration's treatment of the soundness of U.S. currency is baffling. At the other end of the conspiracy spectrum, some argue that the president is deliberately trying to fulfill a transnational globalist agenda. Maybe he's just incompetent.

17. CHRISTIANITY

The idea that Barack Obama is a "secret Muslim" is patently ridiculous. His faith is not in question; his spiritual beliefs are between himself and God. Where and how he worships is nobody else's business.

What is strange is the manner with which he treats Christianity compared to his sycophantic praise of Islam. He launches a "multicultural Ramadan" program but plans a "non-religious" Christmas. He goes around the world effusively glorifying Islam but covers up any symbol or reference to Christianity while speaking at a Catholic university.

18. THE BIRTHER ISSUE

The birth certificate controversy originated in April 2008 when supporters of Hillary Clinton's campaign circulated an e-mail stating, "Barack
Obama's mother was living in Kenya with his Arab-African father late in
her pregnancy. She was not allowed to travel by plane, so Barack Obama
was born there and his mother then took him to Hawaii to register his
birth."

The controversy escalated due to the President's own furtive behavior,
not because of conspiratorial, right-wing birther quacks. Obama stubbornly refused to publish the document that would have taken him no
longer than ten minutes to produce. Even though soldiers risked court-
martial by challenging the Commander in Chief's eligibility to deploy
them, Obama refused to give in. He brushed aside criticism from the right
and the left, refusing to issue his birth certificate. After a continuous ti-
rade led by billionaire Donald Trump, Obama produced his birth certificate in April 2011—three years after the controversy began.

19. RUSSIA

Obama folds like an accordion when it comes to negotiating with Russia. He is simply no match for Putin and Medvedev.

President Obama went to embarrassing lengths to get Russian cooperation in dealing with Iran. He recklessly betrayed our East European
allies by scrapping our missile defense shield and invested a great deal of
his political capital in protracted U.N. negotiations. The result? Russia is
building a nuclear plant for the Iranians while supplying them with mis-

siles and gasoline.

Obama sits idly while Russia establishes a significant military and economic presence in the Western Hemisphere. As Russian submarines patrol off the East Coast, they are evaluating Cuba and Venezuela as possible bases for their bombers. The Russians are also building a nuclear plant for Venezuela as well as munitions factories. Obama went even further to improve Russia's strategic posture by promoting the START treaty, which sacrifices our superior nuclear weapons in exchange for equal reductions of their outdated arsenal.

As the Obama administration stubbornly defies federal court orders to lift oil drilling moratoriums, the Russians are happily sucking oil out of the Gulf of Mexico.

Russia and the rest of the world are exploiting Barack Obama's congenital weakness for everything they can get. Unfortunately for Americans, Obama commands the respect he deserves.

20. BUDGET/DEFICIT/DEBT

Some alcoholics preach temperance by day and pass out on their couches at night. The president is drunk on spending. President Obama frequently cautions against the evils of public debt and has promised to cut the deficit in half by the end of his first term; yet, he rolls out more and more spending, almost quadrupling the deficit in two years.

The point is that President Obama willfully continues his course of out-of-control spending, even though he is well aware of the fact that it will destroy the U.S. economy.

Furthermore, Obama's debt spree could prove disastrous for the rest of the world. Raising debt will raise interest rates for other countries. Printing more money will devalue other currencies tied to the dollar, possibly causing global inflation.

21. MORTGAGE PROGRAMS

President Obama's "Making Homes Affordable" program oversaw record foreclosures. It was designed to help 7 to 9 million borrowers save their homes:

- *if* they haven't lost their jobs,
- *if* they owe less than 105% of the home's value,
- *if* they are "in good standing" (whatever that means),
- *if* they can show the government they are at "imminent risk" of default,
- *if* the bank/lender wishes to participate, and
- *if* the mortgage is owned and/or insured by Fannie Mae or Freddie Mac.

That list certainly whittles down the number of eligible participants. Within a year of enrollment, more than half of the borrowers dropped out of the program citing that it was a bureaucratic nightmare. Why be surprised? Producing red tape is the Obama administration's specialty: Obamacare, the Financial Reform Act, the Gulf oil disaster, Cash for Clunkers and the thousands of other laws and regulations they don't bother to read.

22. GENERALITIES WITHOUT SPECIFICS or "THE MAN WITH-OUT A PLAN"

President Obama is a man of grand visions lacking any grand designs. When the president says he has a plan to address any given issue, he actually means that he has a vague notion of what he would like, and he will leave it up to others to fill in the blanks. He said he wanted to close Gitmo, but he had no idea how it would be done. On health care reform, he signed off on whatever Congress and his apparatchiks slapped together without demonstrating any real knowledge of what was in it. He said he would cut the deficit in half within four years but never submitted a plan for doing so. He proposed a "bold new initiative" for NASA but never offered a destination or timetable for anything. He lives in a rhetorical dreamland mistaking words for deeds, no matter how detached they are from reality.

23. SAN JOAQUIN VALLEY

Obama treats the farmers and residents of the San Joaquin Valley with his trademark indifference. The area is known as "the food basket of the world" because of its tremendous agricultural output. The Environmental Protection Agency (EPA) has determined that it is more important to divert billions of gallons of water away from the valley and into the ocean to protect a fish known as the delta smelt. The entire situation has reached a crisis as unemployment skyrockets, agricultural output plummets, and farms are ruined. Yet, President Obama responds to the farmers' pleas with unsympathetic silence.

24. IRAN

President Obama does not have the fortitude to deal with adversaries effectively. His natural weakness is obvious every time Iran mocks his invitations to negotiate. Mahmoud Ahmadinejad's venomous and taunting rhetoric is backed up with equally venomous and taunting actions, such as building nuclear centrifuges, war gaming, test firing a whole range of missiles and deploying ships into international waters.

Obama's policies toward Iran highlight the ever-shifting lack of focus that colors so many other issues with this administration. Secretary Clinton said the Obama administration sought "sanctions that will bite." Two days later the White House backed away from the tough talk in favor of long, drawn-out negotiations with Russia and China. President Obama did a pitiful job of organizing a coalition to contain Iran in the fourth round of useless, U.N.-backed sanctions. After all of Obama's flimsy efforts, Russia built a nuclear power plant in Iran and, along with China, sold gasoline to the Iranians.

25. CASH FOR CLUNKERS

The Car Allowance Rebate System (CARS), better known as "Cash for Clunkers," offered car buyers a rebate for trading in less fuel-efficient vehicles for more fuel-efficient vehicles. This was supposed to provide a double-whammy of benefits for America: economic stimulus plus a cleaner environment.

The program proved, once again, that centralized economic planning is a bureaucratic failure. Dealerships filled out paperwork on behalf of their customers, sent it in to the Department of Transportation, and, by law, were supposed to get their rebates within ten days. Part of the reason the program was such a disaster was that the Department of Transportation, after careful planning, did not have enough people to review all of the red tape. Two months into the program, only 225 claims processors were reviewing 457,000 applications.

Transportation Secretary Ray LaHood tried to point fingers and blame the dealerships for incorrectly filled-out paperwork, but the system was poorly designed from the start. As a result, car dealerships were overextended and starving for cash. Eventually, many dealerships dropped out of the program rather than continue getting burned by an incompetently planned program.

26. EXTRAVAGANCE

"We can't drive our SUVs and eat as much as we want and keep our homes on 72 degrees at all times."

Obama enjoys the plush benefits of being president. While the Gulf oil disaster was in full swing, so was he...on the golf course. As unemployment climbed higher and higher, the Obamas took luxurious vacations at $20 million estates, only to return home and report that they're just like the rest of us. While foreclosures rose, the White House threw splendid parties with movie stars and celebrities. As bankruptcy filings increased, the First Lady spent more than $10 million on her vacations in one year, including a lavish vacation to Spain's Costa del Sol. While record numbers of Americans filed for food stamps, the Obamas may as well have said, "Let them eat cake."

27. FINANCIAL REFORM

The Financial Regulatory Reform Act can be summarized in seven words: the government can do whatever it wants. Among its many awful provisions, the law allows the government to seize the private property of any business it deems "in danger of default" whose failure would result in "serious adverse effects on financial stability." In the 1942 case of *Wickard v. Filburn*, the Supreme Court decided that if the cumulative effect of the business practices of thousands of small-time operations would have a substantial impact on interstate commerce, then it was fair game to regulate under the Commerce Clause. The government always reaches beyond the constraints allowed by law. Purportedly, this provision of Financial Reform is only supposed to apply to mega-businesses but, after a few years in court, this law will be distorted beyond all boundaries of common sense.

28. APOLOGY TOUR

So far, cravenly supplicating himself before the world in a gesture of weakness has yet to yield one apology in return. If Obama is reelected, he may have the opportunity to grovel before countries he may have missed such as Vanuatu and Moldova.

29. IMMIGRATION

The president said securing the border has been his top priority since he took office. Shortly after Obama took office, Governor Perry (R-TX) requested 1,000 National Guard troops. President Obama said, "We're going to examine whether and if National Guard deployments would make sense and under what circumstances they would make sense." With his characteristic procrastination, he announced he would deploy troops 456 days later.

The president did **not** procrastinate when it came to punishing Arizona for attempting to do what the federal government refused to do. After Arizona passed a tough law attempting to stem the tide of illegal immigration and related drug cartel violence, the Justice Department quickly filed a lawsuit against the State of Arizona. The administration went several steps further by denouncing Arizona as a human rights violator before China, the United Nations and the rest of the world.

The administration has been actively promoting a "backdoor amnesty" program. Immigration Customs Enforcement (ICE) has been conducting "docket reviews" of immigration courts and throwing out cases it considers low priority.

30. HONDURAS

The Obama administration aligned itself with socialists around the world in supporting Honduras's Marxist President Manuel Zelaya, who tried to hold an illegal referendum that would assure his re-election. His attempt was held unconstitutional by the Honduran Supreme Court, legislature, and human rights ombudsman.

Zelaya was eventually ousted in a coup that was roundly condemned by Barack Obama and Hillary Clinton—and other socialists and communists such as Fidel Castro (Cuba), Daniel Ortega (Nicaragua), Hugo Chavez (Venezuela) and Evo Morales (Bolivia).

The Obama administration pressured Honduras to reinstate its Marxist president by withdrawing military aid, threatening to withhold foreign aid, and revoking the diplomatic visas of Honduran officials in the U.S.

31. TERRORISM

The Obama administration's view of terrorism is as garbled as anything else they do. When the underwear bomber was apprehended, the White House said, "The system worked." The next day, they said, "Our system did not work in this instance." The president believes Gitmo is the number one recruiting tool for al-Qaeda, but doesn't shut it down. A gunman shouts *"Allahu Akbar"* before killing twelve people at Fort Hood, but President Obama warns against "jumping to conclusions."

32. WEAKNESS

During the campaign, Vice President Biden said, "he will be tested." Obama has been tested right out of the gate and he has failed from the start. The world didn't bludgeon him with a grand, dramatic conflict; instead, it chewed him up like a nest of termites—little bits at a time. It is evident that he is a pushover for big boys like China and Russia.

The administration makes repeated, repeated, repeated demands on other countries like Israel, Iran, and North Korea that it fails to follow through. When the president makes his twentieth or thirtieth demand that Israel stop construction in East Jerusalem, he squanders the prestige of U.S. diplomacy. Vice President Biden also said, "The world is looking." He was right, and the world has correctly surmised that President Obama is an effete, ineffectual leader who isn't willing to back up his empty demands.

It is even more humiliating that he allows himself to be shoved by tin-horn dictators from Third World banana republics. Instead of leaving the Summit of the Americas during Daniel Ortega's insulting diatribe, Obama disregarded the dignity of the United States and attempted to preserve his own by saying, "I'm grateful that President Ortega did not blame me for things that happened when I was three months old." Presumably, Obama is grateful that Daniel Ortega was merely insulting President Kennedy.

33. ISRAEL

President Obama's stance toward Israel reflects the views of a man who sat in the pews of the Reverend Jeremiah Wright's church for twenty years, or a man who launched his political career in the living room of communist terrorists Bill Ayers and Bernadine Dohrne.

From the beginning of his presidency, Obama has been clear about his commitment to a two-state solution. The White House is willing to use the Iranian threat to coerce Israel into ceding control of the West Bank. While blocking sales of weapons to Israel, the administration approved tens of billions of dollars worth of weapons sales to Arab states. Obama's Department of Defense is also training Palestinian soldiers within Israel.

His ham-handed bullying of the Jewish state is accompanied by his constant nagging and desire to micromanage Israel's internal affairs. Perhaps his multiple gestures of disrespect toward Israeli Prime Minister Netanyahu best illustrate of his disregard for Israel.

34. LACK OF TRANSPARENCY

Transparency was one of the cornerstones of Obama's campaign of "Hope & Change." The day after being sworn into office, he signed three executive orders with the professed purpose of increasing transparency in government.

In practice, he has been anything but transparent. His administration has cloaked its health care negotiations in secrecy, spurned Freedom of Information Act requests, done a sloppy job of disclosing stimulus expenditures, refused requests and court orders to publish the White House visitors lists, held closed-door meetings, refused to release documents related to the Cash for Clunkers program, and repeatedly violated the "sunlight before signing" pledge that would allow citizens to view legislation before it is signed into law.

35. THE GREEN MACHINE

President Obama is using the environment as a pretext for extending the hairy hand of government to all dimensions of American life. From lightbulbs to toilets, almost nothing is beyond its reach.

The economy is mostly fueled by oil, coal, and natural gas. Nevertheless, Obama is determined to force America to make a rapid shift to speculative and less efficient energy sources. His administration ordained an openly socialist "Climate Change Czar" and an openly communist "Green Jobs Czar" to implement his far-fetched vision of a "new economy" with "green jobs" fueled by "renewable energy."

When the entire creed of man-made global warming was exposed as a fraud, the Green Industrial Complex never admitted that a re-examination of data might be justified. Instead, they just kicked the controversy aside and followed their agenda as if nothing happened.

Obama's Environmental Protection Agency (EPA) is running amuck trying to regulate everything from carbon dioxide to farm dust. Two of the agency's noteworthy accomplishments include the colossal failure to perform responsibly during the Gulf oil spill, and the destruction of the agricultural economy of the San Joaquin Valley. With such an atrocious track record, it is certain that Obama's EPA will ruin everything else over which it wishes to seize the power to control.

36. WHIMSICAL ILL-CONCEIVED SCHEMES AND EVER-SHIFTING POLICIES

Society needs fixed policies in order to function efficiently. If the political landscape is unstable, decisions and investments will be delayed until the dust clears.

President Obama makes decisions as if he is having a public brainstorming session without ever committing to any policy. He arbitrarily un-makes decisions as capriciously as he makes them. He decides to defend the Defense of Marriage Act and then he decides not to defend it. He decides to try KSM in New York, then changes his mind again and again. The same goes for releasing torture photos or prosecuting Bush administration officials and CIA employees. His inexplicable blundering of the Gulf oil crisis was a disaster. Whenever a policy becomes inconvenient, the Obama administration takes a mulligan and unveils a new policy that is often a 180-degree turnabout.

The president's inability to make a decision and stick with it has a devastating impact on the economy. Capital investment is sidelined, waiting for the confusion to disappear. Who knows what he will come up with tomorrow? And how quickly will he change his mind? As CEO T. J. Rodgers puts it, "We don't know what the latest, great idea from Obama will be; therefore, we are hunkering down."

37. FOREIGN POLICY SNUBS

President Obama has disgraced the United States numerous times with his shamelessly arrogant mistreatment of traditional allies. Arguably, his most outrageous snub was having the Dalai Lama <u>literally</u> taken out with the trash through a side entrance of the White House. Perhaps snubbing Norway's royal family and the entire nation that honored him with the Nobel Peace Prize is worse. Maybe his worst moment was abruptly leaving Israeli Prime Minister Netanyahu to sit by himself so he could eat dinner with Michelle and the kids. Or was it more undiplomatic to return the bust of Winston Churchill to Great Britain?

There are plenty of other examples to choose from. Obama goes several steps further in sacrificing the prestige of the United States by allowing himself to be snubbed by other countries regularly.

38. PRIVACY

As the Obama administration sees it, your privacy is their business. Naked-image body scanners and humiliating pat-downs at airports barely scratch the surface. Airport imaging technology is being used in vans to search American households and cars. They believe they have the right to collect citizens' electronic data, conduct warrantless searches, track citizens electronically, and snoop through private tax information. President

Obama heartily supports mandatory DNA sampling of anyone who is arrested, regardless of guilt, in order to "tighten the grip around folks."

39. THE TRIAL OF KHALID SHEIKH MOHAMMED (KSM)

Of all of the Justice Department's blunders, announcing the trial of
9/11 mastermind KSM in federal court in lower Manhattan may be the
worst. First of all, it would have been a security nightmare that would have
left New York City vulnerable to another devastating terrorist attack. KSM
would also have the right to subpoena sensitive documents and to use the
trial as a world stage to rally his lunatic followers.

President Obama tried to distance himself from the controversy by
acting as if he had no control over the decision—as if it were solely the responsibility of the attorney general. The decision was so controversial that
the Obama administration kept changing its position on whether to try
him in federal court or by military commission. After a year and a half of
dithering and needless turmoil, the administration felt pressured to move
the trial to a military commission.

40. THE EXECUTIVE JUGGERNAUT

Obama's pervasive "the rules don't apply to me" attitude is evident in
his disregard for the system of checks and balances. He runs his presidency like an executive vigilante unconstrained by constitutional limitations.

He blatantly disregards federal court orders to produce the White
House visitors list or to ease his drilling moratorium in the Gulf of Mexico.
As for the legislative branch of government, if he cannot get what he wants
from Congress, he just ignores the votes of the peoples' elected represen-

tatives and goes around them. For instance, on December 8 2009, the White House warned Congress, "If you don't pass this legislation [Cap and Trade], then...the EPA is going to have to regulate in this area, and it is not going to be able to regulate on a market-based way, *so it's going to have to regulate in a command-and-control way*, which will probably generate even more uncertainty."

There you have it: the end justifies the means. Tyranny will impose its will in a "command-and-control way" no matter what the costs, even though it is fully cognizant that it will "generate even more uncertainty."

If Obama cannot get what he wants by rule of law (the judicial branch) or by the people's elected representatives (the legislative branch), he will reach out and seize it anyway.

41. BAILOUTS

Great industrial enterprises have risen and fallen since America began. In the past, when companies made unwise or stupid decisions, they surrendered to the "creative destruction" of the free enterprise system.

This is no longer the case when the government arbitrarily deems companies "too big to fail," giving the government multiple justifications for inserting itself into the industries and businesses it wishes to control. Obama places his faith in bureaucrats and apparatchiks—self-anointed policy analysts who know better than everybody else how to run the world. Obamanomics allows for "Car Czar" Steve Rattner and Brian Deese, who have zero experience in the auto industry, to call the shots for multibillion-dollar operations from 500 miles away.

42. IMPROV THEATER

Shakespeare famously wrote, "All the world's a stage." The White House is Barack Obama's improv theater. After a series of embarrassingly botched nominations to various posts, one wonders whether the Obama administration had prepared at all. Indeed they had not. In fact, Van Jones did not even bother to fill out the 63–question questionnaire that is standard operating procedure for high-level positions. Placing improperly vetted candidates before confirmation hearings illustrates Obama's penchant for winging it.

The White House wings it in foreign policy as well. On June 3, 2009, President Obama insisted that members of the Muslim Brotherhood be present for his Cairo speech. It requires very little effort to discover an abundance of the Brotherhood's violent, anti-Western rhetoric. Did the Obama administration fail to do due diligence in vetting the Muslim Brotherhood? Given the President's pitiful record of negotiating in the international arena, one wonders if he is actually preparing for his meetings with Russia, India, Germany, et al, or if he is simply acting and reacting at the spur of the moment.

The "Man without a Plan" also has a pattern of expediently assuring the press and the public that a given issue is "top priority" or "priority number one" and that he "will not rest" until the mission is accomplished. The reason Obama never "focused like a laser on jobs" is that he has so many other superlatives and top priorities.

43. THE MINISTRY OF PROPAGANDA

President Obama benefits greatly from his unofficial public relations boosters (such as NBC and ABC). Occasionally, a video surfaces of a fanatical teacher indoctrinating schoolchildren about the "Dear Leader." This pales in comparison to Obama intentionally turning the National Endowment for the Arts (NEA) into a Soviet-style Ministry of Propaganda.

The NEA tried to recruit "a group of artists, producers, promoters, organizers, influencers, marketers, taste-makers, leaders or just plain cool people to join together and work together to promote a more civically engaged America and celebrate how the arts can be used for a positive change!"

The NEA's "positive change" involved giving the arts community marching orders to promote the president's radical agenda, including Obamacare. The NEA was never intended to embellish a president's personality cult or serve as a bullhorn to advance the party line.

44. STEAMROLLING OVER ALL WHO DARE TO DEFY HIM

Obama is at war with anything that criticizes Obama. The administration sends threats and gag orders to insurance companies exercising their 1st Amendment rights, stating, "There will be *zero tolerance* for this type of misinformation." Swiss banks are punished for obeying the laws of their sovereign nation. Secured creditors in the automobile bankruptcies were crushed for asserting their rights against Obama's cronies. Inspector General Gerald Walpin had his integrity impugned for investigating corruption. The media are attacked when they fail to show proper respect to Our Dear Leader. President Obama has the tyrannical disposition of intolerance to all criticism and differences of opinion.

45. NORTH KOREA

Kim Jong Il learned, along with the rest of the world, that Obama's warnings were empty and that he would dither and forestall making tough decisions indefinitely. The administration warned North Korea that missile launches would be deemed provocative. As a result, North Korea conducted many missile launches, tested nuclear bombs, torpedoed a South Korean ship killing sailors and instigated a deadly skirmish with South Korean forces.

46. READ THE BILLS

President Obama, his administration, and his colleagues in Congress do not bother to read the bills they sign into law. As Representative John Conyers (D-MI) stated in July 2009, "I love these members; they get up and say, 'Read the bill.' What good is reading the bill if it's a thousand pages and you don't have two days and two lawyers to find out what it means after you read the bill?"

Perhaps the most seismic legislation in Obama's first two years is Obamacare. Former speaker of the House, Nancy Pelosi (D-CA), told a crowd that Congress must "pass the bill so you can find out what's in it." The president himself said that we would all know what was in the bill when it passed. He signed it thirty-six hours later. Was he able to read and fully comprehend thousands of pages of legalese before signing it into law?

Compared to Obamacare and the Financial Reform law, the Arizona immigration law was a measly sixteen pages. The Obama administration didn't bother to read it either. Attorney General Eric Holder and DHS Secretary Janet Napolitano both testified that they had not bothered to read the law while they were criticizing it. Even after the administration denounced the Arizona law as a human rights violation in talks with Communist China, State Department official P. J. Crowley also admitted that he had not read the law.

47. GROUND ZERO MOSQUE

One has to question Obama's judgment for stepping into a controversy he should have left alone. He used one of his classic strawman arguments by championing Muslims' freedom of religion. None of the demonstrators argued whether Muslims had a right to build the mosque; they just thought it was in poor taste (kind of like staging a cross burning at the Martin Luther King Memorial). They viewed it as a gloating symbol of jihad, memorializing the annihilation of their friends, neighbors, family members and fellow citizens.

The controversy also called attention to Obama's ever-ambiguous loyalties. The president was quick to defend the first amendment rights of Muslims to practice their religion (which was never disputed). Why didn't he defend the demonstrators' first amendment right to protest?

Also, the president did not hesitate to jump into the fray to defend Islam while having done nothing about a $7.2 billion health care bill for 9/11 rescue workers. Which group is he more loyal to?

Furthermore, the administration was indirectly participating in the mosque's construction. Obama's State Department sponsored a $16,000 trip for Feisal Abdul Rauf, Imam of the Ground Zero Mosque, to travel to the Arab Gulf States. Apparently, the purpose of the Imam's trip was to raise funds for the mosque, although the State Department admitted it had no clue about the purpose of the Imam's visit.

48. DITHERING/INDECISIVENESS

Obama is a rigid ideologue who does not have the character, capacity, aptitude or judgment to manage any situation that was not part of his campaign. When faced with a new and unexpected challenge, like the Gulf oil disaster, he stands still like a deer caught in headlights.

President Obama's dithering is as much of a character flaw as his arrogance or his congenital weakness. In the face of tragedy, crisis and unforeseen circumstances, he does...very little. Behind his cool demeanor he seems to be inwardly wincing for fear of not measuring up to the challenge. He retreated from seizing a leadership role in the Gulf oil disaster. Tension mounted until he threw his "just plug the damn hole" tantrum or bragged that he was determining "whose ass to kick." His blasé indifference toward troop deployment in Afghanistan lingered for months as soldiers died and military leadership petrified in a wait-and-see mode. Representative Joe Sestak (D-PA) lobbed very serious and credible criminal allegations against the Obama administration. Typically, they procrastinated for 100 days before giving a lame answer. President Obama claimed that border security was his "top priority" since he took office, but he waited well over a year before addressing the problem (and he addressed it very badly).

His dithering shows lack of involvement and initiative. President Obama treats crises as annoying hindrances to enjoying life as president: golfing with celebrities, throwing parties, and making appearances with his teleprompter.

49. EGO

Barack Obama has a monstrous ego. Only a megalomaniac would celebrate his nomination as being more like a coronation, proclaiming, "This was the moment when the rise of the oceans began to slow and our planet began to heal." Obama tried to soothe his Democratic colleagues who were concerned about a 1994-style midterm election trampling by saying, "Well, the big difference here and in '94 is you've got ME."

The grandiose narcissism permeating this Obamacentric universe poses risks for the other 307,999,999 American citizens. One of the many problems with his overstuffed ego is that he feels entitled to treat allies such as Great Britain and Israel disrespectfully. As an egomaniac with an insecurity complex, his self-image must be fed and validated constantly, making him highly vulnerable to flattery and hypersensitive to criticism.

50. TAKE YOUR PICK

There are many more issues to choose from. You could choose the president's bias for the U.N. and international bodies that are insulated from American voters. You could pick how he personalizes things; is he representing the country or himself? Maybe you're dissatisfied with his treatment of NASA. Perhaps you don't like his masochistic foreign policy. Or maybe you don't like his thin-skinned sensitivity to all who do not praise him appropriately enough.

Read Part III and see how many you can come up with yourself.

PART III

1/20/09

President Obama's Inaugural Address promises to "end petty grievances and false promises." He calls for ethics and transparency in government, "And those of us who manage the public's dollars will be held to account—to spend wisely, reform bad habits, and do our business in the light of day—because only then can we restore the vital trust between a people and their government." It is worth noting that he also says, "We will not apologize for our way of life."[1]

On July 17, 2007, candidate Obama told the Planned Parenthood Action Fund, "The first thing I'd do as president is sign the Freedom of Choice Act. That's the first thing I'd do." Including the oath to uphold the Constitution, how many other presidents have broken TWO campaign promises on the first day in office?

1/21/09

President Obama's first call to a foreign leader is to Mahmoud Abbas, president of the Palestinian National Authority.[2]

Testimony reveals that Treasury Secretary nominee Tim Geithner did not pay $34,000 in taxes.[3] *He blames the software program TurboTax for his oversight. During the first two years of the Obama presidency, Geithner is less forgiving of his fellow citizens as IRS audits increase by 11%.*

37

President Obama meets with Defense Department staff about how to get out of Iraq in sixteen months.[4]

Obama freezes the pay of White House aides making more than $100,000.

The President signs three executive orders:

- The executive order on the Freedom of Information Act will usher a "new era of openness."
- The executive order on Transparency and Openness in Government instructs members of the Administration to be guided by principles of transparency. The Open Government Directive shall be implemented within 120 days.
- The Ethics executive order is designed to close the revolving door between the public and private sectors. White House employees will be barred from working on issues for which they have lobbied in the past.[5]

The National Park Service picks up 100 tons of post-inauguration garbage on the Mall. Washington trucks hauled away at least 130 tons of garbage from the $170 million inauguration.[6]

Fidel Castro praises President Obama as "a man who seems absolutely sincere."[7]

1/22/09

President Obama makes a surprise visit to the pressroom. He becomes irritated and refuses to answer a substantive question about reconciling his ban on lobbyists and hiring a Department of Defense Deputy Secretary who lobbied for Raytheon.[8]

President Obama signs executive orders to close Guantanamo, ban torture and to form an interagency task force to review cases.[9]

President Obama praises *Roe v. Wade* on the thirty-sixth anniversary of the decision.[10]

Obama appoints George Mitchell as Special Envoy to the Middle East and urges Israel to open Gaza borders for commerce and humanitarian aid.[11]

1/23/09

President Obama signs an executive order allowing federal funding for international organizations that do abortion counseling.[12] *As he said on the campaign trail, he doesn't want women to be "punished with a baby."*

President Obama warns Republicans that listening to Rush Limbaugh will not get things done in today's Washington. In response to Representative Eric Cantor's (R-VA) question about a spending proposal, he curtly responds, "I won. I will trump you on that."[13]

Freddie Mac taps the U.S. Treasury for $35 billion in aid.[14]

1/24/09

President Obama warns America of the necessity of his stimulus plan, "If we do not act boldly and swiftly, a bad situation could become dramatically worse." Without the stimulus, he cautions that unemployment could hit 8.5% by April.[15]

Two ex-Guantanamo detainees appear in an al-Qaeda video.[16]

1/25/09

Obama seeks a space weapons ban.[17]

1/26/09

President Obama signs an executive order changing Bush's energy policies "to reverse our dependence on foreign oil while building a new energy economy that will create millions of jobs."[18]

General Motors cuts 2,000 jobs.[19]

Obama goes to Capitol Hill to lobby for his $825 billion stimulus package.[20]

Fannie Mae taps the U.S. Treasury for $16 billion in aid.[21]

Obama kicks off his apology tour by doing his first formal interview with *Al-Arabiya*, saying, "My job to the Muslim world is to communicate that the Americans are not your enemy. We sometimes make mistakes. We have not been perfect." He states that U.S. foreign policy will "start by listening, because all too often the United States starts by dictating— in the past on some of these issues—and we don't always know all the factors that are involved. So let's listen."

To Iran: Obama offers friendship and an extended hand.[22]

The Israeli newspaper *Ha'aretz* claims that Venezuela is actively supporting Hamas and Hezbollah. Allegedly, Venezuela has actually trained Hezbollah militant fighters. Former Clinton advisor Douglas Schoen, co-author of *The Threat Closer to Home: Hugo Chavez and the War Against America*, claims that Chavez "[has] been a supporter of Hamas and Hezbollah and Iran, and he has his own 'axis of evil,' which is designed to undermine and destabilize the United States."[23]

1/27/09

Obama goes to Capitol Hill to lobby for the stimulus. Among other items, it includes $50 million for the National Endowment for the Arts and $335 million for teen education about sexually transmitted diseases (STDs).[24]

$5.2 billion of stimulus funds will be allotted to community organizers, the majority of the chunk will be going to the Association of Community Organizations for Reform Now (ACORN).[25]

The Congressional Budget Office estimates the deficit will equal 10% of GDP, the highest since 1945.[26]

The Department of Treasury bails out twenty-three banks with $386 million.[27]

1/28/09

President Obama meets with CEOs to tout the benefits of the stimulus plan and makes his first trip to the Pentagon.[28]

Russia pauses its plans to deploy missiles to Europe as the President reconsiders the U.S. missile defense shield in Poland and the Czech Republic.[29]

1/29/09

President Obama signs the Lilly Ledbetter Fair Pay Restoration Act only two days after its passage, breaking his "sunlight before signing" pledge to allow citizens to view legislation for five days before signing.[30] *The president is throwing a bone to the labor movement; the Ledbetter Act allows people to go back for decades and sue for wage discrimination.*

President Obama knocks Wall Street bonuses, saying, "And part of what we're going to need is for the folks on Wall Street to show some restraint, discipline and responsibility."[31] *It would be nice if he would lead by example and "show some restraint, discipline and responsibility."*

Russia and China slam the U.S. economy and promote reserve currencies other than the dollar.[32]

President Obama sends a conciliatory letter hoping to change the tone of relations between the U.S. and Iran. He states the desire to pave the way for talks and explicitly remarks that he does not want to overthrow the Islamic regime.[33]

1/30/09

Obama authorizes a "Middle Class Task Force" to be headed by Vice President Joe Biden.[34] *Biden is an obvious choice considering his scant private-sector experience. The rest of the task force contains zero members of the middle class.*

Health and Human Services (HHS) nominee, Tom Daschle, has not paid $128,000 in taxes.[35]

Treasury Secretary Tim Geithner, Fed Chairman Ben Bernanke and the FDIC's Sheila Bair have crafted a two-part bank bailout:

a) buying bad assets and

b) providing guarantees against future losses.[36]

President Obama authorizes $20 million in aid to Gaza.[37]

1/31/09

President Obama lobbies the Senate to pass the stimulus. The President proposes but gives no specifics about a plan to lower mortgage costs, extend loans to business and revive the financial sector to "get credit flowing again." Obama says the stimulus has no earmarks and "we're going to be trimming things that are not relevant to putting people back to work right now." [38] [39]

He also uses his 13-million-person campaign list requesting support for the stimulus plan, "The stakes are too high to allow partisan politics to get in the way."[40] *As if there is nothing at all partisan about using his organizational might to ram through an $862 billion bill.*

Iran responds to President Obama's letter of goodwill saying it demonstrates that capitalist thought and America's domination have failed. Mahmoud Ahmadinejad demands apologies from the U.S. for its "crimes" and expects fundamental changes from Obama.[41]

January unemployment = 7.7%.
Real unemployment = 14%.[42]
("Real unemployment" or "U6 unemployment" includes those who have given up looking for work or are forced to work part time).

2/1/09

In an interview with Matt Lauer, President Obama states that his re-election hinges on whether his policies will turn the economy around, "Look, I'm at the start of my administration. One nice thing about the situation I find myself in is that I will be held accountable. You know, I've got four years. A year from now I think people are going to see that we're starting to make some progress, but there's still going to be some pain out there. If I don't have this done in three years, then there's going to be a one-term proposition."[43]

European leaders at Davos are skeptical of Obama's policies. Germany and France call his auto subsidies and "Buy American Plan" to be protectionist. Europe is also concerned with how Obama will pay for the stimulus. Raising debt will raise interest rates for other countries and printing money will devalue other currencies tied to the dollar, possibly causing global inflation.[44]

Feb 2009

2/2/09

President Obama says he "absolutely" backs Tom Daschle as his HHS nominee.[45] *Daschle withdrew his nomination due to unpaid taxes. This is just one of many of the Obama administration's messy nominations (including Bill Richardson, Nancy Killefer, Charles Freeman, etc.). With so many unvetted and tainted candidates one wonders how seriously they take their responsibilities. If Obama does such a poor job vetting high-level positions, one can only guess what caliber of people he has working behind the scenes within the White House.*

France rejects Obama-style stimulus, "It would be irresponsible…to increase our country's indebtedness."[46]

2/3/09

To support the stimulus package, Obama tells Katie Couric, "We have to act. We have to act now."[47]

Obama caps annual pay at $500,000 for executives at bailed-out Wall Street firms.[48]

President Obama caves to European Union pressure of a trade war unless the "Buy American" provisions are struck from the stimulus plan.[49]

The U.S. warns North Korea that a missile launch would be provocative.[50]

Iran launches a satellite into outer space containing a mouse, worms and two turtles. The West is concerned that Iran can turn this into an intercontinental ballistic missile (ICBM) program.[51]

2/4/09

Obama pushes the stimulus with alarmist language about the necessity of acting immediately. He criticizes Republican tax cut proposals as failed economic theories.[52]

Energy Secretary Steven Chu says California farms and vineyards could vanish by the end of the century due to global warming.[53]

President Obama signs legislation expanding the State Children's Health Insurance Program (SCHIP) at a cost of $32.8 billion.[54]

2/5/09

President Obama is taking steps to increase energy efficiency of household appliances.[55]

Leon Panetta, nominee for Director of CIA, received $700,000 in consulting fees, including a company investing in contractors for National Security agencies.[56]

The White House says DEA pot raids of California medical marijuana shops will discontinue when it appoints a new DEA chief.[57]

2/6/09

President Obama says delaying the stimulus is "inexcusable and irresponsible."[58]

President Obama appoints an Economic Recovery Advisory Board.[59] *"Just today, Senator McCain offered up the oldest Washington stunt in the book – you pass the buck to a commission to study the problem. But here's the thing – this isn't 9/11. We know how we got into this mess. What we need now is leadership that gets us out. I'll provide it, John McCain won't, and that's the choice for the American people in this election." – Candidate Barack Obama.*

Russia gives Kyrgyzstan $2 billion in loans and assistance in exchange for Kyrgyzstan's closing a U.S. Air Force base at Manas, which serves American forces in Afghanistan.[60]

The Israelis intercept an aid ship headed for Gaza, where militants launch two rockets into Israel.[61]

Feb 2009

2/7/09

The U.N. halts aid to Gaza because Hamas is stealing shipments.[62]

2/8/09

The International Monetary Fund (IMF) says that it may run out of cash in six months and that advanced economies are tipping from recession into depression.[63]

2/9/09

In a primetime news conference promoting the stimulus, the President says:

- It will "save or create" 4 million jobs (90% in the private sector), and
- There are no earmarks in the package.[64]

President Obama also takes questions from a pre-selected group of reporters.[65]

Sixteen illegals sue an Arizona rancher for violating their civil rights by holding them up at gunpoint.[66]

GM plans to invest $1 billion in Brazil operations.[67]

2/10/09

Treasury Secretary Geithner unveils his outline for the rescue plan:

- Bank stress tests,
- The Treasury and Fed will leverage about $1 trillion,
- Public/Private funds to buy up toxic assets, and
- The Treasury and Fed will commit $50 billion for loan modifications.
- The plan will also limit executive pay and limit political influence.[68]

Mr. Geithner assures, "We are going to fundamentally reshape our program to repair the financial system." The public need not be worried about the lack of specifics: "We're not going to put out details until we are confident that we've got the right structure that's going to achieve these objectives."[69] *This is classic Obama. He goes around the country promoting a pipe dream of a plan, when the actual plan doesn't exist. How can it be "inexcusable and irresponsible" to vote against a plan without seeing the details? Incidentally, the Dow Jones Industrial Average falls 382 points.*

Las Vegas mayor Oscar Goodman calls for the President to apologize for his anti-Vegas quip.[70]

2/11/09

President Obama claims that if the stimulus passes, the CEO of Caterpillar, Inc., would rehire employees who were laid off (*this news came as a shock to the CEO*). The President further adds that not a single dollar of stimulus funds will go to earmarks.[71]

On consumer protection he affirms, "During these challenging times, the needs of American consumers are a **top priority** of my administration."[72] *The Obama presidency displays a pattern of seat-of-the-pants placating. The administration's answer to most hot-button issues is, "it's a top priority," followed up with inaction.*

The Republicans are shut out of negotiations as the House and Senate reach a deal on the stimulus plan.[73]

President Obama says, "I expect to be judged and should be judged by the results of this program [the stimulus]."[74]

The European bank bailout could plunge the EU into crisis with toxic assets of approximately $24 trillion.[75]

2/12/09

Caterpillar CEO, Jim Owens, contradicts President Obama, saying the stimulus would not allow them to rehire some of the 22,000 laid-off workers; in fact, he said there would be more layoffs.[76]

2/13/09

The Stimulus Bill passes Congress. After weeks of fiery rhetoric, saying it is "irresponsible and inexcusable" to delay its immediate passage, the President takes off for a three-day vacation while the stimulus bill awaits his signature.[77] *According to the Employment Policies Institute, only 8% of Congress majored in economics in college, while 14% studied business or accounting. Surprised?*

2/14/09

President Obama returns a bust of Winston Churchill to the British.[78] *Watch out! There are many outrageous snubs to follow.*

2/15/09

The federal government's obligations exceed the entire world's GDP.[79]

2/16/09

GM says it may need up to $30 billion in aid, while Chrysler says it could use an additional $5 billion.[80]

GM will cut its workforce by 20,000 jobs by 2012.[81]

2/17/09

President Obama signs the stimulus bill, contending it will "save or create" 3.5 million jobs.[82] The Obama administration never clarifies how they measure whether a job is "saved." *By February 24, 2011, the Congressional Budget Office (CBO) will score the average cost of a job "created or saved" at $228,055 per job.*

Health provisions hidden in the stimulus bill include:

- the National Coordinator of Health and Information Technology to reduce costs and "guide" doctors' decisions with electronically delivered protocols, and

- the Federal Coordinating Council for Comparative Effectiveness to apply a cost-effective standard to Medicare.[83]

NOT included in the stimulus bill were President Obama's promises to allow for early withdrawal of 401(k) funds without penalty and to give every employer a $3,000 tax credit for every new full-time employee hired.[84]

According to the Congressional Budget Office (CBO), only 23% of the stimulus will be spent this year.[85] *Then why the urgency?*

GM asks for $16.6 billion while planning to close five plants and cut 47,000 jobs globally; Chrysler is only asking for $5 billion and will cut 3,000 jobs.[86]

President Obama adds 17,000 troops to Afghanistan.[87]

2/18/09

Attorney General Eric Holder declares the U.S. is "essentially a nation of cowards" when it comes to race.[88]

President Obama unveils the Homeowner Stability Initiative (a.k.a. the "backyard bailout"), with the goal of saving 7 to 9 million homes. $75 billion will come from the financial industry's bailout in order to try to keep homeowners out of foreclosure.[89]

The Environmental Protection Agency (EPA) is expected to regulate carbon dioxide as a greenhouse gas.[90]

President Obama wants to double exports in five years.[91] *Exporting what? Jobs?*

The top twenty banks receiving bailouts are lending, says the U.S. Treasury.[92]

The Swiss Bank, UBS, must pay $780 million in fines, penalties, interest and restitution for helping U.S. taxpayers hide money from the IRS. UBS also must provide names and account numbers of its American customers.[93]

2/19/09

CNBC reporter Rick Santelli calls for a Chicago Tea Party in response to President Obama's Homeowner Stability Initiative.[94]

One day after getting a criminal settlement against UBS, the Department of Justice files a civil suit demanding that UBS hand over the names, account numbers and information of 52,000 Americans who do their banking in Switzerland.[95] *The Justice Department is more concerned with guaranteeing constitutional rights to terrorists on the battlefield than respecting Switzerland's sovereignty and the Swiss justice system's due process rights regarding the privacy of account holders.*

Feb 2009

The Swiss SVP party calls the Department of Justice's actions "foreign blackmail" and is calling for diplomatic retaliation against the U.S.[96]

The U.N. announces Iran has enriched sufficient uranium for a nuclear weapon.[97]

President Obama makes his first foreign trip to meet with Canadian Prime Minister Stephen Harper.[98]

Feb 2009

2/20/09

Global Warming?: a satellite glitch has caused scientists to underestimate the size of Arctic sea ice by 193,000 square miles.[99]

President Obama speaks with mayors telling them that stimulus money must not be wasted and that he is assigning staff to ensure "every dollar" is spent wisely.[100]

Secretary of State Hillary Clinton visits China, begging them to keep buying U.S. debt and assuring them that U.S. debt is a reliable investment. She makes it clear that issues regarding Taiwan, Tibet, and human rights will not interfere with other matters.[101] [102]

Secretary Clinton says the U.S. would seek peace with North Korea and provide assistance if they abandon their nuclear program.[103]

2/22/09

President Obama speaks of the stimulus at the National Governors Association, promising "shovels in the ground and cranes in the air."[104]

Obama is working on budget plans to raise taxes on businesses and the wealthy while slashing defense spending.[105]

Americans sue UBS in Switzerland to prevent disclosure of their identities to the U.S. Justice Department.[106]

Feb 2009

2/23/09

President Obama holds a Fiscal Responsibility Summit and says he will cut the deficit in half within four years. He also says he will re-institute the "pay as you go" rule.[107] *"Pay/go" requires Congress to match every spending increase with a corresponding spending cut.*

AIG seeks more U.S. funds as it posts a $60 billion loss. The government already owns 80% of AIG.[108]

Treasury Secretary Geithner announces bank stress tests will begin this week. The government may effectively nationalize banks by converting preferred shares of stock to common stock.[109]

A soldier serving in Iraq denies President Obama's eligibility to deploy him and sues for proof of birth certificate in federal court.[110]

Secretary of State Clinton pledges $900 million to help rebuild Gaza, even though the U.N. just cut off aid to Gaza on February 7, 2009, because Hamas was hijacking aid. The U.S. says the aid will be funneled through non-governmental organizations and the U.N.[111]

2/24/09

President Obama delivers a prime-time address to a joint session of Congress:

- He pledges to cut the deficit in half in four years,

- He will review budgets line by line,

- He says America has a responsibility not to pass debt to its children,

- He says America will double its supply of renewable energy in three years, and

- He says he has identified $2 trillion in budget cuts over the next decade.[112]

The Department of Homeland Security (DHS) affirms Mexican drug cartel violence has spilled over into Texas.[113]

Texas Governor Rick Perry requests 1,000 National Guard troops for the Mexican border.[114]

Mayor Jose Ferriz (Juarez, Mexico) moves his family to El Paso, Texas, after receiving threats.[115]

2/25/09

Senator Robert Byrd (D-WV) criticizes President Obama's "czar" frenzy as a power grab by the executive branch.[116] *"The biggest problems that we're facing right now have to do with George Bush trying to bring more and more power into the executive branch and not go through Congress at all. And that's what I intend to reverse when I'm president of the United States." —Senator Barack Obama, March, 31, 2008. The Romanov Dynasty had eighteen Czars over a period of 304 years. President Obama has crowned thirty-two czars in just a few weeks.*

Feb 2009

Vice President Biden says he is orchestrating an unprecedented oversight effort to "follow the money," ensuring stimulus funds will not be wasted.[117]

President Obama seeks $75.5 billion more for the wars in Iraq and Afghanistan.[118]

Iran tests its first nuclear plant. They refuse to slow down their nuclear program, planning 50,000 centrifuges in the next five years.[119]

2/26/09

President Obama's first budget request:

- includes a $635 billion down payment on the health care overhaul
- plus $750 billion in contingency funds to aid the financial sector
- increases taxes on the "wealthy"
- will spend $3.94 trillion for this year with a $1.75 trillion deficit
- has record outlays of $3.55 trillion for 2010
- decreases Medicare subsidies to insurance companies by $170 billion

- plans to raise $210 billion cracking down on offshore tax havens
- assumes $75 billion revenues from a Cap & Trade system
- increases the Pentagon's budget by 4%
- cuts federal subsidies of student loans by $48 billion
- the budget excludes the costs of running Fannie Mae and Freddie Mac.

Somehow, he says he will cut the budget deficit to $533 billion by 2013.[120] [121]

President Obama also proposes to limit charitable deductions, disputing that charitable giving will decrease. He forecasts that it will raise $179.8 billion over ten years.[122]   *The same man who believes, "I think when you spread the wealth around, it's good for everybody," doesn't bother spreading much of his own wealth. Seven years of tax returns show the Obamas gave less than 1% of their income to charity (for two years), about 1% (for three years), 4.7% in 2005, and 6.1% in 2006. Well, he's certainly more generous with your money than he is with his own.[123]*
As Frank Mayo quipped, "'Liberal' means you're liberal with other people's money."

2/27/09

Attorney General Eric Holder sends strong signals that states should make their own rules about medical marijuana and he will end raids on pot dispensaries in California.[124]

President Obama extends Iraq troop withdrawal timetable to August 31, 2010, with 35,000 to 50,000 troops remaining until the end of 2011.[125]

2/28/09

February's deficit reached a record high of $192.8 billion.[126]

February job losses equal 706,000.[127]

February unemployment = 8.2%.
Real unemployment = 15%.[128]

3/1/09

"Urban Czar" Adolfo Carrion, former Bronx Borough president, is accused of taking thousands of dollars in campaign cash from developers whose projects he approved or funded with taxpayer money.[129]

AIG may get an additional $30 billion in bailout funds.[130]

3/2/09

Kathleen Sebelius is nominated to become Secretary of Health and Human Services (HHS).

Ron Kirk, nominee for U.S. Trade Representative, has to pay $10,000 in back taxes.[131] *Many pages could be written about Obama's botched nominations, but only a few are mentioned in this book. The point is to demonstrate that the administration has a tendency to "wing it," or to jump off the cliff without looking. The fact that they would submit such poorly vetted nominees raises the question of how thoroughly they investigate any responsibility they assume, whether it is a Treasury secretary or a $535 million dollar loan to the failing "green jobs" company Solyndra.*

FDIC Chairman Sheila Bair says the fund it uses to protect customer deposits could be insolvent this year amid the surge in bank failures.[132]

The Obama administration releases its housing plan. The program will only help borrowers:

- *if* they haven't lost their jobs,
- *if* they owe less than 105% of the home's value,
- *if* they are "in good standing" (whatever that means),
- *if* they can show the government they are at "imminent risk" of default,
- *if* the bank/lender wishes to participate, and
- *if* the mortgage is owned and/or insured by Fannie Mae or Freddie Mac.[133]

Secretary of State Hillary Clinton meets with President Abbas of the Palestinian National Authority. Secretary Clinton calls on Israel to allow more aid to Gaza, denounces the demolition of homes in East Jerusalem and vows to work toward a Palestinian state.[134]

Defense Secretary Robert Gates says Iran isn't even close to a nuclear weapon.[135]

President Obama tells Russia that if they will cooperate on resolving the issue of Iran's nuclear program, the U.S. will drop its missile shield plans for Europe.[136] *(i.e., a missile base in Poland and radar base in the Czech Republic).*

3/3/09

President Obama ungraciously meets with British Prime Minister Gordon Brown. For the first time in modern times, there is no formal dinner and no arrangement of a press conference with flags. One is hastily arranged after the British practically beg for it. During the press conference, he looks as if he would prefer being anywhere else.

After receiving incredibly nice and thoughtful gifts from the British, President Obama gives Prime Minister Brown twenty-five American DVDs (which don't even work on European DVD players) and, for his children, two models of the presidential helicopter.

The White House tries to excuse its shabby behavior by claiming that the President is too tired from dealing with domestic policy to properly greet a foreign head of state, even though he happens to be our greatest ally.[137] [138] [139] [140]

President Obama releases billions of dollars for public work projects for the Department of Transportation and the Department of the Interior, declaring that shovels are hitting the ground just fourteen days after signing the stimulus.[141] *On October 12, 2010, Obama admits, "there's no such thing as a shovel-ready project" and in June 2011, he lightheartedly chuckles, "shovel-ready was not as shovel-ready as we expected." Maybe he's shoveling something else.*

The House Omnibus Spending Bill is fraught with unprecedented waste, including 9,000+ earmarks.[142]

The White House attacks Jim Cramer (*a liberal!*), host of CNBC's show

Mar 2009

"Mad Money," for calling Obama's budget "the greatest wealth destruction by a president."[143]

The Obama administration vows to strengthen the Endangered Species Act.[144]

Treasury Secretary Geithner announces plans to limit companies from avoiding U.S. taxation of foreign earnings and crack down on Americans' ability to use offshore tax havens.[145]

Secretary Clinton attacks the Israeli plan to demolish eighty Palestinian homes in East Jerusalem to make way for Jewish families.[146]

3/4/09

United Bank Suisse (UBS) plans to fight the IRS and Department of Justice's demands to provide names and account information of 52,000 American customers. The Swiss believe the issue should be resolved through diplomacy, not American courts. They see the U.S. as tyrannically dictating what the Swiss laws should be.[147]

More than 8.3 million U.S. mortgages are in negative equity.[148]

Secretary Geithner attacks oil and gas tax breaks because of global warming.[149]

President Obama orders an overhaul of the way the government awards contracts to the private sector. He claims it can save $40 billion per year.[150]

The President claims his budget includes $2 trillion in deficit reduction and decreases non-military discretionary spending by 10% over the next ten years.[151]

China will increase military spending by 15%.[152]

Venezuela's Chavez tightens state control of food amid rocketing inflation and food shortages.[153]

3/5/09

President Obama hosts a forum on health care reform. "In this effort every voice must be heard, every idea must be considered. Every option must be on the table. There will be no sacred cows in this discussion," he says.[154] *The President is never too serious about listening to opposing points of view. On September 7, 2009, Representative John Boehner (R-OH) said Obama had not met with Republicans since April.*

Economist Nouriel Roubini claims the U.S. financial system is effectively insolvent.[155]

3/6/09

Secretary Clinton says, "never waste a good crisis" as an opportunity to "invest" in the green economy.[156]

Secretary of State Hillary Clinton meets with Russian Foreign Minister Sergei Lavrov and presents him with a "Reset" button, signifying a desire to reset relations with Russia. There is a translation error: in Russian it says "overcharged."[157]

3/7/09

Mar 2009

The British public is miffed over President Obama's treatment of Gordon Brown. In an interview with the *Sunday Telegraph*, a State Department official says, "There's nothing special about Britain. You're just the same as the other 190 countries in the world. You shouldn't expect special treatment."[158],[159] *Way to make them feel welcome. Maybe he should tell all of his celebrity friends, union backers, campaign donors, and political allies that there's nothing special about them, they are the same as the other 6 billion people on the planet.*

The White House is willing to meet with more moderate elements of the Taliban to resolve the situation in Afghanistan.[160]

3/8/09

On the heels of treating Britain appallingly, Obama is moving to ease travel and trade restrictions with Cuba.[161]

While blasting the Israel lobby, Charles Freeman withdraws from his appointment as chairman of the National Intelligence Council amid controversial financial ties with China and Saudi Arabia.[162]

Israeli intelligence says Iran's nuclear program is probably more advanced than believed.[163]

Iran test fires new air-to-surface missiles.[164]

3/9/09

President Obama issues a memorandum negating all of President Bush's signing statements, telling agencies not to follow them without consulting the Department of Justice in advance.[165] *On March 11, Obama signs his own signing statement.*

President Obama signs an executive order allowing federal funding of embryonic stem cell research.[166]

Secretary of State Clinton announces a $1 million scholarship program for Palestinian students.[167]

3/10/09

President Obama explains his priorities on education with the usual platitudes, allocating $21 billion for school modernization. The administration will also send $79 billion in state fiscal relief.[168]

While visiting Israel, Vice President Biden "condemns" Israeli construction of 1,600 units in East Jerusalem. As a further snub, he keeps Prime Minister Netanyahu waiting for ninety minutes before meeting with him.[169]

Mar 2009

3/11/09

President Obama signs the Omnibus Appropriation Act of 2009 stating, "I am signing an imperfect bill because it is necessary for the ongoing function of government." *Despite its imperfections and more than 8,500 earmarks, Americans can be sure that he fulfilled his promise to go over it line by line.*[170]

Despite denouncing Bush's use of signing statements two days ago, he signs the Omnibus Appropriation Act with his own signing statement saying certain provisions raise constitutional concerns.[171]

2009 deficit spending has already reached $765 billion.[172]

Freddie Mac taps the Treasury for $30.8 billion as its losses deepen.[173]

In preparatory talks preceding the G-20 summit, Obama's chief economic adviser, Larry Summers, encourages other countries to pump stimulus into the world economy. The EU declares they are not inclined to incur further debt.[174]

The U.S. and China work together to smooth relations regarding confrontations between naval vessels.[175] *These negotiations actually worked for three days; see entry for 3/14/09.*

The U.S. finds that an Afghan Taliban leader was formerly a prisoner at Gitmo.[176]

North Korea accuses the U.S. of meddling in their internal affairs and vows to take every necessary measure to defend itself.[177]

3/12/09

Speaking at the Business Roundtable, Obama declares the economy is "not as bad as we think." The President affirms that he supports a free-market–based system and that it is the government's responsibility to "right the ship" then "let private enterprise do its magic."[178] [179]

President Obama is considering Texas Governor Rick Perry's request to deploy National Guard troops along the Texas/Mexico border as drug violence intensifies. The President says, "We're going to examine whether and if National Guard deployments would make sense and under what circumstances they would make sense." Governor Perry believes, "Washington has been an abject failure [in] defending our border…I'm not going to sit back while the feds do not do their job."[180]

Corporate oil booms in low-tax Switzerland. A wave of energy companies have announced plans to move to Switzerland—mainly for its appeal as a low-tax corporate domicile that seems relatively likely to stay out of reach of the claws of Obama's tax-hungry administration.[181]

President Obama meets with China's top diplomat, whom he tells, "The promotion of human rights is an essential aspect of U.S. global foreign policy."[182]

3/13/09

The Obama administration announces it is abandoning the phrase "enemy combatant" and is incorporating international law as the basis for holding terrorist suspects at Guantanamo.[183]

Mar 2009

Chinese Premier Wen Jiabao expresses concern over the safety of U.S. treasuries. "We have lent a huge amount of money to the U.S., so of course we are concerned about the safety of our assets. Frankly speaking, I do have some worries." Since the stimulus is being financed with so much debt, China is concerned that inflation will make treasuries worthless. The administration sought to ease China's fears by reiterating pledges to cut the deficit in half in four years.[184] [185] [186]

Press Secretary Robert Gibbs says, "There's no safer investment in the world than the U.S." Treasury Secretary Geithner called G-20 nations encouraging them to increase funding of the International Monetary Fund (IMF) to $500 billion to combat the financial crisis.[187] [188]

3/14/09

The White House signals to Congress a willingness to tax employee health benefits.[189]

Treasury Secretary Geithner objects to AIG's bonus payments but he concludes they are lawful because they were contracted in 2008.[190]

Russia contemplates Cuba and Venezuela as possible bases to house their strategic bombers.[191]

China accuses U.S. surveillance ships of spying. Chinese boats harass and nearly collide with an unarmed U.S. Navy vessel. The U.S. dispatches a heavily armed escort to aid the surveillance ships.[192] *See entry for 3/11/09.*

President Obama considers his meeting with Brazilian President Lula da Silva successful. Obama remarks, "We have a very strong friendship between the two countries, but we can always make it stronger in areas like energy and biofuels, in the interest in increasing the standards of living in impoverished countries throughout Latin America, expanding trade relationships—you know, the President and I had a wonderful meeting of the minds."[193] *What else did that "meeting of the minds" include? The Gulf oil spill illustrates that the administration takes its marching orders from the George Soros-funded Center for American Progress. Soros's fund owns $900 million of Petrobras, Brazil's national oil company. Brazil is launching a $220 billion program in offshore drilling projects more than twice as deep as the Deepwater Horizon. Plus, the Obama administration granted Brazil $2 billion to explore offshore drilling. Brazil stood to benefit greatly from Obama's drilling moratorium during the Gulf oil disaster. So did George Soros. The administration was determined to impose the drilling moratorium even after a federal judge overturned it.*

Mar 2009

3/15/09

President Obama says the U.S. economy is sound and China should have "absolute confidence" that its sizable investments are safe. He further states that financial regulation will be the main topic at the approaching G-20 summit.

Vice President Biden attributes growing public confidence to the

"Obama Factor."[194]

Does the "Obama Factor" go both ways? When people start to lose confidence, is that also the "Obama Factor?"

Larry Summers, Director of the President's National Economic Council, says it is outrageous that AIG would pay $165 million in executive bonuses.[195]

3/16/09

The American Legion strongly opposes the administration's plan of charging wounded heroes for treatment.[196]

The White House ridicules former vice president Dick Cheney over his criticism that President Obama's revamped policies will make the U.S. more vulnerable. Press Secretary Robert Gibbs makes a double attack: "I guess Rush Limbaugh was busy, so they trotted out the next most popular member of the Republican cabal."[197]

President Obama blasts AIG for its bonus payouts.[198]

3/17/09

The national debt hits $11 trillion.[199]

DHS Secretary Napolitano reveals the term "man-caused disaster" as a substitute for "act of terrorism" because "it demonstrates that we want to move away from the politics of fear."[200]

Vice President Biden says Barack Obama "inherited" a tougher economy than FDR.[201] *The President did not "inherit" anything. He signed up
for the job. In fact, he was elected because he convinced enough Americans that he was knew how to solve economic problems.*

The White House tries to deflect criticism for mishandling AIG, denying knowledge of AIG executive bonus contracts before blessing them
with another $30 billion bailout.[202]

Russia announces support of a supranational reserve currency as an
alternative to the dollar.[203]

Russia announces an ambitious rearmament program in response to
what it considers NATO's expansion. President Obama hopes to "reset"
U.S./Russian relations. On the agenda:

- A nuclear arms control treaty
- Iran's nuclear program
- NATO enlargement
- The U.S. missile defense shield in Eastern Europe.[204]

3/18/09

ACORN will participate in the 2010 Census despite their history of
voter fraud and corruption.[205] *By the way, this month President Obama's
Justice Department dropped its criminal investigation against his buddies
at ACORN.*

The Fed launches a $1.2 trillion effort to revive the economy that will:

Mar 2009

- spend approximately $300 billion buying government bonds and

- spend approximately $750 billion in mortgage-backed securities guaranteed by Fannie and Freddie.[206]

President Obama uses AIG as an example to call for greater regulation over non-banking financial institutions. When asked whether Treasury Secretary Geithner or other members of his administration were at fault, he replies, "The buck stops with me."[207] *He should have said, "The value of the buck stops with me."*

Attorney General Holder signals federal agents will target medical marijuana distributors who violate state and federal law.[208] *Here is the first of many instances where Holder does a 180-degree policy turnaround. See entries for 2/5/09 and 2/27/09.*

Russia confirms signing a contract with Iran to provide S-300 missiles but says the weapons have not yet been delivered. Likely, Russia intends to use the contract as leverage while negotiating with Obama.[209]

A U.N. panel proposes discarding the dollar as the global reserve currency in favor of a shared basket of currencies. America's enormous budget deficits have shaken other central banks' faith in the dollar as a reliable store of value. Russia plans to make a similar proposal at the G-20.[210]

3/19/09

The Senate confirms John Holdren as the Director of the White House Office of Science and Technology (a.k.a. "Science Czar"). *Holdren may be best known for his association with quack scientist Paul Ehrlich. The "Science Czar," who believes the U.S. is the "meanest of wealthy countries," supports abdicating U.S. sovereignty to "'a comprehensive Planetary Regime' that would control all the world's resources, direct global redistribution of wealth, oversee the 'de-development' of the West, control a World Army and taxation regime, and enforce world population limits." Oh yeah, the "population control" includes compulsory abortions and sterilizations.*[211]

Pro-choice fanatic Dawn Johnson, who equates pregnancy to slavery, is confirmed by the Senate to the Department of Justice's Office of Legal Counsel.[212]

Two days after the news surfaced, President Obama is dropping his plan to charge wounded veterans for their service-related injuries.[213]

Senator Chris Dodd says the Obama administration asked him to insert a provision in the stimulus bill that authorized AIG's bonuses.[214]

The dollar falls against other major currencies indicating concern that yesterday's Federal Reserve proposal will spark inflation.[215]

President Obama becomes the first sitting president to appear on the *Tonight Show*. He says that he is a bad bowler, "like the Special Olympics."[216] *He's also a bad economist, "like the Special Olympics."*

Duke basketball Coach Mike Krzyzewski says Obama should spend more time worrying about the economy and less time worrying about basketball.[217]

3/20/09

The Congressional Budget Office (CBO) forecasts a $1.8 trillion deficit this year and $9.3 trillion over the next decade. The White House says budget priorities will not be affected by forecasts of bigger deficits.[218] *But, somehow, he's going to cut the deficit in half in four years.*

3/21/09

"Car Czar" Steve Rattner says GM and Chrysler may need considerably more than $21.6 billion in aid.[219]

3/22/09

President Obama does more cheerleading for the green economy.[220]

In a *60 Minutes* interview, President Obama believes that Dick Cheney's support of Gitmo is based on his lack of faith in the American justice system. Obama says, "I fundamentally disagree with that. Now do these folks deserve Miranda rights? Do they deserve to be treated like a shoplifter down the block? Of course not."[221]

3/23/09

President Obama has a primetime press conference where he blames Bush for everything that is wrong and encourages "investment" in renewable energy.[222]

The White House launches a $500 billion effort to remove toxic assets from banks by attracting private capital, so they can resume lending.[223]

Controversy swirls as Obama accepts an invitation to speak at the commencement ceremony at the University of Notre Dame, a Catholic school.[224]

Amid concerns of inflationary risk, China calls for a new reserve currency with a new global system controlled by the IMF.[225]

3/24/09

The White House seeks the power to seize any and all financial firms (including insurance companies, hedge funds, investment funds, etc.) whose failure could disrupt the broader economy.[226]

The Office of Security Review informs the world that the Obama administration shall henceforth refer to the "Global War on Terror" as "overseas contingency operations."[227]

President Obama and his teleprompter hold a news conference to discuss financial reform. Again, he calls on reporters who were already handpicked in advance.[228] [229] *If Obama is going to read scripted answers to scripted questions, America may as well have elected a sock puppet to the Oval Office.*

3/25/09

Mar 2009

In response to a question about fiscal responsibility and spiraling debt, Budget Director Peter Orszag replies, "I don't know what spiraling debt you're referring to, but we're inheriting a budget situation that is a mess, and that we're working our way out of. And under both budget resolutions, the deficit is reduced in half—by more than half by 2013, and actually then is either stable or declining between 2013 and 2014. So I guess I just—I take issue with the conjecture that we're, you know, there's spiraling debt here."[230]

President Obama appoints Paul Volcker to lead a panel on overhauling the tax code. Peter Orszag, the Budget Director, says they "will be examining ways of being even more *aggressive* on reducing the tax gap" of unpaid taxes. He emphasizes the administration will be "as aggressive as possible."[231]

Postmaster General John Potter says the U.S. Postal Service is running out of money. He is also seeking permission to cut delivery to five days per week.[232]

Bishop John D'Arcy will skip Notre Dame's graduation ceremony in protest of Obama's views regarding the sanctity of life.[233]

Treasury Secretary Timothy Geithner states that he is "quite open" to

China's proposal that the dollar be replaced as the world's reserve currency.

The dollar falls against other major currencies after Secretary Geithner's statement.[234]

EU President Mirak Topolanek condemns U.S. polices for remedying the global recession as "the road to hell."[235]

Secretary Clinton blames Americans' "insatiable" appetite for illegal drugs for the violence in Mexico.[236]

Secretary Clinton warns North Korea that firing missiles for any purpose would be deemed a "provocative act."[237] *"Provocative act?" What exactly will it provoke? Over the next few months North Korea launches many missiles, tests nuclear bombs, torpedoes and sinks a South Korean ship killing sailors and instigates a deadly skirmish with South Korean forces at the border. Despite Secretary Clinton's statement, North Korea behaves with brazen impunity.*

Watch for this pattern of White House inaction on the world stage. The Obama administration habitually grandstands with "tough talk" of deadlines, ultimatums and warnings. When adversaries cross the line in the sand, the administration fights back with ... more empty warnings.

Mar 2009

3/26/09

Treasury Secretary Geithner appears before the House Financial Services Committee to unveil a plan that would radically expand the government's authority to regulate, and even seize, any financial institution it deems "systemically important."[238]

National Intelligence Director Dennis Blair confirms that some Guantanamo inmates may be released on U.S. soil and receive assistance to return to society.[239]

The IRS and Department of Justice intensify their attack on Switzerland. They are giving citizens with Swiss bank accounts a six-month ultimatum to come forward and provide evidence against their bankers and advisers.[240]

A U.N. panel of economists presses for a global currency reserve system to replace the volatile dollar.[241]

Russia plans to create an Arctic military force even though a number of countries have disputed jurisdiction over the mineral-rich region.[242]

Admiral Mike Mullen, chairman of the Joint Chiefs of Staff, says North Korean rockets are capable of reaching Hawaii.[243]

3/27/09

President Obama orders 4,000 more troops to Afghanistan and increases aid to Pakistan.[244]

3/29/09

GM CEO Rick Wagoner resigns at the Obama administration's behest.[245]

Mar 2009

Treasury Secretary Geithner says about $135 billion of uncommitted funds remain in TARP.[246]

DHS Secretary Napolitano has delayed a series of immigration raids at workplaces, apparently, in anticipation of a change in policy.[247]

On *Face the Nation*, President Obama says he does not believe violence on the Mexican border poses an "existential threat" to Americans and that he is considering deploying National Guard troops to the border area. He says the violence has "gotten out of hand," and that he has put together a comprehensive initiative to assist border regions by increasing personnel and surveillance equipment. He continues, "But first we want to see whether some of the steps we've taken can help quell some of the violence...I think the main thing we need is better enforcement."[248] *Obama has been aware of border problems since February 2009. The immigration issue highlights the president's gift for saying what is expedient at any given moment even though he has no intention of backing up his words with action.*

Russia backs a return to the gold standard.[249]

In anticipation of G-20, EU leaders dismiss the Obama administration's support for a large fiscal stimulus plan or a "global new deal."[250]

Defense Secretary Gates says the U.S. is not ready to respond to a North Korean missile launch.[251]

Mar 2009

3/30/09

The Obama administration rejects GM and Chrysler's turnaround plans. Instead of granting their requests for more money, the administration will provide only enough to keep them going for the next sixty days, while the government develops a sweeping restructuring plan.[252]

"Car Czar" Steve Rattner (who has zero experience in the auto industry) makes it clear that the government will only commit funds to Chrysler if they form a partnership with Italian car company Fiat, even though a merger with GM makes more sense to Chrysler executives.[253] *Maybe he should be the Car "Fiat" instead of the Car "Czar."*

The government has also announced a program for a new government-backed warranty program for all new GM and Chrysler vehicles.[254]

Russia and China cooperate on new currency proposals as they move away from the dollar as a medium of exchange.[255]

3/31/09

President Obama's Department of Justice drops its criminal investigation of ACORN's voter fraud and corruption.[256] *"I've been fighting alongside ACORN on issues you care about my entire career. Even before I was an elected official, when I ran Project Vote voter registration drive in Illinois, ACORN was smack dab in the middle of it, and we appreciate your work." —Barack Obama*

HHS nominee Kathleen Sebelius admits errors and pays $7,000 in back

Mar 2009

taxes.[257]

Senate panel testimony reveals that it is not possible to adequately over-see handling of TARP funds due to the Treasury Department's unwill-ingness to disclose bailout details.[258] *So much for transparency.*

Four days prior to going to Prague, President Obama drops plans to have dinner with the Czech president in favor in dining with this wife.[259]

March job losses equal 742,000[260]

U.S. budget deficit hits $192.3 billion for March.[261]

Foreclosures are 46% higher in March than a year ago, 17% above Feb-ruary's total.[262]

March unemployment = 8.6%.
Real unemployment = 15.6%.[263]

4/1/09

Secretary Geithner dodges answering a question about the Treasury's inability to track how banks spend TARP funds. He also predicts we will "see the strongest consensus on coordinated global stimulus you've ever seen in generation…a very powerful consensus on the kind of twenty-first-century rules of the road for our financial systems."[264] *Geithner is wrong again. The rest of the world eventually sees the need to curb government spending through austerity measures.*

Despite President Obama's repeated promises that families making less than $250,000 per year will not experience *any kind* of tax increase, the government levies the largest-ever tobacco tax, which disproportionately affects the poor.[265]

GM requests $2.6 billion from the government to build hybrids.[266]

President Obama gives Queen Elizabeth II an iPod with his speeches and images of himself.[267]

Russian President Dmitry Medvedev argues for the need of a new global currency system to replace the dollar.[268]

President Obama meets with leaders of China, Russia and the U.K. at G-20.

- He promises world leaders he would listen, and not lecture, as they address the financial crisis.
- He and Medvedev announce they reached a deal to re-open nuclear disarmament talks.
- He downplays rumors that the U.S. is feuding with other nations about the need to inject more money into economic stimulus policies.
- Obama and China agree to establish a U.S./China Strategic Economic Dialogue.[269]

4/2/09

London hosts the G-20 summit.

The *Wall Street Journal* reveals that President Obama is willing to resort to Chicago-style mafia politics. When Representative Pete DeFazio (D-OR) voted against the stimulus, he upbraided him behind closed doors: "Don't think we're not keeping score, brother."[270]

U.S. authorities arrest a South Florida accountant for tax evasion for having an account at the Swiss bank UBS. The Department of Justice has opened 100 criminal investigations against Americans with accounts at UBS. UBS maintains Swiss financial privacy laws protect the information sought by the U.S.[271] *Readers will appreciate that he has a flair for ceding U.S. sovereignty to foreign bodies; yet, he does not mind stomping all over other nations when it comes to grubbing for American money that may have escaped his clutches.*

President Obama calls for "transparency and accountability" when it comes to salaries and bonuses of executives.[272] *How about "transparency and accountability" for the Treasury and TARP?*

The U.S. and South Korea warn North Korea not to proceed with a planned satellite launch; Pyongyang threatens a "fiery bolt of retaliatory lightning" if Japan tries to shoot it down.[273]

Israel's Netanyahu warns that the U.S. must end Iran's nuclear program or Israel may attack.[274]

The G-20 Communiqué statement contains provisions too numerous to mention, but here are some highlights. The communiqué resolves to:

- establish a $1.1 trillion program to restore credit, growth and jobs in the world economy

Apr 2009

- take an unprecedented and concentrated fiscal expansion that, by the end of next year, amounts to $5 trillion, raise output by 4 percent and accelerate transition to a green economy

- strengthen financial regulation and supervision to promote propriety, integrity and transparency in order to guard against risk across the financial system

- agree to establish a Financial Stability Board (FSB) to reshape our regulatory systems so that authorities are able to identify and take account of macro-prudential risks

- extend regulation and oversight to all systematically important financial institutions, instruments and markets, including hedge funds

- endorse and implement the Financial Stability Forum's tough new principles on pay and compensation and to support sustainable compensation schemes and social responsibility of all firms

- take actions against non-cooperative jurisdictions, including tax havens. The era of banking secrecy is over

- resist protectionism and promote global trade and investment

- agree to make the best possible use of investment funded by fiscal stimulus programs toward the goal of building a resilient, sustainable and green recovery. It will also make the transition toward clean, innovative, resource efficient, low carbon technologies and infrastructure

- reaffirm its commitment to address the threat of irreversible climate change.[275]

Financially, G-20 agrees to give more than $1 trillion to the IMF and the World Bank. They will also move toward a global currency,

Apr 2009

backed by a global central bank running monetary policy. Point 19 of the G-20 communiqué activates special drawing rights (SDRs) from the IMF that will activate the IMF's power to create money and practice "quantitative easing" on a global scale.[276] [277]

Other G-20 highlights include President Obama bowing before Saudi King Abdullah. Basically, he came out of G-20 with nothing to show for it. When he was asked how the summit would help recession-battered Americans, he could not point to any individual accomplishment beyond general points such as fighting protectionism and making the global economy work together.[278] [279]

President Obama did not miss the opportunity to praise himself with his typical self-flattering delusions, "I would like to think that with my election and the early decisions that we've made, that you're starting to see some restoration of America's standing in the world. And although, as you know, I always mistrust polls, international polls seem to indicate that you're seeing people more hopeful about America's leadership."[280]

4/3/09

During his "town hall" meeting in Strasbourg, France, President Obama says, "In America, there's a failure to appreciate Europe's leading role in the world...there have been times where America's shown arrogance and been dismissive, even derisive." As usual, he only takes softball questions from the audience.[281]

Dick Morris argues that President Obama's signing off on the G-20 communiqué surrenders U.S. sovereignty to an international Financial

Apr 2009

Stability Board that would have the power to regulate ALL firms, including those within the U.S. and place them under the authority of an international governmental agency.[282]

4/4/09

At a NATO press conference, Obama declares, "I believe in American exceptionalism, just as I suspect Brits believe in British exceptionalism and the Greeks believe in Greek exceptionalism."[283]

President Obama fails to win NATO troops for Afghanistan. The U.K. offers to help. Belgium offers thirty-five troops and Spain pledges twelve troops. France rebuffs his request.[284]

President Obama refuses to accept TARP repayments from banks, ostensibly, to maximize control over the financial system.[285]

4/5/09

In Prague, President Obama calls for a world without nuclear arms. "As a nuclear power—as the only nation to have used a nuclear weapon—the U.S. has a moral obligation and responsibility to act."

Obama proposes to reduce America's arsenal, host a summit on nuclear security, seek ratification of the Comprehensive Test Ban Treaty, strengthen the Nuclear Non-Proliferation Treaty and negotiate a new agreement aimed at stopping the production of missile materials.

President Obama says he intends to continue with a missile defense system as long as Iran is a threat. If the Iranian threat is eliminated,

Apr 2009

Obama says, "The driving force for missile defense construction in Europe at this time will be removed."

President Obama also takes the opportunity to single out North Korea, saying all nations must come together to build a global regime, standing shoulder to shoulder to pressure North Korea.

North Korea signals its middle-fingered response by launching a long-range rocket over the Sea of Japan.[286]

4/6/09

GM is speeding up plans for a bankruptcy filing.[287]

Treasury Secretary Geithner declares he may oust executives at banks needing exceptional aid.[288]

With the Obama administration borrowing to finance record deficits, U.S. debt sales will almost triple this year to a record $2.5 trillion according to estimates from Goldman Sachs. 264

Russia, China, Malaysia, Indonesia, Thailand and Kazakhstan are calling for an international currency system to replace the dollar.[289]

President Obama takes his Apology Tour to Turkey, telling a crowd, "The United States is still working through some of our own darker periods in our history...Our country still struggles with the legacies of slavery and segregation, the past treatment of Native Americans...I know that the trust that binds us has been strained, and I know that strain is shared in many places where the Muslim faith is practiced.

Let me say this as clearly as I can: The United States is not at war with Islam."

He further states, "America, like every other nation, has made mistakes and has its flaws, but for more than two centuries it has strived" to seek a more perfect union. *So far, Obama's apology tour has yielded zero apologies from other countries.*

The President's speech infuriates Europeans when he adds that he supports Turkey's bid for EU membership[290] [291] [292]

4/7/09

The apparatchiks at the Department of Homeland Security (DHS) issue a warning about "right-wing extremists" who are concerned about illegal immigration, increasing federal power, restrictions on firearms, abortion, and loss of U.S. sovereignty and singles out returning war veterans as particular threats.

Among those who are dangerous extremists are those who prefer state and local authority to federal authority or those dedicated to a single issue such as abortion or immigration.

The DHS Cheka warns that proposed imposition of firearms restrictions would attract new members of extremists and the high volume of purchases of guns and ammunition in anticipation of said restrictions is cause for deep concern.

Law enforcement agencies are warned to be on the lookout for suspicious persons who have bumper stickers on their cars for Ron Paul or third-party political candidates such as Bob Barr and Chuck Baldwin.

It further warns about individuals with "radical" ideologies based on Christian views, immigration, abortion, or opposition to federal taxes.[293]

Drafting the DHS domestic terrorist memo began almost immediately after President Obama assumed office under an initiative called "Operation Vigilant Eagle," begun in February. DHS had issued an earlier report that it recalled within hours that defined all kinds of "extremists" (white, black, Mexican, Cuban, Christian, Jewish) and several political leanings in its "Domestic Extremism Lexicon."[294] *Perhaps the original plan was to define "domestic terrorists" broadly enough to include just about everybody. Apparently, they were content to scale it back and just label conservatives as "enemies of the state."*

Adhering to the president's desire not to run and micromanage car companies, the Treasury Department "asks" Chrysler Financial to have its top twenty-five executives sign waivers regarding their compensation.[295] In fact, the Obama administration was extremely involved in micromanaging the car companies. The Treasury Department was directly implicated in the decision that led to more than 20,000 non-union GM employees losing their pensions.[296]

Elizabeth Warren of the Congressional Oversight Panel says the financial crisis is far from over. The panel criticizes the U.S. Treasury for failing to identify what measurements it uses to identify whether its rescue plan is working. "If you cannot articulate what the metrics are going out...you don't know if anything succeeded or failed," she says.[297]

Mortgage delinquencies soar as 7% of homeowners are at least thirty

Apr 2009

days behind on their payments. Almost 40% of sub-prime borrowers are at least thirty days behind.[298]

The Obama administration shuts down a China-based network that supplied Iran's nuclear and missile programs with the unwitting aid of some of Wall Street's biggest banks.[299]

Russia says Iran is not a threat to the U.S.; therefore, there is no need for a defense shield in Eastern Europe.[300] *Well, if the Russians say it, it must be true.*

President Obama makes a surprise visit to troops in Iraq.[301]

Vice President Biden says Israel would be ill-advised to attack Iran, although he considers the scenario unlikely.[302]

4/8/09

Somali pirates hijack the *Maersk Alabama*, a ship with more than twenty Americans on board.[303]

North Korea gloats over its rocket launch and warns the U.N. that it would take "strong steps" if it took any action in response to the launch.[304]

4/9/09

President Obama announces electronic health records for veterans.[305]

"And **we will not rest** until we reach a day when not one single veteran falls into homelessness."[306]

President Obama asks Congress for an additional $83.4 billion to fund military operations in Iraq and Afghanistan saying the security situation along the Afghan/Pakistani border is urgent.[307]

Iran claims to install 7,000 uranium centrifuges.[308]

4/10/09

The Fed tells banks not to reveal results of the stress tests.[309]

The Treasury Department takes a hard line trying to force concessions from GM and Chrysler bondholders, banks, and creditors.[310]

President Obama says he's "starting to see progress" toward a recovering economy even as it is "still under severe stress."[311]

4/11/09

For the twelfth straight week, jobless benefits rise by 93,000 to 6.14 million.[312]

Six days after calling for swift punishment of North Korea, the U.N. Security Council has not acted, which presents hard choices for the President, who pledged renewed reliance on the U.N.[313]

Apr 2009

4/12/09

News breaks out that Van Jones, the "Green Jobs Czar," is a radical communist.[314] *This was not another another one of the administration's sloppily vetted appointments. Valerie Jarrett, President Obama's most-trused senior adviser commented, "Van Jones: we were so delighted to be able to recruit him into the White House. We've been watching him really...for as long as he's been active out in Oakland and all of the ways and creative ideas that he has. And so now we have captured that – and we halve all of that energy and enthusiasm in the White House."*

White House Chief of Staff Rahm Emanuel states that the Bush administration officials who devised torture and interrogation policies should not be prosecuted.[315]

China slows its purchases of U.S. bonds.[316]

U.S. Navy SEALs rescue Captain Richard Phillips from Somali pirates.[317]

4/13/09

President Obama allows U.S. telecommunications firms to start providing service for Cubans and lifts restrictions on those with family ties to the island.[318]

4/14/09

Obama speaks at Georgetown University. Prior to the speech, the Obama administration requested that the university hide all symbols and references to Jesus and Christianity, including covering the Christian monogram "IHS" with a piece of black-painted plywood.[319]

President Obama says, "The Recovery Act, the bank capitalization program, the housing plan, the strengthening of the non-bank credit market, the auto plan and our work at the G-20 have been necessary pieces of the recovery puzzle...these actions are starting to generate signs of economic recovery.

"I absolutely agree that our long-term deficit is a major problem that we have to fix, but the fact is that this recovery plan represents only a tiny fraction of that long-term deficit...the key to dealing with our deficit and debt is to get a handle on out-of-control health care costs."[320]

The government is considering swapping some of its $13.4 billion loan to GM for common stock.[321]

Castro criticizes Obama's travel liberalization policy for not going far enough.[322]

4/15/09

President Obama tells a crowd in Miami that he is "amused" by the more than 300 Tea Party rallies across the country.[323]

Officials admit that the National Security Administration's wiretaps, interception of e-mails and phone calls, exceed the limits of the law.[324]

DHS Secretary Napolitano says she was briefed on the controversial report warning of dangerous, domestic, right-wing terrorism before its

Apr 2009

release and she continues to stand by the report.[325] *See the entry for*
April 7, 2009.

French President Sarkozy believes Obama's nuclear efforts lack origi-
nality and substance. He cites Obama's call to "free the world of a nuclear nightmare" as mere fluffy rhetoric and "not a speech about American
security policy."

Sarkozy was particularly miffed by the president's obsequious gestures in Turkey, especially Obama's public call for Turkey's admission to
the EU.[326] *Public criticism like this from a respected world leader marks*
a turning point in the Obama presidency. The rest of the world still takes
the United States seriously, they just don't take Obama seriously.

4/16/09

DHS Secretary Janet Napolitano grants an interview with MSNBC's Joe
Scarborough providing that he is permitted to ask only one question
about the controversial "Domestic Terror" memo and would not be allowed to ask follow-up questions.[327] *"We will continue to work toward*
an unmatched level of transparency, participation and accountability
across the entire administration." – President Barack Obama

J. P. Morgan Chase's CEO Jaime Dimon says he could repay the bank's
$25 Billion TARP loans "tomorrow."[328]

Regulators release some data regarding bank "stress tests," stating that
the results will be made public on May 4, 2009.[329]

Obama needlessly declassifies and releases CIA interrogation memos detailing interrogation techniques the U.S. has used to extract information from terrorists.[330]

The *New York Times* reports that Obama aides "did not rule out legal sanctions for the Bush lawyers who developed the legal basis for the use of techniques." When questioned directly, Obama says he will leave it up to the attorney general to decide. Attorney General Holder formally revokes every legal opinion or memo issued during Bush's presidency that justified interrogation protocols.[331] [332]

Under demands from Latin American and Caribbean leaders, the Obama administration signals greater openness for talks with Cuba; however, the embargo will remain until Castro shows greater respect for democracy and human rights.[333]

In an op-ed meant for circulation in Latin American newspapers, President Obama, once again, apologizes for America while complimenting himself, "Too often, the United States has not pursued and sustained engagement with our neighbors. We have been too easily distracted by other priorities, and have failed to see that our own progress is tied directly to progress throughout the Americas. My administration is committed to the promise of a new day. We will renew and sustain a broader partnership between the United States and the hemisphere on behalf of our common prosperity and our common security."[334]

The White House cancels President Obama's first meeting with Israeli Prime Minister Netanyahu, saying he will not be "in town."[335] *If the*

Apr 2009

president's serial mistreatment of world leaders, such as Gordon Brown and Benyamin Netanyahu, is intentional, then he is too immature to be president. If it is not intentional then, perhaps, he is too incompetent to be president.

4/17/09

The Department of Justice wins a default judgment in federal court against the New Black Panther Party for threatening voters during the 2008 presidential election.[336]

The Environmental Protection Agency (EPA) opens the door for radically expanding the scope of their regulatory authority by concluding that greenhouse gases linked to climate change "endanger public health and welfare," asserting that the science behind man-caused global warming is "compelling and overwhelming."[337]

French President Nicholas Sarkozy characterizes Obama as inexperienced, ill-prepared and "not always up to standard on decision-making and efficiency."[338]

Mahmoud Ahmadinejad declares to Obama, "You are weak. Your hands are empty...7,000 centrifuges are spinning today at Natanz, mocking you."[339]

President Obama is using Israeli fears of a nuclear Iran to coerce Israel into halting settlement construction and giving up control of the West Bank Palestinian territory.[340]

4/18/09

The FBI will begin rapidly expanding their DNA database by collecting samples from millions of people who are arrested or detained, even though they haven't been convicted.[341]

As the May 4 deadline approaches, the U.S. Treasury and financial regulators have no idea how they will disclose the results of the stress tests imposed on nineteen U.S. banks.[342]

Former CIA chief Michael Hayden says that the Obama administration's decision to release four Bush-era interrogation memos threatens national security.[343]

Israel prepares contingency plans to bomb Iran's nuclear sites.[344]

Obama travels from Mexico to Port of Spain, Trinidad and Tobago, for the Summit of the Americas. President Obama states that, "The United States seeks a new beginning with Cuba."[345]

President Obama also uses the Summit of the Americas as a platform to apologize for America once again, "All of us must now renew the common stake that we have in one another. I know that promises of partnership have gone unfulfilled in the past, and that trust has to be earned over time. While the United States has done much to promote peace and prosperity in the hemisphere, we have at times been disengaged, and at times we sought to dictate our terms. But I pledge to you that we seek an equal partnership. There is no senior partner and junior partner in our relations; there is simply engagement based on mutual respect and common interests and shared values. So I'm here to launch a new chapter of engagement that will be sustained throughout my administration."[346]

Obama politely accepts Hugo Chavez's gift of Eduardo Galeano's *Open Veins of Latin America: Five Centuries of the Pillage of a Continent*, a book that blasts America's influence in the Western Hemisphere.[347] *President Obama has a borderline fetish for playing the "gimp" for Third World leftist dictators.*

Obama politely listens to socialist Nicaraguan President Daniel Ortega's fifty-minute venomous scolding regarding what he called U.S. terrorist aggression against Central America.   President Obama is thankful in his response, "I'm grateful that President Ortega did not blame me for things that happened when I was three months old." *Conversely, does that mean that Obama IS grateful that Daniel Ortega insulted President Kennedy?*[348]

4/19/09

Regarding the Tea Party, David Axelrod says, "I think any time you have severe economic conditions there is always an element of disaffection that can mutate into something that's unhealthy."[349] *In other words, it's "unhealthy" when conservatives peacefully protest liberal policies, BUT "dissent is the highest form of patriotism" when liberals burn flags and protest conservatives.*

Opening the door to bank nationalization, the White House and Treasury Department announce that they may convert their loans to nineteen of the nation's largest banks into common stock.[350]

Chief of Staff Rahm Emanuel states that he does not believe officials from the Bush administration should be prosecuted for their interrogation policies, saying that it is not a "time for retribution."[351]

The State Department's special envoy to the Middle East, George Mitchell, rebukes Prime Minister Netanyahu's demand that the Palestinians recognize the legitimacy of Israel's statehood as a precondition to peace negotiations. The State Department releases a statement that it will continue to promote a two-state solution.[352]

4/20/09

President Obama asks his Cabinet to identify $100 million in budget cuts over the next ninety days, equaling. In other words, he is asking his Cabinet to save one dollar for every $35,000 that the government spends. The President says, "None of these savings by themselves are going to solve our long-term fiscal problems, but taken together, they can make a difference and they send a signal that we are serious about how government operates." President Obama acknowledges that Americans have "got to feel confident that their dollars are being spent wisely and I have every confidence that the team that I put together is going to be able to deliver on that efficiency and productivity in the weeks, months and years to come." How will he close the "confidence gap?" "Line by line, page by page, $100 million there, $100 million here, pretty soon, even in Washington, it adds up to real money."[353] *President Obama's private-sector experience does not even include running a cash register. He won't release his college transcripts (probably for good rea-*

Apr 2009

son); did he ever take a course on economics? He spent most of his "public service" career voting "present." How did this man get elected president?

President Obama asks Congress to fund a $100 billion loan to the IMF.[354]

Former vice president Dick Cheney calls on the White House to declassify additional memos that confirm the success of the Bush administration's interrogation tactics, stating, "I know specifically of reports that I read, that I saw that lay out what we learned throughout the interrogation process and what the consequences were for the country."[355]

Mahmoud Ahmadinejad uses the U.N. platform to attack the U.S. and Israel for racism.[356]

4/21/09

President Obama says he is open to prosecuting Bush administration officials for their anti-terror legal advice.[357]

Obama signs the $5.7 billion Edward M. Kennedy Serve America Act, which will more than triple the size of the AmeriCorps program.[358] *And just the day before he was urging his Cabinet to identify cuts.*

President Obama calls Ahmadinejad's comments at the United Nations "appalling and objectionable."[359]

China displays a "fleet parade" to demonstrate its increasing naval strength.[360]

4/22/09

Obama marks Earth Day calling for a "new era of energy exploration in America."[361] *Incidentally, his Earth Day flights consume over 9,000 gallons of fuel.*[362]

Treasury Secretary Geithner states, "Although this crisis in some ways started in the United States, it is a global crisis." *Is Obama outsourcing some of his apology tour?*[363]

4/23/09

Obama is featured on the cover of *Time* magazine for the thirteenth time in the past year.[364]

Treasury Secretary Geithner says the economic downturn may be easing.[365]

President Obama meets with credit card companies to discuss what he believes to be deceptive practices overwhelming consumers with high debt and high interest rates. The President threatens legislation that will force credit card companies to "act responsibly" and enforcement to make them feel the "full weight" of the law.[366] [367]

The Obama administration announces it will release at least forty-four photographs of terrorist-related interrogations on May 28.[368] *President Obama believes that Gitmo is the number one propaganda recruiting tool for al-Qaeda; yet, his administration is under the impression that these photographs will not be used for terrorist propaganda. Somehow,*

Apr 2009

the same people who are committed to killing us are expected to see these pictures and, instead of being outraged, they will develop a deep respect for the United States as we lay bare our own transgressions.

Thankfully the administration reversed itself on May 12, 2009. This is another pervasive characteristic of Obama's management style: reversing unpopular decisions. One of the unfortunate consequences of making decisions that are reversed then further modified is that it produces uncertainty. One has to wonder how serious the administration is when they make a decision for the first time. Another adverse effect of Obama's ambiguous decision making is that he looks weak and frivolous. It appears to the rest of the world that our Chief Executive is unresolved and his decisions do not carry the weight of authority. No wonder miscreants like Kim Jong Il and Mahmoud Ahmadinejad disregard whatever Barack Obama says.

In testimony before the House Appropriations Committee, Attorney General Eric Holder says he is willing to release as much information as possible about "man-caused disaster" and "overseas contingency operations" interrogations. *Who needs WikiLeaks?*[369]

The White House says it does not support an independent panel to investigate the terror-related interrogation techniques.[370]

Apr 2009

4/24/09

The *New York Post* reports that regulators believe they may have to remove Citigroup CEO Vikram Pandit to demonstrate that Washington is willing to get tough with the banks similar to their actions when they ousted GM's CEO, Rick Wagoner.[371]

President Obama calls for student loan reform, the expansion of Pell Grants and Perkins Loans and the discontinuation of providing government subsidies to banks issuing student loans. 340

During their annual meeting, Credit Suisse's Chairman, Walter Kielholz warns against "excessive state intervention regarding the lending policies of banks or the realignment of their structures could have negative implications for the entire sector."[372]

4/26/09

In his weekly radio address, President Obama remarks that "old habits and stale thinking" will not solve our national problems. "To help build a new foundation for the twenty-first century, we need to reform our government so that it is more efficient, more transparent, and more creative. That will demand new thinking and a new sense of responsibility for every dollar that is spent."[373]

China blames the U.S. dollar for the global financial crisis and calls for reform of the global currency system.[374]

National Security Adviser James Jones tells an unflattering and inappropriate Jewish joke while giving the keynote speech at the Washington Institute for Near East Policy.[375] *I'm sure it's a smash hit at the White House when Jones tells unflattering and inappropriate jokes about blacks. Actually, this fits in with a prevailing attitude of immaturity with this administration. The president throws hissy fits when he doesn't get his way and he cannot tolerate criticism or disagreement. He is "out of*

town" when the Israeli prime minister comes to Washington, and he is
"too tired" to extend basic etiquette to the British prime minister. He is
ill prepared when meeting with Nicolas Sarkozy or General McChrystal.
His Chief of Staff, Rahm Emanuel, routinely has profanity-laced explo-
sions and the president himself fails to sound "tough" when he talks about
"whose ass to kick" on national television. He nominates and appoints
improperly vetted people. He conveniently leaves town while giving Eric
Holder the dirty job of announcing that KSM will be tried in lower Man-
hattan— the list goes on. But, he won't allow the Middle East meltdown
or the Japanese catastrophes to hinder his basketball picks. America's debt
crisis and plunging credit rating will not interfere with his posh vacation
at Martha's Vineyard.

Apr 2009

4/27/09

In order to get a good photo op, Air Force One and two fighter jets fly
low over Manhattan causing chaos, panic, and disruption. The FAA
knew that the incident would cause alarm in New York City but, for
some reason, chose not to inform the general public, the media or public officials. Oh yeah, it only cost the taxpayers $328,835.[376]

"Government Motors": GM offers a proposal that would give the federal government and the United Auto Workers effective control and 89%
ownership of the car company.[377]

The bondholders own $27 billion of GM debt and are receiving 10%
of the common stock; the United Auto Workers Union owns $10 bil-
lion of GM debt and is receiving 40% of common stock.[378] *The UAW's*

campaign contributions yielded a good return on their investment!

President Obama has to interrupt his speech for another teleprompter gaffe while speaking to the Council of Advisors on Science and Technology.[379]

President Obama promises major investment in research technology and scientific innovation, saying the U.S. has fallen behind.[380]

The White House asks Congress to change U.S. law to enable the administration to aid the Hamas-allied Palestinian Authority.[381]

4/28/09

Bloomberg reports a tentative agreement that the United Auto Workers will gain effective control and 55% ownership of Chrysler.[382]

Pennsylvania Senator Arlen Specter switches from the Republican to the Democratic Party.[383]

The Treasury Department forecasts that it will borrow $361 billion in the second quarter, more than double its previous projection. They project they will borrow an addition $515 billion in the third quarter.[384]

4/29/09

At a townhall meeting, Obama says, "We've begun the work of remaking America."[385] *Take note: these are ominous words on par with, "We are five days away from fundamentally transforming the United States of*

Apr 2009

America."

During the current outbreak of swine flu, the P.E. teacher-in-chief instructs America on proper hygiene, "Keep your hands washed, cover your mouth when you cough, stay home from work if you are sick, keep your children home from school if they are sick."[386]

On the eve of Chrysler's Chapter 11 bankruptcy filing, "Car Czar" Steve Rattner commands Chrysler, "We need a deal with Fiat today." Even though Chrysler executives think a GM merger is a better idea, key players on the government's Auto Task Force (*whose experience with the car industry is limited to driving them*) will <u>only</u> consider a deal with Fiat.[387]

President Obama supports a merger with Chrysler and Fiat to make "fuel-efficient, clean-energy cars that'll meet the needs of future markets."[388]

Obama also promises that his Cap & Trade plan doesn't compromise jobs for the environment.[389]

On the issue of immigration, he says America cannot continue with a broken system.[390]

In the Fed's April meeting, some Federal Reserve officials have shown a willingness to purchase more mortgage and T-bill securities than the $1.75 trillion than was originally planned.[391]

President Obama holds his third press conference since taking office. Fox News's Major Garrett is snubbed because Fox chose to run with regularly scheduled programming instead of airing the press conference.[392]

4/30/09

Supreme Court Justice David Souter announces his retirement.[393]

Chrysler files Chapter 11 bankruptcy.

President Obama unveils the Chrysler plan that "offers" bondholders 29 cents on the dollar. Smaller firms object to the meager pittance because they are not as prepared to absorb the loss as the larger institutions that have received $100 billion in bailout funds (JP Morgan Chase, Citigroup, Morgan Stanley, and Goldman Sachs).

Nevertheless, he publicly shames and scolds the smaller firms, "While many stakeholders made sacrifices and worked constructively, I have to tell you some did not. In particular, a group of investment firms and hedge funds decided to hold out for the prospect of an unjustified taxpayer-funded bailout. They were hoping that everybody else would make sacrifices, and they would have to make none.

"I don't stand with them. I stand with Chrysler's employees and their families and communities. I stand with Chrysler's management, its dealers, and its suppliers. I stand with the millions of Americans who own and want to buy Chrysler cars. I don't stand with those who held out when everybody else is making sacrifices." *Actually, it appears that President Obama stands with abandoning the rule of law, fleecing secured*

Apr 2009

creditors and rewarding his political cronies for their generous support and contributions.[394]

Again, China reduces its purchases of U.S. debt.[395]

Private-sector employment fell by 611,000 jobs in April; the public sector added 66,000 jobs (mostly temporary, census-related jobs).[396]

Federal tax revenue plunged 34% this month versus last April.[397]

April unemployment = 8.9%.
Real unemployment = 15.8%.[398]

5/1/09

One day after the President talks about where he stands, Michelle Obama steps out in a pair of $540 Lanvin sneakers.[399]

Amid the H1N1 Flu (a.k.a. "Swine Flu") concern, President Obama says, "And throughout this process, my top priority has been the health and the safety of the American people."[400]

5/2/09

The U.S. Treasury is warning Congress that the $12.1 trillion debt ceiling needs to be raised. In the first six months of the fiscal year the federal deficit is running at $956.8 billion, nearly one-seventh of GDP.

Paying the interest on the national debt is projected to be $172 billion

May 2009

next year. The Congressional Budget Office expects interest payments on the debt to more than quadruple in the next decade to $806 billion by 2019.[401]

Chrysler Deal: Perella Weinberg Partners' attorney, Thomas Lauria, claims that his client "was directly threatened by the White House and in essence compelled to withdraw its opposition to the deal under the threat that the full force of the White House press corps would destroy its reputation if it continued to fight." Perella Weinberg's clients are pension plans, college endowments, retirement plans, and credit unions. Small-firm bondholders are dissatisfied with the Obama administration's "offer" of 29 cents on the dollar because, unlike the larger bondholders (JP Morgan Chase, Citigroup, Morgan Stanley, and Goldman Sachs), they are not receiving $100 billion in bailout funds.[402]

The White House confirms Israel's fear that resolving the Iranian nuclear issue is dependent on progress to an independent Palestinian state.[403]

5/4/09

May 2009

The Obama administration announces that it will implement an aggressive program for cracking down on offshore tax havens, targeting wealthy citizens and many U.S.-based multinational corporations who keep their foreign earnings in offshore banks.[404]

With the second-highest corporate tax rate in the world, U.S. companies prefer to keep their profits in the countries where they make them. President Obama believes imposing a 35% tax on foreign profits will somehow incentivize companies to invest in the U.S. The tax plan has been denounced by the U.S. Chamber of Commerce, the National Foreign Trade Council, and the Business Roundtable.[405] *Perhaps these organizations should advise heftier contributions to the President's campaign war chest. GE manages to make a $14 billion profit without paying 1 cent in taxes. Google manages to pay only 2.4% in taxes.*

Chairman of the Joint Chiefs of Staff, Admiral Michael Mullen, believes that China's military buildup is directed at the United States.[406]

5/5/09

President Obama and Vice President Biden prove they're just a couple of regular guys as they go out for fast food at Ray's Hell Burger.[407]

Again, the White House insists that Israel endorse the creation of an independent Palestinian state. Speaking to the American Israel Public Affairs Committee (AIPAC), President Obama demands that Israel halt construction of Jewish settlements.[408]

5/6/09

An internal Justice Department inquiry concludes that Bush administration officials responsible for drafting interrogation protocols committed serious judgmental errors but should not be prosecuted.[409]

Obama's promise that citizens will be able to track every dime of the $787 billion stimulus package may not be fulfilled. They will try to improve *Recovery.gov* by next spring. Meanwhile, the website does show which programs are being funded but it doesn't reveal which contractors are benefiting from the spending.[410]

5/7/09

President Obama cancels an early morning service and a Catholic prayer breakfast for the National Day of Prayer. Instead, he just signs a proclamation honoring the day.[411]

President Obama proposes that Congress slash spending by a mere $17 billion, including tax breaks to oil and gas companies, while granting him an $81 billion increase for his domestic agenda.[412]

Also on the president's wish list is a doubling of funds the IRS to enforce U.S. tax laws with the goal quadrupling funds for tax enforcement within five years.[413] *In other words, taxpayers have to pay for their own shakedown. The President will claw for every dime he can purloin from the citizens.*

5/8/09

President Obama announces a new plan to turn unemployment insurance into job training, saying, "Our unemployment insurance system should no longer be a safety net, but a stepping stone to a new future."[414]

President Obama threatens to take away $6.8 billion in stimulus money from California unless Governor Schwarzenegger and state lawmakers restore wage cuts to <u>unionized</u> home health care workers. The cuts

May 2009

would save California $74 million.[415] *So, in effect, he is punishing states that try to take fiscally responsible measures.*

GM's restructuring plan includes shipping many jobs overseas.[416]

The Federal Reserve reduces its stress test requirements for nineteen of the nation's largest banks.[417]

After performing "stress tests," financial regulators order ten of the nineteen banks to raise a combined $74.6 billion to cushion themselves in case the economy performs worse than expected and to restore faith in the financial system.[418]

5/9/09

At the White House Correspondents Dinner, Obama says, "Most of you covered me, all of you voted for me…Apologies to the Fox table."[419]

The White House releases the $328,000 photo from its flyover of lower Manhattan.[420] *See entry for 4/27/09.*

Hamas does not approve of a two-state solution according to its politburo chief Khaled Meshal.[421] *They believe in a one-state solution: Palestine.*

5/10/09

Former vice president Dick Cheney accuses the White House of not releasing documents proving that rough interrogation techniques yielded intelligence that saved "perhaps hundreds of thousands" of U.S. lives.[422]

5/11/09

The Obama administration projects that the economy will rebound and grow by a 3.5% annual rate by year's end as a result of the stimulus package.[423]

The White House expects a 2009 budget deficit of $1.84 trillion and a 2010 deficit of $1.26 trillion.[424]

President Obama fires NATO Commander General David McKiernan and replaces him with General Stanley McChrystal.[425]

"I will not rest until the dream of health care reform is finally achieved in the United States of America."[426]

5/12/09

While the federal government is borrowing 43 cents of every dollar it spends and 6.35 million people are receiving unemployment...the government is hiring! The executive branch alone is set to increase by 15.6% in 2010 (excluding the Postal Service and Defense Department). The average pay per federal worker will also increase from $72,800 in 2008 to $75,419 in 2010.[427]

The Food and Drug Administration (FDA) slaps General Mills for advertising Cheerios could lower cholesterol 10% which, the government says, would make the breakfast cereal a drug in need of stiffer regulation.[428]

The Obama administration is steeped in serious talks about how it can regulate salaries and compensation across all of the financial industry, regardless of whether the companies received federal bailout money.[429]

The Treasury Department's auto industry task force denies Chrysler's request to spend $134 million in advertising. The Obama administration, which professes it is not interested in managing car companies, is only allowing Chrysler to spend half the amount.[430]

General Motors and Chrysler estimate they may close as many as 3,000 car dealerships.[431]

In a stunning reversal of its previous promise to release forty-four photos of detainees being tortured and interrogated, the Obama administration is now seeking to block their release.[432] *President Obama's policies are often the equivalent of playing checkers with himself. A common theme of his administration is announcing policies that are reversed several times. See entry for 4/23/09.*

May 2009

5/14/09

At a townhall meeting in New Mexico, President Obama denounces credit card companies as dishonest for "all kinds of harsh penalties and fees that you never knew about."[433]

He also calls the budget deficit unsustainable and warns of higher interest rates if the U.S. continues on the path of relying on foreign countries to subsidize its debt. President Obama berates, "We can't keep on just borrowing from China…we have to pay interest on that debt, and that means we are mortgaging our children's future with more and more debt."

President Obama did not discuss his revised 2009 and 2010 budgets of $1.84 trillion (up 5%) and 1.26 trillion (up 7.4%), respectively. While lecturing on the evils of wasteful spending, apparently he was in no mood to lecture about why he is seeking an additional $81 billion for his domestic agenda.[434] *"The problem is, is that the way Bush has done it over the last eight years is to take out a credit card from the Bank of China in the name of our children, driving up our national debt from $5 trillion for the first 42 presidents – #43 added $4 trillion by his lonesome, so that we now have over $9 trillion of debt that we are going to have to pay back – $30,000 for every man, woman and child. That's irresponsible. It's unpatriotic." –Candidate Barack Obama. By his own words, the president is more than twice as "irresponsible" and "unpatriotic" than President Bush.*

Chrysler notifies dealers that it will eliminate 25% of its retail showrooms.[435]

Obama warns Netanyahu not to take any actions against Iran without his authority.[436]

May 2009

5/15/10

The Department of Justice moves to dismiss the New Black Panthers voter intimidation case. *See entry for 4/17/09. The Department of Jus-*

tice has already won the case. Why would the Obama administration want to dismiss a case they already won?

GM announces that it will be dropping 40% of its 6,000 dealers.[437]

President Obama reversed another campaign pledge against trying "man-caused disaster" suspects in civilian court in favor of restoring the Bush administration's military commissions.[438]

5/16/10

Israeli Prime Minister Benjamin Netanyahu arrives in Washington D.C. His top priority is halting Iran's nuclear program.[439]

5/17/09

President Obama gives the commencement address at University of Notre Dame. *Many Catholics believe it is an insult for President Obama to give the commencement at Notre Dame. His views on abortion and embryonic stem cell research oppose Catholic doctrine.*

5/18/09

In the wake of disparaging remarks about Las Vegas, the President dismisses meeting with Nevada Governor Jim Gibbons. Governor Gibbons says, "I am disappointed at the hypocrisy shown by this administration. President Obama is coming to Las Vegas later this month for a political fundraiser, but he will not help the struggling families in Las

Vegas and Nevada who are out of work because of his reckless comments."[440]

Lieutenant General Keith Dayton is the U.S. "security coordinator" responsible for training 1,500 Palestinian military personnel for "immediate deployment." The West Bank Training Initiative will instruct soldiers in logistics, leadership, first aid, maintenance, English, battalion staff training, and driver education.

The U.S. hopes that the Palestinian Authority troops will be trained to fight Hamas. *Oddly enough, the Palestinian Authority and Hamas are currently negotiating an alliance.*[441]

As part of his diplomatic outreach, Obama says he expects serious progress in negotiations with Iran about halting its nuclear program. In light of the attention and respect the Iranian regime has publicly shown President Obama, it is doubtful that they will "unclench their fist" and curb their uranium enrichment, centrifuge or ballistic missile programs.[442]

Brazil and China agree to use their own currencies in all trade transactions instead of using the dollar.[443]

President Obama dictates to Israeli Prime Minister Netanyahu that he must cease building Jewish settlements and seize the "historic opportunity" of peace with the Palestinians.[444]

May 2009

5/19/09

The White House announces its far-reaching fuel-economy emissions initiative for automobiles. It will require 2016 models to get approximately 35.5 miles per gallon. The measure will cost consumers an extra $1,300 per vehicle.[445] [446] *In August 2011, Obama announced he was jacking up fuel efficiency standards to 54.5 miles per gallon by 2025.*

Hamas fires two rockets into Israel.[447]

5/20/09

The White House has started producing its own media and even has its own logo. It gives them the opportunity to conduct interviews, produce, edit and release their own information. *No pesky reporters are allowed in Obama's state-run media!*[448]

Three Indiana pension funds audaciously assert that they have actual legal rights as creditors in Chrysler's Chapter 11. They argue that they are secured creditors and beg for the rule of law to apply.[449]

Amid the president's commanding attitude toward Israeli domestic policy and Hamas's firing two rockets into Israel, Iran test-fires a missile capable of striking Israel. Israelis have dismissed Obama's call to stop building Jewish settlements saying the Palestinians needed to "halt terror first."[450] *Perhaps Israelis should heed DHS Secretary Napolitano's advice and use the term "man-caused disaster;" it would show that they're "not playing into the politics of fear."*

May 2009

5/21/09

Transportation Secretary, Ray LaHood, promotes "a way to <u>coerce</u> people out of their cars." Having joined a "transformational admin-istration" LaHood reports, "I think we can change people's behavior." His transformational transportational vision for America includes "liv-able communities" with trains, busses, bike paths, and walking paths.[451] *This illustrates how out of touch the Obama administration is. They see America as a game of Sim City. Americans are just chess pieces (mostly pawns) to be moved about the board in a game they believe that only the elites are smart enough to win.*

Congressional Democrats deny President Obama the funds needed to close Gitmo. Congress requires that the he provide a <u>detailed</u> plan of what is to be done with the prisoners. So far, the White House is saying that some of them will be tried by military commissions, some will be tried in civilian courts, some will be imprisoned in the U.S. and others will be transferred overseas. President Obama still maintains that our actions at Guantanamo "set back the moral authority that is America's strongest currency in the world."

Former vice president Dick Cheney quipped that the president's policy was "recklessness cloaked in righteousness and would make the American people less safe."[452]

Three months after the bill was signed, *Recovery.gov* still lacks detail and transparency.[453]

5/22/09

President Obama uses the U.S. Naval Academy commencement ceremony as a platform to alter the entire legal framework of anti-terror policies.[454]

President Obama signs into law sweeping reforms of the credit card industry. The new law regulates interest rate increases, late fees, penalties and marketing to consumers under the age of 21.[455]

North Korea prepares to test-fire short-range missiles.[456]

5/24/09

British financial companies are wary of taking on American clients if Obama succeeds with his international tax plans. President Obama's mania for sniffing-out and hunting down every penny of U.S. currency around the globe is having its intended effect of unnerving financial institutions. British bankers believe that the possible legal detriment and the hassle of collecting American taxes is prohibitive. One executive at a large British bank notes, "It's just about manageable under the current system—and that's because we're big. The danger to us is suddenly being hauled over the coals by the IRS for a client that hasn't paid proper taxes. The audit costs will soar. We'll have to pay it but I know plenty of smaller players won't."[457]

Israel's Prime Minister Netanyahu disregards Obama's demand for a settlement freeze.[458]

May 2009

5/25/09

President Obama is welshing, yet again, on his campaign pledge to post bills on the White House website for five days before signing them into law. Last week he signed four bills into law without posting them for more than a day or two.[459]

Iran slaps President Obama's "diplomatic hand" and plans to continue with its nuclear plans. Meanwhile, Iran has deployed six warships into international waters to demonstrate its ability to strangle 40 percent of the world's oil shipping if attacked over its nuclear program.[460] [461] *"Those who bite the hand that feeds them are just as likely to lick the boot that kicks them." —Eric Hoffer*

North Korea successfully tests a nuclear bomb as powerful as Hiroshima less than two months after test firing long-range ballistic missiles. Obama tells reporters, "The United States and the international community must take action in response...We will work with our friends and allies to stand up to this behavior."[462] [463]

5/26/09

President Obama nominates Sonia Sotomayor to the Supreme Court. Sotomayor has said, "I would hope that a wise Latina woman with the richness of her experiences would more often than not reach a better conclusion than a white male who hasn't lived that life."

The nominee believes that terror suspects captured on the battlefield must receive all rights afforded to American citizens under the

Constitution. Those rights do not apply to gun ownership; Judge Sotomayor flatly rejects that the 2nd Amendment protects an individual's right to bear arms.

In a 1999 interview, the La Raza member lamented that America "may never truly be fixed. Racism and economic warfare still crush the dreams of countless second-class citizens. The unfair dimensions of our culture are staggering. You cannot succeed if you are born poor; you simply cannot."[464] [465] [466]

Chrysler applies to the Department of Energy for $448 million to research and develop electric cars.[467]

Concern mounts over the partisanship of the Obama administration's Chrysler car dealership closings. Car dealers who contributed millions of dollars to Republican campaigns are having their dealerships shut down while only one car dealer who contributed to the President's campaign has been closed.

Democratic party insider and former Clinton aide, Mack McClarty, owns a string of dealerships throughout Arkansas and Missouri. None of his dealerships have been closed; yet, suspiciously, several of his competitors have been eliminated.

After deposing Chrysler executives, attorney Leonard Bellavia, who represents a group of Chrysler dealerships, says, "It became clear to us that Chrysler does not see the wisdom of terminating 25% of its dealers. It really wasn't Chrysler's decision. They are under enormous pressure from the President's automotive task force."

Adding to the controversy is the fact that "Car Czar" Steve Rattner is married to Democratic fundraiser Maureen White, the former national finance chairman of the Democratic National Committee.[468]

President Obama is set to name a "Cyber Czar" to ensure cyber security with a particular concern for cyber threats coming from Chinese and Russian cyber-spies.[469]

5/27/09

Prior to President Obama's meeting with Palestinian Authority President Mahmoud Abbas, Secretary of State Hillary Clinton proclaims that Israeli settlement construction must stop.[470]

Richard Fisher, president of the Dallas Federal Reserve Bank, says that China is alarmed by U.S. fiscal and monetary policy and warns the Fed about printing money.[471]

5/28/09

A Justice Department spokesman announces that claims were dropped in the New Black Panther voter intimidation case after "a careful assessment of the facts and the law." Two of the defendants were completely dismissed from the lawsuit with no penalty while the third is simply prohibited from bringing weapons to polling places in future elections.[472]

The hardest hit states are receiving the least stimulus cash. More than three months after the bill was passed into law, the administration has dispensed a measly $4 billion of the $787 billion to states. So far, Michigan has received only $2 million in stimulus funds.[473]

The federal government stands to own more than 70% of the new GM, with the United Auto Workers Union owning 20%.[474]

The President urges Congress to pass health care legislation by the end of the year or the opportunity will be lost.[475]

The White House welcomes Palestinian Authority President Mahmoud Abbas with a renewed demand that Israel stop building Jewish settlements.[476]

Russia is taking security measures against its emboldened nuclear neighbor, North Korea.[477]

5/29/09

May 2009

Reality Check: *Pravda* publishes an article lamenting the death of American capitalism and descent into Marxism.[478] *Pravda was the official newspaper of the Soviet Union.*

President Obama serves more cookies for his cronies who contributed generously to his campaign, bestowing Ambassadorships to the U.K, the Vatican, Ireland, Japan, France, and other exotic locales.[479]

With regard to hurricanes, Obama says, "Our **top priority** is ensuring the public safety. That means appropriate sheltering in place or if necessary, getting as many people as possible out of harm's way prior to landfall."[480]

Bond traders all over the world are underwhelmed by Barack Obama's quadrupling of the budget deficit as their trades drive up yields on U.S. debt.[481]

North Korea launches a new type of short-range, land-to-air missile.[482]

5/30/09

The President and First Lady have "date night," flying to New York City for fine dining and theater.[483]

President Obama supports the troops and their families, "These military families are heroes too. And they are a **top priority** of Michelle and me. And they will always have our support."[484]

President Obama will offer a "personal commitment" to the Islamic world in a much-anticipated speech in Egypt next week.[485]

Obama tells the Palestinian Authority that he foresees a two-state solution with Jerusalem as the capitol of Palestine.[486]

The FBI arrests four men for plotting to blow up Bronx synagogues and using anti-aircraft weaponry to attack military aircraft.[487]

5/31/09

The *New York Times* unveils thirty-one-year-old Brian Deese as the man in charge of reorganizing GM. Mr. Deese is not an economist, has no business background and no experience with the automotive industry.[488] *Maybe he'll run for President some day.*

Treasury Secretary Timothy Geithner *literally* becomes the laughing stock of China as an audience at Peking University laughs when he says that he believes in a strong dollar and that "Chinese financial assets are very safe."[489]

Venezuela has recently purchased Russian shoulder-fired anti-aircraft missiles. Officials are concerned that Venezuela may be collaborating with Colombian FARC terrorists.[490]

May unemployment = 9.4%.
Real unemployment = 16.4%.[491]
Washington D.C.'s unemployment = 5.6%.[492]

6/1/09

President Obama states that the United States cannot impose its values on other countries.[493] *Unless, of course, those countries wish to enforce their own banking laws or build settlements within their own borders.*

In an interview with French Canal Plus network, the President states that the U.S. is one of the largest Muslim countries in the world.[494] *President Obama is correct, as long as you don't include Afghanistan, Albania, Algeria, Azerbaijan, Bangladesh, Burkina Faso, Cameroon, Chad, China, Egypt, Ethiopia, France, Germany, Ghana, Guinea, India, Indonesia, Iran, Iraq, Ivory Coast, Jordan, Kazakhstan, Kenya, Kuwait, Kyrgyzstan, Lebanon, Libya, Malaysia, Mali, Mauritania, Morocco, Mozambique,*

Niger, Nigeria, Oman, Pakistan, Palestinian territories, Philippines, Russia, Saudi Arabia, Senegal, Somalia, Sudan, Syria, Tajikistan, Tanzania, Thailand, Tunisia, Turkey, Turkmenistan, Uganda, United Arab Emirates, Uzbekistan, and Yemen.

Islamic terrorist, Abdulhakim Muhammad, shoots two soldiers at an Army recruiting station in Little Rock, Arkansas. One is killed, the other is critically wounded.[495]

6/2/09

GM files Chapter 11 bankruptcy.

The United Auto Workers (UAW) will get a higher stake in the new GM than other bondholders.[496]

GM plans to close fourteen plants by 2012 and lay off 21,000 workers before the end of 2011.[497]

The *Wall Street Journal* reports that the U.S. government will own 60% of the new GM and restructuring it will cost $30 billion, notwithstanding the $20 billion already dumped into the company.[498]

Amid fears that political decisions will interfere with shrewd business decisions regarding the new car company, the President states, "The federal government will refrain from exercising its rights as a shareholder in all but the most fundamental corporate decisions. When a difficult decision has to be made on matters like where to open a new plant or what type of new car to make, the new GM, not the United

States government, will make that decision."[499]

Hugo Chavez exults, "Hey, Obama has just nationalized nothing more and nothing less than General Motors. Comrade Obama! Fidel, careful or we are going to end up to his right."[500]

Timothy Geithner says that China has expressed "justifiable confidence in the strength and resilience and dynamism of the American economy" and that there is absolutely "no risk" of monetizing our debt.[501] *Does anyone have moral qualms with America's indebtedness to China? The federal government is subsidizing its gluttonous appetite with money borrowed from a country that is built on de facto slavery.*

6/3/09

Fed Chairman Ben Bernanke asserts that our budget deficits threaten our financial stability and cannot continue indefinitely. "Unless we demonstrate a strong commitment to fiscal sustainability in the longer term, we will have neither financial stability nor healthy economic growth," he says.[502]

The White House insists that at least ten members of the Muslim Brotherhood be allowed to attend Obama's speech in Cairo. The organization supports the violent destruction of Israel and has direct links to Hamas.[503] *The Muslim Brotherhood's motto is, "Allah is our objective; the prophet is our leader; the Koran is our law; jihad is our way; dying in the way of Allah is our highest hope."*

Hasan al-Banna, founder of the Muslim Brotherhood, wrote, "It is the nature of Islam to dominate, not to be dominated, to impose its law on all nations, and to extend its power to the entire planet."

The Brotherhood has stated its objective: "Grand Jihad in eliminating and destroying western civilization from within and sabotaging its miserable house by their hands and the hands of their believers so that it is eliminated."

Was the White House unaware of the history of the Muslim Brotherhood? Were they just "winging it" as they did with vetting Van Jones and all of their Executive Branch nominees. If the administration does this little research on the Muslim Brotherhood, how unprepared are they when negotiating at the G-20 or with Russia, China, Brazil, etc.?

Officials discover an al-Qaeda video proposing to smuggle biological weapons into the U.S. through the Mexican border.[504]

6/4/09

Government spending on benefits will skyrocket beyond $2 trillion in 2009. The main contributors to the increased spending are unemployment insurance, social security and a record jump in food stamps.[505] *President Obama and the Democrats fail to understand that they cannot take capital out of the private sector and expect to create wealth.*

Microsoft's CEO Steve Ballmer says his company would have to move jobs overseas if President Obama's tax plan is imposed. Ballmer estimates Obama's plan would cause a 10–15 percent drag on the Dow.[506]

President Obama calls for "a new beginning" in a much-anticipated speech in Cairo, Egypt directed to more than 1 billion Muslims.[507] *The Muslim world must be as puzzled by his obsequious overtures as Americans are. If Obama insists that Islam has been hijacked by a teeny-weenie fraction of terrorists, then why does he feel the need to appeal to the entire Muslim faith? The fact that there are crazed abortion clinic bombers or lunatics from Westboro Baptist Church does not merit an outreach to all of Christendom; in fact, he is willing to cover up Christian symbols when speaking at a Catholic university. How well would it be received if the President insisted that all references to Islam be covered?*

Iran's Ayatollah Ali Khamenei states that Islam's hatred for the U.S. cannot be damped by Obama's "sweet talk" and "slogans." The Ayatollah adds that Israel is "a cancerous tumor in the heart" of the Muslim world.[508]

In a released tape, Osama bin Laden declares, "We either live under the light of Islam or we die with dignity…Brace yourselves for a long war against the world's infidels and their agents."[509]

Germans question whether the President is snubbing them. After his speech in Cairo, he scheduled a short visit to Dresden and Buchenwald, but he is avoiding a trip to Berlin. The U.S. has yet to appoint an ambassador to handle U.S./German interests. German officials were further dismayed when a low-level American administrator was sent to advise and assist with matters concerning GM's bankruptcy. GM's subsidiary, Opel, is a major car manufacturer in Germany and the bankruptcy will have a considerable effect on their economy.[510] [511]

131

6/5/09

Anita Dunn, White House communications director, tells a group of high school students at St. Andrews Episcopal School that one of her two favorite political philosophers is Communist leader Mao Tse Tung, history's greatest mass murderer.[512] *I guess Hitler probably ranks third.*

Since passing the stimulus, the Obama administration has been busy promoting it across the country. Fifty-two of the sixty-six events have been located in states that Obama won in the election.[513]

Four ACORN workers will face a voter fraud trial in Pennsylvania.[514]

President Obama snubs President Sarkozy of France by declining a dinner invitation celebrating the sixty-fifth anniversary of D-Day.[515]

6/6/09

President Obama salutes 9,000 D-Day veterans at Normandy.[516]

6/7/09

To pay for his health care legislation, the President encourages Congress to consider cutting tax exemptions for the wealthiest brackets instead of a broad-based tax.[517]

King Abdullah of Saudi Arabia tells President Obama, "We want from you a serious participation to solve the Palestinian issue and impose the solution if necessary."[518]

President Obama denies all rumors that he is snubbing France or Germany.[519]

6/8/09

With the highest unemployment rate in twenty-five years, the Obama administration believes America's economic situation is worse than previously predicted. *That's another way to blame Bush. Eventually, he will work their way back to blaming Presidents Calvin Coolidge, Grover Cleveland, and William Henry Harrison.*[520]

President Obama wishes to project an image of fiscal responsibility by encouraging Congress to pass "pay as you go" legislation that would prohibit spending increases in some programs without corresponding cuts in other programs.[521]

The $100 billion war-funding bill is swollen with unnecessary, unrelated and unrequested items. The bill contains $4 billion for swine flu treatment and $5 billion to ensure credit for the IMF. The bill also contains expensive equipment not requested by the Pentagon, but is useful for protecting jobs in some lawmakers' districts.[522]

North Korea sentences two American journalists to twelve years of hard labor for "grave crimes." In response, Secretary of State Clinton says that Washington is considering putting North Korea back on the list of states that sponsor terror.[523]

The head of China's largest bank believes the U.S. government should start issuing its debt instruments denominated in Chinese yuan.[524]

6/9/09

Stimulus funds favor large, multinational corporations over local contractors. The government bestows contracts by a process called IDIQ, which skews in favor of large companies. "It's essentially and all-you-can-eat money buffet for big corporations." The General Services Administration defends their actions of granting money to large companies who have IDIQ already in place because the money must move fast in order to stimulate the economy.[525]

North Korea threatens to launch a nuclear "merciless offensive" if sufficiently provoked by "those who touch the country's dignity and sovereignty even a bit."[526]

6/10/09

President Obama himself ousts AmeriCorps Inspector General Gerald Walpin for investigating an Obama-supporting crony who misused $850,000 of grant money. The White House Counsel's office called Walpin on his cell phone and told him he had an hour to resign or he would be fired.[527]

The Reverend Jeremiah Wright says, "Them Jews ain't going to let him talk to me. I told my baby daughter that he'll talk to me in five years when he's a lame duck, or in eight years when he's out of office...They will not let him talk to somebody who calls a spade what it is...I said from the beginning: he's a politician; I'm a pastor. He's got to do what politicians do."[528]

The White House appoints Kenneth Feinberg as "Pay Czar," "Special Master for Compensation" or "Compensation Czar" (*whichever title you prefer*) to oversee payment guidelines of bailout funds.[529]

Citigroup will be converting a large sum of preferred shares into common equity shares, giving the federal government 34% ownership of the bank.[530]

Russia declines the U.S.'s offer to collaborate on a missile defense shield system to contain the threat of Iran. Russia's Foreign Ministry spokesman says, "Only a rejection by the United States of plans to create a … missile defense system in Europe could lay the groundwork for our fully fledged dialogue on questions of cooperation in reacting to potential missile risks."[531]

Russia announces it may swap holding U.S. debt in favor of holding IMF debt.[532]

6/11/09

Jun 2009

The IRS proposes that a special tax can be levied on company-issued cell phones as a "fringe benefit."[533]

The federal government orders five banks to freeze $30 million of the accounts of 27,000 online poker players.[534]

Senators Lindsey Graham, Joe Lieberman and John McCain urge President Obama to classify torture photos to bar their release from a Freedom of Information Act request from the ACLU.[535]

North Korea and Iran have joined forces to build ballistic missiles.[536]

6/12/09

Obama launches a plan to protect oceans, coastlines and the Great Lakes from the effects of climate change, pollution, and overfishing.[537]

In response to U.N. sanctions, North Korea says it will begin uranium enrichment and weaponize its plutonium.[538]

Two Japanese men with mafia ties are stopped at the Swiss/Italian border in possession of $134 billion of fake U.S. bonds.[539] [540]

Ahmadinejad is controversially re-elected as Iran's president.

President Obama says he is hopeful that the presidential debates in Iran would ultimately improve their readiness to negotiate with the U.S.[541]

6/13/09

The U.S. demands that North Korea stop its provocative stance and return to the six-party talks regarding its nuclear program.[542]

6/14/09

Vice President Joe Biden remains cheerful about the results of the stimulus. "The bottom line is that jobs are being created that would not have been there before...Can I claim credit that all of that's due to the recovery package? No. But it clearly has had an impact." *Well, clearly it has had an impact, for instance, every other nation on Earth has lost faith in the stability of our currency.*[543]

Violence erupts in the streets of Iran as Mirhossein Mousavi, who lost the Iranian election, disputed the election result.

The Obama administration maintains it will continue negotiations with Iran despite the questionable election results. Vice President Biden says the U.S. must continue as if Ahmadinejad won the election.[544]

BBC says its broadcast signals covering the election in Iran are being jammed.[545]

Israeli Prime Minister Netanyahu grudgingly accepts the establishment of a Palestinian state subject to conditions that Israel will continue to build Jewish settlements in the West Bank and keep a united Jerusalem.[546]

6/15/09

President Obama breaks yet another campaign pledge, this time at the expense of gay rights groups, by supporting the Defense of Marriage Act.[547]

Market analyst Robert Prechter says the U.S. is dangerously close to losing its AAA bond rating.[548]

The United Kingdom is outraged upon discovering that the United States shipped four Uighur prisoners from Guantanamo Bay to Bermuda without notifying the British government. British officials consider the action a direct slap to the "special relationship" the U.S and the U.K have shared. Said one official, "The Americans were fully aware of the foreign policy understanding we have with Bermuda and they deliberately chose to ignore it. This is not the kind of behavior one expects from an ally."[549]

The U.S. government is threatening British banks that have American customers. Americans who use Lloyd's Bank are told their bank has "no choice" but to "cease acting as your investment manager." The Bank of Scotland's management is informed that U.S. regulations disqualify them from servicing Americans' accounts.

The bankers say that it is inexpedient to open themselves up to the legal liability and administrative burden of collecting taxes on behalf of the United States. They have better things to do than trying to unravel our impossible-to-understand tax code. *Remember, on June 1, 2009, Obama said we cannot impose our values on other countries...unless we're trampling on other countries' banking laws to control our citizens and fund the public chest.*[550]

Amid calls for more protests in Iran, President Obama says he is "deeply troubled" by the government's violence against the protesters. "The democratic process, free speech, the ability of people to peacefully dis-

Jun 2009

sent—all those are universal values and need to be respected." Of the Iranian demonstrators, he says, "The world is watching and inspired by their participation, regardless of what the ultimate outcome of the election was." Nevertheless, he maintains that "tough, direct dialogue" will continue with Iran.[551] [552]

6/16/09

President Obama tries to soothe criticism from both parties over the illegal firing of Inspector General Gerald Walpin. The White House Special Counsel writes to Senate leaders that Walpin was not mentally fit to serve the office, alleging that in meetings Walpin was "confused... disoriented...unduly disruptive" and showed a "lack of candor."[553]

President Obama is proposing a financial plan that will give the government broad powers to regulate and even seize companies whose failure may disrupt the financial markets. One section of his proposal calls for a "resolution regime" for "non-bank financial firms," giving it "broad powers to take action with respect to the financial firm including the authority to take control of the operations of the firm or to sell or transfer all or any part of the assets of the firm."[554] [555]

Obama is "confident" that robust growth of the economy will prevent tax increases. He also repeats his promise to cut the budget deficit by half at the end of his first term.[556]

President Obama tells CNBC that his government is not overregulating the economy. "What we're trying to do is increase transparency and

Jun 2009

openness," he says. *No one is really sure what he means by "transparent" since he refuses to disclose the White House visitor lists, despite two rulings from a federal judge. What he means is that he wants everyone else to be transparent. Incidentally, on January 18, 2011, the President wrote an op-ed for the* Wall Street Journal *admitting that the regulatory environment is too burdensome.*[557] [558]

ABC agrees to be the White House's propaganda wing for the night of June 24, 2009, by broadcasting its nightly news program from the White House to promote government run health care.[559]

Obama attacks Fox News, "I've got one television station that is entirely devoted to attacking my administration."[560] *Obama may be the most thin-skinned president in the history of the Republic. Generally, people who have fragile egos are sensitive for a bloody good reason.*

After their meeting today, Brazil, Russia, India and China call for the end of the dollar as the global reserve currency.[561]

The Pentagon says North Korea will eventually be able to produce weapons that could reach the U.S. mainland.[562]

Iranian authorities are restraining all foreign journalists from reporting from the scenes of protests.[563]

The President believes that Iran should pick its own leaders but repeats his "deep concerns" about unrest; yet, he does not want the U.S. to be seen as "meddling" and worries "when I see violence directed at peaceful protesters, when I see peaceful protest being suppressed."[564] [565] *He doesn't seem to mind "meddling" in Switzerland's right to determine its own banking laws, or in the internal affairs of Israel. This statement is about the furthest Obama, the putative leader of the free world, has strayed from appeasing Iran.*

6/17/09

Gerald Walpin responds emphatically to the White House's letter concerning his fitness to serve: "That's a total lie."[566]

ABC refuses to allow paid-for opposition ads during their news broadcast at the White House promoting Obamacare.[567]

President Obama extends some benefits to same-sex partners.[568]

China is reducing its U.S. Treasury holdings.[569]

6/18/09

The U.S. Treasury announces it will auction a record $104 billion of debt next week.[570]

6/19/09

Obama proposes the creation of an Office of National Insurance to monitor the industry.[571]

Nineteen ambassador nominees' fundraising efforts raised $4.8 million for the president's campaign and inauguration.[572]

Gay rights groups are disgusted that Obama did not give them the same comprehensive rights as others such as comprehensive health care.[573]

The U.S. fortifies Hawaii from a potential North Korean threat.[574]

6/20/09

Post-election protests and violence continues in Iran as police use water cannons, bullets, and brute force to suppress protesters. President Obama takes a hard line by asking them to please stop.[575]

6/21/09

North Korea accuses Obama of plotting nuclear war.[576]

6/22/09

State welfare rolls dramatically increase as unemployment insurance runs out.[577]

Goldman Sachs makes a record bonus payout.[578]

With the ringing endorsement of AARP, Obama announces that pharmaceutical companies will contribute $80 billion over the next decade to help his health care agenda.[579]

Iran begins air force exercises over the Persian Gulf and Gulf of Oman.[580]

Jun 2009

Al-Qaeda says, given the chance, they would use Pakistan's nuclear weapons.[581]

6/23/09

President Obama signs an executive order establishing a White House Council on Automotive Communities and Workers, to aid the transition of auto workers into training for the "green economy" building solar panels, wind turbines and biotech products.[582]

The President signs a bill extending unemployment benefits to those who have been out of work for six or more months.[583]

At his fourth White House news conference, President Obama practices a little stagecraft using planted questioners. Nico Pitney of the *Huffington Post* was asked to pose a question about Iran. Obama responds, "I strongly condemn these unjust actions, and I join with the American people in mourning each and every innocent life that is lost."[584] [585] *How "free" is the press if he gets to cherry pick the questions?*

Of his health care proposal Obama says, "This is legislation that will be paid for. It will not add to our deficits over the next decade. We will find the money through savings and efficiencies within the health care system."[586]

To bolster investment and research into fuel-efficient and electric cars, Ford Motor Company will be receiving a technology loan of $5.9 billion, Nissan will receive $1.6 billion and small manufacturer, Tesla, will

Jun 2009

receive $465 million.[587]

The Senate chooses not to pursue the Waxman-Markey "Cap & Trade" bill.[588]

The Pentagon approves the creation of Cyber Command that will oversee efforts to protect military computer networks.[589]

Russia and Venezuela sign a $4 billion bank deal. Putin says, "We are moving to a high level of political and economic cooperation."[590]

6/24/09

The Supplemental Appropriations Act containing "Cash for Clunkers" is signed into law.

President Obama's ABC network primetime special was nothing more than a cheerleading op for health care reform, shedding no new light on the subject.[591]

Against the background of its own budget crisis, California is poised to issue IOUs in lieu of payments and paychecks.[592]

The House Financial Services Committee has asked Fannie and Freddie to relax rules regarding condo sales.[593]

The European Central Bank has increased $622 billion of money supply into euro-zone money markets.[594]

Jun 2009

6/25/09

President Obama, Nancy Pelosi, and Rahm Emanuel busily try to lobby undecided House votes for the Cap & Trade legislation.[595]

6/26/09

The Senate is proposing a tax on "gold-plated" or "Cadillac" health insurance plans from which, of course, union benefits would be exempt.[596]

The House Passes the Cap & Trade Climate bill, 219–212.

Far leftist President Manuel Zelaya of Honduras flouts the Honduran Constitution by trying to hold an upcoming national referendum paving the way for his unconstitutional re-election. Honduras's Supreme Court, legislature and human rights ombudsman have all declared Zelaya's move illegal.[597]

6/27/09

Iran's Ahmadinejad promises to make the U.S. regret criticism of Iran's post-election crackdown, citing it as proof of the Obama administration's insincerity for requesting frank dialogue.[598]

6/28/09

President Obama announces new standards for light bulbs. Yes, light bulbs. He says, "I know light bulbs may not seem sexy (*how presiden-*

Jun 2009

tial), but this simple action holds enormous promise because 7 percent of all the energy consumed in America is used to light our homes and businesses."[599]

In a military coup, Honduran President Zelaya has been exiled to Costa Rica. Hugo Chavez blames the "Yankee Empire" for Zelaya's expulsion, but the State Department says it still recognizes Zelaya as the legitimate president of Honduras.[600] [601]

President Obama calls the "coup" illegal and pledges to work to restore Zelaya to power (so much for not "meddling" in other countries' affairs).[602] Hillary Clinton and other extreme leftists, including Cuba's Fidel Castro, Venezuela's Hugo Chavez, Nicaragua's Daniel Ortega and Bolivia's Evo Morales, are trying to pressure Honduras's interim government to restore Zelaya to his authoritarian power (*you may know them by the company they keep*).[603] *It is ironic that the Obama administration refrained from taking a strong and immediate public position on the Iranian election crisis in light their active support of the Zelaya regime in Honduras. In both cases, their action or inaction is biased in favor of greater state power.*

6/29/09

Swiss banks are closing Americans' bank accounts. They no longer want to deal with the Obama administration's aggressive onslaught.[604]

6/30/09

Russian Prime Minister Vladimir Putin says that if the U.S. wants to improve relations with Russia, it needs to stop its plans for a European missile defense shield.[605]

The June mortgage delinquency rate hits an all-time high.[606]

The economy loses 467,000 jobs this month.[607]

June budget deficit totals $94.32 billion.[608]

June unemployment = 9.5%.
Real unemployment = 16.5%.[609]

7/1/09

The Department of Justice continues to insist that Switzerland break its own laws and comply with the U.S. tax code. The Swiss believe any exchange of information should be handled through diplomacy.[610]

The Treasury Department gives $135 million to Central Pacific Financial, a small bank that doesn't meet the bailout criteria. Central Pacific was founded by Senator Daniel Inouye (D-HI) and is the bulk of his personal wealth.[611]

California may need to close six state parks to help balance its budget; the federal government is threatening to take them.[612]

7/2/09

In response to unemployment hitting a twenty-six-year high, President

Obama says, "It took us years to get into this mess, and it will take more than a few months to get us out."[613]

Since 2001, spending has tripled for Congressional travel overseas. It has increased tenfold since 1995.[614]

The Marines launch the first large-scale test of the new counterinsurgency strategy in Afghanistan.[615]

North Korea test-fires four more short-range missiles.[616]

Anticipating talks with Russia, President Obama shows poor judgment in his condescending remarks that Prime Minister Vladimir Putin needs to "understand that the Cold War approach to U.S./Russian relationship is outdated" and that Putin has "one foot in the old ways of doing business."[617]

Prime Minister Putin's spokesman acidly replies, "I see that he does not possess full information. After visiting Moscow, President Obama will know the realities better."[618]

7/4/09

North Korea test-fires seven more short-range missiles.[619]

A cyber-attack compromises South Korea and the U.S. Treasury Department, Secret Service, Federal Trade Commission and Transportation Department for several days.[620]

7/5/09

India joins the chorus of nations questioning the dollar's legitimacy as a global reserve currency.[621] *International pressure to scrap the dollar continues to intensify and the President will not even acknowledge it. North Korea, Iran and Venezuela treat Obama with complete disrespect. Russia, China and just about everyone else sees him as a pushover. Vice President Biden promised that by this point in his presidency Obama would be challenged internationally. It appears that the world views him as a frail and effete leader.*

President Medvedev of Russia insists that the U.S. compromise its European defense shield if the Americans wish to move forward with nuclear negotiations.[622]

Vice President Biden says that Israel is a sovereign nation, free to choose its own course in whether or not to attack Iran.[623]

7/6/09

California Controller John Chiang says the state will issue $3.3 billion in IOUs for July.[624]

The administration "clarifies" Vice President Biden's statement, saying that it does not give Israel the "green light [for] any kind of military action."[625]

President Obama and Russian President Dmitri Medvedev reach a "new start" in U.S./Russian relations with agreements on nuclear arms and Afghanistan.[626]

7/7/09

The U.S. signals its support of deposed socialist Manuel Zelaya of Honduras by inviting him to the U.S. to meet with Secretary of State Clinton.[627]

President Obama begins his meeting with Russian President Medvedev and Prime Minister Putin with his characteristic submission, saying, "I think it's very important that I come before you with some humility. I think in the past there's been a tendency for the United States to lecture rather than listen."[628] *Somebody, please, don't let this man open his mouth without a teleprompter present. Does he honestly believe that self-flagellating masochism will be construed as anything other than weakness? He could have just said, "Right now, I'm more interested in hearing what you have to say."*

7/8/09

Democrats are unsure whether to add more stimulus. President Obama says that increasing unemployment is something "we wrestle with constantly," but he admits that continuing to borrow and spend is "potentially counterproductive."[629]

Many states are using stimulus funds to fill short-term budget gaps rather than long-term projects that the stimulus promised.[630]

The Swiss government defends its banking secrecy laws and rebukes the

U.S. Department of Justice over UBS. A spokesman says, "Switzerland will use its legal authority to ensure that the bank cannot be pressured to transmit the information illegally, including if necessary by issuing an order taking effective control of the data at UBS...The IRS now inappropriately seeks to provoke international conflict through this civil proceeding."

Switzerland has offered to renegotiate its tax treaty with the U.S., maintaining that its laws are a matter of diplomacy, not American courtrooms.[631]

G-8 leaders agree to cut greenhouse gas emissions by 80% by 2050 as the climate summit in Copenhagen approaches.[632] *It's easy to take credit for magnificent promises as long as it's some other schlepp way down the road who actually has to accomplish the mission.*

U.S. drones allegedly launch two missile attacks on Taliban targets in Pakistan, killing forty-five.[633]

7/9/09

Counties that supported Obama's candidacy receive twice as much stimulus money than those that did not support him.[634]

AIG seeks clearance to grant millions of dollars in more executive bonuses.[635]

7/10/09

Attorney General Eric Holder is *still* pondering a criminal investigation of Bush-era interrogation tactics.[636]

President Obama meets with the Pope. "Obama told the Pope of his commitment to reduce the number of abortions and of his attention and respect for the positions of the Catholic Church," said a Vatican spokesman.[637]

Russia threatens to deploy missiles near Poland if the U.S. does not modify its Eastern European defense shield.[638]

Russian President Medvedev uses the G-8 summit as a platform to call for the end of the dollar as the world's reserve currency. French President Sarkozy heartily agrees.[639]

The Obama administration withdraws $16.5 million in military aid to Honduras in retaliation for ousting Marxist President Manuel Zelaya.[640]

7/11/09

A report reveals that North Korean computer specialists were ordered to hack and destroy South Korean communications.[641]

7/12/09

President Obama says the stimulus "has worked as intended."[642] *Really? Unemployment was 9.5% last month. On January 24, 2009 he cautioned that unemployment could hit 8.5% by April if the stimulus was not passed.*

More American corporations (Yahoo, Google, McDonald's, Kraft, Proctor & Gamble, etc.) are moving their European headquarters to tax-friendly, business-friendly Switzerland.[643]

A U.S. and allied counterinsurgency has successfully pushed back Taliban soldiers in Afghanistan.[644]

7/13/09

The budget deficit tops $1 trillion for the first time ever.[645]

The White House is trying to come up with a mortgage aid program for the unemployed.[646]

Amtrak unveils its first rail car funded by the stimulus...eighty more to go.[647]

"Car Czar" Steve Rattner resigns.

7/14/09

U.S. Army Major Stefan Frederick Cook requests a temporary restraining order from deployment to Afghanistan. He believes that Barack Obama is not a legitimate president since he was not born in the U.S.[648]

North Korea stole data from South Korean computers in cyber-attacks.[649]

Jul 2009

A House health care bill proposes a 5.4% surtax on millionaires.[650]

Senior adviser to the president, David Axelrod, makes it clear that Obama would like a bipartisan vote on health care, but the Democrats are willing to proceed without Republicans. "Ultimately, this is not about a process, it's about results," says Axelrod.[651] *We use the power of persuasion first. If it doesn't work, we try the persuasion of power."* —SEIU President Andy Stern

7/15/09

Charles Bolden is confirmed as NASA Administrator. In an interview with *Al-Jazeera*, Bolden speaks of President Obama's peculiar wish list for NASA, "When I became the NASA Administrator... he charged me with three things. One was he wanted me to help re-inspire children to want to get into science and math, he wanted me to expand our international relationships, and third, and perhaps foremost, he wanted me to find a way to reach out to the Muslim world and engage much more with dominantly Muslim nations to help them feel good about their historic contribution to science...and math and engineering."[652] *Did he ever mention anything about space exploration?*

President Obama "strongly opposes" any effort by Congress to restore car dealership arrangements with GM or Chrysler. He further states that it would be a "dangerous precedent" to "intervene into a closed judicial bankruptcy proceeding on behalf of one particular group at this point."[653] *Excuse me, the administration spent a great deal of time trying to influence the bankruptcy proceedings.*

States receive $4.7 billion to weatherize homes. President Obama says it is good for America— it will create jobs, insulate more houses, keep utility bills low, etc.[654]

President Obama considers a plan allowing homeowners to rent their homes if they have become delinquent in payments.[655]

Major Cook's deployment orders to Afghanistan have been revoked. *Now the president doesn't have to worry about having to produce his birth certificate in a court of law.*[656] *See entry for 7/14/09.*

The dollar falls as notes from the Federal Reserve's meetings are made public. The Fed believes the economy may not recover for five or six years. "The Fed minutes warned of 'significant downside risks' and a possible slide into deflation, an admission that zero interest rates, $1.75 trillion of Quantitative Easing, and a fiscal deficit above 10% of GDP have so far failed to lift the economy out of a structural slump." It says, "The Committee would need to consider whether further policy stimulus might become appropriate if the outlook were to worsen appreciably."[657]

7/16/09

Vice President Joe Biden proclaims, "We have to go spend money to keep from going bankrupt."[658] *"You cannot spend your way out of recession or borrow your way out of debt." – Daniel Hannan*

Congressional Budget Office (CBO) Director Douglas Elmendorf, after testifying before the Senate Budget Committee, blogs, "Under current law, the federal budget is on an unsustainable path, because federal debt will continue to grow much faster than the economy over the long run."[659]

A community-organizing group called Fund for the Public Interest is offering $11 to $16 per hour for "grassroots" support of health care reform.[660] *Have you ever noticed that left-wing "grassroots" organizations often have hundreds of expensive, pre-fab signs and t-shirts? The Tea Partiers, who are supposedly bankrolled by the big bucks, always have cheaply scrawled, homemade signs.*

The Social Security Administration throws itself a $700,000 party in Phoenix to learn how to reduce stress. The conference features relevant activities like a motivational dance company.[661]

7/17/09

After last month's close vote on the Cap & Trade Climate bill, Federal Election Commission records reveal that House Democratic leaders gave tens of thousands of dollars in campaign cash to Democratic Congressmen whose votes were not secure.[662]

Larry Summers, Director of the White House Economic Council, uses an unusual measurement for his chipper forecast for the economy. The number of Google searches for "economic depression" is down to normal levels.[663]

The White House asks Congress to give it more control over Medicare reimbursement rates.[664]

The House panel passes a health care bill.[665]

President Obama condemns two Indonesian suicide bombings at American hotels that killed eight and wounded fifty.[666]

7/19/09

Once again, Israeli Prime Minister Netanyahu rebuffs President Obama's demand that construction on private property cease in East Jerusalem. "There is no ban on Arabs buying apartments in the western part of the city and there is no ban on Jews buying or building apartments in the eastern part of the city. This is the policy of an open city, an undivided city that has no separation according to religion or national affiliation."[667]

7/20/09

Pork-barrel spending: the government purchases 760,000 pounds of ham for $1.50 per pound, while it can be purchased at Food Lion for $.79 per pound.[668] *Next thing you know, they'll be selling dimes for a nickel.*

At this year's National Governors Association meeting, governors fear that the federal health care plan will be a hugely expensive Medicaid package.[669]

Injecting more uncertainty in a climate of economic confusion, the White House is delaying the release of its congressionally mandated budget update, due in mid-July. They will be putting it off until next month.[670]

The Government Accountability Office (GAO) concludes that the FDA is not competent to come up with "the data to develop a complete and reliable estimate of the resources it needs."[671]

President Obama delays making a decision about Gitmo for another six months.[672]

According to State Department spokesman P. J. Crowley, Israeli construction in East Jerusalem is "the type of issue that should be subject to permanent-status negotiations."[673]

The Army deploys another 22,000 troops to Afghanistan.[674]

Secretary of State Hillary Clinton continues the Obama Apology Tour, this time, for the environment. Before an audience in Mumbai, India, she says, "We acknowledge—now with President Obama—that we have made mistakes in the United States, and we along with other developed countries have contributed most significantly to the problem that we face with climate change."[675]

7/21/09

During a conference call the President urges leftist bloggers to pressure Congress on health care. One blogger asks if it is true that Section

102 would outlaw private insurance. President Obama responds, "You know, I have to say that I am not familiar with the provision you are talking about."[676] *This is the same man who promised, "If you have health insurance, and you like it, and you have a doctor that you like, then you can keep it. Period."*

President Obama inadvertently admits that he had a possibly inappropriate, face-to-face meeting with Doug Elmendorf of the CBO to discuss health care. CBO is supposed to be an independent scorekeeper beyond influence or intimidation.[677]

The Obama administration is upping the pressure to reinstate the overthrown Marxist President Zelaya of Honduras during talks mediated in Costa Rica.[678]

Secretary of State Clinton says she would accept a nuclear-armed Iran surrounded by a "defense umbrella" of armed Persian Gulf states. "But we also have made it clear that we will take action, as I've said time and time again, crippling action, working to upgrade the defense of our partners in the region," she says.[679] *Secretary Clinton points out an interesting foreign policy pattern here: the habit of saying things to countries "time and time again."*

7/22/09

Sergeant James Crowley was called to the scene of a possible burglary committed by a black male in Cambridge, Massachusetts. Unfortunately for Crowley, the suspect was the resident himself, Harvard professor Henry Gates, a close, personal friend of Barack Obama. When questioned, without having the facts, Obama declares, "The Cambridge Police acted stupidly."[680]

President Obama goes on television to promote health care and, according Rahm Emanuel, discuss "how we rescued the economy from the worst recession."[681]

Pakistan objects to intensified U.S. efforts in Afghanistan believing it will force militants across their border.[682]

A member of the Central Committee of Fatah (the dominant political party of the Palestinian Authority) states that Fatah has never recognized Israel's right to exist and it has no intention of ever doing so.[683]

7/23/09

President Obama alleges that doctors intentionally mutilate children: "Right now, doctors a lot of times are forced to make decisions based on the fee payment schedule that's out there…The doctor may look at the reimbursement system and say to himself, 'You know what? I make a lot more money if I take this kid's tonsils out.'"[684]

Sergeant James Crowley refuses to apologize and says the President was "way off base."[685]

President Obama apologizes for his remarks about the Cambridge Police. "Because this has been a ratcheting up and I obviously helped to contribute ratcheting it up, I wanted to make clear in my choice of

words I think I unfortunately gave an impression that I was malign-
ing the Cambridge Police Department or Sergeant Crowley specifically.
And I could have calibrated those words differently."[686] *He should be at
least as harsh on himself by admitting he "talked stupidly."*

Despite the Administration's pressure, Honduras rejects the return of
their ousted former president and professed Marxist, Manuel Zelaya.[687]

North Korea takes umbrage at Secretary Clinton's "vulgar remarks" and
judges "she is by no means intelligent."[688]

7/24/09

President Obama and Education Secretary Arne Duncan announce the
"Race to the Top" education program meant to encourage state reforms.

7/26/09

Secretary Clinton states that Iran does not have the right to have nuclear weapons. She tells *Meet the Press*, "We are going to do everything we
can to prevent you [Iran] from getting a nuclear weapon."[689]

7/27/09

Tens of millions of stimulus dollars are being spent on repairing and
replacing toilets.[690] *Yes, the government is, quite literally, flushing your
money down the toilet.*

Hawaii Health Director Dr. Chiyome Fukino says we can lay our doubts to rest; she has seen Barack Obama's original birth certificate and he is a natural-born citizen. No, really! She's seen it! Hawaii does not release birth certificates to anyone who does not have a tangible interest. *So, in other words, Obama could have cleared up the controversy in about ten minutes instead of waiting more than two years into his presidency.*[691]

Senators Kent Conrad (D-ND) and Chris Dodd (D-CT) received sweetheart mortgage deals according to Countrywide Financial Corp.'s Robert Feinberg. By the way, senators Conrad and Dodd were crucial in drafting the Financial Reform Package signed by President Obama.[692]

Seven terrorists who wanted to "attack the Americans" are arrested for planning to attack a U.S. Marine base in Quantico, Virginia.[693]

Does anyone in Washington read bills? On health care, John Conyers (D-MI) asks, "What good is reading the bill if it's a thousand pages and you don't have two days and two lawyers to find out what it means after you read the bill?"[694]

The President picks out his summer retreat: a $20 million mansion on Martha's Vineyard with a private beach, basketball court and lots of golfing opportunities.[695]

President Obama is denounced as "racist" by 2,000 protesters in Jerusalem.[696]

7/28/09

China's Assistant Finance Minister Zhu Guangyao is "concerned about the security of our financial assets." Treasury Secretary Geithner assures China that the U.S. will shrink the deficit.[697]

The U.S. revokes the diplomatic visas of four Honduran officials as punishment for ousting its socialist president.[698]

7/29/09

Associate Attorney General Thomas J. Perrelli approved the May decision to drop the New Black Panthers case, even though the Justice Department had already won the case. Lawyers were finalizing the paperwork in late April when Obama's political appointees told them to drop the case.[699]

Weak U.S. Treasury auctions raise worries about U.S. debt.[700]

7/30/09

This year's budget deficit hits $1.3 trillion.[701]

BEER SUMMIT! President Obama heals history's deep racial wounds by serving some suds to Sergeant Crowley and Professor Gates. *He should have called Putin, Hu, and Netanyahu to participate in solving problems like adults. World peace could easily be achieved if only President Obama could persuade Mahmoud Ahmadinejad to do a keg stand while Hugo Chavez does belly shots and Kim Jong Il chugs from a beer bong. Maybe they can go to Hooters for all-you-can-eat hot wings.*

The White House charges CEOs for lunch. As President Obama meets with powerful CEOs of Xerox, Coca-Cola, AT&T and Honeywell, the White House staff asks for their credit cards and charges them accordingly for having lunch with President Obama. The White House timidly explains they wished to avoid conflicts of interest but never clarify whether they charged Gordon Brown, Mahmoud Abbas, or any other world leader. It is not known whether he also charged Sergeant Crowley and Professor Gates for the beer they drank.[702] *For someone who is this careful to make a symbolic point, it makes you wonder if those crummy gifts to the Queen and the rude treatment of Netanyahu weren't also intentional.*

Cash for Clunkers is out of cash, but Congress approves another $2 billion for the program.[703]

The price of treasuries increases as the government issues record amounts of debt after a government report forecasting slow growth.[704]

Democratic senators decline to subpoena information proving or disproving corruption allegations against Senators Kent Conrad (D-ND) and Chris Dodd (D-CT).[705] *See entry for 7/27/09.*

The U.S. successfully test-fires missile defenses against North Korea.[706]

Secretary of State Hillary Clinton instructs diplomats to spy and gather information on other countries' representatives to the U.N. Some of the information requested includes personal credit card information, frequent flyer numbers, e-mail accounts, telephone accounts, biometric information, passwords, and personal encryption keys.[707]

Venezuela's Attorney General Luisa Ortega declares freedom of expression "must be limited." She proposes a law that will punish radio stations, newspapers, TV stations and all media outlets that "cause panic...disturb social peace...or manipulate the news with the purpose of transmitting a false perception of the facts."[708]

July unemployment = 9.4%.
Real unemployment = 16.4%.[709]

8/1/09

Chavez shuts down thirty-four radio stations in Venezuela "that now belong to the people, not the bourgeoisie."[710] *Understanding this story is crucially important considering that Mark Lloyd is Obama's "Diversity Czar" at the FCC. Lloyd gushes that Chavez in Venezuela had "really an incredible revolution... The property owners and the folks who then controlled the media in Venezuela...worked to oust him. But he came back with another revolution, and then Chavez began to take very seriously the media in his country."[711] Presumably, the president's appointees closely reflect the views of the president himself.*

The U.K.'s House of Commons Foreign Affairs Committee concludes "that the international effort in Afghanistan since 2001 has delivered much less than it promised and that its impact has been significantly diluted by the absence of a unified vision and strategy grounded in the realities of Afghanistan's history, culture, and politics."[712]

In Cuba, Raul Castro announces he will cut spending on education and health care, calling state spending "simply unsustainable."[713]

8/2/09

Treasury Secretary Geithner refuses to answer *This Week*'s George Stephanopoulos's questions about whether he will rule out middle class tax hikes. Geithner is given several chances to rescue himself; all he can say is, "We have to bring these deficits down very dramatically and that's going to require some very hard choices."[714]

Wall Street is reaping huge gains from trading federal government debt with the Federal Reserve.[715]

8/3/09

For the next several weeks there are scores of townhall meetings with senators and congressmen facing their outraged constituents. It is beyond the scope of this book to cover these meetings in detail. Obamacare and government spending were the themes that were boisterously discussed from Hawaii to Maine. The meetings were all a charade. The Democrats attended the meetings, but they never listened. The die was cast; they already knew what they would do when they returned to Washington.

Tax revenues are set to fall 18% this year, the biggest drop since 1932.[716]

8/4/09

Two Russian nuclear submarines are patrolling off the East Coast of the U.S.[717]

The White House releases a perfectly Orwellian blog concerning "disinformation" (*in other words, "correct information"*) about Obamacare. In order to dispel the truth about the health care overhaul, the White House asks for your help: "There is a lot of disinformation about health insurance reform out there, spanning from control of personal finances to end of life care. These rumors often travel just below the surface via chain e-mails or through casual conversation. Since we can't keep track of all of them here at the White House, we're asking for your help. If you get an e-mail or see something on the Internet about health insurance reform that seems fishy, sent it to flag@whitehouse.gov. *In East Germany they called it "Stasi."*

Another section of the creepy White House e-mail is concerned with "one example that makes it look like the President intends to 'eliminate' private coverage, when the reality couldn't be further from the truth."[718] *That's right, and less than two weeks ago, on July 21, 2009, he admitted he had no idea how private insurance would be affected.*

Four of the top five models sold under the Cash for Clunkers program are built by foreign car companies.[719]

The administration refuses to release government documents related to "Cash for Clunkers."[720]

The Treasury is poised to charge another $75 billion on the government credit card next week.[721]

8/6/09

President Obama gives a health care pep talk to the Democratic senators before they return to their constituents. White House Deputy Chief of Staff, Jim Messina, instructs that if the natives get uppity, "punch back twice as hard." Harry Reid (D-NV) says, "They are just helping us understand the fringe that is trying to mess up our meetings."[722] [723]

The Obama administration is relinquishing the "war on terrorism" evidently to fight the "war of terminology." John Brennan, the "Counter-terrorism Czar," says that we no longer have a need for old-fashioned, outdated terms like "war on terrorism," "jihadists" or "global war." Instead, the President has "a new way of seeing" the conflict. Mr. Brennan ("Czar John"?) chides the yokels for "inflammatory rhetoric, hyperbole, and intellectual narrowness" assuring them that President Obama's views are "nuanced, not simplistic; practical, not ideological."[724] *Here's another term for you: "nuanced." Liberals love to use this term for anything that they don't understand well enough to explain or would rather not explain. Perhaps Mr. Brennan's title should be the "New Way of Seeing Czar."*

Over 34 million Americans are now on food stamps, an all-time record![725]

Fannie Mae has a $14.8 billion loss and asks the U.S. Treasury for another $10.7 billion.[726]

The Senate confirms Justice Sonia Sotomayor to the Supreme Court.[727]

Secretary of State Clinton expresses "great regret" that the United States is not a signatory to the International Criminal Court (ICC) in The Hague.[728] *Critics believe that joining the ICC would cede U.S. sovereignty to a foreign judiciary.*

Venezuela is buying dozens of tanks and artillery from Russia.[729]

8/7/09

At a campaign rally in Virginia, President Obama states, "I don't want the folks who created the mess to do a lot of talking, I want them to just get out of the way so we can clean up the mess. I don't mind cleaning up after 'em but don't do a lot of talking."[730] *It will become clear that he doesn't like for anyone who disagrees with him "to do a lot of talking."*

The Obama administration is still trying to come up with a way to measure whether the war in Afghanistan is being won.[731]

8/8/09

Treasury Secretary Geithner asks Congress to increase the $12.1 trillion debt ceiling, adding, "Congress has never failed to raise the debt limit when necessary."[732] *"It is a sign that we now depend on ongoing financial assistance from foreign countries to finance our government's reckless fiscal policies." –Senator Barack Obama, March 16, 2006.*

Aug 2009

Sonia Sotomayor is sworn in as a Supreme Court Justice.

Sarah Palin says "Death Panels" may be in the final health care bill.[733]

8/9/09

Eric Holder is ready to name a special criminal prosecutor to probe Bush-era interrogation methods.[734]

"Net Neutrality" advocate, Robert McChesney, tells a Canadian Marxist publication, "At the moment, the battle over network neutrality is not to completely eliminate the telephone and cable companies. We are not at that point yet. But the ultimate goal is to get rid of the media capitalists in the phone and cable companies and to divest them from control."[735]

8/10/09

Ministry of Propaganda: The National Endowment for the Arts (NEA), the White House Office of Public Engagement and United We Serve host a conference call with "a group of artists, producers, promoters, organizers, influencers, marketers, taste-makers, leaders or just plain cool people to join together and work together to promote a more civically engaged America and celebrate how the arts can be used for a positive change!" The purpose of the call is "to help lay a new foundation for growth, focusing on core areas of the recovery agenda," with emphasis on health care, energy and the environment.

Yosi Sergant, NEA's communications director, promises, "This is just the beginning. This is the first telephone call of a brand new conversation. We are just now learning how to really bring this community together to speak with the government. What that looks like legally—we're still trying to figure out the laws of putting government websites of Facebook and the use of Twitter. This is all being sorted out. We are participating in history as it's being made, so bear with us as we learn the language so that we can speak to each other safely and we can really work together to move the needle to get stuff done." [736] [737] [738] The Soviets called it "Agitprop," Orwell called it the "Ministry of Truth" in 1984, Obama calls it the "National Endowment for the Arts."

The State Department's Ramadan program is in full gear. The Bureau of International Information Programs (BIIP) website reveals, "On August 10, America.gov will publish a 'Multicultural Ramadan' feature." The BIIP "will publish three articles for Ramadan 2009 addressing the concept of an Islam in America 'brand'; advocacy (civic and political) of the Muslim American community; and community innovation/community building (It sounds a lot like "community organizing"). The writer will contact Muslim American experts in each of these fields. These articles will be available on America.gov in English, Arabic, and Persian."[739]

The White House announces that President Obama has a "winning" strategy for Afghanistan. The President's "winning" strategy involves procrastinating, dithering and refusing to make a decision for several months.[740]

8/11/09

Once again, the Fearmonger-in-Chief accuses doctors of intentionally dismembering people for their own enrichment: "All I'm saying is, let's take the example of something like diabetes, one of—a disease that's skyrocketing, partly because of obesity, partly because it's not treated as effectively as it could be. Right now if we paid a family—if a family care physician works with his or her patient to help them lose weight, modify diet, monitors whether they're taking their medications in a timely fashion, they might get reimbursed a pittance. But if that same diabetic ends up getting their foot amputated, that's $30,000, $40,000, $50,000—immediately the surgeon is reimbursed. Well, why not make sure that we're also reimbursing the care that prevents the amputation, right? That will save us money[741] *He is an outright liar. Fact: Medicare pays a surgeon between $740 and $1,140 for a leg amputation.*

"UPS and FedEx are doing just fine. It's the Post Office that's always having problems." —President Barack Obama[742]

The Taliban has attacked Pakistan's nuclear facilities at least three times in the last two years.[743] *See entry for 6/22/09. Al-Qaeda has expressed their desire to use Pakistan's nuclear facilities.*

Kuwait has arrested six Kuwaitis suspected of being al-Qaeda members plotting to attack a U.S. military base.[744]

Russia is negotiating a Strategic Arms Reduction Treaty with the U.S. The Russians are bargaining for the U.S. discard its plans for a ground-based missile defense in Eastern Europe.[745]

8/12/09

Funding for National Guard deployment along the Mexican border is stalled as the Departments of Defense and Homeland Security fight over who has to pay for it.[746]

The Lockerbie Bomber, Abdelbaset al-Megrahi, is released from a Scottish prison on compassionate grounds on the basis that he had terminal cancer. The Obama administration had secretly participated in releasing Megrahi. Richard LeBaron, deputy head of the U.S. embassy in London, wrote to the Scottish First Minister, "Nevertheless, if Scottish authorities come to the conclusion that Megrahi must be released from Scottish custody, the U.S. position is that conditional release on compassionate grounds would be a far preferable alternative to prisoner transfer, which we strongly oppose."[747]

Anticipating the Copenhagen climate conference, U.N. Secretary-General Ban Ki-moon sounds the alarm, "We have just four months. Four months to secure the future of our planet."[748]

8/13/09

Secretary of State Clinton is going on an eleven-day tour of Africa making women's rights her theme.[749]

The Australian Senate rejects Prime Minister Rudd's Cap and Trade plan.[750]

8/14/09

President Obama says, "We are held hostage at any given moment by health insurance companies that deny coverage, or drop coverage, or charge fees that people can't afford at a time when they desperately need care."[751] *Aren't we also held hostage by a government that has the power to throw us in jail and confiscate our freedom and property?*

The IRS is warning 52,000 Americans who bank in Switzerland that they have until September 23, 2009, to come forward and beg for some measure of clemency. After that, the IRS promises that the penalties will be harsh and severe.[752]

Meanwhile, the Department of Justice is planning to file criminal charges against 150 Americans who bank with UBS.[753]

President Obama cautions America to beware of ratings-hungry cable networks that are covering townhall meetings and inflating stories about Obamacare.[754]

8/15/09

President Obama invokes his own grandmother's death to promote Obamacare.[755]

An association called Healthy Economy Now (HEN) is paying $12 million for an advertising blitz to support Obamacare. HEN is composed of groups and companies that the President has the ability to influence and coerce, such as the American Medical Association, AARP, Pfizer, PhRMA and others.

The money will be paid to the same two advertising agencies that received $343.3 million dollars from the Obama campaign: AKPD and GMMB. By the way, the agency AKPD was started by David Axelrod, the president's senior adviser. Even though AKPD still owes Axelrod $2 million and even though his son still works there, it would be foolish to assume that there is even an appearance of impropriety.[756]

Congressman Joe Sestak (D-PA) sends a letter to President Obama requesting that he increase the number of Cash for Clunkers claims processors from 225 to 1,000.[757] *Part of the reason the program was a disaster was that the Department of Transportation, after careful planning, did not have nearly enough claims processors to review all of the red tape.*

Russia and Venezuela are negotiating arms deals and oil trade.[758]

A car bomb explodes outside NATO headquarters in Kabul.[759]

8/16/09

The Mexican army takes control of Mexican customs at the U.S./Mexico border in a corruption crackdown.[760]

8/18/09

The Obama administration lends $2 billion to Petrobras, Brazil's state-owned oil company, to finance their offshore drilling operations in the Tupi oilfield.[761]

8/19/09

Cash for Clunkers is a good example of the president's top-down management and leadership capabilities. Car dealerships around the country are dropping out of the program because the government isn't reimbursing them for the money they advanced to car buyers. Almost half of New York City's 425 car dealers are now dropping out; so far they have been repaid on about 2% of the contracts they have signed. Dealers in New Mexico are owed about $3.6 million; so far they have received three checks totaling $14,000. The Virginia Automobile Dealers Association says the government has approved just 5% of the deals and less than 3% of those have been reimbursed.

The program says that the dealers will get their rebates within ten days of transaction. Transportation Secretary Ray LaHood blames many of the problems on incorrectly filled-out paperwork. As of August 15, 2009, there were only 225 claims processors reviewing more than 457,000 transactions.[762] [763] [764]

To date, 6.9 million private-sector jobs have been lost while state and local governments have added net 110,000 jobs since the recession began.[765]

Tight budget concerns stifle funding for space exploration.[766] *It's no coincidence since President Obama's chief mission for NASA is "to reach out to the Muslim world and engage much more with dominantly Muslim na-*

*tions to help them feel good about their historic contribution to science...
and math and engineering." See entry for 7/15/09.*

Switzerland agrees to release the names of 4,450 Americans using Swiss banks to the IRS where "tax fraud or the like" is suspected.[767]

Truck bombs in Baghdad kill 95 and wound 563. Evidence suggests collaboration between Iraqi forces and insurgents.[768] [769]

Aug 2009

8/20/09

In a scripted online discussion with religious voters, President Obama wails, "There's been a lot of misinformation" by people who are "bearing false witness." Death panels, care for illegal immigrants, abortions: "these are all fabrications," Obama says. *Somebody should inform him that Representative Zoe Lofgren is telling her constituents that government-funded abortion is, and should be, in the bill.*

President Obama includes Marxist Reverend Jim Wallis in the discussion. Wallis adds, "This call shows how united the faith community is... We are calling on people of faith to make our political representatives understand that the faith community will be satisfied with nothing less than safe, accessible health care for all Americans."[770] [771]

The president discusses health care in a radio interview and says he would "love to have more Republicans engaged and involved in this process," but he promises he would win the fight with or without their support.[772] *So he would love to have Republicans involved so long as they agree with him and don't offer any of their smart-aleck input or ideas.*

Obama says illegal immigrants will receive emergency room care under his plan because of "basic standards of decency."[773]

President Obama brags that Cash for Clunkers is "successful beyond anybody's imagination," and that the dealers were overwhelmed by demand. He promises that the car dealers "will get their money."[774] *It certainly is "beyond anybody's imagination." The dealers weren't overwhelmed, though; the government can't handle the paperwork and they're still waiting for their money*

After the President's many promises to halve the deficit by the end of his first term, the administration raises its ten-year deficit projection to $9 trillion.[775] *While discussing the deficit on the campaign trail, Candidate Obama declared, "The problem is, is that the way Bush has done it over the last eight years is to take out a credit card from the Bank of China in the name of our children, driving up our national debt from $5 trillion for the first 42 presidents—number 43 added $4 trillion by his lonesome, so that we now have over $9 trillion of debt that we are going to have to pay back—$30,000 for every man, woman and child. That's irresponsible! It's unpatriotic!"*

Will President Obama, then, admit that he is irresponsible and unpatriotic?

President Obama goes to Martha's Vineyard for vacation.

The President condemns Scotland for returning the Lockerbie bomber to Libya.[776]

Millions vote in Afghan elections.[777]

Aug 2009

8/23/09

To date, the administration has filled only 43% of the senior policymaking appointments requiring Senate confirmation.[778]

8/24/10

Attorney General Eric Holder appoints John H. Durham as a special prosecutor to investigate CIA interrogations.[779]

AFL-CIO's New York President, Dennis Hughes, is appointed to the Federal Reserve Bank of New York's board of directors.[780]

U.S. and NATO commanders inform President Obama that there are not enough troops to accomplish their mission in Afghanistan.[781]

8/25/09

President Obama calls Federal Reserve chairman Ben Bernanke to Martha's Vineyard to nominate him for a second term.[782]

8/26/09

Four thousand Massachusetts inmates receive $250 stimulus checks.[783]

8/27/09

President Obama will be addressing public school students on September 8, 2009. The Department of Education has sent advance materials to Pre K–6 teachers to prepare a dialogue with students, asking creepy questions like, "What is the President asking me to do?" and "Are we able to do what President Obama is asking of us?"[784]

ABC and NBC refuse to run an advertisement critical of Obamacare.[785] *This isn't surprising since ABC aired an Obama primetime news bonanza in June.*

Atlanta Fed Chief Dennis Lockhart believes the real unemployment rate is 16% when you factor in those who have to work part-time and those who have given up looking for work completely.[786]

Polish press is reporting that President Obama will breach America's promise to Polish and Czech allies in order to appease Russian concerns about the Eastern European defense shield. In March and in July, he suggested to the Russians that he is willing to exchange our defense shield for their cooperation in containing Iran.[787]

Japanese and Korean companies are the biggest beneficiaries of Cash for Clunkers.[788]

The State Department mulls punishing Honduras for ousting socialist President Zelaya by yanking $150 million in U.S. aid.[789]

8/28/09

Senate Bill, S. 773, proposes to give President Obama the power to "declare a cyber-security emergency" and seize control of "non-govern-

Aug 2009

mental" computer networks.[790]

Some voters are surprised to find that their Cash for Clunkers rebates are subject to state taxation.[791]

The United Arab Emirates seizes a North Korean ship bound for Iran. Its deceptively labeled cargo consists of rocket launchers, detonators and munitions.[792]

8/29/09

Venezuelan demonstrators are accused of rebellion. Attorney General Luisa Ortega says, "People who disturb order and the peace to create instability of institutions, to destabilize the government or attack the democratic system, we are going to charge and try them."[793] *This is what Mark Lloyd, an Obama appointee, calls a "really incredible revolution."*

8/30/09

The AFL-CIO and Congressional Democrats support a "Wall Street Tax" of about one-tenth of 1% of every stock transaction.[794]

GM announces a $293 million venture partnering with Chinese auto-maker FAW.[795]

General McChrystal sends his confidential war assessment to Defense Secretary Gates. The General thinks, "Failure to gain the initiative and reverse insurgent momentum in the near-term (next 12 months) while

Afghan security capacity matures risks an outcome where defeating the insurgency is no longer possible." McChrystal has prepared a troop request and is awaiting instructions. Six months after supporting a strategy for "executing and resourcing an integrated civilian-military counterinsurgency strategy" the President has done very little about it.[796] [797] [798] [799]

Aug 2009

8/31/09

The Consumer Product Safety Commission launches "Resale Round-up," a crackdown of new laws making it a crime to sell anything that has been recalled by a manufacturer. It will impose fines as high as $15 million.[800] [801] *Yes, this includes garage sales.*

The government still isn't reimbursing car dealers: $2.878 billion is still owed in the Cash for Clunkers program.[802] [803]

The Department of Homeland Security approves U.S. Customs searches of all electronic data. Customs may copy, download or retain any electronic information without probable cause.[804]

Obama advisers see the need to increase troops in Afghanistan.[805]

"The situation in Afghanistan is serious, but success is achievable and demands a revised implementation strategy, commitment and resolve, and increased unity of effort." —General Stanley McChrystal.

August's budget deficit totals $111.4 billion, making the year-to-date total $1.38 trillion.[806]

For the months (June–August) U.S. bank loans fell at an APR of 14 percent.[807]

August unemployment = 9.7%.
Real unemployment = 16.8%.[808]

9/2/09

Farmers are struggling in the San Joaquin Valley, California, due to the government's uncompromising enforcement of the Endangered Species Act. In order to protect the delta smelt (a fish) the government is channeling billions of gallons of water directly into the ocean, leaving farmers unable to water their crops.[809]

BP discovers a large oil deposit in the Gulf of Mexico.[810]

9/3/09

The IRS will need 16,500 more agents to enforce "acceptable" health insurance plans under Obamacare.[811]

Vice President Biden says the stimulus is working better than expected and has already "saved or created" 500,000 to 750,000 jobs.[812]

$535 million Obama stimulus funds guarantee a loan to Solyndra. After 6 months of due diligence the Department of Energy has determined that Solyndra is a wise investment and will create thousands of "green jobs."[813] *On August 31, 2011, Solyndra filed bankruptcy and laid-*

off 1,100 workers.

To quell controversy, the Administration withdraws its suggestions for teacher-student dialogue after the president's speech before America's public schools on September 8.[814]

It is revealed that "Green Jobs Czar" Van Jones signed a "truther" statement, alleging that the U.S. government attacked itself on 9/11 to justify waging war in the Middle East.[815]

North Korea is on the cusp of successfully enriching uranium. Their other nuclear tests were plutonium-based bombs. With enriched uranium, they will have another means of producing atomic bombs.[816]

Sep 2009

9/4/09

The Obama administration agrees to release some information about White House visitors, but refuses to release information regarding the first eight-months of the Obama presidency.[817] *Transparency?*

Prime Minister Netanyahu offers to freeze Israeli construction at a later date. The White House responds, "We regret the reports of Israel's plans to approve additional settlement construction. As the President has said before, the United States does not accept the legitimacy of continued settlement expansion and we urge it to stop."[818]

9/5/09

Green Jobs Czar Van Jones, resigns in the middle of the night during a three-day weekend.[819]

Venezuela will be shutting down twenty-nine more radio stations in September after shutting down thirty-four in August.[820]

After meeting with Hugo Chavez, Mahmoud Ahmadinijad says, "Helping the oppressed and revolutionary nations and expanding anti-imperialist fronts are the main missions of Iran and Venezuela."[821]

9/6/09

The administration says it did not ask Van Jones to resign.[822]

The U.K. claims that it kept President Obama and Secretary Clinton advised at all times throughout the process of releasing the Lockerbie bomber. "The U.S. was kept fully in touch about everything that was going on with regard to Britain's discussions with Libya in recent years and about Megrahi," said an aide. They claim that the Obama administration's "shock" was due to an unexpected volume of bad publicity.[823]

9/7/09

It turns out that "Green Jobs Czar" Van Jones was improperly vetted. He did not even fill out the sixty-three-question questionnaire that is standard operating procedure for high-level positions.[824] *As with all of their other poorly vetted nominees (Bill Richardson, Tom Daschle, etc.), this shows the Obama administration's inclination for "winging it." Whether they intend to close Guantanamo (without actually having a plan for closing it) or sign laws they have not read, one wonders how seriously they regard the executive function of government.*

In an interview with *Men's Health*, the president likes the idea of taxing sweet drinks. "It's an idea that we should be exploring. There's no doubt that our kids drink way too much soda. And every study that's been done about obesity shows that there is as high a correlation between increased soda consumption and obesity as just about anything else," he says.[825]

Representative John Boehner (R-OH) says the President has not met with Republicans to discuss health care since April.[826]

In defiance of the president's demands, Israel approves the building of 455 units in the West Bank.[827]

Mahmoud Ahmadinejad refuses to compromise on nuclear concessions.[828]

China again expresses alarm that the Fed is printing money, which will seriously decrease the dollar's value. Cheng Siwei, former vice-chairman of the Standing Committee says, "The U.S. spends tomorrow's money today. We Chinese spend today's money tomorrow. That's why we have this financial crisis."[829]

Sep 2009

9/8/09

President Obama appoints Ron Bloom as "Manufacturing Czar."[830] *Bloom reflects the Obama administration's radical Marxist philosophy having said, "We know that the free market is nonsense. We know that the whole point is to game the system, to beat the market, or at least find someone who will pay you a lot of money,'cause they're convinced that there is a free lunch. We know this is largely about power, that it's an adults-only, no limit game. We kind of agree with Mao that political power comes largely from the barrel of a gun."*

Some schools won't show the president's speech and others offer "opt-out" forms.[831]

The United Nations is proposing a global currency to replace the dollar.[832]

9/9/09

President Obama addresses a joint session of Congress to lecture about health care. He says the plan contains both Republican and Democratic ideas. He also states that the $900 billion overhaul will not add "one dime" to the budget deficit. President Obama continues, "There are also those who claim that our reform efforts would insure illegal immigrants. This, too, is false. The reforms I'm proposing would not apply to those who are here illegally." This prompts a hysterical outburst, "You lie!" from Representative Joe Wilson (R-SC).[833] [834] [835]

9/10/09

A man and woman posing as a pimp and prostitute release a video of themselves conspiring with ACORN employees on creative financing for a mortgage that would be used to house underage girls imported from El Salvador for illicit purposes.[836] *In the next few days, several more videos surface from all over the country showing ACORN conspiring in illegal acts.*

9/11/09

Texas Governor Rick Perry calls the Texas Rangers to the Mexican border. So far, the White House has not responded to his two requests for 1,000 National Guard troops.[837]

The Census Bureau severs ties with ACORN for the 2010 census count.[838]

White House Deputy Chief of Staff Jim Messina offers (i.e., —tries to bribe) Andrew Romanoff with his choice of three executive branch jobs in exchange for withdrawing his Senate primary challenge against Obama crony Michael Bennett (D-CO).[839]

The Obama administration and Congressional Democrats are already positioning themselves to pass Obamacare through the "reconciliation" process.[840]

The U.S. will impose tariffs on tires made in China.[841]

Sep 2009

The U.S. changes policy and announces it is ready to have one-on-one talks with North Korea.[842]

9/12/09

1,000,000 people march on Washington protesting government spending and denouncing Obamacare as socialist.[843]

China denounces U.S. tire tariffs as protectionist.[844]

9/13/09

China investigates unfair U.S. trade in chicken and automobile products.[845]

Russia will help Venezuela develop nuclear energy.[846]

9/16/09

The Obama administration believes that Cap & Trade could cost families $1,761 per year.[847]

The White House is collecting and storing data from social-network websites. Marc Rotenberg, president of the Electronic Privacy Information Center, believes the White House should disclose that it is collecting electronic information. "The White House has not been adequately transparent, particularly on how it makes use of new social media techniques."[848]

Sep 2009

Admiral Mike Mullen, chairman of the Joint Chiefs of Staff, supports increasing troops in Afghanistan.[849]

9/17/09

In celebration of the seventieth anniversary of the Soviet invasion of Poland, the Obama administration formally announces that it is dissolving plans for its defense shield in Poland and the Czech Republic.[850] *Keep in mind that Obama betrayed Eastern Europe hoping to convince Russia to cooperate in containing Iran. He was colossally duped. His chump diplomacy resulted in Russia trading arms, fuel and nuclear power plants with Iran.*

Shortly after the announcement placating Russia's request, Prime Minister Vladimir Putin meets with top U.S. corporate executives, including General Electric, a large defense contractor. GE's CEO, Jeff Immelt, is on the president's Economic Recovery Advisory Board.[851]

Also note that under Jeff Immelt's leadership, GE subsidiaries conducted business with the Iranian government while Iran was listed as a state sponsor of terrorism. Iran provides arms and support to radicals in Iraq and Afghanistan to fight Americans.

China is spending hundreds of millions of dollars investing in Cuba.[852]

The President is still procrastinating in his decision about Afghan troop deployment.[853]

The International Atomic Energy Agency (IAEA) says Iran has the capability to make a nuclear bomb.[854]

9/18/09

President Obama wishes to legalize illegals for Obamacare: "Even though I do not believe we can extend coverage to those who are here illegally, I also don't believe we can simply ignore the fact that our immigration system is broken. That's why I strongly support making sure folks who are here legally have access to affordable, quality health insurance under this plan, just like everybody else. If anything, this debate underscores the necessity of passing comprehensive immigration reform and resolving the issue of 12 million undocumented people living and working in this country once and for all."[855]

The *Wall Street Journal* reports that a proposal is being drafted that would give the Fed the power to regulate the salaries of tens of thousands of bank workers. "The Fed's plan would, for the first time, inject government regulators deep into compensation decisions traditionally reserved for the banks' corporate boards and executives."[856]

The homosexual community feels betrayed as the Administration argues in federal court that homosexuals have no right to federal marriage benefits under the 1996 Defense of Marriage Act. The Department of Justice says it is required to defend federal laws when they are challenged.[857] *Note: On February 24, 2011, President Obama and Attorney General Holder reversed course saying they will no longer oppose challenges to the Defense of Marriage Act. I guess they will only defend whichever laws they like at the time. This goes to the root of a very important pattern of the Obama administration: uncertainty. The administration's policies are vague, ill-defined and temporary. Here the issue is gay rights. Tomorrow it will be Afghanistan. The next day, the economy. After that, the trial of KSM, etc.*

The president's decision not to do an interview with Fox last Sunday prompts Chris Wallace to say, "They are the biggest bunch of crybabies I have dealt with in my thirty years in Washington."[858]

Prime Minister Putin welcomes the U.S. decision to scrap its missile defense shield. Next, he is pressing for trade agreements, "I expect that after this correct and brave decision, others will follow, including the complete removal of all restrictions on the transfer of high technology to Russia and activity to widen the membership of the World Trade Organization to (include) Russia, Kazakhstan and Belarus."[859] *Of course Putin praises Obama's "bravery" since he's the beneficiary.*

Mahmoud Ahmadinejad: "The pretext [Holocaust] for the creation of the Zionist regime [Israel] is false…It is a lie based on an unprovable and mythical claim…Confronting the Zionist regime is a national and religious duty."[860]

9/19/09

President Obama stresses that tougher financial regulations need to be imposed globally, "As I told leaders of our financial community in New York City earlier this week, a return to normalcy can't breed complacency. Our government needs to fundamentally reform the rules governing financial firms and markets to meet the challenges of the twenty-first century." He cannot miss the opportunity to take a shot at anyone

Sep 2009

who disagrees with him, "We cannot let the narrow interests of the few come before the interests of all of us."[861]

New York Governor David Paterson defies President Obama's request not to run for re-election.[862] *Note: The administration is very involved with local elections.*

Authorities arrest three terrorists plotting a suicide attack on Grand Central Station.[863]

National Security Advisor James Jones believes Iran is making headway in developing medium-range missiles.[864]

Sep 2009

9/20/09

The President appears on five Sunday talk shows to promote Obamacare: NBC, ABC, CBS, CNN and Univision.[865]

President Obama is willing to consider a bailout bill for newspapers if they will restructure as nonprofit businesses.[866] *What about "letting free enterprise work its magic?"*

Obama says the ACORN controversy is "not something I've followed closely," although he does concede that it should be investigated. He refuses to answer whether he would commit to cutting off federal funding for ACORN.[867]

President Obama is equally reticent to call his insurance mandate a tax. ABC's George Stephanopolous tries his best:

<u>Stephanopolous</u>: Under this mandate, the government is forcing people to spend money, fining you if you don't. How is that not a tax?

<u>Obama</u>: No, but—but, George, you—you can't just make up that language and decide that that's called a tax increase.

<u>Stephanopolous</u>: I don't think I'm making it up. Merriam-Webster's dictionary: 'Tax: a charge, usually of money, imposed by authority on persons or property for public purposes.'

Obama rejected the notion and said that using the dictionary definition showed that he was "stretching."[868]

   Humpty-Dumpty: "When I use a word, it means just what I choose it to mean." —Lewis Carroll, Through the Looking Glass

9/21/09

The Obama administration sends a chilling threat to insurance companies about communicating with their customers about lost benefits under Obamacare. The Centers for Medicaid and Medicare abolish the 1st Amendment rights of all companies that sell private Medicare coverage and stand-alone drug plans to seniors with a gag order stating, "As we continue our research into this issue, we are instructing you to immediately discontinue all such mailings to beneficiaries and to remove any related materials directed to Medicare enrollees from your Web sites."[869]
In Obama's America, as in Chavez's Venezuela, your freedom of speech is the freedom NOT to criticize the government.

Sep 2009

While discussing greenhouse gasses, Secretary of Energy, Steven Chu scolds, "The American public…just like your teenage kids, aren't acting in a way that they should act…The American public has to really understand in their core how important this issue is."[870] *As recently as 2008, Chu commented, "Somehow we have to figure out how to boost the price of gasoline to the levels in Europe."*

FCC Chairman Julius Genachowski proposes regulating the Internet with so-called "net-neutrality," covering all broadband connections, including data connections for smartphones.[871] *For the Marxist roots of "net-neutrality," see entries for 8/9/09 and 12/21/10.*

The Federal Reserve has rejected Secretary Geithner's request for a public review of the books.[872]

President Obama demands that the Pentagon review its nuclear weapons and prepare for dramatic cuts in its arsenal.[873]

Despite Obama's scrapping of the Eastern European defense shield, Russia's top general says they are still considering deploying missiles in Kaliningrad, near the Polish border.[874]

The U.S. will propose a new economic world order at the G-20 summit, with the IMF playing a central role coordinating a "mutual assessment" of policy recommendations directed at balanced growth.[875]

Ousted leftist and Obama favorite, Manuel Zelaya, re-enters Honduras and takes refuge in the Brazilian embassy.[876]

9/22/09

Yosi Sergant resigns after being exposed for initiating the controversial NEA phone call and trying to use the National Endowment for the Arts as a Soviet-style Agitprop Ministry.[877] *Why didn't Attorney General Eric Holder choose to prosecute Sergant under the Hatch Act, which restricts political activity of executive branch employees? After all, Holder has no problem attacking CIA employees.*

Pro-Zelaya demonstrators clash with Honduran forces outside the Brazilian embassy in Tegucigalpa.[878]

9/23/09

"In fiscal year 2009, which ends next week, the U.S. Treasury will have issued $7 trillion in gross issuance. That's in a 12-month period. This issuance was necessary to meet nearly $1.7 trillion in a net marketable borrowing needs, nearly $1 trillion more than what we raised last year," says Karthik Ramanathan, Department of Treasury's acting assistant secretary for financial markets.[879] *America for sale.*

President Obama snubs Britain's Gordon Brown five times to hold a bilateral meeting at the U.N.[880]

President Obama speaks before the U.N. General Assembly, "If the governments of Iran and North Korea choose to ignore international standards...then they must be held accountable. The world must stand together to demonstrate that international law is not an empty promise,

Sep 2009

and that treaties will be enforced."

Later, the president recommends a Security Council resolution that does not mention Iran or North Korea.[881] The most generous explanation of why he failed to mention Iran or North Korea in the Security Council resolution is weakness.

Many believe his speech was "egocentric, apologetic and overly critical of the United States," although it was praised by Mahmoud Ahmadinejad and Hugo Chavez.[882]

General David Petraeus and Admiral Mike Mullen support General McChrystal's assessment of the Afghan war.[883]

Sep 2009

9/24/09

Pittsburgh hosts the G-20 summit.

As unemployment inches up, the federal government's employment has increased 1.3% this year. That's 25,000 employees.[884]

Hong Kong-Shanghai Bank's David Bloom believes the Federal Reserve's monetary policies are responsible for destroying the dollar as the global reserve currency.[885]

A video surfaces of elementary school children being taught pro-Obama songs. "I felt this was reminiscent of 1930s Germany and the indoctrination of children to worship their leader," said an outraged parent. The Burlington, New Jersey, superintendent wrote that the taping was inappropriate.[886] *Apparently, he thought brainwashing schoolchildren into an*

Obama Komsomal was entirely appropriate.

The FBI arrests a Jordanian who tried to blow up a downtown Dallas skyscraper.[887]

Another soldier of Allah tries to bomb a federal building in Springfield, Illinois.

A Brooklyn man and twelve others are charged with supporting al-Qaeda.

Deposed Honduran leftist and Obama favorite, Manuel Zelaya, claims he is being tortured with mind-altering gas, radiation and that Israeli assassins are trying to kill him.[888]

The International Atomic Energy Agency (IAEA) receives evidence of a secret uranium enrichment facility in Qom, Iran. This is in complete violation of the non-proliferation treaty. A U.S. official confirms that it is capable of making bombs.[889] [890]

9/25/09

President Obama credits the G-20 for saving the world economy. "Because of the bold and coordinated action that we took, millions of jobs have been 'saved or created,'" he says. He also talks about tough global financial regulations and climate change.[891]

Thankfully, he condemns Iran for having a secret nuclear facility, saying, "The size and configuration of this facility is inconsistent with a peaceful program."[892]

Sep 2009

9/26/09

President Obama is still requesting meaningful negotiations with Iran about its nuclear program.[893]

Iran is helping Venezuela find uranium deposits.[894]

French President Nicolas Sarkozy gives a blistering critique of President Obama. Sarkozy thinks Obama's goal of nuclear abolition is shallow, especially since it fails to set targets or mandates.

"We live in a real world, not a virtual world, and the real world expects us to take decisions. President Obama dreams of a world without weapons...but right in front of us two countries are doing the exact opposite. Iran since 2005 has flouted five Security Council resolutions. North Korea has been defying council resolutions since 1993. I support the extended hand of the Americans, but what good has proposals for dialogue brought the international community? More uranium enrichment and declarations by the leaders of Iran to wipe a U.N. member state [Israel] off the map."[895]

9/27/09

White House spokesman Adam Abrams says, "Mr. Romanoff was never offered a position with the administration."[896] See entry for 9/11/09.

The White House announces plans for the President to travel to Copenhagen, Denmark to lobby for the 2016 Olympics bid for Chicago.[897]

9/28/09

General McChrystal reveals that he has only spoken to the president once via video teleconference since being appointed Commander of U.S. and ISAF forces in Afghanistan.[898] *Obama has spoken to the NATO Commander just one time in 141 days.*

Iran successfully test-fires its deadliest medium-range missile. The Iranian defense minister says, "Its ultimate result would be that it expedites the Zionist regime's last breath," referring to Israel.[899]

World Bank President Robert Zoellick foresees the end of the dollar's dominance as the world's reserve currency.[900]

9/29/09

SYMBOLISM: In honor of the sixtieth anniversary of history's most murderous Communist regime, the Empire State building is lit-up in red and yellow in honor of red China.[901]

The beleaguered General Motors isn't wasting money; they've made more than $90,000 in political contributions this year.[902] *So the government owns General Motors and then they make political contributions to themselves.*

9/30/09

Banks are still wary of the economic climate as lending declines in the third quarter by 3%, the biggest drop since the statistic has been measured in 1984.[903]

Representative John Boehner (R-OH) rips President Obama for "going off to Copenhagen when we've got serious issues here at home that need to be debated."[904]

In a speech to her supporters in Copenhagen, Michelle Obama says, "As much of a sacrifice as people say this is for me or Oprah or the President to come for these few days, so many of you in this room have been working for years to bring this bid home."[905] *At least she didn't say, "let them eat cake."*

President Obama will take weeks to make a decision on Afghanistan. White House Press Secretary Robert Gibbs says, "When it comes to decisions as important as keeping this country safe and putting our troops into harm's way, the president has made it clear that he will rigorously assess our progress."[906] *It didn't take him forever to promote the Obamacare bill even though he hadn't read it and was thoroughly unfamiliar with some of its key provisions.*

Forty-three soldiers have died since General McChrystal sent his Afghan troop assessment to the White House.[907]

At $3.52 trillion in spending for fiscal year 2009, President Obama has broken all spending records.[908]

The U.S. budget deficit tripled, hitting a record $1.4 trillion for Fiscal Year 2009.[909]

2009 Fiscal Year deficit totals $1.42 trillion.[910]

Stimulus funds allocated = $159 billion

Jobs White House claims it "saved or created" = 640,329

Cost of jobs "saved or created" = $248,309.85[911]

Unemployment = 9.8%.

Real unemployment = 17%.[912]

10/1/09

Operation Fast and Furious: Beginning this month, the Bureau of Alcohol, Tobacco and Firearm's (ATF) Phoenix Field Division Group VII begins its "gunwalking" strategy. According to Sen. Charles Grassley (R-IA), "The purpose was to wait and watch, in hope that law enforcement could identify other members of trafficking network and build a large, complex conspiracy case. Group VII initially began using the new gunwalking tactics in one of its investigations to further the Department's strategy. The case was soon renamed 'Operation Fast and Furious.'"[913] *The ATF sold or facilitated the purchases of at least 2,000 guns and assault weapons to the worst elements in the Mexican gun and drug trade. In other words, the U.S. government, under Barack Obama, enabled drastic violence and the deaths of innumerable innocent people in Mexico. This botched sting operation ended with the death of U.S. Border Patrol Agent Brian Terry.*

President Obama travels to Copenhagen to try to get the 2016 Olympics bid for Chicago, despite the fact that most of the city's residents do not want it. His wife, Oprah Winfrey, Valerie Jarrett, and Arne Duncan join him.[914]

The Transportation Security Administration (TSA) plans to install 150 body- scanning machines at various airport checkpoints.[915]

General Stanley McChrystal outrages the White House with his speech in London. He says that Vice President Biden's recommendations for the Afghan war are chaotic and unworkable. His speech restates themes from his August assessment, "Waiting does not prolong a favorable outcome. This effort will not remain winnable indefinitely, and nor will public support."[916]

10/2/09

The 2016 Olympics bid has been awarded to Rio de Janeiro.[917]

In Copenhagen, the president meets with General McChrystal aboard Air Force One for twenty-five minutes.[918]

The State Department joins Islamic nations in backing a U.N. Human Rights Council resolution censoring speech that some religions and races may find offensive.[919]

The number of banks with 20% of unpaid loans is at an eighteen-year high.[920]

The World Bank claims it could run out of money in twelve months.[921]

10/3/09

The U.N. nuclear agency concludes Iran has enough data to make a nuclear bomb.[922]

The U.N. secretary-general warns that there are only ten days remaining to save the planet from climate change.[923]

10/4/09

While President Obama stalls on making a decision about Afghanistan, ten troops are killed in battle today.[924]

10/5/09

Wishing to appease China, President Obama refuses to meet with the Dalai Lama.[925] *Obama extends an open hand to Ahmadinejad and poses for pictures with Hugo Chavez, but he won't meet with the Dalai Lama?*

Russia, China, Japan, Brazil, European countries, and Arab states are colluding secretly to scrap the dollar as the world's oil trading currency in favor of a basket of currencies.[926]

Although the White House has stated its unwillingness to withdraw from Afghanistan, according to Defense Secretary Gates, the Taliban is gaining momentum in Afghanistan because of the U.S. and NATO's unwillingness to commit more troops.[927] [928]

10/6/09

Obama cowers to Chinese pressure and refuses to meet with the Dalai

Oct 2009

Lama during his visit to Washington.[929]

President Obama stages a massive photo-op with 150 doctors in the White House Rose Garden. Pre-ceremony pictures show White House staff handing out white coats to increase the appearance of legitimacy.[930]

Detained illegal immigrants will now be housed in converted hotels due to overcrowding in jails.[931]

The Obama administration accuses Fox News of being "a wing of the Republican Party."[932]

The United Nations calls for a new global reserve currency.[933]

10/8/09

The Department of Interior blocks sixty oil drilling sites in Utah.[934]

U.S. and NATO Commander, General McChrystal, requests a 40,000 to 60,000-troop increase in Afghanistan.[935] [936]

10/10/09

President Obama wins the Nobel Peace prize just four days after snubbing the Dalai Lama (also a Nobel Peace Laureate). The President was in office for eleven full days before the cutoff date for nominations. He may be the first Nobel recipient to receive the prize simply for his aspirations. 1983 winner, Lech Walesa says, "So soon? Too early. He has no contribution so far."[937] [938] *It is noteworthy that President Obama did not win the Nobel Prize for economics either. Maybe next year.*

Obama attacks the U.S. Chamber of Commerce for not supporting his financial reforms. Unable to concede any validity to those who disagree with him, he states, "Predictably, a lot of the banks and big financial firms don't like the idea of a consumer agency very much. In fact, the U.S. Chamber of Commerce is spending millions on an ad campaign to kill it." The Chamber contends that Obama's reforms would create yet another bureaucracy that would make matters worse for consumers and business.[939]

Washington forbids Arizona Sheriff Joe Arpaio from making immigration arrests.[940]

10/11/09

War on Fox: "We're going to treat them the way we would treat an opponent," says Anita Dunn, the White House communications director.[941] *It's not surprising that a Maoist would scorn dissent.*

10/12/09

Arizona Sheriff Joe Arpaio says that despite the federal government's decision two days ago, he has the authority under Arizona law to keep making arrests.[942]

Oct 2009

10/13/09

Secretary Clinton fails to secure a commitment from Russia regarding tougher sanctions against Iran as Prime Minister Putin warns countries about pressuring Iran regarding their nuclear arms program.[943] [944]

The U.S. has agreed to allow Russia to visit, inspect and count U.S. nuclear missiles and warheads. Secretary Clinton wants the U.S. to be as transparent as possible, "We want to ensure that every question that the Russian military or Russian government asks is answered."[945] *Too bad the transparency pledge wasn't meant for the American people.*

10/14/09

President Obama sets his sights on demonizing the health insurance industry to promote Obamacare. Since Labor Day, over $25 million has been spent campaigning against them.[946]

President Obama endorses sending 50 million senior citizens a $250 bonus check.[947]

10/15/09

President Obama visits New Orleans to inspect post-Katrina progress for four hours. Some residents criticize the "glorified flyover" as too little too late.[948]

Russia warns the U.S. against talking to non-NATO countries, like Ukraine and Georgia, about a missile shield.[949]

Oct 2009

10/16/09

Rumors surface that the President is "disgusted" that the Israelis refuse to stop settlement construction as a precondition to talks with the Palestinian Authority.[950]

Colleen LaRose, a.k.a. "Jihad Jane," is arrested at Philadelphia International Airport and charged with conspiracy to commit murder and terrorism related crimes.[951]

On strengthening ties with Canada and Mexico, the president vows, "We're going to make this a **top priority**..."[952]

10/17/09

President Obama has a 2 ½ hour secret briefing with media allies including Keith Olbermann, Rachel Maddow, and Maureen Dowd.[953] *Wow! General McChrystal only got twenty-five minutes. Also, since the White House attacks Fox as illegitimate, is this their idea of "real news?"*

10/18/09

President Obama continues to stall on the seventy-sixth day since Gen. McChrystal recommended that additional forces were needed.[954] *"All great men are men of quick decision which flows from their intuition, their accumulated knowledge, and previous experience." —Claude Bristol*

Rahm Emanuel contends that Fox is not a news organization because it has a perspective. David Axelrod also says that Fox is "not really a news station" and their programming is "not really news."[955] [956] *Would Axelrod, Emanuel, Dunn, et al, consider ABC and NBC to be "real" news outlets since their networks refused to run paid advertisements critical of Obamacare on 8/27/09?*

Anita Dunn, White House communications director, admits that the Obama campaign controlled the media. Dunn states, "Very rarely did we communicate through the press anything that we didn't absolutely control."[957] *Obviously, controlling the media did not stop when the campaign was over. Also, notice that the White House only considers "legitimate" news operations to be the ones they control.*

10/19/09

REALITY CHECK: *Pravda* publishes yet another article about America's decline into socialism.[958] *Pravda was the official newspaper of the Soviet Union.*

The Administration will not arrest medical marijuana users and suppliers where they comply with the laws of the states in which they operate.[959] *See entries for 2/5/09, 2/28/09, and 3/18/09.*

10/20/09

The White House throws a Latin entertainment extravaganza in a giant tent on the South Lawn.[960]

Oct 2009

10/21/09

Eight months after passage of the stimulus, forty-nine of fifty states have lost jobs.[961]

"Pay Czar" Kenneth Feinberg starts slashing compensation at firms that received government aid.[962]

10/22/09

Democrats seek to increase the debt limit above $13 trillion.[963] *"These deficits are resulting in a dangerous and unprecedented borrowing spree. Total debt during this spree has grown by trillion of dollars…How can the Republican majoritiy in this congress explain to their constituents that trillions of dollars of new debt is good for our economy? How can they explain that they think it's fair to force our children, our grandchildren, our great-grandchildren to finance this debt through higher taxes. That's what it will have to be. Why is it right to increase our nation's dependence on foreign creditors? –Senator Harry Reid, March 2006.*

President Obama lashes out at climate change non-believers.[964]

Former vice president Dick Cheney calls for Obama to stop dithering over Afghanistan.[965]

The White House unveils a Muslim technology fund. The Overseas Private Investment Corporation will provide financing from $25 million to $150 million for chosen projects.[966]

Oct 2009

10/25/09

It turns out that health insurance companies are not quite the greedy profiteers that the White House has portrayed; their profits over the past year are about 2 percent.[967]

10/26/09

IRS Commissioner Doug Shulman unveils his plan for "the globalization of tax administration" which will be a "game changing trend" for the IRS.[968] *You will never be able to outrun the iron claws of the IRS.*

10/28/09

Rocco Landesman, Chairman of the National Endowment for the Arts, praises Barack Obama as "the most powerful writer since Julius Caesar." *This effusive flattery reminds me of Leonid Brezhnev, General Secretary of the Communist Party of the Soviet Union, being awarded the Lenin Prize for Literature.*[969]

President Obama is maybe, kind of, sort of, perhaps, almost ready to unveil an Afghanistan strategy. Right now they are considering a "something for everybody" strategy that would alloy Vice President Biden's wishes with General McChrystal's assessment.

While he continues to "rigorously assesses our progress" in Afghanistan, fifty-three Americans have been killed so far this month.[970] [971] *In light of the fact that Vice President Biden has zero military experience, perhaps he should defer to General McChrystal's judgment.*

10/29/09

Auto publisher Edmunds estimates that Cash for Clunkers cost taxpayers $24,000 per car.[972] *Predictably, the thin-skinned White House attacks Edmunds as savagely as anyone else who disagrees with them.*

Stimulus jobs are overstated. Shabby accounting and fuzzy math have shown that the government is inflating stimulus-related job figures.[973]

10/30/09

Kalpen Modi, White House Associate Director of Public Engagement, is directly implicated in the scandal of attempting to convert the National Endowment for the Arts into Obama's Propaganda Ministry.[974] *Modi is famous for his leading role as a pothead in the "Harold and Kumar" movies. Maybe Oscar Wilde was right: life does imitate art.*

Despite two rulings in federal court, Obama refuses to reveal the full White House visitors list.[975] *We shall see later that he does not feel much need to obey court rulings.*

Hillary on Taxes: Secretary Clinton showed her revulsion for the tax system in Pakistan, "We [the U.S.] tax everything that moves and doesn't move, and that's not what we see in Pakistan."[976]

10/31/09

Liberal Republican Dede Scozzafava withdraws from the race for New York 23rd District Congressional seat due to a challenge from a conservative candidate, Doug Hoffman. White House political director, Patrick Gaspard, is instrumental in convincing Scozzafava to endorse the Democrat.[977] *This situation shows that the White House is inclined to meddle and interfere with regional politics; Gaspard was also the White House's point man in trying to convince New York Govenor David Paterson to withdraw from his reelection campaign.*

Secretary Clinton adopts the position that Israeli settlement expansion in the West Bank should not prevent peace negotiations.[978]

Unemployment soars to 10.2% as the president's stimulus continues to "save or create" jobs.

Real unemployment = 17.4%.[979]

11/1/09

Nov 2009

Despite receiving $2.3 billion in bailout funds, CIT Group, Inc., files for Chapter 11 bankruptcy. CIT is a lender to nearly a million small and medium-sized businesses. They disclose $71 billion in assets and $64.9 billion in debt.[980]

Palestinians accuse the U.S. of changing its position with regard to Secretary Clinton's remarks yesterday and assert that resumption of peace negotiations is impossible as long as Israel expands settlement construction.[981]

11/2/09

The Government Accountability Office (GAO) issues its report of $81.1 billion of TARP bailouts for GM and Chrysler, concluding, "The Treasury is unlikely to recover the entirety of its investment in Chrysler or GM, given that the companies' values would have to grow substantially above what they have been in the past."[982]

"We will not rest until we are succeeding in generating the jobs that this economy needs."[983]

Russian military exercises are war-gaming a nuclear attack on Poland.[984]

Hugo Chavez's socialist revolution has now brought water rationing to Caracas, Venezuela.[985]

11/3/09

Despite President Obama's active campaigning, New Jersey and Virginia elect Republican governors. Hours after the results are in, White House Press Secretary Robert Gibbs says the president is barely interested in the returns and cautions voters not to mistake these returns as any kind of referendum on the president's job.[986]

There are too many examples of ridiculous stimulus spending projects to recount, but here are a couple: $300,000 for a GPS-equipped helicopter to find radioactive rabbit droppings and $11 million for Microsoft to build a bridge connecting its two campuses. By the way, Microsoft is worth over $200 billion.[987] *This is the Obama administration that*

Nov 2009

promised the stimulus would be free of earmarks and that it would review budgets line by line. Apparently, they missed several lines. This puts the Obama administration in a Catch-22. If they actually did as they promised, then they heartily approve of frittering away billions of dollars. If they didn't review it "line by line," then they can't back up their promises.

North Korea claims to have successfully weaponized more plutonium for nuclear bombs.[988]

11/4/09

Iran took the opportunity to celebrate and gloat over the thirtieth anniversary of the U.S. Embassy takeover. Many supporters enjoyed the day shouting, "Death to America!" There were also dissenters of the current regime shouting, "Death to the Dictator!" The dissenters were violently shown their place with bullets, batons and tear gas.[989]

President Obama marks the thirtieth anniversary of the U.S. Embassy takeover by inviting Iran to negotiate.[990]

11/5/09

An Islamic extremist, Major Nidal Hasan, shouts *"Allahu Akbar"* as he fires a barrage of bullets at Fort Hood, killing twelve and wounding thirty.[991]

Americans are stunned to see President Obama's response to the Fort Hood shootings. While speaking at the Tribal Nations Conference, he bathes in the crowd's enthusiasm and even gives "a shout-out to Dr. Joe Medicine Crow," before somberly addressing his nation's

Nov 2009

tragedy. He cautions Americans "against jumping to conclusions."[992]
President Obama must have learned his lessen from the Cambridge, Mas-
sachusetts case. Perhaps if Sergeant Crowley had shouted "Allahu Akbar"
before arresting Dr. Gates, the President probably would not have jumped
to any conclusions.

President Obama weighs in on environmental protection: "So this is
going to be a **top priority** generally improving our environmental quality."[993]

Iran tests an advanced nuclear warhead design that will enhance their
ability to arm missiles with atomic bombs.[994]

11/6/09

President Obama again addresses the tragedy at Fort Hood and also
repeats that Americans should not to jump to conclusions.[995] *For the*
coming weeks, the Administration will exhibit remarkable contortions to
avoid characterizing Major Hasan as an Islamic extremist. When Con-
gresswoman Gabrielle Giffords (D-AZ) was shot, liberals had no problem
high-jumping, long-jumping, triple-jumping, pole-vaulting, and catapult-
ing to all sorts of conclusions from gun control to the evils of talk radio.

President Obama signs a twenty-six-week unemployment extension
bill saying, "Now, it's important to note that the bill I signed will not add
to our deficit. It is fully paid for, and so it is fiscally responsible."[996] *This*
fairytale is 100% true. President Obama was given some magic beans
that grew into a money tree.

Nov 2009

Iranian authorities arrest journalists to suppress information regarding civil unrest.[997]

11/7/09

Freddie Mac posts a $5 billion loss.[998]

11/8/09

Obamacare passes the House.[999]

The *Los Angeles Times* reports that a Democratic consultant received threats from the White House for appearing on Fox. "We better not see you on again…clients might stop using you if you continue," said the un-named White House official. Veteran Democratic pollster and Carter Administration official, Pat Caddell, says he is familiar with the Obama administration's threats to some of his colleagues. Caddell adds, "When the White House gets in the business of suppressing dissent and comment, particularly from its own party, it hurts itself."[1000]

Chavez prepares for war against a U.S.-led attack.[1001]

11/9/09

The U.S. Army was aware of Major Hasan's contact with al-Qaeda. Intelligence agencies intercepted as many as 20 e-mail messages between Hasan and radical cleric Anwar al-Awlaki. In one e-mail inquiring about the appropriateness of jihad, Hasan signs off, "I can't wait to join

Nov 2009

you" in the afterlife. Officials also dismissed colleagues' complaints about Hasan's airing of his political and religious views. Walter Reed officials had repeatedly given Hasan poor evaluations for substandard work. The bureaucratic nightmare of expelling a politically correct employee stymied the process of taking prudent action against their colleague who had "SoA" ("Soldier of Allah") printed on his business cards.[1002] [1003] [1004] [1005]

President Obama is his usual un-transparent self when it comes to jail time for those who violate Obamacare's insurance mandate. When asked, he replies, "I'm not sure that's the biggest question that they're (Congress) asking right now."[1006] *Why didn't the president answer this question? Either he is concealing provisions that he knows will be unpopular or he is callously indifferent to the effects not complying with Obamacare. One would assume he would be mildly curious whether Americans will be incarcerated by his signature legislation. In reality, at this point in the game, the Obamacare legislation is probably as half-baked as every other dish this administration serves*

Attorney General Eric Holder agrees to give the keynote address to the Council on American-Islamic Relations (CAIR). The FBI has severed links to CAIR based on its ties with the Muslim Brotherhood and Hamas.[1007]

The President meets with fifty leaders of the Jewish Federations of North America. While refusing to discuss issues relating to Israel or Iran, he chooses to regale the audience with his dazzling economic policies and his plans for socialized medicine.[1008]

Nov 2009

National Security Advisor James Jones discredits any rumors that the president has finally approved a plan for Afghan troop deployment, "Reports that President Obama has made a decision about Afghanistan are absolutely false. He has not received final options for his consideration, he has not reviewed those options with his national security team, and he has not made any decisions about resources. Any reports to the contrary are completely untrue and come from uninformed sources."[1009] *Tell him to relax and take his time.*

Iran detains Americans for espionage. Three American hikers in Northern Iraq inadvertently crossed the Iranian border and were captured. Meanwhile, the U.S. is giving Iran time to consider a U.N.-brokered deal regarding its nuclear program.[1010] [1011]

President Obama sends a videotaped message to Germany celebrating the fall of the Berlin Wall, without saying the words "Soviet Union" or "communism." He speaks eloquently about how we must help those who still struggle with tyranny today.[1012] *What a difference a year and a half makes. When he was a senator, Barack Obama felt entitled to honor himself with a speech at the Brandenburg Gate, although he did nothing to contribute to the end of communism or the fall of the Berlin Wall. At that time he was unknown in Germany so he had to bribe the audience with a concert, free beer, pizza, and bratwurst. Now that he is president and doesn't need the campaign publicity, he just phoned in a pre-fab speech.*

Nov 2009

11/10/09

Anwar al-Awlaki praises Major Nidal Hasan as a hero on his website.[1013]

The Department of Justice sends a formal request to the News site, *Indymedia.us*, demanding they relinquish the IP addresses of all who visited the site. Pushing the Orwellian envelope even further, the site is ordered "not to disclose the existence of this request" unless authorized by the Department of Justice.[1014] *The first duty of the social compact is to protect us from outside enemies. The second duty is to protect us from inside enemies. Who is left to protect us from our protectors? If Attorney General Holder doesn't bother to read laws he criticizes (like the Arizona immigration law), he should at least read the Bill of Rights.*

William J. Burns, Under Secretary of Political Affairs, outlines the State Department's Middle East goal of a two-state solution by expelling Jews from Judea and Samaria in order to "end the occupation that began in 1967."[1015] *Maybe the Obama administration will provide boxcars to help with the move.*

Nov 2009

11/11/09

Exaggerated, inflated and preposterous claims regarding the success of the president's stimulus spending keep pouring in. According to the *Boston Globe*, the stimulus report of Massachusetts "has so many errors, missing data, or estimates instead of actual job counts that it may be impossible to accurately tally how many people have been employed by the massive infusion of federal money."[1016]

The stimulus itself may be what is "un-stimulating" the economy with government spending sucking capital out of the private sector. The 500 largest non-financial corporations are holding more than $1 trillion in Treasury bills. They are sinking their money in government bonds rather than growing business and creating jobs.[1017]

11/12/09

The Administration is purging the government of undesirable Republican civil servants. The Office of Personnel Management issues a diktat for firing and denying promotions to any political appointees, retroactive for five years.[1018]

•

China warns Obama about meeting with the Dalai Lama. While President Obama obediently complied with China's first directive in October, he has indefinitely postponed meeting with one of the world's greatest living symbols of Peace until his first official meeting with China.[1019]

The Pension Benefit Guaranty Corporation (PBGC), a federal corporation, signals it may need tens of billions of dollars in bailout funds. PBGC is riddled with egregious irresponsibility and stupendous corruption.

PBGC has intentionally lied, mislead and provided false information to Congress and the Inspector General. Records now show that PBGC's deficit is $21.9 billion, not including GM and Chrysler's plans which could balloon into an additional $42 billion.

PBGC also stores citizens' very private personal data. A PBGC contractor stored 1,300 people's financial information and social security numbers on a flash drive that was found on the floor of an Ohio train station.[1020]

11/13/09

The Obama administration announces that Khalid Sheikh Mohammed (KSM), the mastermind who plotted 9/11, will be tried in federal court in New York City.[1021] *This announcement was made almost a week after the Fort Hood shootings. It also dovetails nicely with the President's groveling support of the Ground Zero Mosque. Just in case you need further confirmation of President Obama's spinelessness: it's Friday and he's flying to Asia, leaving Eric Holder to withstand the initial heat.*

President Obama announces that he wants domestic spending cuts to cut the deficit.[1022]

International Atomic Energy Agency (IAEA) inspectors access Iran's recently discovered secret nuclear facility and confirm that it is adequate for nuclear arms manufacturing.[1023]

In Japan, President Obama says that under his leadership the U.S. will be more involved in Asia-Pacific multilateral dialogue, stating, "I know that the United States has been disengaged from these organizations in recent years."[1024] *As one would expect, the president also takes a few moments to personalize his speech and talk about himself. Natch.*

Nov 2009

11/14/09

President Obama bows again, this time before Japanese Emperor Aki-hito.[1025]

China detains and silences dissidents ahead of Obama's visit.[1026]

Anita Dunn, White House communications director, attacks Fox again.[1027] *Yawn.*

11/15/09

Former NYC Mayor Rudy Giuliani attacks the Administration's stance on trying Khalid Sheikh Mohammed in New York, "I do not understand why they cannot try Khalid Sheikh Mohommed in a military tribunal. That also would demonstrate that we are a nation of laws. This is the way we have tried enemy combatants in the past, whether it was the Second World War or the U.S. Civil War."[1028] *What do you expect, Mr. Mayor? President Obama treats the 9/11 tragedy with all the respect and solemnity of a dignitary who eulogized another jihad massacre by giving a "shout-out" to a member of the audience.*

President Obama is greeted by the Chinese people wearing "Oba-Mao" t-shirts.[1029] *They should know.*

At a Far East press conference President Obama is asked a question regarding troop deployment in Afghanistan: "Can you explain to people watching and criticizing your deliberations what piece of information you're still lacking to make that call?" The president chides, "With respect to Afghanistan, Jennifer, I don't think this is a matter of some datum of information that I'm waiting on...Critics of the process... tend not to be folks who... are directly involved in what's happening in Afghanistan. Those who are recognize the gravity of the situation and recognize the importance of us getting it right."[1030] *"An effective leader, once he has all of the relevant facts presented to him, can make a decision rather quickly." —Andrew Carnegie*

The Federal Reserve is endangering the entire global economy according to China's chief banking regulator, Liu Mingkang, who sharply rebukes U.S. fiscal and monetary policy for fostering "dollar carry-trade," a practice in which investors borrow dollars at minimal interest rates and invest them abroad in higher-yielding assets.[1031]

11/16/09

The White House continues to boast stimulus funds are "saving and creating" jobs all over the country. The problem is that they are spending money in places that don't even exist like Arizona's 15th Congressional District or Connecticut's 42nd District (neither of which exists). Representative David Obey (D-WI) remarks, "The inaccuracies on *recovery. gov* that have come to light are outrageous and the Obama administration owes itself, the Congress, and every American a commitment to work night and day to correct the ludicrous mistakes."[1032] *Maybe they can also "save and create" some jobs in Narnia, Oz, Shangri-La and Erewhon.*

As socialized Obamacare approaches, health rationing is already begin-

Nov 2009

ning—starting with mammograms. The United States Preventive Services Task Force is no longer recommending that women in their 40s have annual mammograms. Now they are advising women over fifty to have mammogram check-ups every other year.[1033]

President Obama addresses a group of 400 Chinese students. He tells the audience, "These freedoms of expression and worship and access to information and political participation, we believe, are universal rights. They should be available to all people, including ethnic and religious minorities— whether they are in the United States, China, or any nation. Indeed, it is that respect for universal rights that guides America's openness to other countries; our respect for different cultures; our commitment to international law; and our faith in the future."[1034] *Nice speech, but it rings a bit hollow since Secretary Clinton made it clear on February 20, 2009, that issues like human rights, Tibet and Taiwan would not interfere with the "real business" between the U.S. and China.*

China, the U.S.'s largest creditor, is unimpressed with the fiscal wisdom of Obamacare. Chinese officials use the president's Asian trip as an opportunity to ask very detailed questions. Even though he bowed (again!) to Hu Jintao, they remain skeptical.[1035] [1036] *The Chinese need to stop it with their smarty-pants pencil-work, quit their griping and pay attention to the Prez. On 9/9/09, he told the world that Obamacare would not add "one dime" to the budget deficit. How dare they second-guess the Anointed One?*

11/18/09

President Obama assumes the mantle of fiscal responsibility today. He warns Americans that too much debt may push us into a double-dip recession.[1037]

Senator Grassley (R-IA) asks Attorney General Holder to provide information about Department of Justice lawyers who have previously advocated for terrorist detainees, contending that there may be conflicts of interest.[1038]

Senate Health Care Bill = 2,074 pages
House Health Care Bill = 1,990 pages[1039]

The White House Budget Director estimates that in fiscal year 2009 the government squandered $98 billion in malfeasance, misdirection and fraud.[1040]

President Obama admits that he will be unable to fulfill his promise that Guantanamo prison will close by January 2010.[1041]

Secretary Clinton arrives in Afghanistan.[1042]

Groveling is becoming a habit for President Obama as he bows before communist Chinese Premier Wen Jiabao.[1043]

11/19/09

Umaru Mutallab, father of the "underwear bomber" (*a.k.a. "fruit of the*

Nov 2009

boom"), makes a report to two CIA officers at the U.S. Embassy in Nigeria warning that his son is a potential threat and may be in Yemen. His son, Umar Abdulmutallab, is added to a list of over a half million of those with suspected terrorist connections but he is not added to a "no fly" list.[1044] *After the bomber easily slipped past all security clearances, DHS Secretary Napolitano comforted America by telling us, "the system worked."*

House Speaker Nancy Pelosi (D-CA) announces that any "Wall Street tax" on financial transactions must take effect on an international scale.[1045]

The Senate health care bill includes a 5% tax on elective cosmetic surgery, including botox.[1046] *Now Vice President Biden will have even more opportunity to do his "patriotic duty."*

The White House announces that the president will not reach a decision about Afghan troop deployment before Thanksgiving.[1047]

President Obama returns from Asia having accomplished, well… nothing. The Japanese government will no longer refuel U.S. Navy ships in the Indian Ocean. The President achieved zero concessions from China. The Chinese will not budge on human rights violations, greenhouse gasses, currency valuation, sanctions against Iran or nuclear talks. Hu Jintao hoodwinked Obama into a joint press conference where questions were forbidden (no other President would have been so naively duped).[1048] *On other foreign policy fronts, he is looking more and more like a namby-pamby pushover. Netanyahu ignores him, Ahmadinejad*

and Kim Jong Il simply laugh at him, Putin and Sarkozy don't take him
seriously, Gordon Brown feels rightly snubbed, Chavez is antagonistic,
his Honduran efforts were spayed. As Nero fiddled while Rome burned,
Obama poses for GQ, plays golf and hosts celebrities while the rest of the
world is divesting U.S. currency.

11/20/09

Climategate: one of the greatest swindles in history. Hacked e-mails
from researchers at East Anglia University's Climate Research Unit
(CRU) are made public. CRU's research is the foundation for the U.N.'s
Intergovernmental Panel on Climate Change (IPCC). The researchers'
e-mails show a pattern of collusion, collaboration, and conspiracy to
commit a fraud that would destroy multi-trillions of dollars worth of
wealth-generating capacity. The e-mails reveal:

I—the researchers intentionally manipulated evidence,
II—the researchers' admissions that they lacked evidence proving glob-
al warming,
III—the researchers intentionally suppressed evidence,
IV—the researchers willfully sabotaged evidence to protect their proj-
ect against Freedom of Information requests,
V—the researchers concealed "inconvenient truths" that countered
their bias, like the Medieval Warming Period,
VI—they rigged the peer review process and obstructed the works of
skeptics,
VII—they willfully withheld data from researchers who may have un-

Nov 2009

dermined their cause, and

VIII—they stifled dissenting opinions from entering the IPCC report.[1049]

CRU didn't produce evidence of man-made global warming; instead, they produced man-made evidence of man-made global warming.

Germany joins the ranks of countries concerned about the Federal Reserve's irresponsible monetary policy. Finance Minister Wolfgang Schauble believes that the U.S. is creating a market bubble by devaluing the dollar and inflating away the national debt.[1050]

11/23/09

"**I will not rest** until businesses are investing again, and businesses are hiring again."[1051]

Iran displays war games to deter Western pressure over its nuclear program.[1052]

11/24/09

Completely ignoring the fact that the climate data in the U.N.'s IPCC report is debunked, the president is optimistic that a climate deal can be struck in the upcoming Copenhagen summit.[1053] *In light of recent events regarding "Climategate," one would imagine that dispassionate minds would demand a re-examination of all the facts before the nations of the world commit to anything...unless, of course, global warming is re-*

ally just a pretext for something else—like redistributing wealth.

White House party crashers: Controversy erupts as uninvited guests, Michaele and Tareq Salahi, passed through White House security. The Salahis maintain that there was no wrongdoing on their part.[1054] *Michaele Salahi is a cast member of the television show* The Real Housewives of D.C. *on the Bravo network. Bravo is owned by NBC, which is owned by General Electric. NBC's coverage of Obama has been overwhelmingly biased in his favor. GE and its CEO, Jeff Immelt, have likewise been very generous to the president. Immelt is on the president's Economic Recovery Advisory Board and is the Chairman of the Council on Jobs and Competitiveness. We also know that GE met with Prime Minister Putin after President Obama scrapped the East European defense shield. I'm not trying to promote a conspiracy, but it isn't too much of a stretch for such "good friends" to engineer a profitable publicity stunt.*

Senator Grassley (R-IA) sends a letter to Attorney General Holder demanding that he provide information requested at the November 18, 2009, hearing (that is, which Department of Justice employees previously advocated for terrorist detainees).[1055]

President Obama is seen leaving the White House with a copy of *GQ* magazine featuring none other than himself.[1056]

Britain's Defense Secretary, Bob Ainsworth, publicly criticizes the Commander In Chief for dithering on making his decision about Afghanistan and blames the White House for the British public's declining support of the war.[1057]

The White House announces that President Obama could, just maybe, maybe, maybe make a decision about sending troops to Afghanistan.[1058]

11/25/09

President Obama sends Hajj greetings to the world's Muslims. "Michelle and I would like to send our best wishes to all those performing Hajj this year, and to Muslims in America and around the world who are celebrating Eid al-Adha.[1059] Hajj is the annual pilgrimage Muslims make to Mecca.

With regard to "Climategate," "Global Warming Czarina" Carol Browner, Director of the Office of Energy and Climate Change Policy, says, "We have 2,500 of the world's foremost scientists who are in absolute agreement that this is a real problem and that we need to do something and we need to do something as soon as possible."[1060] *First, she dodges the issue that the scientific conclusions are based on contaminated data. Second, science is about facts, not "consensus." Before Copernicus there was "consensus" that the Earth was the center of the universe——it still didn't make it true. Third, Czarina Carol's motives are suspect. As a member of the Socialist International, her position neatly fits into an agenda that has nothing to do with a cleaner environment.*

Three Navy SEALs capture one of Iraq's most wanted terrorists. Instead of being hailed as heroes, they face court-martial because the terrorist received a bloody lip.[1061]

11/26/09

The International Criminal Court claims it has jurisdiction to prosecute American "war crimes." *See entry for 8/6/09; Secretary Clinton laments that we haven't already ceded sovereignty to this judicial body.*[1062]

World financial markets tumble on news that Dubai is wobbling on a debt crisis.[1063]

11/27/09

President Obama's very own Justice Department concludes that his friends at ACORN can be paid for its contracts prior to the Congressional ban on providing money to the group.[1064] *So, can Bernie Madoff continue to collect management fees from his bilked clients?*

11/29/09

Ben Bernanke cautions that transparency in the Federal Reserve and Congressional oversight by America's elected representatives would impair the economy.[1065] *Yes, if the world really knew what the Fed was up to it probably would upset the applecart.*

In defiance of the U.N., Iran plans to build ten new uranium enrichment plants.[1066]

Nov 2009

11/30/09

The Treasury Department unveils its Home Affordable Foreclosure Alternatives Program which, among other things, gives mortgage companies incentives to allow homeowners to surrender their homes in lieu of foreclosure.[1067]

Unemployment = 10%.
Real unemployment = 17.2%.[1068]

12/1/09

Former Vice President Dick Cheney criticizes the president for projecting weakness, dithering over Afghanistan, trying Khalid Sheikh Mohammed in New York, his disregard for the private sector and his uncertain belief in American exceptionalism.[1069]

After months of dithering, President Obama *finally* announces the deployment of 30,000 troops to Afghanistan (10,000 fewer than General McChrystal's minimum request). One hundred and sixteen Americans died in Afghanistan during the months it took him to make his decision.[1070]

President Obama also tips his hand by setting a timetable, announcing that U.S. troops will begin withdrawing by July 2011.[1071]

Not surprisingly, he uses the troop announcement as another opportunity to scapegoat the Bush administration for the situation in Afghanistan: "Commanders in Afghanistan repeatedly asked for support to deal with the reemergence of the Taliban, but these reinforcements

Dec 2009

did not arrive." Former Defense Secretary Rumsfeld diplomatically called President Obama a liar and disavowed any knowledge of such a request.[1072] *Have you ever noticed that Barack Obama's moral compass always points to someone else?*

12/2/09

"Science Czar" John Holdren testifies before Congress and claims the hacked e-mails exposing scientific fraud at CRU have no effect on the reality of climate change.[1073] *What is truly alarming is the alarmists' reaction to "Climategate." There is a peculiar "Wizard of Oz" quality to Holder, Browner and the rest of the Green Machine's response. In the movie, the dog, Toto, pulls back the curtain and exposes the Wizard as a pudgy, doddering old man. The "Wizard" summons his technological power and bellows, "Pay no attention to the man behind the curtain!" Likewise, the Green Machine continues to howl the same hysterics even though the curtain has been pulled back, exposing them for the frauds they are.*

Russia is building a Kalishnikov AK-103 factory in Venezuela.[1074] *Kalishnikovs are excellent assault weapons and are the weapon of choice for terrorists such as Osama bin Laden.*

12/3/09

Dumbfounded by high unemployment despite the stimulus, the president hosts a "jobs summit." The publicity stunt is a stocked pond of the usual gallery of leftists: liberal economists, union leaders, environmental advocates and some executives from blue-chip companies. Not attending the summit is anyone critical of Obama administration policies, the U.S. Chamber of Commerce and actual small business job creators.[1075] *Obama's guest list reflects his worldview of the factors of production that make an economy work. Since he won't release his college transcripts, it is now safe to assume that he never took economics in college.*

Americans should be grateful that President Obama is solving its economic woes. According to Press Secretary Gibbs, "The President works each and every day on making our economy stronger and putting us in a position to where we're creating jobs, businesses are hiring again. I can certainly assure the American people that that is the chief focus of the President of the United States."

Although President Obama has never even run a cash register in his life he is serious about buckling down on job creation. He proclaims, "Though the job losses we were experiencing earlier this year have slowed dramatically, we're still not creating enough new jobs each month to make up for the ones we're losing."[1076] *By no means is this empty rhetoric. The White House says the stimulus will create more than 3.5 million jobs in 2010. Oops! They meant "create or save."*

On exports by small businesses the president says, "This is going to be a **top priority**."[1077]

According to the *Chicago Tribune*, the president and First Lady have hosted 170 parties and social events since January 20. Throughout the upcoming Holiday Season, they will host seventeen more parties and eleven open houses for some 50,000 guests.[1078]

NASA has refused to comply with Freedom of Information Act requests

Dec 2009

for two years regarding their climate data, ostensibly because their "facts" were compiled by the same *mutatis mutandis* methods as the "Climategate" frauds.[1079]

Prior to the Copenhagen climate summit, India announces it will not commit to limiting its carbon emissions; however, they will consider reductions "if supported by financing and technology transfers."[1080] *Bingo! There's your wealth redistribution.*

Honduras votes against reinstating ousted socialist Manuel Zelaya.[1081]

12/4/09

White House Social Secretary, Desiree Rogers, says, "The Obamas were planning a 'non-religious' Christmas."[1082] *Presumably, this reflects the wishes of President and Mrs. Obama.*

12/6/09

President Obama heads to Capitol Hill to encourage Senate Democrats to support health care reform.[1083]

12/7/09

Circumventing the legislative process, the Environmental Protection Agency (EPA) announces that it will impose mandates on businesses that emit carbon dioxide as a greenhouse gas. Dismissing the recent exposure of scientific fraud, the EPA will now have the power to impose mandates on broad swaths of the economy. Director Jackson says, "There is nothing in the hacked e-mails that undermines the science upon which this decision is based.[1084] [1085] *This should help the president fulfill his campaign promise to bankrupt the coal industry and cause electricity rates to "necessarily skyrocket."*

Judicial Watch files suit against the Obama administration to publish the White House visitors list. The group believes the American people have a right to know who is influencing President Obama and helping to shape policy. The "most transparent administration" vows they will never release the names of visitors from January 20 to September 30, 2009.[1086]

Senator Harry Reid (D-NV) likens opponents of socialized Obamacare to supporters of slavery.[1087] *I wonder if Senator Reid would agree that his gluttonous spending and out-of-control deficits will subject future generations of Americans to involuntary servitude.*

Hugo Chavez purchases thousands of Russian missiles and rocket launchers claiming that Colombia plans to wage war against Venezuela.[1088]

Dec 2009

12/8/09

The White House warns Congress that if it does not pass greenhouse gas regulation, "the EPA is going to have to regulate in this area. And it is not going to be able to regulate on a market-based way, so its' going to have to regulate in a command-and-control way, which will probably generate even more uncertainty."[1089] *There you have it. The White House is telling Congress that it is irrelevant. Apparently, Congress's sole function is to provide the color of legitimacy to Obama's agenda. If it fails to do the administration's bidding, the Great Obama will circumvent the legislative branch and impose his policies anyway. This is how all tyrants view the executive branch of government.*

Global warming enthusiasts continue their state of denial as if the e-mail scandal never occurred. U.N. Secretary-General Ban states publicly that the CRU's fraudulent use of fantasy data has no effect on the truth of global warming.[1090]

The president announces a new multi-billion dollar second stimulus jobs program. According to the president, we must "spend our way out of this recession." He uses the announcement as a platform for his daily assault on Bush.[1091] [1092] *He also blamed President Harding for his Teapot Dome scandal.*

President Obama is in Allentown, Pennsylvania, today as the first stop on a "listening tour" to gather ideas for taxing and spending America into prosperity.[1093]

Moody's, the investment rating agency, says the U.S. is in danger of losing its AAA bond rating.[1094]

The Transportation Security Administration (TSA) committed a major breach by inadvertently revealing online its most closely guarded secrets, including CIA agents, law enforcement and diplomatic officials.[1095]

Federal employees receive a 2% pay raise.[1096]

Facts surface that "Safe Schools Czar" Kevin Jennings hosted an event in 2001 where children were given lessons in "fisting" and children were also given "fisting" kits.[1097]

Five Muslim men from Virginia are arrested in Pakistan for links to terrorism.[1098]

12/9/09

Norwegians are offended by President Obama's arrogant snubs. The president slighted all of the following: King Harald V's invitation for lunch, dinner with the Nobel Committee, a visit to the Peace Center with an exhibition in his honor, a concert in his honor, appearing at a children's event promoting peace, a press conference and TV interviews.[1099 1100]

Congressional Democrats strategize how to raise the debt ceiling an additional $1.8 trillion.[1101] *"I must express my protest against continually increasing the debt without taking positive steps to slow its growth."* –Senator Joe Biden, October 1984.

The administration expects to lose about $30 billion on auto industry bailouts.[1102]

Six million dollars in stimulus funds are awarded to Mark Penn, Hillary Clinton's pollster in 2008. *These stimulus funds saved three jobs![1103] [1104]*

Dec 2009

CONSOL Energy, a coal company, blames environmentalists as they cut 500 jobs.[1105]

12/10/09

President Obama accepts the Nobel Peace Prize.[1106]

12/11/09

The number of federal workers receiving six-figure salaries has risen from 14% to 19% during the recession.[1107]

"Pay Czar" Ken Feinberg caps more bank salaries.[1108]

U.N. security gags journalist Phelim McAleer, a climate-change skeptic, for asking "inconvenient questions."[1109]

12/13/09

In an interview with Oprah Winfrey, "Christmas at the White House," President Obama awards himself the grade of "a good, solid B+."[1110]

Michelle Obama speaks on behalf of her manufactured nutrition crusade. The law she supports, "Healthy, Hunger-Free Kids Act" will subsidize and regulate what children eat before, during and after school and on summer vacations. The First Lady says, "We can't just leave it up to the parents."[1111] *In Obama World, is there any decision that "we can just leave up to the parents?"*

Dec 2009

White House Chief Economic Advisor, Larry Summers, says, "Everybody agrees the recession is over" and "by spring employment growth will start turning positive."[1112] *I'm not so sure that the unemployed agree "the recession is over."*

12/14/09

According to *Timesonline.co.uk*, Iran is working on testing the final component of a nuclear bomb.[1113]

12/15/09

The U.S. will be transporting a limited number of Guantanamo detainees to the Thompson Correctional Center in Thompson, Illinois.[1114]

12/16/09

President Obama passes a $1.1 trillion spending bill laden with more than 5,000 earmarks.[1115] *No doubt, he fulfilled his promise: "And when I'm president, I will go line by line to make sure that we are not spending money unwisely."*

The U.S. national debt has already exceeded the debt limit approved by Congress last February.[1116]

In an interview, the president says America will go bankrupt without health care legislation.[1117]

Dec 2009

Arab states will be launching their own oil-trading currency to displace the U.S. dollar for oil transactions. "The U.S. dollar has failed. We need to de-link," says Nahed Taher, chief executive of Bahrain's Gulf One Investment Bank.[1118]

12/17/09

Secretary Clinton announces that the U.S. will contribute to a $100 billion climate fund agreed to at Copenhagen.[1119]

12/18/09

In Copenhagen, Barack Obama delivers another speech of soaring rhetoric lacking substance and detail, stating that the world must act "boldly and decisively" on climate change.[1120]

China shows a lack of interest in participating in the Copenhagen summit. President Obama and Secretary Clinton call a meeting with Chinese officials but are snubbed when three low-level Chinese delegates arrive to meet with them.[1121]

Zhu Min, deputy governor of the People's Bank of China, states that the dollar's decline is inevitable since the U.S. insists on racking up higher and higher deficits financed by treasuries.[1122]

12/20/09

Senate Democrats announce that they have reached a deal on health care reform.[1123]

President Obama appoints Howard Schmidt as "Cyber Czar" to coordinate cybersecurity.[1124]

12/21/09

A University of Michigan study reveals that banks with political ties were more likely to receive bailouts.[1125]

12/22/09

Representative Bart Stupak (D-MI) says the White House is pressuring him to remain silent about the abortion language in the Senate Health Care Bill.[1126]

12/23/09

President Obama delays his Hawaii vacation plans until socialized Obamacare passes in the Senate.[1127] *Here we see the president's priorities. Later in the Obama presidency, when Standard & Poor's drops the U.S. credit rating, he does not allow bad news and urgent matters to interrupt his vacation to Martha's Vineyard.*

Amid controversy of special deals, giveaways and bribes, Senator Charles Schumer (D-NY) says that every state got special treatment in the Health Care Bill.[1128] *Of course, Schumer is referring only to those states and districts whose senators and representatives supported the leg-*

islation. The rest of the suckers just have to pay for it.

Congressional leaders will forego the traditional conference committee process for approving legislation, opting for a deem-and-pass route.[1129]

The Congressional Budget Office (CBO) disputes claims that the health care bill's Medicare savings "would help finance expanded coverage and postpone the bankruptcy of the medical program for the elderly."[1130]

Treasury Secretary Geithner says the economy and job growth will improve by spring.[1131]

12/24/09

The Senate approves the Obamacare bill. The bill contains everything except principles. It is so bloody awful that it cannot pass on its merits. Instead, Congress has to be bribed into passing it. Here's a tiny fraction of some of the sleazy deals:

- The Cornhusker Kickback has the rest of the country paying for Nebraska's Medicaid,
- Vermont and Massachusetts get similar Medicaid kickbacks,
- Connecticut gets a $100 million hospital,
- Michigan and Nebraska get tax exemptions for their insurance companies,
- Montana, North Dakota, South Dakota, Utah, and Wyoming get increased Medicare payments,
- Florida, Pennsylvania, and New York get protection for their Medi-

Dec 2009

care Advantage patients,

- Louisiana gets a $300 million payoff,
- California gets an extra $300 million in Medicare payments,
- AARP gets $18 million in stimulus money plus favorable treatment for their Medigap coverage plan.[1132]

Congress raises the debt ceiling to $12.4 trillion.[1133]

President Obama leaves for Christmas vacation in Hawaii.[1134]

12/25/09

A terrorist, Umar Abdulmutallab, tries to blow up an airline flight to Detroit with a bomb hidden in his underwear. The plot is thwarted by the brave effort of a Dutch citizen, Jasper Schuringa, who subdued the terrorist. Al-Qaeda claims responsibility for the Christmas Day bomb plot, claiming it is retaliation for U.S. strikes in Yemen.[1135] [1136]

Abdulmutallab is then taken to a hospital. For fifty minutes, he speaks freely about his al-Qaeda ties with FBI agents who are trying to assess whether there are more imminent threats. When he is read his Miranda rights, he immediately refuses to cooperate any further.[1137]

Last October, "Counterterrorism Czar" John Brennan received a briefing on the underwear bombing technique from Saudi Arabia's chief counterterrorism official.[1138]

Dec 2009

12/26/09

Investigators confirm that the bomb plot was hatched by al-Qaeda in

Yemen.[1139]

After receiving reports of the Christmas Day bomb plot, Michael Leiter, head of the National Counter Terrorism Center, decides it would be best not to let the incident interrupt his ski vacation.[1140]

12/27/09

With regard to the Christmas Day bomb plot, DHS Secretary Napolitano tells CNN, "the system worked."[1141]

Napolitano also tells ABC's *This Week*, "Everything went according to clockwork" in describing how passengers, crew and the government responded to the Underwear Bomber.[1142]

Al-Qaeda in Yemen posts a statement online taking responsibility for making Abdulmutallab's bomb.[1143]

Press Secretary Robert Gibbs says that President Obama's transparency pledge was upheld since C-SPAN broadcast Senate health care votes at 2 o'clock in the morning.[1144]

Candidate Obama promised:

- *11/27/07: "Drug and insurance companies will have a seat at the table, they just won't be able to buy every single chair. And we will have a public process for forming this plan. It'll be televised on C-SPAN... but it will be transparent and accountable to the American people."*
- *1/20/08: "... but these negotiations will be on C-SPAN and so the public will be part of the conversation and will see the choices that*

are being made."

- *1/31/08: "... not negotiating behind closed doors but bringing all parties together and broadcasting those negotiations on C-SPAN so the American people can see what the choices are."*

- *3/1/08: "But here's the thing. We're going to do all these negotiations on C-SPAN so the American people will be able to watch these negotiations."*

- *4/25/08: "So I'll put forward my plan but what I'll say is, 'look, if you've got better ideas, I'm happy to listen to them,' but all this will be done on C-SPAN—in front of the public."*

- *May 2008: "The drug and insurance companies are still going to have a lot of power in Washington and they're still going to try to block reforms from taking place so that's why I've said for example that I want the negotiations to be taking place on C-SPAN."*

- *8/21/08: "We will have the negotiations televised on C-SPAN so that people can see who is making arguments on behalf of their constituents and who is making arguments on behalf of the drug companies or the insurance companies."*

- *11/14/08: "We will work on this process publicly. It will be on C-SPAN. It will be streaming over the net."*

12/28/09

Dec 2009

Three days after the bomb plot was thwarted, the president takes his customary stab at the Bush administration and assures the U.S. that all who are responsible will be brought to justice.[1145] [1146]

On the *Today Show*, DHS Secretary Napolitano changes her stance,

"Our system did not work in this instance."[1147]

12/29/09

The CIA had information on Abdulmutallab as early as August, but because of intelligence lapses, he still managed to slip through the cracks.[1148] *Pun not intended.*

The State Department confirms that a U.S. citizen snuck into North Korea on Christmas Day and is being held captive.[1149]

12/30/09

C-SPAN's CEO sends President Obama a letter encouraging him to fulfill his transparency pledge by making health care debates publicly broadcast on C-SPAN.[1150]

Russia's Prime Minister Putin calls for more Russian arms manufacturing capable of penetrating America's missile defense shield. Putin believes that an arms build-up is necessary to keep American from doing "whatever they want." He adds, "To preserve the balance we must develop offensive weapons, not missile defense systems as the United States is doing."[1151] *Remember, President Obama already abandoned our Eastern European defense shield.*

Former Vice President Dick Cheney criticizes Obama for "trying to pretend we are not at war" with terrorists. He continues, "As I've watched the events of the last few days it is clear once again that President Obama is trying to pretend we are not at war. He seems to think if he has a low-key response to an attempt to blow up an airliner and kill hundreds of people, we won't be at war. He seems to think if he gives terrorists the rights of Americans, lets them lawyer up and reads them their Miranda rights, we won't be at war. He seems to think if we bring the mastermind of September 11 to New York, give him a lawyer and trial in civilian court, we won't be at war."[1152]

12/31/09

While the White House claims the stimulus has "created or saved" 2 million jobs, forty-nine of fifty states have lost jobs.[1153]

Taxpayer losses from propping up Fannie Mae and Freddie Mac are projected to exceed $400 billion.[1154]

This month the average government worker earns $26.11 per hour while the average private employee earns $19.41 per hour. Government workers' benefits average $13.49 per hour while private employees' benefits are $8.00 per hour. Total compensation for government employees is 45% higher than the schleps in the private sector.[1155] *"You cannot carry on forever squeezing the productive bit of the economy in order to fund an unprecedented engorgement of the unproductive bit. – Daniel Hannan*

Foreign demand for U.S. Treasury bills falls by a record $53 billion in December. China is worried about Washington's out-of-control spending and has reduced its holdings by $34.2 billion.[1156]

Dec 2009

States see a dramatic drop in tax collections for the fourth quarter.[1157]

Unemployment = 10 percent. [1158]

Real unemployment = 17.3%[1159]

CBS's Mark Knoller compiled a list "Obama's First Year: By the Numbers."

- 411 Speeches, Comments and Remarks
  - 52 addresses or statements specifically about health care
  - Teleprompter used 178 times
- 42 News Conferences
- 5 were formal White House press conferences (4 at prime time)
- 23 Townhall Meetings
- 46 out-of-town trips to 58 cities in 30 states
- 10 foreign trips to 21 countries
- 160 flights on Air Force One
- 193 flights on Marine One
- 28 political fundraisers
- 7 campaign rallies (all for candidates who lost)
- 16% increase in National Debt
- 29 rounds of golf[1160]

1/1/10

The president's $75 billion "Making Homes Affordable" program is not working as planned. Last year saw more than 2 million foreclosures and Moody's projects another 2.4 million for this year.[1]

1/2/10

President Obama confirms that the Christmas Day bomber has ties to al-Qaeda.[2]

1/3/10

"Counterterrorism Czar" John Brennan announces that there is a deal "on the table" for Umar Abdumutallab's cooperation in sharing what he knows about al-Qaeda.[3]

The U.S. and U.K. close their embassies in Yemen amid al-Qaeda threats.[4]

The Obamas leave Honolulu and return to Washington.

1/4/10

The government will spend $340 million advertising the upcoming Census. $80 million will be targeted to racial, ethnic and non-English speaking minorities.[5]

The stimulus should be re-named the "Democratic Stimulus." "The average number of awards per Republican district is 94, while the average number of awards per Democratic district is 152." Also, Democratic districts received approximately twice as much funding as Republican districts.[6]

According to *Recovery.gov*, the average stimulus expenditure per job "saved or created" is $245,807.51.[7] *Since it is impossible to measure whether a job is "saved," it is likely that the cost is much greater. Also, considering that stimulus accounting has proved to be a Gordian knot of irresponsibility, the cost would be higher still.*

The administration awards a lucrative $25 million no-bid contract to a valuable Democratic campaign donor. Vincent Checchi's company received the sweetheart deal to do work in Afghanistan.[8]

President Obama names Amanda Simpson, a transgender appointee, to the Commerce Department.[9]

1/5/10

Operation Fast and Furious: According to a briefing paper from the ATF's Phoenix Field Division, Group VII, US Attorney for the District of Arizona Dennis Burke was briefed on the operation and "concurs with the assessment of his line prosecutors and fully supports the continuation of the investigation." Furthermore, Special Agent in Charge William Newell "has repeatedly met with the USA Burke regarding the on-going status of this investigation and both are in full agreement with the current investigative strategy."[10]

The president meets with House and Senate Democratic leaders telling them he wants the final health care bill to include a tax on "Cadillac" insurance plans. He also makes it perfectly clear that he wants the reform passed before his State of the Union address.[11]

When speaking to his national security advisors about the Underwear Bomber, the president says, "This was a screw up that could have been disastrous. We dodged a bullet but just barely."[12]

Transportation Security Administration (TSA) agents think it's funny to prank airline passengers by placing vials of white powder among their possessions then scaring the passengers into believing they are about to be busted for smuggling drugs.[13]

1/6/10

Umar Abdulmutallab is indicted on six counts.[14]

1/7/10

President Obama takes responsibility for security lapses regarding the Underwear Bomber, "As President, I have a solemn responsibility to protect our nation and our people. And when the system fails it is my responsibility." President Obama discusses his review of events and discloses that the U.S. did have sufficient information to disrupt the al Qaeda plot. Also, the intelligence community leadership did not increase resources on the threat and the watchlist failed.[15]

1/8/10

The president announces $2.3 billion in clean energy manufacturing projects.[16]

The U.S. threatens to impose sanctions and freeze aid to Israel if they fail to advance two-state peace talks.[17]

Twenty-two Republican senators send a letter to President Obama asking that Umar Abdulmutallab be tried in a military court; however, "Counterterrorism Czar" John Brennan does not see any downside to treating the Christmas Day bomber like an ordinary criminal. [18]

Five days after "Counterterrorism Czar" John Brennan announces there is a deal "on the table," Abdulmatallab pleads "not guilty" to all six charges against him.[19]

1/9/10

An early peek at the soon-to-be-released book, *Game Change*, shows that Senate Majority Leader Harry Reid (D-NV) was enthusiastic about the Obama campaign. The Majority Leader compliments him as "a light-skinned African American with no Negro dialect, unless he wanted to have one."[20] *President Obama graciously accepted Senator Reid's apology, but it was not reported whether he used his "Negro dialect" or his "Caucasian dialect."*

1/10/10

NATO Major General Michael Flynn and Representative Mark Kirk (R-IL) say that all 61 freed Gitmo detainees are now major Taliban leaders in southern Afghanistan.[21]

1/11/10

President Obama hosts a meeting with the unions at the White House, including AFL-CIO, SEIU, NEA, Change to Win, the Steelworkers Union, UFCW, Teamsters, AFT, LIUNA, AFSCME and CWA. The White House and the unions agree on union-friendly terms for Obamacare, cutting back on punitive taxes for their "Cadillac" insurance plans.[22] [23]

Even though Russia plans to continue developing nuclear arms, the U.S. continues negotiating START (Strategic Arms Reduction Treaty).[24]

1/12/10

A 7.0 earthquake rocks Haiti today. It takes President Obama thirty minutes to respond to the earthquake; whereas, it took him three days to respond to the Christmas Day bombing attempt.[25] *And it will take him much longer to respond to the Gulf oil disaster.*

1/13/10

President Obama spends all day meeting with House and Senate Democrats on health care legislation.[26]

1/14/10

The national debt has increased more than 16% since President Obama took office. At $12.3 trillion it is $1.7 trillion higher in less than a year.[27]

1/15/10

The administration officially recognizes the Fort Hood shooting as an "act of terrorism."[28] *For some reason, they didn't call it a "man-caused disaster."*

1/16/10

In his weekly radio address, Obama announces new fees for the nation's largest financial institutions to recoup TARP losses.[29] *Does this mean that the private sector banks will be responsible for the TARP losses that were sunk into Fannie and Freddie, too?*

1/17/10

"The **top priority** is to continue to work hard on getting this economy back on track and creating jobs," says Press Secretary Gibbs.[30]

Republican Scott Brown wins the Senate race in Massachusetts.

1/20/10

President Obama accepts part of the blame for losing a Democratic seat in Congress by admitting that he hasn't spent enough time speaking to the American people.[31]

U.N. officials admit that claims of melting Himalayan glaciers are unfounded.[32]

1/22/10

President Obama fails to fulfill his promise to close Gitmo today. *Two weeks ago he said he takes "responsibility to protect our nation and our people." Obama has said on many occasions that the Guantanamo Bay prison facility is al-Qaeda's number one recruiting tool. What gives?*

1/23/10

The President, who raised over $600 million in his campaign and enjoyed vast union support, criticizes the Supreme Court's ruling in *Citizens United v. Federal Election Commission*, allowing corporations to use their profits to support or oppose political candidates.[33]

1/25/10

President Obama meets with his "Middle Class Task Force" and vows to help the middle class.[34] *Unfortunately, the Middle Class Task Force is composed of elitists, none of whom are middle class.*

President Obama praises himself generously while quelling Democrats' fears of the upcoming midterm elections. The Democrats are concerned that they will receive the same type of shellacking they got in 1994. According to Obama, "Well, the big difference here and in '94 is you've got **ME**.[35] *Barack Obama truly is a "Man For All Seasons." He is so self-assured that he campaigned, "I think that I'm a better speechwriter than my speechwriters. I know more about policies on any particular issue than my policy directors. And I'll tell you right now that ... I'm a better political director than my political director."*

President Obama tells Diane Sawyer, "I'd rather be a really good one-term President than a mediocre two-term President." The interview continued with his failure to live up to his transparency pledge. Sort of. He says, "I think your question points out to a legitimate mistake that I made during the course of the year and that is that we had to make so many decisions quickly in a very difficult set of circumstances that after a while, we started worrying more about getting the policy right than getting the process right.

"But I had campaigned on process. Part of what I had campaigned on was changing how Washington works, opening up transparency and I think it is—I think the health care debate as it unfolded legitimately raised concerns not just among my opponents, but also amongst supporters that we just don't know what's going on. And it's an ugly process and it looks like there are a bunch of back room deals."[36] [37] *Reality Check 1: On July 14, 2009, Senior Advisor, David Axelrod, said, "Ultimately this is not about process, it's about results."*

Reality Check 2: in his March 17, 2010, interview with Fox News' Bret

Baier, Obama said, "So you've got a good package in terms of substance. I don't spend a lot of time worrying about what the procedural rules are in the House of the Senate." President Obama, who says he "campaigned on process," dodged all other inquiries about the process of the health care bill. In other words, what he and his advisers are really saying is, "The end justifies the means."

1/26/10

The real cost of the stimulus is $862 billion considering the increased spending on unemployment benefits.[38]

The DHS imposes stringent security regulations on all goods imported to the U.S. Exporters must "tell Washington who sold the goods, who bought them and a host of other information 24 hours before the cargo is loaded on a U.S.-bound vessel, or face fines running to thousands of dollars and possible seizure of the goods."[39]

White House Chief of Staff Rahm Emanuel apologizes for calling a group of activists "f***ing retarded."[40] *Where did they find this guy? Jerry Springer's central casting? Charlie Sheen's sofa? Does Rahm get to sit at the grown-up's table?*

1/27/10

President Obama delivers his second State of the Union address. The most contentious moment occurs when he takes a cheap shot at the Supreme Court. He claims the Court has opened the floodgates of foreign and special interests to influence elections. Cameras capture Justice Alito shaking his head in disgust and mouthing the words "not true." *Obama seems unperturbed by the fact that unions like the AFL-CIO and environmental groups like the Sierra Club also receive donations from foreign entities.*

President Obama also promises, more than a year after taking office, that he will focus on jobs.

There are concerns in the Senate Judiciary Committee related to Department of Justice lawyers (like Neal Katyal and Jennifer Daskal) who stood up for terrorists' rights. Senator Charles Grassley (R-IA) asks Attorney General Holder to quit stonewalling and disclose members of the Obama administration who had previously advocated for the alleged terrorists. The attorney general replies, "I will consider that request.[41]

1/28/10

The White House orders the Justice Department to consider trying Khalid Sheikh Mohammed somewhere other than Manhattan.[42]

Ben Bernanke is re-confirmed as Chairman of the Federal Reserve.[43]

President Obama wants to double exports in five years.[44] *Export what? Jobs?*

"We will not rest until we build an economy that's ready for America's future."[45]

1/29/10

President Obama is seriously considering whether college football's Bowl Championship Series violates antitrust laws.[46]

China protests the U.S.'s sale of $6.4 billion in weapons to Taiwan, warning that it will seriously damage U.S./China relations.[47]

1/30/10

The Department of Justice clears Bush administration lawyers of wrongdoing in the torture memo probe.[48]

President Obama vows to tame the deficit by restoring the "pay as you go" law, freezing discretionary spending, offering middle class tax cuts, cutting redundant and ineffective programs and appointing a bipartisan Fiscal Commission to recommend deficit-reduction strategies.[49]

More evidence emerges demonstrating that the U.N. climate change research is bogus. Reports of glacial melting in the Andes, Alps and Africa cite two articles based only on anecdotal evidence from mountain climbers. Further research shows that the IPCC report based its conclusions on sixteen non-peer reviewed World Wildlife Fund (WWF) articles.[50]

1/31/10

President Obama states in his weekly address, "It is critical to rein in budget deficits...I've called for a bipartisan Fiscal Commission—a panel of Democrats and Republicans who would sit down and hammer out concrete deficit-reduction proposals by a certain deadline. Because we've heard plenty of talk and a lot of yelling on TV about deficits, and it's now time to come together and make the painful choices we need to eliminate those deficits."[51]

The manufacturing sector reported 486 mass layoffs in January affecting 182,261 workers.[52]

White House Press Secretary Robert Gibbs states, "Khalid Sheikh Mohammed will be executed for the crimes he committed."[53] *I thought they wanted to give him a fair trial with the presumption of innocence.*

President Obama bows yet again…to the Mayor of Tampa.[54]

The State Department admits that the no-bid contract it awarded to Vincent Checchi broke Obama's campaign pledge to crackdown on corruption. According to the Associated Press, $242 million of the Pentagon's stimulus projects were given through no-bid contracts.[55]

President Obama is deploying a defensive shield of patriot missiles in the Gulf States capable of shooting down Iranian missiles.[56]

January Unemployment = 9.7%.[57]
Real unemployment = 16.5%.[58]

2/1/10

Warning that the government cannot "continue to spend as if deficits don't have consequences," President Obama unveils a $3.83 trillion budget with a $1.6 trillion deficit. The White House proposal predicts $trillion-plus deficits for the next three years, falling to $700 billion by 2013 and rising again to $1 trillion by the end of the decade. As usual, the White House blames President Bush for these deficits.[59] [60] *So what about his promises to the Chinese to cut budget deficits by the end of his term?*

President Obama acknowledges that he "probably should have" fulfilled his transparency promise with regard to the back room, closed-door deals behind Obamacare which should have been broadcast on C-SPAN.[61]

Obama's "bold new initiative" for NASA doesn't offer a time or a place for a mission of any sort. Part of the president's "bold" initiative seems to be getting rid of space exploration by taking a machete to NASA's Constellation program. "We are proposing cancelling the program, not delaying it," says Peter Orszag, director of the Office of Management and Budget.[62]

The administration says the federal payrolls will swell to 2.15 million employees this year.[63]

With respect to student loan reform, the president states, "This is something that I've made a **top priority**."[64]

The head of the U.N. Climate Change Commission has no personal regrets for the IPCC's fallacious climate reports, "You can't expect me to be personally responsible for every word in a 3,000 page report."[65] *He*

Feb 2010

sounds like a member of Congress. If he denies responsibility for his own commission's reports then, obviously, they need someone who will accept responsibility.

2/2/10

"It keeps me awake at night, looking at all that red ink," says President Obama of the budget deficit.[66]

2/3/10

The president signs an executive order establishing a bipartisan National Commission on Fiscal Responsibility and Reform to make recommendations for deficit reduction strategies. President Obama says debt can "hobble our economy" and "saddle every child in America with an intolerable burden." *"Senator McCain's first answer to this economic crisis was—get ready for it—a commission. That's Washington-speak for 'we'll get back to you later.' ... Folks, we don't need a commission to spend a few years and a lot of taxpayer money to tell us what's going on in our economy. We don't need a commission to tell us gas prices are high or that you can't pay your bills. We don't need a commission to tell us you're losing your jobs. We don't need a commission to study this crisis, we need a President who will solve it—and that's the kind of President I intend to be." – Senator Barack Obama, 9/18/08.[67]*

Government spending will hit the debt ceiling by the end of February.[68]

President Obama insults Las Vegas for a second time, telling a crowd in

New Hampshire, you don't blow a bunch of cash on Vegas when you're trying to save for college."[69] *The president's point is well taken but Nevada has the highest unemployment rate in the country and gambling/tourism is their biggest industry.*

China warns President Obama that meeting with the Dalai Lama will further erode U.S./China relations.[70]

Feb 2010

2/4/10

Moody's again warns that the U.S. AAA credit rating is at risk.[71]

2/5/10

Former Nobel Peace Laureate, Lech Walesa, laments that America has lost its moral leadership. "They don't lead morally and politically anymore. The world has no leadership. The United States was always the last resort and hope for all other nation. There was the hope, whenever something was going wrong, one could count on the United States. Today, we lost that hope."[72]

At the National Prayer Breakfast, President Obama twice referred to Navy corpsman as "corpse man."[73] *He is supposed to be the President of the United States, not a muppet. Too bad he didn't have a phonetic teleprompter.*

China announces tariffs on U.S. chicken products.[74]

Indian film star Shah Rukh Khan claims airport body scanners in London printed and circulated images of his naked body. As a high-profile celebrity and Muslim, Mr. Khan deeply resents this intrusion of his privacy.[75]

2/7/10

Treasury Secretary Geithner says the U.S. will never lose its AAA credit rating, despite projections of $trillion-plus deficits year after year after year.[76]

2/9/10

Reversing their reversal of previous reversals, Khalid Sheikh Mohammed may still be tried in Manhattan. When questioned on the matter, Obama stated, "I have not ruled it out."[77] *The President's official stance on the trial of KSM is that he either will be tried in Manhattan, or he will not be tried in Manhattan—but not both and not neither.*

First Lady Michelle Obama says childhood obesity is a matter of national defense.[78] *"Food is not a private matter!"—Hitler Youth health manual.*

Angry about U.S. arms sales to Taiwan, Chinese military officials are encouraging increased defense spending, redeployments of military assets and selling-off U.S. bonds.[79]

2/10/10

President Obama says he doesn't begrudge huge bonuses to the Wall Street CEOs who, incidentally, contributed heavily to his campaign. He notes that some professional athletes make even more money.[80]

India announces plans to launch a nuclear-capable missile with a 3,100 mile range.[81]

London's Court of Appeal requires the U.K. government to publish CIA intelligence information relating to torture allegations.[82]

2/11/10

Blatantly disregarding one of his cornerstone campaign promises, President Obama says that he is "agnostic" on the subject of raising taxes on the middle class.[83]

The laws of economics are immutable and fixed; however, the laws of man are not. Even if President Obama tried to repeal the law of gravity, marbles would still fall to the floor. Likewise, despite Obama's rhetoric, the immutable laws of economics will not bend to his policies just because he wishes for certain outcomes to be achieved.

The Department of Justice is arguing in favor of warrantless tracking of cell phones claiming Americans have no "reasonable expectation of privacy" regarding their whereabouts.[84]

Mahmoud Ahmadinejad declares that Iran is now a nuclear state.[85]

Feb 2010

2/12/10

Congress raises the debt ceiling to $14.294 trillion.[86] *That's right. Fifty days ago, Congress raised the debt ceiling by $290 billion. Today, they raised it almost $2 trillion!*

The Obama administration breaks contracts and breaks the law when it comes to NASA. They are unilaterally cancelling construction contracts with Boeing and United Space Alliance for the Constellation program. The fact that these companies are heavily invested in standing contracts with the U.S. government is of no concern to the administration. Furthermore, The Consolidated Appropriations for Fiscal Year 2010 expressly forbids the "termination or elimination of any program, project or activity of the architecture for the Constellation program."[87]

Suddenly, the president wishes to present the charade that Obamacare is the result of a bipartisan effort. On February 25, the president will host a health care conference with twelve Democratic and nine Republican members of Congress. The President says he is interested in "listening" to ideas and proposals. *President Obama has approached just about every country on the planet with a message similar to what he told Vladimir Putin, "I think it's very important that I come before you with some humility. I think in the past there's been a tendency for the U.S. to lecture rather than listen." It's too bad Obama assume the same stance of "humility" when dealing with his fellow-countrymen who happen to be Republicans.*

For the last year Representative Tom Price (R-GA), a physician and Chairman of the Republican Study Committee, has requested health care discussions with the President. The White House refused his weekly requests.[88][89]

The White House continues its efforts to advance its energy, environmental, fiscal and domestic policies. Although the President would prefer to enact these measures through Congress, the administration is reviewing ways to impose its agenda through executive orders and directives. [90]

Feb 2010

2/13/10

President Obama signs the increased debt limit into law, raising the debt ceiling from $12.4 trillion to $14.3 trillion.[91] *"Ah, take the Cash, and let the Credit go/Nor heed the rumble of a distant Drum!"* —*The Rubaiyat of Omar Khayyam*

2/14/10

Professor Phil Jones, an instrumental figure in East Anglia University's Climate-Fraud scandal, admits that there has been no global warming since 1995. Professor Jones also admits that the Medieval Warming Period may have been warmer than today, suggesting that temperature changes may not be man-made.[92]

2/15/10

Secretary Clinton calls for more pressure on Iran to halt its nuclear program.[93]

Saudi Arabia's foreign minister doubts sanctions will be very effective in curbing Iran's nuclear ambitions and suggests that more immediate solutions may be appropriate.[94]

The Taliban's top military commander is captured in a joint CIA-Pakistani operation.[95]

The Managing Director of the IMF proposes ditching the dollar in favor of a new world currency.[96]

2/16/10

President Obama gives an $8.3 billion loan to the Southern Co. to help build two nuclear power plants.[97]

2/17/10

On the anniversary of the stimulus bill, Obama insists that it rescued the U.S. economy.[98]

Stimulus Facts:

- The stimulus cost $862 billion.
- The stimulus was supposed to create 3.6 million jobs.
- 3.3 million jobs have been lost since its enactment.
- 67,000 civilian federal employees have been added since the stimulus.
- Those employees cost the taxpayers $270.7 billion.

- Unemployment was 7.6% when the stimulus was signed.

- The stimulus was supposed to keep unemployment under 8%.

- Current unemployment is 9.7%.

- Stimulus funds were provided to 440 congressional districts that don't even exist.

- Each "saved or created" job cost between $225,000 and $250,000.[99]

2/18/10

President Obama meets with fellow Nobel Peace Prize Laureate, the Dalai Lama. In order to appease China, he ensures that the exiled Tibetan leader is treated with the utmost disrespect. To make it perfectly clear that he does not recognize the Dalai Lama as a head of state, the two meet in the White House Map Room instead of the Oval Office. Furthermore, the White House does not allow reporters or photographers to see them together. As a final discourtesy, the Dalai Lama is allowed to exit a side door among heaps of garbage. That's right, the Dalai Lama is <u>literally</u> taken out with the trash![100] [101] *Dissing the Dalai Lama is bad karma. It is possible that Obama wasn't just trying to appease China since his bad manners were consistent with his treatment of Benjamin Netanyahu (Israel), Gordon Brown (Great Britain), Nicolas Sarkozy (France), Vaclav Klaus (Czech Republic) and King Harald V (Norway), to name a few.*

Representative Joe Sestak (D-PA) states in an interview that the White House repeatedly tried to bribe him with a high-ranking job if he withdrew his bid to challenge Senator Arlen Specter in the Pennsylvania primary election. It is a crime for any government official to use his authority "for the purpose of interfering with, or affecting, the nomination or the election of any candidate."[102] [103]

Three months after Senator Grassley's (R-IA) request, Attorney General Holder sends an incomplete, haphazard response addressing the Senate Judiciary Committee's concern that the Department of Justice is employing lawyers who previously represented terrorist detainees. In lock-step with the Obama administration's peculiar brand of transparency, Attorney General Holder admits the Department of Justice employs lawyers who worked for terrorist detainees but refuses to give their names. Holder says there are "at least nine" and that he hasn't bothered to do a complete survey.[104] [105] [106]

Five Muslim soldiers are arrested for conspiring to poison the food supply at Fort Jackson, South Carolina.[107]

The Federal Reserve raises the discount rate.[108]

2/19/10

Apparently, Obama did not mistreat the Dalai Lama severely enough to assuage tempers in China. "The Chinese side demands that the U.S. side seriously consider China's stance, immediately adopt measures to wipe out the baneful impact and stop conniving and supporting anti-China separatist forces that seek Tibet independence" said the Chinese Foreign Ministry.[109]

2/20/10

New GM CEO, Ed Whitacre, receives a $9 million pay package including a $1.7 million base salary.[110]

2/23/10

At a meeting with the Business Roundtable, President Obama tries to refute the label of being a socialist, saying, "Contrary to the claims of some of my critics, I am an ardent believer in the free market."[111]

The FDIC identifies 702 "problem" banks as lending falls.[112]

Reports of Toyota accelerators getting stuck has given Congress the opportunity to stage political theater hearings.[113] *Product recalls happen regularly with Congressional hearings. Now that the U.S. government owns GM and Chrysler, Congress gets to smear its largest competitor. Plus, they can help out their United Auto Workers union pals since Toyota is non-unionized.*

2/24/10

Argentina is once again laying claim to the Falkland Islands. The U.S. refuses to acknowledge Britain's sovereignty over the Islands and refuses to support their right under international law to explore and drill for oil in the region.[114] *In fact, the Assistant Secretary of State for Public Affairs, P.J. Crowley, goes so far as to refer to the Falklands by their Argentine name, "the Malvinas."*

North Korea gives Iran nineteen missiles capable of reaching Western European capitals.[115]

Feb 2010

Ordained minister and Marine Corps veteran, Tony Perkins, is disinvited from speaking at the Military Prayer Breakfast after the White House discovered he publicly disagreed with the administration's "don't ask, don't tell" policy. "It's ironic that this blacklisting should occur because I called for the retention and enforcement of a valid federal statute," says Perkins.[116] *It is also ironic because Obama's Justice Department has been arguing in favor of the Defense of Marriage Act in federal court.*

President Obama outlines another of his many top priorities, "To train our workers for the jobs of tomorrow, we've made education reform a **top priority** in this administration."[117]

Social unrest ignites in Greece in a nationwide strike.[118]

2/25/10

President Obama attends his one and only health care summit broadcast on C-SPAN. Contrary to his statement about listening to other points of view, he does most of the talking. Obama speaks for a total of 119 minutes, seventeen Republicans spoke for 110 minutes and twenty-one Democrats spoke for 114 minutes.

President Obama demonstrates his authority by calling Republicans by their first names instead of their formal titles as duly elected representatives of their constituents. When Senator McCain (R-AZ) complains that the process had taken place secretly behind closed doors, the president dismisses his concerns with, "Look, let me just make this point, John, because we are not campaigning anymore. *The election's over."* On January 25, 2010, Obama admits, *"I had campaigned on process."* So, does this comment mean that when he is in campaign-mode, he is merely paying lip service to process?

The president is annoyed by all criticism. He is particularly irritated by Representative Eric Cantor's (R-VA) sitting behind the three-foot-tall, 2,400-page bill. President Obama accuses him of using it as a cheap prop.[119] *It's pretty odd that he would sign a bill that he considers a "cheap prop." Speaking of "cheap props," maybe Obama would have taken the Republicans more seriously if they had shown up wearing white lab coats (See entry for 10/6/09).*

The entire "summit" was a sham. The president felt forced to attend because he made at least eight campaign promises that health care would be discussed on C-SPAN in the spirit and process of openness and transparency. The plan that the Democrats eventually rammed through was already in place and subsequent actions showed that Republican input was neither wanted nor considered.

The administration considers banning home foreclosures unless the government approves them through the Home Affordable Modification Program.[120]

Secretary of State Clinton compares the situation with Iran's nuclear program to the Cuban Missile Crisis.[121]

2/26/10

For the third time, Senator Grassley (R-IA) demands that Attorney General Holder give a full accounting of Justice Department lawyers who previously represented terrorist detainees. "The administration has made many highly questionable decisions when it comes to national security, chief among them the decisions related to these Guantanamo detainees. First, they want to close the prison at Guantanamo Bay and bring terrorists to U.S. soil. Then, they want to try the mastermind of the deadliest attack against our country on U.S. soil in our civilian courts, and give him more constitutional rights than our own service members who are court-martialed. Americans are concerned about these decisions. They have a right to know who advises the Attorney General and the President on these critical matters. Maybe the third time will be the charm in getting some answers to these questions," Grassley says.[122]

President Obama has appointed SEIU President Andy Stern as a kommissar to his bipartisan debt panel.[123] *Andy Stern sure knows a few things about debt. He has left his union drowning in red ink and its pension plans are in critical status. Stern's mismanagement skills should complement Obama's debt panel perfectly. Like many other elitist union leaders, Stern came from a well-to-do family, has a top-notch Ivy League education and has never had a blue-collar career.*

AIG posts a fourth quarter loss of $8.87 billion.[124]

Dominique Strauss-Kahn of the IMF once again proposes a new reserve currency.[125]

2/27/10

President Obama extends provisions of the Patriot Act which authorize court-approved roving wiretaps that permit surveillance on multiple phones, allow court-approved seizure of records and property in anti-terrorism operations and permit surveillance against non-U.S. citizens engaged in terrorism who may not be part of a recognized terrorist group.[126]

Fannie Mae asks the Treasury for $15.3 billion after its tenth quarterly loss.[127]

Israel approves construction of 600 new units in East Jerusalem.[128]

2/28/10

China's Senior Colonel Liu Mingfu is encouraging a Chinese military build-up and a "sprint to become world number one."[129]

Unemployment = 9.7%.
Real unemployment = 16.8%.[130]

February cost for Afghan war = $6.7 billion
February cost for Iraqi war = $5.5 billion.[131]

Feb 2010

3/1/10

The White House says Democrats will pass health care with Reconciliation.[132] *"Great innovations should not be forced by slender majorities."* —*Thomas Jefferson*

A twenty-one-page White House document surfaces, ominously marked "Internal Draft—NOT FOR RELEASE." The draft details the Obama administration's scheme to annex over 10 million acres of land from Montana to New Mexico. The land in question is ideal for economically viable activities such as ranching, forestry, mining and energy development.[133]

3/2/10

President Obama continues to bribe undecided Democrats to support his ridiculous Obamacare bill. House member Jim Matheson (D-UT) switches his vote to "yes" after the president nominates his brother, Scott Matheson, to the 10th Circuit Court of Appeals.[134]

Government cyber-security officials ponder expanding its Einstein technology to ward off attacks. There is some concern that increased government involvement in private networks will compromise personal privacy.[135]

3/4/10

Representative Bart Stupak (D-MI) says that 12 House Democrats will vote against Obamacare because of provisions that "directly subsidize abortions."[136]

China is waging an undeclared cyber-war against the U.S., the EU and NATO allies. A U.S. official estimates that Chinese cyber-attacks against U.S. government agencies total roughly 1.6 billion per month.[137]

"I'm not gonna rest and my administration is not gonna rest in our efforts to help people who are looking to find a job."[138]

3/5/10

President Obama announces an "entrepreneurship summit" with Muslims.[139] *When the president promised to focus on jobs during the State of the Union address, Americans assumed he meant American jobs.*

The administration is still dithering and flip-flopping on what to do with Khalid Sheikh Mohammed and other 9/11 plotters. Today they are considering military tribunals.[140] *Who knows what they'll recommend tomorrow?*

3/6/10

The Congressional Budget Office (CBO) reports that the president's budget plans grossly underestimate deficits. The report forecasts a National Debt of $20.3 trillion by 2020, with interest payments of $900 billion.[141]

Mar 2010

3/8/10

Representative Eric Massa (D-NY) claims that White House Chief of Staff, Rahm Emanuel, assaulted him in the shower while both men were naked. Allegedly, Emanuel was upset over Massa's wavering support of Obamacare.[142]

President Obama steps up the intensity of his health care overhaul as he further vilifies health insurance companies.[143]

3/9/10

Speaking to an audience about the health care bill, House Speaker Nancy Pelosi (D-CA) says that Congress must "pass the bill so you can find out what's in it, away from the fog of controversy."[144]

The president's briberies of Democrats to support Obamacare keep piling up. The federal government has coincidentally called off an FBI investigation against undecided Representative Alan Mollohan (D-WV), while the liberal media hit squad is attacking the ethics of Representative Stupak (D-MI), who opposes abortion language in the bill.[145]

Americans are tired of hearing politicians and pundits whining about "the incredible pressure" coming from the Speaker or the president. These are the same politicians with generous expense accounts and $175,000 salaries; meanwhile, their constituents have to file for bankruptcy, lose their jobs and face foreclosure.

Politicians who actually have conviction shouldn't feel pressured at all. There is no pressure when one stands for something, has core values and has the integrity to stand by what he/she believes.

Mar 2010

11.4 million people have been receiving unemployment benefits at a cost of $10 billion per month. Under new government guidelines, the unemployed are now eligible to receive benefits for ninety-nine weeks. [146]

3/10/10

President Obama recommends mandatory DNA sampling of anyone who is arrested, regardless of whether charges are filed or convictions are obtained. "It's the right thing to do" to "tighten the grip around folks" who commit crimes.[147] *The administration has demonstrated in many areas that it considers "process" irrelevant (e.g., health care "is not about process, it's about results"). The cornerstone of American criminal law is the presumption of innocence, which the president obviously believes is less important than Big Brother's data collection.*

Representative Darrell Issa (R-CA) calls for an investigation into whether the Obama administration attempted to bribe Representative Joe Sestak (D-PA) with a cushy job in return for not challenging Senator Arlen Specter in the Pennsylvania Democratic Primary. Sestak has repeatedly stated that the White House offered him a high-ranking job. The speculation is that Sestak, a retired Admiral, was offered the job as Secretary of the Navy.[148]

3/11/10

Judicial Watch probes why the Department of Justice and FBI closed their criminal investigation of ACORN's voter fraud. A spokesman says, "The FBI and Department of Justice opened an investigation.

Mar 2010

However, the Obama Justice Department, while noting that ACORN had engaged in 'questionable hiring and training practices,' closed down the investigation in March 2009, claiming ACORN broke no laws."[149] *"I've been fighting alongside ACORN on issues you care about my entire career. Even before I was an elected official, when I ran the Project Vote voter registration drive in Illinois, ACORN was smack dab in the middle of it, and we appreciate your work." —Barack Obama*

With overwhelming bipartisan support, Virginia passes the Health Freedom Bill exempting its residents from complying with any insurance mandate imposed by the federal government.[150]

3/12/10

President Obama delays his trip to Asia to promote Obamacare.[151]

Obama spends White House movie night with Tom Hanks and Steven Spielberg. *Since he charges CEOs to have lunch with him (see entry for 7/30/09), I wonder if he also charges Hollywood celebrities for popcorn and drinks.*[152]

Eric Holder failed to provide full disclosure to the Senate prior to his confirmation as Attorney General. Holder either withheld or overlooked seven legal briefs that he should have disclosed.[153]

A Colorado woman, "Jihad Jaime," is in the custody of the Irish police on terrorism charges.[154]

French President Nicolas Sarkozy accuses Washington of rigging bidding contracts to favor Boeing. "If they want to be heard in the fight against protectionism, they should not set the example of protectionism," he says.[155]

China accuses the U.S. of human rights hypocrisy.[156]

3/14/10

David Axelrod admits the White House still isn't sure about what to do with the 9/11 plotters on CNN's *State of the Union*.[157]

3/15/10

President Obama says he will not campaign for any Democrat who does not support Obamacare.[158]

Mexican "drug cartel hit teams" murder two U.S. citizens. A U.S. consulate employee and her husband were killed in Ciudad Juarez. Their baby daughter, who was in the back seat, survived the attack.[159]

The U.S. and U.K. are coming closer and closer to losing their AAA rating. Under Moody's baseline scenario, the U.S. and U.K. spend more on servicing their national debts than any other AAA-rated country.[160]

Ties between U.S. and Israel are the "worst in thirty-five years." Prime Minister Netanyahu says the construction of 1,600 settlements in East Jerusalem "does not hurt the Arabs of East Jerusalem or come at their expense." Senior Advisor David Axelrod maintains that how Israel chooses to manage its own domestic affairs is an "insult" to the United States.[161]

China decreases its holdings of U.S. Treasuries for the third straight month.[162]

3/16/10

The National Debt has increased by more than $2 trillion since President Obama took office, according to the latest figures from the Treasury Department.[163] *That is roughly $4.8 billion of debt per day, or $200 million per hour, or $3.3 million per minute or $55,115 per second. Remember, that's only debt, not overall spending. Currently the National Debt is $12.6 trillion.*

Unemployment is unlikely to budge according to Treasury Secretary Geithner, Budget Director Orszag and chief economist Christina Romer. Jobless numbers are likely to "remain elevated for an extended period."[164] *In other words, "get used to it; this is the 'new normal.'*

DHS Secretary Napolitano ends $50 million funding for a "virtual" fence along the Mexican border. Secretary Napolitano says that since the program began in 2006, it has been plagued with technical problems and cost overruns. Instead, she says, the money will be allocated to proven methods of stopping illegal immigration.[165]

Utah passes a law protecting its citizens from Obamacare.[166]

In an executive order on the National Export Initiative President Obama writes, "Creating jobs in the United States and ensuring a return to sustainable economic growth is the **top priority** for my administration."[167]

More travelers are complaining that airport body scanners violate their privacy.[168]

Because of Israel's construction of settlements, an American envoy cancels a visit to Jerusalem.[169]

3/17/10

President Obama has a spirited interview with Fox News' Bret Baier regarding the health care bill. Obama gracefully succeeds in dodging all questions related to transparency, the sleazy process and the special deals in his Obamacare legislation. The president tries to smoothe over discussing the pesky details saying, "The final provisions are going to be posted for many days before this thing passes."[170]

When asked by Baier about possible legislative tricks Congress may use to pass the health care bill, the president responds that we need not concern ourselves with "the procedural issues" (in other words, he is more than happy to trample on process). He adds, "By the time the vote has taken place, not only will I know what's in it, you'll know what's in it, because it's going to be posted and everybody's going to be able to evaluate it on the merits."[171] *He lied. After the bill "passed" under Reconciliation, the final provisions were posted for thirty-six hours, not "many days." Even the administration's chief actuary didn't have time to analyze the bill. So much for "sunlight before signing."*

The Democratic Congress passes a $17.7 billion jobs bill consisting of tax breaks for businesses and infrastructure spending.[172]

Idaho passes a law similar to Virginia's shielding its citizens from Obamacare's insurance requirements.[173]

3/18/10

Representative Charles Boustany (R-LA) criticizes the Obamacare bill because it "dangerously expands, in an ominous way the tentacles of the IRS and its reach into every American family." At least 16,500 new IRS agents will be needed to enforce a multitude of Byzantine federal mandates, at least fifteen new tax increases totaling hundreds of billions of dollars and overly complex tax returns.[174][175] *The IRS brownshirts will now have more troops and ammunition at their disposal.*

Vice President Biden tells ABC's Jake Tapper, "You know we're going to control the insurance companies."[176]

President Obama signals his approval of a bill planned by Senators Schumer (D-NY) and Graham (R-SC) that would fast-track illegal immigrants on the path to citizenship.[177]

The Government Accountability Office (GAO) believes it "remains unclear" whether body scanners would have detected the Underwear Bomber.[178]

Secretary Clinton criticizes Russia's plans to build a nuclear power plant in Iran. The purpose of her visit to Moscow is to seek Russia's cooperation in imposing tougher sanctions on Iran and to discuss bi-lateral reductions in U.S./Russian nuclear arsenals.[179] *In order to secure Russian cooperation for containing Iran, Obama scrapped the East European missile defense shield. He failed. Throughout his presidency, Obama is continually bamboozled despite all of his pusillanimous capitulations to "the international community."*

Russia will begin drilling for oil in the Gulf of Mexico. Their rigs will be built near Cuba's coast.[180]

3/19/10

House leaders announce their $940 billion Obamacare compromise bill.[181]

Democrats have implemented the "doc-fix" to make Obamacare look like a fiscally responsible program. Cutting back doctors' fees for Medicare would leave the program with a $59 billion deficit; therefore, the Democrats have decided to address this high-cost issue in separate legislation.[182]

Caterpillar, Inc., the world's largest manufacturer of construction equipment, says the Obamacare bill will cost them $100 million.[183]

Out of the 471 speeches and statements he has given during his 423 days in office, President Obama has given fifty-four on health care.[184]

It is often overlooked that the Obamacare bill will also be nationalizing the student loan industry. According to the Congressional Budget Office (CBO) the government is expected to profit $60 billion. *Why don't they just go ahead and nationalize every other profitable enterprise?*

The only bank in the entire country that stands to benefit from socializing the student loan industry will be the Bank of North Dakota. Budget Committee chairman Senator Kent Conrad (D-ND) had no ethical qualms about cramming this exception into the bill.[185] *Other Democrats didn't object either since they all got their own bribes.*

President Obama joins Mexican President Calderon in slamming Arizona's immigration law.[186]

Secretary Clinton tells the American Israel Public Affairs Committee (AIPAC) that the new Jewish settlements harm the U.S's standing in the peace process and hinder the Obama administration's ability to impose sanctions on Iran. "Our aim is not incremental sanctions, but sanctions that will bite," says Mrs. Clinton.[187]

3/20/10

Prior to the passage of the Patient Protection and Affordable Care Act (a.k.a., "Obamacare"), there was a swarm of news regarding almost every aspect and every facet regarding the bill. The scope and format of this book cannot possibly cover all of the sleazy details regarding the process and the content of this seismic legislative event. Nevertheless, some of the high-water marks will be noted.

The Obama administration's Chief Actuary, Richard Foster, cannot analyze the health care bill before the final vote. "I regret that my staff and

(Mar 2010)

I will not be able to prepare our analysis within this very tight time frame, due to the complexity of the legislation," he says.[188] *Just three days ago the president said, "By the time the vote has taken place, not only will I know what's in it, you'll know what's in it, because it's going to be posted and everybody's going to be able to evaluate it on the merits."*

3/21/10

The House of Representatives passes the Senate amendment to the Patient Protection and Affordable Care Act (a.k.a., "Obamacare") by a vote of 219–212.

The Obama administration is retreating from imposing tough sanctions on Iran, just two days after Secretary Clinton declared to AIPAC, "Our aim is…sanctions that will bite." The White House prefers trying to persuade Russia and China to support a U.N. resolution.[189] *President Obama has made a habit of clamoring for deadlines with Iran that he never enforces. No wonder they don't take him seriously.*

3/22/10

As the U.S. Government risks losing its AAA credit rating, bond traders view government debt as riskier than corporations such as Berkshire Hathaway, Lowe's, Procter & Gamble and Johnson & Johnson by bond traders, according to Bloomberg.[190]

Mar 2010

3/23/10

President Obama again breaks his pledge to allow the public to view legislation for five days before signing into law the massive health care overhaul thirty-six hours after its passage.[191] The bill is impossibly complex and includes all sorts of provisions completely unrelated to health care, such as requiring all businesses to submit tax information for all vendors with whom they do more than $600 in business throughout the year.

Among some of the other provisions are:

- 569 billion in higher taxes,
- $529 billion in cuts to Medicare,
- increasing Medicaid enrollees by 16 million,
- taxing and tracking all gold coin and bullion transactions,
- 17 major insurance mandates,
- 68 grant programs,
- 47 bureaucratic entities,
- 29 demonstration or pilot programs,
- 6 regulatory systems,
- 6 compliance standards
- 2 entitlements, and
- the creation of two new bureaucracies with powers to impose rationing:
  - the Patient-Centered Outcomes Research Institute and
  - the Independent Payments Advisory Board.[192] [193] [194]

Virginia Attorney General Ken Cuccinelli immediately sues the

federal government in Richmond, challenging Obamacare on constitutional grounds.

Florida Attorney General Bill McCollum files a class action lawsuit in the State of Florida challenging Obamacare on constitutional
grounds. Other states included are: Alabama, Colorado, Idaho, Louisiana, Michigan, Nebraska, Pennsylvania, South Carolina, South Dakota,
Texas, Utah, and Washington. Eventually twenty-six states will be part
of the lawsuit.[195]

With the bombastic impoliteness he customarily reserves for allies,
President Obama decides to humiliate Israeli Prime Minister Netanyahu over a disagreement in the Mideast Peace Process. As Netanyahu
explains Israel's policy on construction settlements, the president leaves
the room saying he is going to eat dinner. He tells the Israelis they are
welcome to hang around the White House and see if they can come up
with something more to his liking. "I'm still around," Obama says, "Let
me know if there is anything new." And he withdraws leaving the Israeli
delegation just sitting there.[196] *Hey Mr. President, that's not kosher!*

3/24/10

Obama opposed the inclusion of the Stupak-Pitts amendment to Obamacare so, as promised, he signs a meaningless executive order upholding
prohibitions against federal funding for abortions.[197]

3/25/10

In a speech in Iowa, President Obama taunts Republicans, daring them to try to repeal Obamacare.[198]

An audience member in Iowa City, Iowa, asks him why the public option wasn't included in Obamacare. President Obama replied, "Because we couldn't get it through Congress, that's why."[199]

Fidel Castro congratulates President Obama and hails the passage of Obamacare as "a miracle." The Communist dictator states, "We consider health reform to have been an important battle and a success of his (Obama's) government."[200] *"A friend is one that knows you as you are, understands where you have been, accepts what you have become..."* —*William Shakespeare*

The Congressional Budget Office (CBO) reports that government debt will equal or exceed 90% of GDP by 2020.[201]

This year, Social Security is expected to pay out more in benefits this year than it receives in revenues for the first time since 1983. [202]

3/26/10

A new study shows that Democratic districts receive almost twice as much in stimulus funds as Republican districts. The study also notes that the award of stimulus funding bears no relation to unemployment rates.[203]

AT&T estimates that its first-quarter costs for complying with the new Obamacare law at $1 billion. 3M expects its outlays to approach $90 million.[204]

Transportation Secretary Ray LaHood announces a "major policy revision" giving bicycling and walking equal consideration as motorized transport. "This is the end of favoring motorized transportation at the expense of non-motorized," he says.[205]

The Obama administration plans to solve the foreclosure crisis by having mortgage companies slash or eliminate mortgage payments for unemployed borrowers.[206]

President Obama and Russian President Medvedev agree to cut their long-range nuclear stockpiles by one-third.[207]

Mar 2010

3/27/10

Fuming that AT&T, John Deere, Verizon, and Caterpillar had the gall to publicly disclose their costs of complying with Obamacare, Representative Henry Waxman (D-CA) summons the CEOs to come grovel at his feet in Washington and justify themselves.[208]

President Obama makes 15 recess appointments, including SEIU general counsel Craig Becker to the National Labor Relations Board (NLRB). *Becker is a champion of "card check" laws that would eliminate secret ballots in union elections. Mr. Becker has written that employers should be barred from attending NLRB hearings about union elections and from challenging election results even amid evidence of union misconduct.*[209]

3/28/10

A South Korean warship is sunk by a torpedo, killing several crew members. North Korea is suspected of being responsible for the attack.[210]

3/29/10

President Obama enjoys visiting the blue states as much as he enjoys showering them with stimulus spending. Of the 531 addresses, speeches and remarks since his election only fifteen occurred in red states.[211]

Two Chechen suicide bombers attack the Moscow subway, killing dozens.[212]

3/30/10

IRS Commissioner Doug Shulman says taxpayers will now have to demonstrate that they have health insurance. "We expect to get a simple form that...says this person has acceptable health coverage." The Department of Health and Human Services (HHS) will determine whether the coverage is "acceptable."

With all of the added bureaucratic red tape, Shulman argues that the IRS henchmen "will need resources" to "*serve* the American people."[213] *In other words, the IRS will need another 16,500 agents to help intimidate and harass Americans.*

The CIA believes that Iran is capable of manufacturing nuclear arms.[214]

Mar 2010

3/31/10

Of the eleven bills President Obama has signed into law, only six have been posted on *Whitehouse.gov* and none have been posted for five days.[215] *"When there is a bill that ends up on my desk as a president, you the public will have five days to look online and find out what's in it before I sign it, so that you know what your government's doing." —Candidate Barack Obama*

According to Gallup, March underemployment hits 20.3%. *The "underemployed" are those who are unemployed or working part-time but wanting full-time work.*[216]

USA Today reports, "Paychecks from private business shrank to their smallest share of personal income in U.S. history during the first quarter...At the same time, government-provided benefits—from Social Security, unemployment insurance, food stamps and other programs—rose to a record high."[217]

President Obama reverses a ban on offshore oil drilling for most of the U.S. coastline. "We're announcing the expansion of offshore oil and gas exploration but in ways that balance the need to harness domestic energy resources and the need to protect America's natural resources."[218]

As the White House has blocked weapons sales to Israel, The Jewish Institute for National Security Affairs reports that the Obama administration has approved sales of high-tech military weaponry to Egypt and more than $10 billion of weapons sales to other Arab states.[219]

Russian Prime Minister Putin visits Hugo Chavez to complete a joint venture to drill for oil from Venezuela's Orinoco Belt.[220]

March Unemployment = 9.7%.[221]
Real unemployment = 16.9%.[222]

4/1/10

President Obama says that instead of going to church he receives daily prayers e-mailed to him from pastors around the country.[223]

Verizon announces that it will cost $970 million to comply with the new health care law.[224] Ultimately, consumers will end up bearing the cost.

President Obama is interviewed by CBS on the basketball court this morning. Asked about criticism he has received, he replies, "Well, I think that when you listen to Rush Limbaugh or Glenn Beck, it's pretty apparent, and it's troublesome, but keep in mind that there have been periods in American history where this kind of vitriol comes out. It happens often when you've got an economy that is making people more anxious, and people are feeling like there is a lot of change that needs to take place."[225] *Echoes of candidate Obama's opinion of working-class voters: "And it's not surprising then that they get bitter, they cling to guns or religion or antipathy to people who aren't like them or anti-immigrant sentiment or anti-trade sentiment as a way to explain their frustrations."*

If President Obama had an inkling of self-awareness and personal reflection, he may question that perhaps he is the one who is out-of-step and clinging to a failed, disproven ideology.

May 2010

Afghan President Hamid Karzai accuses the West of engineering election fraud in last year's elections in Afghanistan.[226]

4/2/10

At a townhall meeting, "Doris" tells the President, "We are over-taxed as it is." President Obama takes advantage of the opportunity to straighten Doris out about "a whole lot of misinformation" and that he will "clean up a lot of misapprehensions that people have." After verbally fidgeting for seventeen minutes and twelve seconds, he had imparted more than 2,500 words of disconnected nonsense.[227] *President Obama is clearly uncomfortable whenever he embarks on one of his rambling jags of long-winded gibberish. That's why he needs his teleprompter.*

The Obama administration is shifting its policy for screening air travelers entering the U.S. After the attempted Christmas bombing, "U.S. officials hastily decided that passengers from or traveling through fourteen specified countries would be subjected to secondary searches. Critics have since called the measures discriminatory and overly burdensome, and the administration has faced pressure to refine its approach."[228]

In a pacifying call to Secretary of State Clinton, Afghan President Karzai says he is committed to working with the U.S.[229]

4/3/10

The Obama administration is imposing tough mileage rules for vehicles. Beginning in 2016, new cars and SUVs will have to average 35.5

miles per gallon.[230]

Concern is developing on Obamacare's National Medical Device Registry. The Food and Drug Administration (FDA) now has the power to conduct "postmarket device surveillance activities on implantable medical devices."[231]

4/4/10

President Karzai makes another speech accusing the West of too much meddling in Afghanistan's domestic affairs.[232]

4/5/10

The administration delays its financial report of Social Security and Medicare until it can assess the impact of Obamacare.[233] *Does this mean that the president had not already assessed the impact before signing the bill into law?*

IRS Commissioner Doug Shulman says the IRS will penalize the tax refunds of those who do not have "acceptable" health insurance under Obamacare.[234]

According to the Bureau of Labor Statistics, unemployment for 16 to 29 year-olds is 15.2% —the highest it has been since 1948.[235]

President Obama announces that he is revamping America's entire nuclear strategy and limiting the conditions under which the U.S. would use nuclear weapons.[236]

In a BBC interview, Afghan President Hamid Karzai stands by his statement that the U.S. was responsible for election fraud in Afghanistan.[237]

4/6/10

The Interior Dept.'s Minerals Management Service (MMS) gives BP's Deepwater Horizon oil rig a "categorical exclusion" from an environmental impact analysis, concluding that an oil spill is unlikely.[238]

The U.S. Court of Appeals for the District of Columbia rules that the Federal Communications Commission (FCC) does not have the power to enforce net neutrality. Although the president hasn't read the court's ruling, Press Secretary Robert Gibbs says he is still "committed" to net neutrality.[239]

Defense Secretary Robert Gates defends the administration's nuclear stance today. "Given al-Qaeda's continued quest for nuclear weapons, Iran's ongoing nuclear efforts and North Korea's proliferation, this focus is appropriate and indeed essential, an essential change from previous reviews." As for rogue nations like Iran and North Korea, "All options are on the table when it comes to countries in that category."[240]

4/7/10

Iranian President Mahmoud Ahmadinejad responds to the administration's nuclear stance with his usual lack of respect, "American materialist politicians, whenever they are beaten by logic, immediately put their finger on the trigger like cowboys.

"Mr. Obama, you are a newcomer (to politics). Wait until your sweat dries and get some experience. Be careful not to read just any paper put in front of you or repeat any statement recommended. (American officials) bigger than you, more bullying than you, couldn't do a damn thing, let alone you."[241]

President Obama bans "offensive" terms from the central document outlining his national security strategy. Terms like "Islamic extremism" will not be tolerated.[242]

North Korea sentences an American English teacher to 8 years of hard labor and a $700,000 fine for illegally crossing its border. He is the fourth U.S. citizen to be detained by North Korea this year.[243]

4/9/10

Supreme Court Justice John Paul Stevens announces his retirement.

4/10/10

Polish President Lech Kaczynski and dozens of high-ranking Polish government officials are killed in a plane crash.[244]

In his radio address, the President says, "And one thing we have not done is raise <u>income taxes</u> on families making less than $250,000. That's another promise we've kept." *As we shall see in future days, he is clearly*

May 2010

waffling here. His campaign promise was, "I can make a firm pledge. Under my plan, no family making less than $250,000 a year will see any form of tax increase. Not your income tax, not your payroll tax, not your capital gains taxes, not any of your taxes." [245]

4/11/10

President Obama signs a nuclear reduction treaty with Russia. The treaty would reduce nuclear arsenals by a third and would remove the option of nuclear force against non-nuclear countries.[246]

Wikileaks is prepared to release a video showing an American battle in which ninety-seven Afghan civilians were killed. Julian Assange, Wikileaks founder, claims he is under surveillance and was followed on a flight by two American agents.[247]

4/12/10

Georgia Insurance Commissioner John Oxendine refuses to cooperate with HHS's Obamacare requirements. In a letter to Secretary Sebelius, Oxendine writes, "I am concerned that the high risk pool program will ultimately become the financial responsibility of Georgians in the form of an unfunded mandate ... Unfortunately, I have no confidence in any federal assertion that this so-called temporary program will not burden the taxpayers of Georgia...I cannot commit the State of Georgia to...a scheme which I believe the Supreme Court will hold to be unconstitutional, leads to the further expansion of the federal government, undermines the financial security of our nation, and potentially commits the

State of Georgia to future financial obligations." Oxendine also says, "We don't have to play ball. We can sit back and say we're not going to participate."[248] [249]

White House "Science Czar" John Holdren tells a group of students, "We can't expect to be number one in everything indefinitely."[250]

Secretary of State Hillary Clinton warns that terrorists including al-Qaeda are attempting to possess nuclear materials.[251]

President Obama bows to Chinese Communist dictator Hu Jintao prior to the Nuclear Security Summit. Hu promises that China will partici-pate in negotiations regarding sanctions against Iran, but he is unwill-ing to commit to anything definite or detailed.[252] *Reports are unclear as to whether President Obama kissed the dictator's ring or touched the hem of his garment, but at least he did get an agreement to agree on something.*

May 2010

4/13/10

The Justice Department is arguing in federal court that search warrants signed by judges are not necessary before the FBI or other police agen-cies can read the contents of Yahoo e-mail older than 181 days.[253] *There isn't anything in the 4th Amendment that says the government can con-duct unreasonable searches and seizures after 181 days.*

Democratic House Majority Leader Steny Hoyer (D-MD) doubts Con-gress will pass a budget this year.[254] *They didn't.*

A Texas man pleads guilty to filing false tax returns for "hiding" money at UBS.[255]

4/14/10

President Obama says America gets into conflicts because it is a super-power "whether we like it or not."

Senator John McCain (R-AZ) believes the president's remark is a "direct contradiction to everything America believes in…That's one of the more incredible statements I've ever heard a President of the United States make in modern times. We are the dominant superpower, and we're the greatest force for good in the history of this country, and I thank God every day that we are a dominant superpower."[256]

Sarah Palin comments, "I would hope that our leaders in Washington, D.C., understand we like to be a dominant superpower. I don't understand a world view where we have to question whether we like it or not that America is powerful."[257]

Russia is on schedule to complete a nuclear reactor in Iran by August. The Russians say the nuclear reactor "doesn't threaten the regime of nonproliferation in any way."[258]

The president hails the success of the forty-six-country Nuclear Security Summit. The Summit Communiqué is, predictably, scant on detail but flush with platitudes. For instance, the 46 countries conclude that that nuclear arms in the possession of terrorists is bad. "We have seized the opportunity. The American people will be safer and the world more secure," Obama says.[259]

May 2010

A stringent immigration bill passes the Arizona state legislature.[260]

Lieutenant Colonel Terry Lakin will be court-martialed because he is refusing to obey deployment orders. Lakin believes Obama's presidency is illegitimate and disputes that he is "a natural born citizen of the United States" as required by Article 2 of the Constitution.[261] *Why was he so stubborn about supplying a copy of his #@*& birth certificate?*

4/15/10

President Obama ridicules tea-party protestors saying they should be thankful to him for "cutting taxes."[262] *First, he should know the difference between a tax cut and a tax credit. Second, he is dismissing the protestors' concern over spending, debt and the scope of government power.*

The president says in a speech, "And one thing we haven't done is raise <u>income taxes</u> on families making less than $250,000 a year—another promise that we kept."[263] *He's prevaricating again for the second time in less than a week.*

May 2010

4/16/10

The Securities Exchange Commission (SEC) charges Goldman Sachs with a $1 billion securities fraud suit.

Coincidentally, President Obama and Senator Christopher Dodd (D-CT) are supporting a Financial Regulation bill that, oddly, the CEO and the president of Goldman also support.[264] [265]

Former NY Governor Elliott Spitzer, a Democrat, comments that there is "no coincidence" to the timing of the lawsuit while presenting a financial overhaul bill. Representative Darrell Issa (R-CA) of the House Oversight and Government Reform Committee writes, "It must be nice for Democrats that the SEC's filing against Goldman Sachs so conveniently fits into their political agenda."[266] *President Obama just put the "bully" in "bully pulpit."*

The Environmental Protection Agency (EPA) is offering $2,500 prize money to contestants who make the best video advertising that government regulations are "important to everyone" and how Americans can be more involved in making more regulations.[267]

Two days after the story was made public, the Obama administration withdraws its attempts to read Yahoo users' private e-mails without a search warrant.[268] *Candidate Obama vowed to "strengthen privacy protections for the digital age."*

4/18/10

Treasury Secretary Tim Geithner tells *Meet the Press* that the economy is rebounding faster than expected and that the U.S. is on a path of sustained job creation.[269]

China is investing $20 billion in projects in Venezuela.[270]

President Obama forgoes the Polish president's funeral to play his thirty-second round of golf. Actually, a volcano in Iceland made air travel unsafe. Vice President Biden and Secretary of State Clinton have already visited the Polish Embassy to pay their respects.[271] [272]

4/19/10

Gay rights protesters from GetEQUAL heckle the president's speech in Los Angeles. The activists are upset that the Obama administration allows banning openly gay people from serving in the military.[273]

4/20/10

The police shut down Lafayette Park, across from the White House, and run off reporters as gay rights activists protested the Obama administration's "don't ask, don't tell" policy.[274] *Maybe gay activists have already used up their quota of 1ˢᵗ Amendment rights this week.*

At 11 p.m. an explosion occurs on BP's Deepwater Horizon oil rig in the Gulf of Mexico. Eleven crewmembers are reported missing. The oil spill is just 50 miles off the coast of Louisiana.[275] *During the worst environmental disaster in American history, Americans and the rest of the world get to see Barack Obama's leadership capabilities in a time of crisis.*

4/21/10

Day 1 of the Gulf Oil Disaster

President Obama "categorically" denies that there is any connection between the Financial Reform legislation and having the SEC publicly beat Goldman Sachs to a bloody pulp. Nope.[276]

President Obama contemplates the idea of a value-added tax (VAT).[277] *Afterall, he is "agnostic" on tax increases and he has already twice back-peddled on his famous campaign pledge in the last two weeks.*

The next eight-five days are a good case study of Obama's haphazard mis-management style. President Obama proves incapable of meeting lead-ership challenges arising after January 20, 2009. He is unable to handle emergencies that do not fit into the pre-set ideological agenda he cam-paigned on. Obama responds to any new, unexpected crisis like a deer in headlights. What is widely believed to be a cool demeanor more closely resembles an avoidant defense mechanism. In the face of suddenly aris-ing catastrophe he has no core values from which he reacts. Whether it is rioting over fraudulent Iranian elections, drug cartels swarming north of the Mexican border, or the Gulf oil disaster, his reaction is ... dithering, indolence, and indifference. He simply does not know how to react in a crisis situation. Afterward, his spin-doctors come up with wonderful post hoc justifications for his do-nothingness.

Whether the Obama administration's response is the result of igno-rance, ideology, indifference, indolence or incompetence is a matter to be debated for months and years to come. Regardless of their motivating forces, the inescapable conclusion is that Barack Obama is not someone the United States can rely on in a crisis situation.

May 2010

4/22/10

Day 2 of the Gulf Oil Disaster

High-ranking SEC regulators spend so much office time watching internet porn that they may not have even noticed that the economy tanked.²⁷⁸ *This is the level of mind that is going to enforce and regulate the Financial Reform legislation in front of Congress.*

A search and rescue operation for the eleven missing oil workers continues. The fire is eventually extinguished and the oil rig falls apart into the Gulf of Mexico.²⁷⁹

4/23/10

Day 3 of the Gulf Oil Disaster

Arizona passes an immigration law allowing law enforcement the right to investigate the immigration status of suspects who have been detained for probable cause. The law states, "For any lawful contact made by a law enforcement official or agency of this state or a county, city, town or other political subdivision of this state where reasonable suspicion exists that the person is an alien who is unlawfully present in the United States, a reasonable attempt shall be made, when practicable, to determine the immigration status of the person."

Governor Brewer maintains that Arizona is in a fiscal crisis and can no longer afford the additional burden of welfare state benefits to illegal immigrants. Also, Arizona has been corrupted by violent Mexican drug cartels. She says that the U.S. government has failed in its duty to protect America's border and that "we in Arizona have been more than patient waiting for Washington to act, but decades of inaction and misguided policy have created an unacceptable situation."²⁸⁰

President Obama pounces on the opportunity to pitch woo for His-

May 2010

panic voters by promoting his own design of "comprehensive immigration reform." The president attacks, "Our failure to act responsibly at the federal level will only open the door to irresponsibility by others. That includes, for example, the recent efforts in Arizona."[281] [282] *But hasn't the president himself failed "to act responsibly at the federal level" for the 458 days he's been in office? Obama says securing the border has been his "top priority" since taking office; yet, he has done nothing. For more than a year, Governors Perry and Brewer have vigorously pushed the immigration issue and the president has only offered lip service and high-falutin' rhetoric.*

Vice President Joe Biden foresees rapid job creation in the economy, "Well, I'm here to tell you some time in the next couple of months we're going to be creating between 250,000 jobs a month and 500,000 jobs a month."[283]

The new CEO of the new General Motors, Ed Whitacre, claims that GM has paid off the government bailout loan "in full, with interest, years ahead of schedule."[284] *The government bailout of GM was almost $50 billion. The government also "loaned" GM $6.7 billion. GM paid back the loan with the bailout money.*

Representative Issa (R-CA) encourages the SEC to launch an internal investigation regarding the controversy surrounding their $1 billion suit against Goldman Sachs in coordination with unveiling Congress's financial reform bill.[285]

The Dutch offer ships and a plan for creating sand berms to help avert an oil spill disaster in the Gulf but they are promptly turned away.[286]

4/24/10

Day 4 of the Gulf Oil Disaster

Civil rights groups are poised to oppose the Arizona immigration law as potentially leading to racial profiling. Passage of the Arizona law has sparked national debate on immigration policy.[287]

4/25/10

Day 5 of the Gulf Oil Disaster

The government approves plans to attempt to control the 42,000-gallon-a-day oil spill with remote control, underwater vehicles.[288] [289]

4/26/10

Day 6 of the Gulf Oil Disaster

Underwater robots discover two leaks as the seafood industry grows concerned about this year's catch.[290]

4/27/10

Day 7 of the Gulf Oil Disaster

President Obama criticizes the Arizona immigration law as "poorly

May 2010

conceived." He stokes Hispanic racial fears saying, "But now, suddenly, if you don't have your papers and you took your kid out to get ice cream, you're going to be harassed, that's something that could potentially happen."[291]

DHS Secretary Napolitano announces that the U.S./Mexico border is more secure than it has ever been. She will also be flying unmanned predator drones over the area.[292]

Nobody is fired in the Securities Exchange Commission (SEC) porn scandal. "Of the employees, eight resigned and six were suspended for periods lasting one to fourteen days...Five were issued formal reprimands, six were issued informal counseling or warning letters, and three are currently facing disciplinary action," said Inspector General David Kotz.[293]

Three weeks after a federal appeals court shot down the Federal Communication Commission's (FCC) bid for net neutrality, the House of Representatives passes a version of the financial overhaul that will give the Federal Trade Commission (FTC) greater control over the Internet.[294] *Thankfully, the FTC was not granted this broad, overreaching authority in the final version enacted into law 7/21/10.*

At the first meeting of the National Commission on Fiscal Responsibility and Reform, White House Budget Director Peter Orszag states that deficit spending will "require increased borrowing abroad which will mortgage our future income to foreign creditors."[295]

On free trade agreements the president promises, "That's something

May 2010

that's going to be a **top priority**."[296]

Interior Secretary Ken Salazar pledges "every resource we can to support the massive response effort underway at the Deepwater Horizon." One resource that will be missing is the Interior Department's Chief of Staff, Tom Strickland, as he and his wife take a "work-related" vacation to the Grand Canyon that includes white-water rafting. Strickland is also the Assistant Secretary for Fish and Wildlife and Parks.[297]

4/28/10

Day 8 of the Gulf Oil Disaster

President Obama discloses his true ideology whenever he strays from the teleprompter. While addressing a group of Obama idolators in Quncy, Illinois, he says, "Now, what we're doing, I want to be clear, we're not trying to push financial reform because we begrudge success that's fairly earned. I mean, I do think at a certain point you've made enough money."[298] *What will he do when he has determined <u>you</u> have made enough money? Does he consider the $5.5 million he personally banked last year to be "enough money?" Does he believe that his campaign donors have "enough money?"*

In Dreams from My Father, *Obama admits, "I chose my friends carefully. The more politically active black students. The foreign students. The Chicanos. The Marxist professors and structural feminists and punk-rock performance poets…We discussed neo-colonialism, Franz Fanon, Eurocentrism and patriarchy." This isn't an unusual phase for college students; however, he never discusses a "turning point" or a time when he embraced the ideals of America. He doesn't indicate a time when he dabbled in the theories of Austrian economists, Jeffersonian principles or strict-interpretive constitutionalists.*

Regarding energy security, the president states, "And that's why my energy security plan has been one of the **top priorities** of my Administration since the day I took office."[299]

The Coast Guard is conducting controlled burns of the oil slick that is now 23 miles from the Louisiana coast. Engineers determine that stopping the oil leak could take months.[300] [301]

The controlled burn on the eighth day highlights the government's failure to adhere to their own 1994 response plan that would have required them to have oil booms on hand. They had zero. The government had to call Elastec/American Marine in Illinois to purchase the one boom they had in stock. The company helped by trying to call customers in other countries to try to round up some booms. *Eight days later, remember.*

One boom can burn 1,000 barrels per hour, "raising the possibility that the spill could have been contained at the accident scene" if they had followed their own response plan. One of the authors of that plan, Ron Gouguet, says the Coast Guard already had the pre-approval to start burning; "the whole reason the plan was created was so we could pull the trigger right away."

U.S. Coast Guard Rear Admiral Mary Landry says the government has all the assets it needs.[302]

May 2010

4/29/10

Day 9 of the Gulf Oil Disaster

Jean-Claude Trichet, President of the European Central Bank, tells *Forbes* that global governance is necessary to prevent a future financial crisis.[303]

Nine days since the beginning of the oil disaster in the Gulf of Mexico, President Obama finally sends DHS Secretary Napolitano, Interior Secretary Salazar and the Environmental Protection Agency's Lisa Jackson to try to coordinate a response. Local officials are frustrated by the government's slow response and their disorganized dealings with the Coast Guard and BP.

Experts believe the oil is leaking at the rate of 5,000 barrels per day.

President Obama assures that he is taking the oil spill seriously and is using "every single available resource at our disposal" as the oil creeps into the Mississippi Delta within 3 miles from the coastline.[304] [305]

Wonderful! The president is taking the oil spill seriously. If he were really using "every single available resource at our disposal" he would enlist the foreign aid that has been offered by numerous countries.

4/30/10

Day 10 of the Gulf Oil Disaster

Governor Jan Brewer signs legislation forbidding racial profiling as part of Arizona's immigration enforcement.[306]

May 2010

A Gallup poll shows the federal government is hiring at a faster pace than the private sector.[307]

April's record $82.69 billion budget deficit is the nineteenth monthly budget deficit for the U.S., almost quadrupling last April's deficit. Spending for this month rose to $327.96 billion.[308]

President Obama meets with Elena Kagan as a possible nominee for the Supreme Court.[309]

Residents of Louisiana detect the heavy odor of oil as the president places a moratorium on offshore drilling. Oil is already coming ashore in the southeast corner of Lousiana, threatening the mating season of most species in the region.[310] [311]

Governor Charlie Crist declares a state of emergency for the Florida panhandle due to the Gulf oil spill.[312]

April Unemployment = 9.9%.
Real Unemployment = 17.1%. [313]

5/1/10

Day 11 of the Gulf Oil Disaster

The Department of Health and Human Services (HHS) sends propaganda brochures to millions of seniors titled, "Medicare and the New Health Care Law—What It Means for You."[314] *This is another double standard of Obama World. Recall that on 9/21/09, the administration sent threatening messages to insurance companies for expressing their views of Obamacare to their customers.*

President Obama gives the commencement speech at the University of Michigan.   He cautions the attendees of Tea Party/libertarian sentiments, "What troubles me is when I hear people say that all government is inherently bad. When our government is spoken of as some menacing, threatening, foreign entity, it ignores the fact that in our democracy, government is us."[315] *If "government is us," then we need to start leaving ourselves alone. This is a classic example of the Obama "strawman" technique. He mischaracterizes arguments that don't even exist and then courageously destroys them. No one with a full set of teeth has said, "all government in inherently bad."*

Calling himself a "Muslim soldier," Faisal Shahzad, trained by the Pakistani Taliban, tries to detonate a bomb in Times Square.[316] [317]

Two Brooklyn men are indicted on charges of trying to help al-Qaeda.

May 2010

5/2/10

Day 12 of the Gulf Oil Disaster

President Obama visits the Gulf Coast on the day that experts believe that satellite photos show the oil leak is 25,000 barrels of oil a day.

BP says it may take three months to drill a relief well and that it will pay "all necessary and appropriate clean-up costs," although federal law limits their liability to $75 million.

President Obama responds by disallowing new lease approvals for offshore drilling until the disaster is investigated completely.[318] [319]

Interior Secretary Ken Salazar colorfully explains his view of the proper role of government power, "Our job basically is to keep the boot on the neck of British Petroleum to carry out the responsibilities they have both under the law and contractually to move forward and stop this spill."[320] *"If you want a picture of the future, imagine a boot stamping on a human face—forever."* —George Orwell, *1984*

5/3/10

Day 13 of the Gulf Oil Disaster

Customs agents capture Faisal Shazad, who tried to bomb Times Square on May 1, 2010, as he tries to board a plane to Dubai. He almost escaped; authorities just became aware of his identity this afternoon. [321]

U.S. taxpayers are funding $8 billion of the Greek bailout through IMF funding.[322]

White House Press Secretary Robert Gibbs is arrogant and mocking as he declines to answer a question about why the president has not held a press conference since July 2009. Gibbs echoes Secretary Salazar's sentiment about keeping "our boot on the throat of BP."[323] *Gibbs fails to specify whether the government's henchmen will be wearing their jackboots or hobnailed boots.*

5/4/10

Day 14 of the Gulf Oil Disaster

Record flooding occurs in Kentucky, Tennessee, and Mississippi. Twenty-nine are dead, so far. Half of Tennessee's counties are declared disaster areas.[324] *Red States, no Obama.*

Two recordings surface of Hakimullah Mehsud, leader of the Pakistani Taliban, who was thought to have been killed. In one of the tapes he says their main targets are now U.S. cities.[325]

5/5/10

Day 15 of the Gulf Oil Disaster

Republicans warn that the financial overhaul bill gives the government unprecedented authority to snoop into citizens' privacy through the proposed Office of Financial Research and the Bureau of Consumer Financial Protection.[326]

Freddie Mac seeks another bailout from the Treasury: $10.6 billion.[327]

The State Department e-mails reporters a list of countries which have offered help with the Gulf oil disaster: Canada, Croatia, France, Germany, Ireland, Mexico, the Netherlands, Norway, Romania, South Korea, Spain, Sweden, the U.K.—as well as the U.N.

The Coast Guard says "there is no need right now that the U.S. cannot meet."[328]

May 2010

5/6/10

Day 16 of the Gulf Oil Disaster

The Federal Communications Commission (FCC) won't let a little thing like a federal appeals court halt its quest for "net neutrality." They are now pursuing greater control over the internet through decade-old laws regarding traditional phone networks. Representative John Boehner (R-OH) accuses the FCC of attempting a "government takeover of the Internet."[329] [330]

5/7/10

Day 17 of the Gulf Oil Disaster

The Coast Guard confirms that oil is now washing up on shore.[331]

Despite the president's "relentless response effort," the Obama administration has granted oil and gas companies twenty-seven exemptions since the disaster began.[332]

5/9/10

Day 19 of the Gulf Oil Disaster

Attorney General Eric Holder tells ABC's *This Week* that the Department of Justice is considering suing the state of Arizona over its immigration law. Holder fears, "You'll end up in a situation where people are racially profiled."[333] *Thank God we have Eric the Lionhearted to guide a "nation of cowards when it comes to race."*

At the commencement address at Hampton University, the president complains of "a 24/7 media environment that bombards us with all kinds of content and exposes us to all kinds of arguments, some of which don't always rank all that high on the truth meter...information becomes a distraction, a diversion, a form of entertainment, rather than a tool of empowerment, rather than the means of emancipation...All of this is not only putting new pressures on you, it is putting new pressures on our country and on our democracy."[334] *This is odd timing for such a bizarre statement. The White House is determined to get "net neutrality." He has an FCC Chairman who is undeterred by the ruling of a federal appeals court. FCC "Diversity Czar," Mark Lloyd, salutes Chavez's socialist revolution in Venezuela, which has cracked down and controlled media. It is also peculiar considering his Maoist Communications Director once bragged that his campaign "controlled" news media.*

Prior to giving his commencement address President Obama was on the phone with German Chancellor Angela Merkel, advising her that Europe needs to bail out Greece.[335] *This isn't shocking from a man who believes in stimulus plans and bailouts.*

May 2010

5/11/10

Day 21 of the Gulf Oil Disaster

The Missouri General Assembly approves a statewide referendum for its citizens to decide whether to nullify Obamacare.[336]

Russia is now ready to help Syria build a nuclear power plant.[337]

BP, Transocean and Halliburton executives testify before the Senate to-day. Predictably, there is plenty of wiggling, wriggling, finger pointing and blaming.[338]

5/13/10

Day 23 of the Gulf Oil Disaster

Attorney General Eric Holder admits to the House Judiciary Committee that he hasn't even read the Arizona immigration law that he has already condemned for racial profiling.[339] *Politicians in Washington absolve themselves of the responsibility for reading 2,400 page bills. The Arizona law is only sixteen pages. Can anyone in Washington even read?*

The U.S. Army mulls issuing medals for "courageous restraint" in Afghanistan, i.e., for holding fire to save civilian lives.[340]

Dozens of companies have reported to the Securities Exchange Commission (SEC) that they will suffer heavy losses from Obamacare. *Fortune* magazine writes that even if companies are fined for noncompliance, the fines are "modest when compared to the average cost of health care... Employers may consider exiting the health care market and send employees to the Exchanges...if 50% of people covered by company plans get dumped, federal health care costs will rise by $160 billion in 2016, in addition to the $93 billion in subsidies already forecast by the CBO."[341]

President Obama lampoons Republicans at the Democratic Congressional Campaign Committee's fundraiser, "After they drove the car into the ditch, made it as difficult as possible for us to pull it back, now they want the keys back. No! You can't drive. We don't want to have to go back into the ditch. We just got the car out."[342] *He's right, Republicans did crash the car, but if he considers exploding deficits to be responsible driving then he needs a breathalizer test.*

5/14/10

Day 24 of the Gulf Oil Disaster

The International Atomic Energy Agency (IAEA) confirms Iran's plans for enriching uranium at higher levels. The U.S. sees this as a bonus; it is a good opportunity to beg Russia and China to cooperate with U.N. sanctions.[343]

Lisa Jackson of the Environmental Protection Agency says she has no authority to compel BP to use any particular oil dispersant.[344]

White House Press Secretary Robert Gibbs also plays dodge ball with reporters assuring them that the president's response to the Gulf oil disaster was "comprehensive and fast."[345]

President Obama criticizes corporate executives' testimony before Congress, "You had executives of BP and Transocean and Halliburton falling over each other to point the finger of blame at somebody else."

President Obama who daily falls all over himself "to point the finger of blame" at George W. Bush, adds, "For a decade or more, there has been a cozy relationship between the oil companies and the federal agency that permits them to drill." He later promises the White House would "continue our relentless efforts to stop the leak and contain the damage."[346] *"For a decade or more" is an obvious attempt to blame Bush and deny responsibility, but the fact is that the administrative sloppiness happened under his own watch. At the rate he is going, Obama is establishing the precedent for Bush to blame everything on Clinton, and for Clinton to blame everything on Bush the Elder, and so on.*

5/16/10

Day 26 of the Gulf Oil Disaster

The Department of the Interior's Minerals Management Service (MMS) gave the Deepwater Horizon oil rig an "exemplary" award for its safety history, even though MMS failed to perform its duty of inspecting rigs once a month.[347]

5/17/10

Day 27 of the Gulf Oil Disaster

In human rights talks with China, the Obama administration engages in an exercise of self-flagellation by constantly citing the Arizona immigration law as our own home-cooked racial discrimination. "We brought it up early and often," says Assistant Secretary of State Michael Posner.

Many people were outraged that the administration debased itself before "China (who) murdered millions of its citizens who opposed the government's Communist policies and allows most of its people little or no freedom. We, on the other hand, enforce our immigration laws. No, wait—actually we don't. That's why Arizona had to take a shot at it," writes a blogger.[348]

President Obama's favorite bank, ShoreBank in Chicago, needs propping up. Major banks, such as Goldman Sachs, JPMorgan Chase, GE Capital, and Citibank, will contribute $140 million while the government will contribute tens of millions more. Some companies backing the bailout of ShoreBank say they have been pressured to contribute to a project that they say they would not normally invest in.[349]

President Obama's Kenyan aunt, Zeituni Onyango, is granted asylum today.[350]

Iran signs a deal to export uranium to Turkey and Brazil in a blatant attempt to subvert U.S. attempts to halt Iran's nuclear program. To seal the deal, leaders from all three countries pose triumphantly with raised, clenched hands.[351]

More than two weeks after placing a moratorium on offshore drilling leases until the Gulf oil disaster has been investigated, the administration announces it will appoint a special commission to investigate the oil leak.[352]

May 2010

5/18/10

Day 28 of the Gulf Oil Disaster

After bashing the Arizona immigration law in the media, DHS Secretary Napolitano divulges to Senator John McCain (R-AZ) that she has not bothered to read the bill. Secretary Napolitano's criticism of the law is unhampered by her admitted ignorance of its contents. While testifying before the Senate Homeland Security Committee she continues to attack the law as though she were thoroughly familiar with it.[353]

State Department spokesman P. J. Crowley defends the administration's self-discrediting use of the Arizona immigration law as an example of America's own human rights scarlet letter. Crowley is forced to admit that he has not read the law.

Senate Budget Committee Chairman Kent Conrad (D-ND) blames House Democrats as the reason why Congress will fail to pass a budget this year.[354] *Just four days after slamming the oil companies, one would expect the president to step in and chide Congress for "pointing the finger of blame at somebody else." We're only talking about...the nation's entire budget.*

5/19/10

Day 29 of the Gulf Oil Disaster

Mexico's President Felipe Calderon rails against the Arizona immigration law from the White House lawn.[355] *Maybe the president should*

May 2010

also have invited Daniel Ortega to join in casting aspersions against the United States.

An official signals that the DHS will not assist Arizona in processing illegal immigrants. John Morton, Assisstant. Secretary of DHS for U.S. Immigration and Customs Enforcement (ICE) says, "I don't think the Arizona law, or laws like it, are the solution. The best way to reduce illegal immigration is through a comprehensive federal approach and not a patchwork of state laws. The law, which criminalizes being in the state illegally and requires authorities to check suspects for immigration status is not 'good government.'"

Senator Jeff Sessions (R-AL) wonders why the Obama administration consistently refuses to enforce existing federal immigration laws.[356]

Thirty-two states have borrowed money from the federal government to cover unemployment shortfalls. California has borrowed $6.9 billion, Michigan has borrowed $3.9 billion and Illinois has borrowed $2.2 billion.[357] *The government is rewarding fiscally irresponsible states to the detriment of those that are fiscally responsible.*

5/20/10

Day 30 of the Gulf Oil Disaster

Mexico's President Felipe Calderon addresses the U.S. Congress. Congressional Democrats and administration officials give him a standing ovation when he strongly denounces the Arizona immigration law.[358]

May 2010

The Environmental Protection Agency's Lisa Jackson overrules herself a week after she said she has no authority to dictate what oil dispersants BP must use. Now she is dictating that BP must provide an acceptable dispersant and is giving them seventy-two hours to use it.[359]

5/21/10

Day 31 of the Gulf Oil Disaster

IRS Commissioner Doug Shulman loves the swarm of new regulations provided by Obamacare as he unveils the new 1099-K form. Shulman says, "Better information reporting helps the tax system work better by ensuring that everyone pays what they owe." In 2012, all businesses will be required to furnish information on all with whom they conduct transactions exceeding $600 for the entire year, including tax ID numbers and other information. In other words, your landlord, phone companies, contractors, utilities, office supplies, advertising —all of it must feed the IRS's pointless appetite for paperwork. SMC Business Councils estimates the average small business's compliance costs to prepare a tax return will be about $6,000.

A separate reporting requirement covers all transactions made with credit and debit cards.[360] [361]

It is disturbing that the federal government, which is so lazily negligent in controlling the oil spill, is on a never-ending quest to seek ... more control.

Just a few days after Iran's humiliating uranium-export deal, the U.S. lifts sanctions against three Russian organizations suspected of assisting Iran in achieving its nuclear ambitions. The U.S. also lifts sanctions against a fourth Russian enterprise that is suspected of arms sales to Syria.

There is consensus that the U.S. is trying to appease Russia to join a toothless U.N. Security Council measure.[362] *"It will not be six months before the world tests Barack Obama like they did John Kennedy. The world is looking...Watch. We're going to have an international crisis, a generated crisis, to test the mettle of this guy."* —Senator Joe Biden, while campaigning.

So far the world sees a timid man who is unable to make dauntless decisions.

Press Secretary Robert Gibbs says the president lacks the authority to play a supervisory role in the Gulf oil disaster.[363]

5/22/10

May 2010

Day 32 of the Gulf Oil Disaster

Many European countries are deeply cutting their budgets in "austerity measures."[364] *Less than two weeks ago President Obama was encouraging Europeans to focus on massive fiscal stimulus.*

The U.S. has amassed evidence that Kim Jong-Il ordered the torpedo attack of a South Korean ship on March 28, 2010.[365]

5/23/10

Day 33 of the Gulf Oil Disaster

Representative Joe Sestak (D-PA) on *Meet The Press* sticks to his story and maintains, "I was offered a job, and I answered that," referring to a special deal the administration was willing to give him if he bowed out of the Pennsylvania Senatorial race.[366]

A Republican wins the vacant House seat in President Obama's Hawaiian home district.[367]

Governor Bobby Jindal harshly criticizes BP and the federal government for not having a plan for cleaning up the oil spill at more than a month into the crisis. In despair, Louisianans get their own hands dirty and begin laying down booms and cleaning up the problem themselves.[368]

In regard to BP, Interior Secretary Salazar says, "If we find that they're not doing what they're supposed to be doing, we'll push them out of the way appropriately."[369] *Wait! Just two days ago Robert Gibbs said the president had no authority to play a supervisory role.*

Even liberal Democratic heavy hitters are frustrated and unimpressed with the White House. Donna Brazile criticizes the Obama administration for its weakness and James Carville criticizes its lack of leadership.[370]

May 2010

5/24/10

Day 34 of the Gulf Oil Disaster

The Department of Justice declines special counsel to investigate the administration's alleged bribery of Representative Joe Sestak (D-PA). Congressman Darrell Issa is sharply critical of the Dept.'s decision, saying, "You have a sitting U.S. Congressman who has made a very specific allegation numerous times that someone inside the Obama White House offered him what amounts to a bribe in order to manipulate the Pennsylvania Senate primary."[371]

In his speech to West Point graduates, President Obama seeks "international order" to resolve everything from military issues to climate change to financial markets.[372] *President Obama is always willing to reach across borders and cede U.S. sovereignty but he will not accept international help with the oil spill.*

The Federal Trade Commission (FTC) thinks its job is to overhaul the media and support traditional formats like newspapers. The FTC favors a 5% tax on electronics like laptop computers, kindles and iPads. The FTC also wishes to impose fees on news sites like the Drudge Report or Breitbart in order to redistribute the funds to traditional media.

FTC Chairman Jon Leibowitz strongly resents the new media and in December he complained that online readers get a "free ride instead of paying the full value—or in fact paying anything—for what they're consuming."[373] [374] [375]

The Department of Justice files a motion to dismiss Virginia's chal-

May 2010

lenge to Obamacare, arguing that, "Congress has the authority under the Constitution's Commerce Clause to order Americans to buy health insurance."[376]

A memo surfaces that General David Petraeus has ordered broad expansion of clandestine operations in the Middle East.[377]

Syrian President Assad says that President Obama has failed in his Mideast peace efforts and whatever influence he once possessed has now vanished.[378]

Although the president *literally* bows to China, China is not willing to bow to his light-handed pressure to adjust its exchange rate policy.[379]

U.N. General Secretary Ban Ki-moon expects sanctions against North Korea in the face of overwhelming evidence that they ordered a torpedo attack against a South Korean attack. The U.S. and South Korea join together in a show of military might to "deter future aggression."[380]

Louisiana Governor Bobby Jindal delivers a withering account of BP and the federal government's lack of effort in helping to clean up the Gulf. "We've been frustrated with the disjointed effort to date that has too often meant too little, too late for the oil hitting our coast," he said.

The federal government is dragging its feet in approving a state plan to dredge and build barrier islands and delivering millions of feet in boom. Governor Jindal is ready to build the barrier islands, without federal government authority, and states that he is willing to go to jail for defying their slow-moving bureaucracy.

The White House's response is that they have been taking care of

May 2010

things "since day 1" and that they will hold BP accountable. As the black tide is washing ashore, federal officials state they will need more time to study the idea of erecting artificial barrier islands.[381] [382]

5/25/10

Day 35 of the Gulf Oil Disaster

President Obama has a closed-door meeting with Republican senators that is described as "testy." Senator Pat Roberts (R-KS) says, "The more he talked, the more he got upset. He needs to take a Valium before he comes in and talks to Republicans and just calm down, and don't take anything so seriously. If you disagree with someone, it doesn't mean you're attacking their motives—and he takes it that way and tends then to lecture and then gets upset."[383]

The Obama administration announces that it is deploying 1,200 National Guard troops to the U.S./Mexico border.[384] *This is more evidence of the president procrastinating until a decision absolutely has to be made.*

Once again, Moody's Investors Service warns that the U.S. risks losing its AAA bond rating. Analyst Steven Hess writes that the U.S.'s "ratios of general government debt to GDP and to revenue are deteriorating sharply, and after the crisis they are likely to be higher than the ratios of other AAA-rated countries."[385]

In his latest whimsical, ill-conceived scheme, President Obama is trying to secure an international financial agreement that would require coun-

May 2010

tries to mandate larger banking reserves. With his characteristic flair for ceding U.S. sovereignty to international forums, the proposal is being considered by a committee in Basel, Switzerland (none of whom are accountable to the American electorate). Bankers consider the measure idiotic because it would starve economies of liquidity and constrain growth; whereas, government bureaucrats love the idea of monotone stability and sameness.[386]

President Obama rants to his aides, "Just plug the damn hole!"[387]

Despite the president's previous attempts to foist blame on the Bush administration, evidence surfaces today that it was Obama administration officials who circumvented the standard operating procedures of full environmental and safety reviews of the Deepwater Horizon rig.[388]

5/26/10

Day 36 of the Gulf Oil Disaster

President Obama touts "green jobs" at the Solyndra plant saying it is "leading the way toward a brighter and more prosperous future."[389] *After sucking up $535 million stimulus funds, Solyndra filed bankruptcy and laid-off 1,100 workers.*

Texas Governor Rick Perry's request for National Guard troops along the Texas/Mexico border is still ignored by the White House. The White House said it has yet to decide where to deploy troops along the border. Four hundred and forty days ago the president said, "We're going to examine whether and if National Guard deployments would make sense and under what circumstances they would make sense."[390] [391] *President Obama is still dragging his feet. Either he is incapable of making a decision or he is indifferent about making a decision.*

Representative Issa (R-CA) continues to turn up the heat to probe whether the White House attempted to bribe Representative Joe Sestak (D-PA) to keep him from running for Senate. Issa writes in an e-mail, "Congressman Sestak has continued to repeat his story whenever asked without varying from the original version. The White House however has arrogantly and wrongly assumed that they can sweep this matter under the rug."[392]

Taliban versus Terminology: "Counterterrorism Czar" John Brennan tells an audience, "Describing our enemy in religious terms would lend credence to the lie propagated by al-Qaeda and its affiliates to justify terrorism, that the United States is somehow at war against Islam. The reality, of course, is that we have never been and never will be at war with Islam. After all, Islam, like so many faiths, is part of America."[393]

Secretary State Clinton says North Korea's attack of a South Korean ship is an "unacceptable provocation."[394] *How often does she accept the unacceptable? Four hundred and twenty-seven days ago she also said that North Korea's firing of missiles for any purpose was unacceptable? North Korea ignored her warning (just as the rest of the world ignores the Obama administration) and test-fired several missile launches and tested an atomic bomb.*

The Interior Department's inspector general finds that while Minerals Management Services (MMS) employees enjoy <u>NOT</u> doing their jobs of inspecting offshore rigs, the <u>DO</u> enjoy lots of pornography on their government computers. Other off-the-books job perks include sports tickets and meals from oil and natural gas companies.[395] *Could this be the key to understanding what Congress is actually doing while they are not reading bills?*

Liberal Democrat James Carville unleashes a blistering diatribe against the president for his weak leadership and low aptitude for making decisions. On *Good Morning America*, Mr. Carville was the mouthpiece of America's anguish over the Gulf oil disaster, "The political stupidity is unbelievable. The President doesn't get down here in the middle of this…I have no idea of why they didn't seize this thing. I have no idea why their attitude was so hands off here…The President of the United States could've come down here, he could've been involved with the families of these 11 people (who died in the rig explosion). He could've demanded a plan in anticipation of this…It just looks like he's not involved in this. Man, you got to get down here and take control of this, put somebody in charge of this thing and get this moving. We're about to die down here!"[396] *Well said, Mr. Carville. The American people don't elect a president with the hope that he's going to spend most of his time blaming his predecessor. They elect a president to get things done.*

May 2010

"We will not rest until this well is shut, the environment is repaired and the clean up is complete."[397]

5/27/10

Day 37 of the Gulf Oil Disaster

Senate Democrats block Senator John McCain's (R-AZ) bid to have 6,000 National Guard troops deployed to Arizona.[398] *What else would he expect from a crowd who gave Mexican President Calderon a standing ovation for condemning Arizona?*

Secretary of State Clinton opines that "the rich" need to pay more in taxes. She says, "Brazil has the highest tax-to-GDP rate in the Western Hemisphere and guess what—they're growing like crazy. And the rich are getting richer, but they're pulling people out of poverty."[399]

President Obama holds his first press conference in almost a year. In a sympathy-begging bid bordering on Munchausen Syndrome, he invokes his 12-year-old daughter, Malia, who just so happened to ask him, just this very morning, right before a major press conference, "Did you plug the hole yet, Daddy?"

During the press conference he reflects: "And when you see birds flying around with oil all over their feathers and turtles dying, you know, that doesn't just speak to the immediate economic consequences of this, this speaks to, you know, how we are caring for this incredible bounty that we have." He later says that the magnitude of the oil leak "forces us to do some soul searching." *Excuse me, Mr. President, this is Day 37, not Desiderata. Stop day-dreaming and start cutting red tape. Please refer to James Carville's statement. By the way, birds with oil all over their feathers are incapable of "flying around."*

May 2010

President Obama also announces a six-month moratorium on deepwater wells, a prohibition of Alaska exploration and cancellation of the Atlantic leases that were announced earlier this year.

President Obama accepts the blame, "In the meantime, my job is to get this fixed. And in case anybody wonders, in any of your reporting, in case you were wondering who's responsible, I take responsibility." He also states, "I was wrong in my belief that the oil companies had their act together when it came to worst-case scenarios." *Are you kidding, Mr. President? You've been shifting blame and doing spin control since Day 9 when you finally acknowledged the disaster. You've blamed Bush and you've blamed the "cozy relationship" between the oil companies and the regulators. Saying he was "wrong to believe that the oil companies had their act together" is one of those non-admissions of fault akin to, "I'm sorry you got upset when I called you fat."*[400] [401] [402] [403]

President Obama also needs to accept responsibility for not returning the phone call of Representative Steve Scalise (R-LA) who represents the district most affected by the oil disaster. After Scalise was told the President was too busy to talk to him, the congressman was surprised to see Obama golfing on television and then flying out to California for a Barbara Boxer (D-CA) fundraiser.[404] *President Obama should do some of the aforementioned "soul searching" and find the fortitude to do his job.*

May 2010

5/28/10

Day 38 of the Gulf Oil Disaster

The administration finally comes forth with an explanation for the Joe

Sestak (D-PA) bribery/interference with elections scandal. It has taken the White House 100 days to come up with a story. So the story goes: Rahm Emanuel asked ex-President Bill Clinton to speak with Sestak and talk to him just to gauge whether he is serious about running. Clinton spoke with Congressman Sestak about whether he may be willing to consider options other than running for the Pennsylvania Senate seat—perhaps an unpaid advisory position.[405] *Does anybody really believe this story? Sestak continuously maintained that the White House offered him a job. It is likely that this lame excuse still breaks the law. 18 USC 595 prohibits federal officials from influencing elections. Regardless of what Bill Clinton may have said, Rahm Emanuel (a "federal official") is responsible for initiating the contact.*

This is relevant to other issues prevalent in the Obama presidency. First, it is more of the same sleepy, foot-dragging and dithering. Why did it take them 100 days to craft a simple explanation to a very serious allegation?

Also, if this explanation is true, why didn't they just come right out and say it? It would have taken ten minutes and saved lots of turmoil. It is similar to the Obama birth certificate controversy. It would have only taken the president a few minutes to furnish it, why didn't he? Even if you assume all of this was true, it raises the issue of the White House Communications Director "controlling" the media.

During his brief stop in Louisiana, the president says, "I ultimately take responsibility for solving this crisis. The buck stops with me." President Obama spends three hours in Louisiana. He normally enjoys five hours when he plays eighteen holes of golf.[406] [407]

May 2010

5/29/10

Day 39 of the Gulf Oil Disaster

Does this count as the equivalent of Obama's "3:00 a.m. phone call" that Candidate Hillary Clinton promised?

5/30/10

Day 40 of the Gulf Oil Disaster

The federal government is now telling BP "what to do" regarding the oil spill.[408] *Part of the White House's spin control for its own inertia is to heap as much blame as possible onto BP. BP is unquestionably a malefactor, but the administration's answer to almost any criticism is that they will make BP pay.*

Louisiana Governor Bobby Jindal speaks out against the federal government for its response to Louisiana's proposal to build sand barriers. The governor says, "Yesterday, the Army Corps of Engineers approved six segments out of twenty-four, over forty miles out of a hundred. But here's where our concern was: the federal government only ordered BP to pay for one of those six segments. That's two miles out of a hundred."[409]

5/31/10

Day 41 of the Gulf Oil Disaster

The Israeli Navy confronts a six-ship Gaza flotilla. The purpose of the Israel's Gaza blockade is to prevent arms shipments from reaching Hamas, the terrorist-group-turned-political-party now controlling Gaza. When the Israelis contact the flotilla by radio, they are told to "Shut Up. Go back to Auschwitz." It turns into a violent clash when the Israeli Navy tries to board the boat for inspection. Nine activists are killed and seven Israeli commandos are injured.[410]

The Free Gaza Movement organized the flotilla. Far left and communist members of the Movement include Bill Ayers, Bernadine Dohrn and Jodie Evans (of Code Pink).[411] *Oddly enough, these are some of President Obama's friends. Perhaps this provides some insight into the president's peculiar stances regarding Israel and why he supports a U.N. investigation into Isreal's actions regarding the flotilla.*

Israeli Prime Minister Netanyahu leaves the U.S. immediately to go deal with the crisis, cancelling a meeting with President Obama.[412]

May 2010

Israel is concerned about the Obama administration's backing of a U.N. Mideast Nuclear Non-Proliferation Treaty. The Treaty makes no mention of Iran but calls for Israel to open its sites and facilities for inspection.[413]

President Obama breaks with tradition and spends Memorial Day at the Abraham Lincoln National Cemetery near Chicago. Vice President Biden presides over the ceremonies at Arlington.[414]

The number of Americans on food stamps hits a record high at 40.8 million in May.[415]

90% of the jobs created in May are short-term Census Bureau hires. Even these numbers appear to be inflated because the Obama administration is using the Census Bureau to fraudulently "cook the books" and inflate employment figures. The Census has been hiring, laying off, re-hiring, laying off, and re-hiring workers multiple times. Each hiring counts as a "new" job. [416] [417]

May unemployment = 9.7%.
Real unemployment = 16.6%.[418]

6/1/10

Day 42 of the Gulf Oil Disaster

Press Secretary Robert Gibbs has difficulty answering any questions relating to the Joe Sestak scandal. All of his answers refer to "the memo" that was released.[419]

DHS Secretary Napolitano says she respects privacy concerns but maintains that airport security should still be strict.[420]

6/2/10

Day 43 of the Gulf Oil Disaster

China rejects (i.e., snubs) meeting with Defense Secretary Gates during his trip to Asia. China is still unhappy with U.S. plans to sell Taiwan $6.4 billion in arms.[421]

6/3/10

Day 44 of the Gulf Oil Disaster

President Obama asks Arizona Governor Jan Brewer to support comprehensive immigration reform during an otherwise uneventful meeting. After the meeting the governor says, "People from the staff are coming out to Arizona to brief us on what their projections are going to be in regards to the 1,200 National Guard and the $500 million that he has indicated that he's going to send down there. And we're going to see how that's going to get distributed. He assured us that the majority of resources will be coming to Arizona—yet to be figured out."[422]

Colorado Senate candidate Andrew Romanoff speaks about another White House scandal similar to the Sestak scandal. The allegation is that Romanoff was offered a choice of jobs by Deputy Chief of Staff Jim Messina for not challenging White House favorite, Senator Michael Bennett (D-CO) in the Colorado Democratic primary. Romanoff says he was told a job "might be available." Romanoff states, "At no time was I promised a job, nor did I request Mr. Messina's assistance in obtaining one."[423]

6/4/10

Day 45 of the Gulf Oil Disaster

Israel prepares to intercept another Gaza-bound ship.[424]

Documents surface showing Supreme Court nominee Elena Kagan's

Jun 2010

support for partial-birth abortion and affirmative action. By now, Kagan's contempt for the U.S. military is already well known, as she barred military recruiters from Harvard's career services while she was dean of Harvard law school.[425] [426]

Louisiana Governor Jindal speaks out against President Obama's drilling moratorium. He says it will cost his state as many as 20,000 jobs by the end of the year.[427]

According to Senator Mary Landrieu (D-LA), "If these big rigs ever leave the Gulf... it's not like you can make those every day or every year. Some of them take years to build. If they leave the gulf and go drill under long-term contracts off the coast of Africa, they're not coming home any time soon."[428]

6/5/10

Day 46 of the Gulf Oil Disaster

About 2,000 people rally at the Arizona State Capitol in favor of the immigration law.[429]

The overlaps of red tape are so thick that it is no wonder that the federal response has been so inadequate in the Gulf. The Department of Homeland Security took well over a week to designate the oil spill as an event worthy of the highest priority of federal response. Louisiana fruitlessly pled over and over and over for federal permission to build sand berms.

The *New York Times* reports, "At least a dozen federal agencies have

Jun 2010

taken part in the spill response, making decision-making slow, conflict-ed and confused, as they sought to apply numerous federal statutes." The article further states, "For three weeks, as the giant slick crept closer to shore, officials from the White House, Coast Guard, Army Corps of Engineers, Fish and Wildlife Service, National Oceanic and Atmo-spheric Administration, and Environmental Protection Agency debat-ed the best approach."[430]

6/6/10

Day 47 of the Gulf Oil Disaster

BP CEO Tony Hayward hasn't spoken with President Obama since the rig exploded. "There is no need for that, I have spoken to his key lieu-tenants," Hayward says.[431]

6/7/10

Day 48 of the Gulf Oil Disaster

The U.S. Army arrests Private Bradley Manning for releasing classified information to WikiLeaks.[432]

As part of his "Race to the Top" education initiative, President Obama agreed to speak at a high school graduation in Kalamazoo, Michigan. He tells the students not to make excuses and to take responsibility for their failures and successes.[433] *The President has pretty much monopo-lized excuses already.*

Demonstrators rally to protest the Ground Zero mosque.[434]

Referring to the oil spill, Obama doesn't sound very presidential when he says, "I don't sit around just talking to experts because this is a college seminar, we talk to these folks because they potentially have the best answers, so I know whose ass to kick."[435] *What a poseur! Instead of sounding "tough" he sounded like a mewling eighth grader, simpering in front of the mirror, rehearsing his "manly talk" before standing up to the bully at lunchtime tomorrow.*

6/8/10

Day 49 of the Gulf Oil Disaster

The Treasury Department projects that the U.S. debt will rise to $19.6 trillion by 2015.[436]

The War in Afghanistan is now officially America's longest war.[437]

Russia and China support the U.N. Security Council's fourth round of sanctions against Iran. President Ahmadinejad calls the sanctions "valueless" and should be tossed "in the waste bin like a used handkerchief."
     Russia immediately clarifies that the U.N.'s sanctions do not apply to their contract to sell Iran S-300 missiles.[438]

On tour in South America, Secretary of State Clinton encourages Latin American countries to increase taxes on the rich.
     Clinton also announces on Ecuadoran television that the Department of Justice will sue Arizona because of its immigration law.[439] [440]

6/9/10

Day 50 of the Gulf Oil Disaster

BP is now capturing 15,000 barrels a day from the well and predicts they will be able to capture 20,000 barrels per day by next week.[441]

6/10/10

Day 51 of the Gulf Oil Disaster

Federal Trade Commission (FTC) Chairman Jon Leibowitz eats crow as he testifies before the Senate Judiciary Committee about his idea to tax electronic devices and online news outlets in order to redistribute the funds to traditional media. Leibowitz said, "I think that's a terrible idea."[442] See entry for 5/24/10.

The Senate introduces a bill that would give the president power to press a "kill switch" for the internet.[443] *I'm sure Hugo Chavez and Fidel Castro favor this bill, too.*

6/11/10

Day 52 of the Gulf Oil Disaster

The U.S. plans to support a U.N. commission to investigate the Israeli-Gaza flotilla incident.[444]

The story surfaces that the Obama administration turned away Dutch

Jun 2010

help. Three days after the spill the Dutch government offered ships, booms and plans for creating 60 miles of sand dikes to protect the shoreline from the black tide.

Part of the reason for the rejection is the Jones Act, which disallows foreign vessels from going from U.S. port to U.S. port. The U.S. Maritime Administration could have suspended the Jones Act but, for some reason, did not.[445] *Perhaps maritime labor unions benefited from keeping the Jones Act in place.*

6/13/10

Day 54 of the Gulf Oil Disaster

President Obama urges Congress to pass $50 billion in emergency aid for state and local governments to avoid "massive layoffs of teachers, police and firefighters."[446]

Fannie Mae and Freddie Mac bailouts have already cost taxpayers $145 billion and could go as high as $1 trillion.[447]

Alabama Governor Bob Riley offers a scathing critique of Obama's lack of leadership in the oil disaster. On CNN's *State of the Union*, Riley says, "You can't have a committee making the decisions that are going to impact this entire coastal area." Riley says the Coast Guard plan for protecting the Alabama coast has been stalled for forty-five days while another committee is reviewing it.[448]

6/14/10

Day 55 of the Gulf Oil Disaster

In an outright violation of the law, the administration forces NASA to dismantle its Constellation program that would have taken astronauts to the moon.[449]

The Obama administration seems to be taking its cues from the George Soros-funded Center for American Progress (CAP).

On May 4, CAP recommended the president appoint an independent commission—which he did on May 21.

On May 21, CAP recommended the president appoint a public point person—which he did a week later.

On May 26, CAP recommended the president demand BP set up an escrow account—which he did today.[450]

While President Obama visits the Gulf Coast, Louisiana's Governor Jindal takes leadership and orders the National Guard to start building barrier walls.[451]

Coastal residents are struggling with bureaucratic paperwork to get compensation. The President says, "There are still problems with (the claims). We're gathering up facts, stories right now so that we have an absolutely clear understanding about how we can best present to BP the need to make sure that individuals and businesses are dealt with in a fair manner and a prompt manner."⁴⁵² *BP already understands this. The only thing preventing people from being "dealt with in a fair manner and a prompt manner" is complex paperwork congestion and sloppy administration.*

6/15/10

Day 56 of the Gulf Oil Disaster

Public Policy Polling shows that most Louisianans think George W. Bush did a better job handling Hurricane Katrina than President Obama has handled the oil spill.[453]

Representative John Boehner speaks out about the Gulf oil disaster and cautions the president against political opportunism. The House Minority Leader says, "Even now, nearly two months after disaster first struck, the federal response remains inadequate and disorganized... President Obama should not exploit this crisis to impose a job-killing national energy tax on struggling families and small businesses... There's nothing responsible or reasonable about a job-killing national energy tax that will raise energy costs and destroy more American jobs."[454]

The Obama administration believes the government can contain 90% of the seeping oil by the end of June.[455]

In the president's Address to the Nation, he declares, "Our **top priority** is to recover and rebuild from a recession that has touched the lives of nearly every American."[456]

Jun 2010

6/16/10

Day 57 of the Gulf Oil Disaster

Arizona Governor Jan Brewer denounces Attorney General Eric Holder for holding open the option of suing her state. "I hope (Holder has) read (the law) by now so that he knows what it exactly says," says the Governor.[457] *Secretary Clinton's 6/8/10 announcement on Ecuadoran television has not hit the American news cycle yet.*

New York Law School releases a study showing that if the FCC gains "net neutrality" it could cost the economy $62 billion and 502,00 jobs over the next five years.[458]

Louisiana Governor Jindal has sixteen barges vacuuming oil out of Louisiana's waters.[459]

BP's Chairman, Carl-Henric Svanberg, meets with Obama administration officials for four hours and meets with the president for twenty minutes. The Administration's shakedown results in BP setting up a $20 billion escrow fund to pay claims of Gulf Coast residents.

In a public relations disaster, Svanberg speaks with the press about his meeting, "He's frustrated because he cares about the small people, and we care about the small people. I hear comments that sometimes large oil companies are greedy companies that don't care. But that is not the case with BP. We care about the small people."[460] *Although Swedish is his native language, shouldn't the Chairman of "British" Petroleum speak better English?*

6/17/10

Day 58 after the Gulf Oil Disaster

Day 1 of Recovery Summer

The White House announces "Recovery Summer" to celebrate the achievements of the stimulus bill. Even though 12,000 people lost their jobs last week, Vice President Biden declares the stimulus is "an absolute success."[461]

News surfaces of Secretary of State Clinton's announcement on Ecuadoran television that the Justice Department will be suing Arizona for its immigration law.[462] Displeased, Governor Jan Brewer (AZ) says, "It would seem to me that if they were going to file suit against us they definitely would have contacted us first and informed us before they informed citizens … of another nation."[463]

Increased violence forces park closings in Arizona. The 3,500-acre area spans across 80 miles of the Arizona/Mexico border. The Fish and Wildlife Service claims it was actually closed in October 2006, "due to human safety concerns." *So what? It is still American land that is too dangerous for Americans because of foreign invaders.*

    Sheriff Paul Babeu says the violence against citizens and law enforcement has increased in the last four months. The sheriff states, "We need support from the federal government. It's their job to secure the border and they haven't done it…In fact, President Obama suspended the construction of the fence and it's just simply outrageous."[464]

Jun 2010

In order to argue that Obamacare is constitutional, the administration is forced to argue that the individual mandate to buy health insurance **IS** actually a tax.[465] *Remember that on September 20, 2009, he brushed aside that the notion that Obamacare was a tax. Also remember that he repeatedly campaigned on the promise that people earning under $250,000 per year would not see any tax increase.*

The FCC takes its first formal step toward "net neutrality." There is a 3–2 vote along party lines at the FCC to begin formal consideration to regulating the internet.[466]

The Obama administration is having secret talks with Russia which many officials believe could compromise U.S. missile defense.[467]

Governor Jindal is outraged as the federal government `continues to thwart his clean up effort.[468]

6/18/10

Day 59 of the Gulf Oil Spill

Day 2 of Recovery Summer

Jun 2010

The U.S. Coast Guard shuts down sixteen barges that Governor Jindal has been using to clean up Louisiana's coast and marshland. Given the scope of the problem, Jindal is furious that petty technocrats have side-lined his the barges in order to inspect fire extinguishers, life vests and because they have yet to be able to contact the manufacturers of the barges.[469] *What if the Titanic crew barred passengers from boarding life boats that didn't have fire extinguishers or the proper number of life vests?*

President Obama spends Friday night cheering the Chicago White Sox to a 2–1 victory over the Washington Nationals.[470]

6/19/10

Day 60 of the Gulf Oil Disaster

Day 3 of Recovery Summer

In an op-ed piece, leftish billionaire Mort Zuckerman denounces President Obama, saying the "world sees Obama as incompetent and amateur…Even in Britain, for decades our closest ally, the talk in the press—supported by polls—is about the end of the 'special relationship' with America. French President Nicolas Sarkozy openly criticized Obama for months, including a direct attack on his policies at the United Nations. Sarkozy cited the need to recognize the real world, not the virtual world, a clear reference to Obama's speech on nuclear weapons…Vladimir Putin of Russia has publicly scorned a number of Obama's visions. Relations with the Chinese leadership got off to a bad start with the President's poorly organized visit to China, where his hosts treated him disdainfully and prevented him from speaking to a national television audience of the Chinese people. The Chinese behavior was unprecedented when compared to visits by other U.S. Presidents."

According to Zuckerman, "America right now appears to be unreliable to traditional friends, compliant to rivals, and weak to enemies." He quotes an Asian leader who remarked, "We in Asia are convinced

Jun 2010

that Obama is not strong enough to confront his opponents, but we fear that he is not strong enough to support his friends."[471]

Zuckerman eloquently sums up President Obama's results as a world leader. Obama's character flaw of fundamental weakness is dangerous to U.S. interests.

Arizona Governor Jan Brewer is disgusted that she has not heard from President Obama, as promised, within two weeks (unless you count Secretary Clinton's slip of the tongue in a foreign country). She says, "We are certainly under attack by the drug cartels and by the drug smugglers, the human smugglers. It's out of control. It's totally out of control."[472] *This is another example of the president's management style of "winging it." He has a habit of saying what is politically expedient at the moment and then not following through.*

DHS Secretary Napolitano promotes internet monitoring to fight homegrown terrorism.[473] *Is this message timed to coincide with the FCC's attempt to snatch regulatory power over the internet? It is kind of frightening when one considers that this is the same woman who defines just about every conservative as a potential homegrown terrorist.*

Twenty-five Saudi Guantanamo alumni have returned to terrorism.[474]

Russian President Medvedev is still promoting the end of the dollar as the global reserve currency. Medvedev would like for the ruble to be one of the world's reserve currencies.[475]

Louisiana's Governor Jindal continues to be astonished by the administration's incompetence. In an interview, Governor Jindal says that dealing with the federal government's mismanagement and weak leadership is "the most frustrating thing. Literally, (Wednesday) morning we found out that they were halting all of these barges. These barges work. You've seen them work. You've seen them suck oil out of the water." The governor continues, "The Coast Guard came and shut them down. You got men on the barges in the oil, and they have been told by the Coast Guard, 'Cease and desist. Stop sucking up that oil.'"[476]

Coast Guard Capt. Roger Laferriere defends the Coast Guard's idiotic 'cease and desist' order by saying, "Safety is my number one priority." Capt. Laferriere goes on to say, "We have exhausted all our east coast supply of skimming vessels. We are now looking at Norway, France, Spain and other European vessels." *All were offered two months ago.* He adds that regulations are a major challenge. The Coast Guard has worked with the president and Admiral Allen to get the Jones Act waived. *Take your time, Mr. President. No rush.*

"Pay Czar" Kenneth Feinberg is dispatched to Louisiana to improve the ridiculously bureaucratic mess of processing the claims of people who have lost their livelihoods. Czar Kenneth says, "We'll decide who will get paid. We're going to get them paid immediately."

Meanwhile, BP has to reject claims because, surprise, the claimants do not have the proper paperwork—tickets, deposit slips, bank statements and tax returns.[477]

6/20/10

Day 61 of the Gulf Oil Disaster

Day 4 of Recovery Summer

President Obama's seven-person Gulf Oil Spill Commission includes one optics engineer, one environmental scientist and three members who have called for an end to offshore drilling. The remaining two members are policy analysts.[478]

6/21/10

Day 62 of the Gulf Oil Disaster

Day 5 of Recovery Summer

Labor Secretary Hilda Solis says that illegals have a right to fair wages. In a public service announcement, Solis says, "Remember: every worker in America has a right to be paid, fairly, whether documented or not. So, call us, it is free and confidential."[479]

While speaking about immigration, Senator Jon Kyl (R-AZ) describes for his constituents a meeting he had with President Obama, "The problem is, he (the president) said, if we secure the border, then you all won't have any reason to support comprehensive immigration reform. In other words, they're holding it hostage."[480]

The Kaiser Foundation's research shows that those who have to buy their own health insurance have seen their premiums skyrocket by 20% since the passage of Obamacare.[481]

More than a third of the 1.24 million borrowers who entered Obama's mortgage modification plan have left the program because of its failure to help.[482]

President Obama urges world leaders not to focus on cutting deficits. As usual, they ignore him. German Economy Minister Rainer Bruederle says, "It's urgently necessary for monetary stability that public budgets return to balance. This is something we should also tell our American friends."

German Finance Minister Wolfgang Schaeuble chimes in, "Nobody can seriously dispute that excessive public debts, not only in Europe, are one of the main causes of this crisis."[483]

Canadian Prime Minister Stephen Harper appeals to world leaders to cut their budget deficits in half by 2013.

The White House jeers at BP CEO Tony Hayward's attendance at a yacht race while defending Obama's golf game. Spokesman Bill Burton says, "I think that a little time to himself on Father's Day weekend probably does us all good as American citizens."[484] *Father's Day weekend may also be a good time for fathers to spend with their children.*

6/22/10

Day 63 of the Gulf Oil Disaster

Day 6 of Recovery Summer

President Obama comments that General McChrystal showed "poor judgment" in some offhanded remarks he made in a *Rolling Stone* interview.

The General said his first meeting with Obama was disappointing because President Obama was unprepared.

An aide to the General also described National Security Advisor James Jones as a "clown" stuck in 1985.[485] *President Obama is weak. His generals don't respect him. World leaders don't respect him. Governors don't respect him. Business leaders don't respect him. Crackpot, Third World tinhorn dictators don't respect him.*

Business leaders warn that Obama's policies are strangling economic growth. Ivan Seidenberg, CEO of Verizon Wireless and Chairman of the Business Roundtable says Democratic taxes, policies and regulations are preventing growth and "harm our ability ... to grow private sector jobs." He further states, "By reaching into virtually every sector of economic life, government is injecting uncertainty into the marketplace and making it harder to raise capital and create new businesses."[486]

Federal Judge Martin Feldman lifts the Obama administration's moratorium on deepwater drilling and "immediately prohibited" the U.S. from enforcing the ban. In his opinion the judge says, "The court is unable to divine or fathom a relationship between the findings and the immense scope of the moratorium. The blanket moratorium, with no parameters, seems to assume that because one rig failed and although no one yet full knows why, all companies and rigs drilling new wells over 500 feet also universally present an imminent danger."

The Interior Department was dishonest in the material it presented to the Court. It claimed its report was based on "peer reviewed" evidence by "experts identified by the National Academy of Engineering." The Interior Department mischaracterized the opinion of the experts.

Jun 2010

As it turns out, they never saw anything that suggested a moratorium; eight of the experts say they opposed the moratorium.[487]

Interior Secretary Salazar remains undeterred by the ruling. He says he will find a way to reimpose the drilling moratorium.[488] *I guess he wants to "put his boot on the neck" of the federal courts, too.*

Eventually, Judge Feldman compels the Interior Department to pay the plaintiffs' legal fees and rules that the Department act on pending offshore drilling applications.

A *New York Times*/CBS poll shows that 59% of Americans think the Obama administration does not have a "clear plan" for dealing with the oil spill.[489]

6/23/10

Day 64 of the Gulf Oil Disaster

Day 7 of Recovery Summer

Thirteen hundred prisoners fraudulently receive millions of dollars from the first-time homebuyer tax credit program.[490] *It makes you wonder how much other fraud is riddled throughout the system.*

Venezuela seizes eleven U.S.-owned oil rigs. The Venezuelan government owed the U.S. company Helmerich & Payne $43 million as of June 14. The company said they would stop drilling unless Venezuela started paying them. Last year, Venezuela took over another American oil company's rigs while still owing $35 million.[491]

General McChrystal is dismissed from his command in Afghanistan.[492]

The federal government shuts down sand berm dredging in Louisiana. Governor Jindal and Plaquemines Parish President Billy Nungesser are increasingly irritated by the federal government's lack of direction, leadership and misplaced priorities. Nunngesser writes to the President, "Once again, our government resource agencies, which are intended to protect us, are now leaving us vulnerable to the destruction of our coastline and marshes by the impending oil."[493]

6/24/10

Day 65 of the Gulf Oil Disaster

Day 8 of Recovery Summer

"Counteterrorism Czar" John Brennan storms out of meeting with editors of *The Washington Times* after a question regarding an earlier remark about calling jihad a "legitimate tenet of Islam." Czar John, who has a history of being obsessed with terminology, defends the administration's goal that describing al-Qaeda in terms of Islam gives them legitimacy.

Douglas Feith, Bush's undersecretary of defense for policy, says, "What Brennan has done in this speech, I think, he's bent over backwards to avoid using the term 'Islam' at all and makes discussions of what we're really up against artificial, unrealistic and strategically unhelpful. I think they need to be a little bolder and a little more honest and a little more assertive in making this extremely important distinction. To say Islam has nothing to do with it is ridiculous."[494]

In anticipation of the G8 and G-20 meetings, President Obama encourages other nations not to cut their debt too much or too quickly. Treasury Secretary Geithner tells BBC that the world "cannot depend as much on the U.S. as it did in the past."[495]

6/25/10

Day 66 of the Gulf Oil Disaster

Day 9 of Recovery Summer

Vice President Biden celebrates Day 9 of Recovery Summer telling an audience, "There's no possibility to restore 8 million jobs lost in the Great Recession."[496]

DHS Secretary Napolitano tells an audience, "The plain fact of the matter is the border is as secure now as it has ever been, but we know we can always do more." She further explains, "You're never going to totally seal that border."[497] *Admittedly, this is a bad example, but the Soviet Union effectively sealed the largest border in the world.*

Governor Jan Brewer (AZ) responds to Obama's failure to respond to her within two weeks of their meeting. In a YouTube video taken 80 miles from the border, she unveils the president's response: signs warning Americans to stay away from the area since it is full of illegal drug and human trafficking. The governor says, "This is an outrage. Washington says 'our border is as safe as it has ever been.' (Pointing to the sign) Does this look safe to you?"[498]

The Obama administration has knocked the closing of the Guantanamo prison to a low priority. It probably will not close before the end of Obama's first term.[499]

The White House and Congressional Democrats are tweaking small details of overhauling the financial system and will soon be ready to move forward.[500]

The IRS issues a diktat to the people of Louisiana warning them that the government will pursue them for whatever BP payments they have received.[501] *"Aside from the incident, Mrs. Lincoln, what did you think of the play?"*

6/26/10

Day 67 of the Gulf Oil Disaster

Day 10 of Recovery Summer

Toronto hosts the G-20 summit.

Vice President Biden rolls the Recovery Summer bandwagon to a Milwaukee custard shop for an impromptu visit. When he asks the manager, "What do we owe you?" the manager replies, "Lower our taxes and we'll call it even." The vice president sharply retorts, "Why don't you say something nice instead of being a smartass all the time?"[502]

President Obama wishes to levy a special bank tax as part of his financial reform.[503]

President Obama prefers golf to the Gulf. He has played seven times since the Gulf oil disaster began.[504] *We will **not** rest until this well is shut, the environment is repaired and the clean up is complete. 5/26/10.*

6/27/10

Day 68 of the Gulf Oil Disaster

Day 11 of Recovery Summer

President Obama says he cannot wait until next year to start cutting the deficit. He says, "Somehow people say, why are you doing that, I'm not sure that's good politics. I'm doing it because I said I was going to do it and I think it's the right thing to do. People should learn that lesson about me because next year when I start presenting some very difficult choices to the country, I hope some of these folks who are hollering about deficits and debt step-up because I'm calling their bluff. We'll see how much of that, how much of the political arguments that they're making right now are real and how much of it was just politics."[505] *Does he seriously believe people are bluffing when they say the deficit is too big? Remember this quotation. When the time comes next year, he proposes a budget with $6 billion in cuts (a bit over one-tenth of 1%) and underestimates deficits by $2 trillion.*

Americans will have to tighten their belts in the coming year as the president vows to cut the soaring budget deficits. He plans to present

Americans with "some very difficult choices" next year. He dispels any notion that he is unserious about deficit cutting by adding, "I'm serious about it."[506] *Those who talk too much tend to do little else. The president mistakes words for deeds.*

CIA Director Leon Panetta says his agency believes Iran has enough low-enriched uranium to build two nuclear weapons if they can further enrich it. Russian President Medvedev calls the news "worrying."[507]

At the end of G-20, Obama says, "A strong and durable recovery also requires countries not having an undue advantage."[508] *He has certainly ripped-apart our advantage.*

Although he encouraged other nations to follow his example and spend, they have chosen austerity measures to halve their deficits by 2013.[509]

6/28/10

Day 69 of the Gulf Oil Disaster

Day 12 of Recovery Summer

Jun 2010

The Supreme Court affirms 5–4 the fundamental right to bear arms. Justice Alito writes the opinion of the Court, "It is clear that the Framers … counted the right to keep and bear arms among those fundamental rights necessary to our system of ordered liberty."[510] *"To preserve liberty, it is essential that the whole body of the people always possess arms, and be taught alike, especially when young, how to use them." —Richard*

Henry Lee, Founding Father

Governor Jan Brewer (R-AZ) meets with White House officials to discuss the administration's proposal for addressing Arizona's immigration mess. The White House refuses to provide Arizona authorities with hard copies of their Powerpoint presentation. Brewer says the administration proposes to remedy Arizona's immigration woes with 525 National Guardsmen for six months.[511]

Banks forecast that the Federal Reserve will be 'monster' money-printing soon.[512] *In a speech in 2002, Fed Chairman Ben Bernanke said, "The U.S. government has a technology, called a printing press, that allows it to produce as many U.S. dollars as it wishes at essentially no cost."*

President Obama has named the White House "Ethics Czar" Norm Eisen for Ambassadorship to the Czech Republic. Among his duties as "Ethics Czar" was insuring transparency.[513]

Ten Russian agents are apprehended in the New York area and charged with conspiracy to act as agents of a foreign government.[514]

The state of Alabama uses snare booms to keep oil from washing up on their beaches. The Fish and Wildlife Service orders them removed because they endanger turtles. Alabama has also hired 400 workers to patrol beaches and scoop up oil. OSHA steps in and mandates that workers be limited to working twenty minutes per hour.[515]

Jun 2010

6/29/10

Day 70 of the Gulf Oil Disaster

Day 13 of Recovery Summer

President Obama convenes a bipartisan meeting with twenty senators to promote energy and climate change. Senator Lamar Alexander (R-TN) tells the President, "The priority should be fixing the oil spill. That's what any meeting about energy should be about." President Obama does not like the Senator's insolence and shoots back, "That's just your talking point." Senator Alexander rejoins, "No, it's my opinion."[516] *Testy aren't we, Mr. President? Does Obama really think that the senator is merely trying to score cheap points during the worst environmental disaster this country has known?*

Refer back to Sen. Pat Roberts' comments on 5/25/10. Or his "bipartisan" C-SPAN chat. Or when he bellowed, "Plug the damn hole!" Does the president throw these kinds of immature hissy fits when he meets with foreign leaders? Could that be why he is so universally disrespected?

On the flip side: why doesn't the president bring his trademark submissiveness to the table when negotiating with Republicans? Perhaps President Obama should open talks with Tea Party members of Congress saying, "I come to you in a spirit of humility to listen and not dictate."

The U.S. finally, after seventy days, accepts international help with the oil spill. Since the beginning of the disaster, more than thirty countries and international organizations have offered to help with the spill.[517]

6/30/10

Day 71 of the Gulf Oil Disaster

Day 14 of Recovery Summer

The National Debt rises $166 billion in <u>just one day</u>. In this one day alone, each U.S. household is saddled with an extra $1,500 in debt. This is only the third-largest daily increase in debt. The first and second largest one-day increases in the national debt have also occurred under President Obama.[518]

The 2010 budget deficit surpassed $1 trillion today.[519]

The National Debt reaches its highest level since World War II.[520]

While much of Europe is pursuing deficit-cutting austerity measures, the Obama administration spends, spends, spends. The Congressional Budget Office (CBO) releases a report projecting the National Debt could rise to 87% of GDP by 2020, 109% of GDP by 2025 and 185% of GDP by 2035.[521]

The U.S. workforce shrinks by 652,000 this month.[522]

Fannie Mae suffers a $1.2 billion quarterly loss.[523] *Actually, it is the taxpayers who will be suffering the loss.*

The U.S. Postal Service delivers a $3.5 billion loss for this past quarter. The deficit is largely due to higher workers' compensation costs and retiree health benefits. To help cut costs, the USPS will be seeking Congressional approval to cut Saturday service.[524]

The Federal Reserve's monetary policy and the Obama administration's fiscal policy provoke weakened confidence in the stability and value of the dollar. In the past twelve months China has cut its holdings of U.S. Treasuries by $100 billion.[525]

June unemployment = 9.5%.[526]
Real unemployment = 16.5%.[527]

7/1/10

Day 72 of the Gulf Oil Disaster

Day 15 of Recovery Summer

President Obama speaks about immigration reform, inviting Republicans to sit at the table and hash out the issue. Anticipating the Republican argument that the borders must be secured first, he says, "Our borders are just too vast for us to be able to solve the problem only with fences and border patrols." He understands the frustrations of states like Arizona, but says their efforts to pass immigration laws are "ill-conceived." *President Obama is determined to do every thing he can with regard to immigration except enforce the law.*

President Obama also says that being American "is not a matter of blood or birth." *Hmmm...actually being an American is a matter of blood or birth. The only other way to become an American is through naturalization.*[528] [529]

The Transportation Security Administration (TSA) is blocking certain websites from its computers. The five types of banned websites are: chat/messaging, criminal activity, extreme violence, gaming and controversial opinion.[530] *What is "controversial opinion?" TSA is part of the Department of Homeland Security. It could be anything given the fact that DHS Secretary Napolitano thinks that people with Ron Paul stickers are potential terrorists (she says she stands by the memo).*

Since other government agencies have had porn scandals, why aren't sex sites blocked from the TSA?

The United Nations issues a report calling for the end of the dollar as the global reserve currency in favor of special drawing rights with the IMF.[531]

7/2/10

Day 73 of the Gulf Oil Disaster

Day 16 of Recovery Summer

The government may have to turn sick people away from Obamacare. The law has set up $5 billion to take care of high-risk patients between now and January 1, 2014. If the money runs out, the administration has not ruled out reducing benefits or redistributing funds between state pools.[532]

Various skimmers and tankers are still available but unused for Gulf oil clean up. The Environmental Protection Agency (EPA) is unwilling to relax its regulations and allow them to be used. [533]

7/3/10

Day 74 of the Gulf Oil Disaster

Day 17 of Recovery Summer

General David Petraeus arrives in Afghanistan to take control of NATO forces. General Petraeus's doctrine refers to "Islamic insurgents," "Islamic extremists" and "Islamic subversives" as the enemy. The White House has a policy of not using the terms "Muslim" or "Islam" with regard to terrorists.[534]

A giant oil skimmer from Taiwan, dubbed "A Whale," arrives in the Gulf for test runs. The skimmer can process 21 million gallons of oil-contaminated water per day. A frustrated Louisiana Governor Jindal thinks the world's largest oil skimmer should be put to immediate use.[535]

7/5/10

Day 76 of the Gulf Oil Disaster

Day 19 of Recovery Summer

Private Bradley Manning is charged with transferring and transmitting classified data to WikiLeaks.[536]

7/6/10

Day 77 of the Gulf Oil Disaster

Day 20 of Recovery Summer

The Justice Department files a suit against Arizona for its immigration law. The lawsuit states, "In our constitutional system, the federal government has pre-eminent authority to regulate immigration matters."[537] *Really? All that Article 1 section 8 of the Constitution says is that Congress has the power "to establish a uniform Rule of Naturalization." That's it. If the Obama administration believes it has "pre-eminent authority" why haven't they sued left-wing municipalities that have designated themselves as "sanctuary cities?" Afterall, this is also a challenge to federal authority. The simple fact is that Obama will do whatever he must to pander to the Hispanic vote as long as it does not entail enforcing the law.*

This really isn't surprising given the fact that Obama's brand of justice includes prosecuting CIA employees and Navy SEALs while dropping criminal investigations of ACORN and dismissing a slam-dunk victory in the New Black Panthers voter intimidation case.

President Obama circumvents the Senate by making a recess appointment of ultra-leftist physician Dr. Donald Berwick to run Medicare and Medicaid. Dr. Berwick has spoken of the need to ration health care, the need to "reduce the total supply of high-technology medical and surgical care" and has expressed his admiration of the U.K.'s system of socialized medicine. Dr. Berwick asserts, "Any health care funding plan that is just, equitable, civilized and humane must redistribute wealth...

excellent health care is by definition redistributional."[538] [539] *Dr. Berwick's medical ideology is outside American mainstream thought. It's unsurprising that President Obama would bypass the traditional confirmation route in order to install another Marxist.*

Christian Adams, a former attorney at the Department of Justice, testifies before the U.S. Commission on Civil Rights that he and other attorneys at the civil rights division were instructed to drop cases with black defendants and white victims. He claims that Department of Justice lawyers were ordered to dismiss the New Black Panthers voter-intimidation case because of race. The Justice Department had already won a judgment against the New Black Panthers members in April 2009, but political appointees ordered them to file a dismissal. Adams says his superiors were "motivated by a lawless hostility toward equal enforcement of the law."[540] [541]

President Obama meets with Israeli Prime Minister Netanyahu to discuss Mideast peace. The U.S. wants Israel to commit to a two-state solution; Israel wants the Palestinian Authority to drop their preconditions to the negotiation process.

Israel is also concerned that the U.S. may back a U.N. investigation into the recent Gaza flotilla incident.[542]

In Iran today, a son is pleading for help as his mother is awaiting death by stoning. Also, Iran's Ministry of Culture and Islamic Guidance is trying to "cut-back" on Western decadence by allowing only certain haircuts to be given in barbershops.[543] [544]

7/7/10

Day 78 of the Gulf Oil Disaster

Day 21 of Recovery Summer

To defend against cyber-attacks, the National Security Agency (NSA) is launching an internet power grab with a program called "Perfect Citizen." The NSA will engage in domestic eavesdropping by placing sensors throughout the Web.[545]

Rhode Island has been enforcing "Arizona style" immigration checks for years. Rhode Island police officers routinely ask about immigration status during traffic stops when reasonable suspicion exists. In the case, *Estrada v. Rhode Island*, the U.S. Court of Appeals for the for the First Circuit upheld the Rhode Island procedures, reasoning that the Supreme Court has "held that a police officer does not need independent reasonalbe suspician to question an individual about her immigration status."[546] [547]*Not only did Arizona try to craft a bill that tries to conform to Constitutional requirements, but they seem to have case law to support their position also. Obama's Justice Department doesn't see the need to punish a reliable blue state, however.*

President Obama reflects on why Israeli citizens don't embrace him, "Some of it may just be the fact that my middle name is Hussein, and that creates suspicion."[548]

The federal government criticizes Louisiana Governor Jindal's proposal to erect barrier islands. Jindal says, "This is the same bureaucracy that has turned down every other plan. They don't have an alternative. Their resolution is [to] let the oil come into the bay."[549] *This is a pattern of Obama-style mismanagement. He criticizes whatever is put before him without offering a plan of his own.*

7/8/10

Day 79 of the Gulf Oil Disaster

Day 22 of Recovery Summer

"My administration **will not rest** until every American who is able and ready and willing to work can find a job."[550]

The EU and the U.S. agree to share bank data under the pretext of fighting terrorism.[551]

The Obama administration loses its appeal regarding the drilling moratorium in the Fifth Circuit Court of Appeals. Interior Secretary Ken Salazar assures that he is determined to impose a drilling moratorium anyway.[552]

7/11/10

Day 82 of the Gulf Oil Disaster

Day 25 of Recovery Summer

President Obama's National Commission on Fiscal Responsibility and

Reform calls the current budgetary trend a cancer "that will destroy the country from within" unless it is reversed. Erskine Bowles, the Democratic leader of the Commission, says, "We can't grow our way out of this. We could have decades of double-digit growth and not grow our way out of this enormous debt problem. We can't tax our way out…The reality is we've got to do exactly what you all do every day as governors. We've got to cut spending or increase revenues or do some combination of that."[553]

Democratic Governors sense doom in the upcoming elections due to the Obama administration's immigration stance while Attorney General Holder says the Department of Justice may sue Arizona more than once.

    DHS Secretary Napolitano meets with Arizona Gov. Brewer. They do not discuss the lawsuit, but only discuss the Governor's request for National Guard troops.[554]

7/12/10

Day 83 of the Gulf Oil Disaster

Day 26 of Recovery Summer

The Chinese bond rating agency Dagong Global Credit Rating Co. has stripped the U.S. from its AAA bond rating, knocking it down to AA. U.K., Germany and France have also lost their AAA bond ratings.[555]

Russian President Dmitry Medvedev announces that Iran is close to nuclear weapons.[556]

7/13/10

Day 84 of the Gulf Oil Disaster

Day 27 of Recovery Summer

Evidence grows over the inefficiency, waste and mismanagement of stimulus spending. Jill Zuckerman of the Department of Transportation says that, so far, the states have spent about $5 million of the $28 billion allotted for road projects and signs.[557]

Airlines and travelers are increasingly dismayed with the time consumption and privacy invasion of full-body scanners.[558]

President Obama plans to cut the U.S. nuclear stockpile by up to 40% by 2021.[559]

7/14/10

Day 85 of the Gulf Oil Disaster

Day 28 of Recover Summer

Abortion is now being funded under Obamacare. HHS Secretary Sebelius will be giving $160 million to Pennsylvania and $85 million to Maryland that will go into each states high-risk insurance pools that will cover any abortion that is legal.[560] [561]

Jul 2010

The Stimulus Bill has given HHS Secretary Sebelius the power to issue a diktat requiring each American to have his/her obesity rating included in electronic medical records that all Americans are supposed to have under the Stimulus law.[562] *"And that after this is accomplished, and the* **Brave New World** *begins, When all men are paid for existing and no man must pay for his sins..." —Rudyard Kipling*

The Department of Justice states that it will not sue "sanctuary cities" that refuse to cooperate with federal immigration authorities and enforce federal laws.[563] *It should be called the "Department of Selective Justice." Arizona is punished for drafting a law that tries to comply with federal law while "sanctuary cities" are rewarded for brazenly flouting federal law.*

The Dodd-Frank financial reform bill contains many provisions unrelated to the financial crisis it was designed to prevent. For instance, it makes it easier to put unions, activists and environmental groups on corporate boards of directors. The bill creates over 20 "offices of minority and women inclusion" and imposes "fair employment tests" on financial institutions, designed for racial and gender balance.

The Federal Reserve will now be charged with regulating all large, complex financial institutions.[564] [565]

Michelle Obama is in Panama City, FL certifying that the Florida Gulf Coast is a "wonderful place to visit" this year.[566] *Although the Obamas will be vacationing in Maine later this week.*

7/15/10

Day 86 of the Gulf Oil Disaster

Day 29 of Recovery Summer

BP tests a cap that has successfully stopped the oil flow.[567]

President Obama kicks back in Maine to enjoy his seventh vacation.[568] *Some people thought he should have gone to the Gulf Coast.*

7/16/10

Day 30 of Recovery Summer

Secretary of State Clinton announces $500 million in aid to Pakistan. Right now Pakistan supports negotiations between the Afghan government and the Taliban. The White House is also considering talks with the Taliban through third parties.[569] [570]

7/19/10

Day 33 of Recovery Summer

TARP Inspector General Neil Barofsky thinks the Department of Treasury's "dramatic and accelerated dealership closings" were probably unnecessary.[571] *But it was a convenient method for running Republican donors out of business while helping out Democratic contributors.*

Chinese Major General Zhu Chenghu tells the Communist Party media, "If the United States truly wants to take into account the overall interests of the Sino-U.S. relationship, then it must on no account send its USS Washington to the Yellow Sea."[572] *On November 24, 2010, the U.S. sends the USS George Washington to the Yellow Sea for naval exercises with South Korea.*

7/20/10

Day 34 of Recovery Summer

Agriculture Secretary Vilsack demands the resignation of Rural Development Director Shirley Sherrod for a video that surfaced on YouTube. In the video, Sherrod discusses a case she had where she considered discriminating against a white farmer. Sherrod insists it was taken out of context and that Secretary Vilsack should view the entire speech she gave. "They were not interested in hearing the truth. No one wanted to hear the truth," Sherrod says.[573] *Eventually Shirley Sherrod's reputation was vindicated when the entire video was made public. Her speech was about her own transformation of seeing beyond black and white.*

7/21/10

Day 35 of Recovery Summer

President Obama signs Financial Reform into law. Say 'hello' to 533 new regulations.[574] *Why did Congress bother passing a Financial Reform Bill of 2,000 pages? If they wanted powers this broad they simply should have passed a bill saying, "Congress can do whatever it wishes."*

James Gattuso of the Heritage Fountation outlines a tiny fraction of troublesome issues with the Financial Reform Law include:

- it creates a protected class of "too big to fail" firms,
- it provides for seizure of private property without meaningful judicial review. Due process is whittled down to the minimum, giving the Treasury almost total power to intervene in companies it deems "in danger of default" whose failure would result in "serious adverse effects on financial stability,"
- it creates permanent bailout authority,
- it establishes a $50 billion fund to pay for bailouts,
- it provides an "open line of credit" for additional government funding,
- it authorizes regulators to guarantee the debt of solvent banks,
- it establishes the Bureau of Consumer Financial Protection which will be part of the Federal Reserve...meaning that it will be very powerful autonomous bureaucracy that is unaccountable to Congress or elected officials,
- it subjects non-financial firms to financial regulations, and
- it does nothing to address problems with Fannie Mae and Freddie Mac.[575]

E-mails show that Agriculture Secretary Vilsack hastily fired Shirley Sherrod.[576] *Perhaps President Obama would agree that his Agriculture Secretary "acted stupidly" in firing Sherrod. Maybe they can all have a "beer summit" sometime.*

Gold coin dealers are angry that Obamacare tracks and taxes coin and bullion transactions.[577]

TARP Inspector General Neil Barofsky says that housing commitments grew by $700 billion in the last year, increasing the total to $3.7 trillion. Barofsky attributes the bulk of the increase is due to Fannie and Freddie bailouts.

Also under fire is the Home Affordable Modification Program designed to keep homeowners out of foreclosure. Earlier entries in this section indicate that the program has been pretty useless as participants continue to leave the program. Of the $50 billion allotted to mortgage modification programs, about $248 million has been spent.[578]

Thousands of Louisianans stage a "Rally for Economic Survival" calling for the Obama administration to end the drilling moratorium.[579] *The White House doesn't care about destroying farmers and farm workers in the San Joaquin Valley, why should they care about oil workers?*

7/22/10

Day 36 of Recovery Summer

The White House supports the Paycheck Fairness Act that requires U.S. businesses to collect and provide data regarding sex, race and national origin of employees.[580] If businesses have to comply with this, in addition to heaps of all the other stupid regulations, when will they have time to do actual work?

"Pay Czar" Kenneth Feinberg will cite seventeen businesses for "ill-advised" payments totaling $1.6 billion during the financial crisis.[581]

President Obama signs another bill extending unemployment benefits through November 30.[582]

7/23/10

Day 37 of Recovery Summer

The White House is predicting a $1.47 trillion deficit, with government borrowing equaling 41 cents for every dollar it spends and estimates 2011 unemployment to be 9%.[583]

Attendance to the president's birthday party in Chicago will require a $30,000 donation to the Democratic National Committee. President Obama will be fundraising for Illinois Senate candidate Alexi Giannoullas.[584]

Of the $5.55 billion of government bailout money it received, Goldman Sachs put $4.3 billion in thirty-two entities, including overseas banks, hedge funds and pensions.[585]

China's central bank, once again, calls for moving away from the dollar as the world's global reserve currency to a basket of diverse currencies.[586]

7/25/10

Day 39 of Recovery Summer

WikiLeaks publishes more than 91,000 secret documents of the Afghan war. The leaked information spans from January 2004 to December 1, 2009.[587]

7/26/10

Day 40 of Recovery Summer

Evidence reveals that the administration actively participated in the release of the Lockerbie bomber. Richard LeBaron, deputy head of the U.S. embassy in London, communicated with the Scottish First Minister Alex Salmond. In an August 12, 2009, letter, LeBaron wrote, "Nevertheless, if Scottish authorities come to the conclusion that Megrahi must be released from Scottish custody, the U.S. position is that conditional release on compassionate grounds would be a far preferable alternative to prisoner transfer, which we strongly oppose."[588] *This is another snub because the U.S. denounced the U.K. when Megrahi was released.*

President Obama tells ABC that his family is "not that far removed from what most Americans are going through."[589] *In one year, Michelle Obama spent over $10 million in taxpayer money to fund her lavish vacations, including posh hotels, the best liquor, expensive massages and other perks.*[590]

Michelle Obama's vacation plans include a five-day trip to Spain, followed by a weekend on Florida's Gulf Coast and a ten-day vacation in

Martha's Vineyard.[591]

7/27/10

Day 41 of Recovery Summer

The Defense Department cannot account for $8.7 billion of the $9.1 billion for the Development Fund for Iraq that is supposed to support construction projects.[592]

A report reveals that the U.S. Coast Guard did a sloppy job responding to the Deepwater Horizon explosion. They did not follow their own firefighting procedures that contributed to the sinking of the oil rig.[593] *They sure were sticklers for following every other agency procedure that slowed down and halted an effective response to the Gulf oil disaster. They didn't mind stopping Gov. Jindal's barges from cleaning up the Louisiana coast.*

7/28/10

Day 42 of Recovery Summer

The Securities Exchange Commission (SEC) proclaims that under the new Financial Reform law, it is exempt from having to comply with releasing information to the public under the Freedom of Information Act. President Obama says this law is one of the cornerstones to "increase transparency in financial dealings."[594]

Federal judge, Susan Bolton, issues a temporary injunction against key parts of the Arizona immigration law.[595]

Representative Kevin Brady (R-TX) has produced a mind-boggling flow chart of the 2,801 page Obamacare bill. The chart shows a bewildering multitude of arrows and lines. Brady says they were unable to fit the entire bill onto one chart. "This portrays only about one-third of the complexity of the final bill. It's actually worse than this."[596]

7/29/10

Day 43 of Recovery Summer

U.S. Citizenship and Immigration Services (USCIS) staffers have schemed and plotted various ways for the administration to bequeath amnesty on illegal immigrants without having to go through the fussy process of having America's elected representatives in Congress voting on it. The scheme states, "In the absence of comprehensive immigration reform, UCSIS can extend benefits and/or protections to many individuals and groups by issuing new guidance and regulations, exercising discretion with regard to parole-in-place, deferred action and the issuance of Notices to Appear." The staffers seek to "reduce the threat of removal" (i.e. deportation) for illegal immigrants who have been caught.

Senator Charles Grassley (R-IA) says, "This memo gives credence to our concerns that the administration will go to great lengths to circumvent Congress and unilaterally execute a backdoor amnesty plan."[597]

Under the guise of fighting terrorism, the White House seeks greater power for the FBI to tap internet activity without having to get a search warrant or court order.[598]

Press Secretary Robert Gibbs vilifies Rush Limbaugh for denouncing the administration's auto bailouts.[599]

7/30/10

Day 44 of Recovery Summer

President Obama says it is time for Representative Charlie Rangel (D-NY) to step down and retire "with dignity."[600]

7/31/10

Day 45 of Recovery Summer

The Obama administration is deploying 1,200 National Guard troops to the U.S./Mexico border in the same confused, ineffective manner with which they handled the Gulf oil disaster. The troop deployment will not be immediate, but will occur over the period between August 1 and September 30. Senator John McCain (R-AZ) says, "This Administration seems to promise a lot and then when you get into the fine print, it just doesn't happen." McCain and other interested parties "have not been briefed, and we have asked for briefing both in writing and verbally, and the answer is, 'we'll get back to you.'"

A total of 524 troops will be will be temporarily stationed in Arizona (they asked for 6,000), 250 in Texas (they requested 1,000 troops 523 days ago), 224 in California and 72 in New Mexico. It is believed that a high number of troops will be relegated to desk jobs.[601] *In other words, nobody really knows at which time how much of what is going where to do whatever.*

Arizona's Pinal County Sheriff Paul Babeu complains that the federal government is strangling the state's efforts to gain control of immigration, "What's very troubling is the fact that at a time when we in law enforcement and our state need help from the federal government, instead of sending help they put up billboard-size signs warning our citizens to stay out of the desert in my county because of dangerous drug and human smuggling and weapons and bandits and all these other things and then, behind that, they drag us into court with the ACLU."[602]

Obamacare gives HHS Secretary Sebelius the power to make judgments that cannot be challenged administratively or through the courts. Denial of due process is the very definition of tyranny.

Perhaps as many as 117 million people will have to change their health plans by 2013. The Congressional Budget Office (CBO) says that families who buy their insurance privately will have to pay an additional $2,100 annually. Those whose health insurance is deemed too good (i.e. a "Cadillac plan") will pay a 40% excise tax. Oh yeah, there is also an additional 3.8% tax on investment income for individuals making more than a $250,000 profit on the sale of a house.[603]

The Environmental Protection Agency (EPA) is considering cracking down on farm dust.[604] *This sounds ridiculous but it is absolutely true.*

The deep thinkers at the EPA begin clamping down in an effort that will be very expensive for farmers.

July budget deficit = $165.04 billion,.[605]

The number of July food stamp recipients reaches a record high of 41.8 million Americans.[606]

July unemployment = 9.5%.[607]
Real unemployment = 16.5%.[608]

8/2/10

Day 47 of Recovery Summer

Treasury Secretary Geithner predicts that unemployment may go up for a couple of months and then come down. Geithner also believes that the Bush tax cuts should be allowed to expire and that "the rich" are always griping about taxes. *Apparently, Geithner believes that taking capital out of the private economy and putting it in the hands of government will create wealth and generate productivity.*

Critics charge that President Obama's unwillingness to extend the Bush tax cuts contributes to the climate of economic uncertainty and is keeping employment down.[609]

Senators Tom Coburn (R-OK) and John McCain (R-AZ) release a report of the 100 stupidest and most wasteful stimulus spending projects. Among them is a $300,000 grant to Wake Forest University to study whether yoga can reduce hot flashes in breast cancer survivors. About the projects, Senator McCain says, "I think none of them really have any meaningful impact on creating jobs. And, of course, some are more egregious than others but all of them are terrible."[610]

Pakistani President Asif Ali Zardari rebukes U.K. Prime Minister David Cameron's comments that Pakistan must do more to prevent "the export of terror." Zardari claims the West is losing the war against the Taliban because it has become nonchalant about the seriousness of the war.[611]

Aug 2010

8/4/10

Day 49 of Recovery Summer

Prop C passes in Missouri. Missouri voters went to the polls to register their dissatisfaction with Obamacare's health insurance mandate by a margin of 3:1. Prop C is a measure that exempts Missouri from Obamacare.[612] *Nancy Pelosi said they had to pass the bill before citizens could see what's in it. Well, they've seen it.*

The administration uses Andy Griffith in an ad campaign extolling the virtues of Obamacare. Obamacare is so unpopular that they had to launch a $700,000 promotion after it passed.[613]

For the first time in more than eighteen months, the president speaks with Senate Republican leader Mitch McConnell.[614]

Despite their many statements to the contrary, it turns out that many government agencies can and do store electronic images from body scanners.[615]

The State Department scrubs a fifteen-month-old snippet of advice from its website intended for travelers to Spain, "Racist prejudices could lead to the arrest of Afro-Americans who travel to Spain." The U.S. Embassy in Madrid said, "We are in no way suggesting Spanish police are racist."[616] *No, you weren't suggesting it, you were blatantly saying it.*

With "Recovery Summer" more than halfway over, Vice President Joe Biden's April 23 prediction of creating a half-million jobs a month has yet to materialize.

8/5/10

Day 50 of Recovery Summer

In Orlando, U.S. Marshals are busted storing more than 35,000 naked body images from the controversial airport body scanners.[617] *The Transportation Security Administration (TSA) outright lied when it said the body scan technology did not allow storage of images.*

GM, now owned largely by the federal government, is making political contributions to the same politicians who draft and vote on laws. GM donated $36,000 to the Congressional Black Caucus Foundation.[618]

Chief White House economist Christina Romer resigns. An insider says, "She has been frustrated. She doesn't feel that she has a direct line to the President. She would be giving different advice than Larry Summers, who does have a direct line to the President."[619]

Justice Elena Kagan is confirmed to the Supreme Court today.

First Lady Michelle Obama begins her lavish five-day vacation in the Costa del Sol in Spain. The First Lady arrived in Air Force Two (round trip $147,563) with her daughter, forty of her closest friends and seventy Secret Service agents. They have booked sixty rooms at the Ritz-Carlton Hotel Villa Padierna in Marbella. Apparently, the First Diva hasn't been "proud of her country" for the second time in her life yet since she chose to vacation outside the U.S. With all of the president's talk about sacrificing for the common good, one can hardly imagine what her original travel plans must have been.[620] [621] *She could have met up with BP's Carl-Henric Svanberg and talked about how much she cared about the "small people."*

8/8/10

Day 53 of Recovery Summer

Approximately 16% of the babies born in Texas are from parents who are here illegally. That translates to about 60,000 babies a year being granted birthright citizenship.[622]

First Lady Michelle Obama visits King Juan Carlos and Queen Sofia in their summer residence in Mallorca, Spain.[623]

8/9/10

Day 54 of Recovery Summer

President Obama goes to Texas to attack former President Bush. *Why not? He attacks him at all times no matter where he goes.* The president says that it is important that he continues to attack Bush often to re-mind Americans of what he inherited from President Bush.[624]

Texas Governor Rick Perry issues President Obama a hand-delivered invitation to tour the Texas/Mexico border and evaluate the difficult border security situation. During his thirty-four-second meeting with President Obama at the Austin airport, the governor tried to hand him an envelope; he was directed to give the letter to presidential advisor Valerie Jarrett.

In his letter, Perry wrote, "Drug cartels and related forces are wag-ing war in Northern Mexico, their tactics include death threats, torture, car bombings, kidnappings, assassinations and beheadings."[625] [626]

Freddie Mac asks for another $1.8 billion.[627] *Are you keeping up with how many times Freddie and Fannie have bellied-up to the Treasury's counter? Probably not.*

8/10/10

Day 55 of Recovery Summer

The Federal Reserve will try to spur economic growth by buying more government debt.[628] *This means that they will print a whole bunch of money to buy the bonds, a.k.a. "inflation."*

Some Democrats are upset that Congress stripped $12 billion from the food stamp budget to fund a bill for school districts to keep teachers employed.[629]

Al-Qaeda is recruiting Iraqi militia troops by offering them higher pay.[630]

8/11/10

Day 56 of Recovery Summer

Federal workers earn double their private counterparts in salary and benefits. According to the Bureau of Economic Analysis, federal workers earn an average pay plus benefits of $123,049 while the average private worker earns a total of $61,051. Considering that their compensation has outstripped the private sector for 9 straight years, the gap is likely to get bigger and bigger.[631]

In the interest of promoting true diversity, Greg Gutfeld is raising funds to build a Muslim-themed gay bar next door to the Ground Zero Mosque. He proposes naming the bar "Suspicious Packages" and he promises to offer a menu of 72 "virgin" non-alcoholic drinks.[632]

Russia's LUKOIL and China's state-run Zhuhai Zhenrong resume selling gasoline to Iran. Although Russia and China signed the U.N. sanctions against Iran, they exempted themselves from oil/gas sanctions.[633] *See, I told you those sanctions were toothless (see entry for 6/8/10). Barack*

Aug 2010

Obama is the gift that keeps on giving. The world recognizes that they get four years to play him for a chump. Think about all of the slack that President Obama has given Iran. Instead of assuming the mantle of leadership, he accommodated every interested party in favor of the mob consensus of U.N. sanctions. This is where all of that accommodating got him.

8/12/10

Day 57 of Recovery Summer

As the Senate passes a $600 million Border Security Bill, the president issues a statement saying that securing the border has been a **"top priority"** since he took office.[634] *Really?*

Home foreclosures are up 6% from last year. 1727

8/13/10

Day 58 of Recovery Summer

President Obama strongly defends the Ground Zero Mosque. He successfully inserts himself into a controversy he should have successfully avoided. In his fawning speech, Obama recognizes the rituals of Ramadan that "remind us of the principles that we hold in common, and Islam's role in advancing justice, progress, tolerance and the dignity of all human beings." *He stops just short of calling it "the Religion of Peace."*

The president continues, "As a citizen and as President, I believe that Muslims have the same right to practice their religion as anyone else in this country."[635] [636] *This is the president using the Straw Man argument again. Everyone acknowledges that Muslims have the right to practice their 1st Amendment freedoms. People just think it's tacky and/ or antagonistic that they wish to build a mosque there. President Obama should understand that most Americans don't share his talent for submissiveness.*

Russia announces that it will be putting the finishing touches on Iran's nuclear power plant. On August 21st they will be loading the uranium for the reactor.[637]

8/15/10

Day 60 of Recovery Summer

During his twenty-seven-hour stop to the Florida Panhandle, Obama informs the nation that the Gulf Coast is "open for business."[638] *Does that mean that oil rig employees can go back to work?*

8/17/10

Day 62 of Recovery Summer

Suspicion over "death panels" arises after passage of Obamacare. The Food and Drug Administration (FDA) is considering revoking its approval for the breast cancer drug Avastin, which it approved in 2008. The FDA advisory panel cited "effectiveness," but "cost-effectiveness" seems to be the more likely issue since Avastin costs about $8,000 per

Aug 2010

month.[639]

Progressive drones from MoveOn.org announce that Target must be punished for making a political donation to Minnesota Republican primary candidate, Tom Emmer. MoveOn's intimidation campaign smears Target for being anti-gay.[640]

U.S. bankruptcies reach an almost five-year high.[641]

China's military build-up seems to be geared toward a possible regional war with Taiwan. Their arsenal of missiles, warheads and aircraft carriers may be designed to attack U.S. ships in case America were to become involved.[642]

8/18/10

Day 63 of Recovery Summer

The Ground Zero Mosque developer rejects New York Governor David Paterson's offer to find a different location for construction of the controversial mosque.[643]

9/11 rescue workers criticize President Obama for championing the cause of the Ground Zero Mosque and not doing anything about a $7.2 billion health care bill for 9/11 rescue workers. Representative Peter King (R-NY) says, "It is offensive to have mosque two blocks from Ground Zero, but it's also offensive to let firefighters die with pulverized glass in their lungs."[644]

8/19/10

Day 64 of Recovery Summer

One of the backers for the Ground Zero Mosque states that the $100 million project is just in the beginning stages of fundraising. Oz Sultan says they will first look at available sources of funds in the U.S. When asked if they would also be looking for foreign sources, Sultan says, "I can't comment on that."

The State Department is sponsoring a $16,000 trip for the Imam of the controversial Ground Zero Mosque. U.S. taxpayers will pick up the tab as the Obama administration pays for Imam Feisal Abdul Rauf to travel to Bahrain, Qatar and the United Arab Emirates. It is expected that the Imam will raise funds for the mosque but the State Department admits it really does not have a clue about the purpose of his visit.[645]

Two weeks after Mrs. Obama's lavish trip to the Costa del Sol, the First Family leaves for the posh shores of Martha's Vineyard.[646] *I'm sure every president gets some work done on his vacations, but this is the same guy who told Americans they must sacrifice. President Obama once remarked, "We can't drive our SUVs and eat as much as we want and keep our homes on 72 degrees at all times." What is he sacrificing? Maybe he should stay in his office and work once in a while. Actually, maybe it would be better for us if he didn't. Ignore what I said, Mr. President, get back to your golf game.*

8/20/10

Day 65 of Recovery Summer

Secretary of State Clinton submits a report to the U.N. citing Arizona as a human rights violator. Clinton believes this will somehow allow the U.S. to serve as a "model" to the rest of the world.[647] *So, Secretary Clinton believes Arizona is comparable to China, Zimbabwe, North Korea, and Iran?*

Immigration and Customs Enforcement (ICE) Director John Morton has ordered officials to dismiss deportation cases of illegal immigrants who have not committed serious crimes. Morton also proposes to prohibit police from using routine misdemeanor traffic stops as a means for referring illegal immigrants to ICE. Morton defends his policy saying, "Congress provides enough money to deport a little less than 400,000 people. My perspective is those 400,000 people shouldn't be the first 400,000 people in the door but rather 400,000 people who reflect some considered enforcement policy based on a rational set of objectives and priorities."[648] *Morton's defense makes sense on the surface. The policy also snugly fits with the agenda of the administration that handles illegal immigration with billboards in the desert, underserving state governments in an untimely manner and prefers comprehensive immigration reform to enforcing its own laws.*

Also, refer back to the USCIS memo outlining a scheme for backdoor amnesty (7/29/10). That memo combined with these actions heightens suspicion that the Obama administration clearly has an immigration agenda that is at odds with the desire of American citizens.

Nearly 50% of participants have dropped out of the president's mortgage assistance program citing that it is a bureaucratic nightmare.[649]

The FDIC closes Chicago's ShoreBank. ShoreBank's assets will be bought by the Urban Partnership Bank, which is backed by Goldman Sachs, General Electric and JPMorgan Chase.[650] *All of these companies backed the Obama campaign.*

Aug 2010

8/21/10

Day 66 of Recovery Summer

Airport searches at Boston's Logan International Airport are now a little more aggressive with the palms-first, slide-down the body frisking.[651]

8/22/10

Day 67 of Recovery Summer

As supporters and opponents of the Ground Zero Mosque stage demonstrations in New York City, Daisy Khan, wife of Ground Zero Mosque Imam Feisal Abdul Rauf, compares opposition to the mosque with persecution of Jews. Mrs. Khan says, "We are deeply concerned because this is like a metastasized anti-Semitism. It's beyond Islamophobia. It's hate of Muslims."[652] [653]

A tape has surfaced where Imam Rauf said in 2005, "We tend to forget, in the West, that the United States has more Muslim blood on its hands than al-Qaeda has on its hands of innocent non-Muslims" at the

University of South Australia.[654]

8/23/10

Day 68 of Recovery Summer

The Gun Owners of America (GOA) severs its ties with the "net-neutrality" group "Save the Internet." Save the Internet has deep associations with Marxist media-hound Robert McChesney, ACORN, SEIU, MoveOn.org and other far left organizations. GOA communications director Erich Pratt says, "Back in 2006 we supported net neutrality, as we had been concerned that AOL and others might continue to block pro-second amendment issues. The issue has now become one of government control of the Internet, and we are 100% opposed to that."[655]

While on vacation, President Obama spends part of the day playing basketball with UBS Group Americas Chairman and CEO Robert Wolf and his two teenage sons.[656] *This is very strange. The Obama administration very aggressively pursued criminal and civil penalties against UBS. The White House had a campaign of continuous threats demanding that UBS violate Swiss banking laws and furnish names and information on all Americans banking in Switzerland. Now the president is enjoying a leisurely game of hoops with one of UBS's top executives and his kids while he's on vacation. Stranger still is the fact that he appointed Wolf to his Economic Recovery Advisory Board on February 6, 2009.*

8/24/10

Day 69 of Recovery Summer

Airport body scanning technology is now available in mobile vans called "Z Backscatter Vans" (ZBVs) manufactured by American Science and Engineering. The company's vice president of marketing, Joe Reiss, says they have been used in Afghanistan and Iraq. Reiss says the ZBVs are also roaming the streets of America being driven by law enforcement agencies. Privacy groups are, to say the least, upset that the government is now driving around searching peoples' homes and cars without warrants.[657]

Law enforcement in Washington D.C. is using "pre-crime" technology to fight crime. Software developed by the University of Pennsylvania sifts through enormous amounts of data to determine who, when and where a crime may take place.[658] [659]

The Obama administration grovels ever more cravenly before the U.N. Human Rights Council. The State Department issues a report saying that minorities are still victims of discrimination and considerable progress is still needed. They cite the Arizona immigration law as an example of how human rights are being trampled in the United States.

The Bush administration refused to submit a report declining to be judged by countries with appalling human rights records.[660]

The federal government has adopted a nationwide strategy of dismissing deportation cases for non-criminal illegal immigrants. Critics see this as "<u>backdoor amnesty</u>."[661] *This is another example of President Obama*

Aug 2010

refusing to enforce the law. Keep in mind that while the Obama administration is freeing illegal aliens, they are suing Arizona and threatening to sue them again. Immigration is a perfect example of one of Obama's patterns on so many issues. When he is called to do his job he stalls... procrastinates... and stalls until the issue is immediate, in which case, he capitulates with the bare minimum of attention. Texas Governor Rick Perry asked for border help over a year and a half ago and got much less than he asked for. Arizona Governor Jan Brewer's request was answered with signs in the desert warning Americans that it was not safe in their own country. President Obama also ignored both governors' requests to come and view the border.

Vice President Biden ridicules Republicans and denounces the Bush tax cuts. Biden believes the tax cuts are economically destructive and "it's a Wall Street tax cut, not a Main Street tax cut."[662]

Four-Star General James Conway says that announcing a deadline for operations in Afghanistan is the equivalent of "giving our enemy sustenance."[663] *The Commander in Chief doesn't seem to be in control of his own military. The fact that his own generals, like McChrystal, regard him so dismissively projects the image of weakness that the rest of the world's leaders have already concluded.*

8/25/10

Day 70 of Recovery Summer

The Environmental Protection Agency (EPA) is trying to advance the global warming agenda even though it got shot down in Congress. The EPA wants to federalize the air-permitting process and require states to comply with the EPA's latest, greatest interpretation of the Clean Air Act. Forty years after its passage, the EPA is re-interpreting the Clean Air Act and requiring states to "tailor" their laws to conform to its dictates.

Texas Attorney General Greg Abbott and Texas Commission on Environmental Quality Chairman Bryan Shaw eloquently rebuke the EPA: "In order to deter challenges to your plan for centralized control of industrial development through the issuance of permits for greenhouse gases, you have called upon each state to declare its allegiance to the EPA's recently enacted greenhouse gas regulations—regulations that are plainly contrary to U.S. laws… To encourage acquiescence with your unsupported findings you threaten to usurp state enforcement authority and to federalize the permitting program of any state that fails to pledge their fealty to the EPA. On behalf of the State of Texas, we write to inform you that Texas has neither the authority nor the intention of interpreting, ignoring or amending its laws in order to compel the permitting of greenhouse gas emissions."[664] *Candidate Obama promised that under his energy plan, "electricity rates would necessarily skyrocket." He's just trying to keep that promise.*

8/26/10

Day 71 of Recovery Summer

The Obama administration suspends prosecution of the USS Cole bomber, Abd al-Rahim al-Nashiri. In a filing in the U.S. Court of Appeals for the District of Columbia, the Department of Justice says, "No charges are either pending or contemplated with respect to al-Nashiri in the near future."[665]

The Department of Justice delivers a second ultimatum to Sheriff Joe Arpaio demanding he explain his policies regarding the arrest and detention of illegal immigrants.[666]

Mort Zuckerman calls this "the most fiscally irresponsible government in U.S. history, current federal budget trends are capable of destroying this country."[667]

8/27/10

Day 72 of Recovery Summer

Arizona Governor Jan Brewer demands an apology from the administration for calling the state a human rights violator before the U.N.[668]

Economic adviser Austan Goolsbee, tells a group of reporters, "We have a series of entities that do not pay corporate income tax. Some of which are really giant firms, you know Koch Industries is a multibillion dollar business." The billionaire Koch brothers have been contributing to Republican Congressional candidates.[669] *How is it that this Administration official is familiar with Koch's private and confidential tax returns? Could it be that the White House is using private tax information to target political opponents? The administration feels no need to answer questions*

Aug 2010

about this apparent, illegal tax snooping.

The Ground Zero Mosque is looking into raising $70 million dollars in tax-free debt to build the mosque.[670]

8/30/10

Day 75 of Recovery Summer

Opposition to Obamacare prompts HHS Secretary Sebelius to tell ABC News that the Obama administration has "a lot of re-education to do."[671] *This is how leftists think: they are unable to accept that people can have informed opinions and have valid reasons for rejecting their silly ideals and notions of government-sponsored happiness. History shows that very bad things happen when leftists use the term "reeducation."*

Record numbers of Americans are on government assistance. More than 50 million Americans are on Medicaid at a cost of $273 billion, almost 10 million receive jobless benefits at a cost of $160 billion (the government has extended benefits to last as long as ninety-nine weeks), 40 million Americans are receiving food stamps at a cost of $70 billion and the 4.4 million people on welfare costs $22 billion. These programs alone cost $525 billion.[672] *"Recovery Summer" was launched to praise the achievements of the Stimulus, which Vice President Biden calls an "absolute success."*

8/31/10

Aug 2010

Day 76 of Recovery Summer

Climate change is again debunked for the fraud that it is. The InterAcademy Council (IAC) skewers the U.N.'s Intergovernmental Panel on Climate Change (IPCC) in a review. The IAC finds that there was "little evidence" to substantiate the IPCC's claims about climate change and the IPCC's "substantive findings" were based on little proof. Of the many, many, many flaws and sham science conducted by the IPCC was its false claim that Himalayan glaciers could melt my 2035. The IPCC's claim that the glaciers were melting came from a 1999 magazine article. The Indian scientist featured in the article later said that the interview was merely his musings and speculations unsupported by scientific evidence or research.[673] *Al Gore's only rebuttal to skeptics was his oft-repeated apoplectic hysteria, "The debate is over!" That's right Al, the debate IS over. Man-made climate change is a hoax; the debate is over.*

President Obama declares that America has completed its mission in Iraq.[674]

Home foreclosures rise to a record high.[675]

August unemployement = 9.6%.[676]
Real unemployment = 16.7%.[677]

9/1/10

Day 77 of Recovery Summer

So far the federal government's border security for Arizona consists of 30 National Guard troops and 15 billboards warning American citizens to beware of foreign invaders in their own country. The signs say, "DANGER—PUBLIC WARNING, TRAVEL NOT RECOMMENDED. Visitors may Encounter Armed Criminals and Smuggling Vehicles Traveling at High Rates of Speed. Stay Away From Trash, Clothing, Backpacks and Abandoned Vehicles."[678]

The Department of Justice files a civil rights lawsuit against Sheriff Joe Arpaio. The Sheriff is surprised because he and his county's lawyers have been cooperating with the feds.[679]

9/6/10

Day 82 of Recovery Summer

The president unveils his $50 billion stimulus plan, mainly devoted to infrastructure. He also believes that America should have a special infrastructure bank.[680]

9/7/10

Day 83 of Recovery Summer

President Obama opposes extending the Bush tax cuts for the top

Sep 2010

bracket of income earners.[681]

The controversial airport scanners may be upgraded to address privacy concerns. The companies that developed the technology have software upgrades that can show a generic figure that highlights areas of the body that need to be checked.[682]

9/8/10

Day 84 of Recovery Summer

Thusfar, in just 19 months, President Obama has added more to the National Debt than the first 40 Presidents combined. George Washington through Ronald Reagan racked-up $2.1907 trillion; whereas, President Obama in just 19 months has increased the National Debt by $2.5620 trillion—a difference of $355.3 billion.[683]

9/9/10

Day 85 of Recovery Summer

HHS Secretary Sebelius sends a scorching letter to America's Health Insurance Plans' president, Karen Ignagni, who lobbies for private health insurers. Health insurers have notified their customers that rising premiums are caused by increased costs imposed by Obamacare.

Sebelius writes, "There will be <u>zero tolerance</u> for this type of misinformation and unjustified rate increases." She continues, "It is my hope we can work together to stop misinformation and misleading marketing from the start."[684] *Perhaps Secretary Sebelius should banish Ignagni to a "re-education" labor camp. The soft tyranny and coercive threats are frightening. The administration has no right to impose gag orders limiting the free speech rights of whoever disagrees with them. Silencing critics is a standard feature of Marxist dictatorships. Perhaps they should have "zero tolerance" for Secretary Sebelius as she becomes a greater and greater embarrassment. See entries for 9/21/09 and 5/1/10.*

To date, not a single Democrat has run a campaign ad mentioning Obamacare.[685]

9/10/10

Day 86 of Recovery Summer

In his press conference, President Obama repeats his defense of the Ground Zero Mosque.

Obama also attacks Republicans for opposing his economic agenda, "Republicans (are) holding middle class tax relief hostage because they're insisting we've got to give tax relief to millionaires and billionaires, which would cost, over the course of 10 years, $700 billion and economists say is probably the worst way to stimulate the economy." *Attacking and demonizing Republicans is a moot point since Democrats control both houses of Congress. The fact of the matter is that Obama is unable to persuade members of his own party to go along with him.*

Senator Mitch McConnell (R-KY) responds, "President Obama spent a lot of time blaming others and talking about more government spending. But Americans want to know that Washington is going to stop the reckless spending and debt, the burdensome red-tape and job-killing taxes."[686]

9/11/10

Day 87 of Recovery Summer

Thousands of demonstrators crowd New York City supporting and opposing the Ground Zero Mosque.[687]

9/13/10

Day 89 of Recovery Summer

DHS will test iris scanners that can detect identities from six feet away. The test subjects will be illegal immigrants.[688]

9/14/10

Day 90 of Recovery Summer

President Obama will be penning a new children's book, <u>Of Thee I Sing: A Letter to My Daughters</u>, which will be released November 16th.[689] *So what else does he do when he's not vacationing, playing golf and figuring out basketball picks?*

In order to absorb the costs imposed by the new Financial Reform law, Bank of America announces that it will be charging customers new monthly fees.[690]

There is a bill in Congress that would give the president "kill switch" authority over the internet and would give DHS broader authority to police the internet.[691]

9/15/10

Day 91 of Recovery Summer

President Obama and the First Lady attend the Congressional Hispanic Caucus Institute gala. During his speech he quotes the Declaration of Independence omitting "the Creator." Instead, he says, "All men are created equal, endowed with certain inalienable rights."[692]

9/16/10

Day 92 of Recovery Summer

Census data shows that approximately 44 million people in the U.S. lived below the poverty line in 2009, the largest number since the census has been tracking poverty in 1951. The poverty line is drawn at earning less than $22,000 for a family of four.[693]

Los Angeles is a good case study of the ineffectiveness of stimulus spending. Wendy Greuel, the city's Controller, says, "I'm disappointed that we've only created or retained 55 jobs after receiving $111 million." The L.A. Department of Public Works "saved or created" forty-five jobs with $70.65 million in Stimulus funds, while the L.A. Department of Transportation created only nine jobs with $40.8 million.[694] *There you have it: 109 jobs "saved or created" with $222.45 million, an average of $2,040,000 per job "saved or created."*

The White House's fixation on ridiculous terminology continues. "Science Czar" John Holdren eschews the terms like "global warming" or "climate change" in favor of "global climate disruption."[695]

The State of Texas sues the Environmental Protection Agency (EPA) for trying to enforce its climate change/greenhouse gas agenda. Texas says that the regulations are based on the "thoroughly discredited" and "factually flawed" report of the U.N.'s Intergovernmental Panel on Climate Change (IPCC).[696] *Research conducted at East Anglia University provided the backbone of the IPCC report. When the controversy over East Anglia University's fraudulent research was exposed, the Obama administration and other attendees at the Copenhagen summit just carried on and pretended it never happened. Later, the InterAcademy Council (IAC) conducted an independent assessment of the IPCC report. IAC found the report to be riddled with bogus claims, falsehoods and quack research.*

Press Secretary Robert Gibbs slams *Forbes* magazine and Dinesh D'Souza for an opinion article about the roots of Obama's anti-British outlook.[697] *How thin-skinned are these people? They attack Fox, Forbes, "fishy e-mails," insurance companies that send discrediting letters, etc. They really do have "zero tolerance" for anything outside the monolithic party line.*

Sep 2010

9/17/10

Day 93 of Recovery Summer

President Obama appoints Elizabeth Warren as "Consumer Czar" to the Consumer Financial Protection Bureau, which was set up by the Financial Reform law.[698]

9/19/10

Day 95 of Recovery Summer

Russia has reportedly sold seventy-two cruise missiles to Syria.[699]

9/20/10

Day 96 of Recovery Summer

Major health insurers stop offering new child-only policies rather than comply with Obamacare.[700]

The Gulf oil leak is declared to be permanently sealed.[701]

9/21/10

Day 97 of Recovery Summer

Secretary Clinton promises the U.N. $50 billion to buy cooking stoves for impoverished nations.[702]

The Obama administration is arguing before a federal appeals court that it has a right to place GPS tracking device on cars without court warrants.[703]

American CEOs are being more outspoken in their remarks about President Obama. Most of their criticism regards the uncertain economic environment, taxes and the president's ignorance of business in general. "We don't know what the latest great idea from Obama will be; therefore, we are hunkering down...It is amateur hour in Washington. The guy hasn't a clue about the economy, how jobs are created, how wealth is created," says T. J. Rodgers of Cypress Semiconductors. Intel's CEO Paul Otellini states, "I think this group does not understand what it takes to create jobs." These sentiments are echoed by Verizon CEO Ivan Seidenberg who believes Obama is creating an "increasingly hostile environment for job creation."[704] *What do they expect? He has never owned, run or worked in a business. He doesn't understand wealth creation except that he takes for granted that it is "somehow" created.*

9/22/10

Day 98 of Recovery Summer

Larry Summers, Director of the National Economic Council, and TARP chief Herb Allison announce their resignations.[705] [706]

In order to break-even on General Motors, shares of stock would need to sell for $134 per share.[707]

Gay rights activists heckle the president at a fundraiser. They are protesting the military's "don't ask/don't tell" policy and advocating for increased AIDS funding.[708]

9/23/10

The Last Day 99 of Recovery Summer (Autumnal Equinox)

On the last day of Recovery Summer, Americans are still feeling the full force of the president's "stimulus package" in a place very near their wallets.

President Obama blasts Israel before the U.N. General Assembly, "We continue to emphasize that America does not accept the legitimacy of continued Israeli settlements." He calls for the establishment of a "viable, independent Palestinian state with contiguous territory that ends the occupation that began in 1967, and realizes the potential of the Palestinian people."[709] *The president fails to mention that "the occupation that began in 1967" was the result of Islamic states trying to wipe Israel off the map.*

9/24/10

U.S. delegates walk out on Iranian President Ahmadinejad's speech to the U.N. The Iranian President accuses the U.S. of orchestrating 9/11.[710]

9/26/10

Expiration of the Israeli settlement freeze stalls peace talks.[711]

Sep 2010

9/27/10

Hundreds of anti-war protesters demonstrate outside the offices of the FBI in Chicago and Minneapolis. The FBI has been conducting searches aimed at groups they believe are supportive of terrorist organizations including Revolutionary Armed Forces of Colombia (FARC), the Popular Front for the Liberation of Palestine (PFLP) and Hezbollah.[712]

Russia and China celebrate the completion of an oil pipeline linking the two countries.[713]

China imposes a chicken tariff on the U.S.[714]

9/28/10

The FBI investigates ex-SEIU labor leader Andy Stern in a corruption probe.[715]

Senator Max Baucus (D-MT) sends a letter to IRS Commissioner Doug Shulman prodding him to audit and investigate 501(c) groups and political opponents. Liberals are using threats to try to muzzle conservative groups from making political donations. Since the Supreme Court decision in *Citizens United v. FEC*, Democrats have tried to neuter opposing business interests while promoting union influence.[716]

9/29/10

As elections approach, President Obama is talking more about Jesus.[717]

Sep 2010

9/30/10

The federal government ends Fiscal Year 2010 $2 trillion deeper in debt.[718]

Food stamp recipients are at an all time high, 42.9 million Americans, or 14% of the country, are now on food stamps.[719]

Treasury Secretary Geithner says the economy still needs support from the government.[720]

Members of Congress decide to go home and campaign even though they still haven't passed a budget. Members have also decided to play it safe and not take a stand on tax cuts until after the election.[721] *President Obama stomps his feet and throws a temper tantrum when the Bush tax cuts weren't repealed and he takes cheap shot after cheap shot at Republicans in budget talks. Take not of this date. Druing his 20 months in office President Obama had his party in complete control of Congress. They never passed a budget.*

The Association of American Medical Colleges announces that post-Obamacare doctor shortages will be 50% lower in 2015 than they originally forecast.[722]

American helicopters kill Pakistani soldiers mistaken for Taliban fighters. Pakistan retaliates by closing a key supply crossing.[723]

September unemployment = 9.6%.[724]

Real unemployment = 17.1%.[725]

Sep 2010

10/1/10

Rahm Emanuel steps down as White House Chief of Staff and is replaced by Pete Rouse.[726]

10/2/10

HHS Secretary Sebelius says it is "flat-out wrong" that McDonald's cannot afford Obamacare and may have to cancel health insurance coverage for 29,500 employees unless it can get a waiver. McDonald's offers low-cost, low-benefit "mini-med" plans for its low-wage employees. The *Wall Street Journal* says, "If only for the sake of her own credibility, at some point Ms. Sebelius is going to have to try to persuade people who actually know something about the industries she regulates."[727]

Mexican pirates attack two Americans on Falcon Lake, which straddles the Texas/Mexico border. David Hartley is shot in the head and killed as the couple flees for their lives.[728]

The CIA is using aerial drones in Pakistan to attack Taliban safe havens.[729]

10/3/10

Venezuela confiscates land from the British food company, Vestey, for the "acceleration of the agrarian revolution." Since Chavez took office, Venezuela has nationalized over 6.2 million acres of land.[730]

Chavez also says Venezuela's civilian militia will be armed full-time

Oct 2010

because it is crucial to its national defense.[731]

A key party defection deposes Pakistan's ruling coalition. The political turmoil will surely benefit Muslim extremists.[732]

10/5/10

At a fundraiser in Minnesota, Vice President Biden says he will "strangle" Republicans who complain about the deficit.[733] *He also challenged them to a cage match.*

10/6/10

Nancy Pelosi offers a bizarre solution for revving up the economy: food stamps. She says that for every dollar a person receives in food stamps, $1.79 is put back into the economy. She says, "It is the biggest bang for the buck when you do food stamps and unemployment insurance. The biggest bang for the buck."[734] *The Speaker is breaking new ground in economic theory as she has cracked the code of how to get something from nothing.*

Newt Gingrich calls Democrats "the party of food stamps" while Republicans are "the party of paychecks."[735]

Senator Charles Grassley (R-IA) announces that the Treasury Inspector General for Tax Administration will investigate remarks by President Obama's chief economist, Austan Goolsbee.[736] *On August 27, 2010, Goolsbee made an offhanded remark about Koch Industries' tax return, suggesting that he had illegally viewed Koch's tax returns. The*

Koch brothers have gained some notoriety for funding the president's political opponents.

Recipients of 352 stimulus projects have not disclosed $162 million of stimulus funds.[737]

The National Commission on the BP Deepwater Horizon Oil Spill and Offshore Drilling issues a report stating that the U.S. was slow to react to the Gulf oil disaster.[738]

10/7/10

72,000 stimulus payments have gone to dead people while 17,000 went to prisoners.[739]

Thirty companies, including McDonald's, get waivers from Obamacare.[740] *See entry for 10/2/10.*

After 42 days of stalling/dithering, Press Secretary Robert Gibbs explains that Austan Goolsbee's highly suspicious comments are "not in any way based on any review of tax filings."[741] *In that case he's psychic! Maybe Mr. Goolsbee should apply his paranormal gifts to economic policy.*

A casting call goes out in advance of the president's MTV/BET/CMT townhall meeting. Applicants are required to provide "a short description of your political views."[742] *Maoist Communications Director Anita Dunn bragged that the Obama campaign "controlled the media." President, Obama still controls the media by staging pre-screened audiences with cherry-picked questions that he answers with his teleprompter.*

10/8/10

President Obama names Thomas Donilon to replace James Jones as National Security Adviser. Donilon has vast experience in being a top lobbyist for Fannie Mae, Citigroup, Goldman Sachs and Apollo Investments. Representative Cliff Stearns (R-FL) remarks, "Now that we're in a post-9/11 environment we need a National Security Advisor who has a history of expertise with security issues to protect us against terrorists and not a lobbyist who has a history of running our economy into the ditch as Senior Vice President and General Counsel for Fannie Mae and as a lobbyist for Goldman Sachs."[743]

The dollar falls below 82 yen for the first time in fifteen years.[744]

10/9/10

Treasury Secretary Geithner calls for the International Monetary Fund (IMF) to supervise currencies closely. Part of Geithner's concern is that China manipulates its exchange rate to keep yuan artificially low.[745]

10/11/10

The carefree Federal Reserve has no clue where quantitative easing (i.e., printing money) will lead. Former economic adviser Christina Romer says the Fed is in unchartered territory and it is uncertain what will be accomplished by printing more magic make-believe money.[746]

For the second straight year, Barack Obama does NOT win the Nobel

Prize for economics.

10/12/10

General Electric (GE) has laid-off 18,000 workers while receiving $24.9 million in stimulus grants. President Obama's favorite corporate crony has also paid $0 in corporate income taxes despite earning $14 billion in global profits, $5 billion of which came from the U.S.[747]

President Obama admits to the *New York Times* that he looks like "the same old tax-and-spend Democrat" and that "there's no such thing as a shovel-ready project." *Obama's rhetoric may be the only thing that requires shoveling.*

He also likened the presidency to his campaign, "The mythology has emerged somehow that we ran this flawless campaign, I never made a mistake, that we were master communicators, everything worked in lockstep. And somehow now, as president, things are messy and they don't always work as planned and people are mad at us. That's not how I look at stuff, because I remember what the campaign was like. And it was just as messy and just as difficult."[748] *Wait a minute. Candidate Obama used his successful campaign to try to soothe voters' concerns over his lack of executive ability and experience. Now we find out that it was just as messy as the last nineteen months.*

10/14/10

President Obama attributes racial tension to "tribal attitudes" which surface in a climate of economic hardship. He states, "Our strength

[Oct 2010]

comes from unity, not division."[749] *People used to think our strength came from our freedom.*

Iranian President Ahmadinejad joins crowds of Hezbollah supporters in an intentionally provocative appearance at the Lebanese/Israeli border.[750]

10/15/10

Obamacare is raising health insurance premiums around the country. In Connecticut, new rates jump from 19% to 47%, depending on the policy.[751]

For the second straight year, 58 million recipients will not receive a social security increase.[752]

Federal Reserve Chairman Ben Bernanke foresees that another round of quantitative easing (a.k.a. "printing money") is likely.[753] *Perhaps Bernanke should take a cue from Nancy Pelosi and start printing food stamps instead.*

Russia agrees to build a nuclear power plant in Venezuela. Since seizing control of Venezuela, Chavez has purchased billions of dollars worth of military equipment from Russia, including submarines, helicopters and attack aircraft.[754]

The U.S. Treasury Department backs down from labeling China as a "currency manipulator" prior to the G-20 summit next month.[755] *By law, countries that manipulate their currencies are subject to U.S. trade retaliation. If Obama doesn't do something soon he may face pressure from unions and manufacturers.*

10/16/10

As Immigration and Customs Enforcement (ICE) continues its agenda of <u>backdoor amnesty</u>. In Houston, Tx,   ICE's "docket review" proce-dure of immigration courts has increased deportation case dismissals by more than 700%![756]

At a Boston fundraiser, President Obama explains the resistance of voters to embracing the Democratic agenda, "People out there are still hurting very badly, and they are still scared. And so part of the reason that our politics seems so tough right now, and facts and science and argument does not seem to be winning the day all the time, is because we're hard-wired not to always think clearly when we're scared."[757] *He should've just finished his statement saying, "the benighted bumpkins cling to their guns and their religion..."*

10/17/10

White House Adviser David Axelrod says that next year the adminis-tration's focus will be "to generate more growth and jobs."[758] *How many times have they said this? He's been in office for more than a year and a half, why hasn't this been the focus since Day 1? Why are they waiting until next year for this to be the focus?*

10/18/10

The Treasury Department releases data showing that since Barack Obama took office 637 days ago, he has increased the National Debt by more than $3 trillion.[759] *He's racking up debt at the rate of $4.7 billion per day, or $200 million per hour, or $3.3 million per minute, or $55,000 per second. Remember, this isn't just the spending; this is the debt on top of all of the other spending.*

Obamacare is already hurting American workers. Today, Boeing Corp. is asking its 90,000 *non-union* workers to pay much higher premiums for their health insurance. In a letter sent to employees, Boeing writes, "The newly enacted health care reform legislation, while intended to expand access to care for millions of uninsured Americans, is also adding cost pressure as requirements of the new law are phased in over the next several years."[760] *Wait until they find out they're paying much more for much lower quality care.*

For the second time, the president gives a speech misquoting the Declaration of Independence, leaving out "the Creator." President Obama says "that each of us are endowed with certain inalienable rights."[761]

10/19/10

The United Steelworkers Union (part of AFL-CIO) has asked (*i.e., "pressured"*) the government to probe China for allegedly giving out illegal subsidies for green energy. China is retaliating by halting shipments of rare earth minerals, which are critical in manufacturing high-tech

Oct 2010

products.[762] *At least we'll be protecting union jobs.*

10/20/10

DHS Secretary Napolitano unveils new body scanners at JFK airport. During the demonstration of the new scanners, Secretary Napolitano refused to volunteer.[763]

President Obama will be cancelling a trip to a Sikh Temple during his visit to India. Mortals must cover their heads with scarves before entering the shrine. He is afraid that pictures of him wearing a headscarf will fuel rumors that he is a secret Muslim.[764]

10/21/10

Obama attends a $30,400 per guest fundraiser with Google executives.[765] *The president has no problem with tax dodgers as long as they are his friends, cronies and supporters. Google paid only a 2.4 percent tax rate. They have played an international shell game of income shifting techniques such as the "Double Irish" and the "Dutch Sandwich" to avoid paying Uncle Sam. As long as the money flows into his campaign coffers, that's fine with him. President Obama who remarked, "At some point I do think you've earned enough money" apparently doesn't think that applies to his contributors.*[766]

Treasury Secretary Geithner says his focus on upcoming meetings with G-20 finance ministers will be "rebalancing" the world economy so that it is less reliant on U.S. consumers. Geithner also wishes to stress that the U.S. will not be monetizing its debt.[767]

10/22/10

WikiLeaks releases 400,000 military documents detailing Iraqi torture and U.S. misdeeds.[768]

10/24/10

Treasury Secretary Geithner is meeting with other G-20 finance ministers. They have decided to give emerging countries such as China, Brazil, India and Turkey a bigger place at the IMF table. Geithner and others hope that with this latest move China will now be more willing to be more flexible with its currency policy.[769]

10/25/10

President Obama campaigns for Democrats in midterm elections. Well, except for one Democrat: Rhode Island gubernatorial candidate Frank Caprio. Obama is returning a favor to ex-Republican-turned-Independent Lincoln Chafee. Chafee endorsed Obama in 2008. Democrat Caprio said Obama can "take his endorsement and shove it!"

Elsewhere in Rhode Island, the president used more car analogies to take potshots at Republicans, saying, "We can't have special interests sitting shotgun. We gotta have middle class families up in front. We don't mind the Republicans joining us. They can come for the ride, but they gotta sit in back."[770]

Oct 2010

In the first day of trading since Secretary Geithner's meeting with other finance ministers, the dollar falls again to a fifteen-year low against the Japanese yen.[771] *Maybe Secretary Geithner didn't do a very good job trying to convince people that the U.S. will not monetize the debt.*

President Karzai of Afghanistan confirms that he is receiving money from Iran. Karzai uses the news conference as an opportunity to launch an anti-Western rant and accuse the U.S. of exporting killing to Afghanistan.[772]

This year China is on track to invest $30 billion in Brazil, up from $400 million last year. Approximately $20 billion will be going to the oil sector.[773]

Cuba will be expanding its private sector. Yes, communist Cuba realizes it needs free markets. They will be charging entrepreneurs 25% to 50% income taxes.[774]

Oct 2010

10/26/10

President Obama admits to civil rights ambulance chaser Reverend Al Sharpton that the midterm elections will be a referendum on his agenda.[775]

10/27/10

Just a few days after President Obama's high-dollar fundraiser with Google executives, the Federal Trade Commission (FTC) drops its investigation of Google's data-mining privacy transgressions.[776] *Move along, folks. There's no influence peddling here, there's nothing suspicious about it at all. Just like suing Goldman Sachs when they unveiled the Financial Reform Bill. Everything is completely above-board.*

Democrats request that the Pentagon produce records relating to potential Republican challengers. The Democratic National Committee is specifically requesting Pentagon files on governors of the following states: Sarah Palin (Alaska), Mitt Romney (Massachussetts), Haley Barbour (Mississippi), Tim Pawlenty (Minnesota), Mike Huckabee (Arkansas), Mitch Daniels (Indiana), and Bobby Jindal (Louisiana). They also seek information on ex-House Speaker Newt Gingrich (Georgia) and Senator John Thune (South Dakota).[777]

Preliminary preparations for the president's trip to India include forty aircraft, including Air Force One, six armored cars, two command posts and three Marine One choppers.[778]

Oct 2010

10/28/10

DHS Secretary Napolitano says the military will be working with civilian cybersecurity. Anticipating criticism from privacy rights groups, Secretary Napolitano says, "That means that we have to, on the civilian side, be particularly cognizant of privacy issues, of civil liberties issues, and we have built that into the memorandum."[779] *Relax. The federal government never oversteps its boundaries.*

10/31/10

Christians are attacked in Iraq. Muslim fanatics attack a Syriac Catholic Church, killing at least fifty-eight people and two priests.[780] *We're waiting for Obama to make a statement telling us not to jump to conclusions.*

October unemployment = 9.6%.[781]
Real unemployment = 17%.[782]

11/1/10

In full campaign mode, the president calls Republicans "enemies." He tries to energize the Latino vote, saying, "If Latinos sit out the election instead of (saying) 'we're going to punish our enemies and we're going to reward our friends who stand with us on issues that are important to us'—if they don't see that kind of upsurge in voting in this election, then I think it's going to be harder."[783]

The Fed signals "QE 2," another round of quantitative easing. Estimates are that the Fed will pump anywhere from $500 billion to $1 trillion into the economy."[784]

11/2/10

The Democrats lose big in the midterm elections. They narrowly retain control of the Senate by a margin of 53 to 47. Republicans scored an enormous victory in the House with the final result being 242 Republican seats to 193 Democrat seats. The nation now has twenty-nine

Nov 2010

Republican governors to twenty Democrat governors (and one Independent). Republicans now control twenty-six state legislatures, Democrats control fifteen, and eight are split (Nebraska is non-partisan). The race is widely believed to be a referendum on President Obama and his agenda. President Obama clings to a predictably self-flattering delusion that he was working too hard to broadcast his message effectively. *Even though on October 26, 2010, he admitted to the Reverend Al Sharpton that the midterm elections would be a referendum on his presidency.*

A presidential advance team is in India with helicopters, a ship and security instruments.[785]

11/3/10

General Motors will not have to pay taxes on future profits of $45.4 billion due to tax-loss carry-forward provisions.[786]

China and other emerging economies view the Fed's "QE 2" as a hostile attempt to drive down the dollar that would spark currency wars.[787]

11/4/10

The geniuses at the Federal Reserve announce they will be pumping $600 billion into the economy over the next 8 months for more "quantitative easing."[788]

China sees the Fed's policy as a dangerous threat to the world economy. Xia Bin, advisor to the Chinese central bank, says, "As long as the world exercises no restraint in issuing global currencies such as the dollar—and this is not easy—then the occurrence of another crisis is inevitable, as quite a few wise Westerners lament." China's foreign minister says, "Many countries are worried about the impact of the policy on their countries" and that the U.S. "owes us some explanation on their decision of quantitative easing."[789] [790]

Brazil's finance minister says it may retaliate in a currency war and adds, "Everybody wants the U.S. economy to recover, but it does no good at all to just throw dollars from a helicopter." Brazil's central bank president blames the U.S.'s excess liquidity as creating "risks for everyone."[791] [792]

Germany's finance minister Wolfgang Schaeuble says that Bernanke's "QE 2" will create problems for Germany as well. Schaeuble tells reporters, "With all due respect, U.S. policy is clueless. It's not that the Americans haven't pumped enough liquidity into the market. Now to say let's pump more into the market is not going to solve their problems."[793] [794]

South Africa's finance minister thinks the Fed's policy "undermines the spirit of multilateral co-operation that G-20 leaders have fought so hard to maintain during the current crisis." Furthermore, he believes it is a betrayal of an agreement among G-20 finance ministers to refrain from uncoordinated policies. [795]

Since President Obama took office, every major economy throughout the world has expressed shaken faith in the U.S. economy and has called for the end of the dollar as the global reserve currency. Americans have reason to suspect that some of these countries would love to see an end to U.S. domination, but all of them have valid concerns for protecting their

Nov 2010

own economies from the reckless fiscal and monetary policies rippling out of Washington. The Dubious Duo of Geithner and Bernanke have devastated American financial credibility and prestige. The rest of the world now scorns and derides the dollar. Only this Administration would have a Treasury Secretary who is laughed at on a foreign visit. No other Fed Chairman his been ever been so universally and publicly disrespected.

11/5/10

In the aftermath of the Democrats' electoral defeat, Obama resorts to his usual modus operandi of taking personal responsibility without actually taking personal responsibility. He tells *60 Minutes'* Steve Kroft, "I think that's a fair argument. I think that, over the course of two years we were so busy and so focused on getting a bunch of stuff done that we stopped paying attention to the fact that leadership isn't just legislation. That it's a matter of persuading people. And giving them confidence and bringing them together and setting a tone."

Here's the really good part: "Making an argument that people can understand, I think that we haven't always been successful at that. And I take personal responsibility for that. And it's something that I've got to examine carefully as I go forward."[796] *The president blames the election disaster on his being too busy to communicate effectively; he does not acknowledge that his appalling polices played any role. This also illustrates a mindset that is too shallow to recognize its own arrogance. President Obama does not credit the American people for honestly rejecting policies that they fully understand. No. The only way that people of intelligence can disagree with him is if they do not receive his message*

Nov 2010

properly. The rest of the clodhoppers are just "not thinking clearly." See
entry for 10/16/10.

AARP jacks up its own employees' health insurance premiums, citing
rising medical costs and Obamacare as the causes.[797] *Why is it that*
groups who lobbied most strongly for Obamacare, like the AARP and
unions, are either hurt by it or seek exemptions from it?

11/6/10

President Obama arrives in India today with unmatched extravagance.
His 3-day visit to India is the start of his ten-day Asian tour. An Indian newspaper estimates the president's three-day visit to India will
cost about $200 million per day. The White House claims this figure
is grossly inflated, but will not provide its own estimate. Other reports
claim the presidents's trip will be accompanied by an armada of thirty-
four warships, including an aircraft carrier that will patrol the sea-lanes
of the Indian Coast (the Pentagon calls this claim ludicrous). Outlays
for the president's visit include an entourage of 3,000 people, two jets
with advanced security systems, a convoy of over forty cars, thirteen
heavy-lift aircraft, three Marine One helicopters, security, hotel rooms
and meals.[798 799]

In preparation for Obama's visit to the Gandhi Museum, all coco-
nuts are removed from the trees to eliminate the chance of a falling
coconut hitting the president. For the his visit to the Gandhi Museum,
U.S. engineers build a one kilometer long, 12'x12', bomb-proof tunnel.
The tunnel will be air-conditioned, equipped with security cameras and

Nov 2010

manned by security and both ends.[800][801]   *The President is treating him-*
self to this luxurious flamboyance while the U.S. unemployment rate is
9.6%. It's hard to believe that this is the same White House that ridiculed
BP's CEO Tony Hayward for attending a yacht race.

Now that Republicans will be the majority party in the House, Obama
calls for compromise; however, he himself is unwilling to compromise
on extending the Bush tax cuts. On the brighter side, he says that Democrats and Republicans see the need to control spending.[802] *Indeed, his*
very own Fiscal Responsibility Commission that he appointed calls for
spending cuts (see 7/11/10). Future events will reveal that Obama's re-
marks to rein in spending are mere rhetoric not borne of any real convic-
tion.

Once again, Mort Zuckerman weighs in with another piece of elegant
writing titled, *America's Love Affair With Obama Is Over.* Zuckerman
doubts whether Obama has the proper aptitude and character to be
president. He writes, "He came across as a young man in a grown-up's
game—impressive but not presidential. A politician but not a leader,
managing American policy at home and American power abroad with
disturbing amateurishness. Indeed, there was a growing perception of
the inability to run the machinery of government and to find the right
people to manage it. A man who was once seen as a talented and even
charismatic rhetorician is now seen as lacking real experience or even
the ability to stop America's decline. 'Yes we can,' he once said, but now
America asks, 'Can he?'"

Zuckerman also calls into question the president's judgment, "Why
did Obama put his health plan so far ahead of the economy?... His rush

Nov 2010

to do it sparked a broad resistance that has only spread since the bill was passed. The public sensed that health care was a victory for Obama, and maybe for the Democrats, but not for the country...A significant majority, some 58 percent, now wish to repeal the entire bill."[803]

11/7/10

Ahead of the G-20 summit, Treasury Secretary Geithner is promoting a framework that would limit countries' trade balances.[804]

The rest of the world is still in a furor over the Fed's decision to dump $600 billion in "quantitative easing" (pronounced: **prin**-ting **muhn**-ee). The Russians are outraged by "QE 2" and insist that the Fed consult with other countries before making stupid decisions.

Jean-Claude Juncker, Luxembourg's Prime Minister and Chairman of the EU's finance ministers, says, "I don't think it's a good decision. You're fighting debt with more debt."

Germany's criticism was particularly scorching. Finance Minister Schauble tells a reporter, "I seriously doubt that it makes sense to pump unlimited amounts of money into markets. There is no lack of liquidity in the U.S. economy, which is why I don't recognize the economic argument behind this measure."

Even Sarah Palin chimed in about QE 2's inflationary impact and that "it's far from certain this will even work."[805] *Sarah Palin's two cents' worth is chump change compared to Bernanke's $600 billion. Oh, by the way, President Obama defends QE 2 and thinks it's a great idea. But then again, at the last G-20 he was the only world leader who promoted stimulus spending instead of austerity cuts.*

11/8/10

President Obama's National Commission on Fiscal Responsibility and Reform issues recommendations that infuriate conservatives and liberals. The Commission targets tax breaks, like the mortgage interest deduction, and sacred cows like Medicare, Defense and Social Security.[806]

President Obama will be the first person in history using a teleprompter to address the Indian Parliament. Some Indians are disappointed; one official said, "We thought Obama is a trained orator and skilled in the art of mass address with his continuous eye contact."[807]

The President resumes his customary stature of groveling weakness in Mumbai, India. He publicly declares the decline of U.S. dominance in the world when he says the U.S. no longer has the standing to "meet the rest of the world economically on our terms."[808] *Even if he believes it to be true, why would he publicly show his hand for all the world to see?*

The Chinese Finance Vice Minister joins the rest of the world in criticizing QE 2, "As a major reserve currency issuer, for the U.S. to launch a second round of quantitative easing at this time, we feel that it did not recognize its responsibility to stabilize global markets and did not think about the impact of excessive liquidity on emerging markets."[809]

11/9/10

Vice President Biden meets with Earl Devaney about government transparency...behind closed doors.[810]

Nov 2010

In Indonesia today, the president tries to score some points in the world's most populous Muslim country by criticizing Israel.[811] *Obama said Israel's construction of East Jerusalem settlements was unhelpful to the peace process...It seems that Jew-baiting in front of 205 million Muslims would also be unhelpful. He also took a shot at his own country saying Americans must stop mistrusting Islam.*

China's Dagong Global Credit Rating Co. downgrades U.S. Treasuries again from AA to A+ due to the Fed's recent policy of quantitative easing. The bond markets were unpersuaded as yields held even.[812]

11/10/10

The number of federal workers earning more than $150,000 has doubled in the twenty-two months since Barack Obama was sworn into office. The President would like to give them and the other 2.1 million federal workers a 1.4% raise.[813]

The Association of Flight Attendants Union denounces the Transportation Safety Administration's (TSA) aggressive pat-down screenings. A spokeswoman for the union says, "We don't want them in uniform going through this enhanced screening where their private areas are being touched in public. They actually make contact with the genital area."[814]

Despite Candidate Obama's campaign promise, the administration supports the "don't ask, don't tell" policy of banning homosexuals from the military. In the case of *Log Cabin Republicans v. United States*, the Department of Justice argues before the Supreme Court that it is not a

Nov 2010

matter for courts to decide.[815]

For Veteran's Day (which is actually tomorrow), President Obama lays a wreath at during a ceremony at a U.S. Army base in South Korea.[816]

Transocean, Ltd., owner of the Deepwater Horizon oil rig, is upset that federal regulators have not begun forensic testing on the blowout preventer mechanism from the oil spill. The equipment was recovered two months ago and the evidence is corroding as regulators inexplicably stall their investigation.[817]

7 scientific experts complain that the Interior Department lied and intentionally misrepresented their findings to support the six-month moratorium of offshore oil drilling. The scientists say their reports were manipulated to suit the Interior Department's own ends.[818]

11/11/10

Seoul hosts the G-20 summit.

The Fed's QE 2 dominates the G-20 summit. China reiterates its criticism saying the U.S. "should not force others to take medicine for its own disease."[819]

On other fronts, President Obama fails to reach a free trade agreement with South Korea. Germany tramples President Obama's wish to curb trade imbalances between nations. The Germans believe that trade imbalances should reflect economic competition, not political covenants. The President is also unable to build support for pressur-

Nov 2010

ing China to change its currency policy. While trying to save face, he served up one of his usual rhetorical dishes of meaningless fried air and word salad, saying, "I think that you will see at this summit a broad-based agreement from all countries, including Germany, that we need to ensure balanced and sustainable growth."[820] *After the midterm election whipping, he was hoping to use his Asia trip and this G-20 summit as a platform to cast himself as a great world leader.*

11/12/10

TSA Administrator John Pistole and DHS Secretary Napolitano meet with travel industry executives and pilot associations to discuss the increasing public outrage over airport screening techniques. Some travelers are dissatisfied that their children either have to have a naked image body scan or be groped inappropriately.[821] [822]

Louisiana Governor Bobby Jindal releases his book *Leadership in Crisis*. Jindal describes Obama as a disconnected chief executive of reptilian political instincts who is more concerned about image and appearance. When Jindal complained that the drilling moratorium would kill Louisiana jobs, Obama replied that national polls supported the ban. Jindal writes, "The human element seemed invisible to the White House" and "they're not connected to reality on the ground." The administration retorts from the same old playbook, "From Day One President Obama has directed his administration to work with state and local governments to respond to and help gulf communities recover from the BP oil spill."[823] *The administration claims to have been involved "from day 1" on everything from immigration to unemployment. If this is true, then what does it say about their aptitude to govern?*

11/13/10

Doctors are getting very nervous as Medicare looks to cut benefits by 23%.[824]

11/14/10

The Obama administration has allowed 111 waivers to Obamacare, thusfar. Not surprisingly, unions are heavily favored.[825]

In Yokohama, President Obama tells Russian President Medvedev that ratification of the START treaty will be his **top priority**.[826] *President Obama may be telling the truth. Addressing deficit spending, unemployment, the economy and immigration have certainly not been his top priority.*

11/17/10

The Transportation Safety Administration (TSA) is hit with lawsuits over naked body scanners and aggressive groping.[827]

TSA is now threatening to impose $11,000 fines on anyone who refuses to submit to their searches. "I'm not going to change those policies," declares TSA Administrator John Pistole. DHS Secretary Napolitano insists that people who have a problem with their searches simply should not fly.[828] [829] *Maybe bureaucrats who disregard the 4th Amend-*

ment shouldn't be in positions of authority.

Fox News Chairman Roger Ailes comments during an interview about President Obama's lackluster results at the G-20 summit. Ailes tells Howard Kurtz, "The President has not been very successful. He just got kicked from Mumbai to South Korea, and he came home and attacked Republicans for it. He had to be told by the French and the Germans that his socialism was too far left for them to deal with."[830]

Senator Jay Rockefeller (D-WV) wishes he could personally censor media outlets without affording them due process rights. At a Cable and Broadcast subcommittee hearing, the Senator says, "There's a little bug inside of me which wants to get the FCC to say to FOX and to MSNBC: 'Out. Off. End. Goodbye.' It would be a big favor to political discourse, our ability to do our work here in Congress and to the American people to be able to talk with each other and have some faith in government and, more importantly, in the future."[831] *Maybe the Senator will be able silence critics and to crush opposing viewpoints if "net neutrality" passes.*

President Obama and Congressional leaders were supposed to meet today on whether to extend the Bush tax cuts. The meeting is rescheduled for 11/30/10.

General Motors IPO raises $20.1 billion, the largest in U.S. history. The federal government's share in the car company should fall to about 33%.[832]

Nov 2010

11/18/10

Despite a federal court's ruling, FCC Chairman Julius Genachowski is tweaking plans to pursue "net neutrality" which he hopes to advance in the next several weeks.[833]

While Congress is in recess, the administration is working on the biggest arms deal in U.S. history. Without having to be bothered by the concerns of another branch of government, the Commander in Chief is trying to sell $60 billion worth of fighter jets and attack helicopters to Saudi Arabia.[834]

11/19/10

President Obama announces that NATO countries have agreed to a defense shield system to protect all NATO members.[835]

Pascal Lamy, Director General of the World Trade Organization, warns that currency wars could lead to 1930s-style protectionism.[836]

11/20/10

An SEIU affiliate, 1199 SEIU United Healthcare Workers East, in New York is dropping health coverage for 6,000 children of its members because of financial problems posed by the New York State Health Department and Obamacare. The union administers its own health insurance funds but claims the state is making them buy coverage from a third party. "The state is not forcing 1199 to do anything regarding its employee health insurance," says a state official.[837]

11/21/10

An American scientist has toured a North Korean uranium enrichment facility that he says is highly sophisticated and was built in secret with remarkable speed.[838]

11/22/10

Members of a stimulus panel meet at the Ritz-Carlton Hotel in Phoenix, AZ to discuss "fraud, waste and abuse of Recovery Act funds."[839] *For starters they could stay at the Red Roof Inn.*

The Obama administration has bought approximately one-fourth of Ford and GM's total output of hybrid vehicles. $300 million in stimulus money plus other funds were used to buy the 14,584 cars.[840]

Nov 2010

11/23/10

The Transportation Security Administration (TSA) allows certain government officials to be exempt from its unpleasant screening procedures while traveling commercially.[841] *"All animals are equal but some animals are more equal than others"—George Orwell, Animal Farm*

The controversial full body scanners are now being used in some courthouses.[842]

North and South Korean forces clash along their disputed border, killing two South Korean soldiers and two South Korean civilians. North Korea's casualties are unknown. North Korea threatens to continue strikes against the South.[843] [844]

11/24/10

A Pennsylvania Zionist group called Z Street claims that the IRS is unfairly targeting pro-Israel groups in challenging their 501(c)(3) status. The IRS challenged Z Street's legitimacy to receive tax-exempt status by asking, "Does your organization support the existence of the land of Israel?" and "Describe your organization's religious belief system toward the land of Israel."[845]

China and Russia officially quit using the dollar when trading with each other. The new policy is not directed at challenging the dollar, but at protecting their own economies from being demolished by Washington's inexplicable policies.[846]

President Obama asks China to keep North Korea on a short leash. The U.S. is sending an aircraft carrier, the USS George Washington, to the Yellow Sea for naval exercises with South Korea.[847] *See earlier comment, 7/22/10.*

11/26/10

A Somali-born U.S. citizen tries to detonate what he believes to be a bomb during a crowded Christmas tree lighting in Portland, Oregon.[848]

Nov 2010

11/28/10

WikiLeaks dumps 250,000 U.S. diplomatic cables that are embarrassing for the whole world but particularly the U.S. The leaked secret documents contain American diplomats' disparaging and brutally candid assessments of world leaders and previously undisclosed details of nuclear and antiterrorism activity. Among other things, they also show the Obama administration attempted to pay or coerce other governments into receiving Gitmo prisoners.[849]

11/29/10

President Obama calls for a two-year freeze in federal pay, a move that would save taxpayers more than $5 billion. Union leaders express predictable mock outrage while Representative Darrell Issa (R-CA) calls it "long overdue."[850]

Nov 2010

The U.N. Climate Summit in Cancun, Mexico begins with an invocation of the ancient jaguar moon-goddess Ixchel. Christiana Figueres, Executive Secretary of the U.N. Framework Convention on Climate Change, informs attendees that Ixchel is also "the goddess of reason, creativity and weaving. May she inspire you— because today you are gathered in Cancun to weave together the elements of a solid response to climate change, using both reason and creativity as your tools."[851] *The rest of the summit is about what one would expect after such an opening. 190 countries agreed to agree on something definite at some indefinite future date. Predictably, no one mentioned that the entire U.N.Climate Change structure is based on corrupted data and fraudulent information.*

11/30/10

U.S. November budget deficit = $150.4 billion

November unemployment = 9.8%.

Real unemployment = 17%.[852]

12/1/10

The Federal Reserve releases some details of the $3.3 trillion in aid it gave to U.S. and <u>foreign</u> banks. Many of the loans were for short durations but were renewed many times. Over time the Fed lent to Citigroup ($2.2 trillion), Merrill Lynch ($2.1 trillion), Morgan Stanley ($2 trillion), Bear Stearns ($960 billion), Bank of America ($887 billion), Goldman Sachs ($615 billion), JPMorgan Chase ($178 billion) and Wells Fargo ($154 billion).

The Federal Reserve showered its generosity on many foreign banks, too. A few highlights include: UBS ($165 billion), Deutsche Bank ($97 billion) and the Royal Bank of Scotland ($92 billion).

The Fed is remaining secretive about collateral pledged by recipients of $885 billion.

The Fed also bought $1.25 trillion in mortgages from Fannie Mae and Freddie Mac. *Talk about "cash for clunkers..."*

Non-banking institutions also benefited from the Fed's largesse. Harley-Davidson borrowed $2.3 billion and a group of independent Caterpillar dealers borrowed $733 million. The Fed secretly bailed out General Electric (GE) to the tune of $16 billion. *By the luckiest of coincidences, GE just happens to be the most commonly held stock by members*

Dec 2010

of Congress.[853] [854] [855]

President Obama announces that he is willing to delay his vacation plans to Hawaii to sort out a deal with Republicans regarding the Bush tax cuts.[856]

WikiLeaks cables demonstrate the shocking extent of corruption in Russia. The government is so enmeshed with criminal enterprises that, in some instances, it is impossible to distinguish them.[857]

The U.S. is still willing to go further to stabilize Europe's finances by giving more money to the International Monetary Fund (IMF).[858]

12/2/10

Julius Genekowski of the Fedeal Communications Commission (FCC) proposes to regulate the internet (*Still!*). This time he believes he has a "sound legal basis" for butting into peoples' lives. The draft document the FCC submitted contains over 550 footnotes and is labeled "Non-Public, for internal use only," meaning that no one can see it unless the rules are approved on 12/21/10.[859]   *"Transparency" is their motto.*

The freedom-crushing FCC now wants to regulate news programming to promote "diversity." Commissioner Michael Copps wants to indroduce a "public values test" that broadcasters must take every four years. The broadcasters' license renewals would be contingent upon criteria that meet the federal government's approval.[860]

Barack Obama's war on personal freedoms is also extending to tram-

Dec 2010

pling the 4th Amendment. Without warrants the federal government is tracking its citizens' credit card transactions, store loyalty cards, travel reservations, etc. The government has the ability to do all of this in real time. Government agents use "hotwatch" orders by issuing their own subpoenas. At some later date they get orders from judges that the surveillance not be disclosed.

The federal government also refuses to disclose how many Americans' telephones, e-mail accounts, text messages and all other communications it has tracked and intercepted under the Foreign Intelligence Survellance Act (FISA).[861] [862] *Are we citizens of the State or subjects of the State? This is especially daunting considering the DHS memo that labels almost any conservative as a potential domestic terrorist.*

12/3/10

The Transportation Safety Administration (TSA) goes from a policing agency to a police-state agency. TSA is compiling a "watch list" of those who dare to question its ominous power. For instance, CNN reporter Drew Griffin made the list for filing reports critical of the TSA.[863]

WikiLeaks cables reveal that the U.S. tried to influence the Copenhagen climate accord with bribes, threats and coercion. The purpose of the Obama administration's nasty behavior was to overwhelm any opposition to the climate change agenda.[864] *Why would the Obama administration take such aggressive action after the East Anglia University and IPCC scandals exposed the global warming industrial complex for the fraud and hoax that it is?*

At a dinner party in Bahrain, Iranian Foreign Minister Manouchehr Mottaki snubs Secretary of State Clinton <u>twice</u> by refusing to shake Mrs. Clinton's extended hand or even acknowledge her presence.[865]

President Obama makes a surprise trip to Afghanistan to visit the troops.[866]

12/4/10

The Senate blocks President Obama's tax plan. He accuses Republicans of holding the middle-class hostage.[867] *If the president were truly interested in raising revenues, why doesn't he consider lowering the capital gains tax? In the April 16, 2008 Democratic debate, he admits that lower capital gains rates increase revenues to the Treasury. He famously said he wanted to raise capital gains rates for purposes of "fairness,"*

12/5/10

Newt Gingrich remarks that the WikiLeaks cables demonstrate the Obama administration's "shallow, amateurish" approach to national security.[868]

12/6/10

Dec 2010

President Obama is humiliated by having to cave to Republican pressure regarding extension of the Bush tax cuts. One of Obama's marquee campaign pledges was that he would make "the rich" pay more in taxes. The tax cuts were extended to all. The President tries to downplay it by calling it a compromise, but he was routed.[869]

DHS Secretary Napolitano will be launching the "If You See Something, Say Something" campaign which will be played via telescreen at checkout lines in 588 Wal-marts in 27 states. The idea is to prod the American public into playing an active role in notifying authorities of suspected terrorists and criminals.[870]

Despite President Obama's freeze on federal pay, 1.1 million federal workers will receive more than $2.5 billion in raises. Obama's "freeze" only applies to cost-of-living expenses, not regularly scheduled pay increases. Most workers will continue to receive their regularly scheduled pay increases.[871]

It is estimated that more than 500 Taliban members have returned to fighting after being detained by U.S. forces.[872]

12/7/10

At a press conference today, the president is visibly upset that the Republicans scored a victory over extending the Bush tax cuts. On the verge of throwing a full-fledged hissy fit, he says, "The middle-class tax cuts were being held hostage to the high-end tax cuts. I think it's tempting not to negotiate with hostage-takers—unless, the hostage gets harmed—and then people will question the wisdom of that strategy. In this case the hostage was the American people and I was not willing to see them get harmed."[873] *President Obama should blame himself and his own party. They decided to play politics and kick the can down the road*

Dec 2010

rather than vote on the tax cuts before the election. If the Democrats had been a little more courageous, he would not be throwing his undignified tantrum on national television.

The president tries to save face amid his smoldering defeat. Obama says that Republicans should not view him as a pushover, "I will be happy to see the Republicans test whether or not I'm itching for a fight on a whole range of issues. I suspect they will find I am." *Note that Barack Obama plays a submissive role when dealing with socialists, dictators and Islamic extremists; yet, the only time his temper actually flares, the only time he actually wants to joust is when he faces off with opponents who profess beliefs in the free market.*

President Obama also lashes out at his Democratic critics who feel he has forsaken one of his basic campaign pledges. The president calls them "sanctimonious," willing to "have the satisfaction of having a purist position and no victories for the American people."[874]

The Obamacare health waivers now number 222. His union friends are still getting their special treatment, as well.[875]

150 terrorists released from Gitmo are either confirmed or strongly suspected of resuming terrorist activities.[876]

Dec 2010

12/8/10

Congress blocks the closing of Gitmo and the transfer of detainees to the U.S.[877]

12/10/10

President Obama makes one of the worst blunders of his entire presidency. In order to lessen the humiliation of his tax compromise with Republicans, he embarrasses himself even further by having a joint press conference with ex-President Bill Clinton. *He looks like the little boy President bringing Dad to the party to stand up for him and answer his questions for him. Evidently, Obama needs to defer to someone with the gravitas that he himself lacks. The President makes himself look even weaker when he turns the forum over to Clinton and says he does not want to keep Michelle waiting.*[878] [879]

12/12/10

D.C. Metro Police will be coordinating random bag searches with the Transportation Security Administrations (TSA). The TSA has a long-standing policy of disregarding 4th Amendment rights.[880]

Venezuela acquires 1,800 shoulder-fired anti-aircraft missiles from Russia in the last year. The U.S. fears they may be funneled to the Marxist FARC forces in Colombia.[881]

12/13/10

Virginia U.S. District Judge Henry Hudson rules Obamacare's insurance mandate   unconstitutional, saying it goes beyond Congress's powers to regulate interstate commerce. In his opinion, Judge Hudson states, "At its core, this dispute is not simply about regulating the business of insurance—or crafting a scheme of universal health insurance coverage—it's about an individual's right to choose to participate." He adds, "No Supreme Court decision has authorized Congress to compel an individual to involuntarily enter the stream of commerce by purchasing a commodity in the private market."[882]

For the umpteenth time, Moody's warns that the U.S. is in danger of losing its AAA debt rating.[883]

Democrats characterize President Obama's caving in to Republicans as a lily-livered response. Obama promises that he will fight the Republicans aggressively when they take over the House of Representatives.[884]

North Korea warns that South Korea's continued military exercises could bring a nuclear response.[885]

12/14/10

Operation Fast and Furious: U.S. Border Patrol Agent Brian Terry is murdered by Mexican drug smugglers with guns purchased from Operation Fast and Furious.

Democrats roll out a $1.1 trillion, 1,900-page omnibus spending bill in the lame duck Congress.[886]

Hugo Chavez asks the Venezuelan Congress to give him power to rule by decree for 1 year.[887]

Dec 2010

12/15/10

The Senate plans to work on ratifying the new START treaty with Russia.

Vice President Biden attacks Senator Jim DeMint and other Republicans critical of the START treaty, "Get out of the way. There's too much at stake." The START treaty will reduce our nuclear stockpiles from 2,200 to 1,550.[888] *Evidently, Vice President Biden doesn't think any sort of deliberative process is necessary.*

IRS audits have increased by 11% in 2010.[889]

German computer consultants sabotage the Iranian nuclear program with the Stuxnet computer virus. Iran's program is expected to suffer a two-year setback.[890]

12/16/10

President Obama's "Making Work Pay" tax credit means that workers must pay the government. More than 13 million taxpayers will be receiving tax bills for receiving too much money from the program.[891]

TSA screeners at Los Angeles, Chicago and Newark airports miss guns and bombs.[892]

President Obama breaks his five-day public viewing pledge by signing the tax law within hours of the Congressional vote.[893]

12/17/10

DHS Secretary Napolitano says that the Department of Homeland Security will begin battling climate change.[894]

Venezuela's National Assembly of Socialist Loyalists has voted to extend President Chavez's request for dictatorial powers to eighteen months.[895]

12/20/10

The *Washington Post* reports that the government is creating a vast domestic spying system. "The system collects, stores and analyzes information about thousands of U.S. citizens and residents, many of whom have not been accused of any wrongdoing." Much like the Soviet NKVD, the FBI is compiling a database with thousands of names and personal information of its own citizens. The goal is to have every state and local law enforcement agency report to Washington.[896] [897] *Remember, on 4/7/09, DHS Secretary Napolitano and the Obama administration disclosed in a secret memo that just about anyone critical of the government is a potential domestic terrorist and enemy of the state. Plus, he supports a federalized DNA database, even for detainees who haven't been charged or convicted of any crime, the Feds issue their own "hotwatch" warrants, the U.S. Marshals store naked body scans and so on and so on.*

The FCC launches unprecedented steps to bypass elected representatives in controlling the inner workings of the Internet.[898]

British Police conduct a large-scale anti-terrorist sweep, apprehending

Dec 2010

12 suspects accused of plotting terror attacks within the U.K.[899]

Hugo Chavez imposes "net neutrality" for Venezuela. The socialist dictator has imposed restrictions on all messages showing "disrespect for public authorities," that "incite or promote hatred" or create "anxiety."[900]

12/21/10

Thumbing their nose at federal courts, the administration's Federal Communications Commission (FCC) celebrates step 1 of controlling the Internet by adopting "net neutrality." Senator Jim DeMint (R-SC) is determined to reverse the FCC's "Internet takeover."

President Obama has been a longtime fan of net neutrality and he is only too happy for his Administration to circumvent Congress to get what he wants. The roots of "net neutrality" began with Marxist professor Robert McChesney. In 2009, McChesney told SocialistProject, "But the ultimate goal is to get rid of the media capitalists in the phone and cable companies and to divest them from control." McChesny told another Marxist publication, "Any serious effort to reform the media system would have to necessarily be part of a revolutionary program to overthrow the capitalist system itself."[901] [902]

Attorney General Holder fears "radical citizens." The Attorney General says, "The threat has changed from simply worrying about foreigners coming here to worrying about people in the United States." Holder says that 126 people have been indicted on terrorism-related charges in the last twenty-four months; fifty of them are Americans.[903]

Dec 2010

Thirty-two states will be borrowing billions from the federal government to cover unemployment benefits.[904]

12/22/10

In an interview with ABC, Director of National Intelligence James Clapper, is completely ignorant of the U.K.'s major arrest of terrorists just two days ago.[905]

President Obama says the economy will be his "singular focus" for the next two years. 23 months into his presidency, he says the economy is past the "crisis point." The government needs to be a "good partner" with the private sector and get rid of regulations that stand in the way of economic progress.[906] *This time he is serious. All of those other times he said the economy was **top priority** and that jobs were **number 1**—all of that was just little league compared to right now. He's serious this time. Honestly. He really is going to "focus like a laser beam" this time. You can count on it.*

More and more Americans are leaving the president's mortgage relief program. As of this month, 774,000 homeowners (more than half) have dropped out of the foreclosure-relief program.[907]

Critics must be punished. A Sacramento-based airline pilot posted videos on YouTube showing the laxity of the Transportation Safety Administration (TSA). The pilot showed that under the TSA system the flight crew must submit to the troublesome screening process while the ground crews who service the planes are allowed access by simply swip-

Dec 2010

ing a card. The pilot's video narrates, "As you can see, airport security is kind of a farce. It's only smoke and mirrors so you people believe there is actually something going on here." The pilot's insolence is punishable by civil penalties from the TSA.[908]

President Obama begins his vacation in Hawaii.[909]

12/23/10

North Korea threatens a "sacred war" with South Korea with a veiled nuclear threat. South Korea says it will launch a "merciless counterattack" if it is attacked again.[910]

The Senate ratifies the new START treaty for U.S./Russian nuclear disarmament. The terms of the treaty require each country to cut its warheads by 30% and allow mutual inspections. Critics claim the U.S. got the short-end of the bargain because the Russians would be disarming mostly-obsolete missiles while the U.S. will be required to disarm a superior arsenal.[911] [912] [913] [914]

12/24/10

President Obama is again willing to flex the executive branch's muscles while disregarding Congress. The EPA will unilaterally restrict emissions on new power plants and oil refineries.[915]

Dec 2010

12/25/10

The Obamas celebrate Christmas with a Christmas tree ornament commemorating renowned Communist mass-murderer and atheist Mao
Tse Tung.

12/26/10

DHS Secretary Napolitano tells CNN's *State of the Union* that the U.S.
needs to tighten security on "soft targets" like hotels, shopping malls
and train stations. The Secretary also says that the invasive airport security procedures will not change in the "foreseeable future."[916]

After several days of rocket attacks on southern Israel, the Israeli foreign minister says that peace is impossible under current conditions.[917]

12/27/10

President Obama congratulates the Philadelphia Eagles for signing star
quarterback Michael Vick, saying everyone deserves a second chance.[918]
*Why would he insert himself into a controversy on behalf of a man who
murdered dogs for amusement? Incidentally, why is the president so obsessed with sports? To paraphrase Duke basketball coach Mike Krzyzewski, he needs to spend his time worrying about the economy instead of
sports.*

The 111th Congress added more to the National Debt than the first 100
Congresses combined. Each American is stuck with a $10,429 bill for

the past two years (*not including interest*).[919]

12/28/10

MSNBC host Chris Matthews, while discussing President Obama's birth certificate, asks, "Why has the President himself not demanded they put out the original documents?"[920]

The Chinese military build-up is now a viable threat to the Pacific region. China now has an anti-ship missile capable of sinking U.S. aircraft carriers. Japan is now shifting its military focus to meet a potential threat from China.[921]

12/29/10

Even though Congress did not pass the Cap and Trade Bill, President Obama is determined to ram his environmental agenda down America's throats. Beginning 1/2/11, the Environmental Protection Agency (EPA) will require permits for companies releasing greenhouse gases (including carbon dioxide).[922]

Executives at the Professional Golfers' Association (PGA) admire President Obama's free time. PGA producer John Kim said of Obama's fifty-plus rounds since taking office, "That's more than me! But then again, my job is ... golf. Wait, that doesn't seem right."[923]

Hugo Chavez disapproves of President Obama's ambassadorial nominee to Venezuela, Larry Palmer. Chavez taunts the U.S., "If the govern-

Dec 2010

ment is going to expel our ambassador there, let them do it. If they're going to cut diplomatic relations, let them do it." Soon afterward, the State Department revokes the visa of Venezuelan Ambassador Bernardo Alvarez.[924] [925]

12/30/10

A Chinese Defense Minister says, "In the coming five years, our military will push forward preparations for military conflict in every strategic direction…The modernization of the Chinese military cannot depend on others, and cannot be bought. In the next five years, our economy and society will develop faster, boosting comprehensive national power. We will take the opportunity and speed up modernization of the military."[926]

Obama makes a recess appointment of a new ambassador to Syria. The Bush administration severed ties following the Syrian assassination of the anti-Syrian Lebanese leader Rafik Hariri.[927]

12/31/10

Obama's goon squad tramples 1st and 4th Amendment rights in Hawaii. A local TV film crew tries to catch a glimpse of the president. Secret Service agents turn them away from the compound where he is staying. When the crew leaves, Secret Service agents and police follow them. As the crew parks in a gas station, the brownshirts surround the vehicle and command them not to film them and to turn off the camera. An officer reaches into the van and destroys the camera. The Secret Service refuses to respond.[928] *Is he the President or Der Führer?*

Dec 2010

Christians are attacked at a Coptic Church in Alexandria, Egypt. At least twenty-one people are killed. President Hosni Mubarak strongly condemns the attack saying that it bears the hallmark of "foreign hands" seeking to destabilize Egypt.[929]

Personal bankruptcy filings total 1.53 million, up 9% from 2009.[930]

CBS's Mark Knoller has compiled a list, "Obama's 2010: By the Numbers":

	2010	Since Taking Office
Speeches, Statements And Remarks	492	883
News Conferences and Press Availabilities	27	68
White House Press Conferences	6	11
Town Hall Meetings	17	40
Domestic Trips	65 over 104 days	111 over 176 days
Vacation Trips	6 for 32 days	10 for 58 days
Foreign Trips	6 trips/8countries	16 trips/25 countries

Dec 2010

Flights on Air Force One	172	328
Flights on Marine One	196	386
Interviews	107	254
Golf	29 rounds	57 rounds

Unemployment was 10% in the beginning of 2010 and 9.8% at the end of 2010.

The national debt was $12.3 trillion in the beginning of 2010 and $14 trillion at the end of 2010. It took President Obama and the 111th Congress just seven months to increase the National Debt an extra $1 trillion.[931][932]

Energy and food prices climb dramatically in December. Home heating oil has jumped 12.3% and fresh and dry vegetables have skyrocketed 22.8%.[933]

More than 1 million homes are repossessed in 2010.[934]

December unemployment = 9.4%.
Real unemployment = 16.7%.[935]

Dec 2010

1/1/11

Ten thousand people will become eligible for Medicare each day for the next nineteen years. The system could become bankrupt by 2017.[1]

Bloodshed, turmoil and social unrest surround the disputed election of President Laurent Gbagbo of the Ivory Coast. Gbagbo refuses to take President Obama's phone call to discuss options for a peaceful resolution.[2]

1/2/11

Austan Goolsbee, the president's Chief Economic Adviser, says it would be catastrophic for Congress not to raise the debt ceiling. The federal government will soon hit the current debt ceiling of $14.3 trillion, which was raised less than a year ago.[3] *It is even more irresponsible to rack up mountains of debt without any assurances that your credit limit will be raised. It is as childish for the White House to demand the right to saddle future generations with debt as it would be for the U.S. to demand that China buy our debt.*

1/4/11

DHS Secretary Napolitano says that Israeli-style airport security would not work in the U.S. The Israelis use profiling to screen travelers. Napolitano says the Israeli method may be practical in a country of 7.3 million but not for a nation of 308 million.[4]

1/5/11

The House introduces H.R. 2, "Repealing The Job-Killing Health Care Law Act."[5]

The Federal Communications Commission (FCC) "asks" software app developers to create apps that let users know when their service providers are interfering with content.[6]

Robert Gibbs resigns as White House Press Secretary. *Now journalists will no longer have to suffer the beratings of an oaf with half their IQ and ability.*

China's military technology is advancing faster than previously thought. Not only have they developed a ballistic missile capable of attacking aircraft carriers and warships, but they may have developed a radar-evading fighter plane.[7]

The World Bank is trying to promote the use of Chinese currency by issuing yuan-denominated bonds for the first time. The World Bank issues two-year bonds and raises $76 million.[8]

1/6/11

Treasury Secretary Geithner is asking congress to raise the debt ceiling. The debt ceiling was last raised less than eleven months ago on February 13, 2010.[9] *Apparently, $2 trillion wasn't enough.*

While food and energy prices are soaring, Americans filing for first-time unemployment jumps from 410,000 last week to 445,000 this week, the biggest one-week jump in six months.[10]

The Defense Department is facing budget cuts by 2015. Defense Secretary Gates says, "What had been a culture of endless money…will become a culture of savings and restraint." The Army will cut active duty soldiers by 27,000 and the Marines by 15,000 to 20,000.[11]

The Pentagon plans to send an additional 1,400 Marines to Afghanistan for a spring surge. Commanders are hoping to defeat an anticipated Taliban offensive before President Obama's mandated troop reduction in July.[12]

1/7/11

President Obama hails the success of the 9.4% unemployment rate. The president chirps, "The trend is clear—the pace of hiring is beginning to pick up…We've got a big hole that we're digging ourselves out of."[13]

The White House is drafting the "National Strategy for Trusted Identities in Cyberspace" to create Internet IDs for Americans.[14]

French President Nicolas Sarkozy condemns the "religious cleansing" of Christians throughout the Middle East.[15] *Just as nature abhors a vacuum, the world abhors a lack of moral authority. Thank you, President Sarkozy, for filling that void.*

China gives the Euro a thumbs-up. The central bank's Deputy Governor Yi Gang says, "The Euro and the European financial markets are an important part of the global financial system and were, are and will be one of the most important investment areas for China's foreign-exchange reserves."[16]

1/8/11

A mentally ill gunman, Jared Lee Loughner, shoots and critically wounds Representative Gabrielle Giffords (D-AZ). Loughner's shooting spree killed a federal judge and five others. Seventeen people were wounded during the rampage.[17] *The liberal press and politicians immediately blamed Sarah Palin and conservatives for creating an anti-government climate. By the way, these are the same people who warned the public "not to jump to conclusions" after Major Nidal Hassan shouted "Allahu Akbar" while killing Americans at Fort Hood.*

Liberals stuck to their motto and "didn't let a good crisis go to waste." Some Democrats exploited the tragedy to advocate for more gun control. Ironically, their arguments contradict their counter-arguments to things like sex and violence on TV, video games and music (i.e.—"you can't pin the actions of a diseased mind on Ozzy Osborne, Judas Priest, etc.").

1/9/11

For the eleventy-thousandth time, the Obama administration criticizes Israel's settlement construction in East Jerusalem.[18] *President Obama has given birth to a secondary problem regarding the diktats he issues to Israel. Regardless of the wisdom of the president's agenda, every time Israel (or North Korea, Iran, EU, etc.) laughingly defies his demands, he*

Jan 2011

squanders U.S. prestige. Spending his political capital as profligately as he spends borrowed money from China lightens the weight of his words.

The Defense Department reassesses its estimates of China's military. China unveils its stealth fighter jet during Defense Secretary Gates's visit. Gates says, "They clearly have potential to put some of our capabilities at risk. We have to pay attention to them, we have to respond appropriately with our own programs."[19]

1/10/11

Now that the federal government has mandated that citizens have health insurance, they are now trying to decide what it should cover.[20]

Arizona's Pima County Sheriff Clarence Dupnik identifies Rush Limbaugh as the cause of Saturday's shooting. Dupnik, a Democrat, believes, "(Limbaugh) attacks people, angers them against government, angers them against elected officials and that kind of behavior in my opinion is not without consequences…The vitriol affects the (unstable) personality that we are talking about. You can say, 'Oh no, it doesn't,' but my opinion is that it does."[21] *Candidate Obama encouraged supporters to "argue with your neighbors… get in their face." The future President also told his backers, "If they bring a knife to the fight, we bring a gun."*

China snubs Defense Secretary Gates's invitation to discuss nuclear strategy. Gates tries to recover his composure by telling reporters that he is "pleased" that China will "consider and study" his plan for a nuclear dialogue.[22] *This is yet another unimpressive agreement to agree.*

1/11/11

The Fed plans to buy up roughly $75 billion of Treasuries per month, plus another $30 billion from its mortgage holdings.[23]

Home values have dropped 26% since June 2006.[24] *Waiting for the stimulus to take effect is like Waiting for Godot.*

President Obama declares, "We don't have a stronger friend and stronger ally than Nicolas Sarkozy and the French people."[25] *Nothing against France, but after all the times Obama has snubbed Britain and Israel, he's probably right.*

Defense Secretary Gates warns that North Korea will have the technology to strike the continental U.S. within five years.[26]

1/12/11

The President is putting together his *re-election* campaign. Fundraising should begin some time in March or April. He expects to raise about $1 billion to campaign for a second term.[27]

The Heritage Foundation and the *Wall Street Journal* rank Hong Kong as the world's freest economy. The U.S. ranks ninth, behind Singapore, Australia, New Zealand, Switzerland, Canada, Ireland and Denmark.[28]

European Union leaders expand the euro-zone bailout fund in an attempt to calm markets.[29]

1/13/11

Vice President Biden travels to Baghdad to cheer the new Iraqi government and "celebrate the progress they made." Iraqis greet the vice president's convivial visit with three bombings, killing two people and gunmen killing a jewelry shop owner.[30] [31]

Lebanese officials from Hezbollah pull out of the government. Lebanon's government completely falls apart, plunging the nation and the region into a realm of tense uncertainty.[32]

Tunisia also collapses into chaos and violence as rioters revolt against the government.[33]

1/14/11

Standard & Poors and Moody's, once again, warn that the U.S. is in danger of losing its AAA credit rating.[34]

States will be paying the federal government $1.3 billion in interest for loans they borrowed to shore up their unemployment benefits.[35]

A Mexican gunman fires across the Texas/Mexico border at American highway workers.[36]

The Russian parliament amends the START treaty allowing Russia to withdraw if it feels threatened by the West.[37]

President Obama eases travel restrictions on Cuba.[38]

1/15/11

Washington has officially pawned the U.S.A. with a national debt topping $14 trillion. It looks like this: $14,000,000,000,000.00. Each American is now in hock for $45,300 (*interest not included*).[39] *Fourteen trillion $1 bills, laid end-to-end, would wrap around the Earth almost 55,000 times. That would be a wall of dollar bills, approximately 180 feet high, wrapping around the Earth.*

DHS Secretary Napolitano scraps the Bush administration's "Virtual Fence" to protect the U.S./Mexico border. The program was supposed to incorporate radar technology with border enforcement. Secretary Napolitano determines the "Virtual Fence" under-delivers given its costs. Her new plan "will utilize existing, proven technology tailored to the distinct terrain and population density of each border region, including commercially available Mobile Surveillance Systems, Unmanned Aircraft Systems, thermal imaging devices, and tower-based Remote Video Surveillance Systems."[40]

As rioting accelerates, the Tunisian President flees the country while the Prime Minister takes over as interim president.[41]

1/16/11

Chinese President Hu Jintao continues the international onslaught against the dollar as the international reserve currency. Hu asserts, "The monetary policy of the United States has a major impact on global liquidity and capital flows and therefore, the liquidity of the U.S. dollar should be kept at a reasonable and stable level." He believes the current system "is a product of the past," but thinks it will take a while for the Chinese yuan to be accepted as a viable international currency.[42]

Venezuela's oil reserves surpass Saudi Arabia.[43]

The Tunisian government is still in chaos as lawless hordes run amuck. The outbreak of violence includes a gun battle at the Presidential Palace.[44]

1/17/11

Without government aid, the city of Detroit may be forced to close half of its public schools. As revenues decline, the city is obligated to honor its contract with the teachers' union.[45]

Dick Cheney enjoys a few "I told you so" moments in an interview. The former vice president says, "I think he's learned that what we did was far more appropriate than he ever gave us credit for while he was a candidate. So I think he's learned from experience. And part of that experience was the Democrats having a terrible showing last election."[46]

The White House rolls out the "red" carpet hosting Communist Chinese President Hu Jintao. President Obama throws a lavish state dinner in honor of the Chinese president's four-day visit.[47]

1/18/11

Two years into his presidency, Obama orders a review of government regulations that have hampered economic growth. In an op-ed in The *Wall Street Journal*, he writes that some regulations have placed "unreasonable burdens on business—burdens that have stifled innovation and have had a chilling effect on growth and jobs."[48]

U.S. states are facing a $2.5 trillion shortfall in pension funding. A big part of the problem is that politicians have spent decades overpromising workers benefits to get elected and leaving the mess for future generations to clean up.[49]

The World Economic Forum in Davos, Switzerland says the world needs $100 trillion in credit over the next ten years.[50]

1/19/11

Over 1,000 waivers have been granted from Obamacare.[51]

298 banks have been shut down since President Obama took office.[52]

H.R. 2, "Repealing the Job-Killing Health Care Law Act," passes the House by a vote of 245-189.[53]

The Arab League warns that chaos in Tunisia is an indication of general unrest throughout the Arab world.[54]

President Obama begins today's talks with Hu Jintao with a call for improved human rights in China. Hu responds that each nation must respect the other's core interests.[55]

President Obama emphasized the benefits of China's economic improvement at a press conference, "We welcome China's rise. I absolutely believe that China's peaceful rise is good for the world and it's good for America. We just want to make sure that that rise occurs in a way that reinforces international norms and international rules, and enhances security and peace, as opposed to it being a source of conflict either in the region or around the world."[56]

PART IV

Contents

TRANSPARENCY

1/20/09—Obama calls for transparency in his inaugural address.

1/21/09—Obama signs an executive order on Transparency and Openness in Government.

4/2/09—Obama calls for "transparency and accountability" when it comes to executive bonuses and salaries.

4/26/09—President Obama says "old habits and stale thinking" will not solve our national problems and that "we need to reform our government so that it is more efficient, more transparent, and more creative."

5/6/09—*Recovery.gov* is doing a poor job of allowing citizens to "track every dime" of the stimulus.

5/21/09—*Recovery.gov* still lacks the detail and transparency that was promised.

6/16/09—Obama refuses to disclose White House visitor lists to MSNBC, despite two rulings from a federal judge that the records be made public.

6/16/09—Obama tells CNBC, "What we're trying to do is increase transparency and openness."

8/4/09—The Obama administration refuses to release government documents related to Cash for Clunkers.

9/4/09—The Obama administration agrees to release some information about White house visitors, but the first eight months will remain secret.

10/30/09—Despite two federal court rulings, Obama still refuses to reveal the full White House guest list.

12/3/09—In the wake of Climategate, NASA refuses to comply with Freedom of Information Act requests regarding climate data.

12/7/09—Judicial Watch files suit demanding the White House visitor list, believing Americans have a right to know who is working with Obama to shape policy.

12/27/09—Press Secretary Robert Gibbs says the president is upholding his Obamacare transparency pledge since C-SPAN is broadcasting Senate health care votes at two o'clock in the morning.

12/30/09—C-SPAN's CEO sends Obama a letter encouraging him to fulfill his transparency pledge by making health care debates publicly broadcast on C-SPAN.

2/1/10—Obama admits that he "probably should have" kept his transparency promise regarding health care.

3/23/10—Obama again breaks his pledge of allowing the public to view legislation for five days before signing bills into law. He signs Obamacare thirty-six hours after its passage.

3/31/10—Despite his "sunlight before signing" transparency pledge, of the eleven bills Obama has signed into law, only six have been posted on *White-*

house.gov and none have been posted for five days.

7/29/10—The SEC proclaims that under the new Financial Reform law, it is exempt from having to comply with releasing information to the public under the Freedom of Information Act. Obama said the law will "increase transparency in financial dealings."

11/9/10—Vice President Biden meets with Earl Devaney about government transparency ... behind closed doors.

12/16/10—Obama breaks his five-day public viewing pledge again by signing the tax law within hours of the Congressional vote.

BIRTH CERTIFICATE

2/23/09—A soldier denies Obama's eligibility and sues for proof of birth.

7/14/09—An Army major requests a temporary restraining order from deployment to Afghanistan, citing Obama is not a legitimate President since he is not a natural born citizen.

7/15/09—Instead of answering the major's challenge, the major's deployment orders are revoked; therefore, negating any legal standing for Obama to produce birth documents.

7/27/09—Hawaii's health director says America can relax; she's seen the birth certificate.

4/14/10—Lieutenant Colonel Terry Lakin will be court-martialed for refusing to obey deployment orders. Lakin believes Obama is not a "natural born citizen."

12/28/10—MSNBC host Chris Matthews discusses Obama's birth certificate, "Why has the President himself not demanded they put out the original documents?"

CHRISTIANITY

4/14/09—Obama speaks at Georgetown University and requires them to hide all symbols and references to Christianity.

5/7/09—Obama signs a proclamation acknowledging the National Day of Prayer and cancels attending a church service and a prayer breakfast.

8/20/09—Obama panders to religious voters that people "are bearing false witness" that Obamacare includes death panels, care for illegals, and abortions.

12/4/09—White House Social Secretary, Desiree Rogers, says, "The Obamas were planning a 'non-religious' Christmas."

12/25/09—The Obamas celebrate their "non-religious" Christmas with a tree ornament commemorating renowned communist mass-murderer and atheist Mao Tse Tung.

2/24/10—Ordained minister and Marine Corps veteran, Tony Perkins, is disinvited from speaking at the Military Prayer Breakfast for disagreeing with Obama's "don't ask, don't tell" policy.

4/1/10—Obama says that instead of going to church he receives daily prayers e-mailed to him from pastors around the country.

9/15/10—Obama misquotes the Declaration of Independence, conspicuously omitting that all men are endowed by "their Creator" with certain unalienable rights.

9/29/10—As elections approach, Obama is talking more about Jesus.

10/18/10—Obama again quotes the Declaration of Independence, leaving out "the Creator."

10/31/10—Muslim fanatics in Iraq kill Fifty-eight Christians and two priests.

12/31/10—At least twenty-one Christians are killed at a Coptic church in Alexandria, Egypt.

1/7/11—French President Nicolas Sarkozy condemns the "religious cleansing" of Christians throughout the Middle East.

TOP PRIORITY

2/11/09—Obama says the needs of consumers are his top priority.

4/9/09— "We will not rest" until veterans are no longer homeless.

5/1/09—Obama addresses swine flu concerns, "And throughout this process, my top priority has been the health and the safety of the American people."

5/11/09—"I <u>will not rest</u>" until Obamacare is passed.

5/29/09—Obama says, "Our <u>top priority</u> is public safety" with regard to hurricanes.

5/30/09—Obama says military families are heroes, too, and they are a <u>top priority</u>.

7/15/09—When Obama appoints Charles Bolden as NASA administrator, he tells him <u>his foremost mission</u> is "to reach out to the Muslim world and engage much more with dominantly Muslim nations to help them feel good about their historic contribution to science … and math and engineering."

11/2/09—"We <u>will not rest</u>" until the economy is generating jobs.

11/5/09—Obama says environmental protection is a <u>top priority</u>.

11/23/09—"I <u>will not rest</u> until businesses are investing again, and businesses are hiring again."

12/3/09—Obama says that boosting exports by small businesses is a <u>top priority</u>.

1/21/10—Press Secretary Gibbs says, "The President works each and every day on making our economy stronger and putting us in a position to where we're creating jobs, businesses are hiring again. I can certainly assure the American people that that is <u>the chief focus</u> of the President of the United States."

1/28/10—"We <u>will not rest</u> until we build an economy that's ready for America's future."

2/1/10—Student loan reform "is something that I've made a <u>top priority</u>."

2/24/10—"To train our workers for the jobs of tomorrow, we've made education reform a <u>top priority</u> in this administration."

3/4/10—"I'm <u>not gonna rest</u> and my administration is <u>not gonna rest</u> in our efforts to help people who are looking to find a job."

3/16/10—"Creating jobs in the United States and ensuring a return to sustainable economic growth is the <u>top priority</u> for my administration."

4/27/10—Free trade agreements are a <u>top priority</u>.

4/29/10—"And that's why my energy security plan has been one of the <u>top priorities</u> of my administration since the day I took office."

5/26/10—"We <u>will not rest</u> until this well is shut, the environment is repaired and the cleanup is complete."

6/15/10—"Our <u>top priority</u> is to recover and rebuild from a recession that has touched the lives of nearly every American."

6/19/10—Press Secretary Gibbs says, "The <u>top priority</u> is to continue to work hard on getting this economy back on track and creating jobs."

7/8/10—"My administration <u>will not rest</u> until every American who is able and ready and willing to work can find a job."

8/12/10—Obama says securing the border has been a <u>top priority</u> since he took office.

11/13/10—Obama promises Russian President Medvedev that ratification of the START treaty will be his <u>top priority</u>.

12/22/10—Twenty-three months into his Presidency, Obama says the economy will be his "<u>singular focus</u>" for the next two years.

ABORTION

1/20/09—Obama says he would sign the Freedom of Choice Act.

1/22/09—Obama praises *Roe v. Wade* on its thirty-sixth anniversary of the decision.

1/23/09—Obama signs an executive order allowing international funding of abortion counseling.

3/19/09—Pro-choice fanatic Dawn Johnson, who equates pregnancy to slavery, joins the Department of Justice's Office of Legal Council.

7/10/09—Obama assures the Pope "of his commitment to reduce the number of abortions and of his attention and respect for the positions of the Catholic Church."

12/22/09—Representative Bart Stupak (D-MI) says the White House is pressuring him to remain silent about the abortion language in the Senate Health Bill.

3/4/10—Representative Bart Stupak (D-MI) says that twelve House Democrats will vote against Obamacare because of provisions that "directly subsidize abortions."

3/24/10—Obama signs a meaningless executive order upholding prohibitions against federal funding for abortions in Obamacare.

7/14/10—Abortion is now funded under Obamacare. HHS Secretary Sebelius is giving $160 million to Pennsylvania and $85 million to Maryland that will go into each states' high-risk insurance pools which will cover any abortion that is legal.

MEDIA ATTACKS

1/23/09—Obama attacks Rush Limbaugh.

3/3/09—The White House attacks liberal Jim Cramer for criticizing the president's budget.

3/16/09—The White House attacks Dick Cheney and Rush Limbaugh.

3/27/09—Press Secretary Gibbs paraphrases the president's opinion of criticism, "I think it's important to engage your critics … because not only will you occasionally change their mind but, more importantly, sometimes they will change your mind."

4/29/09—Obama snubs Fox's Major Garrett at his third primetime press conference because Fox chose to run regularly scheduled programming.

6/16/09—Obama refers to Fox: "I've got one television station that is entirely devoted to attacking my administration."

8/14/09—Obama warns the public to beware of ratings-hungry cable networks that are covering townhall meetings and inflating stories about Obamacare.

9/18/09—Obama's refusal to do an interview with Fox prompts Chris Wallace to say, "They are the biggest bunch of crybabies I have dealt with in my thirty years in Washington."

10/6/10—The Obama administration calls Fox News "a wing of the Republican Party."

10/11/09—War on Fox: "We're going to treat them the way we would treat an opponent," says White House Communications Director Anita Dunn.

10/15/09—White House Communications Director Anita Dunn proclaims Communist mass-murderer Mao Tse Tung as one of her two favorite political philosophers.

10/18/09—Rahm Emanuel says Fox is not a news organization because it has a perspective.

10/18/09—David Axelrod says Fox is not really a news station.

11/8/09—The *Los Angeles Times* reports that the White House is threatening Democratic consultants who appear on Fox.

11/14/09—White House Communications Director Anita Dunn attacks

Fox.

4/1/10—Obama tells CBS, "Well, I think that when you listen to Rush Limbaugh or Glenn Beck, it's pretty apparent, and it's troublesome, but keep in mind that there have been periods in American history where this kind of vitriol comes out."

5/9/10—At a commencement address Obama complains of "a 24/7 media environment that bombards us with all kinds of content and exposes us to all kinds of arguments, some of which don't always rank all that high on the truth meter ... information becomes a distraction, a diversion, a form of entertainment, rather than a tool of empowerment, rather than the means of emancipation ... All of this is not only putting new pressures on you, it is putting new pressures on our country and our democracy."

7/29/10—Press Secretary Gibbs vilifies Rush Limbaugh for denouncing Obama's auto bailouts.

9/16/10—Press Secretary Gibbs attacks Forbes for an opinion piece by Dinesh D'Souza.

PROPAGANDA

6/16/09— ABC will broadcast its nightly news from the White House to promote government run health care on June 24, 2009.

6/17/09—ABC refuses to allow paid-for advertisements that oppose Obamacare during its White House news broadcast.

6/24/09—Obama's ABC primetime newscast is little more than a one-man pep rally for Obamacare.

8/10/09—The National Endowment for the Arts (NEA) uses its budget to solicit artists to create propaganda promoting the Obama agenda. They promise to communicate more clandestinely until they figure out the legalities.

8/27/09—ABC and NBC refuse to run advertisements critical of Obamacare.

9/22/09—Yosi Sergant resigns from the NEA after his Soviet-style Agitprop is exposed. ("Agitprop" is the Soviet term for "agitation + propaganda").

10/17/09—Obama has a 2-½ hour secret briefing with media allies including Keith Olbermann, Rachel Maddow, and Maureen Dowd.

10/18/10—White House Communications Director Anita Dunn admits that during the campaign, "Very rarely did we communicate through the press anything that we didn't absolutely control."

10/28/09—The NEA chairman praises Obama as "the most powerful writer since Julius Caesar."

10/30/09—Hollywood actor turned White House aide Kalpen Modi is directly implicated in the Obama Agitprop scandal.

4/16/10—The Environmental Protections Agency (EPA) is offering $2,500 prize money to contestants who make the best video advertising that government regulations are "important to everyone" and how Americans can be more involved in making more regulations.

5/1/10—The Department of Health and Human Services (HHS) sends propaganda brochures to millions of seniors titled, "Medicare and the New Health Care Law—What It Means for You."

IMMIGRATION

2/9/09—Illegal immigrants sue an Arizona rancher for civil rights violations.

2/24/09—Juarez, Mexico's mayor moves his family to El Paso, Texas, for safety.

2/24/09—DHS affirms Mexican drug cartel violence has spilled over into Texas.

2/24/09—Texas Governor Rick Perry requests 1,000 National Guard troops.

3/12/09—Obama says he is considering Governor Perry's proposal, saying, "We're going to examine whether and if National Guard deployments would make sense and under what circumstances they would make sense."

3/29/09—DHS delays a series of workplace immigration raids.

3/29/09—Obama believes Mexican border violence has gotten out of hand but does not pose an "existential threat" to Americans.

3/29/09—Obama's remedy for the border he has never visited: "I think the main thing we need is better enforcement. And so this week we put forward a comprehensive initiative to assist those border regions that are being threatened by these drug cartels."

3/29/09—Obama says he is considering deploying U.S. troops to the border.

4/29/09—Obama says America cannot continue with a broken immigration system.

6/3/09—Officials discover an al-Qaeda video proposing to smuggle biological weapons into the U.S. through the Mexican border.

8/12/09—Funding for National Guard deployment along the Mexican border is stalled as the Department of Defense and the Department of Homeland Security feud over whose budget will pay for it.

8/16/09—The Mexican army takes control of customs at the U.S./Mexico border in a corruption crackdown.

9/9/09—Obama says Obamacare will not insure illegal immigrants.

9/11/09—Texas Governor Perry calls the Texas Rangers to the Mexican border. After six and a half months, Obama still has not responded to his request for National Guard troops.

9/18/09—Obama wants to extend Obamacare to illegals under the guise of immigration reform.

10/6/09—Detained illegal immigrants will now be housed in converted hotels due to overcrowding in jails.

10/10/09—Washington strips Arizona Sheriff Joe Arpaio of his authority to make immigration arrests.

10/11/09—Sheriff Arpaio says that he still has authority under Arizona law to keep making arrests.

3/15/10—Mexican "drug cartel hit teams" murder a U.S. Consulate employee and her husband in Ciudad Juarez. Their baby survived the attack.

3/16/10—DHS Secretary Napolitano ends $50 million funding for the "virtual fence" along the border, citing that it is costly, unreliable, and ineffective.

3/18/10—Obama signals his approval of a bill that would fast-track illegal immigrants to citizenship.

3/19/10—Obama joins Mexican President Calderon in slamming Arizona's immigration bill.

4/14/10—A strict immigration bill passes the Arizona state legislature.

4/23/10—Arizona passes an immigration law allowing law enforcement the right to investigate the immigration status of suspects who have been otherwise detained for probable cause.

4/23/10—Obama attacks Arizona's law as irresponsible.

4/27/10—Obama panders to Hispanic fears, saying, "But now, suddenly, if you don't have your papers and you took your kid out to get ice cream, you're going to be harassed, that's something that could potentially happen."

4/27/10—DHS Secretary Napolitano announces that the U.S./Mexico border is more secure than it has ever been.

4/30/10—Arizona Governor Brewer signs legislation forbidding racial profiling as part of her state's immigration enforcement.

5/9/10—Attorney General Holder tells ABC that the DOJ is considering suing the state of Arizona over its immigration law.

5/13/10—Attorney General Holder testifies that he hasn't even read the Arizona immigration law.

5/17/10—In human rights talks with China, the Obama administration exercises more self-flagellation by constantly citing the Arizona immigration law as our own home-cooked racial discrimination. "We brought it up early and often," says Assistant Secretary of State Michael Posner.

5/18/10—State Department spokesman P. J. Crowley defends the Obama administration's fetish for self-humiliation by mischaracterizing the Arizona law to the Chinese. Crowley also admits that he has not bothered to read the Arizona law.

5/18/10—DHS Secretary Napolitano has been bashing the Arizona law in the media. Today she testifies that she also has not read the law and is unburdened by any knowledge of what she is talking about.

5/19/10—Mexico's President Calderon rails against the Arizona immigration law from the White House lawn.

5/19/10—<u>Backdoor Amnesty</u>: John Morton, assistant secretary of DHS for Immigration and Customs Enforcement (ICE), says they will not do their job and assist Arizona in processing illegal immigrants. Morton tows the Party line and pitches for comprehensive immigration reform.

5/19/10—Senator Jeff Sessions (R-AL) publicly inquires why the Obama administration consistently refuses to enforce existing federal immigration laws.

5/20/10—Mexico's President Calderon receives a standing ovation from Congressional Democrats when he condemns Arizona while addressing the U.S. Congress.

5/25/10—Obama announces he is deploying 1,200 National Guard troops to the U.S./Mexico border (456 days after Governor Perry's request).

5/27/10—Senate Democrats block Senator McCain's (R-AZ) bid to have 6,000 National Guard troops deployed to Arizona

6/3/10—Obama meets with Arizona Governor Brewer and tries to get her to support comprehensive immigration reform. Obama promises to send staff to Arizona to brief them on a plan for border control.

6/5/10—About 2,000 people rally at the Arizona State Capitol in favor of the immigration law.

6/8/10—Secretary Clinton announces on Ecuadoran television that the DOJ will be suing Arizona over its immigration law.

6/16/09—Governor Brewer denounces Attorney General Holder for holding open the option of suing her state. "I hope [Holder has] read [the law] by now so that he knows what it exactly says," says Brewer (Secretary Clinton's disclosure in Ecuador hasn't hit the American news cycle yet).

6/17/10—Increased violence forces park closings in Arizona.

6/17/10—Secretary Clinton's Ecuadoran announcement hits the American media. Governor Brewer is surprised that the DOJ is so cowardly and discourteous that it would inform another country before informing Arizona.

6/19/10—Governor Brewer is incensed that Obama has not contacted her within two weeks of their meeting as promised. She says, "We are certainly under attack by the drug cartels and by the drug smugglers, the human smugglers. It's out of control. It's totally out of control."

6/21/10—Labor Secretary Hilda Solis says illegals have a right to fair wages. In a public service announcement, Solis says, "Remember: every worker in America has a right to be paid, fairly, whether documented or not. So call us, it is free and confidential."

6/21/10—Senator John Kyl (R-AZ) describes a meeting with Obama, "'The problem is,' he said, 'if we secure the border, then you all won't have any reason to support comprehensive immigration reform.' In other words, they're holding it hostage."

6/25/10—DHS Secretary Napolitano tells an audience, "The plain fact of the matter is the border is as secure now as it has ever been, but we know we can always do more."

6/25/10—Governor Brewer responds to Obama's failure to take action with a YouTube video showing that the federal government has posted signs in Arizona to stay away from certain areas because it is too dangerous.

6/28/10— Governor Jan Brewer (R-AZ) meets with White House officials to discuss the administration's proposal for addressing Arizona's immigration mess. The White House refuses to provide Arizona authorities with hard copies of their Powerpoint presentation. Brewer says the administration proposes to remedy Arizona's immigration woes with 525 National Guardsmen for six months.[1]

7/1/10—Pitching for his immigration reform, Obama says, "Our borders are just too vast for us to be able to solve the problem only with fences and border patrols."

7/1/10—Obama calls the Arizona immigration law "ill-conceived."

7/6/10—The DOJ files suit against Arizona for its immigration law.

7/7/10— For several years, Rhode Island has enforced tough immigration laws in a manner similar to Arizona's controversial law.

7/11/10—DHS Secretary Napolitano meets with Governor Brewer. They discuss Governor Brewer's request for National Guard troops, but not the DOJ's lawsuit.

7/28/10—Federal Judge Susan Bolton issues a temporary injunction against key parts of the Arizona immigration law.

7/29/10—U.S. Citizenship and Immigration Services (USCIS) staffers have drafted a memo for circumventing Congress and granting *"backdoor amnesty"* in case Obama does not get comprehensive immigration reform.

7/31/10—Obama commandeers the border deployment of 1,200 National Guard troops with the same degree of incompetence and confusion he used to mismanage the Gulf oil disaster. In other words, nobody really knows at which time how much of what is going where to do whatever.

8/6/10—16 percent of babies born in Texas are from parents who are here illegally. That equates to 60,000 babies a year being granted birthright citizenship.

8/9/10—Texas Governor Perry meets with Obama for thirty-four seconds and hand-delivers an invitation to tour the border. Perry's request is ignored.

8/12/10—As the Senate passes a $600 million Border Security Bill, Obama issues a statement saying that securing the border has been a "top priority" since he took office.

8/20/10—Secretary of State Clinton submits a report to the U.N. citing Arizona as a human rights violator. Secretary Clinton believes the U.S. can serve as a "model" to the rest of the world.

8/24/10—The federal government's *"backdoor amnesty"* program of not deporting illegal immigrants is in full swing across the nation. ICE is enforcing "*backdoor amnesty*" by ordering officials to dismiss deportation cases of illegal immigrants.

8/24/10—Obama submits a report to the U.N. Human Rights Council stating that minorities are still victims of discrimination and considerable progress is still needed. The report cites Arizona's immigration law as an example of how human rights are trampled in the U.S.

8/26/10—The DOJ delivers a second ultimatum to Sheriff Joe Arpaio demanding he explain his policies regarding the arrest and detention of illegal immigrants.

8/27/10—Governor Brewer demands an apology from the Obama administration for calling Arizona a human rights violator.

9/1/10—So far the federal government's border security for Arizona consists of thirty National Guard troops and fifteen billboards warning Americans to beware of foreign invaders in their own country.

9/1/10—The DOJ files a civil rights lawsuit against Sheriff Joe Arpaio. The sheriff is surprised because he and his county's lawyers have been cooperating with the feds.

10/2/10—Mexican pirates attack two Americans on Falcon Lake, which straddles the Texas/Mexico border. David Hartley is shot in the head as the couple flees for their lives.

10/16/10—ICE continues its *backdoor amnesty* program so successfully that deportation case dismissals are up by 700 percent in Houston, TX since it began a few weeks ago.

1/11/11—A Mexican gunman fires across the Texas/Mexico border at American highway workers.

ENVIRONMENTAL RUBBISH

1/26/09—Obama signs an executive order reversing Bush energy policies.

2/4/09—Energy Secretary Chu says California agriculture will vanish due to global warming.

2/5/09—Obama takes steps to regulate household appliances.

2/18/09—The Environmental Protection Agency (EPA) plans to regulate carbon dioxide as a greenhouse gas.

2/20/09—A satellite glitch reveals Arctic Ice has been grossly underestimated by 193,000 square miles.

2/24/09—Obama says America will double its supply of renewable energy in three years.

3/3/09—Obama vows to strengthen the Endangered Species Act.

3/23/09—Obama calls for greater "investment" in green energy.

4/17/09—The EPA opens the door to radically expanding its authority to regulate all greenhouse gases.

4/22/09—Obama calls for a "new era of energy exploration in America."

4/22/09—Obama's Earth Day flights use 9,000 gallons of jet fuel.

4/29/09—Obama supports a Chrysler/Fiat merger to make energy efficient cars of the future.

4/29/09—Obama promises his Cap & Trade system doesn't compromise jobs for the environment.

5/19/09—The White House announces its fuel-economy emissions standards for automobiles that, by 2016, will cost consumers an extra $1,300 per vehicle.

5/26/09—Chrysler applies to the Department of Energy for $448 million to research and develop electric cars.

6/16/09—Obama tells CNBC that he is not over-regulating the economy

6/23/09—For research into fuel-efficient electric cars, Ford will receive a $5.9 billion loan, Nissan a $1.6 billion loan, and Tesla a $465 million loan.

6/23/09—Obama signs an executive order to train out-of-work auto workers for jobs in the "green economy."

6/26/09—The House passes Cap & Trade by 219–212.

6/29/09—Obama announces new standards for light bulbs.

7/8/09—G-8 leaders agree to cut greenhouse gas emissions by 80 percent by 2050.

7/15/09—States receive $4.7 billion to weatherize homes. Obama says it is good for America; it will create jobs, insulate more houses, keep utility bills low, etc.

7/20/09—Secretary Clinton carries the apology tour baton to India and apologizes for the U.S.'s responsibility for climate change.

8/12/09—Prior to the Copenhagen summit, U.N. Secretary-General Ban says "We have just four months to secure the future of our planet."

9/2/09—The government refuses to curtail its idiotic environmental enforcement scheme of protecting the delta smelt fish while the agricultural economy of the San Joaquin Valley in California is being wiped out.

9/3/09—$535 million Obama stimulus funds guarantee a loan to Solyndra. After 6 months of due diligence the Department of Energy has determined that Solyndra is a wise investment and will create thousands of "green jobs." *On August 31, 2011, Solyndra filed bankruptcy and laid-off 1,100 workers.*

9/5/09—Obama's openly communist "Green Jobs" Czar, Van Jones, resigns.

9/6/09—The Obama administration says it did not ask Jones to resign.

9/16/09—The Obama administration believes that Cap & Trade could cost families $1,761 per year.

9/21/09—Energy Secretary Chu says Americans are basically spoiled brats who need to be disciplined by the government. Chu says, "The American public ... just like your teenage kids, aren't acting in a ways that they should act."

9/25/09—Obama talks about climate change at the G-20.

10/8/09—The Department of Interior blocks sixty drilling sites in Utah.

10/23/09—Obama lashes out at climate change non-believers.

11/20/09—E-mails leaked from East Anglia University's Climate Research Unit (CRU) demonstrate that the whole climate change myth is a hoax. The researchers manipulated evidence, suppressed evidence, sabotaged evidence, concealed evidence, rigged the peer review process, obstructed skeptics, and withheld data that would undermine their cause and stifled dissent. In short, the whole thing is a fraud.

11/24/09—Completely ignoring the exposure of fraud less than a week ago, Obama is hopeful that a climate deal can be struck in the upcoming Copenhagen summit.

11/25/09—"Global Warming Czarina" Browner is also in denial about the recent revelations of the climate hoax, citing that 2,500 of the "world's foremost scientists" are in agreement. She does not address that they agree on contaminated data.

12/2/09—"Science Czar" Holdren believes the Climategate e-mails have no effect on the "reality" of man-made climate change.

12/3/09—In the wake of Climategate, NASA refuses to comply with Freedom of Information Act requests regarding climate data, ostensibly because their "facts" were compiled with the same sloppy *mutatis mutandis* methods employed by the CRU.

12/7/09—The Environmental Protection Agency (EPA) announces that it will impose mandates on businesses that emit carbon dioxide as a greenhouse gas.

12/8/09—If Congress does not pass greenhouse gas regulation, Obama promises that he will circumvent America's elected representatives and impose his will through the EPA.

12/8/09—U.N. Secretary-General Ban states publicly that CRU's outright scientific fraud of using fantasy data has no effect on the truth of global warming.

12/9/09—CONSOL Energy, a coal company, blames environmentalists as they cut 500 jobs.

12/11/09—U.N. security gags journalist Phelim McAleer, a climate change skeptic, for asking "inconvenient questions."

12/17/09—Secretary Clinton announces the U.S. will contribute to a $100 billion climate fund agreed to at Copenhagen.

12/18/09—Obama delivers a speech in Copenhagen with generous amounts of soaring rhetoric but lacking substance and detail, stating the world must act "boldly and decisively" on climate change.

1/8/10—Obama announces $2.3 billion in clean energy manufacturing projects.

1/20/10—U.N. officials admit that claims of melting Himalayan glaciers are unfounded.

1/30/10—More evidence emerges that the U.N.'s Intergovernmental Panel on Climate Change (IPCC) report is based on false and bogus information.

2/1/10—The head of the U.N.'s climate change commission does not regret the IPCC's fallacious report, saying he can't be responsible for everything.

2/14/10—Professor Phil Jones of CRU admits there has been no global warming since 1995.

3/31/10—Obama reverses a ban on offshore drilling "but in ways that balance the need to harness domestic energy resources and the need to protect America's natural resources."

4/3/10—The Obama administration is imposing strict mileage regulations for vehicles. Beginning in 2016, new cars and SUVs will have to average 35.5 miles per gallon.

4/6/10—The Interior Department's Minerals Management Service (MMS) gives BP's Deepwater Horizon oil rig a "categorical exclusion" from an environmental impact analysis, concluding that an oil spill is unlikely.

4/16/10—The EPA is offering $2,500 prize money to contestants who make the best video advertising that government regulations are "important to

everyone" and how Americans can be more involved in making more regulations.

4/20/10—At 11 p.m. an explosion occurs on BP's Deepwater Horizon oil
rig. President Obama's mismanagement of the Gulf oil disaster was such a
debacle that it merits its very own section.

5/7/10—Despite the Obama administration's "relentless response effort" in
the Gulf, they have granted oil and gas companies twenty-seven exemptions
since the disaster began.

5/26/10— President Obama touts "green jobs" at the Solyndra plant saying
it is "leading the way toward a brighter and more prosperous future." *After
sucking up $535 million stimulus funds, Solyndra filed bankruptcy and laid-
off 1,100 workers.*

7/31/10—The EPA is considering cracking down on farm dust.

8/24/10—Obama uses the EPA to accomplish what he couldn't convince
elected members of Congress to do. The EPA tries to advance the climate
change agenda by trying to federalize the air-permitting process. Texas is
fighting back and refusing to cooperate.

8/31/10—Climate Change is again debunked for the fraud that it is. A review by the InterAcademy Council (IAC) skewers the U.N.'s Intergovernmental Panel on Climate Change (IPCC). The only warming that occurs
is the complete incineration of the IPCC and the climate change platform.

9/16/10—Texas sues the EPA for trying to enforce its climate change/greenhouse gas agenda. Part of the brief states that the EPA's agenda is based on the "thoroughly discredited," "factually flawed" sham science churned out by enviro-hacks and hucksters.

9/16/10—"Science Czar" John Holdren eschews terms like "global warming" and "climate change" in favor of "global climate disruption."

11/22/10—The Obama administration has bought approximately one-fourth of Ford and GM's total output of hybrid vehicles. $300 million in stimulus money plus other funds were used to buy 14,584 cars.

11/29/10—The U.N. Climate Summit in Cancun, Mexico, begins with an invocation of the ancient jaguar moon-goddess Ixchel. That's about the most interesting thing that happened.

12/17/10—Secretary Napolitano says the DHS will begin battling climate change.

12/24/10—The EPA will unilaterally restrict emissions on new power plants and oil refineries.

1/2/11—The EPA now requires permits for companies releasing greenhouse gases (including carbon dioxide).

GULF OIL DISASTER

3/31/10—Obama reverses a ban on offshore drilling "but in ways that balance the need to harness domestic energy resources and the need to protect America's natural resources."

4/6/10—The Interior Department's Minerals Management Service (MMS) gives BP's Deepwater Horizon oil rig a "categorical exclusion" from an environmental impact analysis, concluding that an oil spill is unlikely.

4/20/10—At 11 p.m. an explosion occurs on BP's Deepwater Horizon oil rig.

4/22/10—The search and rescue operation for eleven missing workers continues. The fire is extinguished and the oil rig falls into the ocean.

4/23/10—The Dutch government offers ships, booms and plans for creating sixty miles of sand barriers. The Obama administration tells them, "No, thanks."

4/25/10—The government approves plans to attempt to control the 42,000-gallon a day oil spill with remote control, underwater vehicles.

4/26/10—Underwater robots discover two leaks.

4/27/10—Interior Secretary Salazer pledges "every resource we can to support the massive response effort underway at the Deepwater Horizon."

4/27/10—The Interior Secretary's chief of staff, Tom Strickland, and his wife take a "work-related" vacation to the Grand Canyon that includes whitewater rafting. Strickland is also the Assistant Secretary for Fish and Wildlife and Parks.

4/28/10—The Coast Guard is conducting controlled burns of the oil slick that is now twenty-three miles from the Louisiana coast.

4/28/10—The government failed to adhere to their own 1994 response plan, which would have required them to have oil booms on hand. They had none, but they are trying to locate some now.

4/28/10—Coast Guard Rear Admiral Landry says the government has all the assets it needs to control the spill.

4/29/10—Obama finally sends DHS Secretary Napolitano, Interior Secretary Salazar and the Environmental Protection Agency's (EPA) Lisa Jackson to try to coordinate a response.

4/29/10—Obama assures that he is taking the oil spill seriously and is using "every single available resource at our disposal."

4/30/10—Oil is already coming ashore in Louisiana and residents detect the heavy odor of oil.

4/30/10—Florida Governor Crist declares a state of emergency for the Florida panhandle.

5/2/10—President Obama visits the Gulf Coast and disallows new lease approvals for offshore drilling until the disaster is investigated completely.

5/2/10—BP says it may take three months to drill a relief well and that it will pay "all necessary and appropriate clean up costs."

5/2/10—Interior Secretary Salazar promises to "keep the boot on the neck of British Petroleum."

5/3/10—Press Secretary Gibbs affirms that the Obama administration will keep "our boot on the throat of BP."

5/5/10—The list of countries that have offered help so far: Canada, Croatia, France, Germany, Ireland, Mexico, Netherlands, Norway, Romania, South Korea, Spain, Sweden, U.K. The U.N. has also offered to help.

5/5/10—The Coast Guard claims "There is no need right now that the U.S. cannot meet."

5/5/10—The Coast Guard confirms that oil is now washing up on shore.

5/11/10—BP, Transocean, and Halliburton executives testify before the Senate.

5/14/10—Press Secretary Gibbs tries to cover up the Obama administration's pathetic response by saying their response was "comprehensive and fast."

5/14/10—The EPA's Lisa Jackson says she has no authority to compel BP to use a particular oil dispersant.

5/16/10—MMS had given the Deepwater Horizon rig an "exemplary" award for its safety history, even though MMS failed to perform its duty of inspecting rigs once a month.

5/17/10—More than two weeks after placing a moratorium on offshore drilling leases until the Gulf oil disaster had been investigated, the Obama administration announces it will appoint a special commission to investigate the oil leak.

5/21/10—Press Secretary Gibbs says Obama lacks the authority to play a supervisory role in the Gulf oil disaster.

5/23/10—Louisiana Governor Jindal harshly criticizes BP and the federal government for not having a plan for cleaning up the oil spill at more than a month into the crisis. In despair, Louisianans get their own hands dirty and begin laying down booms and cleaning up the problem themselves.

5/23/10—In regard to BP, Secretary Salazar says, "If we find that they're not doing what they're supposed to be doing, we'll push them out of the way appropriately."

5/23/10—Even liberal Democratic heavy hitters are frustrated and unimpressed with the White House. Donna Brazile criticized the Obama administration for its weakness and James Carville criticized its lack of leadership.

5/24/10—Governor Jindal delivers a withering account of BP and the federal government's lack of effort in cleaning up the Gulf. "We've been frustrated with the disjointed effort to date that has too often meant too little, too late for the oil hitting our coast," he said.

5/24/10—As the federal government dithers with delivering oil booms, Governor Jindal is willing to build barrier islands.

5/24/10—The White House says they have been taking care of things "since Day 1" and they will hold BP accountable.

5/25/10—Obama rants, "Just plug the damn hole!"

5/25/10—Despite Obama's "Blame Bush" reflex, it turns out that it was his own administration's officials who circumvented the standard operating procedures of full environmental and safety reviews.

5/26/10—The Interior Department's inspector general finds that MMS employees have enjoyed lots of Internet pornography on their government computers as well as sports tickets and meals from those they are supposed to regulate.

5/26/10—Liberal Democrat James Carville unleashes a scathing critique of Obama's mishandling of the oil spill, basically calling him stupid, uncaring, uninvolved, lazy, and incompetent.

5/27/10—Obama makes his most pathetic public appearance to date. He personalizes the oil spill and takes responsibility without actually taking responsibility.

5/27/10—Obama does not return the call of Representative Steve Scalise (R-LA) whose district is hardest hit by the oil disaster. Instead, Obama plays golf and fundraises in California.

5/28/10—Obama spends three hours in Louisiana and says he takes responsibility for solving the crisis.

5/30/10—The federal government has changed course and is now telling BP "what to do" regarding the oil spill.

5/30/10—Governor Jindal discusses the government's incompetent response to the oil spill, such as trying to protect two out of 100 miles of shoreline.

6/4/10—Governor Jindal says Obama's drilling moratorium may cost as many as 20,000 jobs.

6/4/10—Senator Mary Landrieu (D-LA) criticizes the moratorium, pointing out that if the oil rigs leave the Gulf, they may never return.

6/5/10—The red tape is thicker than the oil polluting the Gulf. Government bureaucracies are fighting and overruling each other resulting in nothing getting done.

6/6/10—BP CEO Tony Hayward hasn't spoken to Obama since the day the rig exploded.

6/7/10—Obama makes an effete attempt at sounding "tough," saying he's trying to find out "whose ass to kick."

6/9/10—BP is capturing 15,000 barrels a day from the well.

6/11/10—The story surfaces that Obama turned away help from the Dutch.

6/13/10—Alabama Governor Bob Riley says that federal government bureaucracy and inertia is quashing any reasonable attempt to handle the disaster.

6/14/10—Governor Jindal takes leadership and orders the National Guard to start building walls.

6/14/10—Coastal residents struggle with a tangled mess of meaningless government paperwork in order to get compensated by BP.

6/15/10—Representative Boehner (R-OH) blasts Obama's response as "inadequate and disorganized."

6/15/10—Polls show that Louisianans think George W. Bush did a better job handling Hurricane Katrina than Obama has handled the oil spill.

6/16/10—BP's Chairman Carl-Henric Svanberg meets Obama and talks about how BP and the government care about "the small people."

6/16/10—Governor Jindal has sixteen barges vacuuming oil out of Louisiana's waters.

6/17/10—Governor Jindal is outraged when he finds out the federal government plans to thwart his cleanup efforts.

6/18/10—The Coast Guard shuts down Governor Jindal's sixteen barges to inspect them for fire extinguishers, life vests and manufacturer's verifications.

6/19/10—In an interview, Governor Jindal appears disturbed and perturbed that the federal government is stupid enough to halt a program that works.

6/19/10—"Pay Czar" Feinberg is dispatched to Louisiana to try to improve the ridiculously disorganized mess of processing claims.

6/20/10—Obama's seven-person Gulf Oil Spill Commission includes one optics engineer, one environmental scientist, and three members who have called for an end to offshore drilling. The remaining two are policy analysts.

6/22/10—Federal Judge Martin Feldman lifts the Obama administration's moratorium on drilling. He found that the Interior Department misrepresented and mischaracterized its evidence for ordering the moratorium.

6/22/10—Secretary Salazar vows that he will find a way to reimpose the drilling moratorium regardless of a federal judge's order.

6/22/10—A New York Times/CBS poll shows that 59 percent of Americans think Obama does not have a "clear plan" for dealing with the oil spill.

6/23/10—The federal government halts Governor Jindal's sand berm dredging efforts.

6/25/10—The IRS issues a diktat to the people of Louisiana warning them that the government will pursue them for the BP payments they have received!

6/28/10—Alabama uses snare booms to keep oil from washing ashore. The Fish and Wildlife Service orders them removed because they endanger turtles. Alabama also hired 400 workers to patrol beaches and scoop up oil. OSHA steps in and mandates that workers are limited to working twenty minutes per hour.

6/29/10—After seventy days, the U.S. finally accepts international help. So far, more than thirty countries and international organizations have offered to help.

7/2/10—Various skimmers and tankers are still available but unused for the Gulf oil cleanup; however, the EPA is unwilling to relax its regulations and allow them to be used.

7/3/10—A giant oil skimmer from Taiwan arrives in the Gulf for test runs. The skimmer can process 21 million gallons of oil-contaminated water per day. A frustrated Governor Jindal thinks it should be put to immediate use.

7/7/10—The federal government criticizes Governor Jindal's proposal to erect barrier islands. Jindal says, "This is the same bureaucracy that has turned down every other plan. They don't have an alternative. Their resolution is to let the oil come into the bay."

7/8/10—The Obama administration loses its appeal regarding the drilling moratorium in the 5th Circuit Court of Appeals. Secretary Salazar assures that he is determined to impose the moratorium anyway.

7/15/10—BP tests a cap that has successfully stopped the oil flow.

7/21/10—Thousands of Louisianans stage a "Rally for Economic Survival" calling for Obama to end the drilling moratorium.

7/27/10—A report shows that the Coast Guard did a sloppy job responding to the Deepwater Horizon explosion and did not even follow their own firefighting procedures, which contributed to the sinking of the rig.

9/20/10—The Gulf oil leak is declared permanently sealed.

10/6/10—The National Commission on the BP Deepwater Horizon Oil Spill and Offshore Drilling issues a report stating that the U.S. was slow to react to the Gulf oil disaster.

11/10/10—The owners of the Deepwater Horizon rig are upset that federal regulators have not begun forensic testing on the blowout preventer mechanism. The equipment was recovered two months ago and the evidence is corroding as regulators inexplicably stall their investigation.

11/10/10—Seven scientific experts complain that the Interior Department lied and intentionally misrepresented their findings to support the six-month moratorium of offshore oil drilling. The scientists say their reports were manipulated to suit the Interior Department's own ends.

11/12/10—Governor Jindal releases a book characterizing Obama as detached and uninvolved. Jindal says Obama was more concerned with projecting the right image and the political impact of the oil spill than he was with actually helping people.

HEALTH CARE

2/17/09—The stimulus bill has many hidden sections pertaining to health care.

3/5/09—Obama hosts a health care forum and says he will consider every voice and idea. History shows that he only considered "every voice" that agrees with him.

3/14/09—The White House is willing to tax employee health care benefits.

3/16/09—The White House plans to charge wounded veterans for treatment of their service-related injuries.

3/19/09—After receiving bad press, Obama drops his plan to charge wounded veterans.

4/9/09—Obama announces electronic health records for veterans.

4/14/09—Obama says controlling health care costs is the key to controlling the debt and deficit.

5/28/09—Obama urges Congress to pass health care legislation by the end of the year.

6/22/09—With the endorsement of AARP, Obama announces pharmaceutical companies will contribute $80 billion to Obamacare.

6/23/09—The President says Obamacare "will not add to our deficits over the next decade."

7/14/09—Senior Advisor David Axelrod says Obama would like bipartisan support for health care, but Democrats are willing to proceed without Republicans. Axelrod says, "Ultimately, this is not about process, it's about results."

7/16/09—A community-organizing group called Fund for the Public Interest is offering $11 to $16 per hour for "grassroots" support of health care reform.

7/17/09—The White House asks Congress for more control over Medicare reimbursement rates.

7/21/09—When asked if the health care law would outlaw private insurance, Obama replies, "You know, I have to say that I am not familiar with the provision you are talking about."

7/22/09—Obama appears on television to promote Obamacare.

7/23/09—Obama alleges that doctors intentionally mutilate children with procedures such as unnecessary tonsillectomies.

8/4/09—The Orwellian Obama administration requests that citizens notify the White House of any "disinformation" they hear about Obamacare, including "fishy e-mails."

8/6/09—Obama gives a health care pep talk to senators before they return home to face hordes of tea partiers and uppity natives.

8/8/09—Sarah Palin says "death panels" may be in the final health care bill.

8/11/09—Obama again accuses doctors of maiming and dismembering patients merely for profit. This time he accuses doctors of unnecessarily chopping off diabetics' feet.

8/14/09—Obama says health insurance companies hold Americans hostage.

8/15/09—An association of the usual leftists and browbeaten companies called "Healthy Economy Now" launches an Obamacare advertising blitz.

8/15/09—Obama invokes his own grandmother's death to promote Obamacare.

8/20/09—Obama panders to religious voters claiming that people "are bearing false witness" that Obamacare includes death panels, care for illegals, and abortions.

8/20/09—Obama says he would appreciate Republican support, but promises he will steamroll over them anyway.

8/20/09—Obama says illegal immigrants will receive emergency room care under his plan.

9/3/09—The IRS will need 16,500 more agents to enforce "acceptable" health insurance plans under Obamacare.

9/7/09—Representative Boehner (R-OH) says Obama has not met with Republicans to discuss health care since April.

9/9/09—Obama lectures a joint session of Congress about Obamacare saying it "will not add one dime to the budget deficit," nor will it insure illegal immigrants.

9/11/09—The White House and Congressional Democrats are already positioning themselves to pass Obamacare through the "reconciliation" process.

9/18/09—Obama cloaks extending Obamacare to illegals under the guise of immigration reform.

9/20/09—Obama appears on five Sunday talk shows to promote Obamacare.

9/20/09—Obama says the insurance mandate in Obamacare is <u>not</u> a tax.

9/21/09—The Obama administration sends a chilling threat to insurance companies for communicating information to their customers that fails to flatter the Obama administration sufficiently.

10/6/09—Obama stages a massive photo op with 150 doctors in the White House Rose Garden. Pre-ceremony pictures show White House staff handing out white coats to increase the appearance of legitimacy.

10/25/09—Health insurance companies' profits over the past year are about 2 percent.

11/9/09—Obama minimizes the issue of jail time to be served for citizens failing to meet Obamacare's insurance mandate.

11/16/09—Health rationing begins with the Preventative Services Task Force advising women in their forties that they no longer need annual mammograms; instead, women in their fifties should have them every other year.

12/7/09—Senator Harry Reid (D-NV) likens opponents of socialized Obamacare to supporters of slavery.

12/16/09—Obama says America will go bankrupt without Obmamacare.

12/20/09—Senate Democrats announce they have reached a deal on health care reform.

12/22/09—Representative Bart Stupak (D-MI) says the White House is pressuring him to remain silent about the abortion language in the Senate Health Bill.

12/23/09—Obama delays his Hawaiian vacation until Obamacare passes the Senate.

12/23/09—Amid controversy of special deals, giveaways and bribes, Senator Charles Schumer (D-NY) says that every state got special treatment in the Health Bill (of course, he was referring only to states with Democratic senators and congressmen).

12/23/09—Congressional leaders will forego the traditional conference committee process for approving legislation, opting for the deem-and-pass route.

12/24/09—Obamacare passes the Senate. The bill is fraught and laden with bribes, kickbacks, corrupt deals, and pork.

12/30/09—C-SPAN's CEO sends Obama a letter encouraging him to fulfill his transparency pledge by making health care debates publicly broadcast on C-SPAN.

1/5/10—Obama tells Congressional Democratic leaders that he wants to include a tax on "Cadillac" insurance plans.

1/11/10—Obama meets with SEIU, AFL-CIO, Teamsters, NEA, and other unions to hash out union-friendly terms in Obamacare.

1/13/10—Obama spends all day meeting with Congressional Democrats.

2/12/10—Obama announces that he will meet with both parties to discuss Obamacare on C-SPAN. It's really just window dressing since the deal is pretty much sealed anyway.

2/25/10—Obama attends his one and only bipartisan health care meeting broadcast on C-SPAN. Obama talks down to Republicans and doesn't seriously consider one word they say. Why should he? He already has his deal.

3/1/10—The White House says Democrats will pass Obamacare through the "reconciliation" process.

3/2/10—Obama bribes Representative Jim Matheson (D-UT) to support Obamacare by nominating his brother to the 10th Circuit Court of Appeals.

3/4/10—Representative Bart Stupak (D-MI) says twelve House Democrats will vote against Obamacare because of provisions that "directly subsidize abortions."

3/8/10—Rahm Emanuel, while completely naked, assaults Representative Eric Massa (D-NY), also completely naked, in the shower over Massa's wavering stance on Obamacare.

3/8/10—Obama stokes the embers of the debate by continuing to demonize insurance companies.

3/9/10—Obama bribes Representative Alan Mollohan (D-WV) for his Obamacare vote by calling off an FBI investigation against Mollohan.

3/9/10—House Speaker Nancy Pelosi tells an audience that Congress must "pass the bill so you can find out what's in it, away from the fog of controversy."

3/12/10—With overwhelming bipartisan support, Virginia passes the Health Freedom Bill that exempts its residents from complying with any insurance mandate imposed by the federal government.

3/12/10—Obama delays his trip to Asia to promote Obamacare.

3/15/10—Obama says he will not campaign for any Democrat who does not support Obamacare.

3/16/10—Utah passes a law protecting its citizens from Obamacare.

3/17/10—Idaho passes a law shielding its citizens from Obamacare's insurance mandate.

3/17/10—In a Fox interview, Obama will not discuss specifics of Obamacare and dismisses the importance of process. He comforts the nation saying, "By the time the vote has taken place, not only will I know what's in it, you'll know what's in it because it's going to be posted and everybody's going to be able to evaluate it on the merits."

3/18/10—Vice President Biden tells ABC, "You know, we're going to control the insurance companies."

3/19/10—Obamacare will also nationalize student loans. The only bank in the country that stands to benefit is the Bank of North Dakota— a fine plate of pork for Senate Budget Committee Chairman Kent Conrad (D-ND).

3/19/10—House leaders announce their $940 billion Obamacare compromise bill.

3/19/10—Caterpillar, Inc., estimates Obamacare will cost them $100 million.

3/19/10—Democrats have implemented the "doc fix" to try to make Obamacare look fiscally responsible.

3/21/10—The House passes Obamacare by 219–212.

3/23/10—Obama again breaks his pledge of allowing the public to view legislation for five days before signing bills into law by signing Obamacare thirty-six hours after its passage.

3/23/10—Virginia immediately sues challenging Obamacare on constitutional grounds.

3/23/10—Florida Attorney General also challenges Obamacare on constitutional grounds in a class action suit with other states. The number eventually totals twenty-six states.

3/24/10—Obama signs a meaningless executive order upholding prohitions against federal funding for abortions in Obamacare.

3/25/10—In a speech in Iowa, Obama dares Republicans to try to repeal Obamacare.

3/25/10—When an audience member asks why Obamacare doesn't include the public option, he replies, "Because we couldn't get it through Congress, that's why."

3/25/10—Fidel Castro congratulates Obama on passage of Obamacare.

3/26/10—AT&T estimates that its costs for complying with Obamacare will be $1 billion. 3M expects outlays of $90 million.

3/30/10—IRS Commissioner Shulman says the IRS will now be responsible for making sure taxpayers have "acceptable" health insurance.

4/1/10—Verizon announces that it will cost $970 million to comply with Obamacare.

4/3/10—Obamacare gives the Food and Drug Administration (FDA) power to conduct "postmarket device surveillance activities on implantable medical devices."

4/12/10—Georgia Insurance Commissioner John Oxendine sends a letter to Department of Health and Human Services (HHS) Secretary Sebelius refusing to comply with Obamacare's unconstitutional requirements.

5/1/10—HHS sends propaganda brochures to millions of seniors titled, "Medicare and the New Health Care Law—What It Means for You."

5/11/10—The Missouri General Assembly approves a statewide referendum for its citizens to decide whether to nullify Obamacare.

5/13/10—Fortune reports that it will be cheaper for employers to dump employees into the Obamacare Exchanges. "If 50 percent of people covered by company plans get dumped, health care costs will rise by $160 billion in 2016, in addition to the $93 billion in subsidies already forecast by the CBO."

5/21/10—IRS Commissioner Shulman swoons over the swarms of new tax regulations provided by Obamacare. He unveils the new 1099-K form. All businesses will be required to furnish information on all with whom they conduct yearly transactions exceeding $600.

5/24/10—The Department of Justice (DOJ) files a motion to dismiss Virginia's challenge to Obamacare, arguing that, "Congress has the authority under the Constitution's Commerce Clause to order Americans to buy health insurance."

6/17/10—In order to argue that Obamacare is constitutional, the Obama administration is forced to argue that the individual mandate to buy health insurance IS A TAX.

6/21/10—Kaiser Foundation research shows that those who have to buy their own health insurance have seen their premiums skyrocket by 20 percent since the passage of Obamacare.

7/6/10—Obama circumvents the Senate with the recess appointment of ultra-leftist Dr. Donald Berwick to run Medicare and Medicaid.

7/14/10—Abortion is funded under Obamacare. HHS Secretary Sebelius is giving $160 million to Pennsylvania and $85 million to Maryland that will go into each states' high-risk insurance pools which will cover any abortion that is legal.

7/14/10—The Stimulus Law has given power to HHS Secretary Sebelius to issue a diktat requiring each American to have his/her obesity rating included in electronic medical records that all Americans are supposed to have under the law.

7/31/10—Obamacare gives HHS Secretary Sebelius the power to make judgments that cannot be challenged administratively or through the courts.

7/31/10—Employees with really good plans (a.k.a. "Cadillac plans") will have to pay a 40 percent excise tax on their health insurance.

8/4/10—Prop C passes in Missouri. Missouri voters went to the polls to register their dissatisfaction with Obamacare by a margin of 3:1.

8/4/10—Obama uses commercials with Andy Griffith in his continuing campaign to try to persuade voters to like what he has already forced.

8/30/10—Opposition to Obamacare prompts HHS Secretary Sebelius to tell ABC that the Obama administration has "a lot of re-education to do."

9/9/10—HHS Secretary Sebelius sends a threatening letter to insurers who notify their customers of rate increases due to Obamacare. Sebelius writes, "There will be zero tolerance for this type of misinformation and unjustified rate increases."

9/9/10—In the upcoming midterm elections, not a single Democrat has run a campaign mentioning Obamacare.

9/20/10—Major health insurers stop offering new child-only policies because Obamacare requirements make it not worth pursuing.

9/30/10—The Association of American Medical Colleges announces that post-Obamacare doctor shortages will be 50 percent lower in 2015 than originally forecast.

10/2/10—HHS Secretary Sebelius says it is "flat-out wrong" that McDonald's cannot afford Obamacare. McDonald's offers "mini-med" programs for its low-wage employees. The *Wall Street Journal* says, "If only for the sake of her own credibility, at some point Ms. Sebelius is going to have to try to persuade people who actually know something about the industries she regulates."

10/15/10—Obamacare is raising health insurance premiums around the country. For example, in Connecticut, new rates jump from 19 to 47 percent, depending on the policy.

10/18/10—Boeing is asking its 90,000 *non-union* workers to pay much higher premiums. In a letter, Boeing writes, "The newly enacted health care reform legislation, while intended to expand access to care for millions of uninsured Americans, is also adding cost pressure as requirements of the new law are phased in over the next several years."

11/5/10—AARP increases its own employees' health insurance premiums, citing medical costs and Obamacare.

11/13/10—Doctors are getting very nervous as Medicare looks to cut benefits by 23 percent.

11/14/10—The Obama administration has allowed 111 waivers to Obamacare. Unions are heavily favored.

11/20/10—An SEIU affiliate in New York is dropping health coverage for

6,000 children of its members because of financial problems posed the State of New York and Obamacare.

12/7/10—Obamacare health waivers now number 222. His union friends are still being treated well.

12/12/10—A federal judge in Virginia rules Obamacare's insurance mandate unconstitutional.

1/5/11—The House introduces H.R. 2, "Repealing the Job-Killing Health Care Law Act."

1/10/11—Now that the federal government has mandated that citizens have health insurance, they are now trying to decide what should be covered.

1/19/11—H.R. 2, "Repealing the Job-Killing Health Care Law Act," passes the House by a vote of 245–189.

1/19/11—Over 1,000 waivers have been granted from Obamacare.

STIMULUS

1/24/09—Obama warns unemployment could reach 8.5 percent without the stimulus.

1/26/09—Obama lobbies Congress for the stimulus.

1/27/09—Obama lobbies Congress for the stimulus.

1/27/09—The bill allots $5.2 billion to "community organizing" groups, the majority of which will be going to ACORN.

1/27/09—Obama tries to sell the stimulus to CEOs.

1/31/09—Obama lobbies Senate to pass the stimulus.

2/1/09—European leaders are concerned about how Obama will pay for the stimulus.

2/2/09—France rejects the notion of an Obama-style stimulus for itself saying, "It would be irresponsible .. to increase our country's indebtedness."

2/3/09—Obama tells Katie Couric of the urgency of its passage.

2/4/09—Obama criticizes Republicans for not supporting the stimulus.

2/6/09—Obama says delaying stimulus is "inexcusable and irresponsible."

2/9/09—Obama says the stimulus will "save or create" 4 million jobs (90 percent in the private sector).

2/9/09—Obama says there are no earmarks in stimulus.

2/10/09—Treasury Secretary Geithner unveils the stimulus plan.

2/10/09—Obama says, **"As President, I expect to be judged—and should be judged—by the results of this program [the stimulus]."**

2/11/09—Republicans are excluded from stimulus process.

2/11/09—Obama falsely claims that Caterpillar, Inc., will rehire if the stimulus is passed.

2/11/09—Obama again says there are no earmarks in the stimulus.

2/12/09—Caterpillar's CEO rejects Obama's claim that stimulus will spark rehiring; in fact, he will probably lay off an additional 22,000 workers despite the stimulus.

2/13/09—The stimulus bill passes Congress.

2/17/09—Obama signs the stimulus bill into law even though it omits key promises made to taxpayers.

2/20/09—Obama tells mayors that "every dollar" of stimulus will be spent wisely.

2/22/09—Obama promises governors "shovels on the ground and cranes in the air."

3/3/09—Obama declares shovels are hitting the ground just fourteen days after stimulus passed.

3/19/09—Senator Dodd (D-CT) says the White House told him to include provisions in the Stimulus Bill that authorized AIG bonuses.

4/10/09—Obama is "starting to see progress" toward recovery.

4/15/09—Obama says the stimulus and other actions are generating signs of economic recovery.

4/20/09—Obama asks Congress to give $100 billion to the IMF.

4/23/09—Treasury Secretary Geithner says the downturn may be easing.

5/6/09—*Recovery.gov* is doing a poor job of allowing citizens to track every dime of the stimulus.

5/8/09—Obama threatens to take away $6.8 billion in stimulus money from California for cutting $74 million to *unionized* home health care workers.

5/11/09—The Obama administration projects the economy will rebound by year's end because of the stimulus.

5/28/09—The hardest-hit states receive the least stimulus funds.

6/5/09—The government has staged sixty-six events promoting the stimulus thus far.

6/9/09—Stimulus funding favors large, multi-national corporations over local contractors.

6/14/09—Vice President Biden brags about the results of the stimulus.

6/16/09—Obama is "confident" that robust growth of the economy will prevent tax increases.

7/2/09—After unemployment hits a twenty-six-year high, Obama says, "It took us years to get into this mess, and it will take more than a few months to get us out."

7/8/09—Many states are using stimulus funds to fill short-term budget gaps rather than long-term projects that the stimulus promised.

7/9/10—Counties that supported Obama receive twice as much stimulus money as those that did not.

7/12/09—President Obama says the stimulus has worked as intended.

7/16/09—Vice President Biden says, "We have to go spend money to keep from going bankrupt."

7/27/09—Tens of millions of stimulus dollars are being spent on repairing and replacing toilets.

8/26/09—Four thousand Massachusetts inmates receive $250 stimulus checks.

9/23/09—Vice President Biden says the stimulus is working better than expected and has already "saved or created" 500,000 to 750,000 jobs.

9/30/09—Obama breaks all spending records with $3.52 trillion for fiscal year 2009.

10/21/09—Eight months after passage of the stimulus, forty-nine of fifty states have lost jobs.

10/29/09—Shabby accounting practices and fuzzy math show that the government is inflating its stimulus-related job figures.

11/11/09—Preposterous stimulus claims keep mounting. The whole mechanism of accounting is too disheveled to assess its effects in many places.

11/16/09—The stimulus continues to "save or create" jobs that do not exist in places that do not exist like Arizona's 15th District or Connecticut's 42nd District.

12/3/09—Dumbfounded by high unemployment despite the miracle stimulus, Obama hosts a "jobs summit." The publicity stunt is a stocked pond of the usual leftists.

12/8/09—Obama unveils a multibillion-dollar second stimulus saying America must "spend our way out of recession."

12/9/09—$6 million in stimulus funds go to Mark Penn, Hillary Clinton's pollster. It "saved" three jobs!

12/13/09—White House Chief Economist Larry Summers says, "Everybody agrees the recession is over" and "by spring employment growth will start turning positive."

12/23/09—Treasury Secretary Geithner says the economy and job growth will improve by spring.

1/4/10—According to *Recovery.gov*, the average stimulus expenditure per job "saved or created" is $245,807.51.

1/4/10—The average number of stimulus projects in Democratic districts is 152 versus 94 for Republican districts. Democratic districts receive approximately twice as much funding as Republican districts.

1/8/10—Obama announces $2.3 billion in clean energy manufacturing projects.

1/26/10—The real cost of the stimulus is $862 billion considering the increased spending on unemployment benefits (future interest payments not included).

2/17/10—On the anniversary of the stimulus bill, Obama insists that it rescued the U.S. economy.

3/26/10—Another study shows that Democratic districts receive almost twice as much stimulus funding as Republican districts. Also, stimulus funding bears no relation to unemployment rates.

4/18/10—Treasury Secretary Geithner says the economy is rebounding faster than expected and that the U.S. is on a path of sustained job creation.

4/23/10—Vice President Biden foresees rapid job creation in the economy: "Well, I'm here to tell you some time in the next couple of months we're going to be creating between 250,000 jobs and 500,000 jobs a month."

6/1/10—Obama is using the Census Bureau to "cook the books" and inflate employment figures. The Census hires, lays off, re-hires and lays off workers multiple times. Each re-hire is counted as a "new job."

6/17/10—The White House announces "Recovery Summer" to celebrate the achievements of the stimulus package.

6/21/10—President Obama urges world leaders **not** to focus on cutting deficits. As usual, they ignore him.

6/21/10—Germany's economy minister says, "It's urgently necessary for monetary stability that public budgets return to balance. This is something we should also tell our American friends."

6/21/10—German Finance Minister Schaeuble responds, "Nobody can seriously dispute that excessive public debts, not only in Europe, are one of the main causes of this crisis."

6/25/10—Vice President Biden tells an audience, "There's no possibility to restore 8 million jobs lost in the Great Recession."

6/26/10—As Vice President Biden celebrates Recovery Summer, he asks a custard shop manager what he owes. The manager replies, "Lower our taxes and we'll call it even." Biden irately yells, "Why don't you say something nice instead of being a smartass all the time?"

7/14/10—The Stimulus Law has given power to HHS Secretary Sebelius to issue a diktat requiring each American to have his/her obesity rating included in electronic medical records that all Americans are supposed to have under the law.

9/6/10—Obama unveils another $50 billion stimulus plan, mainly devoted to infrastructure. He believes America should have a special infrastructure bank.

9/16/10—Los Angeles is a good case study of the ineffectiveness of the stimulus. The average cost for each job "saved or created" is $2,040,000.

9/23/10—Recovery Summer Ends.

10/6/10—Recipients of 352 stimulus projects have not disclosed $162 million of stimulus funds.

10/7/10—72,000 stimulus payments have gone to dead people.

10/7/10—17,000 stimulus payments have gone to prisoners.

10/12/10—General Electric (GE) has laid off 18,000 workers while receiving $24.9 million in stimulus grants. Obama's favorite corporate crony has also paid $0 in corporate income taxes despite earning $14 billion in global profits, $5 billion of which came from the U.S.

10/12/10—Obama admits to the *New York Times* that "there's no such thing as a shovel-ready project."

10/17/10—White House Advisor David Axelrod says that next year Obama's focus will be "to generate more growth and jobs."

11/22/10—Members of a Stimulus Panel meet to discuss "fraud, waste and abuse of Recovery Act funds." The panel meets at the Ritz-Carlton hotel in Phoenix.

11/22/10—The Obama administration has bought approximately one-fourth of Ford and GM's total output of hybrid vehicles. $300 million in stimulus money plus other funds were used to buy 14,584 cars.

12/22/10—Twenty-three months into his presidency, Obama says the economy will be his "singular focus" for the next two years.

1/7/11—Obama hails the success of the 9.4 percent unemployment rate. He chirps, "The trend is clear—the pace of hiring is beginning to pick up … We've got a big hole that we're digging ourselves out of."

BUDGET

2/22/09—Obama is working on a budget that raises taxes and slashes defense.

2/24/09—Obama pledges to review the budget line by line.

2/24/09—Obama says he has identified $2 trillion of budget cuts over the next ten years.

2/26/09—Obama submits his first budget requ3/4/09—Obama says he has redesigned the way contracts are awarded and will save $40 billion per year.

3/4/09—He also says he will reduce the deficit $2 trillion over ten years.

3/4/09—Obama will decrease non-military discretionary spending by 10 percent over ten years.

3/11/09—Obama signs the Omnibus Appropriation Act with 8,500 earmarks.

3/20/09—The White House says budget priorities will not be affected by forecasts of bigger deficits.

4/20/09—Obama asks his Cabinet to identify $100 million in budget cuts.

7/16/09—Congressional Budget Office (CBO) Director Elmendorf says, "Under current law, the federal budget is on an unsustainable path, because federal debt will continue to grow much faster than the economy over the long run."

7/16/09—Vice President Biden says, "We have to go spend money to keep from going bankrupt."

7/20/09—The White House is delaying the release of its congressionally mandated budget update.

9/30/09—Obama breaks all spending records with $3.52 trillion for fiscal year 2009.

12/16/09—Obama passes a $1.1 trillion spending bill laden with more than 5,000 earmarks.

2/1/10—Obama warns that the U.S. cannot "continue to spend as if deficits don't have consequences."

2/1/10—Obama presents a $3.83 trillion budget with a $1.6 trillion deficit.

2/3/10—Obama says debt can "hobble our economy" and "saddle every child in America with an intolerable burden."

2/3/10—Obama signs an executive order establishing a Commission on Fiscal Responsibility.

3/6/10—The CBO reports that Obama's budget plans grossly underestimate deficits. The report forecasts a National Debt of $20.3 trillion by 2020, with interest payments of $900 billion.

4/13/10—Democratic House Majority Leader, Steny Hoyer (D-MD), doubts Congress will pass a budget this year. *They never did pass a budget.*

5/18/10—Senate Budget Committee Chairman Kent Conrad (D-ND) blames House Democrats as the reason why Congress will fail to pass a budget this year.

6/21/10—President Obama urges world leaders not to focus on cutting deficits. As usual, they ignore him.

6/21/10—Germany's economy minister says, "It's urgently necessary for monetary stability that public budgets return to balance. This is something we should also tell our American friends."

6/21/10—German Finance Minister Schaeuble responds, "Nobody can seriously dispute that excessive public debts, not only in Europe, are one of the main causes of this crisis."

7/23/10—The White house is predicting a $1.47 trillion deficit, with government borrowing equaling 41 cents for every dollar it spends and estimates 2011 unemployment to be 9 percent.

9/30/10—Members of Congress go home to campaign even though the still haven't passed a budget.

12/14/10—Democrats roll out a $1.1 trillion, 1,900-page omnibus spending bill in the lame duck Congress.

DEFICIT

1/27/09—The Congressional Budget Office (CBO) estimates the deficit will equal 10 percent of GDP.

2/23/09—Obama says he will cut the deficit in half within four years.

2/24/09—Obama pledges to cut the deficit in half within four years.

2/24/09—Obama says he has identified $2 trillion in budget cuts over ten years.

3/20/09—The CBO forecasts a $1.8 trillion deficit this year.

3/25/09—Budget Director Orszag disagrees that U.S. debt is spiraling out of control.

3/25/09—Orszag also assures the deficit will be reduced by more than half by 2013.

4/14/09—Obama says controlling health care costs is the key to controlling the debt and deficit.

5/7/09—Obama proposes slashing spending by $17 billion...while also raising spending by $81 billion.

5/11/09—The White House projects a 2009 deficit of $1.84 trillion and a 2010 deficit of $1.26 trillion.

5/14/09—Obama warns of the dangers of running budget deficits.

6/3/09—Fed Chairman Bernanke warns that budget deficits threaten financial stability.

6/16/09—Obama declares he will cut the deficit in half by the end of his first term.

7/8/09—Obama says that continuing to borrow and spend is "potentially counterproductive."

7/12/09—The budget deficit tops $1 trillion for the first time ever.

7/16/09—CBO Director Elmendorf says, "Under current law, the federal budget is on an unsustainable path, because federal debt will continue to grow much faster than the economy over the long run."

7/16/09—Vice President Biden says, "We have to go spend money to keep from going bankrupt."

7/28/09—Treasury Secretary Geithner assures China the U.S. will shrink its deficit.

7/30/09—The budget deficit hits $1.3 trillion.

8/20/09—The Obama administration raises its ten-year deficit projection to $9 trillion.

9/9/09—Obama says Obamacare "will not add one dime to the budget deficit."

9/23/09—The Treasury handed out a gross issuance of $7 trillion for fiscal year 2009.

9/30/09—Obama breaks all spending records with $3.52 trillion for fiscal year 2009.

10/7/09—The U.S. budget deficit tripled, hitting a record $1.4 trillion for fiscal year 2009.

11/6/09—After signing the umpteenth unemployment extension, Obama says, "Now it's important to note that the bill I signed will not add to our deficit."

11/13/09—Obama announces that he wants domestic spending cuts to cut the deficit.

11/18/09—Obama warns America that too much debt may cause a double-dip recession.

1/30/10—Obama vows to tame the deficit.

1/31/10—Obama recognizes, "It is critical to rein in budget deficits" and calls for a Fiscal Commission to recommend deficit-reducing proposals.

2/1/10—Obama warns that the U.S. cannot "continue to spend as if deficits don't have consequences."

2/1/10—Obama presents a $3.83 trillion budget with a $1.6 trillion deficit.

2/1/10—Obama predicts $trillion-plus deficits for the next three years, falling to $700 billion by 2013 and rising again to $1 trillion by the end of the decade.

2/2/10—Barack Obama: "It keeps me awake at night, looking at all that red ink."

2/3/10—Obama says debt can "hobble our economy" and "saddle every child in America with an intolerable burden."

2/3/10—Obama signs an executive order establishing a Commission on Fiscal Responsibility.

3/6/10—The CBO reports that Obama's budget plans grossly underestimate deficits. The report forecasts a National Debt of $20.3 trillion by 2020, with interest payments of $900 billion.

4/27/10—Budget Director Orszag states, "Deficit spending will require increased borrowing abroad which will mortgage our future income to foreign creditors."

6/21/10—President Obama urges world leaders not to focus on cutting deficits. As usual, they ignore him.

6/21/10—Germany's economy minister says, "It's urgently necessary for monetary stability that public budgets return to balance. This is something we should also tell our American friends."

6/21/10—German Finance Minister Schaeuble responds, "Nobody can seriously dispute that excessive public debts, not only in Europe, are one of the main causes of this crisis."

6/27/10—Obama gives a great speech about the importance of cutting the deficit, how much it means to him and how he cannot wait to start slashing and cutting.

6/30/10—The national debt rises by $166 billion in just one day. Each household is saddled with an extra $1,500 in debt. This is only the third-largest daily increase in debt. The first and second largest one-day increases also occurred under Obama's steermanship.

6/30/10—The 2010 budget deficit surpasses $1 trillion today.

7/11/10—Obama's Debt Commission says debt is destroying the country and that "we can't grow our way out of this. We could have decades of double-digit growth and not grow our way out of this enormous debt problem. We can't tax our way out."

7/23/10—The White House is predicting a $1.47 trillion deficit, with government borrowing equaling 41 cents for every dollar it spends and estimates 2011 unemployment to be 9 percent.

10/5/10—Vice President Biden says he will "strangle" Republicans who complain about the deficit.

DEBT

2/24/09—Obama says America has a duty not to pass debt along to children.

2/24/09—Obama says he has identified $2 trillion in budget cuts over ten years.

3/17/09—The national debt hits $11 trillion.

3/20/09—The Congressional Budget Office (CBO) forecasts $9.3 trillion deficits over the next decade.

4/14/09—Obama says controlling health care costs is the key to controlling the debt and deficit.

5/2/09—The Treasury tells Congress to raise the $12.1 trillion debt ceiling.

5/2/09—The CBO projects next year's interest payments on the debt will be $172 billion.

8/8/09—Treasury Secretary Geithner asks Congress to raise the debt ceiling, adding, "Congress has never failed to raise the debt limit when necessary."

12/9/09—Congressional Democrats strategize how to raise the debt ceiling an additional $1.8 trillion.

12/16/09—The U.S. national debt has already exceeded the debt limit approved by Congress last February.

12/24/09—Congress raises the debt ceiling to $12.4 trillion.

1/14/10—The national debt has increased more than 16 percent since the President took office. At $12.3 trillion, it is $1.7 trillion higher in less than a year.

2/1/10—Obama warns that the U.S. cannot "continue to spend as if deficits don't have consequences."

2/2/10—Barack Obama: "It keeps me awake at night, looking at all that red ink."

2/3/10—Obama says debt can "hobble our economy" and "saddle every child in America with an intolerable burden."

2/3/10—Obama signs an executive order establishing a Commission on Fiscal Responsibility.

2/13/10—After seven weeks, Congress raises the debt ceiling, AGAIN, to $14.3 trillion.

2/26/10—Obama appoints SEIU President Andy Stern to his debt panel.

3/16/10—The national debt has increased by more than $2 trillion since Obama took office, according to the Treasury Department.

3/25/10—The CBO reports that government debt will equal or exceed 90 percent of GDP by 2020.

6/8/10—The Treasury Department projects that the U.S. National Debt will be $19.6 trillion by 2015.

6/21/10—President Obama urges world leaders not to focus on cutting deficits. As usual, they ignore him.

6/21/10—Germany's economy minister says, "It's urgently necessary for monetary stability that public budgets return to balance. This is something we should also tell our American friends."

6/21/10—German Finance Minister Schaeuble responds, "Nobody can seriously dispute that excessive public debts, not only in Europe, are one of the main causes of this crisis."

6/30/10—The national debt rises by $166 billion in <u>just one day</u>. Each household his saddled with an extra $1,500 in debt. This is only the third-largest daily increase in debt. Their first and second largest one-day increases also occurred under Obama's steermanship.

6/30/10—The CBO projects that the National Debt could rise to 87 percent of GDP by 2020, 109 percent of GDP by 2025 and 185 percent of GDP by 2035.

7/11/10—Obama's Debt Commission says debt is destroying the country and that "we can't grow our way out of this. We could have decades of double-digit growth and not grow our way out of this enormous debt problem. We can't tax our way out."

9/8/10—In just nineteen months, Obama has added more to the national debt than the first forty presidents combined.

9/30/10—The federal government ends Fiscal Year 2010 $2 trillion deeper in debt.

10/18/10—The Treasury Department releases data showing that since Obama took office, the National Debt has increased by more than $3 trillion.

12/27/10—The 111th Congress added more to the national debt than the first 100 Congresses combined. Each American is stuck with a $10,429 bill for the past two years.

1/2/11—Chief Economic Advisor Austan Goolsbee says it would be catastrophic for Congress not to raise the debt ceiling.

1/6/11—Treasury Secretary Geithner is asking Congress to raise the debt ceiling. The debts ceiling was raised less than eleven months ago on February 12, 2010.

1/15/11—Washington has officially pawned the U.S.A. with a national debt topping $14 trillion. It looks like this: $14,000,000,000,000.00. Each American is now in hock for $45,300.

TAXES

2/26/09—Obama will allow Bush tax cuts to expire in 2011.

3/14/09—The White House is willing to tax employee health care benefits.

3/25/09—Paul Volcker and Peter Orszag will lead a panel to discuss overhauling the tax code.

4/1/09—The government enacts the largest-ever tobacco tax.

5/7/09—Obama wants to double funds to the IRS, with a quadrupling of funds within five years.

6/4/09—Microsoft's CEO says it will have to move jobs overseas if Obama's tax plan is imposed.

6/6/09—To pay for Obamacare, Obama wants to cut tax exemptions for the wealthiest brackets instead of a broad-based tax.

6/11/09—The IRS proposes a tax on company-issued cell phones as a "fringe benefit."

6/16/09 - Obama is "confident" that robust growth of the economy will prevent tax increases.

6/26/09—As Vice President Biden celebrates Recovery Summer, he asks a custard shop manager what he owes. The manager replies, "Lower our taxes and we'll call it even." Biden irately yells, "Why don't you say something nice instead of being a smartass all the time?"

8/2/09—Treasury Secretary Geithner refuses to answer whether he would rule out tax hikes, saying, "We have to bring these deficits down very dramatically and that's going to require some very hard choices."

8/30/09—The AFL-CIO and Congressional Democrats support a "Wall Street Tax" of about one-tenth of 1 percent of every stock transaction.

9/7/09—Obama voices his support for taxing sweet drinks.

9/11/09—The U.S. will impose tariffs on tires made in China.

9/20/09—Obama says the insurance mandate in Obamacare is not a tax.

10/26/09—IRS Commissioner Shulman unveils his plan for "the globalization of tax administration."

10/30/09—Secretary Clinton tells the Pakistanis, "We tax everything that moves and doesn't move, and that's not what we see in Pakistan."

11/19/09—House Speaker Nancy Pelosi (D-CA) announces that any "Wall Street Tax" must take effect on an international scale.

1/16/10—Obama announces new fees for the nation's largest financial institutions to recoup TARP losses.

2/11/10—Obama says he is "agnostic" on the subject of middle-class tax hikes.

3/30/10—IRS Commissioner Shulman says the IRS will now be responsible for making sure taxpayers have "acceptable" health insurance.

4/2/10—At a townhall meeting, "Doris" tells Obama that "we are over-taxed as it is." Obama gives a seventeen-minute lecture of rambling, incoherent nonsense.

4/5/10—IRS Commissioner Shulman says the IRS will penalize the tax refunds of those who do not have "acceptable" insurance under Obamacare.

4/21/10—Obama considers the idea of a value-added tax (VAT).

5/21/10—IRS Commissioner Shulman swoons over the swarms of new tax regulations provided by Obamacare. He unveils the new 1099-K form. All businesses will be required to furnish information on all with whom they conduct yearly transactions exceeding $600.

5/27/10—Secretary Clinton opines that "the rich" need to pay more in taxes.

6/8/10—On tour in South America, Secretary Clinton encourages Latin American countries to increase taxes on the rich.

6/17/10—In order to argue that Obamacare is constitutional, the Obama administration is forced to argue that the individual mandate to buy health insurance IS A TAX.

6/25/10—During the Gulf oil disaster, the IRS issues a diktat to the people of Louisiana warning them that they will pursue them for the BP payments they have received!

6/26/10—As Vice President Biden celebrates Recovery Summer, he asks a custard shop manager what he owes. The manager replies, "Lower our taxes and we'll call it even." Biden irately yell, "Why don't you say something nice instead of being a smartass all the time?"

6/26/10—Obama wishes to levy a special bank tax as part of his financial reform.

7/21/10—Gold coin dealers are surprised that Obamacare tracks and taxes gold transactions.

8/2/10—Treasury Secretary Geithner believes the Bush tax cuts should expire and that "the rich" are always griping about taxes.

9/7/10—Obama opposes extending the Bush tax cuts for the top bracket.

9/10/10—Obama savages Republicans for holding middle-class taxpayers hostage in the Bush Tax cut debate.

9/30/10—Members of Congress go home to campaign. They are playing it safe by leaving Washington without voting on whether to extend the Bush tax cuts.

11/6/10—Now that Republicans will control the House, Obama calls for an era of compromise…except he will not budge on extending the Bush tax cuts.

11/17/10—Obama and Congressional leaders delayed a meeting on extending the Bush tax cuts until November 30, 2010.

12/4/10—The Senate blocks Obama's tax plan. President Obama accuses Republicans of holding the middle class hostage.

12/7/10—Obama is visibly upset that Republicans scored a victory by extending the Bush tax cuts.

12/13/10—Democrats characterize Obama's caving in to Republicans as weak.

12/15/10—IRS audits have increased by 11 percent in 2010.

FEDERAL RESERVE

3/18/09—The Fed launches a $1.2 trillion effort to revive the economy.

4/10/09—The Fed tells banks not to reveal results of stress tests.

4/29/09—The Fed shows a willingness to purchase more mortgage and T-bill securities than the $1.75 trillion that was originally planned.

5/27/09—The president of the Dallas Federal Reserve Bank says China is alarmed by U.S. fiscal and monetary policy and warns the Fed about printing money.

6/2/09—Treasury Secretary Geithner says there is absolutely "no risk" of the U.S. monetizing the debt.

6/3/09—Fed Chairman Bernanke warns that budget deficits threaten financial stability.

6/15/09—Technical analyst Robert Prechter says the U.S. is in danger of losing its AAA rating.

7/15/09—The dollar falls as notes from the Federal Reserve meeting are made public.

8/24/09— Dennis Hughes, president of the AFL-CIO's New York chapter, is appointed to the Federal Reserve Bank of New York's board of directors.

8/25/09—Obama calls Fed chairman Ben Bernanke to Martha's Vineyard to nominate him for a second term.

9/18/09—The *Wall Street Journal* reports that there is a proposal being drafted which would give the Fed unprecedented authority to regulate the salaries of tens of thousands of bank workers.

9/21/09—The Fed rejects Secretary Geithner's request for a public review of the books.

11/29/09—Chairman Bernanke cautions that transparency in the Federal Reserve and Congressional oversight would impair the economy.

12/8/09—Moody's says America is in danger of losing its AAA bond rating.

1/28/10—Ben Bernanke is re-confirmed as chairman of the Federal Reserve.

2/4/10—Moody's again warns that America risks losing its AAA bond rating.

2/7/10—Treasury Secretary Geithner says the U.S. will never lose its AAA credit rating, despite deficit spending without end.

3/15/10—Moody's warns that the U.S. is getting closer to losing its AAA rating.

5/25/10—Moody's again warns that the U.S. risks losing its AAA rating.

6/28/10—Banks forecast that the Federal Reserve will be "monster" money-printing soon.

7/12/10—The U.S. loses its AAA credit rating with China's Dagong Global

Credit Rating Company. The company has also downgraded Germany, France and the U.K.

7/14/10—Under the Financial Reform Bill, the Fed will be in charge of regulating all large, complex financial institutions.

8/10/10—The Fed will try to spur growth by buying more government debt.

10/11/10—The Fed has no clue where quantitative easing (i.e., printing money) will lead. Former economic advisor Christina Romer says the Fed is in unchartered territory and it is uncertain what will be accomplished by printing more money.

10/15/10—Fed Chairman Bernanke foresees another round of "quantitative easing."

10/21/10—Treasury Secretary Geithner informs the world's finance ministers that the U.S. will not be monetizing its debt.

11/1/10—The Fed signals "QE2," another round of quantitative easing. Almost every country in the world is outraged by the new quantitative easing program. The condemnations are too numerous to chronicle in this section, but many can be found in Part III.

11/9/10—China's Dagong Global Credit Rating Company downgrades U.S. Treasuries again from AA to A+ due to the Fed's recent policy of quantitative easing.

12/1/10—The Fed releases some details of the $3.3 trillion in aid it gave to U.S. and *foreign* banks. The Fed also bought $1.25 trillion in mortgages from Fannie Mae and Freddie Mac.

12/12/10—For the umpteenth time, Moody's warns that the U.S. is in danger of losing its AAA debt rating.

1/11/11—The Fed plans to buy up roughly $75 billion of Treasuries per month—plus another $30 billion from its mortgage holdings.

1/14/11—Standard & Poor's and Moody's, once again, warn that the U.S. is in danger of losing its AAA credit rating.

BAILOUTS

1/23/09—Freddie Mac taps Treasury for $35 billion.

1/26/09—Fannie Mae taps Treasury for $16 billion.

1/27/09—The Treasury bails out twenty-three banks.

2/3/09—Obama caps executive pay at $500K for bailed out Wall Street firms.

2/18/09—Obama unveils Homeowner Stability Initiative ("backyard bailout").

2/23/09—AIG seeks more U.S. funding.

3/1/09—AIG gets another $30 billion bailout.

3/11/09—Freddie Mac taps Treasury for $30.8 billion.

3/14/09—AIG executives receive $165 million in bonuses.

3/19/09—Senator Dodd (D-CT) says the White House told him to include provisions in the Stimulus Bill that authorized AIG bonuses.

3/23/09—Obama launches a $500 billion effort to buy banks' toxic assets.

6/10/09—"Pay Czar" Feinberg will oversee payment of bailout funds.

7/1/09—The Treasury Department bails out Central Pacific Financial, a small bank that does not meet its criteria. The bank was founded by Senator Inouye (D-HI) and is the bulk of his personal wealth.

8/6/09—Fannie Mae asks the U.S. Treasury for another $10.7 billion

9/20/09—Obama is willing to consider a bailout for newspapers if they will restructure as nonprofit businesses.

10/21/09—"Pay Czar" Feinberg slashes compensation at firms that received government aid.

11/1/09—Despite receiving $2.3 billion in bailout funds, CIT Group files Chapter 11 bankruptcy.

11/12/09—The Pension Benefit Guaranty Corporation may need tens of billions in bailout funds.

12/21/09—A University of Michigan study reveals that banks with political ties received more bailouts.

12/31/09—Taxpayer losses from propping up Fannie Mae and Freddie Mac are projected to exceed $400 billion.

2/27/10—Fannie Mae asks the U.S. Treasury for $15.3 billion.

5/5/10—Freddie Mac asks the U.S. Treasury for $10.6 billion

5/17/10—Obama's favorite bank, ShoreBank in Chicago, needs propping up. The Obama administration pressures Goldman Sachs, JPMorgan Chase, GE Capital, and Citibank to "contribute" $140 million while the government will provide tens of millions more.

6/13/09—Obama urges Congress to pass $50 billion in emergency aid for state and local governments to avoid "massive layoffs of teachers, police, and firefighters."

6/13/09—Fannie Mae and Freddie Mac bailouts have already cost taxpayers $145 billion and could go as high as $1 trillion.

8/9/10—Freddie Mac asks for another $1.8 trillion.

8/20/10—The FDIC closes Chicago's ShoreBank. Its assets will be bought by the Urban Partnership Bank, which is backed by Obama cronies Goldman Sachs, General Electric, and JPMorgan Chase.

12/21/10—Thirty-two states will be borrowing billions from the federal government to cover unemployment benefits.

WALL STREET

1/27/09—The Treasury bails out twenty-three banks.

1/29/09—Obama knocks Wall Street bonuses.

2/3/09—Obama caps executive pay at $500k for bailed out Wall Street firms.

3/1/09—AIG gets another $30 billion bailout.

3/14/09—AIG executives receive $165 million in bonuses.

3/17/09 –The White House tries to deflect criticism for its mishandling of AIG.

3/18/09—Obama demonizes AIG as an excuse to impose greater regulation on non-banking financial institutions.

3/19/09—Senator Dodd (D-CT) says the White House told him to include provisions in the Stimulus Bill that authorized AIG bonuses.

3/23/09—Obama launches a $500 billion effort to buy banks' toxic assets.

3/24/09—The Obama administration seeks the power to seize financial firms whose failure could disrupt the broader economy.

3/26/09—Treasury Secretary Geithner testifies that he plans to regulate and even seize and business deemed "systemically important."

4/2/09—Obama calls for "transparency and accountability" when it comes to executive bonuses and salaries.

4/5/09—Treasury Secretary Geithner says he may oust executives at banks needing aid.

4/19/09—Obama and the Treasury Department say they may convert their loans to the nineteen largest banks to common stock.

5/12/09—The Obama administration wants to regulate salaries across all of the financial industry regardless of whether they received bailout money.

6/10/09—The government takes a 34 percent stake in Citigroup.

6/16/09—Obama is proposing a plan that will give the government broad power to regulate and seize banks and financial firms whose failure could affect the broad market.

6/16/09—Obama tells CNBC that his not over-regulating the economy

6/22/09—Goldman Sachs makes a record bonus payout.

7/9/09—AIG seeks clearance to grant millions of dollars in more executive bonuses.

9/18/09—The *Wall Street Journal* reports that there is a proposal being drafted that would give the Fed unprecedented authority to regulate the salaries of tens of thousands of bank workers.

9/19/09—Obama stresses that tougher financial regulation need to be imposed globally.

10/10/09—Obama attacks the U.S. Chamber of Commerce and anyone else who criticizes his financial reforms.

12/11/09—"Pay Czar" Feinberg caps more bank salaries.

12/21/09—A University of Michigan study reveals that banks with political ties received more bailouts.

2/10/10—Obama doesn't begrudge huge bonuses to Wall Street CEOs. He notes that some professional athletes make even more money.

4/16/10—The Securities Exchange Commission (SEC) charges Goldman Sachs with a $1 billion securities fraud suit

4/16/10—Coincidentally, Obama and Senator Dodd (D-CT) are supporting a Financial Reform bill.

4/21/10—Obama "categorically" denies that there is any connection to the Financial Reform legislation and the SEC lawsuit.

4/22/10—Many high-ranking SEC regulators spend more time looking at Internet porn than doing their jobs.

4/27/10—Nobody is fired in the SEC porn scandal.

4/28/10—Obama discusses financial reform, "Now, what we're doing, I want to be clear, we're not trying to push financial reform because we begrudge success that's fairly earned. I mean, I do think at a certain point you've made enough money."

5/5/10—Republicans warn that the financial reform bill gives the government unprecedented authority to snoop into citizens' privacy through the proposed Office of Financial Research and the Bureau of Consumer Financial Protection.

5/25/10—Obama is trying to secure an international financial agreement that would require countries to mandate larger banking reserves.

6/22/10—Business leaders warn that Obama's policies are strangling economic growth. Verizon CEO Ivan Seidenberg says, "By reaching into virtually every sector of economic life, government is injecting uncertainty into the marketplace and making it harder to raise capital and create new businesses."

6/26/10—Obama wishes to levy a special bank tax as part of his financial reform.

7/8/10—The EU and the U.S. agree to share bank data under the pretext of fighting terrorism.

7/14/10—The Financial Reform Bill makes it easier to put unions, activists and environmental groups on corporate boards. The bill creates over twenty "offices of minority and women inclusion" and imposes "fair employment tests" on financial institutions.

7/14/10—Under the Financial Reform Bill, the Fed will be in charge of regulating all large, complex financial institutions.

7/21/10—Obama signs the Financial Reform Bill into law. For a tiny explanation of how awful it is, refer to Part III.

7/22/10—Obama supports the Paycheck Fairness Act that requires businesses to collect and provide data regarding sex, race, and national origin of employees.

7/23/10—Of the $5.55 billion of government bailout money received, Goldman Sachs put $4.3 billion in thirty-two entities, including overseas banks, hedge funds, and pensions.

7/29/10—The SEC proclaims that under the new Financial Reform law, it is exempt from having to comply with releasing information to the public under the Freedom of Information Act. Obama said the law will "increase transparency in financial dealings."

8/20/10—The FDIC closes Chicago's ShoreBank. Its assets will be bought by the Urban Partnership Bank, which is backed by Obama cronies Goldman Sachs, General Electric, and JPMorgan Chase.

10/12/10—General Electric (GE) has laid off 18,000 workers while receiving $24.9 million in stimulus grants. Obama's favorite corporate crony has also paid $0 in corporate income taxes despite earning $14 billion in global profits, $5 billion of which came from the U.S.

10/21/10—Obama attends a $30,400 per guest fundraiser with Google executives.

10/27/10—Six days after Obama's fundraiser, the Federal Trade Commission (FTC) drops its investigation of Google's data-mining transgressions.

AUTO INDUSTRY

1/26/09—GM cuts 2,000 jobs.

2/9/09—GM will invest $1 billion in a Brazilian operation.

2/16/09—GM says it could use $30 billion in aid.

2/16/09—GM will cut 20,000 jobs by 2012.

2/16/09—Chrysler says it could use $5 billion in aid.

2/17/09—GM asks for 16.6 billion and will cut five plants and 47,000 jobs.

2/17/09—Chrysler asks for $5 billion and will cut 3,000 jobs.

3/21/09—"Car Czar" Steve Ratner says GM and Chrysler may need more than $21.6 billion in aid.

3/29/09—The Obama administration pressures GM CEO Rick Wagoner to resign.

3/30/09—The Obama administration rejects GM and Chrysler's turn-around plans.

3/30/09—The administration demands that Chrysler partner with Italian company Fiat.

3/30/09—The government will be backing GM and Chrysler warranties.

4/1/09—GM requests $2.6 billion to build hybrids.

4/7/09—The Treasury Department "asks" Chrysler executives to sign waivers regarding their compensation.

4/10/09—The Treasury Department tries to force concessions from GM and Chrysler bondholders, banks, and creditors.

4/14/09—The government considers swapping its $13.4 billion loan to GM for common stock.

4/27/09—GM proposes a plan giving the federal government and the United Auto Workers 89 percent control of the company.

4/28/09—There is a tentative agreement to give the United Auto Workers 55 percent ownership of Chrysler.

4/29/09—Obama supports a Chrysler/Fiat merger to make energy efficient cars of the future.

4/29/09—"Car Czar" Steve Ratner demands that Chrysler close a deal with Fiat today.

4/30/09—Chrysler files for Chapter 11 bankruptcy protection.

4/30/09—Obama unveils a plan that "offers" Chrysler bondholders 29 cents on the dollar.

5/2/09—Small-firm bondholders are threatened and coerced by the Obama administration's insulting "offer."

5/8/09—GM's restructuring plan includes shipping many jobs overseas.

5/12/09—The Treasury denies Chrysler's request to spend $134 million on advertising.

5/14/09—Chrysler notifies dealers it will close 25 percent of its dealerships.

5/15/09—GM announces it will be closing 40 percent of its dealerships.

5/20/09—Three Indiana pension funds assert their rights as creditors in the Chrysler bankruptcy.

5/26/09—Chrysler applies to the Department of Energy for $448 million to research and develop electric cars.

5/26/09—The Obama administration disproportionately closes car dealerships that contributed to Republican campaigns.

5/28/09—The federal government stands to own more than 70 percent of GM with the United Auto Workers Union owning 20 percent.

5/31/09—Thirty-one-year-old Brian Deese is in charge of dismantling GM.

6/2/09—GM files for Chapter 11 bankruptcy protection.

6/2/09—The United Auto Workers union will get a higher stake in the new GM than other bondholders.

6/2/09—GM will close fourteen plants by 2012 and lay off 21,000 workers before the end of 2011.

6/2/09—The *Wall Street Journal* reports that the government will own 60 percent of the new GM.

6/2/09—Hugo Chavez welcomes Obama to the Marxist camp for nationalizing GM.

6/16/09—Obama tells CNBC that his not over-regulating the economy

6/23/09—For research into fuel-efficient electric cars, Ford will receive a $5.9 billion loan, Nissan a $1.6 billion loan, and Tesla a $465 million loan.

6/23/09—Obama signs an executive order to train out-of-work auto workers for jobs in the "green economy."

7/13/09—"Car Czar" Steve Rattner resigns.

7/15/09—Obama "strongly opposes" any effort to restore car dealership arrangements with GM or Chrysler.

8/30/09—GM announces a $293 million venture partnering with Chinese automaker FAW.

9/29/09—GM has made over $90,000 in political donations this year.

11/2/09—The Government Accountability Office (GAO) reports that the U.S. Treasury is unlikely to recoup all of its $81.1 billion of TARP bailouts for GM and Chrysler.

2/20/10—New GM CEO Ed Whitacre receives a $9 million pay package including a $1.7 million base salary.

4/23/10—New GM CEO Whitacre claims GM has paid the government bailout loan "in full, with interest, years ahead of schedule."

7/19/10—TARP Inspector General Neil Barofsky thinks the Treasury Department's "dramatic and accelerated dealership closings" were probably unnecessary.

8/5/10—GM, largely owned by the government, makes political contributions to the same politicians who regulate its existence.

11/3/10—GM will not have to pay taxes on future profits of $45.4 billion due to tax-loss carry-forward provisions.

11/17/10—GM's initial public offering raises $20.1 billion. The government's share

of the car company should fall to about 33 percent.

11/22/10—The Obama administration has bought approximately one-fourth of Ford and GM's total output of hybrid vehicles. $300 million in stimulus money plus other funds were used to buy 14,584 cars.

DEPARTMENT OF JUSTICE

2/18/09 —Attorney General Holder calls America "a nation of cowards" when it comes to race.

2/19/09—The Department of Justice (DOJ) demands that the Swiss bank UBS handover all private information regarding its U.S. customers.

3/31/09—The DOJ drops its investigation of ACORN voter fraud.

4/16/09—The Obama administration needlessly declassifies CIA interrogation memos.

4/16/09—The Obama administration considers legal sanctions against Bush lawyers who drafted interrogation memos.

4/17/09—The DOJ wins a default judgment against the New Black Panthers in its voter intimidation case.

4/20/09—Dick Cheney asks the White House to declassify memos showing the Bush interrogation techniques saved lives.

4/21/09—Obama says he is open to prosecuting Bush officials for their anti-terror legal advice.

4/23/09—Obama will release forty-four photos of terrorist-related interrogations.

4/23/09—Attorney General Holder will release any and all information relating to terrorism and the war on terror.

4/23/09—The White House says it does not support an independent panel to investigate terror-related interrogation techniques.

5/6/09—A DOJ inquiry determines that Bush officials committed serious errors but should not be prosecuted.

5/10/09—Dick Cheney accuses the White House of not releasing documents showing that Bush interrogation techniques saved lives.

5/12/09—The Obama administration now wants to block the release of interrogation photos.

5/15/09—The DOJ moves to dismiss the New Black Panthers voter intimidation case.

5/28/09—The DOJ claims it dropped the New Black Panther voter intimidation case after "a careful assessment of the facts and the law."

7/9/09—Attorney General Holder is still contemplating whether to launch a criminal investigation of Bush-era interrogation tactics.

8/9/09—Attorney General Holder is ready to name a special criminal prosecutor to probe Bush-era interrogation methods.

8/24/09—Attorney General Holder appoints John H. Durham as a special prosecutor to investigate CIA interrogations.

11/9/09—Attorney General Holder agrees to give the keynote address to the Council on American-Islamic Relations (CAIR), which has links to the Muslim Brotherhood and Hamas.

11/10/09—The DOJ sends a request to a news site requesting the IP addresses of all who have visited the site and orders them "not to disclose the existence of this request."

11/13/09—The DOJ announces that Khalid Sheik Mohammed (KSM), the 9/11 mastermind, will be tried in federal court in New York City.

11/18/09—Senator Grassley (R-IA) asks Attorney General Holder to provide information regarding DOJ lawyers who previously advocated for terrorist detainees, contending there may be a conflict of interest.

11/24/09—Senator Grassley (R-IA) sends a letter to Attorney General Holder demanding that he provide the previously requested information regarding DOJ employees who represented terrorists.

11/27/09—Obama's DOJ concludes that his friends at ACORN can be paid for its contracts prior to the Congressional ban on providing money to the group.

12/1/09—Dick Cheney criticizes Obama for projecting weakness, dithering over Afghanistan, trying KSM in New York, his disregard of the private sector and his uncertain belief in American exceptionalism.

1/28/10—The White House asks the DOJ to consider trying KSM somewhere else.

1/30/10—The DOJ clears Bush administration lawyers in the interrogation probe.

1/31/10—Press Secretary Gibbs states, "KSM will be executed for the crimes he committed."

2/9/10—Obama will not rule out trying KSM in Manhattan.

2/11/10—The DOJ argues in favor of warrantless tracking of cell phones, claiming Americans have no "reasonable expectation of privacy."

2/18/10—Three months after the request, Attorney General Holder sends Senator Grassly (R-IA) an incomplete, haphazard response that "at least nine" lawyers at the DOJ previously represented terrorists. Holder refuses to release their names and hasn't bothered to do a complete survey anyway.

2/26/10—For the third time, Senator Grassley (R-IA) demands Attorney General Holder provide a full accounting of DOJ lawyers who represented terrorists.

3/4/10—The Obama administration is dithering and flip-flopping on what to do with KSM. Today they are considering military tribunals.

3/11/10—Judicial Watch probes the DOJ's highly questionable decision to drop the ACORN voter fraud investigation.

3/12/10—Attorney General Holder failed to provide full disclosure to the Senate prior to his confirmation as attorney general.

4/13/10—The DOJ argues in federal court that search warrants are not necessary for law enforcement to read the contents of Yahoo e-mails older than 181 days.

4/16/10—After the story is made public, the DOJ withdraws its attempts to read Yahoo users' private e-mail without search warrants.

5/9/10—Attorney General Holder tells ABC that the DOJ is considering suing the State of Arizona over its immigration law.

5/13/10—Attorney General Holder testifies that he hasn't even read the

Arizona immigration bill.

5/24/10—The DOJ refuses to appoint special counsel to investigate the Joe Sestak bribe/election fraud scandal.

6/8/10—Secretary Clinton announces on Ecuadoran television that the DOJ will be suing Arizona over its immigration law.

6/30/10—Former DOJ lawyer, Christian Adams, says they were ordered to dismiss the New Black Panthers voter intimidation case for racially motivated reasons.

7/6/10—The DOJ files suit against Arizona for its immigration law.

7/6/10—Former DOJ lawyer Christian Adams testifies before the U.S. Commission on Civil Rights that he and other attorneys at the civil rights division were instructed to drop cases with black defendants and white victims.

7/14/10—The DOJ states that it will not sue sanctuary cities that refuse to cooperate with federal immigration authorities and enforce federal laws.

8/26/10—The DOJ suspends prosecution of the USS *Cole* bomber, Abd al-Rahim al-Nashiri. The DOJ tell the U.S. Court of Appeals, "No charges are either pending or contemplated with respect to al-Nashiri in the near future."

8/26/10—The DOJ delivers a second ultimatum to Sheriff Joe Arpaio demanding he explain his policies regarding the arrest and detention of illegal immigrants.

9/1/10—The DOJ files a civil rights lawsuit against Sheriff Joe Arpaio. The sheriff is surprised because he and his county's lawyers have been cooperating with the feds.

9/21/10—Obama's DOJ argues in a federal appeals court that it has the right to place GPS tracking devices on cars without warrants.

12/21/10—Attorney General Holder fears "radical citizens." Holder says, "The threat has changed from simply worrying about foreigners coming here to worrying about people in the United States."

PRIVACY

4/7/09—The Department of Homeland Security (DHS) sends out a memo that basically warns that anyone who is a conservative is a potential terrorist.

4/15/09—The National Security Administration admits it has exceeded the boundaries of the law by tapping e-mails, phone calls, and wiretaps.

4/18/09—FBI is expanding its DNA database to include people who are arrested and detained, but not necessarily convicted.

8/31/09—DHS approves U.S. Customs searches of all electronic data. Customs may now copy, download, or retain any electronic information without probable cause.

9/16/09—The White House is collecting and storing all sorts of data from social network websites, such as Facebook.

10/1/09—The Transportation Security Administration (TSA) plans to install 150 body-scanning machines at various airport checkpoints.

11/10/09—The DOJ sends a formal request to the news site, *Indymedia.us*, demanding they relinquish the IP addresses of all who visited the site. The government orders Indymedia "not to disclose the existence of this request."

11/12/09—The Pension Benefit Guaranty Corporation lost 1,300 citizens' very private personal financial data and social security information. It was found on a flash drive in an Ohio train station.

1/5/10—TSA agents prank travelers by placing vials of white powder among their belongings, and then scare them into believing they are being arrested for drug smuggling.

2/11/10—The DOJ argues in favor of warrantless tracking of cell phones, claiming Americans have no "reasonable expectation of privacy."

2/27/10—Obama extends provisions of the Patriot Act that allow the government to snoop.

3/10/10—Obama recommends mandatory DNA sampling of anyone who is arrested, regardless of whether charges are filed or convictions are obtained. "It's the right thing to do" to "tighten the grip around folks" who commit crimes.

3/16/10—More travelers complain that TSA body scanners violate their privacy.

3/18/10—The Government Accountability Office (GAO) believes it "remains unclear" whether body scanners would have detected the Underwear Bomber.

4/3/10—Obamacare gives the Food and Drug Administration (FDA) power to conduct "post-market device surveillance activities on implantable medical devices."

4/13/10—The DOJ argues in federal court that search warrants are not necessary for law enforcement to read the contents of Yahoo e-mails older than 181 days.

4/16/10—After the story is made public, the DOJ withdraws its attempts to read Yahoo users' private e-mail without search warrants.

5/5/10—Republicans warn that the financial reform bill gives the government unprecedented authority to snoop into citizens' privacy through the proposed Office of Financial Research and the Bureau of Consumer Financial Protection.

6/1/10—DHS Secretary Napolitano says she respects privacy concerns but maintains that airport security should still be strict.

6/19/10— DHS Secretary Napolitano promotes Internet monitoring to fight homegrown terrorism.

7/8/10—The EU and the U.S. agree to share bank data under the pretext of fighting terrorism.

7/13/10—Airlines and travelers are increasingly dismayed with the time consumption and privacy invasion of full-body scanners and aggressive pat-downs.

7/14/10—The Stimulus Law allows HHS Secretary Sebelius to issue a diktat requiring each American to have his/her obesity rating included in electronic medical records that all Americans must have under the law.

7/22/10—Obama supports the Paycheck Fairness Act that requires businesses to collect and provide data regarding sex, race, and national origin of employees.

7/29/10—Under the guise of fighting terrorism, the White House seeks greater power for the FBI to tap Internet activity without a warrant.

8/4/10—Despite their many statements to the contrary, it turns out that many government agencies can and do store electronic images from body scanners.

8/5/10—U.S. Marshals in Orlando are caught storing more than 35,000 naked body images captured from the controversial airport body scanners.

8/21/10—TSA pat-downs get a lot "friskier" using the palms-first, slide-down-the-body technique.

8/24/10—Airport body-scanning technology is now available in mobile vans, called "ZBVs." ZBVs can conduct warrantless searches by spying into people's homes and cars. They are currently roaming the streets of America, being driven by law enforcement agencies.

8/24/10—Washington D.C. is using "pre-crime" technology which is based on software algorithms that sift through enormous amounts of data to determine who, when, and where a crime may take place.

8/27/10—Obama's chief economist, Austan Goolsbee, proves that the Obama administration illegally snoops into citizens' confidential tax information when he cites tax data from Koch industries.

9/7/10—The TSA's airport scanners may be upgraded to address privacy concerns by showing a generic figure that highlights areas of the body that need to be checked.

9/13/10—DHS will test iris scanners that can detect identities from six feet away.

9/21/10—Obama's DOJ argues in a federal appeals court that the government has the right to secretly place GPS tracking devices on cars without warrants.

10/20/10—DHS Secretary Napolitano unveils new body scanners at JFK Airport but declines to volunteer for a demonstration.

10/27/10—DHS Secretary Napolitano says the military will be working with civilian cyber-security.

11/10/10—The Association of Flight Attendants Union denounces the TSA's aggressive pat-down screenings saying, "We don't want them in uniform going through this enhanced screening where their private areas are being touched in public. They actually make contact with the genital area."

11/12/10—TSA Administrator Joe Pistole and DHS Secretary Napolitano meet with travel industry executives and pilot associations to discuss increasing public outrage over airport screening techniques. People are also upset over inappropriate groping of children or taking naked body images of children.

11/17/10—The TSA is being hit with lawsuits over their naked image scanning and aggressive groping.

11/17/10—TSA is now threatening to impose $11,000 fines on anyone who refuses to submit to their searches.

11/23/10—The controversial full-body scanners are now being used in some courthouses.

11/23/10—The TSA allows certain government officials to be exempt from its unpleasant screening procedures while traveling commercially.

11/25/10—DHS stations approximately 300 surveillance cameras in downtown Houston.

12/2/10—Government agents use "hot watch" orders by issuing their own subpoenas. Without warrants, the federal government can track credit card transactions, store loyalty cards, travel reservations, etc. They have the ability to track all of this in real time.

12/2/10—The federal government refuses to disclose how many Americans' telephones, e-mail accounts, text messages, and other communications it has tracked and intercepted.

12/3/10—The TSA goes from a policing agency to a police-state agency. TSA is compiling a "watch list" of those who dare to question its ominous authority. For instance, CNN reporter Drew Griffin made the list for filing reports critical of the TSA.

12/6/10—DHS Secretary Napolitano will be launching the "If You See Something, Say Something" campaign.

12/12/10—The D.C. Metro Police will be coordinating random bag searches with the TSA.

12/16/10—TSA screeners at Los Angeles, Chicago, and Newark airports miss guns and bombs.

12/20/10—The *Washington Post* reports that the government is creating a vast domestic spying system, "The system collects, stores and analyzes information about thousands of U.S. citizens and residents, many of whom have not been accused of any wrongdoing." The FBI is compiling a database with thousands of names and personal information of its own citizens. The goal is to have every state and local law enforcement agency report to Washington.

12/22/10—An airline pilot posts a video on YouTube showing the laxity of TSA security. While flight crews and passengers are going through the strict screening process, ground crews just swipe a card. The TSA may punish the pilot for his insolence.

12/26/10—DHS Secretary Napolitano says the U.S. needs to tighten security on "soft targets" like hotels, shopping malls, and train stations. She also says that the invasive airport security procedures will not change.

12/29/10—Tammy Banovac protested TSA's invasive search procedures by stripping down to her bra and panties. She is now banned from flying.

1/7/11—The White House is drafting the "National Strategy for Trusted Identities in Cyberspace" to create Internet IDs for Americans.

DEMISE OF THE DOLLAR AS THE WORLD RESERVE CURRENCY

1/29/09—Russia and China call for end of dollar as the global reserve currency.

3/17/09—Russia calls for a supranational currency to replace the dollar.

3/18/09—A U.N. panel proposes to ditch the dollar as a global reserve currency.

3/23/09—China calls for a new reserve currency to be controlled by the IMF.

3/25/09—Treasury Secretary Geithner is "quite open" to China's proposal that the dollar be replaced as the reserve currency.

3/26/09—A U.N. panel of economists calls for an end to the dollar's dominant role.

4/1/09—Russia argues for the need of a global currency to replace the dollar.

4/2/09—The G-20 will move toward replacing the dollar as the world reserve currency.

4/5/09—Russia, China, Malaysia, Indonesia, Thailand, and Kazakhstan call for an international currency system to replace the dollar.

4/26/09—China blames the dollar for the global financial crisis and calls for reform of the global currency system.

5/18/09—Brazil and China agree to use their own currencies in all trade transactions instead of using the dollar.

6/8/09—The head of China's largest bank believes the U.S. government should start issuing its debt instruments denominated in Chinese yuan.

6/10/09—Russia may swap holding U.S. debt in favor of holding IMF debt.

6/16/09—Brazil, Russia, India, and China call for the end of the dollar as the global reserve currency.

7/5/09—India joins the international chorus questioning the dollar's legitimacy as a reserve currency.

7/9/09—President Medvedev uses the G-8 summit as a platform to call for the end of the dollar as the world's reserve currency. French President Sarkozy heartily agrees.

9/8/09—The U.N. proposes a global currency to replace the dollar.

9/24/09—Hong Kong-Shanghai Bank's David Bloom believes the Federal

Reserve's monetary policies are responsible for destroying the dollar as the global reserve currency.

9/28/09—World Bank President Robert Zoellick foresees the end of the dollar's dominance as the world's reserve currency.

10/5/09—Russia, China, Japan, Brazil, European countries, and Arab states are colluding to scrap the dollar as the world's oil trading currency in favor of a basket of currencies.

10/6/09—The U.N. calls for a new global reserve currency.

12/16/09—Arab states will be launching their own oil-trading currency to displace the U.S. dollar for oil transactions. "The U.S. dollar has failed. We need to de-link."

12/18/09—The deputy governor of the Bank of China says that the dollar's decline is inevitable since the U.S. insists on racking up higher and higher deficits financed by the U.S. Treasury.

2/15/10—The managing director of the International Monetary Fund (IMF) proposes ditching the dollar in favor of a new world currency.

2/26/10—Dominique Strauss-Kahn of the IMF again proposes a new global reserve currency.

6/19/10—Russian President Medvedev calls for the end of the dollar as the global reserve currency; he would like for the ruble to be one of the reserve currencies.

7/1/10—The U.N. issues a report calling for the end of the dollar as the global reserve currency in favor of special drawing rights (SDRs) with the IMF.

7/23/10—China's central bank, once again, calls for moving away from the dollar as the world's global reserve currency to a basket of diverse currencies.

11/1/10—After the Federal Reserve announced its intention to launch another round of quantitative easing, almost every major country denounced the dollar as a sound and legitimate currency. The condemnations are too numerous for this section, but many of them can be found in Part III.

11/24/10—China and Russia officially quit using the dollar when trading with each other. The new policy is not directed at challenging the dollar but at protecting their own economies.

1/5/11—The World Bank is trying to promote the use of Chinese currency by issuing yuan-denominated bonds for the first time.

1/16/11—Chinese President Hu Jintao continues the international onslaught against the dollar as the reserve currency. Hu asserts, "The monetary policy of the United States has a major impact on global liquidity and capital flows and therefore, the liquidity of the U.S. dollar should be kept at a reasonable and stable level."

APOLOGY TOUR

1/20/09—In his Inaugural Address, Obama says, "We will not apologize for our way of life."

1/26/09—In his *Al-Arabiya* interview, Obama says, "We sometimes make mistakes. We have not been perfect." The U.S. will "start by listening, because all too often the United States starts by dictating..."

4/2/09—Obama bows before the King of Saudi Arabia.

4/3/09—Obama tells a group in Strasbourg, France, "There have been times where America's shown arrogance and been dismissive, even derisive."

4/4/09—Obama thinks American exceptionalism isn't very exceptional.

4/5/09—Obama reminds the world that the U.S. is the only country that ever used nuclear arms.

4/6/09—Obama debases the U.S. in Turkey.

4/16/09—In an op-ed circulated throughout Latin America, Obama writes that, prior to his administration, the U.S. has not been properly engaged. Of course, he apologizes.

4/18/09—Obama apologizes for the U.S. at the Summit of the Americas.

4/22/09—Treasury Secretary Geithner accepts responsibility for the global economic crisis.

7/7/09—When meeting with Medvedev and Putin, Obama says, "I think it's very important that I come before you with some humility. I think in the past there's been a tendency for the United States to lecture rather than listen."

7/20/09—Secretary Clinton carries the apology tour baton to India and apologizes for the U.S.'s responsibility for climate change.

11/13/09—In Japan, Obama pledges greater involvement with Asia-Pacific multilateral dialogue, stating, "I know that the United States has been disengaged from these organizations in recent years."

11/13/09—Obama bows before Japanese Emperor Akihito.

11/16/09—Obama bows to China's Hu Jintao.

11/24/09—Obama bows before communist Chinese Premier Wen Jiabao.

1/20/10—After one year, Obama's apology strategy has not yielded any apologies from other countries.

1/31/10—President Obama bows yet again…to the mayor of Tampa.

4/12/10—Obama bows before communist China's Hu Jintao.

5/17/10—In human rights talks with China, the Obama administration exercises more self-flagellation by constantly citing the Arizona immigration law as our own home-cooked racial discrimination. "We brought it up early and often," says Assistant Secretary of State Michael Posner.

8/24/10—Obama submits a report to the U.N. Human Rights Council stating that minorities are still victims of discrimination and considerable progress is still needed. The report cites Arizona's immigration law as an example of how human rights are trampled in the U.S.

11/9/10—Obama tells a crowd in Indonesia that Americans must stop mistrusting Islam.

TERRORISM

3/13/09—The U.S. is abandoning the phrase "enemy combatant."

3/17/09—DHS reveals the term "man-caused disaster" instead of "terrorism."

3/24/09—The Obama administration shall now refer to the "Global War on Terror" as "overseas contingency operations."

4/7/09—DHS sends out a memo that basically warns that anyone who is a conservative is a potential terrorist.

5/19/09—Hamas fires two rockets into Israel.

5/30/09—The FBI arrests four men plotting to blow up Bronx synagogues and use anti-aircraft weaponry to attack military aircraft.

6/1/09—An Islamic terrorist shoots two soldiers in Little Rock, Arkansas.

6/3/09—Officials discover an al-Qaeda video proposing to smuggle biological weapons into the U.S. through the Mexican border.

6/4/09—Osama bin Laden says, "We either live under the light of Islam or we die with dignity…brace yourselves for a long war against the world's infidels and their agents."

6/15/09—The U.K. is outraged when the U.S. ships four Uighur prisoners from Gitmo to Bermuda without notifying British authorities.

6/22/09—Al-Qaeda says they would use Pakistan's nuclear weapons.

7/17/09—Obama condemns two Indonesian suicide bombings at American hotels that killed eight and wounded fifty.

7/27/09—Seven terrorists who wanted to "attack the Americans" are arrested for planning to attack a U.S. Marine base in Quantico, Virginia.

8/6/09—Counterterrorism Czar Brennan chides the yokels for the "intellectual narrowness" of using terms like "jihadists" or "war on terrorism."

8/11/09—News surfaces that the Taliban has tried to attack Pakistan's nuclear installations three times in the last two years.

8/11/09—Kuwait has arrested six nationals suspected of being al-Qaeda members plotting to attack a U.S. military base.

8/12/09—The Lockerbie bomber, Abdelbaset al-Megrahi, is released from a Scottish prison on compassionate grounds (with the conscious support of American diplomats).

8/15/09—A car bomb explodes outside NATO headquarters in Kabul.

8/19/09—Truck bombs in Baghdad kill ninety-five and wound 563.

8/20/09—President Obama condemns Scotland for releasing the Lockerbie bomber.

8/28/09—The United Arab Emirates seizes a North Korean ship bound for Iran. Its deceptively labeled cargo consists of rocket launchers, detonators, and munitions.

9/6/09—The British maintain that Obama and Secretary Clinton were advised at all times prior to the release of the Lockerbie bomber.

9/19/09—Authorities arrest three terrorists plotting a suicide attack on Grand Central Station.

9/24/09—The FBI arrests a Jordanian who tried to blow up a downtown Dallas skyscraper.

9/24/09—Another "Soldier of Allah" tries to bomb a federal building in Springfield, Illinois.

9/24/09—A Brooklyn man and twelve others are charged with supporting al-Qaeda.

10/16/09—"Jihad Jane" is arrested at Philadelphia International Airport and charged with conspiracy to commit murder and terrorism related crimes.

11/5/09—Islamic extremist, Major Nidal Hasan, shouts *"Allahu Akbar"* as he fires a barrage of bullets at Fort Hood, killing twelve and wounding thirty.

11/5/09—Obama marks the solemn occasion by bantering with a crowd, giving a "shout out" to Dr. Joe Medicine Crow and warning America "against jumping to conclusions."

11/6/09—Obama again addresses the tragedy at Fort Hood and tells Americans not to jump to conclusions.

11/10/09—Anwar al-Awlaki praises Major Nidal Hasan as a hero on his website.

11/13/09—The DOJ announces that Khalid Sheikh Mohammed (KSM), the 9/11 mastermind, will be tried in federal court in New York City.

11/18/09—Senator Grassley (R-IA) asks Attorney General Holder to provide information regarding DOJ lawyers who previously advocated for terrorist detainees, contending there may be a conflict of interest.

11/19/09—Umaru Mutallab, father of the "underwear bomber," warns two CIA officers at the U.S. Embassy in Nigeria that his son is a potential threat and may be in Yemen.

11/24/09—Senator Grassley (R-IA) sends a letter to Attorney General Holder demanding that he provide the previously requested information regarding DOJ employees who represented terrorists.

12/8/09—Five Americans are arrested on an anti-terror raid in Pakistan.

12/25/09—Umar Abdulmutallab tries to low up an airline flight to Detroit.

His father tried to warn U.S. officials six weeks ago.

12/25/09—Abdulmutallab speaks freely with the FBI for fifty minutes. He refuses to cooperate after he is read his Miranda rights.

12/26/09—Investigators confirm that the bomb plot was hatched by al-Qaeda in Yemen.

12/26/09—Michael Leiter, head of the National Counterterrorism Center, doesn't let the failed bombing interrupt his ski vacation.

12/27/09—DHS Secretary Napolitano tells CNN, "The system worked."

12/27/09—DHS Secretary Napolitano tells ABC, "Everything went according to clockwork," describing how passengers, crew and the government responded.

12/27/09—Al-Qaeda in Yemen posts a statement taking responsibility for making Abdulmutallab's bomb.

12/28/09—DHS Secretary Napolitano tells NBC, "Our system did not work in this instance."

12/20/09—Dick Cheney criticizes Obama for "trying to pretend we are not at war" with terrorists.

1/2/10—Obama announces the Christmas Day bomber has ties to al-Qaeda.

1/3/10—The U.S. and U.K. close their embassies in Yemen amid al-Qaeda threats.

1/3/10—"Counterterrorism Czar" John Brennan announces there is a deal "on the table" for Abdulmutallab's sharing what he knows about al-Qaeda.

1/5/10—Referring to Abdulmutallab, Obama tells his national security advisors, "This was a screw up that could have been disastrous. We dodged a bullet, but just barely."

1/6/10—Abdulmutallab is indicted on six counts.

1/7/10—Obama says he takes responsibility for the failure of the security system.

1/8/10—Twenty-two Republican senators send Obama a letter asking that Abdulmutallab be tried in a military court.

1/8/10—Five days after "Czar John" announces a "deal on the table," Abdulmutallab pleads "not guilty."

1/10/10—NATO Major General Michael Flynn and Representative Mark Kirk (R-IL) say that all sixty-one freed Gitmo detainees are now major Taliban leaders in southern Afghanistan.

1/15/10—The Obama administration officially recognizes the Fort Hood shooting as an "act of terrorism."

1/31/10—Press Secretary Gibbs states, "KSM will be executed for the crimes he committed."

2/9/10—Obama will not rule out trying KSM in Manhattan.

2/15/10—The Taliban's top military commander is captured in a joint CIA-Pakistani effort.

2/18/10—Five Muslim soldiers are arrested for conspiring to poison the food supply at Fort Jackson, South Carolina.

2/18/10—Three months after the request, Attorney General Holder sends Senator Grassly (R-IA) an incomplete, haphazard response that "at least nine" lawyers at the DOJ previously represented terrorists. Holder refuses to release their names and hasn't bothered to do a complete survey anyway.

2/26/10—For the third time, Senator Grassley (R-IA) demands Attorney General Holder provide a full accounting of DOJ lawyers who represented terrorists.

3/4/10—The Obama administration is dithering and flip-flopping on what to do with KSM. Today they are considering military tribunals.

3/12/10—"Jihad Jaime," a Colorado woman, is in the custody of the Irish police on terrorism charges.

3/18/10—The Government Accountability Office (GAO) believes it "remains unclear" whether body scanners would have detected the Underwear Bomber.

3/29/10—Two Chechen suicide bombers attack the Moscow subway, killing dozens.

4/2/10—After the Christmas Day bomb plot, officials profiled passengers traveling out of fourteen countries. Not anymore. The Obama administration has shifted to a more politically correct policy.

4/7/10—Obama bans "offensive" terms for outlining national security strategy—terms like "Islamic extremism."

4/12/10—Secretary Clinton warns that terrorists, including al-Qaeda, are attempting to possess nuclear materials.

5/1/10—Faisal Shahzad, a self-proclaimed "Muslim soldier" who was trained by the Pakistani Taliban, tries to detonate a bomb in Times Square.

5/1/10—Two Brooklyn men are indicted on charges of trying to help al-Qaeda.

5/3/10—U.S. Customs agents capture Faisal Shazad trying to board a plane to Dubai. Authorities just became aware of his identity this afternoon.

5/4/10—Two recordings surface of Hakimullah Mehsud, leader of the Pakistani Taliban, who was thought to have been killed. In one of the tapes he says their main targets are now U.S. cities.

5/26/10—"Counterterrorism Czar" Brennan obsesses again over terminology. He objects to describing the enemy in religious terms like, "Islamic," "Muslim," "jihadist," and the like.

5/31/10—The Israeli navy confronts a six-ship Gaza flotilla organized by the Free Gaza Movement (composed of American communists and Islamic extremists). After the Israelis are told to "shut up. Go back to Auschwitz," the clash violently ended with nine activists killed.

6/11/10—The U.S. plans to support a U.N. commission to investigate the Israeli-Gaza flotilla incident.

6/19/10—Twenty-five Saudi Guantanamo alumni have returned to terrorism.

6/24/10—"Counterterrorism Czar" Brennan throws a hissy fit when *Washington Times* reporters question his judgment of whether jihad is a "legitimate tenet of Islam." Czar John storms out of the meeting.

7/8/10—The EU and the U.S. agree to share bank data under the pretext of fighting terrorism.

7/16/10—Pakistan supports negotiations between the Afghan government and the Taliban. The White House is also considering talks with the Taliban through third parties.

7/29/10—Under the guise of fighting terrorism, the White House seeks greater power for the FBI to monitor Internet activities without search warrants.

8/2/10—Pakistani President Zardari claims the West is losing the war against the Taliban because it has become nonchalant about the seriousness of the war.

8/10/10—Al-Qaeda is recruiting Iraqi militia troops by offering them higher pay.

8/26/10—The DOJ suspends prosecution of the USS *Cole* bomber, Abd al-Rahim al-Nashiri. The DOJ tell the U.S. Court of Appeals, "No charges are either pending or contemplated with respect to al-Nashiri in the near future."

10/31/10—Fifty-eight Christians and two priests are killed in Iraq.

11/26/10—A Somali-born U.S. citizen tries to detonate what he believes to be a bomb during a crowded Christmas tree lighting in Portland, Oregon.

12/20/10—British police conduct a large-scale anti-terrorist sweep, apprehending twelve suspects accused of plotting terror attacks within the U.K.

12/22/10—In an ABC interview, director of National Intelligence James Clapper, is completely ignorant of the U.K.'s major arrest of terrorists just two days ago.

ISLAM

1/21/09—Obama's first call to a foreign leader is Mahmoud Abbas of the Palestinian Authority.

1/24/09—Ex-Gitmo detainees appear in al-Qaeda videos.

1/26/09—Obama launches his apology tour during his first formal interview. He tells *Al-Arabiya*, "We sometimes make mistakes. We have not been perfect," and that the U.S. will "start by listening, because all too often the United States starts by dictating."

1/26/09—Hamas and Hezbollah have been training in Venezuela.

3/9/09—Secretary Clinton offers $1 million scholarship to Palestinian students.

3/13/09—The U.S. is abandoning the phrase "enemy combatant."

4/6/09—Obama debases the U.S. in Turkey.

4/19/09—Special Envoy George Mitchell rebukes Netanyahu's demand that Palestinians recognize Israel's sovereign legitimacy.

4/19/09—The State Department releases memos that it supports a two-state solution.

4/27/09—Obama asks Congress to change the law to allow the Obama administration to aid the Hamas-backed Palestinian Authority.

5/9/10—Hamas does not approve of a two-state solution with Israel.

5/18/09—The U.S. is training 1,500 Palestinian military personnel.

5/19/09—Hamas fires two rockets into Israel.

5/30/09—Obama announces his "personal commitment" to the Islamic world.

5/30/09—The FBI arrests four men plotting to blow up Bronx synagogues and using anti-aircraft weaponry to attack military aircraft.

6/1/09—Obama states that the U.S. is one of the largest Muslim nations in the world.

6/1/09—An Islamic terrorist shoots two soldiers in Little Rock, Arkansas.

6/3/09—Obama insists that at least ten members of the Muslim Brotherhood be present during his speech in Cairo.

6/4/09—Obama calls for "a new beginning" between the U.S. and the Muslim world during his speech in Cairo.

6/4/09—Iran's Ayatollah Khamenei says Islam's hatred for the U.S. cannot be damped by Obama's "sweet talk" and "slogans."

6/4/09—Osama bin Laden says, "We either live under the light of Islam or we die with dignity...brace yourselves for a long war against the world's infidels and their agents."

6/22/09—Al-Qaeda says they would use Pakistan's nuclear weapons.

7/15/09—When Obama appoints Charles Bolden as NASA administrator, he tells him his foremost mission is "to reach out to the Muslim world and engage much more with dominantly Muslim nations to help them feel good about their historic contribution to science ... and math and engineering."

7/17/09—Obama condemns two Indonesian suicide bombings at American hotels that killed eight and wounded fifty.

8/10/09—The State Department launches a "multicultural Ramadan" program which sounds a lot like "community organizing" for Islam in America.

8/11/09—News surfaces that the Taliban has tried to attack Pakistan's nuclear installations three times in the last two years.

8/11/09—Kuwait has arrested six nationals suspected of being al-Qaeda members plotting to attack a U.S. military base.

8/12/09—The Lockerbie bomber, Abdelbaset al-Megrahi, is released from a Scottish prison on compassionate grounds (with the conscious support of American diplomats).

8/15/09—A car bomb explodes outside NATO headquarters in Kabul.

8/19/09—Truck bombs in Baghdad kill ninety-five and wound 563.

8/20/09—President Obama condemns Scotland for releasing the Lockerbie bomber.

9/19/09—Authorities arrest three terrorists plotting a suicide attack on Grand Central Station.

9/24/09—The FBI arrests a Jordanian who tried to blow up a downtown Dallas skyscraper.

9/24/09—Another "Soldier of Allah" tries to bomb a federal building in Springfield, Illinois.

9/24/09—A Brooklyn man and twelve others are charged with supporting al-Qaeda.

10/2/09—The State Department joins Islamic nations in backing a U.N. Human Rights Council resolution censoring speech that some religions and races find offensive.

10/16/09—"Jihad Jane" is arrested at Philadelphia International Airport and charged with conspiracy to commit murder and terrorism related crimes.

10/23/10—The White House unveils a Muslim technology fund which will provide financing from $25 million to $150 million for chosen projects.

11/5/09—Islamic extremist, Major Nidal Hasan, shouts *"Allahu Akbar"* as he fires a barrage of bullets at Fort Hood, killing twelve and wounding thirty.

11/5/09—Obama marks the solemn occasion by bantering with a crowd, giving a "shout-out" to Dr. Joe Medicine Crow and warning America "against jumping to conclusions."

11/6/09—Obama again addresses the tragedy at Fort Hood and tells Americans not to jump to conclusions.

11/9/09—Attorney General Holder agrees to give the keynote address to the Council on American-Islamic Relations (CAIR), which has links to the Muslim Brotherhood and Hamas.

11/13/09—The DOJ announces that Khalid Sheik Mohammed, the 9/11 mastermind, will be tried in federal court in New York City.

11/25/09—Obama sends Hajj greetings to the world's Muslims.

12/25/09—Umar Abdulmutallab tries to blow up an airline flight to Detroit. His father tried to warn U.S. officials six weeks ago.

12/26/09—Investigators confirm that the bomb plot was hatched by al-Qaeda in Yemen.

12/27/09—Al-Qaeda in Yemen posts a statement taking responsibility for making Abdulmutallab's bomb.

1/2/10—Obama announces the Christmas Day bomber has ties to al-Qaeda.

1/3/10—The U.S. and U.K. close their embassies in Yeman amid al-Qaeda threats.

1/3/10—"Conterterrorism Czar" John Brennan announces there is a deal "on the table" for Abdulmutallab's sharing what he knows about al-Qaeda.

2/15/10—The Taliban's top military commander is captured in a joint CIA-Pakistani effort.

2/18/10—Five Muslim soldiers are arrested for conspiring to poison the food supply at Fort Jackson, South Carolina.

3/4/10—President Obama announces an "entrepreneurship summit" with Muslims.

3/12/10—"Jihad Jaime," a Colorado woman, is in the custody of the Irish police on terrorism charges

3/29/10—Two Chechen suicide bombers attack the Moscow subway, killing dozens.

3/30/10—Obama tells the Palestinian Authority that he foresees a two-state solution with Jerusalem as the capital of Palestine.

3/31/10—As Obama has blocked weapons sales to Israel, he has approved sales of high-tech military weaponry to Egypt and more than $10 billion of weapons sales to other Arab states.

5/1/10—Faisal Shahzad, a self-proclaimed "Muslim soldier" who was trained by the Pakistani Taliban, tries to detonate a bomb in Times Square.

5/1/10—Two Brooklyn men are indicted on charges of trying to help al-Qaeda.

5/4/10—Two recordings surface of Hakimullah Mehsud, leader of the Pakistani Taliban, who was thought to have been killed. In one of the tapes he says their main targets are now U.S. cities.

5/24/10—Syrian President al-Assad says that Obama has failed in his Mideast peace efforts and whatever influence he once possessed has now vanished.

5/26/10—"Counterterrorism Czar" Brennan obsesses again over terminology. He objects to describing the enemy in religious terms like, "Islamic," "Muslim," "jihadist," and the like.

5/31/10—The Israeli navy confronts a six-ship Gaza flotilla organized by the Free Gaza Movement (composed of American communists and Islamic extremists). After the Israelis are told to "shut up. Go back to Auschwitz," the clash violently ended with nine activists killed.

6/7/10—Demonstrators rally to protest the Ground Zero Mosque.

6/11/10—The U.S. plans to support a U.N. commission to investigate the Israeli-Gaza flotilla incident.

6/19/10—Twenty-five Saudi Guantanamo alumni have returned to terrorism.

6/24/10—"Counterterrorism Czar" Brennan throws a hissy fit when *Washington Times* reporters question his judgment of whether jihad is a "legitimate tenet of Islam." Czar John storms out of the meeting.

7/16/10—Pakistan supports negotiations between the Afghan government and the Taliban. The White House is also considering talks with the Taliban through third parties.

8/2/10—Pakistani President Zardari claims the West is losing the war against the Taliban because it has become nonchalant about the seriousness of the war.

8/10/10—Al-Qaeda is recruiting Iraqi militia troops by offering them higher pay.

8/13/10—Obama makes a characteristically supplicating speech in support of the Ground Zero Mosque.

8/18/10—The Ground Zero Mosque developer rejects Governor Paterson's offer to find a different location for construction of the controversial mosque.

8/18/10—9/11 rescue workers criticize Obama for championing the cause of the Ground Zero Mosque while doing nothing about the health care bill allotted for 9/11 rescue workers.

8/19/10—A backer of the Ground Zero Mosque says he will begin fundraising for the $100 million project in the U.S. He will not comment on whether he will be looking to foreign sources.

8/19/10—The State Department sponsors the Ground Zero Mosque's Imam Feisal Abdul Rauf's trip to the Mideast. The $16,000 trip will enable the Imam to raise funds for the Ground Zero Mosque.

8/22/10—Supporters and opponents of the Ground Zero Mosque gather and demonstrate.

8/27/10—The Ground Zero Mosque is looking into raising $70 million dollars in tax-free debt to build the mosque.

9/10/10—Obama steps out again to defend the Ground Zero Mosque.

9/11/10—Thousands of demonstrators crowd New York City supporting and opposing the Ground Zero Mosque.

10/20/10—Obama cancels a trip to a Sikh Temple because he is afraid that photos of him in a headscarf will be used to characterize him as a Muslim.

10/31/10—Fifty-eight Christians and two priests are killed in Iraq.

11/9/10—Obama criticizes Israel in Indonesia, the world's most populous Muslim country. He also says the U.S. must stop mistrusting Islam.

11/26/10—A Somali-born U.S. citizen tries to detonate what he believes to be a bomb during a crowded Christmas tree lighting in Portland, Oregon.

1/7/11—French President Nicolas Sarkozy condemns the "religious cleansing" of Christians throughout the Middle East.

GUANTANAMO/GITMO

1/22/09—Obama signs an executive order to close Gitmo.

1/24/09—Ex-Gitmo detainees appear in an al-Qaeda video.

3/11/09—The U.S. discovers an Afghan Taliban leader was formerly at Gitmo.

3/13/09—The U.S. is looking to international law as a basis for holding detainees.

3/26/09—The Obama administration plans to release Gitmo inmates into the general population and provide them with assistance to help get them on their feet.

5/15/09—Obama is in favor of restoring military commissions.

5/21/09—Congressional Democrats deny Obama the funds to close Gitmo.

5/21/09—Dick Cheney criticizes Obama's desire to close Gitmo.

6/15/09—The U.K. is outraged when the U.S. ships four Uighur prisoners from Gitmo to Bermuda without notifying British authorities.

7/20/09—Obama delays making a decision about Gitmo for another six months.

11/18/09—Obama admits he will be unable to fulfill his promise to close Gitmo.

12/15/09—The administration announces it will be transporting a limited number of Guantanamo detainees to the Thompson Correctional Center in Thompson, Illinois.

1/10/10—NATO Major General Michael Flynn and Representative Mark Kirk (R-IL) say that all sixty-one freed Gitmo detainees are now major Taliban leaders in southern Afghanistan.

1/22/10—Obama fails to fulfill his promise to close Gitmo.

6/19/10—Twenty-five Saudi Guantanamo alumni have returned to terrorism.

6/25/10—Obama has lowered the priority of closing Gitmo. It probably will not close before the end of his term.

12/8/10—One hundred and fifty terrorists released from Gitmo are either confirmed or are strongly suspected of resuming terrorist activities.

12/8/10—Congress blocks the closing of Gitmo and the transfer of detainees to the U.S.

AFGHANISTAN

2/17/09—The U.S. adds 17,000 troops.

2/25/09—Obama requests $75.5 billion for the Afghan and Iraqi wars.

3/7/09—The White House is willing to meet "moderate" elements of the Taliban.

3/11/09—The U.S. discovers that an Afghan Taliban leader was formerly at Gitmo.

3/27/09—Obama deploys 4,000 more troops to Afghanistan.

4/4/09—Obama fails to win NATO troops for Afghanistan.

4/9/09—Obama asks for $83.4 billion for Afghan/Iraq wars.

5/11/09—Obama fires NATO Commander, General David McKiernan and replaces him with General Stanley McChrystal.

7/2/09—The Marines launch the first large-scale test of the new counterinsurgency strategy.

7/12/09—The U.S. and allied counterinsurgency has successfully pushed back Taliban soldiers.

7/20/09—Another 22,000 troops are deployed to Afghanistan.

8/7/09—The Obama administration is still trying to come up with a way to measure whether the war in Afghanistan is being won.

8/10/09—The White House announces Obama has a "winning" strategy for Afghanistan.

8/15/09—A car bomb explodes outside NATO headquarters in Kabul.

8/20/09—Millions vote in Afghan elections.

8/24/09—U.S. and NATO commanders inform Obama that there are not enough troops to accomplish their mission in Afghanistan.

8/30/09—General McChrystal sends his war assessment to Defense Secretary Gates, stating, "Failure to gain the initiative and reverse insurgent momentum in the near-term … risks an outcome where defeating the insurgency is no longer possible."

8/31/09—Obama advisors agree on the need to increase troops in Afghanistan.

8/31/09—General McChrystal believes, "The situation in Afghanistan is serious, but success is achievable and demands a revised implementation strategy, commitment and resolve, and increased unity of effort."

9/16/09—Admiral Mike Mullen supports increasing troops in Afghanistan.

9/17/09—There is still no word from Obama about the increased troop deployment.

9/23/09—General David Petreaus and Admiral Mike Mullen support General McChrystal's assessment of the Afghan war.

9/28/09—General McChrystal reveals that he has only spoken to President Obama once via video teleconference since being appointed commander in Afghanistan.

9/30/09—43 soldiers have died since General McChrystal sent his Afghan troop assessment to the White House.

9/30/09—Press Secretary Gibbs says that Obama is nowhere near making a decision regarding McChrystal's troop assessment in Afghanistan.

10/1/09—General McChrystal delivered a speech saying Vice President Biden's recommendations for the war are chaotic and unworkable.

10/1/09—General McChrystal also says, "Waiting does not prolong a favorable outcome. This effort will not remain winnable indefinitely, and nor will public support."

10/2/09—General McChrystal is summoned to Copenhagen to meet with Obama for twenty-five minutes (he is there trying to get the Olympics bid for Chicago).

10/4/09—While Obama stalls on making a decision about General McChrystal's plan, ten troops are killed in battle today.

10/5/09—Defense Secretary Gates believes the Taliban is gaining momentum because the U.S. and NATO are unwilling to commit more troops.

10/8/09—U.S. and NATO Commander, General McChrystal, requests a 40,000 to 60,000 troop increase in Afghanistan.

10/18/09—Seventy-six days since Gen. McChrystal recommended additional forces, Obama is still thinking about it.

10/22/09—Dick Cheney calls for Obama to stop dithering over Afghanistan.

10/28/09—Fifty-three Americans have been killed this month while Obama dithers on his decision to deploy troops.

11/9/09—National Security advisors emphatically report that Obama has not made a decision regarding troop deployment to Afghanistan.

11/15/09—Obama cannot answer a question about why he is stalling and dithering on the decision to deploy (or not deploy) troops to Afghanistan.

11/18/09—Secretary Clinton arrives in Afghanistan.

11/19/09—The White House announces that Obama will not reach a decision about Afghan troop deployment before Thanksgiving.

11/24/09—Britain's Defense Secretary criticizes Obama for dithering on making a decision about Afghanistan.

11/26/09—The International Criminal Court claims it has jurisdiction to prosecute American "war crimes."

12/1/09—Dick Cheney criticizes Obama for projecting weakness, dithering over Afghanistan, trying Khalid Sheik Mohammed in New York, his disregard of the private sector and his uncertain belief in American exceptionalism.

12/1/09—After months of dithering, Obama *finally* announces the deployment of 30,000 troops to Afghanistan, 10,000 fewer than McChrystal's minimum request. One hundred and sixteen Americans died in the ninety-one days Obama dithered before making his decision.

12/1/09—Obama announces a timetable for troop withdrawal from Afghanistan: July 2011.

1/10/10—NATO Major General Michael Flynn and Representative Mark Kirk (R-IL) say that all sixty-one freed Gitmo detainees are now major Taliban leaders in southern Afghanistan.

4/1/10—Afghan President Hamid Karzai accuses the West of engineering election fraud in last year's elections in Afghanistan.

4/2/10—In a pacifying call to Secretary Clinton, Karzai says he is committed to working with the U.S.

4/4/10—Karzai makes another speech accusing the West of too much meddling in Afghanistan's domestic affairs.

4/5/10—In a BBC interview, Karzai stands by his statement that the U.S.

was responsible for election fraud in Afghanistan.

5/13/10—The Army considers giving medals for "courageous restraint," that is, not firing their weapons.

6/8/10—Afghanistan is now officially America's longest war.

6/22/10—A *Rolling Stone* article quotes General McChrystal saying his first meeting with Obama was disappointing because he was unprepared.

6/22/10—Obama believes McChrystal showed "poor judgment" in his interview.

6/23/10—General McChrystal is dismissed from his command in Afghanistan.

7/3/10—General David Petraeus arrives in Afghanistan to take control of NATO forces.

8/2/10—Pakistani President Zardari claims the West is losing the war against the Taliban because it has become nonchalant about the seriousness of the war.

8/24/10—General James Conway says that announcing a deadline for operations in Afghanistan is the equivalent of "giving our enemy sustenance."

10/25/10—Afghanistan's President Karzai confirms that he is receiving money from Iran. Karzai also launches an anti-Western rant and accuses the U.S. of exporting killing to Afghanistan.

12/6/10—It is estimated that more than 500 Taliban members have returned to fighting after having been detained by U.S. forces.

1/6/11—The Pentagon plans to send an additional 1,400 marines to Afghanistan for a spring surge. Commanders are hoping to defeat an anticipated Taliban offensive before Obama's mandated troop reduction in July.

PAKISTAN

3/27/09—Obama increases aid to Pakistan.

6/22/09—Al-Qaeda says it would use Pakistan's nuclear weapons.

7/8/09—U.S. drones allegedly launch two missile attacks on Taliban targets killing forty-five.

7/21/09—Pakistan objects to intensified efforts in Afghanistan believing it will force Taliban militants across their border.

8/11/09—News surfaces that the Taliban has tried to attack Pakistan's nuclear installations three times in the last two years.

12/8/09—Five Americans are arrested on an anti-terror raid in Pakistan.

2/15/10—The Taliban's top military commander is captured in a joint CIA-Pakistani effort.

7/16/10—Secretary Clinton announces $500 million in aid to Pakistan.

10/2/10—The CIA is using aerial drones in Pakistan to attack Taliban safe havens.

7/16/10—Pakistan supports negotiations between the Afghan government and the Taliban. The White House is also considering talks with the Taliban through third parties.

8/2/10—Pakistani President Zardari claims the West is losing the war against the Taliban because it has become nonchalant about the seriousness of the war.

9/30/10—American helicopters kill Pakistani soldiers mistaken for Taliban fighters. Pakistan retaliates by closing a key supply crossing.

10/3/10—A key party defection deposes Pakistan's ruling coalition.

IRAQ

2/25/09—Obama requests $75.5 billion for both wars.

2/27/09—Obama offers troop withdrawal by August 31, 2010.

4/7/09—Obama makes a surprise visit to troops in Iraq.

4/9/09—Obama asks for $83.4 billion for Afghan/Iraq wars.

8/19/09—Truck bombs in Baghdad kill ninety-five and wound 563.

11/25/09—Three Navy SEALs capture one of Iraq's most wanted terrorists.

Instead of being hailed as heroes, they are court-martialed because the terrorist received a bloody lip.

8/10/10—Al-Qaeda is recruiting Iraqi militia troops by offering them higher pay.

8/31/10—Obama declares that America has completed its mission in Iraq.

10/27/10—The Inspector General for Iraqi Reconstruction finds that the Defense Department is unable to account for $8.7 billion of the $9 billion it received from Iraqi oil sales.

10/31/10—Fifty-eight Christians and two priests are killed in Iraq.

1/13/10—Vice President Biden travels to Baghdad to cheer the new Iraqi government and "celebrate the progress they made." Iraqis greet the Vice President's convivial visit with three bombings, killing two people and gunmen killing a jewelry shop owner.

IRAN

1/26/09—Obama offers friendship to Iran.

1/29/09—Obama sends a conciliatory goodwill letter to Iran.

1/31/09—Iran venomously snubs Obama's goodwill letter.

2/3/09—Iran launches a satellite into outer space.

2/19/09—The U.N. announces Iran has enriched sufficient uranium for a nuclear weapon.

2/25/09—Iran tests its first nuclear plant.

3/2/09—Defense Secretary Gates says Iran is not close to a nuclear weapon.

3/8/09—Iran test fires new surface-to-air missiles.

3/8/09—Israeli intelligence thinks Iran's nuke program is more advanced than believed.

3/18/09—Russia contracts to provide Iran with S-300 missiles.

4/2/09—Israel warns the U.S. must end Iran's nuclear program or Israel may attack.

4/7/09—The Obama administration shuts down a China-based network supplying Iran with nuclear and missile programs.

4/9/09—Iran installs 7,000 nuclear centrifuges.

4/17/09—Ahmadinejad openly mocks Obama: "You are weak. Your hands are empty...7,000 centrifuges are spinning today at Natanz, mocking you."

4/18/09—Israel prepares contingency plans to bomb Iran's nuclear sites.

4/20/09—Iran attacks the U.S. and Israel for racism.

5/18/09—Obama expects to make serious progress in curbing Iran's nuclear ambitions.

5/20/09—Iran test-fires a missile capable of reaching Israel.

5/25/09—Iran plans to continue its nuclear program.

5/25/09—Iran deploys six warships into international waters demonstrating its ability to control 40 percent of the world's oil shipping.

6/4/09—Iran's Ayatollah Khamenei says "Israel is a cancerous tumor in the heart" of the Muslim world.

6/10/09—Russia declines U.S. efforts to design a defense shield to contain Iran.

6/11/09—North Korea and Iran join forces to build ballistic missiles.

6/12/09—Ahmadinejad is controversially reelected as Iranian president.

6/13/09—Violence erupts in Iran over disputed election results.

6/13/09—The BBC says Iran is jamming their broadcast signals from Tehran.

6/13/09—The U.S. plans to continue negotiations with Iran despite election results.

6/15/09—Obama goes out on a limb and says he is "deeply troubled" by the Iranian government's violence against its own people, but he insists negotiations will continue.

6/16/09—Iranian authorities muzzle all foreign journalists from reporting from scenes of protests.

6/16/09—Obama believes Iran should pick its own leaders and does not want the U.S. to be seen as "meddling."

6/20/09—Amid violent government suppression of protest, Obama politely asks the Iranian government to stop.

6/22/09—Iran begins air force exercises over the Persian Gulf and the Gulf of Oman.

6/23/09—Obama tells a cherry-picked journalist at a press conference that he condemns Iran's actions.

6/27/09—Ahmadinejad promises to make the U.S. regret criticism of Iran's post-election crackdown.

7/21/09—Secretary Clinton says she would accept a nuclear-armed Iran surrounded by a "defense umbrella" of armed Gulf States.

7/26/09—Secretary Clinton states Iran does not have the right to have nuclear weapons, saying, "We are going to do everything we can to prevent you (Iran) from getting a nuclear weapon."

8/28/09—The United Arab Emirates seizes a North Korean ship bound for Iran. Its deceptively labeled cargo consists of rocket launchers, detonators, and munitions.

9/5/09—After meeting with Chavez, Ahmadinejad declares, "Helping the oppressed and revolutionary nations and expanding anti-imperialist fronts are the main missions of Iran and Venezuela."

9/7/09—Ahmadinejad refuses to compromise on nuclear concessions.

9/17/09—The International Atomic Energy Agency (IAEA) says Iran has the capability to make a nuclear bomb.

9/18/09—Ahmadinejad issues a bizarre Holocaust denial.

9/19/09—National Security Advisor James Jones believes Iran is making headway in developing medium-range missiles

9/23/09—Before the U.N., Obama calls for the international community to hold Iran and North Korea accountable for their actions.

9/23/09—Obama recommends a U.N. Security Council resolution that fails to mention Iran and North Korea.

9/24/09—The IAEA publishes evidence of an illegal, secret uranium enrichment facility in Qom, Iran.

9/26/09—Obama is still requesting meaningful negotiations with Iran about their nuclear program.

9/26/09—President Sarkozy criticizes Obama for being a pushover when it comes to Iran and North Korea. Sarkozy also believes Obama's viewpoint on nuclear arms is shallow.

9/26/09—Iran is helping Venezuela find uranium deposits.

9/28/09—Iran successfully test-fires its deadliest medium-range missile. Iran's defense minister says, "Its ultimate result would be that it expedites the Zionist regime's last breath."

10/3/09—The U.N. nuclear agency concludes Iran has enough data to make a nuclear bomb.

10/13/09—Secretary Clinton fails to secure a commitment from Russia regarding tougher sanctions against Iran.

10/13/09—Prime Minister Putin warns countries about pressuring Iran regarding their nuclear arms program.

11/4/09—Iran celebrates and gloats over the thirtieth anniversary of the U.S. Embassy hostage takeover.

11/4/09—Obama marks the thirtieth anniversary of the U.S. Embassy takeover by inviting Iran to negotiate.

11/5/09—Iran tests an advanced nuclear warhead design that will enhance their ability to arm missiles with atomic bombs.

11/6/09—Iranian authorities arrest journalists to suppress information regarding civil unrest.

11/9/09—Three American hikers stray into Iran and are arrested for espionage.

11/9/09—The U.S. is giving Iran time to consider a U.N.-brokered deal regarding its nuclear program.

11/13/09—IAEA inspectors toured Iran's secret nuclear facility and confirmed that it is adequate for nuclear arms manufacturing.

11/23/09—Iran displays war games to deter Western pressure over its nuclear program.

11/29/09—In defiance of the U.N., Iran plans to build ten new uranium enrichment plants.

12/14/09—Iran is working on testing the final component of a nuclear bomb.

1/31/10—Obama deploys a defensive shield of patriot missiles in the Persian Gulf states capable of shooting down Iranian missiles.

2/11/10—Ahmadinejad declares that Iran is now a nuclear state.

2/15/10—Secretary Clinton calls for more pressure on Iran to halt its nuclear program.

2/15/10—Saudi Arabia's foreign minister doubts sanctions will be effective in curbing Iran's nuclear ambitions.

2/24/10—North Korea gives Iran nineteen missiles capable of reaching Western European capitals.

2/25/10—Secretary Clinton compares Iran's nuclear program to the Cuban Missile Crisis.

3/18/10—Secretary Clinton criticizes Russia's plans to build a nuclear power plant in Iran.

3/19/10—Secretary Clinton tells a Jewish group that Israel's settlements hinder the peace process and the U.S.'s ability to impose sanctions on Iran. "Our aim is not incremental sanctions, but sanctions that will bite."

3/21/10—The White House backs off from Secretary Clinton's comment, now preferring to deal with Iran by persuading Russia and China to back a U.N. resolution.

3/30/10— The CIA believes that Iran is capable of manufacturing nuclear arms.

4/6/10—After Obama's statement about revamping America's nuclear policy, Defense Secretary Robert Gates says that for rogue nations like Iran and North Korea "all options are on the table."

4/7/10—In response to America's policy change, Ahmadinijad mocks Obama's weakness saying, "[American officials] bigger than you, more bullying than you, couldn't do a damn thing, let alone you."

4/14/10—Russia is on schedule to complete a nuclear reactor in Iran by August.

5/14/10—The IAEA confirms Iran's plans for enriching uranium at higher levels.

5/17/10—Iran signs a deal to export uranium to Turkey and Brazil in a blatant attempt to subvert U.S. attempts to halt Iran's nuclear program. The leaders pose triumphantly for a picture with raised, clenched hands.

5/21/10—The U.S. lifts sanctions against three Russian organizations sus-pected of assisting Iran in achieving its nuclear ambitions. The U.S. also lifts sanctions against a fourth Russian enterprise that is suspected of arms sales to Syria.

5/31/10—Obama backs the U.N. Mideast Nuclear Non-Proliferation Trea-ty. The treaty makes no mention of Iran but calls for Israel to open its sites and facilities for inspection.

6/8/10—Russia and China support the U.N. Security Council's fourth round of sanctions against Iran. Ahmadinejad calls the sanctions "valueless" and should be tossed "in the waste bin like a used handkerchief."

6/8/10—Russia immediately clarifies that the U.N.'s sanctions do not apply to their contract to sell Iran S-300 missiles.

6/27/10—The CIA believes Iran has enough low-enriched uranium to build two nuclear weapons if they can further enrich it.

7/12/10—Russian President Medvedev announces that Iran is close to hav-ing nuclear weapons.

8/11/10—Russia and China resume selling gasoline to Iran. Although Rus-sia and China signed the U.N. sanctions against Iran, they exempted them-selves from highly profitable oil/gas sanctions.

8/13/10—Russia announces that it will be putting the finishing touches on

Iran's nuclear power plant. On August 21, 2010, they will be loading uranium for the reactor.

9/24/10—As Ahmadinejad accuses the U.S. of orchestrating 9/11, U.S. delegates walk out.

10/14/10—Ahmadinejad joins crowds of Hezbollah supporters in an intentionally provocative appearance at the Lebanese/Israeli border.

10/25/10 – Afghanistan's President Karzai confirms that he is receiving money from Iran.

12/3/10—At a dinner party in Bahrain, the Iranian Foreign Minister snubs Secretary of State Clinton <u>twice</u> by refusing to shake Mrs. Clinton's extended hand or even acknowledge her presence.

12/15/10—German computer consultants sabotage the Iranian nuclear program with the Stuxnet computer virus. Iran's program is expected to suffer a two-year setback.

NORTH KOREA

2/3/09—The U.S. warns North Korea that a missile launch would be provocative.

2/20/09—Secretary Clinton seeks peace with North Korea and will provide aid if they avoid nukes.

3/11/09—North Korea accuses U.S. of meddling and vows to take every necessary measure to defend itself.

3/25/09—Secretary Clinton warns North Korea that firing missiles for any purpose would be deemed a "provocative act."

3/26/09—Admiral Mullen says North Korean rockets can reach Hawaii.

3/29/09—Defense Secretary Gates says the U.S. is not ready to respond to a North Korean missile launch.

4/2/09—The U.S. and South Korea warn North Korea not to proceed with a satellite launch.

4/2/09—North Korea threatens Japan with a "fiery bolt of retaliatory lightning" if they attempt to interfere with its satellite launch.

4/5/09—Obama says the world must stand together against rogue states like North Korea.

4/5/09—North Korea's middle-fingered response to President Obama is launching long-range rockets over the Sea of Japan.

4/5/09—The U.N. calls to punish North Korea.

4/8/09—North Korea warns the U.N. against any reprisal against its rocket launch.

4/11/09—The U.N. still hasn't done anything about North Korea's rocket launches.

5/22/09—North Korea plans to test-fire short-range missiles.

5/25/09—North Korea successfully tests a nuclear bomb. President Obama says, "The United States and the international community must take action in response ... We will work with our friends and allies to stand up to this behavior."

5/29/09—North Korea launches a new type of short-range, land-to-air missile.

6/7/09—Two American journalists are sentenced to twelve years for "grave crimes."

6/9/09—North Korea declares it will launch a nuclear attack if sufficiently provoked.

6/11/09—North Korea and Iran join forces to build ballistic missiles.

6/12/09—North Korea ignores U.N. sanctions and begins uranium enrichment and weaponizing plutonium.

6/13/09—The U.S. demands that North Korea cease its provocative stance and return to six-party talks.

6/16/09—The Pentagon says North Korea will eventually be able to produce weapons that could reach the U.S. mainland.

6/19/09—The U.S. fortifies Hawaii against an attack from North Korea.

6/21/09—North Korea accuses Obama of plotting nuclear war.

7/2/09—North Korea test fires four more short-range missiles.

7/8/09—North Korea is responsible for a recent spate of cyber-attacks against South Korea and the United States.

7/11/09—North Korean computer specialists were ordered to hack and destroy South Korean communications.

7/23/09—North Korea states that Secretary Clinton "is by no means intelligent."

7/30/09—The U.S. successfully test-fires missile defenses against North Korea.

8/28/09—The United Arab Emirates seizes a North Korean ship bound for Iran. Its deceptively labeled cargo consists of rocket launchers, detonators, and munitions.

9/3/09—North Korea is on the cusp of successfully enriching uranium.

9/11/09—The U.S. changes its policy and announces it is ready to have one-on-one talks with North Korea.

9/23/09—Before the U.N., Obama calls for the international community to hold Iran and North Korea accountable for their actions.

9/23/09—Obama recommends a U.N. Security Council resolution that fails to mention Iran and North Korea.

9/26/09—President Sarkozy criticizes Obama for being a pushover when it comes to Iran and North Korea. Sarkozy also believes Obama's viewpoint on nuclear arms is shallow.

11/3/09—North Korea claims to have successfully weaponized more plutonium for nuclear bombs.

12/29/09—The State Department confirms that a U.S. citizen snuck into North Korea on Christmas Day and is being held captive.

2/24/10—North Korea gives Iran nineteen missiles capable of reaching Western European capitals.

3/28/10—A North Korean torpedo sinks a South Korean warship, killing several crewmembers.

4/6/10—After Obama's statement about revamping America's nuclear policy, Defense Secretary Gates says that for rogue nations like Iran and North Korea "all options are on the table."

4/7/10—North Korea sentences an American English teacher to eight years of hard labor for illegally crossing the border. He is the fourth U.S. citizen to be detained by North Korea.

5/24/10—U.N. Secretary-General Ban expects sanctions against North Korea for the torpedo attack against South Korea.

5/24/10—The U.S. and South Korea join together in a show of military might to "deter future aggression."

5/26/10—Secretary Clinton says North Korea's attack of a South Korean ship is an "unacceptable provocation."

11/21/10—An American scientist has toured a North Korean uranium enrichment facility that he says is highly sophisticated and was built in secret with remarkable speed.

11/23/10—North and South Korean forces clash along their disputed border, killing two South Korean soldiers and two South Korean civilians. North Korea's casualties are unknown. North Korea threatens to continue strikes against the South.

11/24/10—The U.S. asks China to keep North Korea on a short leash. The U.S. is also sending the aircraft carrier, the USS *George Washington*, to the Yellow Sea for naval exercises with South Korea.

12/13/10—North Korea warns that South Korea's continued military exercises could bring a nuclear response.

12/23/10—North Korea threatens a "sacred war" with South Korea with a veiled nuclear threat. South Korea says it will launch a "merciless counterattack" if it is attacked again.

1/11/11—Defense Secretary Gates warns that North Korea will have the technology to strike the continental U.S. within five years.

ISRAEL

1/30/09—Obama authorizes $20 million in aid for Gaza.

2/6/09—Israel intercepts an aid ship headed for Gaza; militants from Gaza launch two rockets at Israel.

2/7/09—U.N. halts aid to Gaza due to Hamas stealing shipments.

2/23/09—Secretary Clinton pledges $900 million to rebuild Gaza.

3/2/09—Secretary Clinton meets with Palestinian National Authority, vows to work toward a Palestinian state.

3/2/09—Secretary Clinton calls on Israel to allow more aid to Gaza.

3/2/09—Secretary Clinton denounces Israeli construction in East Jerusalem.

3/3/09—Secretary Clinton attacks Israeli construction plans for East Jerusalem.

3/10/09—While visiting Israel, Vice President Biden "condemns" Israel's East Jerusalem construction.

3/10/09—Vice President Biden keeps Prime Minister Netanyahu waiting for ninety minutes.

3/15/09—The U.S. again denounces Israeli construction in East Jerusalem.

4/2/09—Israel warns the U.S. must end Iran's nuclear program or Israel may attack.

4/7/09—Vice President Biden says Israel would be ill-advised to attack Iran.

4/16/09—Obama cancels his first meeting with Prime Minister Netanyahu because he will not be "in town."

4/17/09—Israel believes Obama is using the Iranian threat to coerce Israel into ceding control of the West Bank.

4/18/09—Israel prepares contingency plans to bomb Iran's nuclear sites.

4/19/09—Special Envoy George Mitchell rebukes Netanyahu's demand that Palestinians recognize Israel's sovereign legitimacy.

4/19/09—The State Department releases memos that it supports a two-state solution.

4/26/09—National Security Advisor James Jones tells an inappropriate Jewish joke at a speech on Near East policy.

4/27/09—Obama asks Congress to change the law to enable the Obama administration to aid the Hamas-backed Palestinian Authority.

5/2/09—The White House confirms that it is using the Iranian threat to coerce a two-state solution.

5/5/09—The White House insists that Israel support a two-state solution.

5/5/09—The White House insists that Israel halt construction of Jewish settlements.

5/9/10—Hamas does not approve of a two-state solution with Israel.

5/14/09—Obama warns Netanyahu not to take any action against Iran without his approval.

5/18/09—The U.S. is training 1,500 Palestinian military personnel.

5/18/09—Obama personally dictates to Netanyahu that Israel must halt settlements.

5/19/09—Hamas fires two rockets into Israel.

5/20/09—Iran test-fires a missile capable of reaching Israel.

5/20/09—Israelis dismiss Obama's call to halt settlements.

5/24/09—Prime Minister Netanyahu disregards Obama's demand for a settlement freeze.

5/27/09—Secretary Clinton demands that Israel must stop settlement construction.

5/28/09—The White House hosts Palestinian President Mahmoud Abbas and demands Israel stop building Jewish settlements.

3/30/10—Obama tells the Palestinian Authority that he foresees a two-state solution with Jerusalem as the capital of Palestine.

6/4/09—Iran's Ayatollah Khamenei says "Israel is a cancerous tumor in the heart" of the Muslim world.

6/14/09—Netanyahu accepts the establishment of a Palestinian state subject to strenuous conditions.

7/5/09—Vice President Biden says that Israel is a sovereign nation, free to choose their own course in whether or not to attack Iran.

7/6/09—The White House "clarifies" Vice President Biden's statement saying that it does not give Israel the "green light [for] any kind of military action."

7/19/09—Prime Minister Netanyahu rebuffs another White House demand to stop construction of Jewish settlements.

7/20/09—State Department spokesman P. J. Crowley says Israeli construction in East Jerusalem is "the type of issue that should be subject to permanent-status negotiation."

7/22/09—A member of the Palestinian Fatah party states that Fatah has never recognized Israel's right to exist and it will never do so.

7/27/09—Two thousand protesters in Jerusalem denounce Obama as "racist."

9/4/09—Netanyahu offers to freeze settlements at some later date. The White House disapproves.

9/7/09—In defiance of Obama's demands, Israel approves the building of 455 units in the West Bank.

9/28/09—Iran successfully test-fires its deadliest medium-range missile. Iran's defense minister says, "Its ultimate result would be that it expedites the Zionist regime's last breath."

10/16/09—Obama is "disgusted" that the Israelis refuse to stop settlement constructions as a pre-condition to talks with the Palestinian Authority.

10/31/09—Secretary Clinton adopts the position that Israeli settlement expansion in the West Bank should not prevent peace negotiations.

11/1/09—Palestinians accuse the U.S. of changing its position with regard to Secretary Clinton's remarks yesterday.

11/10/09—Obama meets with American Jewish leaders. Although he does not discuss Iran or Israel, he does brag about Obamacare.

11/9/09—William Burns outlines the State Department's goal of a two-state solution expelling Jews from Judea and Samaria.

1/8/10—Obama threatens to impose sanctions and freeze aid to Israel if they fail to advance two-state peace talks.

2/27/10—Israel approves construction of 600 new units in East Jerusalem.

3/15/10—Ties between U.S. and Israel are the "worst in thirty-five years." David Axelrod maintains that Israel's settlement construction is an "insult" to the U.S.

3/16/10—An American envoy cancelled a trip to Jerusalem over Israel's settlement constructions.

3/19/10—Secretary Clinton tells a Jewish group that Israel's settlements hinder the peace process and the U.S.'s ability to impose sanctions on Iran. "Our aim is not incremental sanctions, but sanctions that will bite."

3/21/10—The White House backs off from Secretary Clinton's comment, now preferring to deal with Iran by persuading Russian and China to back a U.N. resolution.

3/23/10—Obama leaves Israeli Prime Minister Netanyahu and his team sitting alone in a room in the White House. He says he is going to eat dinner with his family. He tells them they are welcome to hang around the White House if they want and, if they come up with anything important, they can let him know.

3/31/10—As Obama has blocked weapons sales to Israel and has approved sales of high-tech military weaponry to Egypt and more than $10 billion of weapons sales to other Arab states.

5/31/10—The Israeli navy confronts a six-ship Gaza flotilla organized by the Free Gaza Movement (composed of American communists and Islamic extremists). After the Israelis are told to "shut up. Go back to Auschwitz," the clash violently ends with nine activists killed.

5/31/10—Prime Minister Netanyahu leaves the U.S. immediately to go deal with the flotilla crisis.

5/31/10—Obama backs the U.N. Mideast Nuclear Non-Proliferation Treaty. The treaty makes no mention of Iran but calls for Israel to open its sites and facilities for inspection.

6/4/10—Israel prepares to intercept another Gaza-bound ship.

6/11/10—The U.S. plans to support a U.N. commission to investigate the Israeli-Gaza flotilla incident.

7/6/10—Obama meets with Netanyahu to discuss Mideast peace. Obama wants Israel to commit to a two-state solution.

7/7/10—Obama says he believes Israelis may not like him because his middle name is "Hussein."

9/23/10—President Obama blasts Israel before the U.N. General Assembly, "We continue to emphasize that America does not accept the legitimacy of continued Israeli settlements." He calls for the establishment of a "viable, independent Palestinian state with contiguous territory that ends the occupation that began in 1967, and realizes the potential of the Palestinian people."

11/9/10—Obama criticizes Israel in Indonesia, the world's most populous Muslim country.

11/24/10—A group called Z Street claims the IRS is unfairly targeting pro-Israel groups in challenging their 501(c)(3) tax-exempt status by asking such questions as, "Does your organization support the existence of the land of Israel?" and "Describe your organization's religious belief system toward the land of Israel."

12/26/10—After several days of rocket attacks on southern Israel, the Israeli foreign minister says that peace is impossible under current conditions.

1/9/11—Once again, the Obama administration criticizes Israel's settlement construction in East Jerusalem.

VENEZUELA

1/26/09—Evidence exists that Venezuela sponsors Hamas and Hezbollah, even offering training for their soldiers.

3/4/09—Chavez tightens his control over Venezuela's food supply.

4/18/09—Obama politely accepts Hugo Chavez's gift of Eduardo Galeano's *Open Veins of Latin America: Five Centuries of the Pillage of a Continent*, a book that blasts America's influence in the Western Hemisphere.

5/31/09—Venezuela purchases shoulder-fired anti-aircraft missiles from Russia.

6/2/09—Hugo Chavez welcomes Obama to the Marxist camp for nationalizing GM.

6/23/09—Russia and Venezuela sign a $4 billion bank deal. Putin says, "We are moving to a high level of political and economic cooperation."

7/30/09—Venezuela's Attorney General Luisa Ortega declares freedom of expression "must be limited" by punishing media outlets critical of the regime.

8/1/09—Chavez shuts down thirty-four radio stations "that now belong to the people, not the bourgeoisie."

8/6/09—Venezuela is buying dozens of tanks and artillery from Russia.

8/15/09—Russia and Venezuela are negotiating arms deals and oil trade.

8/29/09—Protestors criticizing the government are accused of rebellion and will be tried.

9/5/09—After meeting with Chavez, Ahmadinejad declares, "Helping the oppressed and revolutionary nations and expanding anti-imperialist fronts are the main missions of Iran and Venezuela."

9/5/09—Venezuela plans to shut down twenty-nine more radio stations.

9/13/09—Russia will help Venezuela develop nuclear energy.

9/26/09—Iran is helping Venezuela find uranium deposits.

11/2/09—Venezuelans now experience socialist-style water rationing.

11/8/09—Chavez prepares for war against a U.S.-led attack.

12/2/09—Russia is building a Kalishnikov AK-103 factory in Venezuela.

12/7/09—Venezuela purchases thousands of Russian missiles and rocket launchers claiming that Colombia plans to wage war.

3/31/10—Putin visits Chavez to complete a joint venture to drill for oil from Venezuela's Orinoco Belt.

4/18/10—China is investing $20 billion in projects in Venezuela.

6/23/10—Venezuela seizes eleven U.S.-owned oil rigs.

10/3/10—Venezuela confiscates huge swaths of land from the British food company, Vestey, for the "acceleration of the agrarian revolution." Since Chavez took office, Venezuela has nationalized over 6.2 million acres of land.

10/15/10—Russia agrees to build a nuclear power plant in Venezuela.

12/12/10—Venezuela acquires 1,800 shoulder-fired, anti-aircraft missiles from Russia in the last year. The U.S. fears they may be funneled to the Marxist FARC forces in Colombia.

12/14/10—Hugo Chavez asks the Venezuelan Congress to give him power to rule by decree for one year.

12/17/10—Venezuela's National Assembly of socialist loyalists has voted to extend President Chavez's request for dictatorial powers to eighteen months.

12/20/10—Hugo Chavez imposes "net neutrality" for Venezuela. The socialist imposes restrictions on all messages showing "disrespect for public authorities" that "incite or promote hatred" or create "anxiety."

12/29/10—Chavez refuses to accept Obama's ambassadorial nonimee, Larry Palmer. Chavez says, "If the government is going to expel our ambassador, then let them do it. If they're going to cut diplomatic relations, let them do it." Soon afterward, the State Department revoked the Venezuelan ambassador's visa.

1/16/11—Venezuela's oil reserves surpass Saudi Arabia.

RUSSIA

1/28/09—Russia halts plans to deploy Eastern European missiles, anticipating that President Obama will scrap the U.S. missile defense shield.

1/29/09—Russia calls for the end of the dollar as the global reserve currency.

2/6/09—Russia pays Kyrgyzstan $2 billion to close a U.S. Air Force base.

3/2/09—Obama offers to scrap Eastern European defense shield for Russian cooperation with Iran.

3/6/09—Secretary Clinton meets the Russian foreign minister with a "reset" button that was mistranslated as "overcharged."

3/14/09—Russia evaluates Cuba and Venezuela to base their strategic bombers.

3/17/09—Russia announces plans to expand rearmament.

3/17/09—Russia calls for a supranational currency to replace the dollar.

3/18/09—Russia contracts to provide Iran with S-300 missiles.

3/26/09—Russia is launching a military force to occupy the mineral-rich Arctic region.

3/29/09—Russia supports a return to the gold standard.

3/30/09—Russia and China cooperate on currency proposals.

4/1/09—Russia argues for the need of a global currency to replace the dollar.

4/1/09—Obama and Medvedev plan to re-open disarmament talks.

4/5/09—Russia, China, Malaysia, Indonesia, Thailand, and Kazakhstan call for an international currency system to replace the dollar.

4/7/09—Russia says the U.S. does not need a defense shield in Eastern Europe because Iran is not a threat to the U.S.

5/31/09—Venezuela purchases shoulder-fired, anti-aircraft missiles from Russia.

6/10/09—Russia may swap its ownership of U.S. debt in favor of IMF debt.

6/10/09—Russia declines U.S. efforts to design a defense shield to contain Iran.

6/16/09—Brazil, Russia, India, and China call for the end of the dollar as the global reserve currency.

6/23/09—Russia and Venezuela sign a $4 billion bank deal. Putin says, "We are moving to a high level of political and economic cooperation."

6/30/09—Vladimir Putin says if the U.S. wants to improve its relations with

Russia, it must not build a European missile defense shield.

7/5/09—President Medvedev insists that the U.S. compromise its European defense shield if the Americans wish to move forward with nuclear negotiations.

7/6/09—President Obama meets with President Medvedev to reach a "new start" in U.S./Russian relations.

7/7/09—When meeting with Medvedev and Putin, Obama says, "I think it's very important that I come before you with some humility. I think in the past there's been a tendency for the United States to lecture rather than listen."

7/10/09—Russia threatens to deploy missiles near Poland if the U.S. does not modify its Eastern European defense shield.

7/10/09—President Medvedev uses the G-8 summit as a platform to call for the end of the dollar as the world's reserve currency. French President Sarkozy heartily agrees.

8/4/09—Two Russian nuclear submarines are patrolling off the East Coast.

8/6/09—Venezuela is buying dozens of tanks and artillery from Russia.

8/11/09—Russia is trying to get the U.S. to discard its European defense shield in order to proceed with negotiations in the Strategic Arms Reduction Treaty (START).

8/15/09—Russia and Venezuela are negotiating arms deals and oil trade.

8/27/09—Polish press reports that the U.S. will breach its East European defense shield agreement to appease Russia.

9/13/09—Russia will help Venezuela develop nuclear energy.

9/17/09—The White House formally announces that it is dissolving plans for its East European defense shield. Shortly after the announcement, Putin meets with Obama corporate cronies like GE's Jeff Immelt (GE is a big defense contractor).

9/18/09—After the U.S. scrapped its plans for a defense shield, Putin is now pursuing trade agreements.

9/21/09—Obama demands that the Pentagon review its nuclear weapons and prepare for dramatic cuts in its arsenal.

9/21/09—Even though Obama scrapped the East European missile shield, Russia's top general says they still may deploy missiles in Kaliningrad, near Poland.

9/26/09—French President Sarkozy believes Obama's view of nuclear disarmament is shallow.

10/5/09—Russia, China, Japan, Brazil, European countries, and Arab states are colluding to scrap the dollar as the world's oil trading currency in favor of a basket of currencies.

10/13/09—Secretary Clinton fails to secure a commitment from Russia regarding tougher sanctions against Iran.

10/13/09—Prime Minister Putin warns countries about pressuring Iran regarding their nuclear arms program.

10/13/09—Secretary Clinton agrees to allow Russia to inspect our nuclear weapons facilities. She says the U.S. wants to be as transparent as possible with Russia.

10/15/09—Russia warns the U.S. against talking to Ukraine and Georgia about a missile shield.

11/2/09—Russian military exercises are war-gaming a nuclear attack on Poland.

12/2/09—Russia is building a Kalishnikov AK-103 factory in Venezuela.

12/7/09—Venezuela purchases thousands of Russian missiles and rocket launchers claiming that Colombia plans to wage war.

12/30/09—Putin calls for more Russian arms manufacturing capable of penetrating America's missile defense shield.

1/11/10—Even though Russia plans to continue developing nuclear arms, the U.S. continues negotiating START.

3/18/10—Russia will begin drilling for oil in the Gulf of Mexico. Oil rigs will be built near Cuba's coast.

3/18/10—Secretary Clinton criticizes Russia's plans to build a nuclear power plant in Iran.

3/26/10—Obama and Medvedev agree to cut their long-range nuclear stockpiles by one-third.

3/31/10—Putin visits Chavez to complete a joint venture to drill for oil from Venezuela's Orinoco Belt.

4/11/10—Obama signs a nuclear reduction treaty with Russia requiring each nation to reduce its stockpiles by a third.

4/14/10—Russia is on schedule to complete a nuclear reactor in Iran by August.

5/11/10—Russia is ready to help Syria build a nuclear power plant.

5/21/10—The U.S. lifts sanctions against three Russian organizations suspected of assisting Iran in achieving its nuclear ambitions. The U.S. also lifted sanctions against a fourth Russian enterprise which is suspected of arms sales to Syria.

6/8/10—Russia and China support the U.N. Security Council's fourth round of sanctions against Iran. Ahmadinejad calls the sanctions "valueless" and should be tossed "in the waste bin like a used handkerchief."

6/8/10—Russia immediately clarifies that the U.N.'s sanctions do not apply to their contract to sell Iran S-300 missiles.

6/19/10—Russian President Medvedev calls for the end of the dollar as the global reserve currency; he would like for the ruble to be one of the reserve currencies.

6/28/10—Ten Russian agents are apprehended in the New York area and charged with conspiracy to act as agents of a foreign government.

7/13/10—Obama plans to cut the U.S. nuclear stockpile by up to 40 percent by 2021.

8/11/10—Russia and China resume selling gasoline to Iran. Although Russia and China signed the U.N. sanctions against Iran, they exempted themselves from highly profitable oil/gas sanctions.

8/13/10—Russia announces that it will be putting the finishing touches on Iran's nuclear power plant. On August 21, 2010, they will be loading uranium for the reactor.

9/19/09—Russia has reportedly sold seventy-two cruise missiles to Syria.

9/27/10—Russian and China celebrate the completion of an oil pipeline linking the two countries.

10/15/10—Russia agrees to build a nuclear power plant in Venezuela.

11/1/10—After the Federal Reserve announces its second round of "quantitative easing," Russia and almost every other country strongly disapproves of the U.S. monetary policy. The denunciations are too numerous to mention in this section but can be found in Part III.

11/13/10—Obama promises Russian President Medvedev that ratification of the START treaty will be his top priority.

11/24/10—China and Russia officially quit using the dollar when trading

CHRISTOPHER HALL 661

with each other. The new policy is not directed at challenging the dollar, but at protecting their own economies.

12/15/10—Democrats are scrambling to ratify the START treaty. Vice President Biden tells Republicans, "Get out of the way. There's too much at stake."

12/23/10—The Senate ratifies the START treaty. Critics claim the U.S. got the short end of the stick because the U.S. will be dismantling a superior arsenal.

1/14/11—The Russian parliament amends the START treaty allowing Russia to withdraw if it feels threatened by the West.

CHINA

1/29/09—China calls for the end of dollar as the global reserve currency.

2/20/09—Secretary Clinton begs China to keep buying U.S. debt.

2/20/09—Secretary Clinton says China's human rights violations will not affect U.S./China relations.

3/4/09—China increases military spending 15 percent.

3/11/09—U.S. and China negotiate to deter naval confrontations.

3/12/09—Obama tells China that human rights issues are essential to U.S. foreign policy.

3/13/09—China voices concern over U.S. debt and the value of Treasuries.

3/14/09—Chinese and U.S. vessels face off in a naval confrontation.

3/15/09—Obama declares the U.S. economy is sound and China should be confident that its investment in our economy is safe.

3/23/09—China calls for a new reserve currency to be controlled by the IMF.

3/25/09—Treasury Secretary Geithner is "quite open" to China's proposal that the dollar be replaced as a reserve currency.

3/30/09—Russia and China cooperate on currency proposals.

4/1/09—Obama and China agree to establish a strategic economic dialogue.

4/5/09—Russia, China, Malaysia, Indonesia, Thailand, and Kazakhstan call for an international currency system to replace the dollar.

4/7/09—The Obama administration shuts down a China-based network supplying Iran with nuclear and missile programs.

4/12/09—China slows its purchases of U.S. bonds.

4/21/09—China stages a naval "fleet parade" to demonstrate its military might.

4/26/09—China blames the dollar for the global financial crisis and calls for reform of the global currency system.

4/30/09—China reduces its purchases of U.S. debt.

5/4/09—Admiral Mike Mullen says China's military buildup is directed at the United States.

5/18/09—Brazil and China agree to use their own currencies in all trade transactions instead of using the dollar.

5/27/09—The president of the Dallas Federal Reserve Bank says China is alarmed by U.S. fiscal and monetary policy and warns the Fed about printing money.

5/31/09—Chinese students laugh at Treasury Secretary Geithner when he says, "Chinese financial assets are very safe."

6/2/09—Treasury Secretary Geithner says China expresses confidence in the U.S. economy and there is "no risk" of monetizing the debt.

6/7/09—The head of China's largest bank believes the U.S. should start issuing debt denominated in Chinese yuan.

6/16/09—Brazil, Russia, India and China call for the end of the dollar as the global reserve currency.

6/17/09—China continues to cut back on U.S. Treasuries.

7/28/09—China's Assistant Finance Minister is "concerned about the security of our financial assets." Treasury Secretary Geithner assures China the U.S. will shrink the deficit.

9/7/09—China voices its alarm that the U.S. is printing money.

9/11/09—The U.S. will impose tariffs on tires made in China.

9/12/09—China denounces the tire tariffs as protectionist.

9/13/09—China investigates unfair U.S. trade in chicken and automobile products.

9/14/09—Obama postpones meeting with the Dalai Lama.

9/17/09—China is investing hundreds of millions of dollars in Cuba.

9/29/09—In honor of the sixtieth anniversary of history's most murderous Communist regime, the Empire State building is lit up in red and yellow.

10/5/09—Obama refuses to meet with the Dalai Lama this week. The move is criticized as an effort to appease China.

10/5/09—Russia, China, Japan, Brazil, European countries, and Arab states are colluding to scrap the dollar as the world's oil trading currency in favor of a basket of currencies.

11/12/09—China warns Obama about meeting with the Dalai Lama.

11/14/09—China detains and silences dissidents ahead of Obama's visit.

11/15/09—Chinese citizens greet President Obama wearing "Oba-Mao" t-shirts.

11/15/09—China's chief banking regulator rebukes U.S. fiscal and monetary policy for fostering "dollar carry-trade."

11/16/09—Obama tells 400 Chinese students that the Western concept of universal rights should be available to all.

11/16/09—China is unimpressed with the fiscal wisdom of Obamacare.

11/19/09—Obama returns from Asia accomplishing, well, nothing.

12/18/09—China shows a lack of interest in participating in the Copenhagen summit.

12/18/09—China snubs Obama and Secretary Clinton by sending three low-level officials to meet with them.

12/18/09—The deputy governor of the Bank of China says that the dollar's decline is inevitable since the U.S. insists on racking up higher and higher deficits financed by the U.S. Treasury.

12/31/09—China is worried about Washington's out-of-control spending and has reduced its holdings by $34.2 billion.

1/29/10—China protests the U.S.'s sale of $6.4 billion in weapons to Taiwan.

2/3/10—China warns Obama that meeting with the Dalai Lama will further erode U.S./China relations.

2/5/10—China announces tariffs on U.S. chicken products.

2/9/10—Angry about U.S. arms sales to Taiwan, China considers increased defense spending, redeploying military assets and selling off U.S. bonds.

2/18/10—Obama meets with the Dalai Lama. He demonstrates that he does not recognize the Dalai Lama as a head of state; he meets him in the White House Map Room. Obama literally treated the Dalai Lama like trash, forcing him to exit a side door among heaps of garbage.

2/19/10—China is outraged that Obama failed to mistreat the Dalai Lama poorly enough. "The Chinese side demands that the U.S. side seriously consider China's stance, immediately adopt measures to wipe out the baneful impact and stop conniving and supporting anti-China separatist forces that seek Tibet independence."

2/28/10—China's Senior Colonel Liu Mingfu encourages Chinese military buildup and a "sprint to become world number one."

3/4/10—China is waging a cyber-war against the U.S., the EU, and NATO allies. Chinese cyber-attacks against U.S. agencies are roughly 1.6 billion per month.

3/12/10—China accuses the U.S. of human rights hypocrisy.

3/15/10—China decreases its holding of U.S. Treasuries for the third straight month.

4/12/10—Hu Jintao promises Obama that he will participate in negotiations about sanctions against Iran; however, he is unwilling to commit to anything.

4/18/10—China is investing $20 billion in projects in Venezuela.

5/17/10—In human rights talks with China, the Obama administration exercises more self-flagellation by constantly citing the Arizona immigration law as our own home-cooked racial discrimination. "We brought it up early and often," says Assistant Secretary of State Michael Posner.

5/24/10—China will not adjust its exchange rate policy, despite Obama's light-handed pressure.

6/2/10—China rejects (i.e.—snubs) meeting with Defense Secretary Gates during his trip to Asia.

6/8/10—Russia and China support the U.N. Security Council's fourth round of sanctions

against Iran. Ahmadinejad calls the sanctions "valueless" and should be tossed "in the waste bin like a used handkerchief."

6/30/10—The Federal Reserve's monetary policy and the Obama administration's fiscal policy provoke weakened confidence in the stability and value of the dollar. In the past twelve months China has cut its holdings of U.S. Treasuries by $100 billion.

7/12/10—The U.S. loses its AAA credit rating with China's Dagong Global Credit Rating Company.

7/20/10—Chinese General Zhu Chenghu tells the Communist Party media, "If the U.S. truly wants to take into account the overall interests of the

Sino-U.S. relationship, then it must on no account send its USS [*George*] *Washington* to the Yellow Sea."

7/23/10—China's central bank, once again, calls for moving away from the dollar as the world's global reserve currency to a basket of diverse currencies.

8/11/10—Russia and China resume selling gasoline to Iran. Although Russia and China signed the U.N. sanctions against Iran, they exempted themselves from highly profitable oil/gas sanctions.

8/17/10—China's military buildup may be geared for a regional war with Taiwan. Their arsenal of missiles, warheads, and aircraft carriers may be designed to attack U.S. ships if America were to become involved.

9/27/10—China imposes chicken tariffs on the U.S.

9/27/10—Russian and China celebrate the completion of an oil pipeline linking the two countries.

10/9/10—Treasury Secretary Geithner calls for the IMF to supervise China's currency, believing that they are keeping their currency artificially low.

10/15/10—The Treasury Department backs down from labeling China as a "currency manipulator" prior to the G-20 summit.

10/19/10—The United Steelworkers has asked the government to probe China for allegedly giving out illegal subsidies for green energy.

10/19/10—China is retaliating by halting shipments of rare earth minerals that are critical in manufacturing high-tech products.

10/24/10—G-20 gives China a bigger place at the IMF table. Treasury Secretary Geithner hopes that this move will make China more willing to be flexible with its currency rates.

10/25/10—China is on track to invest $30 billion in Brazil, up from $400 million last year. Approximately $20 billion will be going to the oil sector.

11/1/10—After the Federal Reserve announces its second round of "quantitative easing," China and almost every other country strongly disapproves of the U.S. monetary policy. The denunciations are too numerous to mention in this section but can be found in Part III.

11/24/10—China and Russia officially quit using the dollar when trading with each other. The new policy is not directed at challenging the dollar, but at protecting their own economies.

11/24/10—The U.S. is asking China to keep North Korea on a short leash. The U.S. is sending the aircraft carrier, the USS *George Washington*, to the Yellow Sea for naval exercises with South Korea. See entry for 7/20/10.

12/28/10—China's military buildup is now a viable threat to the Pacific region. China now has an anti-ship missile capable of sinking U.S. aircraft carriers.

12/29/10—A Chinese defense minister says, "In the coming five years, our military will push forward preparations for military conflict in every strategic direction ... In the next five years, our economy and society will develop faster, boosting comprehensive national power. We will take the opportunity and speed up modernization of the military."

1/5/11—The World Bank is trying to promote the use of Chinese currency by issuing yuan-denominated bonds for the first time.

1/5/11—China's military technology is advancing faster than previously thought. Not only have they developed a ballistic missile capable of attacking aircraft carriers and warships, but they have developed a radar-evading stealth fighter plane.

1/9/11—The Defense Department reassesses its estimate of China's military. Secretary Gates says, "They clearly have potential to put some of our capabilities at risk. We have to pay attention to them; we have to respond appropriately with our own programs."

1/10/11—China snubs Defense Secretary Gates's invitation to discuss nuclear strategy. Gates tries to recover his composure by telling reporters that he is "pleased" that China will "consider and study" his plan for a nuclear dialogue.

1/16/11—Chinese President Hu Jintao continues the international onslaught against the dollar as the reserve currency. Hu asserts, "The monetary policy of the United States has a major impact on global liquidity and capital flows and therefore, the liquidity of the U.S. dollar should be kept at a reasonable and stable level."

1/17/11—Obama rolls out the "red" carpet hosting communist Chinese President Hu Jintao. Hu is treated to a lavish state dinner in honor of his visit to the U.S.

1/18/11—Obama addresses human rights concerns with President Hu. Hu responds that each nation must respect the other's core interests.

BRAZIL

3/14/09—Obama meets with Brazilian President Lula da Silva.

5/18/09—Brazil and China agree to use their own currencies in all trade transactions instead of using the dollar.

6/16/09—Brazil, Russia, India, and China call for the end of the dollar as the global reserve currency.

8/18/09—The Obama administration lends $2 billion to Petrobras, Brazil's state-owned oil company, to finance their offshore drilling operations.

10/5/09—Russia, China, Japan, Brazil, European countries, and Arab states are colluding to scrap the dollar as the world's oil trading currency in favor of a basket of currencies.

5/17/10—Iran signs a deal to export uranium to Turkey and Brazil in a blatant attempt to subvert U.S. attempts to halt Iran's nuclear program. The leaders pose triumphantly for a picture with raised, clenched hands.

10/25/10—China is on track to invest $30 billion in Brazil, up from $400 million last year. Approximately $20 billion will be going to the oil sector.

11/1/10—After the Federal Reserve announces its second round of "quantitative easing," Brazil and almost every other country strongly disapproves of the U.S. monetary policy. The denunciations are too numerous to mention in this section but can be found in Part III.

HONDURAS

6/26/09—President Zelaya tries to hold a national referendum on an unconstitutional reelection of himself. The Honduran Supreme Court, legislature, and human rights ombudsman have all declared Zelaya's move illegal.

6/28/09—Zelaya is ousted in a military coup. Obama, Secretary Clinton and other leftists such as Fidel Castro, Hugo Chavez, Daniel Ortega, and Evo Morales condemn Zelaya's exile.

7/7/09—The U.S. signals its support of deposed socialist Manuel Zelaya by inviting him to the U.S. to meet with Secretary of State Clinton.

7/10/09—The Obama administration withdraws $16.5 million in military aid to Honduras in retaliation for ousting Marxist President Zelaya.

7/21/09—The Obama administration is pressuring Honduras to reinstate Zelaya during mediation talks in Costa Rica.

7/23/09—Despite Obama's pressure, Honduras refuses to reinstate Zelaya.

7/28/09—The U.S. revokes the diplomatic visas of four Honduran officials as punishment for ousting the socialist Zelaya.

8/27/09—The State Department considers punishing Honduras by yanking $150 million in U.S. aid.

9/21/10—Zelaya takes refuge in the Brazilian embassy.

9/22/09—Honduran forces clash with pro-Zelaya forces outside the Brazilian embassy.

9/24/09—Zelaya claims Israeli assassins are trying to kill him and that he is being tortured with radiation and mind-altering gas.

12/3/09—Honduras votes against reinstating Zelaya.

ENGLAND

2/14/09—Obama returns bust of Winston Churchill to the Brits.

3/3/09—Obama meets with Prime Minister Gordon Brown and treats him shabbily.

3/7/09—With regard to the White House's discourteous treatment of Prime Minister Brown, a State Department official tells a British journalist, "There's nothing special about Britain. You're just the same as the other 190 countries in the world. You shouldn't expect special treatment."

4/1/09—Obama gives Queen Elizabeth an iPod with his speeches.

6/15/09—The U.K. is outraged when the U.S. ships four Uighur prisoners from Gitmo to Bermuda without notifying British authorities.

8/12/09—The Lockerbie bomber, Abdelbaset al-Megrahi, is released from a Scottish prison on compassionate grounds (with the conscious, behind-the-scenes support of American diplomats).

8/20/09—President Obama condemns Scotland for releasing the Lockerbie bomber.

9/6/09—The British maintain that Obama and Secretary Clinton were advised at all times prior to the release of the Lockerbie bomber.

9/23/09—Obama snubs Britain's Gordon Brown five times regarding a bilateral meeting at the U.N.

2/24/10—Obama backs Argentina in refusing to acknowledge legitimate British sovereignty over the Falkland Islands.

12/20/10—British police conduct a large-scale anti-terrorist sweep, apprehending twelve suspects accused of plotting terror attacks within the U.K.

12/22/10—In an ABC interview, director of National Intelligence James Clapper, is completely ignorant of the U.K.'s major arrest of terrorists just two days ago.

FRANCE

2/2/09—France rejects Obama-style stimulus.

4/15/09—Sarkozy characterizes Obama as unoriginal, unsubstantial, and overrated.

4/15/09—Sarkozy is miffed that Obama publicly called for Turkey's admission to the EU.

4/16/09—Sarkozy characterizes Obama as inexperienced, ill prepared and "not always up to standard on decision-making and efficiency."

6/5/09—Obama snubs France's President Sarkozy by declining a dinner invitation celebrating the sixty-fifth anniversary of D-Day.

7/9/09—President Medvedev uses the G-8 summit as a platform to call for the end of the dollar as the world's reserve currency. French President Sarkozy heartily agrees.

9/26/09—President Sarkozy criticizes Obama for being a pushover when it comes to Iran and North Korea. Sarkozy also believes Obama's viewpoint on nuclear arms is shallow.

3/12/10—President Sarkozy accuses Washington of protectionism in their contract-bidding process.

11/1/10—After the Federal Reserve announces its second round of "quantitative easing," France and almost every other country strongly disapproves of the U.S. monetary policy. The denunciations are too numerous to mention in this section but can be found in Part III.

1/7/11—French President Nicolas Sarkozy condemns the "religious cleansing" of Christians throughout the Middle East.

1/11/11—Obama declares, "We don't have a stronger friend and stronger ally than Nicolas Sarkozy and the French people."

GERMANY

6/4/09—Germans feel snubbed that Obama's visit is so short after his Cairo speech. The U.S. still has not appointed an ambassador, and the U.S. has only sent a low-level government employee to explain the effects of the GM bankruptcy on the German economy.

11/9/10—Obama sends a message to Germany celebrating the fall of the Berlin Wall. He never mentions the "Soviet Union" or "communism."

11/20/09—Germany chimes in over America's irresponsible monetary policy. Finance Minister Schauble believes the U.S. is creating a market bubble by devaluing the dollar and inflating away its debt.

5/9/10—Obama advises Chancellor Merkel that Europe needs to bail out Greece.

6/21/10—President Obama urges world leaders not to focus on cutting deficits. As usual, they ignore him.

6/21/10—Germany's economy minister says, "It's urgently necessary for monetary stability that public budgets return to balance. This is something we should also tell our American friends."

6/21/10—German Finance Minister Schaeuble responds, "Nobody can seriously dispute that excessive public debts, not only in Europe, are one of the main causes of this crisis."

11/1/10—After the Federal Reserve announces its second round of "quantitative easing," Germany and almost every other country strongly disapproves of the U.S. monetary policy. The denunciations are too numerous to mention in this section but can be found in Part III.

SWITZERLAND

2/18/09—The Department of Justice fines Swiss UBS $780 million for helping taxpayers shield assets.

2/19/09—The Department of Justice demands UBS hand over account information of American customers.

2/19/09—The Swiss party SVP accuses U.S. of "foreign blackmail."

3/4/09—The Swiss think banking issues should be resolved diplomatically, not judicially.

3/26/09—The IRS and Department of Justice provide U.S. citizens with an ultimatum to come forth and provide evidence against Swiss banks.

6/29/09—Swiss banks are closing Americans' bank accounts. They no longer want to deal with the Obama administration's aggressive onslaught.

7/1/09—The Department of Justice continues to insist that the Swiss break their own laws to accommodate the U.S. tax code.

7/8/09—The Swiss government continues to defy the U.S. Department of Justice and the IRS. The Swiss believe they are a sovereign nation with the right to exercise their own laws.

8/14/09—The IRS and Department of Justice issue another ultimatum to Americans banking in Switzerland.

8/19/09—Switzerland agrees to release the names of 4,450 Americans using Swiss banks to the IRS where "tax fraud and the like" is suspected.

4/13/10—A Texas man pleads guilty of filing false tax returns for "hiding" money at UBS.

G-20

3/11/09—U.S. encourages G-20 countries to launch Obama-style stimulus.

3/25/09—The EU president condemns U.S. proposals of a global stimulus as "the road to hell."

3/29/09—EU leaders dismiss the Obama administration's call for a "global new deal" of increased stimulus.

4/1/09—Obama tells world leaders he will listen and not lecture.

4/2/09—The G-20 issues its communiqué.

4/2/09—The G-20 will move toward replacing the dollar as the world's reserve currency.

4/2/09—Obama comes out of G-20 with nothing really to show for it.

7/8/09—G-8 leaders agree to cut greenhouse gas emissions 80 percent by 2050.

7/9/09—President Medvedev uses the G-8 summit as a platform to call for the end of the dollar as the world's reserve currency. French President Sarkozy heartily agrees.

9/21/09—The U.S. will propose a new economic world order at the upcoming G-20.

9/25/09—Obama credits the G-20 for saving the world economy, encourages tough international financial regulations and talks about climate change.

5/25/10—Obama is trying to secure an international financial agreement which would require countries to mandate larger banking reserves.

6/21/10—President Obama urges world leaders not to focus on cutting deficits. As usual, they ignore him.

6/21/10—Germany's economy minister says, "It's urgently necessary for monetary stability that public budgets return to balance. This is something we should also tell our American friends."

6/21/10—German Finance Minister Schaeuble responds, "Nobody can seriously dispute that excessive public debts, not only in Europe, are one of the main causes of this crisis."

6/24/10—In anticipation of G-20 meetings, Obama encourages other nations not to cut their debt too much or too quickly.

6/24/10—Treasury Secretary Geithner says the world "cannot depend as much on the U.S. as it did in the past.

6/27/10—Obama says, "A strong and durable recovery also requires countries not having an undue advantage."

10/21/10—Treasury Secretary Geithner tells the world's finance ministers he wants to focus on "rebalancing" the world economy so that it is less reliant on U.S. consumers.

10/21/10—Geithner also emphasizes that the U.S. will not be monetizing its debt.

10/24/10—G-20 finance ministers give China, Brazil, India, and Turkey a bigger place at the IMF table.

11/7/10—Ahead of the G-20 summit, Treasury Secretary Geithner is promoting a framework that would limit countries' trade balances.

11/7/10—Almost every country in the G-20 expresses its furor and outrage over the Federal Reserve's new program of quantitative easing. The comments and criticisms are too numerous to mention in this section, but many can be found in Part III.

11/11/10—The Fed's QE2 dominates the G-20 summit. Amid the howling chorus of harsh criticism, China says the U.S. "should not force others to take medicine for its own disease."

11/17/10—Roger Ailes commented on Obama's lackluster results at the

G-20 summit, "The President has not been very successful. He just got kicked from Mumbai to South Korea, and he came home and attacked Republicans for it. He had to be told by the French and the Germans that his socialism was too far left for them to deal with."

FOREIGN POLICY SNUBS

This is only a partial list of some of the most egregious snubs. Obama has snubbed Israel regularly. Insane rhetoric coming from Venezuela, Iran, and North Korea are almost daily occurrences.

China:

9/14/09—Obama postpones meeting with the Dalai Lama.

10/5/09—Obama refuses to meet with the Dalai Lama this week. The move is criticized as an effort to appease China.

12/18/09—China snubs Obama and Secretary Clinton by sending three low-level officials to meet with them.

2/18/10—Obama meets with the Dalai Lama. He demonstrates that he does not recognize the Dalai Lama as a head of state; he meets him in the White House Map Room. Obama literally treated the Dalai Lama like trash, forcing him to exit a side door among heaps of garbage.

6/2/10—China rejects (i.e., snubs) meeting with Defense Secretary Gates during his trip to Asia.

1/10/11—China snubs Defense Secretary Gates's invitation to discuss nuclear strategy. Gates tries to recover his composure by telling reporters that he is "pleased" that China will "consider and study" his plan for a nuclear dialogue.

Czech Republic:

3/31/09—Obama cancels plans to have dinner with the Czech president while he is in Prague in favor of having dinner with his wife.

France:

6/5/09—Obama snubs France's President Sarkozy by declining a dinner invitation celebrating the sixty-fifth anniversary of D-Day.

Germany:

6/4/09—Germans feel snubbed that Obama's visit is so short after his Cairo speech. The U.S. still has not appointed an ambassador and it has only sent a low-level government employee to explain the effects of the GM bankruptcy on the German economy.

Iran:

12/3/10—At a dinner party in Bahrain, the Iranian foreign minister snubs Secretary of State Clinton <u>twice</u> by refusing to shake Mrs. Clinton's extended hand or even acknowledge her presence.

Israel:

3/10/09—Vice President Biden keeps Prime Minister Netanyahu waiting for ninety minutes.

4/16/09—Obama cancels his first meeting with Prime Minister Netanyahu because he will not be "in town."

3/23/10—Obama leaves Israeli Prime Minister Netanyahu and his team sitting alone in a room in the White House. He says he is going to eat dinner with his family. He tells them they are welcome to hang around the White House if they want and, if they come up with anything important, they can let him know.

Nicaragua:

4/18/09—Obama sits politely as communist Daniel Ortega blasts the United States.

Norway:

12/9/09—Nobel Laureate Obama snubs lunch with Norway's King Harald V, dinner with the Nobel Committee, the Nobel Peace Center with an exhibition in his honor. He manages to snub the rest of the country by refusing to appear at a children's event, a press conference and TV interviews.

Spain:

8/4/10—The State Department advises travelers that, "Racist prejudices could lead to the arrest of Afro-Americans who travel to Spain."

The U.K.:

2/14/09—Obama returns bust of Winston Churchill to the Brits.

3/3/09—Obama meets with Gordon Brown and treats him shabbily.

3/7/09—A State Department official says there's nothing special about Britain and they're just like any other country.

6/15/09—The U.K. is outraged when the U.S. ships four Uighur prisoners from Gitmo to Bermuda without notifying British authorities.

9/6/09—The British maintain that Obama and Secretary Clinton were advised at all times prior to the release of the Lockerbie bomber.

9/23/09—Obama snubs Britain's Gordon Brown five times regarding a bilateral meeting at the U.N.

2/24/10—The Obama administration refuses to acknowledge the legitimacy British sovereignty over the Falkland Islands.

Endnotes

2009

1   Barack Obama's Inaugural Address," New York Times, January 20, 2009, http://www. nytimes.com/2009/01/20/us/politics/20text-obama.html.

2   "Obama's first call abroad to Palestin: Official," The Vancouver Sun, January 21, 2009   http://www.vancouversun.com/Life/Obama+first+call+abroad+Palesti ne/1202283/story.html,

3   Deborah Solomon, "Geithner Apologizes, Calls for 'Dramatic Action," Wall Street Journal, January 21, 2009, http://online.wsj.com/article/SB123254915519002447.html.

4   "Obama Faces Doubters On Economic Plan," CBS News, January 24, 2009, http://www. cbsnews.com/stories/2009/01/24/politics/100days/main4750909.shtml?tag=contentMain;c ontentBody

5   Brian Montopoli, "Obama Freezes Pay For White House Employees, Limits Lobbyists," CBS News, January 21, 2009, http://www.cbsnews.com/8301-503544_162-4744108-503544. html?tag=contentMain%3bcontentBody.

6   Paul Dvorak, "The Trash Was Historic Too," Washington Post, January 21, 2009, http:// www.washingtonpost.com/wp-dyn/content/article/2009/01/21/AR2009012103900.html.

7   Graham Keeley, "Fidel Castro praises Barack Obama as 'absolutely sincere'," Times On-line, January 21, 2009, http://www.timesonline.co.uk/tol/news/world/us_and_ameri-cas/us_elections/article5565856.ece.

8   Jonathan Martin & Carrie Budoff Brown, "Obama Flashes irritation in press room," Politico, January 22, 2009, http://www.politico.com/news/stories/0109/17831.html.

9   "Obama signs order to close Guantanamo Bay facility," CNN, January 22, 2009, http:// articles.cnn.com/2009-01-22/politics/guantanamo.order_1_detention-guantana-mo-bay-torture?_s=PM:POLITICS.

10   Brian Montopoli, "Obama: On Roe Anniversary, I Remanin Committed To Choice," CBS News, January 22, 2009, http://www.cbsnews.com/8301-503544_162-4747731-503544. html?tag=contentMain%3bcontentBody.

11   "Obama urges action on Gaza borders," Al-Jazeera, January 22, 2009, http://english. aljazeera.net/news/americas/2009/01/2009122205033617751.html.

12   "Obama reverses abortion-funding policy," CNN, January 23, 2009, http://articles. cnn.com/2009-01-23/politics/obama.abortion_1_abortion-counseling-family-planning-family-planning?_s=PM:POLITICS.

13   "Obama: Quit Listening to Rush Limbaugh if You Want to Get Things Done," Fox News, January 23, 2009, http://www.foxnews.com/politics/2009/01/23/obama-quit-listening-rush-limbaugh-want-things/.

14   "Freddie Mac Seeks Up to $35 Billion More in Aid," New York Times, January 23, 2009, http://dealbook.nytimes.com/2009/01/23/freddie-mac-seeks-up-to-35-billion-more-in-aid/.

15   Jeff Poor, "FNC's Kelly: What Happened to Eased Unemployment Promised with Obama Stimulus?," Media Research Center Network, May 26, 2009, http://www.mrc.org/ bmi/articles/2009/FNCs_Kelly_What_Happened_to_Eased_Unemployment_Promised_ with_Obama_Stimulus.html.

16   "Two ex-Guantanamo inmates appear in Al-Qaeda video," AFP, January 24, 2009, http://www.google.com/hostednews/afp/article/ALeqM5hZfIcWnHqBz4kQR90lC_pXa-HeW4Q

17   Andrea Shalal-Esa, "Challenges loom as Obama seeks space weapons ban," Reuters, January 25, 2009, http://www.reuters.com/article/idUSTRE50O15X20090125.

18   "Obama Lays Out New Energy Plan," CBS News, January 26, 2009, http://www.cbsnews.com/stories/2009/01/26/politics/100days/main4753112.shtml?tag=contentMain;contentBody.

19   Ibid.

20   Ibid.

21   Dawn Kopecki, "Fannie to Tap U.S. for as Much as $16 Billion in Aid (Update 2)," Bloomberg, January 26, 2009, http://www.bloomberg.com/apps/news?pid=newsarchive&sid=aS99YT_58YqY&refer=worldwide,,,.

22   "Full Transcript of Obama's Al-Arabiya interview," MSNBC, January 27, 2009, http://www.msnbc.msn.com/id/28870724/,,,.

23   "Venezuela denies Hamas, Hezbollah ties," Press TV, January 28, 2009, http://edition.presstv.ir/detail/83951.html.

24   Brian Montopoli, "Day 8: Obama Tries To Win Over Stimulus Skeptics," CBS News, January 27, 2009, http://www.cbsnews.com/8301-503544_162-4758072-503544.html?tag=contentMain%3bcontentBody.

25   Matthew Vadum, "ACORN's Stimulus," American Spectator, January 27, 2009, http://spectator.org/archives/2009/01/27/acorns-stimulus#.

26   Paul Sherman, "U.S. Federal Deficit To Top 10% of GDP at End of 2009," Capital Beat, January 27, 2009, http://capitalbeat.com/?p=781.

27   "Obama Woos GOP Over Stimulus Plan," CBS News, January 27, 2009, http://www.cbsnews.com/stories/2009/01/27/politics/100days/economy/main4755065.shtml?tag=contentMain;contentBody.

28   Kevin Hechtkopf, "Day 9: Obama Pushes Stimulus Plan, Meets With Joint Chiefs," CBS News, January 28, 2009, http://www.cbsnews.com/8301-503544_162-4761131-503544.html.

29   Tony Halpin and Tom Baldwin, "Russia 'stops missile deployment in Europe because of Obama,'" Times Online, January 28, 2009, http://www.timesonline.co.uk/tol/news/world/europe/article5602899.ece.

30   Chelsea Schilling, "Obama racks up list of broken promises, Just 2 months into term, president abandons numerous commitments," World Net Daily, March 12, 2009, http://www.wnd.com/?pageId=91286.

31   Brian Montopoli, "Obama Calls Wall Street Bonuses "Shameful," CBS News, January 29, 2009, http://www.cbsnews.com/8301-503544_162-4762719-503544.html.

32   Marc Champion and Andrew Batson, "Russia, China Blame Woes on Capitalism," Wall Street Journal, January 29, 2009, http://online.wsj.com/article/SB123315961511224575.html.

33   Robert Talt and Ewen MacAskill, "Revealed: the letter Obama team hope will heal Iran rift," The Guardian, January 29, 2009, http://www.guardian.co.uk/world/2009/jan/28/barack-obama-letter-to-iran.

34   Brian Montopoli, "Transcript: The President's Remarks On The Middle Class Task Force," CBS News, January 30, 2009, http://www.cbsnews.com/8301-503544_162-4764713-503544.html.

35   Jake Tapper, "Bumps in the Road: Obama's HHS Secretary Nominee Faces Tax Ques-

tions Over Car and Driver," ABC News, January 30, 2009, http://blogs.abcnews.com/politicalpunch/2009/01/bumps-in-the-ro.html.

36   Damian Paletta, Jonathan Weisman and Deborah Solomon, "U.S. Eyes Two-Part Bailout for Banks," Wall Street Journal, January 30, 2009, http://online.wsj.com/article/SB123326820233830623.html.

37   "Obama Authorizes $20 Million in Aid to Gaza Palestinians," Voice of America, January 30, 2009, http://www.voanews.com/english/news/a-13-2009-01-30-voa17-68810337.html.

38   Matt Spetalnick and Jeff Mason, "Obama pushes economic plan; cloud over health pick," Reuters, January 31, 2009, http://www.reuters.com/article/idUSTRE50P6MB20090131?sp=true.

39   Kevin Hechtkopf, "Day 12-13: Obama Pushes Stimulus Plan, Attends Comedy Dinner," CBS News, February 2, 2009, http://www.cbsnews.com/8301-503544_162-4770204-503544.html.

40   Marc Ambinder, "Obama Sends E-Mail To DNC/OFA List," The Atlantic, February 2, 2009, http://www.theatlantic.com/politics/archive/2009/02/obama-sends-e-mail-to-dnc-ofa-list/264/.

41   "Iran says Obama's offer to talk shows US failure," Breitbart, January 31, 2009, http://www.breitbart.com/article.php?id=CNG.073ba2ee2f1f00668848a4655420fedc.411.

42   "Unemployment Rate," Portal Seven, http://portalseven.com/employment/unemployment_rate.jsp.

43   Nicholas Ballasy, "Obama: My Presidency Will Be 'A one-Term Proposition' If Economy Doesn't Turn In 3 Years," CNS News, August 5, 2011, http://www.cnsnews.com/news/article/flashback-obama-my-presidency-will-be-one-term-proposition-if-economy-doesnt-turn-3.

44   Nelson D. Schwartz, "In time of crisis, looking to U.S. with wariness and hope," New York Times, February 1, 2009, http://www.nytimes.com/2009/02/01/business/worldbusiness/01iht-webglobal.19850861.html?_r=1.

45   Aliza Marcus and Edwin Chen, "Obama 'Absolutely' Backs Daschle After Tax Errors (Update2)," Bloomberg, February 2, 2009, http://www.bloomberg.com/apps/news?pid=newsarchive&sid=ak8vFBzQdnQw&refer=worldwide.

46   "Paris rejects 'Obama-style' stimulus program," New York Times, February 2, 2009, http://www.nytimes.com/2009/02/02/business/worldbusiness/02iht-frecon.4.19867327.html.

47   Brian Montopoli, "Day 15: Obama Takes Stimulus Fight To Public As Nominees Drop Out," CBS News, February 3, 2009, http://www.cbsnews.com/8301-503544_162-4773738-503544.html.

48   Jeff Mason, "U.S. sets executive pay limits for bailout companies," Reuters, February 3, 2009, http://www.reuters.com/article/idUSTRE5125P420090204.

49   David Charter, Rory Watson and Phillip Webster, "President Obama to water down 'Buy American' plan after EU trade war threat," Times Online, February 3, 2009, http://www.timesonline.co.uk/tol/news/world/europe/article5655115.ece.

50   "NKorean missile launch would be 'provocative':US," Breitbart, February 3, 2009, http://www.breitbart.com/article.php?id=CNG.5462250a30747f03350e1ee540485670.611&show_article=1.

51   "Missile Chronology," NTI, June 30, 2010, http://www.nti.org/b_aboutnti/b_index.

html.

52   Brian Faler, "Obama Pushes Congress to Complete Stimulus Package (Update1)," Bloomberg, February 4, 2009, http://www.bloomberg.com/apps/news?pid=newsarchive&sid=aj.gxocTEf9k&refer=worldwide.

53   Jim Tankersley, "California farms, vineyards in peril from warming, U.S. energy secretary warns," Los Angeles Times, February 4, 2009, http://articles.latimes.com/2009/feb/04/local/me-warming4.

54   Brian Montopoli, "Day 16: Obama Expands Children's Health Care, Limits Executive Pay," CBS News, February 4, 2009, http://www.cbsnews.com/8301-503544_162-4776422-503544.html.

55   Brian Montopoli, "Day 17: Obama Gets More Aggressive On Stimulus," CBS News, February 5, 2009, http://www.cbsnews.com/8301-503544_162-4778878-503544.html.

56   Glenn R. Simpson, "CIA Nominee Panetta Received $700,000 in Fees," Wall Street Journal, February 5, 2009, http://online.wsj.com/article/SB123378062602049003.html.

57   Ibid.

58   Brian Montopoli, "Day 18: Obama Pushes Hard On Stimulus," CBS News, February 6, 2009, http://www.cbsnews.com/8301-503544_162-4781514-503544.html.

59   "Obama Announces Economic Advisory Board," February 6, 2009, http://www.whitehouse.gov/the_press_office/ObamaAnnouncesEconomicAdvisoryBoard/.

60   Caroline B. Glick, "Obama's New World Order and Israel," Jewish World Review, February 10, 2009, http://www.jewishworldreview.com/0209/glick021009.php3.

61   Josef Federman, "UN halts aid to Gaza, cites Hamas disruption," Pakistan Defence, February 7, 2009, http://www.defence.pk/forums/world-affairs/21232-un-halts-aid-gaza-cites-hamas-disruption.html.

62   Ibid.

63   Edmund Conway, "IMF may run out of cash to fight crisis in six months, Strauss-Khan warns," The Daily Telegraph, February 8, 2009, http://www.telegraph.co.uk/finance/financetopics/financialcrisis/4560897/IMF-may-run-out-of-cash-to-fight-crisis-in-six-months-Strauss-Khan-warns.html.

64   Kevin Hechtkopf, "Senators Hail Stimulus Deal, But GOP Oppostion Remains," CBS News, February 11, 2009, http://www.cbsnews.com/8300-503544_162-503544-75.html?categoryId=10299.

65   "Obama's Press List Membership shall have its privileges," Wall Street Journal, February 12, 2009, http://online.wsj.com/article/SB123431418276770899.html.

66   Jerry Seper, "16 illegals sue Arizona rancher," Washington Times, February 9, 2009, http://www.washingtontimes.com/news/2009/feb/09/16-illegals-sue-arizona-rancher/.

67   "General Motors to Invest $1 Billion in Brazil Operations," Latin American Herald Tribune, February 9, 2009, http://www.laht.com/article.asp?CategoryId=12396&ArticleId=320909.

68   "Costly bank rescue plan aims to increase trust," Politico, February 10, 2009, http://www.politico.com/news/stories/0209/18659.html.

69   John Ydstie, "Lack of TARP-2 Details Pushes Dow Down," National Public Radio, February 10, 2009, http://www.npr.org/templates/story/story.php?storyId=100534817&ft=1&f=1001.

70   Oskar Garcia, "Mayor: Obama should apologize for Vegas trips quip," Breitbart, Febru-

ary 10, 2009, ttp://www.breitbart.com/article.php?id=D9694E2O0.

71   Brian Montopoli, "Day 23: Obama Lauds Stimulus Compromise," CBS News, February 11, 2009, http://www.cbsnews.com/8301-503544_162-4794188-503544.html.

72   Mark Knoller, "How Many "Top Priority" Issues Does Obama Have?," CBS News, August 13, 2010, http://www.cbsnews.com/8301-503544_162-20013622-503544.html.

73   Connie Hair, "Republicans Shut Out of Stimulus Conference Negotiations," Human Events, February 11, 2009, http://www.humanevents.com/article.php?id=30667.

74   February 11, 2001, http://www.youtube.com/watch?v=GpF5VO2XbDI.

75   Bruno Waterfield, "European bank bail-out could push EU into crisis," The Daily Telegraph, February 11, 2009, http://www.telegraph.co.uk/finance/financetopics/financialcrisis/4590512/European-banks-may-need-16.3-trillion-bail-out-EC-dcoument-warns.html.

76   Jake Tapper, "D'oh! Caterpillar CEO Contradicts President on Whether Stimulus Will Allow Him to Re-Hire Laid Off Workers," ABC News, February 12, 2009, http://blogs.abcnews.com/politicalpunch/2009/02/doh-caterpillar.html."

77   Brendan Scott and Ana Maria Alaya, "What's The Rush?," New York Post, February 15, 2009, http://www.nypost.com/p/news/national/item_ANAXdDX43gF8ywcWXdNYwN;jsessionid=4296D162CB473876495965D5BB0C0C56.

78   Tim Shipman, "Barack Obama sends bust of Winston Churchill on its way back to Britain," The Daily Telegraph, February 14, 2009, http://www.telegraph.co.uk/news/worldnews/barackobama/4623148/Barack-Obama-sends-bust-of-Winston-Churchill-on-its-way-back-to-Britain.html

79   Jerome Corsi, "Federal obligation exceed world GDP: Does $65.5 trillion terrify anyone yet?, WorldNetDaily, February 15, 2009, http://www.wnd.com/index.php?fa=PAGE.view&pageId=88851.

80   Kevin Krolicki, "GM needs up to $30B in aid to avoid failure," National Post, February 16, 2009, http://www.nationalpost.com/cars/needs+avoid+failure/1299377/story.html

81   Ibid.

82   Brian Montopoli, "Day 29: Obama Signs Stimulus, OKs Troop Increase," CBS News, February 17, 2009, http://www.cbsnews.com/8300-503544_162-503544-18.html?keyword=cbs&tag=contentMain;contentBody.

83   Betsy McCaughey, "Ruin Your Health With the Obama Stimulus Plan," Bloomberg, February 9, 2009, http://www.bloomberg.com/apps/news?pid=newsarchive&refer=columnist_mccaughey&sid=aLzfDxfbwhzs.

84   Chelsea Schilling, "Obama racks up list of broken promises, Just 2 months into term, president abandons numerous commitments," WorldNetDaily, March 12, 2009, http://www.wnd.com/?pageId=91286.

85   Matt Cover, "Only 23 Percent of Stimulus Will be Spent This Fiscal Year, Congressional Budget Office Find," CNS News, February 17, 2009, http://www.cnsnews.com/news/article/43708.

86   "GM, Chrysler file plans, ask for more money," MSNBC, February 17, 2009, http://www.msnbc.msn.com/id/29243150/.

87   "17,000 U.S. Troops Headed For Afghanistan," CBS News, February 17, 2009, http://www.cbsnews.com/stories/2009/02/17/politics/100days/iraqafghanistan/main4807791.shtml.

88   Devlin Barrett, "Holder: US is a nation of cowards on racial matters," Breitbart, February 18, 2009, http://www.breitbart.com/article.php?id=D96E53483&show_ar-

ticle=1.

89   "Obama Unveils $75B Mortgage Relief Plan," CBS News, February 18, 2009, http://www.cbsnews.com/stories/2009/02/18/politics/100days/economy/main4808886.shtml

90   John M. Broder, "E.P.A. Expected to Regulate Carbon Dioxide," New York Times, February 19, 2009, http://www.nytimes.com/2009/02/19/science/earth/19epa.html?_r=1.

91   Helene Cooper, "Obama Sets Ambitious Export Goal," New York Times, January 28, 2009, http://www.nytimes.com/2010/01/29/business/29trade.html.

92   "Top 20 banks receiving US aid are lending: Treasury," Breitbart, February 18, 2009, http://www.breitbart.com/article.php?id=CNG.4af01da7b3cc07f873e6956875508 2f5.c41&show_article=1.

93   "Swiss bank to pay U.S. $780 million," UPI, http://www.upi.com/Business_News/2009/02/18/Swiss-bank-to-pay-US-780-million/UPI-98221235008225/.

94   http://www.youtube.com/watch?v=zp-Jw-5Kx8k.

95   Lynnley Browning, "UBS Pressed for 52,000 Names in 2nd Inquiry," New York Times, February 20, 2009, http://www.nytimes.com/2009/02/20/business/worldbusiness/20ubs.html?_r=1&hp=&adxnnl=1&adxnnlx=1235084414-RBbVDgzSaixxNaeu6P1i9w.

96   Lisa Jucca and Jonathan Lynn, "UPDATE 5-Swiss bank secrecy under threat after UBS tax deal," Reuters, February 19, 2009, http://www.reuters.com/article/idUSTHO9568982009 0219?feedType=RSS&feedName=rbssFinancialServicesAndRealEstateNews&rpc=22&sp=true.

97   David Byers, James Hider, "Binyamin Netanyahu to be Israel's next Prime Minister," TimesOnline, February 20, 2009, http://www.timesonline.co.uk/tol/news/world/middle_east/article5772433.ece.

98   Brian Montopoli, "Day 31: Obama makes First Foreign Trip, To Canada," CBS News, February 19, 2009, http://www.cbsnews.com/8301-503544_162-4813873-503544.html.

99   Alex Morales, "Arctic Sea Ice Underestimated for Weeks Due to Faulty Sensor," Bloomberg, February 20, 2009, http://www.bloomberg.com/apps/news?pid=newsarchive&sid=aIe 9swvOqwIY.

100   Brian Montopoli, "Day 32: Obama Warns Mayors Not To Waste Stimulus Money," CBS News, February 20, 2009, http://www.cbsnews.com/8301-503544_162-4816743-503544.html.

101   "Clinton wraps Asia trip by asking China to buy US debt," Breitbart, February 20, 2009, http://www.breitbart.com/article.php?id=CNG.42a44b0f5d9cf5c9762e80574e79a3d5.831&show_article=1.

102   "Clinton softens her tone on China," New York Times, February 20, 2009, http://www.nytimes.com/2009/02/20/world/asia/20iht-clinton.4.20337969.html?_r=1.

103   Ibid.

104   Kevin Hechtkipf, "Days 33-34: Obama Hosts Governors At The White House," CBS News, February 23, 2009, http://www.cbsnews.com/8301-503544_162-4828776-503544.html.

105   Lori Montgomery and Ceci Connolly, "Obama's First Budget Seeks To Trim Deficit, Plan Would Cut War Spending, Increase Taxes on the Wealthy," Washington Post, February 21, 2009, http://www.washingtonpost.com/wp-dyn/content/article/2009/02/21/AR2009022100911_pf.html.

106   Lynnley Browning, "Rich Americans Sue UBS to Keep Names Secret," CNBC, February 25, 2009, http://www.cnbc.com/id/29385606.

107   Brian Montopoli, "Day 35: Obama Vows To Cut Deficit In Half," CBS News, February 23, 2009, http://www.cbsnews.com/8301-503544_162-4823030-503544.html.
108   David Faber, "AIG Seeks More US Funds As Firm Faces Record Loss," CNBC, February 23, 2009, http://www.cnbc.com/id/29353282.
109   Linda Shen, "Obama Bank Nationalization Is Focus of Speculation (Update3)," Bloomberg, February 23, 2009, http://www.bloomberg.com/apps/news?pid=newsarchive&sid=an GxzRYhVF_Y&refer=worldwide.
110   Bob Unruh, "Soldier questions eligibility, doubts president's authority, 'As and officer, my sworn oath to support and defend our Constitution requires this,'" WorldNetDaily, February 23, 2009, http://www.wnd.com/index.php?fa=PAGE.view&pageId=89837.
111   Helene Cooper, "U.S. to give $900 Million in Gaza Aid, Officials Say," New York Times, February 24, 2009, http://www.nytimes.com/2009/02/24/washington/24gaza.html?_r=1.
112   Kevin Hechtkopf, "Day 36: Recapping Obama's Address To Congress," CBS News, February 25, 2009, http://www.cbsnews.com/8301-503544_162-4828635-503544.html.
113   Brandi Grissom, "Homeland Security official affirms Mexican drug cartel violence has spilled over into Texas," El Paso Times, February 24, 2009, http://www.elpasotimes.com/newupdated/ci_11770847
114   Diana Washington Valdez, "Gov. Perry wants U.S. troops guarding border," El Paso Times, February 25, 2009, http://www.elpasotimes.com/news/ci_11779431.
115   Diana Washington Valdez, "After threats, Juarez mayor in El Paso," El Paso Times, February 24, 2009, http://www.elpasotimes.com/newupdated/ci_11770841.
116   John Bresnahan, "Byrd: Obama in power grab," Politico, February 25, 2009, http://www.politico.com/news/stories/0209/19303.html.
117   Stephen Smith, "Biden Vows To "Follow The Money,"" CBS News, February 25, 2009, http://www.cbsnews.com/8301-503544_162-4827236-503544.html.
118   Tony Capaccio, "Obama to Seek $75.5 Billion More for Wars in 2009 (Update2)," Bloomberg, February 25, 2009, http://www.bloomberg.com/apps/news?pid=newsarchive&sid=aN3Z5Oo3eStg&refer=worldwide.
119   Parisa Hafezi and Hossein Jaseb, "Iran says no slowdown in its nuclear work," Reuters, February 25, 2009, http://www.reuters.com/article/2009/02/25/us-iran-nuclear-work-idUSLP58564820090225?feedType=RSS&feedName=topNews&rpc=22&sp=true,,,.
120   Caren Bohan and Jeff Mason, "WRAPUP-7-Obama sees soaring deficits, pushes big goals, Reuters, February 26, 2009, http://www.reuters.com/article/idUSN2644850320090226?sp=true.
121   Roger Runningen and Brian Faler, "Obama Budget Has Contingency for More Aid to Banks (Update1)," Bloomberg, February 26, 2009, http://www.bloomberg.com/apps/news?pid=washingtonstory&sid=aY8vuevw1NKs.
122   Stephen Dinan and David Sands, "Charity tax limits upset many," Washington Times, February 27, 2009, http://www.washingtontimes.com/news/2009/feb/27/charity-tax-challenged-by-political-friends/.
123   J.P. Freire, "Obama made $5m in 2009 and tells us we've made enough?," Washington Examiner, April 28, 2010, http://washingtonexaminer.com/blogs/beltway-confidential/obama-made-5m-2009-and-tells-us-we039ve-made-enough.
124   Bob Egelko, "U.S. to yielf marijuana jurisdiction to states," San Francisco Chronicle, February 27, 2009, http://www.sfgate.com/cgi-bin/article.cgi?file=/c/a/2009/02/27/MN2016651R.DTL.

125   Steven Thomma, "Obama to extend Iraq withdrawal timetable; 50,000 troops to stay," McClatchy, February 27, 2009, http://www.mcclatchydc.com/2009/02/27/62930/obama-to-extend-iraq-withdrawal.html

126   "U.S. budget deficit reaches $765 billion in 5 months," The Economic Times, March 12, 2009, http://articles.economictimes.indiatimes.com/2009-03-12/news/28409973_1_budget-deficit-economic-assumptions-tax-revenues.

127   Richard Leong and Nick Olivari, "U.S. private sector axes 742,000 jobs in March," Reuters, April 1, 2009, http://www.reuters.com/article/idUSTRE5303F820090401.

128   "Unemployment Rate," Portal Seven, http://portalseven.com/employment/unemployment_rate.jsp.

129   Banjamin Lesser and Greg B. Smith, "Buildings sprang up as donations rained down on Bronx Bourough President Adolfo Carrion," New York Daily News, March 1, 2009, http://www.nydailynews.com/ny_local/bronx/2009/02/28/2009-02-28_buildings_sprang_up_as_donations_rained_.html.

130   Hugh Son and Rebecca Christie, "AIG May Get $30 Billion in Additional U.S. Capital (Update2)," Bloomberg, March 1, 2009, http://www.bloomberg.com/apps/news?pid=newsarchive&sid=a9tDCRpMNHkI&refer=worldwide.

131   Brian Montopoli, "Day 42: Obama Taps Sebelius For HHS," CBS News, March 2, 2009, http://www.cbsnews.com/8301-503544_162-4839548-503544.html.

132   Alison Vekshin, "Bair Says Insurance Fund Could Be Insolvent This Year (Update1), Bloomberg, March 4, 2009, http://www.bloomberg.com/apps/news?pid=newsarchive&sid=alsJZqIFuN3k&refer=homehttp://www.bloomberg.com/apps/news?pid=washingtonstory&sid=alsJZqIFuN3k.

133   Dick Morris and Eileen McGann, Catastrophe (New York: HarperCollins Publishers, 2010), 95-100.

134   Brian Montopoli, "Day 44: Obama Overhauls Contracts, Picks FEMA Head, Unveils Mortgage Program," CBS News, March 4, 2009, http://www.cbsnews.com/8301-503544_162-4843585-503544.html.

135   "Obama 'ready to drop shield plans for Russian help on Iran,'" Rianovosti, March 2, 2009, http://en.rian.ru/russia/20090302/120375219.html.

136   Ibid.

137   Brian Montopoli, "Day 43: Obama Meets With Brown, Talks Stocks," CBS News, March 3, 2009, http://www.cbsnews.com/8301-503544_162-4841753-503544.html.

138   Iain Martin, "President Barack Obama dislikes Britain, but he's keen to meet the Queen," The Daily Telegraph, March 6, 2009, http://blogs.telegraph.co.uk/news/iainmartin/9105397/President_Barack_Obama_dislikes_Britain_but_hes_keen_to_meet_the_Queen/.

139   Ian Drury, "To my special friend Gordon, 25 DVDs: Obama gives Brown a set of classic movies. Let's hope he like the Wizard of Oz," The Daily Mail, March 6, 2009, http://www.dailymail.co.uk/news/worldnews/article-1159627/To-special-friend-Gordon-25-DVDs-Obama-gives-Brown-set-classic-movies-Lets-hope-likes-Wizard-Oz.html.

140   "Barack Obama too tired to give proper welcome to Gordon Brown," The Daily Telegraph, March 7, 2009, http://www.telegraph.co.uk/news/worldnews/northamerica/usa/barackobama/4953523/Barack-Obama-too-tired-to-give-proper-welcome-to-Gordon-Brown.html.

141   Julianna Goldman and Kim Chipman, "Obama Releases Billions for Public Works Projects," Bloomberg, March 3, 2009, http://www.bloomberg.com/apps/news?pid=newsarchive&sid=a7PZO..IJU.s&refer=worldwide.

142 Brian Riedl, "Omnibus Spending Bill: Huge Spending and 9,000 Earmarks Represent Business as Usual," The Heritage Foundation, March 3, 2009, http://www.heritage.org/research/reports/2009/03/omnibus-spending-bill-huge-spending-and-9000-earmarks-represent-business-as-usual.

143 SteveK, "White House Knocks Jim Cramer For Calling Obama Budge "Greatest Wealth Destruction By a President," TVNewser, March 3, 2009, http://www.mediabistro.com/tvnewser/white-house-knocks-jim-cramer-for-calling-obama-budget-greatest-wealth-destruction-by-a-president_b23066.

144 Brian Montopoli, "Day 43: Obama Meets With Brown, Talks Stocks," CBS News, March 3, 2009, http://www.cbsnews.com/8301-503544_162-4841753-503544.html.

145 Stephen Ohlemacher, "Geithner: Obama to fight intenational tax dodgers," Breitbart, March 3, 2009, http://www.breitbart.com/article.php?id=D96MN08G1&show_article=1.

146 Liz hazelton, "Hillary Clinton attacks Israeli plan to demolish 80 Palestinian homes in East Jerusalem 'to make way for Jewish families,'" The Daily Mail, March 3, 2009, http://www.dailymail.co.uk/news/worldnews/article-1158870/Hillary-Clinton-attacks-Israeli-plan-demolish-80-Palestinian-homes-East-Jerusalem-make-way-Jewish-families.html.

147 Kevin Drawbaugh and Corbett B. Daly, "UBS exec criticizes U.S. effort to get account data," Reuters, March 4, 2009, http://www.reuters.com/article/idUSTRE5236OL20090304?feedType=RSS&feedName=topNews.

148 Dan Levy, "More Than 8.3 Million U.S. Mortgages Are Under Water (Update3), Bloomberg, March 4, 2009, http://www.bloomberg.com/apps/news?pid=newsarchive&sid=amoql5AqN9z4&refer=worldwide.

149 Tom Doggett, "US Treasury secretary attacks oil, gas tax breaks," Reuters, March 4, 2009, http://in.reuters.com/article/idINN0454844120090304.

150 Brian Montopoli, "Day 44: Obama Overhauls Contracts, Picks FEMA Head, Unveils Mortgage Program," CBS News, March 4, 2009, http://www.cbsnews.com/8301-503544_162-4843585-503544.html.

151 Ibid.

152 Richard Spencer, "China to increase defence spending by 15 per cent," The Daily Telegraph, March 4, 2009, http://www.telegraph.co.uk/news/worldnews/asia/china/4936931/China-to-increase-defence-spending-by-15-per-cent.html

153 Jeremy McDermott, "Venezuela's Hugo Chavez tightens state crontrol of food amid rocketing inflation and food shortages," The Telegraph, March 4, 2009, http://www.telegraph.co.uk/news/worldnews/southamerica/venezuela/4938993/Venezuelas-Hugo-Chavez-tightens-state-control-of-food-amid-rocketing-inflation-and-food-shortages.html

154 Brian Montopoli, "Day 45: Obama Hosts Health Care Reform Forum," CBS News, March 5, 2009, http://www.cbsnews.com/8301-503544_162-4847215-503544.html.

155 Nouriel Roubini, "The U.S. Financial System Is Effectively Insolvent," Forbes, March 4, 2009, http://www.forbes.com/2009/03/04/global-recession-insolvent-opinions-columnists-roubini-economy.html.

156 Pete Harrison, "Never waste a good crisis, Clinton says on climate," Reuters, March 7, 2009, http://in.reuters.com/article/idINTRE5251VN20090306.

157 "Russian media teases Clinton over 'reset' button," Breitbart, March 7, 2009, http://www.breitbart.com/article.php?id=CNG.9ca28ad2530b0d0029e1304762eca18f.8c1.

158 Tim Shipman, "Barack Obama 'too tired' to give proper welcome to Gordon Brown," The Daily Telegraph, March 7, 2009, http://www.telegraph.co.uk/news/worldnews/

northamerica/usa/barackobama/4953523/Barack-Obama-too-tired-to-give-prop-er-welcome-to-Gordon-Brown.html.

159   David Saltonstall, "London aghast at President Obama over gifts given to Prime Minister Brown," New York Daily News, March 7, 2009, http://www.nydailynews.com/news/politics/2009/03/06/2009-03-06_london_aghast_at_president_obama_over_gi.html.

160   Brian Montopoli, "Days 47-48: Obama Signals Openness To Talking To Taliban," CBS News, March 9, 2009, http://www.cbsnews.com/8301-503544_162-4854934-503544.html.

161   Rory Carroll, "Obama will use spring summit to bring Cuba in from the cold," The Guardian, March 8, 2009, http://www.guardian.co.uk/world/2009/mar/08/cuba-obama-administration.

162   Ben Smith, "Freeman hits 'Israel lobby' on way out," Politico, March 11, 2009, http://www.politico.com/news/stories/0309/19856.html.

163   "Iran using nuclear talks to buy time for bomb: Israel," Breitbart, March 8, 2009, http://www.breitbart.com/article.php?id=CNG.0083ee8504ebab02aaef67ccd951d391.d81&show_article=1.

164   Thomas Ferraro, "Iran test-fires new missile – media," Reuters, March 8, 2009, http://in.reuters.com/article/idINIndia-38404720090308.

165   Chelsea Schilling, "Obama racks up list of broken promises, Just 2 months into term, president abandons numerous commitments," WorldNetDaily, March 12, 2009, http://www.wnd.com/?pageId=91286.

166   Michelle Levi, "Day 49: President Obama's Schedule," CBS News, March 9, 2009, http://www.cbsnews.com/8301-503544_162-4853606-503544.html.

167   Matthew Kalman, "Clinton Announces Million-Dollar Scholarship Program for Palestinian Students," The Chronicle of Higher Education, March 9, 2009, http://chronicle.com/article/Clinton-Announces/42530.

168   Brian Montopoli, "Day 50: Obama Lays Out Education Priorities," CBS News, March 10, 2009, http://www.cbsnews.com/8301-503544_162-4857327-503544.html.

169   Janine Zacharia, "U.S. condemns Israel's plans to build housing in east Jerusalem," Washington Post, March 9, 2009, http://www.washingtonpost.com/wp-dyn/content/article/2010/03/09/AR2010030900497.html.

170   Henry J. Pulizzi, "Obama Backs Spending Bill, Pushes for New Rules," Wall Street Journal, March 11, 2009, http://online.wsj.com/article/SB123676768335693459.html.

171   Brian Montopoli, "Day 51: Obama (Reluctantly) Signs Spending Bill," CBS News, March 11, 2009, http://www.cbsnews.com/8301-503544_162-4860371-503544.html

172   Christopher S. Rugaber, "Budget Deficit Reaches $765B in 5 months," Breitbart, March 11, 2009, http://www.breitbart.com/article.php?id=D96RVTCO0&show_article=1.

173   Dawn Kopecki, "Freddie to Tap $30.8 Billion in Aid as Losses Deepen (Update2), Bloomberg, March 11, 2009, http://www.bloomberg.com/apps/news?pid=newsarchive&sid=abhCNOyyZPnc&refer=worldwide.

174   David Charter and Phillip Webster, "'Difficult' Americans hamper G20 efforts to secure a global deal," TimesOnline, March 11, 2009, http://www.timesonline.co.uk/tol/news/politics/article5884398.ece.

175   Foster Klub, "Top US, China diplomats work to smooth relations," Jakarta Post, March 11, 2009, http://www.thejakartapost.com/news/2009/03/11/top-us-china-diplomats-work-smooth-relations.html.

176   "Afghan Taliban Leader Was At Gitmo," The Right Perspective, March 11, 2009, http://

www.therightperspective.org/2009/03/11/afghan-taliban-leader-was-at-gitmo/.

177   "N. Korea Accuses Obama's Government of Interference," Fox News, March 11, 2009, http://www.foxnews.com/story/0,2933,508587,00.html.

178   Jim Kuhnhenn, "Obama: Economic crisis 'not as bad as we think,'" Breitbart, March 12, 2009, http://www.breitbart.com/article.php?id=D96SP30G5&show_article=1.

179   "White House objects to UN calling US 'deadbeat,'" Breitbart, March 12,2009, http://www.breitbart.com/article.php?id=D96SLVQ85&show_article=1.

180   Spencer S. Hsu, "Obama Considering Guard Troops on Texas-Mexico Border," Washington Post, March 12, 2009, http://voices.washingtonpost.com/44/2009/03/12/obama_considering_guard_troops.html.

181   Sam Cage, "Corporate oil booms in low-tax Switzerland," Reuters, March 12, 2009, http://www.reuters.com/article/idUSL312427120090312?feedType=RSS&feedName=rbssEnergyNews&rpc=22.

182   Brian Montopoli, "Day 52: Obama Says Not to Waste Stimulus," CBS News, March 12, 2009, http://www.cbsnews.com/8301-503544_162-4862756-503544.html.

183   Randall Mikkelsen, "U.S. drops 'enemy combatant' as basis for detention," Reuters, March 13, 2009, http://www.reuters.com/article/2009/03/13/idUSWAT011142

184   Michael Wines, "China's Leader Says He Is 'Worried' Over U.S. Treasuries," New York Times, March 14, 2009, http://www.nytimes.com/2009/03/14/business/worldbusiness/14china.html.

185   Andrew Batson and Andrew Browne, "Wen Voices Concern Over China's U.S. Treasurys," Wall Street Journal, March 13, 2009, http://online.wsj.com/article/SB123692233477317069.html.

186   Susanne Walker, "Treasuries Fall as Stocks Rise, China Comments on debt Safety," Bloomberg, March 13, 2009, http://www.bloomberg.com/apps/news?pid=newsarchive&sid=aP7DPb6vb0Eo&refer=worldwide.

187   Andrew Batson and Andrew Browne, "Wen Voices Concern Over China's U.S. Treasurys," Wall Street Journal, March 13, 2009, http://online.wsj.com/article/SB123692233477317069.html.

188   Susanne Walker, "Treasuries Fall as Stocks Rise, China Comments on debt Safety," Bloomberg, March 13, 2009, http://www.bloomberg.com/apps/news?pid=newsarchive&sid=aP7DPb6vb0Eo&refer=worldwide.

189   Jackie Calmes and Robert Pear, "Administration Is Open to Taxing Health Benefits," New York Times, March 15, 2009, http://www.nytimes.com/2009/03/15/us/politics/15health.html.

190   Glenn Somerville, "Treasury objects to AIG bonus payments," Reuters, March 15, 2009, http://www.reuters.com/article/idUSTRE52D1ZR20090314.

191   "Russia weights Cuba, Venezuela bases: report," Reuters, March 14, 2009, http://www.reuters.com/article/idUSTRE52D1ZR20090314.

192   Tim Reid, "US warships head for South China Sea after standoff," TimesOnline, March 14, 2009, http://www.timesonline.co.uk/tol/news/world/us_and_americas/article5898650.ece.

193   Kevin Hechtkopf, "Days 54-55: Obama Meets With Brazil's President, Names FDA Chief," CBS News, March 15, 2009, http://www.cbsnews.com/8300-503544_162-503544.html?keyword=Luiz+Inacio+Lula+Da+Silva.

194   "Obama says US economy sound, reassures investors," Jakarta Post, March 15, 2009, http://www.thejakartapost.com/news/2009/03/15/obama-says-us-economy-

sound-reassures-investors.html.

195   Adam Nagourney, "Bracing for a Backlash Over Wall Street Bailouts," New York Times, March 16, 2009, http://www.nytimes.com/2009/03/16/us/politics/16assess.html.

196   Craig Roberts, "The American Legion Strongly Opposed to President's Plan to Charge Wounded Heroes for Treatment," InfoWars, March 16, 2009, http://www.infowars.com/the-american-legion-strongly-opposed-to-presidents-plan-to-charge-wounded-heroes-for-treatment/.

197   Matt Spetalnick, "White House ridicules Cheney over criticism of Obama," Reuters, March 16, 2009, http://www.reuters.com/article/idUSTRE52F72H20090316.

198   Carol E. Lee, "Biden: Economy tougher than FDR's," Politico, March 17, 2009, http://www.politico.com/news/stories/0309/20101.html.

199   Manu Raju, "National debt hits record $11 trillion," Politico, March 17, 2009, http://www.politico.com/news/stories/0309/20139.html.

200   Bret Baier, "Terrorism Is a 'Man-Caused' Disaster?," Fox News, March 17, 2009, http://www.foxnews.com/on-air/special-report/2009/03/18/terrorism-man-caused-disaster.

201   Carol E. Lee, "Biden: Economy tougher than FDR's," Politico, March 17, 2009, http://www.politico.com/news/stories/0309/20101.html.

202   Jake Tapper, "Obama Administration: We Didn't Find Out About AIG Bonuses Until This Month," ABC News, March 17, 2009, http://blogs.abcnews.com/politicalpunch/2009/03/obama-adminis-1.html

203   Ira Iosebashvili, "At G20, Kremlin to Pitch New Currency," Moscow Times, March 17, 2009, http://www.themoscowtimes.com/business/article/at-g20-kremlin-to-pitch-new-currency/375364.html.

204   Andrew Osborn, "Kremlin Signals a Harder Line on Relations With the U.S.," Wall Street Journal, March 18, 2009, http://online.wsj.com/article/SB123730715570057705.html.

205   Cristina Corbin, "ACORN to Play Role in 2010 Census," Fox News, March 18, 2009, http://www.foxnews.com/politics/2009/03/18/acorn-play-role-census/.

206   "Fed launches bold $1.2T effort to revive economy," China Daily, March 19, 2009, http://www.chinadaily.com.cn/world/2009-03/19/content_7593655.htm.

207   Brian Montopoli, "Day 57: Obama Celebrates St. Patrick's Day," CBS News, March 17, 2009, http://www.cbsnews.com/8301-503544_162-4872652-503544.html.

208   Devlin Barrett, "Attorney General Signals Shift In Medical Marijuana Policy," Huffingtonpost, March 18, 2009, http://www.huffingtonpost.com/2009/03/18/attorney-general-signals-_n_176592.html.

209   "Reports: Russia confirms Iran missile contract," USA Today, March 18, 2009, http://www.usatoday.com/news/world/2009-03-18-russia-iran-missiles_N.htm.

210   Jeremy Gaunt, "U.N. panel says world should ditch dollar," Reuters, March 18, 2009, http://www.reuters.com/article/idUSTRE52H2CY20090318.

211   Ben Johnson, "Obama's Biggest Radical," FrontPageMag, February 27, 2009, http://archive.frontpagemag.com/readArticle.aspx?ARTID=34198.

212   Andrew McCarthy, "Lawyer's Lawyer, Radical's Radical," National Review, March 9, 2009, http://nrd.nationalreview.com/article/?q=YzcyODUwNjAwNzg3YTYyZjBiOWU3ZTQwZmYzOGIwOGQ.

213   Bob McCarthy, "Obama Drops Plans to Soak Wounded Veterans," Bobmccarty.com, March 19, 2009, http://bobmccarty.com/2009/03/19/obama-drops-plans-to-soak-wounded-veterans/.

214   Ryan J. Donmoyer, "Dodd Blames Obama Administration for Bonus Amendment (Update2), Bloomberg, March 19, 2009, http://www.bloomberg.com/apps/news?pid=washingtonstory&sid=aT_tMXRy2vDs.

215   "Fed launces bold $1.2T effort to revive economy," China Daily, March 19, 2009, http://www.chinadaily.com.cn/world/2009-03/19/content_7593655.htm.

216   Jonathan Martin, "Obama apologizes for remark," Politico, March 20, 2009, http://www.politico.com/news/stories/0309/20268.html.

217   "Duke Coach to Obama: Worry About the Economy, Not NCAA Picks," Fox News, March 19, 2009, http://www.foxnews.com/politics/2009/03/19/duke-coach-obama-worry-economy-ncaa-picks/.

218   "U.S. Budget Deficit Forecast to Hit $1.8 Trillion This Year," Fox News, March 20, 2009, http://www.foxnews.com/politics/2009/03/20/budget-deficit-forecast-hit-trillion-year/.

219   John Hughes, "GM, Chrysler May Need More Aid Than Requested, Rattner Says," Bloomberg, March 21, 2009, http://www.bloomberg.com/apps/news?pid=newsarchive&sid=aV8LR4i3muGE&refer=worldwide.

220   Brian Montopoli, "Obama: 'We Need Some Inventiveness,'" CBS News, March 23, 2009, http://www.cbsnews.com/8301-503544_162-4885397-503544.html.

221   "EDITORIAL: Stop Mirandizing terrorists," Washington Times, June 12, 2009, http://www.washingtontimes.com/news/2009/jun/12/stop-mirandizing-terrorists/.

222   Brian Montopoli, "Day 64: Obama Holds Prime Time News Conference," CBS News, March 24, 2009, http://www.cbsnews.com/8301-503544_162-4890909-503544.html.

223   Brian Montopoli, "Obama: 'We Need Some Inventiveness,'" CBS News, March 23, 2009, http://www.cbsnews.com/8301-503544_162-4885397-503544.html.

224   Christopher Wilson, "Obama faces Notre Dame backlash," MSNBC, March 23, 2009, http://firstread.msnbc.msn.com/_news/2009/03/23/4436211-obama-faces-notre-dame-backlash.

225   Jamil Anderlini, "China calls for new reserve currency," Financial Times, March 23, 2009, http://www.ft.com/cms/s/0/7851925a-17a2-11de-8c9d-0000779fd2ac.html#axzz1B70PmkaT.

226   Binyamin Appelbaum and David Cho, "U.S. Seeks Expanded Power to Seize Firms," Washington Post, March 23, 2009, http://www.washingtonpost.com/wp-dyn/content/article/2009/03/23/AR2009032302830_pf.html.

227   Al Kamen, "The End of the Global War on Terror," Washington Post, March 23, 2009, http://voices.washingtonpost.com/44/2009/03/23/the_end_of_the_global_war_on_t.html?hpid=news-col-blog.

228   Ron Rournier, "Analysis: Teleprompter telegraphs Obama caution," Breitbart, March 23, 2009, http://www.breitbart.com/article.php?id=D974P3SG0&show_article=1.

229   Michael Calderone, "Obama skips major papers: No NYT, WaPo, WSJ, USA Today," Politico, March 23, 2009, http://www.politico.com/blogs/michaelcalderone/0309/Who_got_questions_at_2nd_presser.html?showall.

230   Peter Orszag, "Press Briefing," Whitehouse.gov, March 25, 2009, http://www.whitehouse.gov/sites/default/files/omb/assets/blog/032509_Orszag_Press_Briefing.pdf.

231   Roger Runningen and Ryan J. Donmoyer, "Obama Asks Volcker to Lead Panel on Tax-Code Overhaul (Update4)," Bloomberg, March 25, 2009, http://www.bloomberg.com/apps/news?pid=newsarchive&sid=a8yCQsJfpb24&refer=home.

232   "Postal chief says post office running out of money," Breitbart, March 25, 2009, http://www.breitbart.com/article.php?id=D97582V00&show_article=1.

233   "Bishop to skip Notre Dame graduation over Obama's views," CNN, March 24, 2009, http://www.cnn.com/2009/POLITICS/03/24/obama.bishop/index.html.

234   Ben Smith, "Geithner 'open' to china proposal," Politico, March 25, 2009, http://www.politico.com/blogs/bensmith/0309/Geithner_open_to_China_proposal.html?showall.

235   Tony Barber and Edward Luce, "EU leader condemns US 'road to hell,'" Financial Times, March 25, 2009, http://www.ft.com/cms/s/0/1d3fa8fa-1975-11de-9d34-0000779fd2ac.html#axzz1B70PmkaT.

236   Arshad Mohammed, "U.S. to blame for much of Mexico violence: Clinton," Reuters, March 25, 2009, http://www.reuters.com/article/2009/03/25/us-usa-mexico-idUSTRE52O5RF20090325?feedType=RSS&feedName=topNews&rpc=22&sp=true.

237   "Clinton: N. Korea Plan to Fire Missile 'Provocative,'" Fox News, March 25, 2009, http://www.foxnews.com/politics/2009/03/25/clinton-n-korea-plan-missile-provocative/.

238   Tom Braithwaite and Francesco Guerrera, "US reveals sweeping regulatory overhaul," Financial Times, March 26, 2009, http://www.ft.com/cms/s/0/9d8a6dd2-1a11-11de-9f91-0000779fd2ac.html#axzz1B70PmkaT.

239   "Terror inmates may be released in US: intel chief," Breitbart, March 26, 2009, http://www.breitbart.com/article.php?id=CNG.18e9e5692442aa61d7510553b5ffc14e.e01&show_article=1.

240   Devlin Barrett, "IRS squeezes Swiss bank clients for evidence," Sign On San Diego, March 26, 2009, http://www.signonsandiego.com/news/2009/mar/26/ubs-secrets-clients-032609/.

241   "UN panel touts new global currency reserve system," Breitbart, March 26, 2009, http://www.breitbart.com/article.php?id=CNG.18e9e5692442aa61d7510553b5ffc14e.8b1&show_article=1.

242   "Russia plans to create Arctic military force," Breitbart, March 27, 2009, http://www.breitbart.com/article.php?id=D976C8E01&show_article=1.

243   "North Korean rocket could reach Hawaii: US admiral," Breitbart, March 26, 2009, http://www.breitbart.com/article.php?id=CNG.92e661444313b232e8931de00c29c73b.de1&show_article=1.

244   Brian Montopoli, "Day 67: Obama Announces New Afghanistan Strategy," CBS News, March 27, 2009, http://www.cbsnews.com/8301-503544_162-4898442-503544.html.

245   Mike Allen and Josh Gerstein, "GM CEO resigns at Obama's behest," Politico, March 29, 2009, http://www.politico.com/news/stories/0309/20625.html.

246   George Stephanopoulus, "Geithner of TARP Money: 'We Have Roughly $135 Billion Left,'" ABC News, March 29, 2009, http://blogs.abcnews.com/george/2009/03/geithner-on-tar.html.

247   Spencer S. Hsu, "DHS Signals Policy Changes Ahead for Immigration Raids," Washington Post, March 29, 2009, http://www.washingtonpost.com/wp-dyn/content/article/2009/03/29/AR2009032901109_pf.html.

248   Michelle Levi, "Obama Considering Sending U.S. Troops To Mexican Border," CBS News, March 29, 2009, http://www.cbsnews.com/8301-503544_162-4900882-503544.html.

249   Ambrose Evans-Pritchard, "Russia backs return to Gold Standard to solve financial crisis," The Telegraph, March 29, 2009, http://www.telegraph.co.uk/finance/financetopics/g20-summit/5072484/Russia-backs-return-to-Gold-Standard-to-solve-financial-crisis.html.

250   Jonathan Oliver and Bohan Pancevski, "Brown snubbed over tax, Germans wreck 'global new deal,'" TimesOnline, March 29, 2009, http://www.timesonline.co.uk/tol/news/politics/G20/article5993184.ece.

251   Bill Sammon, "Gates: U.S. Not Prepared to Respond to North Korea Missile Launch," Fox News, March 29, 2009, http://www.foxnews.com/politics/2009/03/29/gates-prepared-respond-north-korea-missile-launch/.

252   Paul Tharp, "Today's Target: Detroit, White House Gets Tough," New York Post, March 30, 2009, http://www.nypost.com/p/news/business/item_iGWcRefnrJwV3RW0zn8UxH;jsessionid=D445A922C951DA12AE54C6EF4ACCE6BA.

253   Greg Gardner, "Obama Forced Chrysler Into Bankruptcy," Sweetness & Light, June 7, 2009, http://sweetness-light.com/archive/obama-forced-chryslers-bankruptcy.

254   Ed Morrissey, "Unveiling the Government Car Warranty," Hotair, March 30, 2009, http://hotair.com/archives/2009/03/30/unveiling-the-government-car-warranty/.

255   "Russia, China cooperate on new currency proposals," Breitbart, March 30, 2009, http://www.breitbart.com/article.php?id=CNG.7e6cab4fec704a0fdd135ecdac0067 3b.9c1&show_article=1.

256   "Obama Justice Department Shut Down Federal ACORN Investigation According to Documents Obtained by Judicial Watch," Breitbart, March 11, 2010, http://www.breitbart.com/article.php?id=xprnw.20100311.DC69102.

257   Erica Werner, "Sebelius admits errors, pays $7,000 in back taxes," Breitbart, March 31, 2009, http://www.breitbart.com/article.php?id=D979CMGO0&show_article=1.

258   Chris Adams, "Watchdogs: Treasury won't disclose bank bailout details," McClatchy, March 31, 2009, http://www.mcclatchydc.com/2009/03/31/65195/watchdogs-treasury-wont-disclose.html.

259   Rosie Johnston, "Does curtailed programme spell snub for Obama's Czech hosts?," Cesky Rozhlas, March 31, 2009, http://www.radio.cz/en/section/curraffrs/does-curtailed-programme-spell-snub-for-obamas-czech-hosts.

260   Richard Leong and Nick Olivari, U.S. private sector axes 742,000 jobs in March, Reuters, April 1, 2009, http://www.reuters.com/article/idUSTRE5303F820090401.

261   "U.S. Budget Deficit Hits $192.3B In March," CBS News, April 10, 2010, http://www.cbsnews.com/stories/2009/04/10/politics/100days/main4935470.shtml.

262   Stephanie Armour, "Foreclosures 46% higher in March than a year ago," USA Today, April 16, 2009, http://www.usatoday.com/money/economy/housing/2009-04-16-foreclosures_N.htm.

263   "Unemployment Rate," Portal Seven, http://portalseven.com/employment/unemployment_rate.jsp.

264   Stephen Smith, "Geithner On Ousting CEOs, Reviving Economy," CBS News, April 1, 2009, http://www.cbsnews.com/8301-503983_162-4911030-503983.html.

265   Calvin Woodward, "PROMISES, PROMISES: Obama tax pledge up in smoke," Breitbart, April 1, 2009, http://www.breitbart.com/article.php?id=D979POSG0&show_article=1.

266   Kevin Krolicki, "GM asks U.S. gov't for $2.6 bln to build hybrids," Reuters, April 1, 2009, http://www.reuters.com/article/idINN0152247120090402?rpc=44.

267   Jake Tapper, "What Does One Get a Queen?," ABC News, April 1, 2009, http://blogs.abcnews.com/politicalpunch/2009/04/what-does-one-g.html.

268 "Asian countries call for global currency," WikiNews, April 6, 2009, http://en.wikinews.org/wiki/Asian_countries_call_for_global_currency.

269 Brian Montopoli, "Day 72: Obama's Whirlwind Day Of Diplomacy," CBS News, April 1, 2009, http://www.cbsnews.com/8301-503544_162-4911556-503544.html.

270 Karl Rove, "The President Is 'Keeping Score,' Chicago politics has moved into the White House," Wall Street Journal, April 2, 2009, http://online.wsj.com/article/SB123862834153780427.html.

271 Pascal Fletcher, "UPDATE 3-US accuses UBS client of tax evasion, more to come," Reuters, April 2, 2009, http://www.reuters.com/article/idUSN0227011520090402.

272 Brian Montopoli, "Day 73: Obama Wraps Up At G20," CBS News, April 2, 2009, http://www.cbsnews.com/8301-503544_162-4915041-503544.html.

273 Demetri Sevastopulo, Mure Dickie and Christian Oliver, "N Korea warned over missile launch," Financial Times, April 2, 2009, http://www.ft.com/intl/cms/s/0/99bd5ac4-1fa3-11de-a7a5-00144feabdc0.html#axzz1WTSDXKqL.

274 Matt Drudge, "New Israeli PM Netanyahu wastes little time," DrudgeReport, April 2, 2009, www.drudgereport.com.

275 "RAW DATA: G-20 Communique Statement," Fox News, April 2, 2009, http://www.foxnews.com/politics/2009/04/02/raw-data-g-communique-statement/

276 Jane Wardell, "G-20 to give $1 trillion to IMF, World Bank," Breitbart, April 2, 2009, http://www.breitbart.com/article.php?id=D97ADJJO0.

277 Ambrose Evans-Pritchard, "The G20 moves the world a step closer to a global currency," The Telegraph, April 3, 2009, http://www.telegraph.co.uk/finance/comment/ambroseevans_pritchard/5096524/The-G20-moves-the-world-a-step-closer-to-a-global-currency.html.

278 Brian Montopoli, "Day 73: Obama Wraps Up At G20," CBS News, April 2, 2009, http://www.cbsnews.com/8301-503544_162-4915041-503544.html.

279 Ralph Peters, "O's Amateur hour, Appeasing Islamists in Turkey," New York Post, April 8, 2009, http://www.nypost.com/p/news/opinion/opedcolumnists/item_cB9ec23XV3KArRGjtqnjSO;jsessionid=6DA53BB84825EBE3581098725A89CC57.

280 Flor Miguez, "Obama's first year in office." Commonsensepoliticsusa.com, January 27, 2010, http://commonsensepoliticsusa.wordpress.com/2010/01/27/obamas-first-year-in-office-its-the-economy-stupid/.

281 Kevin Hechtkopf, "Obama Reaches Out To The World," CBS News, April 3, 2009, http://www.cbsnews.com/8301-503544_162-4916458-503544.html.

282 Sher Zieve, "Obama Begins Turnover of USA Sovereignty to International Body," Canada Free Press, April 3, 2009, http://www.canadafreepress.com/index.php/article/9908.

283 James Fallows, "More on Obama, exceptionalism, and impromptu speaking," The Atlantic, April 5, 2009, http://www.theatlantic.com/technology/archive/2009/04/more-on-obama-exceptionalism-and-impromptu-speaking/9876/.

284 Michael Evans and David Charter, "Barack Obama fails to win NATO troops he wants for Afghanistan," TimesOnline, April 4, 2009, http://www.timesonline.co.uk/tol/news/world/us_and_americas/article6032342.ece.

285 Stuart Varney, "Obama Wants to Control the Banks, There's a reason he refuses to accept repayments of TARP money," Wall Street Journal, April 4, 2009, http://online.wsj.com/article/SB123879833094588163.html.

286 Jonathan Martin and David S. Cloud, "Obama calls for 'world without' nukes," Politico, April 5, 2009, http://www.politico.com/news/stories/0409/20901.html.

287 Jeff Green, "GM Said to Speed Bankruptcy Plans as Board Crafts Savings Goals," Bloomberg, April 6, 2009, http://www.bloomberg.com/apps/news?pid=newsarchive&sid=af2zdGPHQ0NU&refer=worldwide.

288 Jesse Westbrook, "Geithner May Oust Executives at Banks Needing 'Exceptional' Aid," Bloomberg, April 6, 2009, http://www.bloomberg.com/apps/news?pid=newsarchive&sid=aMWnzAPdYvl8&refer=worldwide.

289 "Asian countries call for global currency," WikiNews, April 6, 2009, http://en.wikinews.org/wiki/Asian_countries_call_for_global_currency.

290 "Obama makes Surprise Visit To Iraq," CBS News, April 9, 2010, http://www.cbsnews.com/stories/2009/04/07/politics/100days/iraqafghanistan/main4925411.shtml.

291 Ralph Peters, "O's Amateur hour, Appeasing Islamists in Turkey," New York Post, April 8, 2009, http://www.nypost.com/p/news/opinion/opedcolumnists/item_cB9ec23XV3KArRGjtqnjSO;jsessionid=6DA53BB84825EBE3581098725A89CC57.

292 James Kirchick, "Squanderer in chief," Los Angeles Times, April 28, 2009, http://articles.latimes.com/2009/apr/28/opinion/oe-kirchick28.

293 "Homeland Security on guard for 'right-wing extremists,'" WorldNetDaily, April 12, 2009, http://www.wnd.com/?pageId=94803.

294 Audrey Hudson, "Homeland agency pulled back extremism dictionary," Washington Times, May 5, 2009, http://www.washingtontimes.com/news/2009/may/05/homeland-pulled-back-extremism-dictionary/.

295 David Cho, Peter Whoriskey and Amit R. Paley, "Pay Rule Led Chrysler to Spurn Loan, Agency Says," Washington Post, April 20, 2009, http://www.washingtonpost.com/wp-dyn/content/article/2009/04/20/AR2009042002156.html.

296 Matthew Boyle, "Private emails detail Obama admin involvement in cutting non-union worker pensions post-GM bailout," The Daily Caller, June 22, 2011, http://dailycaller.com/2011/06/22/private-emails-detail-obama-admin-involvement-in-cutting-non-union-worker-pensions-post-gm-bailout/.

297 Charles Herman and Alice Gomstyn, "Financial Crisis 'Far From Over,' Panel Says," ABC News, April 7, 2009, http://abcnews.go.com/Business/Economy/story?id=7283059&page=1.

298 Helen Chernikoff, "Mortgage delinquencies soar in the U.S.," Reuters, April 7, 2009, http://www.reuters.com/article/idUSTRE5363EV20090407.

299 Joanna Chung and Daniel Dombey, "US moves on Iran nuclear trade," Financial Times, April 8, 2009, http://www.ft.com/cms/s/0/bd57f0ca-239f-11de-996a-00144feabdc0.html#axzz1BNiCwPv5.

300 "Iran poses no threat to US: Russia," Breitbart, April 8, 2009, http://www.breitbart.com/article.php?id=CNG.89f94643ff57e11b42acfa11b92f8e26.fd1&show_article=1.

301 "Obama makes Surprise Visit To Iraq," CBS News, April 9, 2010, http://www.cbsnews.com/stories/2009/04/07/politics/100days/iraqafghanistan/main4925411.shtml.

302 "Biden: New Israel would be 'ill-advised' to attack Iran," Breitbart, April 7, 2009, http://www.breitbart.com/article.php?id=CNG.89f94643ff57e11b42acfa11b92f8e26.ed1.

303 Daniel Wallis, "Pirates hijack ship with 20 Americans onboard," Reuters, April 8, 2009, http://www.reuters.com/article/idUSTRE53721Z20090408?feedType=RSS&feedName=domesticNews&rpc=22&sp=true.

304 Jon Herskovitz, "North Korea celebrates launch, makes new threat," Reuters, April 8, 2009, http://www.reuters.com/article/idUST26328320090408.

305   Michelle Levi, "Obama Announces Electronic Health Records For Vets," CBS News, April 9, 2009, http://www.cbsnews.com/8301-503544_162-4931789-503544.html.

306   www.marklevinshow.com.

307   "Obama asks Congress for extra $83.4 bln for military," Reuters, April 9, 2009, http://www.reuters.com/article/idUSN0930196920090409.

308   "Iran claims to install 7,000 centrifuges," Breitbart, April 9, 2009, http://www.breitbart.com/article.php?id=CNG.648c7f446c0adbd8abd546a57259eed4.271&show_article=1.

309   Bradley Keoun and Scott Lanman, Fed Said to Order Banks to Stay Mum on 'Stress Test' Results," Bloomberg, April 10, 2009, http://www.bloomberg.com/apps/news?pid=newsarchive&sid=aEX9sBcofMYY&refer=worldwide.

310   John D. Stoll, Jeffrey McCracken and Kate Linebaugh, "U.S. Squeezes Auto Creditors," Wall Street Journal, April 10, 2009, http://online.wsj.com/article/SB123932036083306929.html.

311   "U.S. Budget Deficit Hits $192.3B In March," CBS News, April 10, 2009, http://www.cbsnews.com/stories/2009/04/10/politics/100days/main4935470.shtml.

312   Elizabeth Hester and Linda Shen, "Stress-Tested Banks may Struggle as Bad Assets Triple (Update4)," Bloomberg, April 24, 2009, http://www.bloomberg.com/apps/news?pid=newsarchive&sid=aj2.3MlNetzM.

313   Joe Lauria, North Korea Crisis Tests Obama's Reliance on U.N.," Wall Street Journal, April 11, 2009, http://online.wsj.com/article/SB123941001784910263.html.

314   Aaron Klein, "Will a 'red' help blacks go green?," WorldNetDaily, April 12, 2009, http://www.wnd.com/?pageId=94771.

315   "Obama: Holder Will Decide Whether To Prosecute Torture Authors, Supports Bipartisan Truth Commission," Thinkprogress, April 21, 2009, http://thinkprogress.org/politics/2009/04/21/37726/obama-holder-prosecutions/.

316   Keith Bradsher, "China Slows Purchases of U.S. and Other Bonds," New York Times, April 13, 2009, http://www.nytimes.com/2009/04/13/business/global/13yuan.html.

317   Michelle Levi, "Days 82 and 83: Pirates, Praise and PWDs," CBS News, April 13, 2009, http://www.cbsnews.com/8301-503544_162-4940096-503544.html.

318   Matt Spetalnick, "Obama opens crack in U.S. embargo against Cuba," Reuters, April 13, 2009, http://www.reuters.com/article/idUSTRE53C3O620090413?feedType=RSS&feedName=topNews&rpc=22&sp=true.

319   Jim Iovino, "Jesus Missing From Obama's Georgetown Speech, White House asked university to cover symbol," NBC, April 16, 2009, http://www.nbcwashington.com/news/local-beat/Jesus-Missing-From-Obamas-Georgetown-Speech.html.

320   "Obama: 'Instant Gratification' Fueled Bust," CBS News, April 14, 2009, http://www.cbsnews.com/stories/2009/04/14/politics/politico/main4943656.shtml.

321   Linda Sandler, Rebecca Christie and Jeff Green, "Auto Team Considers Swapping GM Loan fro Equity (Update2)," Bloomberg, April 14, 2009, http://www.bloomberg.com/apps/news?pid=newsarchive&sid=ad9_AOTWnbnQ&refer=home.

322   "Castro criticizes Obama's Cuba measures; Moves fall short of lifting 'cruel' embargo," As In The Days of Noah, April 15, 2009, http://asinthedaysofnoah.blogspot.com/2009/04/castro-criticizes-obamas-cuba-measures.html.

323   Sam Youngman, "Obama 'amused' by Tea Party rallies," The Hill, April 15, 2009, http://thehill.com/homenews/administration/92625-obama-amused-by-tea-party-rallies.

324   Eric Lichtblau and James Risen, "Official Say U.S. Wiretaps Exceeded Law," New York Times, April 16, 2009, http://www.nytimes.com/2009/04/16/us/16nsa.html

325   Eli Lake, "Napolitano stands by controversial report," Washington Times, April 16, 2009,   http://www.washingtontimes.com/news/2009/apr/16/napolitano-stands-rightwing-extremism/.

326   Charles Bremmer, "World Agenda: Nicolas Sarkozy puts Barack Obama in the doghouse," TimesOnline, April 16, 2009, http://www.timesonline.co.uk/tol/news/world/world_agenda/article6098836.ece.

327   "One Question Napolitano," Politico, April 16, 2009, http://www.politico.com/blogs/anneschroeder/0409/One_Question_Napolitano.html

328   Elizabeth Hester, "Dimon Says He's Eager to Repay 'Scarlet Letter' TARP (Update3)," Bloomberg, April 16, 2009, http://www.bloomberg.com/apps/news?pid=newsarchive&sid=aQfH3nZz9azc&refer=worldwide.

329   Mark Felsenthal and Karey Wutkowski, "W.S. lays groundwork for bank stress test release," Reuters, April 16, 2009, http://www.reuters.com/article/idUSTRE53F-4NX20090416.

330   Mike Allen, "Obama consulted widely on memos," Politico, April 16, 2009, http://www.politico.com/news/stories/0409/21338.html.

331   "Obama: Holder Will Decide Whether To Prosecute Torture Authors," Thinkprogress, April 21, 2009, http://thinkprogress.org/2009/04/21/obama-holder-prosecutions/.

332   "CIA Off The Hook For Past Waterboarding," CBS News, April 16, 2009, http://www.cbsnews.com/stories/2009/04/16/politics/100days/main4950212.shtml.

333   Pascal Fletcher, "U.S. says ready to talk to Cuba," Reuters, April 16, 2009, http://www.reuters.com/article/idUSTRE53F7B620090416.

334   Ed Hornick, "Obama to latin America: Time for a 'new direction,'" Political Ticker, April 16, 2009, http://politicalticker.blogs.cnn.com/2009/04/16/obama-to-latin-america-time-for-a-new-direction/.

335   Jason Koutsoukis, "Obama's stance worries Israelis," The Age, April 18, 2009, http://www.theage.com.au/world/obamas-stance-worries-israelis-20090417-aa90.html

336   Tina Korbe, "The New Black Panther Party Case: A Timeline," Heritage Foundation, July 16, 2010, http://blog.heritage.org/2010/07/16/the-new-black-panther-party-case-a-timeline/.

337   H. Josef Hebert, "EPA takes first step toward climate change regs," Breitbart, April 17, 2009, http://www.breitbart.com/article.php?id=D97KBAC00&show_article=1.

338   Bruce Crumley, "Sarkozy's Comments on Leaders Draw Shock, Denial," Time, April 18, 2009, http://www.time.com/time/world/article/0,8599,1892375,00.html.

339   "Sarkozy Insults EU Colleagues and US Leader at Lunch," Gates of Vienna, April 17, 2009, http://gatesofvienna.blogspot.com/2009/04/gates-of-vienna-news-feed-4172009.html#15993.

340   Jason Koutsoukis, "Obama's stance worries Israelis," The Age, April 18, 2009, http://www.theage.com.au/world/obamas-stance-worries-israelis-20090417-aa90.html

341   "FBI, States Vastly Expand DNA Databases," Huffingtonpost, April 18, 2009, http://www.huffingtonpost.com/2009/04/18/fbi-states-vastly-expand_n_188626.html.

342   Robert Schmidt, "Bank Regulators Clash Over U.S. Stress-Tests Endgame (Update1)," Bloomberg, April 18, 2009, http://www.bloomberg.com/apps/news?pid=newsarchive&sid=aQM1Cmt7cY24&refer=worldwide.

343   "Ex-CIA chief: Obama risks national security," CNN, April 19, 2009, http://edition.cnn.

com/2009/POLITICS/04/19/cia.torture.chief/index.html.

344 Sheera Frenkel, "Israel stands ready to bomb Iran's nuclear sites," TimesOnline, April 18, 2009, http://www.timesonline.co.uk/tol/news/world/middle_east/article6115903.ece.

345 Kevin Hechtkopf, "Day 88: Obama Pledges 'New Beginning' With Cuba," CBS News, April 17, 2009, http://www.cbsnews.com/8301-503544_162-4960423-503544.html.

346 Flor Miguez, "Obama's first year in office," CommonSensePoliticsUSA, April 18, 2009, http://commonsensepoliticsusa.wordpress.com/2010/01/27/obamas-first-year-in-office-its-the-economy-stupid/.

347 Jake Tapper and Sunlen Miller, "Chavez Gifts Obama With Book That Assails U.S. for Exploiting Latin America," ABC News, April 18, 2009, http://blogs.abcnews.com/politicalpunch/2009/04/chavez-gifts-ob.html.

348 Major Garrett, "Obama Endures Ortega Diatribe," Fox News, April 18, 2009, http://www.foxnews.com/politics/2009/04/18/obama-endures-ortega-diatribe/.

349 Peter Hamby, "Axelrod suggests 'Tea Party' movement is 'unhealthy,'" Political Ticker, April 19, 2009, http://politicalticker.blogs.cnn.com/2009/04/19/axelrod-suggests-tea-party-movement-is-unhealthy/.

350 Edmund L. Andrews, "U.S. May Convert Banks' Bailouts to Equity Share," New York Times, April 19, 2009, http://www.nytimes.com/2009/04/20/business/20bailout.html.

351 Caren Bohan, "Obama doesn't rule out charges over interrogations," Reuters, April 21, 2009, http://www.reuters.com/article/2009/04/21/us-security-usa-obama-idUSTRE53J6MS20090421.

352 Akiva Elder-Haaretz, "U.S." Palestinians Need Not Recognize Israel as Jewish State Before Talks," Matzav, April 19, 2009, http://matzav.com/us-palestinians-need-not-recognize-israel-as-jewish-state-before-talks.

353 Huma Khan, "Obama Asks For $100 Million in Budget Cuts: Is it Just a Drop in the Bucket?," ABC News, April 20, 2009, http://abcnews.go.com/blogs/politics/2009/04/obama-asks-for/.

354 "Obama asks congress to back IMF boost," Breitbart, April 20, 2009, http://www.breitbart.com/article.php?id=CNG.e43b9036d7e888689f940591f2b4c7cd.b31&show_article=1.

355 Matt Drudge, "Cheney Calls For More CIA Reports To Be Declassified," DrudgeReport, April 21, 2009, http://www.drudgereportarchives.com/data/2009/04/21/20090421_013927_flashcm.htm.

356 "Ahmadinejad Attacks Israel, U.S. at U.N. Racism Conference," Fox News, April 20, 2009, http://www.foxnews.com/story/0,2933,517151,00.html.

357 Caren Bohan, "Obama doesn't rule out charges over interrogations," Reuters, April 21, 2009, http://www.reuters.com/article/2009/04/21/us-security-usa-obama-idUSTRE53J6MS20090421

358 Brian Montopoli, "Obama Signs National Service Bill," CBS News, April 21, 2009, http://www.cbsnews.com/8301-503544_162-4960344-503544.html.

359 Ibid.

360 Ben Blanchard and Lucy Hornby, "China displays resurgent naval strength," Reuters, April 21, 2009, http://af.reuters.com/article/worldNews/idAFTRE53K11O20090421.

361 "On Earth Day, Obama Talks Up Wind Power," CBS News, April 22, 2009, http://www.cbsnews.com/stories/2009/04/22/tech/main4961315.shtml.

362 Mark Knoller, "Obama Earth Day Flights Burned More Than 9,000 Gallons of Fuel," CBS

News, April 22, 2009, http://www.cbsnews.com/8301-503544_162-4962384-503544.
html?CMP=OTC-RSSFeed&source=RSS&attr=PoliticalHotsheet_4962384.

363 "US needs rest of world economy to recover: Geithner," Breitbart, April 22, 2009,
http://www.breitbart.com/article.php?id=CNG.9867c5035cd3c8b80d71014626f10
fc8.3d1&show_article=1.

364 Matt Drudge, "Obama graces cover of 'Time' for 13th time in past year," DrudgeReport, April 22, 2009, www.drudgereport.com.

365 "U.S. Treasury's Geithner says downturn may be easing – FT," Reuters, April
24, 2009, http://www.reuters.com/article/2009/04/23/financial-geithner-ft-
idUSLN67924120090423.

366 Caren Bohan, ""Obama to attend meeting with credit card firms," Reuters, April
24, 2009, http://www.reuters.com/article/2009/04/23/financial-geithner-ft-
idUSLN67924120090423.

367 "Obama Pushes Stronger Credit Card Rules," CBS News, April 23, 2009, http://www.
cbsnews.com/stories/2009/04/23/politics/100days/economy/main4963448.shtml.

368 "Obama to release interrogation photos," UPI, April 23, 2009, http://www.upi.
com/Top_News/2009/04/23/Obama-to-release-interrogation-photos/UPI-
94901240542264/.

369 Devlin Barrett, "Holder won't selectively release terror memos," Breitbart, April 23,
2009, http://www.breitbart.com/article.php?id=D97OCRP01&show_article=1.

370 Jennifer Loven, "White House: No independent interrogations probe," Breitbart, April
23, 2009, http://www.breitbart.com/article.php?id=D97ODIOG0&show_article=1.

371 Mark Decambre, "CEO STRESSED OUT," New York Post, April 24, 2009, http://www.
nypost.com/p/news/business/item_eYGJs3oUJZg5loUDPQHXJL;jsessionid=EC9
6F887E5F4421A7AADE08CE797181C.

372 "Credit Suisse warns of 'excessive' state action," Breitbart, April 24, 2009, http://www.
breitbart.com/article.php?id=CNG.d81974e1cbbbefa036fc5a30929876c4.b1.

373 Brian Montopoli, "Days 96-97: Obama Gets In Some Golf," CBS News, April 27, 2009,
http://www.cbsnews.com/8301-503544_162-4975765-503544.html?tag=contentMain%3bc
ontentBody.

374 "China calls for reform of global monetary system," Breitbart, April 26, 2009, http://
www.breitbart.com/article.php?id=CNG.d0b05e03449a3458184c8c136bfcc595.
f01&show_article=1.

375 Jeff Dunetz, "National Securtiy Adviser Jones: Jews Are Greedy Merchants," RedState,
April 26, 2009, http://www.redstate.com/jeffdunetz/2010/04/26/national-security-
adviser-jones-jews-are-greedy-merchants/.

376 Kenneth Bazinet, Alison Gendar and Christina Boyle, "Feds knew Air Force One photo-op flyover might spark panic in the city – but didn't give a hoot," New York Daily News,
April 29, 2009, http://www.nydailynews.com/ny_local/2009/04/29/2009-04-29_feds_knew_
flyover_might_spark_panic.html.

377 Robert Schoenberger, "Government, UAW to own 89% of GM if restructuring deal
works," The Plain Dealer, April 27, 2009, http://www.cleveland.com/business/index.
ssf/2009/04/government_uaw_to_own_89_perce.html.

378 Tom Suhadolnik, "Obama's Pinstripe Revolution," American Thinker, May 6, 2009,
http://www.americanthinker.com/2009/05/obamas_pinstripe_revolution.html.

379 Alexander Burns, "Obama gets ahead of prompter," Politico, April 27, 2009, http://www.
politico.com/politico44/perm/0409/obama_gets_ahead_of_prompter_3813cbcb-

1e4a-44c6-b1e7-26017e7b70c2.html.

380 "Obama Promises Major Investment In Science," CBS News, April 30, 2009, http://www.cbsnews.com/stories/2009/04/27/politics/main4970918.shtml.

381 "Report: US seeks to aid Hamas-backed gov't," Ynet News, April 27, 2009, http://www.ynetnews.com/articles/0,7340,L-3707195,00.html.

382 John Lippert and Mike Ramsey, "UAW Said to Get 55% Chrysler Ownership, Board Seats (Update1), Bloomberg, April 28, 2009, http://www.bloomberg.com/apps/news?pid=newsarchive&sid=al89RU9gWof8&refer=home.

383 Edwin Chen and Roger Runningen, "Obama, on 100th Day, Says He Is 'Remaking America' (Update3)," Bloomberg, April 29, 2009, http://www.bloomberg.com/apps/news?pid=newsarchive&sid=aEOXy3xJPVoU&refer=worldwide.

384 Luke Funk, "Air Force Jets Over Manhattan Spark Panic," My Fox, April 27, 2001, http://www.myfoxny.com/dpp/news/090427_Jet_Circles_Lower_Manhattan.

385 Edwin Chen and Roger Runningen, "Obama, on 100th Day, Says He Is 'Remaking America' (Update3)," Bloomberg, April 29, 2009, http://www.bloomberg.com/apps/news?pid=newsarchive&sid=aEOXy3xJPVoU&refer=worldwide.

386 Susan Jones, "Obama Tells Americans, 'Wash Your Hands,'" CNS News, April 29, 2009, http://www.cnsnews.com/node/47352.

387 Greg Gardner, "Obama Forced Chrysler into Bankruptcy," Sweetness & Light, June 7, 2009, http://sweetness-light.com/archive/obama-forced-chryslers-bankruptcy.

388 Edwin Chen and Roger Runningen, "Obama, on 100th Day, Says He Is 'Remaking America' (Update3)," Bloomberg, April 29, 2009, http://www.bloomberg.com/apps/news?pid=newsarchive&sid=aEOXy3xJPVoU&refer=worldwide.

389 Ibid.

390 Ibid.

391 Brian Blacksone, "Fed Open to Buying More Securities," Wall Street Journal, May 21, 2009,   http://online.wsj.com/article/SB10001424052970203771904574177673022851160.html.

392 "Garrett on White House 'retribution' against Fox," Politico, May 2, 2009, http://www.politico.com/blogs/michaelcalderone/0509/Garrett_on_White_House_retribution_against_Fox.html.

393 "Supreme Court Justice Souter To Retire," National Public Radio, April 30, 2009, http://www.npr.org/templates/story/story.php?storyId=103694193.

394 Jake Tapper, "White House Denies Charge By Attorney that Administration Threatened to Destroy Investment Firm's Reputation," ABC News, May 2, 2009, http://blogs.abcnews.com/politicalpunch/2009/05/bankruptcy-atto.html.

395 "China has 'canceled US credit card': lawmaker," Google, April 30, 2009, http://www.google.com/hostednews/afp/article/ALeqM5i4estRSYeFBIII9kezxnP4jgoGZQ.

396 Kevin G. Hall, "Job losses slow, but is it from government hiring?" McClatchy, May 8, 2009, http://www.mcclatchydc.com/2009/05/08/67789/job-losses-slow-but-is-it-from.html.

397 "IRS Tax Revenue Down," USA Today, May 26, 2009, http://www.usatoday.com/money/perfi/taxes/2009-05-26-irs-tax-revenue-down_N.htm.

398 "Unemployment Rate," Portal Seven, http://portalseven.com/employment/unemployment_rate.jsp.

399 Amy Diluna, "First Lady Michelle Obama steps out in Lanvin sneakers and they're only $540," New York Daily News, May 1, 2009, http://articles.nydailynews.com/2009-05-

01/entertainment/17922541_1_lanvin-fancy-footwear-first-lady-michelle-obama.

400 Mark Knoller, "How Many 'Top Priority' Issues Does Obama Have?," CBS News, August 13, 2010, http://www.cbsnews.com/8301-503544_162-20013622-503544.html.

401 Graham Bowley and Jeck Healy, "Worries Rise on the Size of U.S. Debt," New York Times, May 4, 2009, http://www.nytimes.com/2009/05/04/business/economy/04debt.html?_r=1&hpw.

402 Jake Tapper, "White House Denies Charge By Attorney that Administration Threatened to Destroy Investment Firm's Reputation," ABC News, May 2, 2009, http://blogs.abcnews.com/politicalpunch/2009/05/bankruptcy-atto.html.

403 "White House links Iran nukes to Palestinian state," Israel Today, May 4, 2009, http://www.israeltoday.co.il/default.aspx?tabid=178&nid=18709.

404 John D. McKinnon and Jesse Drucker, "Firms Face New Tax Curbs," Wall Street Journal, May 4, 2009, http://online.wsj.com/article/SB124140022601982149.html.

405 Ryan J. Donmoyer, "Ballmer Says Tax Would Move Microsoft Jobs Offshore (Update3)," Bloomberg, June 3, 2009, http://www.bloomberg.com/apps/news?pid=newsarchive&sid=aAKluP7yIwJY.

406 "China military build-up seems U.S.-focused: Mullen," Reuters, May 4, 2009, http://uk.reuters.com/article/2009/05/04/us-usa-china-military-idUK-TRE54363X20090504.

407 Ben Feller, "Obama, Biden wait in line to buy hamburgers," Breitbart, May 5, 2009, http://www.breitbart.com/article.php?id=D9808DQO0.

408 Tom Baldwin, "Barack Obama hints at tougher line on Israel," TimesOnline, May 5, 2009, http://www.timesonline.co.uk/tol/news/world/middle_east/article6229180.ece.

409 David Johnston and Scott Shane, "Interrogation Memos: Inquiry Suggests No Charges," New York Times, May 6, 2009, http://www.nytimes.com/2009/05/06/us/politics/06inquire.html?_r=1&hp,,,.

410 Matt Kelley, "Details thin on stimulus contracts," USA Today, May 6, 2009, http://www.usatoday.com/tech/news/techpolicy/2009-05-06-stimulus_N.htm.

411 Julia Duin, "Obama to be prayer day no-show," Washington Times, May 6, 2009, http://www.washingtontimes.com/news/2009/may/06/prayer-day-no-show/.

412 Roger Runningen and Brian Faler, "Obama Proposes Saving $17 Billion by Cutting Programs (Update3)," Bloomberg, May 7, 2009, http://www.bloomberg.com/apps/news?pid=newsarchive&sid=aFoD4LsL9QPE&refer=worldwide.

413 "Obama seeks to double tax law enforcement budget," Reuters, May 7, 2009, http://www.reuters.com/article/idUSTRE5464DP20090507.

414 "Obama vows to retrain unemployed," Breitbart, May 8, 2009, http://www.breitbart.com/article.php?id=CNG.1c433b2fde51ec190e5ff5ada161b7e5.e1&show_article=1.

415 Evan Halper, "U.S. threatens to rescind stimulus money over wage cuts," Los Angeles Times, May 8, 2009, http://articles.latimes.com/2009/may/08/local/me-health-cuts8.

416 Peter Whoriskey, "Under Restructuring, GM To Build More Cars Overseas," Washington Post, May 8, 2009, http://www.washingtonpost.com/wp-dyn/content/article/2009/05/07/AR2009050704336.html.

417 David Enrich, Dan Fitzpatrick and Marshall Eckblad, "Banks Won Concessions on Tests," Wall Street Journal, May 9, 2009, http://online.wsj.com/article/SB124182311010302297.html.

418   David Enrich, Robin Sidel and Deborah Solomon, "Fed Sees Up to $599 Billion in Bank Losses," Wall Street Journal, May 8, 2009, http://online.wsj.com/article/SB124172137962697121.html.

419   Jeff Poor, "Obama Blasts Fox News: 'I've Got One Television Station that is Entirely Dovoted to Attacking My Administration,' NewsBusters, June 16, 2009, http://www.newsbusters.org/blogs/jeff-poor/2009/06/16/obama-blasts-fox-news-ive-got-one-television-station-entirely-devoted-att.

420   "$328K 'Scare' Force One Flyover Photo Released," WCBSTV, May 18, 2009, http://newyork.cbslocal.com/2011/05/18/air-force-one-aborts-first-attempt-to-land-in-connecticut/air-force-one/.

421   "Hamas: We won't accept two-state solution," Haaretz, May 9, 2009, http://www.haaretz.com/news/hamas-we-won-t-accept-two-state-solution-1.275703.

422   "Cheney: Interrogations saved 'hundreds of thousands' of lives," Breitbart, May 10, 2009, http://www.breitbart.com/article.php?id=CNG.dc9a9389e3e13c60bc16c36307b899fb.111&show_article=1.

423   Brendan Murray, "White House Sees 3.5% Growth by Year-End, Exceeding Forecasts," Bloomberg, May 11, 2009, http://www.bloomberg.com/apps/news?pid=newsarchive&sid=afNxR8Ary_Nk&refer=worldwide,,,.

424   David Lightman, "Deficits soar even with rosy Obama budget assumptions," McClatchy, May 11, 2009, http://www.mcclatchydc.com/2009/05/11/67948/deficits-soar-even-with-rosy-obama.html.

425   Toby Harnden, "US replaces NATO commander in Afghanistan war overhaul," The Telegraph, May 11, 2009, http://www.telegraph.co.uk/news/worldnews/asia/afghanistan/5310230/US-replaces-Nato-commander-in-Afghanistan-war-overhaul.html.

426   www.marklevinshow.com

427   Declan McCullagh, "It's A Good Time To Work For Uncle Sam," CBS News, May 12, 2009, http://www.cbsnews.com/8301-503983_162-5007862-503983.html.

428   "FDA Blasts General Mills Over Cheerios Claim," WCBSTV, May 12, 2009, http://wcbstv.com/health/cheerios.general.mills.2.1007986.html.

429   Deborah Solomon and Damian Paletta, "U.S. Eyes Bank Pay Overhaul," Wall Street Journal, May 13, 2009, http://online.wsj.com/article/SB124215896684211987.html.

430   Jean Halliday, "Obama halves Chrysler's Planned Marketing Budget," Advertising Age, May 11, 2009, http://adage.com/article?article_id=136552.

431   Soyoung Kim and John Crawley, "GM, Chrysler to cut up to 3,000 dealers: sources," Reuters, May 13, 2009, http://www.reuters.com/article/idUSTRE54C64K20090513.

432   Josh Gerstein, "Obama reverses on releasing detainee photos," Politico, May 13, 2009, http://www.politico.com/news/stories/0509/22470.html.

433   "The President on Credit Card Tactics: 'Enough is Enough,'" White House, May 14, 2009,   http://www.whitehouse.gov/blog/The-President-on-Credit-Card-Tactics-Enough-is-Enough/.

434   Brian Faler, "House Passes War Bill Amid Criticism of Obama Policy (Update1)," Bloomberg, May 14, 2009, http://www.bloomberg.com/apps/news?pid=newsarchive&sid=a_sJT3FrgY_o&refer=worldwide.

435   Poornima Gupta, "Chrysler to terminate 25 percent of U.S. dealers," Reuters, May 14, 2009,   http://www.reuters.com/article/idUSTRE54D3FM20090514?feedType=RSS&feedName=topNews&rpc=22&sp=true.

436   Natasha Mozgovaya and Aluf Benn, "Obama warns Netanyahu: Don't surprise me with

Iran strike," Haaretz, May 14, 2009, http://www.haaretz.com/print-edition/news/obama-warns-netanyahu-don-t-surprise-me-with-iran-strike-1.275993.

437 Chris Isidore, "GM whacks 1,100 dealers," CNNMoney, May 15, 2009, http://money.cnn.com/2009/05/15/news/companies/gm_dealers/index.htm.

438 David Gardner, "Barack Obama U-turn over military terror trials," MailOnline, may 16, 2009, http://www.dailymail.co.uk/news/article-1182228/Barack-Obama-U-turn-military-terror-trials.html.

439 Jeffrey Heller, "At odds with Obama, Netanyahu heads to U.S.," Reuters, May 16, 2009, http://www.reuters.com/article/idUSTRE54F2J920090516.

440 "President Obama refuses to meet with Governor Gibbons about tourism comments," KTNV, May 18, 2009, http://www.ktnv.com/Global/story.asp?S=10383051.

441 David Bedein, "The Philadelphia Bulletin: US Admits Training Palestinian Armed Forces While PA Negotiates With Hamas," Israel Behind the News, May 18, 2009, http://israelbehindthenews.blogspot.com/2009/05/philadlephia-bulletin-us-admits.html.

442 Ross Colvin, "Obama says he wants progress with Iran by year's end," Reuters, May 18, 2009, http://www.reuters.com/article/2009/05/18/us-usa-iran-obama-idUSTRE-54H4QX20090518.

443 Jonathan Wheatley, "Brazil and China eye plan to axe dollar," Financial Times, May 18, 2009, http://www.ft.com/intl/cms/s/0/996b1af8-43ce-11de-a9be-00144feabdc0.html#axzz1XspKP6nx.

444 Steven R. Hurst, "Obama prods Netanyahu, Iran in Mideast foray," Breitbart, May 18, 2009, http://www.breitbart.com/article.php?id=D988V98O0&show_article=1.

445 "Obama unveils mpg rule, gets broad support," MSNBC, May 19, 2009, http://www.msnbc.msn.com/id/30810514/ns/us_news-environment/t/obama-unveils-mpg-rule-gets-broad-support/#.Tl2dMHPs6Go.

446 Jayne O'Donnell and James R. Healey, "Safety could suffer if we boost mileage by making cars smaller," USA Today, May 19, 2009, http://www.usatoday.com/money/autos/2009-05-19-auto-safety-small-cars_N.htm.

447 Tzvi Ben Gedalyahu, "Rocket Attack on Sderot home," Israel National News, May 19, 2009, http://www.israelnationalnews.com/News/News.aspx/131444.

448 Kristina Wong, "Do You Want Your OTV?," ABC News, May 20, 2009, http://blogs.abcnews.com/politicalpunch/2009/05/do-you-want-you.html.

449 "Feds to inject $7.5B more into GMAC," The Detroit News, May 20, 2009, http://www.detnews.com/article/20090520/AUTO01/905200376/Feds-to-inject-$7.5B-more-into-GMAC.

450 Ali Akbar Dareini, "Iran tests missile with range that can hit Israel," Breitbart, May 20, 2009, http://www.breitbart.com/article.php?id=D98A4CQG2&show_article=1.

451 Terence P. Jeffrey, "Obama's Transportation Secretary Says He Wants to 'Coerce People Out of Their Cars,'" CNS News, May 25, 2009, http://www.cnsnews.com/news/article/48578.

452 Matt Spetalnick, "Obama: Some Guantanamo prisoners to go to U.S.," Reuters, May 21, 2009, http://www.reuters.com/article/2009/05/21/us-guantanamo-obama-idUS-TRE54K11020090521.

453 Alec MacGillis, "Tracking Stimulus Spending May Not Be as Easy as Promised," Washington Post, May 21, 2009, http://www.washingtonpost.com/wp-dyn/content/article/2009/05/20/AR2009052003535.html.

454   "Upholding values will shield US from terror: Obama," Breitbart, May 22, 2009, http://www.breitbart.com/article.php?id=CNG.bd0713f4765981d1edbe5b522ce08354.3e1&show_article=1.

455   Kathy Chu, "Obama signs into law credit card reform," USA Today, May 22, 2009, http://www.usatoday.com/money/perfi/credit/2009-05-21-obama-credit-card-reform-law_N.htm.

456   "N.Korea may be planning missile tests: report," Breitbart, May 22, 2009, http://www.breitbart.com/article.php?id=CNG.686d42207318a92c2bfc6b3df68c90a5.381&show_article=1.

457   Louise Armitstead, "British banks revolt against Obama tax plan," The Telegraph, May 24, 2009, http://www.telegraph.co.uk/finance/newsbysector/banksandfinance/5374095/British-banks-revolt-against-Obama-tax-plan.html.

458   Adam Entous, "Netanyahu defies Obama on Israeli settlement freeze, Reuters, May 24, 2009, http://www.reuters.com/article/2009/05/24/us-israel-palestinians-settlements-idUSTRE54N12320090524.

459   Stephen Dinan, "Obama ducks promise to delay bill signings," Washington Times, May 26, 2009, http://www.washingtontimes.com/news/2009/may/26/obama-vow-to-delay-signing-is-subject-to-interpret/.

460   "Iran sends warships to Gulf of Aden – navy," Reuters, May 25, 2009, http://in.reuters.com/article/2009/05/25/idINIndia-39868320090525.

461   Parisa Hafezi and Zahra Hosseinian, "Iran's Ahmadinejad rejects Western nuclear proposal," Reuters, May 25, 2009, http://www.reuters.com/article/idUSTRE54O25V20090525?feedType=RSS&feedName=topNews&rpc=22&sp=true.

462   Justin McCurry and Tania Branigan, "North Korea tests nuclear weapon 'as powerful as Hiroshima bomb,'" The Guardian, May 25, 2009, http://www.guardian.co.uk/world/2009/may/25/north-korea-hiroshima-nuclear-test.

463   Bill Varner, "UN Security Council Condemns North Korea Nuclear Test (Update1), Bloomberg, May 25, 2009, http://www.bloomberg.com/apps/news?pid=newsarchive&sid=aKS4lyOHwn9k&refer=worldwide.

464   Charlie Savage, "A Judges View of Judging Is on the Record," New York Times, May 14, 2009, http://www.nytimes.com/2009/05/15/us/15judge.html.

465   Nathan Figler, "Sotomayor: Gun Ownership 'Unconstitutional,'" JumpingPools, May 26, 2009, http://jumpinginpools.blogspot.com/2009/05/sotomayor-gun-ownership.html.

466   Joe Kovacs, "Sonia Sotomayor 'La Raza member,'" WorldNetDaily, May 27, 2009, http://www.wnd.com/index.php?fa=PAGE.view&pageId=99420.

467   "UPDATE 1-Chrysler submits $448 million electric car plan," Reuters, May 26, 2009, http://uk.reuters.com/article/idUKN2651474920090526.

468   Mark Tapscott, "Furor grows over partisan car dealer closings," Washinton Examiner, May 26, 2009, http://washingtonexaminer.com/blogs/beltway-confidential/2009/05/furor-grows-over-partisan-car-dealer-closings.

469   Ellen Nakashima, "Obma Set to Create A Cybersecurity Czar With Broad Mandate," Washington Post, May 26, 2009, http://www.washingtonpost.com/wp-dyn/content/article/2009/05/25/AR2009052502104.html.

470   Mark Landler and Isabel Kershner, "Israeli Settlement Growth Must Stop, Clinton Says," New York Times, May 28, 2009, http://www.nytimes.com/2009/05/28/world/middleeast/28mideast.html.

471 Ambrose Evans-Pritchard, "China warns Federal Reserve over 'printing money,'" The Telegraph, May 24, 2009, http://www.telegraph.co.uk/finance/financetopics/financialcrisis/5379285/China-warns-Federal-Reserve-over-printing-money.html.

472 Jerry Seper, "Career lawyers overruled on voting case," Washington Times, May 29, 2009, http://www.washingtontimes.com/news/2009/may/29/career-lawyers-overruled-on-voting-case/?feat=home_cube_position1.

473 Brad Heath, "Stimulus projects bypass hard-hit states," USA Today, May 27, 2009, http://www.usatoday.com/news/nation/2009-05-27-contracts_N.htm.

474 "GM Bankruptcy Could Take 90 Days Or More: Official," CNBC, May 28, 2009, http://www.cnbc.com/id/30980818.

475 Phillip Elliott, "Obama says health care changes must come this year," Breitbart, May 28, 2009, http://www.breitbart.com/article.php?id=D98FI7I00.

476 Farah Stockman, "Obama, Abbas talk peace," Boston Globe, May 28, 2009, http://www.boston.com/news/politics/politicalintelligence/2009/05/obama_abbas_tal.html.

477 Oleg Shchedrov, "Russia fears Korea conflict could go nuclear – Ifax," Reuters, May 27, 2009, http://in.reuters.com/article/2009/05/27/idINIndia-39913120090527.

478 Stanislav Mishin, "American capitalism gone with a whimper," Pravda, April 27, 2009, http://english.pravda.ru/opinion/columnists/27-04-2009/107459-american_capitalism-0/.

479 Jonathan D. Salant and Julianna Goldman, "Obama Offers Prime Posts to Top Campaign Contributors (Update1)," Bloomberg, May 29, 2009, http://www.bloomberg.com/apps/news?pid=washingtonstory&sid=adfv4RHV3Kmk.

480 Mark Knoller, "How Many 'Top Priority' Issues Does Obama Have?," CBS News, August 13, 2010, http://www.cbsnews.com/8301-503544_162-20013622-503544.html.

481 Liz Capo McCormich and Daniel Kruger, "Bond Vigilantes Confront Obama as Housing Falters (Update3)," Bloomberg, May 29, 2009, http://www.bloomberg.com/apps/news?pid=newsarchive&sid=akW9GQw.X9KM&refer=worldwide.

482 "N. Korea fires new type of short-range missile off east coast: source," Yonhap News, May 29, 2009, http://english.yonhapnews.co.kr/northkorea/2009/05/29/66/0401000000AEN20090529008200320F.HTML

483 "GOP takes aim at Barack and Michelle Obama's NYC trip," Politico, May 31, 2009, http://www.politico.com/news/stories/0509/23122.html.

484 Mark Knoller, "How Many 'Top Priority' Issues Does Obama Have?," CBS News, August 13, 2010, http://www.cbsnews.com/8301-503544_162-20013622-503544.html.

485 "Obama speech to offer personal commitment to Muslims," Breitbart, May 30, 2009, http://www.breitbart.com/article.php?id=CNG.0d36e60ce28699094108bce0f5e6b839.21&show_article=1.

486 Aaron Klein, "Obama promises Arabs Jerusalem will be theirs," WorldNetDaily, may 30, 2009, http://www.wnd.com/?pageId=99664.

487 Michael Daly, Alison Gendar and Helen Kennedy, "FBI arrest four in alleged plot to bomb Bronx synagogues, shoot down plane," New York Daily News, May 20, 2009, http://articles.nydailynews.com/2009-05-20/news/17924045_1_synagogues-car-bombs-cell-phones.

488 David E. Sanger, "The 31-Year-Old in Charge of Dismantling G.M.," New York Times, June 1, 2009, http://www.nytimes.com/2009/06/01/business/01deese.html.

489 "Geithner backs strong dlr, says China's assets safe," Reuters, May 31, 2009, http://www.reuters.com/article/2009/06/01/usa-china-dollar-idINPEK12423320090601.

490   Juan O. Tamayo, "U.S. officials raise alarm about new Venezuelan missiles," McClatchy, May 31, 2009, http://www.mcclatchydc.com/2009/05/31/69148/us-officials-raise-alarm-about.html

491   "Unemployment Rate," Portal Seven, http://portalseven.com/employment/unemployment_rate.jsp.

492   "Boom Town," Wall Street Journal, June 10, 2009, http://online.wsj.com/article/SB124458850503399823.html#mod=djemEditorialPage.

493   "Obama says US cannot impose its values: BBC interview," Breitbart, June 1, 2009, http://www.breitbart.com/article.php?id=CNG.9ea937445ae71bcf5056c436c0955d4d.1731&show_article=1.

494   "Transcript of the Interview of the Presideent by Laura Haim Canal Plus," WhiteHouse.gov, June 1, 2009, http://www.whitehouse.gov/the_press_office/Transcript-of-the-Interview-of-the-President-by-Laura-Haim-Canal-Plus-6-1-09/.

495   Richard Esposito, Pierre Thomas and Jack Date, "Recruiter Shooting Suspect Under FBI Investigation," ABC News, June 1, 2009, http://abcnews.go.com/Politics/story?id=7730637&page=1.

496   Christopher Neefus, "UAW Bondholders to Receive More Equity in GM than Others," Free Republic, June 2, 2009, http://www.freerepublic.com/focus/f-news/2262842/posts.

497   Ibid.

498   Neil King, Jr. and Sharon Terlep, "GM Collapses Into Government's Arms," Wall Street Journal, June 2, 2009, http://online.wsj.com/article/SB124385428627671889.html.

499   David Lightman, "Can a government of politicians keep politics out of GM?," McClatchy, June 1, 2009, http://www.mcclatchydc.com/2009/06/01/69220/can-a-government-of-politicians.html#ixzz0vjoJDv5Q.

500   "Venezuela Chavez says 'Comrade' Obama more left-wing," Reuters, June 2, 2009, http://www.reuters.com/article/idUSTRE5520GX20090603?feedType=RSS&feedName=ObamaEconomy&virtualBrandChannel=10441.

501   Rebecca Christie, "Geithner Says China Has Confidence in U.S. Economy (Update3)," Bloomberg, June 2, 2009, http://www.bloomberg.com/apps/news?pid=newsarchive&sid=aSMi3X3PNBFU&refer=worldwide.

502   Craig Torres and Brian Faler, "Bernanke Warns Deficits Threaten Financial Stability (Update4)," Bloomberg, June 3, 2009, http://www.bloomberg.com/apps/news?pid=newsarchive&sid=agmj05AcqWHo&refer=worldwide.

503   Marc Ambinder, "'Brotherhood' Invited To Obama Speech by U.S.," The Atlantic, June 3, 2009, http://www.theatlantic.com/politics/archive/2009/06/-brotherhood-invited-to-obama-speech-by-us/18693/.

504   "Al-Qaeda eyes bio attack from Mexico," Washington Times, June 3, 2009, http://www.washingtontimes.com/news/2009/jun/03/al-qaeda-eyes-bio-attack-via-mexico-border/?feat=home_cube_position1.

505   Dennis Cauchon, "Benefit spending soars to new high," USA Today, June 4, 2009, http://www.usatoday.com/news/washington/2009-06-03-benefits_N.htm.

506   Ryan J. Donmoyer, "Ballmer Says Tax Would Move Microsoft Jobs Offshore (Update3)," Bloomberg, June 3, 2009, http://www.bloomberg.com/apps/news?pid=newsarchive&sid=aAKluP7yIwJY.

507   Ross Colvin and David Alexander, "Obama seeks to change Muslim perceptions of U.S.," Reuters, June 4, 2009, http://www.reuters.com/article/idUSTRE55344S2009060

4?feedType=RSS&feedName=topNews&rpc=22&sp=true.

508   Zahra Hosseinian and Fredrik Dahl, "Iran says Obama 'sweet talk' not enough for Muslims," Reuters, June 4, 2009, http://uk.reuters.com/article/idUKTRE55319W20090604.

509   "Bin Laden calls for long war against 'infidels,'" Reuters, June 4, 2009, http://uk.reuters.com/article/idUKTRE55333D20090604?sp=true.

510   Nicholas Kulish, "Rift With Germany Is Next on Diplomatic Agenda," New York Times, June 4, 2009, http://www.nytimes.com/2009/06/05/world/europe/05germany.html.

511   Charles Bremner, "Barack and Michelle Obama decline dinner with the Sarkozys," TimesOnline, June 5, 2009, http://www.timesonline.co.uk/tol/news/world/europe/article6434141.ece.

512   "Obama's Aide and Mao," Media Research Center, http://www.mrc.org/specialreports/2010/omittingforobama/AnitaDunn.aspx.

513   Eamon Javers, "A political pattern to stimulus tour," Politico, June 5, 2009, http://www.politico.com/news/stories/0609/23379.html.

514   Joe Mandak, "4 ACORN ex-workers to face vote fraud trial in Pa.," Breitbart, June 5, 2009, http://www.breitbart.com/article.php?id=D98KJNH80&show_article=1.

515   Charles Bremner, "Barack and Michelle Obama decline dinner with the Sarkozys," TimesOnline, June 5, 2009, http://www.timesonline.co.uk/tol/news/world/europe/article6434141.ece.

516   Mike Allen, "Obama salutes fading D-Day vets- minus one," Politico, June 6, 2009, http://www.politico.com/news/stories/0609/23430.html.

517   Laura Litvan and Ryan Donmoyer, "Democrats Weigh Health Mandate as Obama Urges Taxing Wealthy," Bloomberg, June 7, 2009, http://www.bloomberg.com/apps/news?pid=newsarchive&sid=aj5HHIKfogR8&refer=worldwide.

518   "Saudi urges Obama to impose Mideast solution – paper," Reuters, June 7, 2009, http://in.reuters.com/article/idINIndia-40143320090607.

519   "Obama hits back at Euro snub rumors," Breitbart, June 6, 2009, http://www.breitbart.com/article.php?id=CNG.f81c21b2e705813bf48fa8f9241d53af.201&show_article=1.

520   "US Unemployment Rate Gallops Ahead of Expectations," Voice of America, June 7, 2009,   http://www.voanews.com/english/news/a-13-2009-06-07-voa22-68693307.html.

521   Caren Bohan, "UPDATE 2-Obama seeks fiscal responsibility mantle," Reuters, June 9, 2009, http://www.reuters.com/article/idUSN0938720120090609.

522   Jeremy Pelofsky, "U.S. war funding bill brims with unrelated extras," Reuters, June 8, 2009, http://www.reuters.com/article/idUSN08333615

523   Jack Kim, "North Korea jails U.S. journalists, warns U.N.," Reuters, June 8, 2009, http://www.reuters.com/article/idUSSP46862120090608.

524   Malcolm Moore, "Top Chinese banker Guo Shuqing calls for wider use of yuan," The Telegraph, June 8, 2009, http://www.telegraph.co.uk/finance/financetopics/financialcrisis/5473491/Top-Chinese-banker-Guo-Shuqing-calls-for-wider-use-of-yuan.html.

525   Michael Jamison, "State firms cry foul over stimulus projects," Billings Gazette, June   9,   2009,   http://billingsgazette.com/news/state-and-regional/montana/article_227518f3-11f6-5999-b9b5-2c04143378ba.html.

526   "North Korea would use nuclear weapons in a 'merciless offensive,'" The Independent, June 9, 2009, http://www.independent.co.uk/news/world/asia/north-korea-would-

use-nuclear-weapons-in-a-merciless-offensive-1700590.html.

527 Byron York, "What's behind Obama's sudden attempt to fire the AmeriCorps inspector general?" Washington Examiner, June 10, 2009, http://washingtonexaminer.com/blogs/beltway-confidential/2009/06/whats-behind-obamas-sudden-attempt-fire-ameri-corps-inspector-gener.

528 David Squires, "Rev. Jeremiah Wright says 'Jews' are keeping him from President Obama," Daily Press, June 10, 2009, http://www.dailypress.com/news/dp-local_wright_0610jun10,0,7603283.story.

529 David Cho, Zachary A. Goldfarb and Tomoeh Murakami Tse, "U.S. Targets Excessive Pay for Top Executives," Washington Post, June 11, 2009, http://www.washingtonpost.com/wp-dyn/content/article/2009/06/10/AR2009061001416_pf.html.

530 "Citi Sets Plan to Convert $58 Billion in Stock," Deal Book, June 10, 2009, http://dealbook.blogs.nytimes.com/2009/06/10/citi-sets-plan-to-convert-58-billion-in-stock/?ref=business.

531 Conor Sweeney, "Russia snubs U.S. call to consider hosting radar," Reuters, June 11, 2009, http://www.reuters.com/article/idUSTRE55A2Y020090611.

532 Alex Nicholson and Dakin Campbell, "Russia May Swap Some U.S. Treasuries for IMF Debt (Update1)," Bloomberg, June 10, 2009, http://www.bloomberg.com/apps/news?pid=newsarchive&sid=ahoIPyEdpHUI.

533 Martin Vaughan and Amol Sharma, "Tax Man's Target: The Mobile Phone," Wall Street Journal, June 12, 2009, http://online.wsj.com/article/SB124473141538306335.html.

534 Russell Goldman, "Feds Freeze Poker Champ's Winnings," ABC News, June 11, 2009, http://abcnews.go.com/print?id=7808131.

535 "Senators Call on Obama to Resolve Dispute With Pelosi Over 'Torture Photos,'" Fox News, June 11, 2009, http://www.foxnews.com/politics/2009/06/11/senators-obama-resolve-dispute-pelosi-torture-photos/.

536 Jim Wolf, "North Korea, Iran joined on missile work: U.S. general," Reuters, June 11, 2009, http://www.reuters.com/article/idUSTRE55A4E720090611.

537 Doug Palmer, "Obama Launches ocean protection plan," Reuters, June 12, 2009, http://www.reuters.com/article/idUSTRE55B6CJ20090612.

538 "US tells North Korea to end 'provocative' actions," Reuters, June 13, 2009, http://uk.reuters.com/article/2009/06/13/idUKN1392693.

539 Shunichi Ozasa and Makiko Kitamura, "Japan Probes Report Two Seized With Unde-clared Bonds," Bloomberg, June 12, 2009, http://www.bloomberg.com/apps/news?pid=newsarchive&sid=ayy1QKcwcGN0.

540 "Mafia blamed for $134 bn fake Treasury bills," Financial Times, June 18, 2009, http://www.ft.com/intl/cms/s/0/82091ec2-5c2f-11de-aea3-00144feabdc0.html#axzz1YY498M8w.

541 David Alexander, "Obama 'excited' by Iran's robust election debate," Reuters, June 12, 2009, http://www.reuters.com/article/idUSTRE55B4SG20090612.

542 "US tells North Korea to end 'provocative' actions," Reuters, June 13, 2009, http://uk.reuters.com/article/2009/06/13/idUKN1392693.

543 "Biden sees stimulus working, but not quickly," MSNBC, June 14, 2009, http://www.msnbc.msn.com/id/31355497/ns/business-stocks_and_economy/t/biden-sees-stimulus-working-not-quickly/#.Tl4MVHPs6Go.is89

544 Parisa Hafezi and Fredrik Dahl, "Mousavi seeks to overturn Iran election result," Reuters, June 14, 2009, http://www.reuters.com/article/2009/06/14/us-iran-election-idUSEVA14340720090614.

545 "BBC says election broadcasts disrupted from Iran," Breitbart, June 14, 2009, http://www.breitbart.com/article.php?id=CNG.de58ae79bab547316b950e6d9851e 28a.4b1&shois90 w_article=1.

546 James Hilder, "Netanyahu defies Obama with harsh conditions for Palestinian 'entity,'" TimesOnline, June 15, 2009, http://www.timesonline.co.uk/tol/news/world/middle_ east/article6498930.ece.

547 "Gays decry Obama's stand on gay marriage case," 365Gay, June 15, 2009, http://www.365gay.com/news/gays-decry-obamas-stand-on-gay-marriage-case/.

548 John Parry, "U.S. likely to lose AAA rating: Prechter," Reuters, June 15, 2009, http://www.reuters.com/article/idUSTRE55E6BM20090615.

549 Kim Sengupta, "America's 'Bermuda solution' angers Britain," The Independent, June 13, 2009, http://www.independent.co.uk/news/world/americas/americas-bermuda-solution-angers-britain-1704147.html.

550 Louise Armitstead, "Lloyds Bank hit by Obama tax purge," The Telegraph, June 13, 2009, http://www.telegraph.co.uk/finance/newsbysector/banksandfinance/5526129/ Lloyds-Bank-hit-by-Obama-tax-purge.html.

551 Parisa Hafezi, "Protesters plan more mass rallies in Iran," Reuters, June 15, 2009, http://www.reuters.com/article/idUSEVA14340720090615?sp=true.

552 Nicholas Johnston, "Obama Says 'Dialogue' With Iran Will Continue After Election," Bloomberg, June 16, 2009, http://www.bloomberg.com/apps/news?pid=newsarchive &sid=aJ5vKNSLGKgQ.

553 Judson Berger, "Fired IG Calls White House Explanation 'Baseless,' Says He's Being Targeted," Fox News, June 17, 2009, http://www.foxnews.com/politics/2009/06/17/ fired-ig-calls-white-house-explanation-baseless-says-hes-targeted/.

554 Jim Puzzanghera, "Obama to propose strict new regulation of financial industry," Los Angeles Times, June 16, 2009, http://articles.latimes.com/2009/jun/16/business/fi-financial-regs16.

555 John Berlau, "Nationalization Review," The American Spectator, June 23, 2009, http://spectator.org/archives/2009/06/23/nationalization-review.

556 Brian Faler and Nicholas Johnston, "Obama Says 'Robust' Growth Will Prevent Tax Increases (Update1)," Bloomberg, June 16, 2009, http://www.bloomberg.com/apps/new s?pid=newsarchive&sid=akaJVOByDsHg.

557 Bill Dedman, "Obama blocks list of visitors to White House," MSNBC, June 16, 2009, http://www.msnbc.msn.com/id/31373407/ns/politics-white_house/.

558 John Harwood, "Obama: US Not Overregulating; Iran Election Won't Alter Policy," CNBC, June 17, 2009, http://www.cnbc.com/id/31391532/Obama_US_Not_Over-regulating_Iran_Election_Won_t_Alter_Policy.

559 Matt Drudge, "ABC Turns Programming Over To Obama; News To Be Anchored From Inside White House," DrudgeReport, June 16, 2009, http://www.drudgereportarchives. com/data/2009/06/16/20090616_161307_flashaot.htm.is91

560 Jeff Poor, "Obama Blasts Fox News: 'I've Got One Television Station that is Entirely Devoted to Attacking My Administration," NewsBusters, June 16, 2009, http://newsbusters.org/blogs/jeff-poor/2009/06/16/obama-blasts-fox-news-ive-got-one-television-station-entirely-devoted-att.

561 Vladimir Isachenkov, "Russia Challenges Dollar, China Offers Loans," CBN News, June 16, 2009, http://www.cbn.com/cbnnews/world/2009/June/Russia-Challenges-

Dollar-China-Offers-Loans/.

562   Lara Jakes, "Pentagon: NKorea Missiles could threaten US," Breitbart, June 16, 2009, http://www.breitbart.com/article.php?id=D98RR9180&show_article=1.

563   "Iran bars foreign media from reporting on streets," Breitbart, June 16, 2009, http://www.breitbart.com/article.php?id=D98RP8GO2&show_article=1.

564   "Obama: Iran supreme leader worried about election," Breitbart, June 16, 2009, http://www.breitbart.com/article.php?id=D98RSCDG4&show_article=1.

565   Jay Solomon and Peter Spiegel, "Obama Says Iran Must Pick Its Own Leaders," Wall Street Journal, June 16, 2009, http://online.wsj.com/article/SB124510480449716609.html.

566   Judson Berger, "Fired IG Calls White House Explanation 'Baseless,' Says He's Being Targeted," Fox News, June 17, 2009, http://www.foxnews.com/politics/2009/06/17/fired-ig-calls-white-house-explanation-baseless-says-hes-targeted/.

567   Matt Drudge, "ABC Refuses Opposition Ads During White House Special," DrudgeReport, June 17, 2009, http://www.drudgereportarchives.com/data/2009/06/18/20090618_044552_flashaot1.htm

568   Ed O'Keefe, "Obama Extends Benefits To Same-Sex Partners," Washington Post, June 17, 2009, http://voices.washingtonpost.com/federal-eye/2009/06/eye_opener_same-sex_partners_g.html?hpid=topnews.

569   "China sells US bonds to 'show concern,'" Breitbart, June 17, 2009, http://www.breitbart.com/article.php?id=CNG.6cc88b76aff9be3f90f62526a3107ec9.31&show_article=1.

570   "Treasury to Auction $104 Billion In Debt Next Week, a Record," CNBC, 6/18/09, http://www.cnbc.com/id/31429270.

571   Erik Holm, "Obama's Insurance Proposal May Grab Power From States (Update1)," Bloomberg, June 19, 2009, http://www.bloomberg.com/apps/news?pid=washingtonstory&sid=apCXAt_EyyMg.

572   Huma Khan, "Study: 19 Ambassador Nominees Bundled $4.8 Million for President's Campaign, Inauguration," ABC News, June 19, 2009, http://blogs.abcnews.com/politicalpunch/2009/06/study-19-ambassador-nominees-bundled-48-million-for-presidents-campaign-inauguration.html.

573   "As Criticism of Obama Mounts within Gay Community, Gay Rights Pioneer Cleve Jones Calls for March for Equality on Washington," DemocracyNow, June 19, 2009, http://www.democracynow.org/2009/6/19/as_criticism_of_obama_mounts_within.

574   Yochi J. Dreazen, "U.S. Fortifies Hawaii to Meet Threat From Korea," Wall Street Journal, June 19, 2009, http://online.wsj.com/article/SB124535285705228571.html.

575   "Iran police clash with protesters," BBC, June 20, 2009, http://news.bbc.co.uk/2/hi/middle_east/8110582.stm.

576   "N.Korea accuses Obama of nuclear war plot," Breitbart, June 21, 2009, http://www.breitbart.com/article.php?id=CNG.33b78ee19629f3815e9f9ef7e17315dc.281&show_article=1.

577   Sara Murray, "Numbers On Welfare See Sharp Increase," Wall Street Journal, June 22, 2009, http://online.wsj.com/article/SB124562449457235503.html

578   Phillip Inman, "Goldman to make record bonus payout," The Observer, June 21, 2009, http://www.guardian.co.uk/business/2009/jun/21/goldman-sachs-bonus-payments.

579 Michael A. Fletcher and Ceci Connolly, "Obama Announces Agreement With Drug Companies," Washington Post, June 22, 2009, http://www.washingtonpost.com/wp-dyn/content/article/2009/06/22/AR2009062200349.html.

580 "Iran starts airforce manoeuvres in Gulf," Reuters, June 22, 2009, http://www.reuters.com/article/idUSHOS233576.

581 Inal Ersan, "Al Qaeda says would use Pakistani nuclear weapons," Reuters, June 22, 2009, http://www.reuters.com/article/idUSTRE55L12V20090622?feedType=RSS&feedName=topNews&rpc=22&sp=true.

582 John Seewer, "Obama wants new council to help auto industry," Breitbart, June 23, 2009, http://www.breitbart.com/article.php?id=D990GHH00&show_article=1.

583 Carl Hulse and David M. Herszenhorn, "Democrats Call Off Climate Bill Effort," New York Times, July 22, 2009, http://www.nytimes.com/2010/07/23/us/politics/23cong.html?_r=1.

584 Dana Milbank, "Washington Sketch: Welcome to 'The Obama Show,'" Washington Post, June 24, 2009, http://www.washingtonpost.com/wp-dyn/content/article/2009/06/23/AR2009062303262.html.

585 John Whitesides and Jeff Mason, "Obama harshly condemns Iran crackdown on protesters," Reuters, June 23, 2009, http://www.reuters.com/article/idUSTRE55M0RI20090623?sp=true.

586 Ibid.

587 Kevin Krolicki, "Ford, Nissan, Tesla to get U.S. technology loans," Reuters, 6/23/2009, http://www.reuters.com/article/idUSTRE55M39120090623.

588 Carl Hulse and David M. Herszenhorn, "Democrats Call Off Climate Bill Effort," New York Times, July 22, 2009, http://www.nytimes.com/2010/07/23/us/politics/23cong.html?_r=1.

589 Andrew Gray, "Pentagon approves creation of cyber command," Reuters, June 23, 2009, http://www.reuters.com/article/2009/06/23/idUSN2388687.

590 "Russia, Venezuela sign $4 bln joint bank deal," Breitbart, June 23, 2009, http://www.breitbart.com/article.php?id=CNG.1debc0c644600c07a24e054a4ded5f8d.71&show_article=1.

591 Jeff Poor, "ABC ObamaCare Special Turns Into Presidential Filibuster," Media Research Center, June 25, 2009, http://www.mrc.org/bmi/articles/2009/ABC_ObamaCare_Special_Turns_Into_Presidential_Filibuster.html.

592 Dan Whitcomb and Clara Linnane, "California set to issue IOUs as fiscal crisis weighs," Reuters, June 24, 2009, http://www.reuters.com/article/idUSTRE55O07Q20090625?sp=true.

593 "Fannie, Freddie asked to relax condo loan rules: report," Reuters, June 22, 2009, http://www.reuters.com/article/idUSTRE55L39120090622.

594 Geoffrey T. Smith, "ECB Lends Record $622 Billion in Bid to Ease Crisis," Wall Street Journal, June 25, 2009, http://online.wsj.com/article/SB124583774423646701.html?mod=googlenews_wsj.

595 Lisa Lerer, "Al Gore not coming to D.C.," Politico, June 25, 2009, http://www.politico.com/news/stories/0609/24193.html.

596 Ryan J. Donmoyer and Holly Rosenkrantz, "Unions' Health Benefits May Avoid Tax Under Proposal (Update1)," Bloomberg, June 26, 2009, http://www.bloomberg.com/apps/news?pid=newsarchive&sid=aDvu77pZr7k4.

597 Jose De Cordoba, "Honduras Lurches Toward Crisis Over Election," Wall Street Jour-

nal, June 26, 2009, http://online.wsj.com/article/SB124597369604957305.html.

598   Michael Weissenstein, "Iran pledges 'crushing' response to US critiques," Breitbart, June 27, 2009, http://www.breitbart.com/article.php?id=D9938GKO0&show_article=1.

599   Liz Sidoti, "White House Announces New Lighting Standards," HuffingtonPost, June 29, 2009, http://www.huffingtonpost.com/2009/06/29/white-house-announces-new_n_222479.html.

600   "Ousted Honduran president flown to Costa Rica: television," Breitbart, June 28, 2009, http://www.breitbart.com/article.php?id=TX-PAR-LYV63&show_article=1.

601   "Honduran leader forced into exile," BBC, June 28, 2009, http://news.bbc.co.uk/2/hi/americas/8123126.stm.

602   Arshad Mohammed and David Alexander, "Obama says coup in Honduras is illegal," Reuters, June 29, 2009, http://www.reuters.com/article/idUKTRE55S5J220090629?sp=true.

603   Mary Anastasia O'Grady, "Honduras Defends Its Democracy," Wall Street Journal, June 29, 2009, http://online.wsj.com/article/SB124623220955866301.html.

604   Warren Giles, "Swiss Banks Shun Americans as U.S. Compels Disclosure," Bloomberg, June 30, 2009, http://www.bloomberg.com/apps/news?pid=newsarchive&sid=akWgh.6sIgTQ.

605   "Russian PM calls on US to shelve missile shield-Ifax," London South East, July 3, 2009, http://www.lse.co.uk/FinanceNews.asp?ArticleCode=enjpkyod7dsreis&ArticleHeadline=Russian_PM_calls_on_US_to_shelve_missile_shieldIfax.

606   Eileen AJ Connelly, "Mortgage delinquency rate hits all time high in 2Q," Breitbart, August 17, 2009, http://www.breitbart.com/article.php?id=D9A4Q7H00.

607   Jim Geraghty, "Obama: Stop Blaming Me for the Economy, I Just Got Here in January," National Review, July 2, 2009, http://www.nationalreview.com/campaign-spot/6888/obama-stop-blaming-me-economy-i-just-got-here-january.

608   Martin Crutsinger, "Budget Deficit Tops $1 Trillion For First Time," HuffingtonPost, July 13, 2009, http://www.huffingtonpost.com/2009/07/13/budget-deficit-tops-1-tri_n_230822.html.

609   "Unemployment Rate," Portal Seven, http://portalseven.com/employment/unemployment_rate.jsp.

610   "US demands UBS comply in tax evasion case," SwissInfo, July 1, 2009, http://www.swissinfo.ch/eng/Specials/Swiss_banking_secrecy_under_fire/News/US_demands_UBS_comply_in_tax_evasion_case.html?cid=7422.

611   Paul Kiel and Binyamin Appelbaum, "After Call From Senator's Office, Small Hawaii Bank Got U.S. Aid," Washington Post, July 1, 2009, http://www.washingtonpost.com/wp-dyn/content/article/2009/06/30/AR2009063004229_pf.html.

612   "Feds could seize Calif. Parks if closed by budget," Breitbart, July 1, 2009, http://www.breitbart.com/article.php?id=D995Q9I00&show_article=1.

613   Jim Geraghty, "Obama: Stop Blaming Me for the Economy, I Just Got Here in January," National Review, July 2, 2009, http://www.nationalreview.com/campaign-spot/6888/obama-stop-blaming-me-economy-i-just-got-here-january.

614   Brody Mullins and T.W. Farnam, "Congress's Travel Tab Swells," Wall Street Journal, July 2, 2009, http://online.wsj.com/article/SB124650399438184235.html.

615   Rajiv Chandrasekaran, "Marines Deploy on Major Mission," Washington Post, July 2, 2009, http://www.washingtonpost.com/wp-dyn/content/article/2009/07/01/

AR2009070103202_pf.html.

616   Jack Kim and Miyoung Kim, "North Korea ups tension with short-range missiles," Reuters, July 2, 2009, http://www.reuters.com/article/2009/07/02/us-korea-north-idUSTRE5612OE20090702.

617   "Obama not fully informed on Russia: Putin spokesman," Reuters, July 3, 2009, http://www.reuters.com/article/idUSTRE5621OD20090703.

618   Ibid.

619   Saeromi Shin, "North Korea Test-Fires Seven Missiles, Drawing Condemnation," Bloomberg, July 4, 2009, http://www.bloomberg.com/apps/news?pid=newsarchive&sid=ayZKFRte_kus.

620   Lolita C. Baldor, "Federal Web sites knocked out by cyber attack," Breitbart, July 7, 2009, http://www.breitbart.com/article.php?id=D999VT9O0&show_article=1.

621   Mark Deen and Isabelle Mas, "India Joins Russia, China in Questioning U.S. Dollar Dominance," Bloomberg, July 3, 2009, http://www.bloomberg.com/apps/news?pid=newsarchive&sid=aR7yfqUwTb4M.

622   "Russia calls on U.S. to compromise on missile defense," Reuters, July 5, 2009, http://www.reuters.com/article/idUSTRE5611DV20090705.

623   "Biden: Israel free to set own course on Iran," MSNBC, July 5, 2009, http://www.msnbc.msn.com/id/31751832/.

624   Kevin Hassett, "California's Nightmare Will Kill Obamanomics," Bloomberg, July 6, 2009, http://www.bloomberg.com/apps/news?pid=newsarchive&sid=aTKrn1jUJwdE.

625   "US not giving Israel 'green light to attack Iran," Breitbart, July 6, 2009, http://www.breitbart.com/article.php?id=CNG.b1bda39889783bf24189b0a92f01fc43.821&show_article=1.

626   Hans Nichols and Roger Runningen, "Obama Lauds Putin's 'Extraordinary Work' in Visit to Mend Ties," Bloomberg, July 7, 2009, http://www.bloomberg.com/apps/news?pid=washingtonstory&sid=al7IO7sebEWA.

627   Matthew Lee, "Ousted Honduran president expected in Washington," Breitbart, July 6, 2009, http://www.breitbart.com/article.php?id=D99971O00&show_article=1.

628   Jake Tapper, "President Obama on Putin," ABC News, July 7, 2009, http://blogs.abcnews.com/politicalpunch/2009/07/president-obama-on-putin-i-thought-it-was-important-to-listen/comments/page/2/.

629   Matthew Benjamin, "Democrats Split on Stimulus as Job Losses Mount, Deficit Soars," Bloomberg, July 8, 2009, http://www.bloomberg.com/apps/news?pid=washingtonstory&sid=aIHpsBT0JHFc.

630   Matt Kelley, "Report: States aren't using stimulus funds as intended," USA Today, July 8, 2009, http://www.usatoday.com/news/nation/2009-07-07-stimulus_N.htm.

631   Lisa Jucca, "Swiss to stop UBS handing over data in U.S. tax row," Reuters, July 8, 2009, http://www.reuters.com/article/idUSTRE5672DM20090708?feedType=RSS&feedName=businessNews&rpc=23&sp=true.

632   Phillip Webster, "G8 leaders claim historic breakthrough on new deal to tackle global warming," TimesOnline, July 9, 2009, http://www.timesonline.co.uk/tol/news/world/europe/article6670327.ece.

633   Ishtiaq Mahsud, "2 suspected US missile attacks kill 45 in Pakistan," Breitbart, July 8, 2009, http://www.breitbart.com/article.php?id=D99ACQNO0.

634   Brad Heath, "Billion in aid go to areas that backed Obama in '08," USA Today, July 9,

2009, http://www.usatoday.com/news/washington/2009-07-08-redblue_N.htm.

635   Brady Dennis and David Cho, "AIG Seeks Clearance For More Bonuses," Washington Post, July 10, 2009, http://www.washingtonpost.com/wp-dyn/content/article/2009/07/09/AR2009070902702_pf.html.

636   Daniel Klaidman, "Obama doesn't want to look back, but Attorney General Eric Holder may probe Bush-era torture anyway," Newsweek, July 10, 2009, http://www.thedailybeast.com/newsweek/2009/07/10/independent-s-day.html.

637   Phillip Pullella and Jeff Mason, "Obama tells pope he wants to reduce abortions in U.S.," Reuters, July 10, 2009, http://www.reuters.com/article/idUSTRE5693XC20090710?feedType=RSS&feedName=topNews&rpc=22&sp=true.

638   Oleg Shcherdrov, "Medvedev threatens U.S. over missile shield," Reuters, July 10, 2009, http://www.reuters.com/article/2009/07/10/us-g8-summit-nuclear-medvedev-idUSTRE5693VW20090710.

639   "Medvedev sees single currency dream in G8 coin gift," Breitbart, July 10, 2009, http://www.breitbart.com/article.php?id=CNG.4eb2c06b46ea42dece225df0a3ec3799.641&show_article=1.

640   Simon Gardner, "Honduras pressure mounts, U.S. wants deal 'now,'" Reuters, July 21, 2009, http://www.reuters.com/article/idUSN2124095620090721.

641   "Report: N. Korean hackers Ordered to 'Destroy' S. Korean Computer Networks," Fox News, July 11, 2009, http://www.foxnews.com/story/0,2933,531637,00.html.

642   Edwin Chen, "Obama Says Economic Stimulus Plan Worked as Intended (Update2), Bloomberg, July 11, 2009, http://www.bloomberg.com/apps/news?pid=newsarchive&sid=a0StZd9y2rCY.

643   Stacy-Marie Ishmael, "Swiss tax rules lure McDonald's from UK," Financial Times, July 13, 2009, http://ftalphaville.ft.com/blog/2009/07/13/61546/swiss-tax-rules-lure-mcdonalds-from-uk/.

644   "Taliban pushed back, long way to go: Obama," Reuters, July 12, 2009, http://www.reuters.com/article/idUSTRE56A2Q420090712?feedType=RSS&feedName=topNews&rpc=22&sp=true.

645   Martin Crutsinger, "Budget Deficit Tops $1 Trillion For First Time," HuffingtonPost, July 13, 2009, http://www.huffingtonpost.com/2009/07/13/budget-deficit-tops-1-tri_n_230822.html.

646   Patrick Rucker and David Lawder, "U.S. mulling mortgage aid for unemployed," Reuters, July 14, 2009, http://www.reuters.com/article/2009/07/14/us-financial-mortgage-exclusive-idUSTRE56D04920090714.

647   "Amtrak Unveils First Rail Car Funded by Stimulus," Way of the Rail, July 30, 2009, http://www.wayoftherail.com/2009/07/30/canadian-pacific/amtrak-unveils-first-rail-car-funded-by-stimulus/.

648   Lily Gordon, "Soldier balks at deploying; says Obama isn't president," Columbus Ledger-Enquirer, July 14, 2009, http://www.ledger-enquirer.com/2009/07/14/776335/soldier-balks-at-deploying-says.html.

649   Jae-Soon Chang, "SKorean police: Hackers extracted data in attacks," Physorg, July 14, 2009, http://www.physorg.com/news166768093.html.

650   Donna Smith, "House bill to hit millionaires with 5.4 pct surtax," Reuters, July 14, 2009, http://www.reuters.com/article/2009/07/14/usa-healthcare-millionaires-idUSWEN055320090714.

651   Edwin Chen, "Obama Open to Partisan Vote on Health-Care Over-

haul, Aides Say," Bloomberg, July 14, 2009, http://www.bloomberg.com/apps/news?pid=newsarchive&sid=a4.kYDWV9erc.

652 "NASA Chief: Next Frontier Better Relations With Muslim World," Fox News, July 5, 2009, http://www.foxnews.com/politics/2010/07/05/nasa-chief-frontier-better-relations-muslims/.

653 Brian Faler, "Obama Opposes House Plan to Protect Chrysler, GM Dealerships," Bloomberg, July 15, 2009, http://www.bloomberg.com/apps/news?pid=newsarchive&sid=aioxPp9w.vzM.

654 Phillip Rawls, "States awash in stimulus money to weatherize homes," Breitbart, July 15, 2009, http://www.breitbart.com/article.php?id=D99F72OO0&show_article=1.

655 "Obama mulls rental option for some homeowners-sources," Reuters, July 14, 2009, http://www.reuters.com/article/idUSN1429265720090714?rpc=77.

656 Chelsea Schilling and Joe Kovacs, "Bombshell: Orders revoked for soldier challenging prez," WorldNetDaily, July 14, 2009, http://www.wnd.com/index.php?fa=PAGE.view&pageId=104009.

657 Ambrose Evan's Pritchard, "Fed's volte face sends the dollar tumbling," The Telegraph, July 15, 2009, http://www.telegraph.co.uk/finance/currency/7893238/Feds-volte-face-sends-the-dollar-tumbling.html.

658 Penny Starr, "Joe Biden: 'We Have to Go Spend Money to Keep From Going Bankrupt,'" CNS News, July 16, 2009, http://www.cnsnews.com/node/51162.

659 Douglas Elmendorf, "The Long-Term Outlook," Congressional Budget Office, July 16, 2009, http://cboblog.cbo.gov/?p=328.

660 "HIRING! 'Grassroots' work to promote Obama's healthcare pays $11-16 per hour," Free Republic, July 16, 2009, http://www.freerepublic.com/focus/f-news/2293869/posts.

661 Joseph Rhee and Brian Ross, "Social Security Execs Boogie Down at lavish Phoenix Conference," ABC News, July 15, 2009, http://abcnews.go.com/Blotter/story?id=8084663&page=1.

662 "Big Dem cash dump on eve of climate vote," Politico, July 17, 2009, http://www.politico.com/blogs/glennthrush/0709/Big_Dem_cash_dump_on_eve_of_climate_vote.html?showall.

663 Eamon Javers, "Larry Summers cites Google search as progress," Politico, 7/17/09, http://www.politico.com/news/stories/0709/25083.html.

664 Charles Babingon, "White House wants more power to set Medicare rates," Breitbart, July 17, 2009, http://www.breitbart.com/article.php?id=D99GD8QG2&show_article=1.

665 "House panel passes health bill, critics slam cost," Reuters, July 17, 2009, http://www.reuters.com/article/idUSTRE56G4LQ20090717?feedType=RSS&feedName=domesticNews&rpc=22&sp=true.

666 "Obama condemns 'outrageous attacks' on Indonesia," Breitbart, July 17, 2009, http://www.breitbart.com/article.php?id=D99G8OAO4&show_article=1.

667 Patrick Goodenough, "'"Jerusalem Is Not a Settlement,' Netanyahu Reminds Obama Administration,'" CNS News, July 20, 2009, http://www.cnsnews.com/news/article/51247.

668 "Stimulus Has Million In Spending On Actual Pork, Ham," HuffingtonPost, July 21, 2009, http://www.huffingtonpost.com/2009/07/21/stimulus-has-millions-in-_n_241826.html.

669   Kevin Sack and Robert Peat, "Governors worried by healthcare bill costs," The Boston Globe, July 20, 2009, http://www.boston.com/news/nation/articles/2009/07/20/governors_balk_over_what_healthcare_bill_will_cost_states/.

670   Tom Raum, "White House putting off budget update," Breitbart, July 20, 2009, http://www.breitbart.com/article.php?id=D99I8E485.

671   Matthew Perrone, "GAO: FDA can't estimate its own budget needs," Breitbart, July 20, 2009, http://www.breitbart.com/article.php?id=D99I9O3O0&show_article=1.

672   "Gitmo review delayed 6 months," Washington Times, July 21, 2009, http://www.washingtontimes.com/news/2009/jul/21/gitmo-review-delayed-6-months/.

673   Jonathan Ferziger, "Obama Presses Israel to Halt Plans Funded by Rennert (Update1)," Bloomberg, July 27, 2009, http://www.bloomberg.com/apps/news?pid=newsarchive&sid=aSiB6pijo7_I.

674   "US Army to increase soldier numbers by 22,000," The Telegraph, July 20, 2009, http://www.telegraph.co.uk/news/worldnews/northamerica/usa/5873636/US-Army-to-increase-by-22000-soldiers.html.

675   Patrick Goodenough, "Clinton Accepts Blame for 'Global Warming' Role, Ponders Link Between Climate Change and Family Planning," CNS News, July 20, 2009, http://www.cnsnews.com/node/51260.

676   Conn Carroll, "Morning Bell: Obama Admits He's 'Not Familiar' With house Bill," Heritage Foundation, July 21, 2009, http://blog.heritage.org/2009/07/21/morning-bell-obama-admits-hes-not-familiar-with-house-bill/.

677   Ed Morrissey, "Why did Obama meet with the CBO?," HotAir, July 21, 2009, http://hotair.com/archives/2009/07/21/why-did-obama-meet-with-the-cbo/.

678   Simon Gardner, "Honduras pressure mounts, U.S. wants deal 'now,'" Reuters, July 21, 2009, http://www.reuters.com/article/idUSN2124095620090721.

679   "Clinton stirs Israeli fears US will accept nuclear Iran," Breitbart, July 22, 2009, http://www.breitbart.com/article.php?id=CNG.5fce011c9a76f3468914821101a3f8a5.381&show_article=1.

680   Ben Smith, "Obama: Cambridge police acted 'stupidly,'" Politico, July 22, 2009, http://www.politico.com/blogs/bensmith/0709/Obama_Cambridge_police_acted_stupidly.html.

681   "Obama goes prime-time to pitch healthcare," UPI, July 22, 2009, http://www.upi.com/Top_News/2009/07/22/Obama-goes-prime-time-to-pitch-healthcare/UPI-38611248259706/.

682   Eric Schmitt and Jane Perlez, "Pakistan Objects to U.S. Expansion in Afghan War," Sarasota Herald-Tribune, July 22, 2009, http://www.heraldtribune.com/article/20090722/ZNYT03/907223015?Title=Pakistan-Objects-to-U-S-Expansion-in-Afghan-War.

683   Khaled Abu Toameh, "Fatah has never recognized Israel," Jerusalem Post, July 22, 2009, http://www.jpost.com/MiddleEast/Article.aspx?id=149571.

684   "Obama: Doctors Taking tonsils Out For Money Instead of Diagnosing It As Allergies," Real Clear Politics, July 22, 2009, http://www.realclearpolitics.com/video/2009/07/22/obama_doctors_taking_tonsils_out_for_money_instead_of_diagnosing_it_as_allergies.html.

685   "Gates Arresting Officer: Obama 'Way Off Base,'" WBZTV, July 23, 2009, http://wbztv.com/local/obama.comment.cambridge.2.1097782.html.

686   Steve Holland, "Obama regrets remarks in racially charged case," Reuters, July 24, 2009, http://www.reuters.com/article/idUSN2447761120090724?feedType=RSS&feedNa

me=domesticNews&rpc=22&sp=true.

687 "Honduran regime rejects plan for president's return," Breitbart, July 23, 2009, http://www.breitbart.com/article.php?id=CNG.97a31b1d5a5db1905fc6db2713c125a7.91&show_article=1.

688 Glenn Kessler, "N. Korea Escalates War of Words, Calls Clinton Vulgar, Unintelligent, Washington Post, July 23, 2009, http://www.washingtonpost.com/wp-dyn/content/article/2009/07/23/AR2009072300299_pf.html.

689 Sue Pleming, "Clinton says Iran's nuclear pursuit is 'futile,'" Reuters, July 26, 2009, http://www.reuters.com/article/idUSN2651064120090726.

690 Geoff Earle, "Money Down The Toilet: Stimulus Millions Go To Pots," New York Post, July 27, 2009, http://www.nypost.com/p/news/national/item_5JsxHUH6v5ABlGORMWhZHO;jsessionid=2B117B788081D782C15E850E983ECCDC#ixzz0yRfjnsBm.

691 "State declares Obama birth certificate real, again," Breitbart, July 27, 2009, http://www.breitbart.com/article.php?id=D99N5J4O0&show_article=1.

692 Larry Margasak, "Dodd, Conrad told deals were sweetened," Breitbart, July 27, 2009, http://www.breitbart.com/article.php?id=D99N143G3&show_article=1.

693 "North Carolina Man Pleads Guilty in Terror Plot," Anti-Defamation League, February 10, 2011, http://www.adl.org/main_Terrorism/north_carolina_jihad_plot.htm.

694 Nicholas Ballasy, "Conyers Sees No Point in Members Reading 1,000-Page health Care Bill – Unless They Have 2 Lawyers to Interpret It for Them," CNS News, July 27, 2009, http://www.cnsnews.com/node/51610.

695 Tim Reid, "$20 m holiday home at Blue Heron Farm suits Barack Obama to a tee," TimesOnline, July 28, 2009, http://www.timesonline.co.uk/tol/news/world/article6729772.ece.

696 Aaron Klein, "Obama slammed as 'racist' at Jerusalem rally," WorldNetDaily, July 27, 2009, http://www.wnd.com/index.php?fa=PAGE.view&pageId=105173.

697 Rob Delaney and Rebecca Christie, "U.S. Assures 'Concerned' China It will Shrink Deficit," Bloomberg, July 28, 2009, http://www.bloomberg.com/apps/news?pid=washingtonstory&sid=aaVGe5smuZAU.

698 Morgan Lee and Juan Carlos Llorca, "US revokes visas of 4 Honduran officials," Breitbart, July 28, 2009, http://www.breitbart.com/article.php?id=D99NM95O0&show_article=1.

699 Jerry Seper, "No. 3 at Justice OK'd Panther reversal," Washington Times, July 30, 2009, http://www.washingtontimes.com/news/2009/jul/30/no-3-at-justice-okd-panther-reversal/?feat=home_cube_position1.

700 "Weak Treausury Auctions Raise Worries About US Debt Burden," CNBC, July 29, 2009, http://www.cnbc.com/id/32201716.

701 "US deficit climbs to 1.3 trillion dollars," Google, August 6, 2009, http://www.google.com/hostednews/afp/article/ALeqM5hAAhDJ_IAwKglPuq8VnzLGW4Rblg.

702 Eamon Javers, "W.H. makes CEOs pay for lunch," Politico, July 30, 2009, http://www.politico.com/news/stories/0709/25627.html.

703 Neil King, Jr. and Andrew Grossman, "New Cash Steered to Clunkers," Wall Street Journal, August 1, 2009, http://online.wsj.com/article/SB124903908261696593.html.

704 Sara Lepro, "Signs of weakness in economy boost Treasurys," Breitbart, July 31, 2009, http://www.breitbart.com/article.php?id=D99PKIR83&show_article=1.

705 Larry Margasak, "Democrat resists subpoenaing VIP mortgage records," Breitbart, July

30, 2009, http://www.breitbart.com/article.php?id=D99OUTF03&show_article=1.

706 "Pictured: U.S. missile defense test hailed a success as North Korea tensions rise," Daily Mail, August 1, 2009, http://www.dailymail.co.uk/news/worldnews/article-1203370/Pictured-U-S-missile-defence-test-hailed-success-North-Korea-tensions-rise.html.

707 "US Diplomats Told to Spy on Other Countries at United Nations," SpiegelOnline, Novermber 28, 2010, http://www.spiegel.de/international/world/0,1518,731587,00.html.

708 Christopher Toothaker, "Venezuela: 'Freedom of expression must be limited,'" Breitbart, July 30, 2009, http://www.breitbart.com/article.php?id=D99P3IKO0&show_article=1.

709 "Unemployment Rate," Portal Seven, http://portalseven.com/employment/unemployment_rate.jsp.

710 Raymond Colitt and Ana Isabil Martinez, "Venezuela begins shutdown of 34 radio stations," Reuters, August 1, 2009, http://www.reuters.com/article/2009/08/01/venezuela-media-idUSN0146551720090801.

711 Seton Motley, "Video: FCC 'Diversity' Czar on Chavez's Venezuela: 'Incredible… Democratic Revolution,'" NewsBusters, August 28, 2009, http://newsbusters.org/blogs/seton-motley/2009/08/28/video-fcc-diversity-czar-chavezs-venezuela-incredible-democratic-revol.

712 "Afghan mission falls short of expectations: Lawmakers," Breitbart, August 1, 2009, http://www.breitbart.com/article.php?id=CNG.6c394a230bece3a4943ecb703a1405f3.e01&show_article=1.

713 Will Weissert, "Raul Castro: Cuba won't undo communist system," Breitbart, August 1, 2009, http://www.breitbart.com/article.php?id=D99QE9CG0&show_article=1.

714 Mary Bruce, "Geithner Won't Rule Out New Taxes for Middle Class," ABC News, August 2, 2009, http://blogs.abcnews.com/george/2009/08/geithner-wont-rule-out-new-taxes-for-middle-class.html.

715 Henny Sender, "Wall Street profits from trades with Fed," Free Republic, August 2, 2009, http://www.freerepublic.com/focus/f-news/2306776/posts.

716 "Feds see biggest tax revenue drop since 1932," MSNBC, August 3, 2009, http://www.msnbc.msn.com/id/32275055/.

717 Mark Mazzetti and Thom Shanker, "Russian Subs Patrolling Off East Coast of U.S.," New York Times, August 4, 2009, http://www.nytimes.com/2009/08/05/world/05patrol.html?_r=1.

718 Macon Phillips, "Facts Are Stubborn Things," The White House Blog, August 4, 2009, http://www.whitehouse.gov/blog/Facts-Are-Stubborn-Things/.

719 Angela Greiling Keane and Holly Rosenkrantz, "Four of Top 'Clunkers' Model Purchases Are Foreign (Update3)," Bloomberg, August 4, 2009, http://www.bloomberg.com/apps/news?pid=newsarchive&sid=am1mj6R6tAcg.

720 Michelle Malkin, "Obama lied, transparency died, Pt. 10,001: No Cash for Clunkers disclosure," michellemalkin.com, August 4, 2009, http://michellemalkin.com/2009/08/04/obama-lied-transparency-died-pt-100001-no-cash-for-clunkers-disclosure/.

721 Rebecca Christie, "U.S. Treasury to Sell $75 Billion in Long-Term Debt (Update2)," Bloomberg, August 5, 2009, http://www.bloomberg.com/apps/news?pid=newsarchive&sid=acHzsgcOptGI.

722 Donna Smith and Jackie Frank, "Obama gives healthcare pep talk as Senate leaves,"

Reuters, August 6, 2009, http://www.reuters.com/article/idUSTRE56M0HE20090806
?feedType=RSS&feedName=domesticNews&rpc=22&sp=true.

723 Carrie Budoff Brown, "White House to Democrats: 'Punch back twice as hard,'" Politico, August 6, 2009, http://www.politico.com/news/stories/0809/25891.html.

724 "White House: 'War on terrorism' is over," Washington Times, August 6, 2009, http://www.washingtontimes.com/news/2009/aug/06/white-house-war-terrorism-over/.

725 Julie Hirschfeld Davis, "Senate confirms Sotomayor for Supreme Court," Breitbart, August 6, 2009, http://www.breitbart.com/article.php?id=D99TIOQO0&show_article=1.

726 "Fannie Mae suffers massive loss, seeks more aid," Google, August 6, 2009, http://www.google.com/hostednews/afp/article/ALeqM5i0PRnWFbBMa9QOmgJk-2tA4nlxjyA.

727 Julie Hirschfeld Davis, "Senate confirms Sotomayor for Supreme Court," Breitbart, August 6, 2009, http://www.breitbart.com/article.php?id=D99TIOQO0&show_article=1.

728 Daniel Schwammenthal, "Prosecuting American 'War Crimes,'" Wall Street Journal, November 26, 2009, http://online.wsj.com/article/SB10001424052748704013004574519253095440312.html.

729 "Venezuela to buy Russian arms, tanks: Chavez," Breitbart, August 5, 2009, http://www.breitbart.com/article.php?id=CNG.8c34a75248ddd401e7db0815cb13f5d1.111.

730 "Obama: 'Don't Want The Folks Who Created The Mess to Do A Lot Of Talking,'" Breitbart.tv, August 7, 2009, http://www.breitbart.tv/obama-dont-want-the-folks-who-created-the-mess-to-do-a-lot-of-talking/.

731 David Sanger, Eric Schmitt and Thom Shanker, "White House Struggles to Gauge Afgan Success," New York Times, August 6, 2009, http://www.nytimes.com/2009/08/07/world/asia/07policy.html?_r=1.

732 Corey Boles and Michael R. Crittenden, "Geithner Asks Congress to Increase Federal Debt Limit," Wall Street Journal, August 8, 2009, http://online.wsj.com/article/SB124970470294516541.html.

733 Jordan Fabian, "Sarah Palin: 'Death panels' may be in final healthcare reform bill," The Hill, August 8, 2009, http://thehill.com/blogs/blog-briefing-room/news/73371-palin-death-panels-may-be-in-final-health-bill.

734 Greg Miller and Josh Meyer, "Criminal investigation into CIA treatment of detainees expected," Los Angeles Times, August 9, 2009, http://www.latimes.com/news/nation-world/nation/la-na-cia-interrogate9-2009aug09,0,34626.story.

735 "'Net Neutrality' Is Socialism, Not Freedom," Washington Examiner, October 20, 2009, http://washingtonexaminer.com/node/156326.

736 Patrick Courrielche, "The National Endowment for the Art of Persuasion?," Big Hollywood, August 25, 2009, http://bighollywood.breitbart.com/pcourrielche/2009/08/25/the-national-endowment-for-the-art-of-persuasion-patrick-courrielche/.

737 John Nolte, "Propaganda, Health Care and ACORN: Full Context of NEA Conference Call Reveals Disturbing Pattern," Big Hollywood, September 21, 2009, http://bighollywood.breitbart.com/jjmnolte/2009/09/21/propaganda-health-care-and-acorn-full-context-of-nea-conference-call-reveals-disturbing-pattern/.

738 Huma Khan, "After 'Inappropriate' NEA Conference Call, White House Pushes New Guidelines," ABC News, September, 22, 2009, http://abcnews.go.com/blogs/poli-

tics/2009/09/after-inappropriate-nea-conference-call-white-house-pushes-new-guidelines/.

739   Pamela Geller, "Obama's State Department Submits to Islam," American Thinker, August 18, 2009, http://www.americanthinker.com/2009/08/obamas_state_department_submit.html.

740   "White House says Obama strategy will win Afghan war," Reuters, August 10, 2009, http://www.reuters.com/article/idUSTRE57A03T20090811.

741   Tom Blumer, "Surgical Strike: Surgeons' Group Blasts Obama's $30K-$50K Foot/Leg Amputation Claim," NewsBusters, August 13, 2009, http://newsbusters.org/blogs/tom-blumer/2009/08/13/surgical-strike-surgeons-group-blasts-obamas-30k-50k-leg-amputation-clai.

742   Caroline Baum, "Obama Goes Postal, Lands in Dead-Letter Office," Bloomberg, August 17, 2009, http://www.bloomberg.com/apps/news?pid=newsarchive&sid=aJ01reSCujDQ.

743   Chidanand Rajghatta, "Jihadis thrice attacked Pakistan nuclear sites," Times of India, August 11, 2009, http://timesofindia.indiatimes.com/news/world/pakistan/Revealed-Jihadis-thrice-attacked-Pakistan-nuclear-sites/articleshow/4879235.cms.

744   "Kuwait says it foiled Qaeda attack on US base," Breitbart, August 11, 2009, http://www.breitbart.com/article.php?id=CNG.e975259b386fc683f1e88d0b03ec7004.bd1&show_article=1.

745   Dmitry Solovyov, "Russia sees U.S. space threat, builds new rocket," Reuters, August 11, 2009, http://www.reuters.com/article/idUSTRE57A25Z20090811.

746   "Funding stalls putting Guard soldiers on U.S. border," USA Today, August 12, 2009, http://www.usatoday.com/news/washington/2009-08-12-%20border-guard_N.htm.

747   Jason Allardyce and Tony Allen-Mills, "White House backed release of Lockerbie bomber Abdel Baset al-Megrahi," The Australian, July 26, 2010, http://www.theaustralian.com.au/news/world/white-house-backed-release-of-lockerbie-bomber-abdel-baset-al-megrahi/story-e6frg6so-1225896741041.

748   Tony Hake, "UN: Four months to secure the future of our planet," Examiner.com, August 14, 2009, http://www.examiner.com/weather-in-denver/un-four-months-to-secure-the-future-of-our-planet.

749   "Clinton heads to Liberia to show women power," Breitbart, August 12, 2009, http://www.breitbart.com/article.php?id=CNG.66fa5ac30a5f2e10d66fb4e51be7512e.81&show_article=1.

750   Gemma Daley, "Australian Senate Rejects Rudd's Cap and Trade Emissions Plan," Bloomberg, August 12, 2009, http://www.bloomberg.com/apps/news?pid=newsarchive&sid=aHo_TW08Y3to.

751   "Obama slams TV over health care 'ruckus,'" Breitbart, August 14, 2009, http://www.breitbart.com/article.php?id=CNG.228e42c5948115405d6f3ec5d1ad6b50.1a1&show_article=1.

752   Laura Saunders, "Tax-Cheat Showdown: Fess Up or Stay Quiet?," Wall Street Journal, August 14, 2009, http://online.wsj.com/article/SB125020653689430645.html.

753   Lynnley Browning, "US Builds Crime Cases on Clients of UBS," CNBC, August 14, 2009, http://www.cnbc.com/id/32413524.

754   "Obama slams TV over health care 'ruckus,'" Breitbart, August 14, 2009, http://www.breitbart.com/article.php?id=CNG.228e42c5948115405d6f3ec5d1ad6b50.1a1&sh

ow_article=1.

755 Liz Sidoti, "Obama invokes grandmother's death in health debate," Breitbart, August 15, 2009, http://www.breitbart.com/article.php?id=D9A3KRQG0&show_article=1.

756 Timothy J. Burger, "Obama Campaign Ad Firms Signed On to Push Health-Care Overhaul," Bloomberg, August 15, 2009, http://www.bloomberg.com/apps/news?pid=news archive&sid=aV3dLt6wmZH4.

757 Angela Greiling Keane, "Car Dealers Will Get Clunkers Money, LaHood Says (Update3)," Bloomberg, August 19, 2009, http://www.bloomberg.com/apps/news?pid=ne wsarchive&sid=agl7R9EceOTw.

758 Katya Golubkova, "Russia, Venezuela edge closer to oil deal, talk arms," Reuters, August 15, 2009, http://www.reuters.com/article/idUSTRE57E19G20090815?feedType =RSS&feedName=environmentNews&rpc=22&sp=true.

759 "As Afghans vote, US raises the stakes in war," Breitbart, August 16, 2009, http://www.breitbart.com/article.php?id=CNG.7ab069c9afb660253e9107028a479c85. b21&show_article=1.

760 "Mexican Army takes over customs on US border," Breitbart, August 16, 2009, http://www.breitbart.com/article.php?id=CNG.18f81af5666e40153a84161ef1da2a77.21 &show_article=1.

761 "Obama Underwrites Offshore Drilling, Wall Street Journal, August 18, 2009, http://online.wsj.com/article/SB10001424052970203863204574346610120524166.html.

762 Dan Strumpf, "NY dealers pull out of clunkers program," Breitbart, August 19, 2009, http://www.breitbart.com/article.php?id=D9A63RC81&show_article=1.

763 Angela Greiling Keane, "Car Dealers Will Get Clunkers Money, LaHood Says (Update3)," Bloomberg, August 19, 2009, http://www.bloomberg.com/apps/news?pid=ne wsarchive&sid=agl7R9EceOTw.

764 "'Clunkers' program runs out of gas," Washington Times, August 20, 2009, http://www.washingtontimes.com/news/2009/aug/20/clunkers-program-runs-out-gas.

765 Michael Cooper, "Government Jobs Have Grown Since Recession," New York Times, August 19, 2009, http://www.nytimes.com/2009/08/20/us/20states.html.

766 "Tight budget quashes US space ambitions: panel," Breitbart, August 19, 2009, http://www.breitbart.com/article.php?id=CNG.1d64c1d955288aef25c4e96c9d9139b1.24 1&show_article=1.

767 Jason Rhodes and Kim Dixon, "Swiss to reveal UBS accounts to settle U.S. tax battle," Reuters, August 19, 2009, http://www.reuters.com/article/idUSLJ59987220090819.

768 "95 killed on Iraq's deadliest day since U.S. handover," CNN, August 19, 2009, http://articles.cnn.com/2009-08-19/world/iraq.violence_1_iraqi-security-forces-iraqi-interior-ministry-official-truck-bomb?_s=PM:WORLD.

769 "Iraqi security forces collaborated with bombers: FM," Breitbart, August 22, 2009, http://www.breitbart.com/article.php?id=CNG.38b8a40bdeef850d50a01aea146fda20.361& show_article=1.

770 Steven Thomma, "Fighting false health care claims, Obama repeats one of his own," McClatchy, August 19, 2009, http://www.mcclatchydc.com/2009/08/19/74035/fighting-false-health-care-claims.html.

771 Guy Benson, "Obama 'Bearing False Witness' on Abortion," National Review, August 20, 2009, http://www.nationalreview.com/media-blog/30240/obama-bearing-false-witness-abortion/guy-benson.

772 "Obama: Republican conspiracy out to kill health reform," Washington Times, August

20, 2009, http://www.washingtontimes.com/news/2009/aug/20/obama-gop-conspiracy-out-kill-health-reform/.

773 "Obama: 'Basic Standard Of Decency' Allows Illegals To Be Treated," Real Clear Politics, August 20, 2009, http://www.realclearpolitics.com/video/2009/08/20/obama_basic_standard_of_decency_allows_illegals_to_be_treated.html.

774 Ken Thomas and Stephen Manning, "Obama admin. To end cash for clunkers on Monday," Breitbart, August 20, 2009, http://www.breitbart.com/article.php?id=D9A6RBR00&show_article=1.

775 Jeff Mason, "Obama to raise 10-year deficit to $9 trillion," Reuters, August 21, 2009, http://www.reuters.com/article/newsOne/idUSTRE57K4XE20090821.

776 James Kirkup, Auslan Cramb and Alex Spillius, "Barack Obama leads condemnation of Scotland for freeing Lockerbie bomber," The Telegraph, August 20, 2009, http://www.telegraph.co.uk/news/uknews/terrorism-in-the-uk/6062496/Barack-Obama-leads-condemnation-of-Scotland-for-freeing-Lockerbie-bomber.html.

777 "Afghanistan's Elections," Washington Post, August 20, 2009, http://www.washingtonpost.com/wp-srv/special/world/afghanistan-election/.

778 Peter Baker, "Obama's Team Is Lacking Most of Its Top Players," New York Times, August 23, 2009, http://www.nytimes.com/2009/08/24/us/politics/24confirm.html?_r=1&hp.

779 Carrie Johnson, "Prosecutor to Probe CIA Interrogations," Washington Post, August 25, 2009, http://www.washingtonpost.com/wp-dyn/content/article/2009/08/24/AR2009082401743_pf.html.

780 Neil Irwin, "Denis Hughes Named Chairman of New York Fed's Board of Directors," Washington Post, August 25, 2009, http://www.washingtonpost.com/wp-dyn/content/article/2009/08/24/AR2009082403124.html.

781 Helene Cooper, "U.S. Military Says Its Force in Afghanistan Is Insufficient," New York Times, August 24, 2009, http://www.nytimes.com/2009/08/24/world/asia/24military.html.

782 "Obama ends frenetic vacation," Breitbart, August 30, 2009, http://www.breitbart.com/article.php?id=CNG.3c4f86ce84d6de5a63599166b04e1920.901&show_article=1.

783 Laura Crimaldi, "Feds: Stimulus money sent to 4,000 cons," Boston Herald, August 26, 2009, http://www.bostonherald.com/news/regional/view/20090826feds_stimulus_money_sent_to_4000_cons_herald_report_spurs_probe/srvc=home&position=also.

784 "President Obama's Address to Students Across America September 8, 2009, Docstoc, September 1, 2009, http://www.docstoc.com/docs/10582301/President-Obama?s-Address-to-Students-Across-America-September-8-2009,,,Obama.

785 Joshua Rhett Miller, "ABC, NBC Won't Air Ad Critical of Obama's Health Care Plan," Fox News, August 27, 2009, http://www.foxnews.com/politics/2009/08/27/abc-nbc-wont-air-ad-critical-obamas-health-care-plan/.

786 "Real US unemployment rate at 16 pct: Fed official," Breitbart, August 26, 2009, http://www.breitbart.com/article.php?id=CNG.4452bed82adf3124e5884678e236d7fb.361&show_article=1.

787 Conn Carroll, "Obama Officially Abandons Missile Defense in Europe," Heritage Foundation, August 27, 2009, http://blog.heritage.org/2009/08/27/obama-officially-abandons-missile-defense-in-europe/.

788 John Crawley, "Japanese, Koreans gain most from cash for clunkers," Reuters, August 26, 2009, http://www.reuters.com/article/idUSTRE57P5C220090826.
789 "U.S. moves toward formal cut off of aid to Honduras," Reuters, August 27, 2009, http://www.reuters.com/article/idUSN27328207.
790 Declan McCullagh, "Bill would give president emergency control of Internet," Cnet, August 28, 2009, http://news.cnet.com/8301-13578_3-10320096-38.html.
791 Shawn Neisteadt, "Some Surprised By 'Clunker' Tax," Keloland, August 24, 2009, http://www.keloland.com/NewsDetail6162.cfm?Id=0,89084.
792 Bill Varner, "UAE Seizes North Korean Weapons Shipment to Iran (Update2), Bloomberg, August 28, 2009, http://www.bloomberg.com/apps/news?pid=newsarchive&sid=ap9U2VfbfCBs.
793 Venezuela accuses protesters of attempting 'rebellion,'" Breitbart, August 29, 2009, http://www.breitbart.com/article.php?id=CNG.476dd184fc2bc70d989c0182943b0833.991&show_article=1.
794 Alexander Bolton, "AFL-CIO, Dems push new Wall Street tax," The Hill, August 30, 2009, http://thehill.com/homenews/house/56789-afl-cio-dems-push-new-wall-street-tax.
795 Fang Yan and Edmund Klamann, "GM to form China venture, invest $293 million," Reuters, August 30, 2009, http://www.reuters.com/article/idUSTRE57T0IV20090830
796 Bob Woodward, "McChrystal: More Forces or 'Mission Failure,'" Washington Post, September 21, 2009, http://www.washingtonpost.com/wp-dyn/content/article/2009/09/20/AR2009092002920_pf.html.
797 Rajiv Chandrasekaran and Karen DeYoung, "Changes in Afghanistan, Washington May Require Shift in U.S. War Strategy," Washington Post, September 21, 2009, http://www.washingtonpost.com/wp-dyn/content/article/2009/09/20/AR2009092002878_pf.html.
798 Susan Jones, "43 U.S. Troops Have Died in Afghanistan Since Gen. McChrystal Called for Reinforcements," CNS News, September 30, 2009, http://www.cnsnews.com/news/article/54807.
799 Mark Tran, "Afghanistan strategy must change, US commander McChrystal says," The Guardian, August 31, 2009, http://www.guardian.co.uk/world/2009/aug/31/general-mcchrystal-afghanistan-bull.
800 "Feds Crack Down on 'Garage Sales,'" Education News, August 31, 2009, http://ednews.org/articles/feds-crack-down-on-garage-sales-.html.
801 Diane Macedo, "New government Policy Imposes Strict Standards on Garage Sales Nationwide," Fox News, September 18, 2009, http://www.foxnews.com/us/2009/09/18/new-government-policy-imposes-strict-standards-garage-sales-nationwide/.
802 Don Jorgensen, "Dealers Still Waiting For Clunker Cash," Keloland, August 31, 2009, http://www.keloland.com/NewsDetail6162.cfm?Id=89419.
803 "Car Dealers Still Waiting On 'Clunkers' Cash," Edmunds, August 31, 2009, http://townhall-talk.edmunds.com/direct/view/.f1c306b/3580.
804 Jaikumar Vijayan, "Privacy Office approves laptop searches without suspicion at U.S. borders," Computerworld, August 31, 2009, http://www.computerworld.com/s/article/9137315/Privacy_Office_approves_laptop_searches_without_suspicion_at_U.S._borders.
805 Adam Entous and Arshad Mohammed, "Obama aides see need for more troops in Afghanistan," Reuters, August 31, 2009, http://af.reuters.com/article/worldNews/

idAFN3143955820090831.

806   Martin Crutsinger, "Federal deficit hits $1.38T through August," Breitbart, September 11, 2009, http://www.breitbart.com/article.php?id=D9AL936G2.

807   Ambrose Evans- Pritchard, "US credit shrinks at Great Depression rate prompting fears of double-dip recession," The Telegraph, September 14, 2009, http://www.telegraph.co.uk/finance/financetopics/recession/6190818/US-credit-shrinks-at-Great-Depression-rate-prompting-fears-of-double-dip-recession.html.

808   "Unemployment Rate," Portal Seven, http://portalseven.com/employment/unemployment_rate.jsp.

809   "California's Man-Made Drought," Wall Street Journal, September 2, 2009, http://online.wsj.com/article/SB10001424052970204731804574384731898375624.html.

810   Eduard Gismatullin, "BP Makes 'Giant' Oil Discover in Gulf of Mexico (Update4)," Bloomberg, September 2, 2009, http://www.bloomberg.com/apps/news?pid=newsarchive&sid=a44RUTBIl_3Q.

811   Byron York, "Health care reform means more power for the IRS," Washington Examinier, September 2, 2009, http://washingtonexaminer.com/politics/2009/09/healthcare-reform-means-more-power-irs.

812   "Biden: Stimulus Working Better Than Expected," Fox News, September 3, 2009, http://www.foxnews.com/politics/2009/09/03/biden-stimulus-working-better-expected/.

813   Department of Energy, "Timeline of DOE's review of the Solyndra Loan Guarantee Application," http://energy.gov/sites/prod/files/Solar%20Background%20Document%201.pdf.

814   "White House Withdraws Call for Students to 'Help' Obama," Fox News, September 3, 2009, http://www.foxnews.com/politics/2009/09/03/white-house-withdraws-students-help-obama/.

815   Amanda Carpenter, "Green jobs czar signed 'truther' statement in 2004," Washington Times, September 3, 2009, http://www.washingtontimes.com/weblogs/back-story/2009/sep/03/green-jobs-czar-signed-truther-statement-in-2004/.

816   Jonathan Thatcher, "North Korea says in last stage of enriching uranium," Reuters, September 3, 2009, http://uk.reuters.com/article/2009/09/03/uk-korea-north-idUK-TRE5826I520090903.

817   Bill Dedman, "Obama yields on most White House visitor logs," MSNBC, September 4, 2009, http://www.msnbc.msn.com/id/32447886/ns/politics-white_house/.

818   Sheera Frenkel, "US fury as Israel defies settlement freeze call," TimesOnline, September 5, 2009, http://www.timesonline.co.uk/tol/news/world/middle_east/article6822540.ece.

819   "Obama did not order Van Jones' resignation, adviser says," CNN, September 6, 2009, http://www.cnn.com/2009/POLITICS/09/06/obama.adviser.resigns/index.html.

820   "Chavez minister vows more Venezuela radio closings," Reuters, September 5, 2009, http://uk.reuters.com/article/idUKN0520744720090905.

821   "Ahmadinejad, Chavez back 'revolutionary' nations," Breitbart, September 5, 2009, http://www.breitbart.com/article.php?id=CNG.87b8890481f4f1f90eb45fabbef1e661.141&show_article=1.

822   "Obama did not order Van Jones' resignation, adviser says," CNN, September 6, 2009, http://www.cnn.com/2009/POLITICS/09/06/obama.adviser.resigns/index.html.

823   Simon Walters, "No. 10 turns on Obama and Clinton for criticizing decision to release Lockerbie bomber," Daily Mail, September 6, 2009, http://www.dailymail.co.uk/news/article-1211495/No-10-turns-Obama-Clinton-criticising-decision-release-

Lockerbie-bomber.html.

824 "White House: Van Jones Did Not Fill Out 63-Question, Seven-Page Questionnaire," Breitbart.tv, September 7, 2009, http://www.breitbart.tv/white-house-van-jones-did-not-fill-out-63-question-seven-page-questionnaire.

825 David Saltonstall, "President Obama says 'sin tax' on sodas is food for thought, despite Gov. Paterson's failed proposal," New York Daily News, September 8, 2009, http://www.nydailynews.com/news/politics/2009/09/08/2009-09-08_president_obama_says_sin_tax_on_sodas_is_food_for_thought.html.

826 Molly K. Hooper, "Boehner: GOP leaders haven't met Obama for health talks since April," The Hill, September 9, 2009, http://thehill.com/blogs/blog-briefing-room/news/57859-boehner-gop-leaders-havent-met-obama-for-health-talks-since-april.

827 Jonathan Ferziger, "Barak Approves Construction of 455 West Bank Homes (Update3)," Bloomberg, September 7, 2009, http://www.bloomberg.com/apps/news?pid=news archive&sid=aO1TKptOIJhQ.

828 Ladane Nasseri and Ali Sheikholeslami, "Ahmadinejad Rules Out Nuclear Concessions, Urges Obama Debate," Bloomberg, September 7, 2009, http://www.bloomberg.com/apps/news?pid=newsarchive&sid=aa7mTee2kpoU.

829 Ambrose Evans-Pritchard, "China alarmed by US money printing, The Telegraph, September 6, 2009, http://www.telegraph.co.uk/finance/economics/6146957/China-alarmed-by-US-money-printing.html.

830 Nia-Malika Henderson, "President Obama announces another czar, Ron Bloom," Politico, September 8, 2009, http://www.politico.com/news/stories/0909/26824.html.

831 Doug Stanglin, "Some Schools Won't Show Obama TV Address, Others Offer an Opt-Out," USA Today, September 4, 2009, http://content.usatoday.com/communities/ondeadline/post/2009/09/68498425/1.

832 Edmund Conway, "UN wants new global currency to replace dollar," The Telegraph, September 7, 2009, http://www.telegraph.co.uk/finance/currency/6152204/UN-wants-new-global-currency-to-replace-dollar.html.

833 Molly K. Hooper, "Boehner: GOP leaders haven't met Obama for health talks since April," The Hill, September 9, 2009, http://thehill.com/blogs/blog-briefing-room/news/57859-boehner-gop-leaders-havent-met-obama-for-health-talks-since-april.

834 Laurie Kellman, "Rep. Joe Wilson's outburst criticized by colleagues," Washington Examiner, September 10, 2009, http://washingtonexaminer.com/politics/2009/09/rep-joe-wilsons-outburst-criticized-colleagues.

835 Julianna Goldman and Mike Dorning, "White House Resists Offering Details on Financing Health Plan," Bloomberg, September 11, 2009, http://www.bloomberg.com/apps/news?pid=newsarchive&sid=aqbQf_x.Zd1g.

836 "ACORN fires 2 after hidden-camera footage aired," Breitbart, September 10, 2009, http://www.breitbart.com/article.php?id=D9AKORB81&show_article=1.

837 "Texas governor sends Rangers to Mexico border," MSNBC, September 11, 2009, http://www.msnbc.msn.com/id/32793136/ns/us_news-security#.Tl-zIHPs6Go.

838 Hope Yen, "Census Bureau severs ties with ACORN in 2010 count," Breitbart, September 11, 2009, http://www.breitbart.com/article.php?id=D9ALCUJO0&show_article=1.

839 Tom Fitton, "Smoking Gun in White House-Romanoff Bribery Scandal?," Right Side News, June 4, 2010, http://www.rightsidenews.com/2010060410458/us/politics-and-economics/smoking-gun-in-white-house-romanoff-bribery-scandal.html.

840   Sam Youngman, "Obama sets stage for Using budget maneuver to pass health reform," The Hill, September 10, 2009, http://thehill.com/homenews/administration/58233-obama-sets-stage-for-using-budget-maneuver-to-pass-health-reform.

841   Peter Whoriskey and Anne Kornblut, "U.S. to Impose Tariff on Tires From China," Washington Post, September 11, 2009, http://www.washingtonpost.com/wp-dyn/content/article/2009/09/11/AR2009091103957_pf.html.

842   Lindsey Ellerson, "US Shifts Policy, Willing to Meet 1-on-1 With North Korea," ABC News, September 11, 2009, http://blogs.abcnews.com/politicalpunch/2009/09/us-shifts-policy-willing-to-meet-1on1-with-north-korea.html.

843   David Gardner, "A million march to US Capitol to protest against 'Obama the socialist,'" The Daily Mail, September 14, 2009, http://www.dailymail.co.uk/news/worldnews/article-1213056/Up-million-march-US-Capitol-protest-Obamas-spending-tea-party-demonstration.html.

844   Chris Buckley, "China blasts U.S. tire duties as protectionist blow," Reuters, September 12, 2009, http://www.reuters.com/article/idUSTRE58B1O320090912?feedType=RSS&feedName=topNews&rpc=22&sp=true.

845   "China Probes 'Unfair Trade' in U.S. Chicken and Auto Products," Bloomberg, September 13, 2009, http://www.bloomberg.com/apps/news?pid=newsarchive&sid=a9igRzOC55wE.

846   Daniel Cancel, "Venezuela to Develop Nuclear Energy With Russian Help (Update1)," Bloomberg, September 13, 2009, http://www.bloomberg.com/apps/news?pid=newsarchive&sid=aElQ3UEU9eYM.

847   Declan McCullagh, "Obama Admin: Cap and Trade Could Cost Families $1,761 A Year," CBS News, September 15, 2009, http://www.cbsnews.com/8301-504383_162-5314040-504383.html.

848   Audrey Hudson, "W.H. collects Web users' data without notice," Washington Times, September 16, 2009, http://www.washingtontimes.com/news/2009/sep/16/obama-wh-collects-web-users-data/.

849   "US military chief wants more troops for Afghan war," China Daily, September 16, 2009, http://www.chinadaily.com.cn/world/2009-09/16/content_8697110.htm.

850   "U.S. scraps missile defense shield plans," CNN, September 17, 2009, http://edition.cnn.com/2009/WORLD/americas/09/17/united.states.missile.shield/index.html.

851   Timothy P. Carney, "Obama helps strengthen General Electric-Putin ties," Washington Examiner, September 17, 2009, http://washingtonexaminer.com/blogs/beltway-confidential/obama-helps-strengthen-general-electric-putin-ties.

852   Tom Lasseter, "'Old friends' Cuba, China strengthen ties," McClatchey, September 16, 2009, http://www.mcclatchydc.com/2009/09/16/75560/old-friends-cuba-china-strengthen.html.

853   Viola Gienger and Indira A.R. Lakshmanan, "Obama Delays Afghanistan Troop Decision as Criticism Deepens," Bloomberg, September 16, 2009, http://www.bloomberg.com/apps/news?pid=newsarchive&sid=aOsI6x5z.3b0.

854   "Nuke agency says Iran can make bomb," Breitbart, September 17, 2009, http://www.breitbart.com/article.php?id=D9AP714G0&show_article=1.

855   Stephen Dinan, "Obama: Legalize illegals to get them health care," Washington Times, September 18, 2009, http://www.washingtontimes.com/news/2009/sep/18/obamas-ties-immigration-to-health-care-battle/?feat=home_cube_position1.

856   "Fed plans to approve banking salaries: report," Google, September 17, 2009, http://

www.google.com/hostednews/afp/article/ALeqM5j3JObwETrLtj7GTDl8avD6ha-nEOQ.

857   Jeremy Pelofsky, "Obama admin: dismiss gay couple benefits lawsuit," Reuters, September 18, 2009, http://www.reuters.com/article/2009/09/18/us-obama-gaymarriage-massachusetts-idUSTRE58H57T20090918.

858   "Snubbed By Obama, Fox News's Chris Wallace Calls White House 'Biggest Bunch of Crybabies I've Ever Seen,'" HuffingtonPost, September 19, 2009, http://www.huffingtonpost.com/2009/09/19/snubbed-by-obama-fox-news_n_292254.html.

859   "Russia's Putin says U.S. shield decision positive," Reuters, September 18, 2009, http://in.reuters.com/article/idUSTRE58H1O320090918.

860   Parisa Hafezi and Firouz Sederat, "Iranian president raises stakes against Israel," Reuters, September 18, 2009, http://in.reuters.com/article/idINIndia-42553620090918.

861   Nicholas Johnston, "Obama Says Financial regulations Must Be Strengthened Globally," Bloomberg, September 19, 2009, http://www.bloomberg.com/apps/news?pid=newsarchive&sid=aNRS9zQAgnBQ.

862   Raymond Hernandez and Jeff Zeleny, "Paterson Says He Will Run, Rejecting Call From Obama," New York Times, September 20, 2009, http://www.nytimes.com/2009/09/20/nyregion/20paterson.html.

863   Dina Temple-Raston, "Officials: NYC Plot Operational, Not Just Aspirational," National Public Radio, September 29, 2009, http://www.npr.org/templates/story/story.php?storyId=113290720.

864   Peter Graff, "U.S. Afghanistan commander's troops request ready," Reuters, September 19, 2009, http://www.reuters.com/article/idUSTRE58I11O20090919.

865   "Obama Plans Back-to-Back TV Interviews Sunday," New York Times, September 14, 2009,   http://thecaucus.blogs.nytimes.com/2009/09/14/obama-may-do-back-to-back-tv-interviews-sunday/.

866   Michael O'Brien, "Obama open to newspaper bailout bill," The Hill, September 20, 2009,   http://thehill.com/blogs/blog-briefing-room/news/59523-obama-open-to-newspaper-bailout-bill.

867   "Obama on ACORN: 'Not Something I've Followed Closely' Won't Commit to Cut Federal Funds," ABC News, September 20, 2009, http://blogs.abcnews.com/george/2009/09/obama-on-acorn-not-something-ive-followed-closely.html.

868   Kimberly Schwandt, "Obama, Stephanopoulos Spare Over Definition of 'Tax,'" Fox News, September 20, 2009, http://www.foxnews.com/politics/2009/09/20/obama-stephanopoulos-spar-definition-tax/.

869   Ricardo Alonso-Zaldivar, "HHS investigates Humana for Medicare mailer warning seniors on health overhaul," Minneapolis Star Tribune, September 21, 2009, http://www.startribune.com/lifestyle/health/59990947.html?elr=KArksLckD8EQDUoaEyqyP4O:DW3ckUiD3aPc:_Yyc:aUnciatkEP7DhUsl.

870   Ian Talley, "Steven Chu: Americans Are Like 'Teenage Kids' When It Comes to Energy," Wall Street Journal, September 21, 2009, http://blogs.wsj.com/environmental-capital/2009/09/21/steven-chu-americans-are-like-teenage-kids-when-it-comes-to-energy/.

871   Ryan Singel, "FCC Backs Net Neutrality – And Then Some," Wired, September 21, 2009, http://www.wired.com/epicenter/2009/09/net-neutrality-announcement/.

872   Craig Torres and Robert Schmidt, "Fed Rejects Geithner Request for Study of Governance, Structure," Bloomberg, September 21, 2009, http://www.bloomberg.com/apps/ne

ws?pid=newsarchive&sid=adjvXg1zP.zY.

873   Julian Borger, "Barack Obama ready to slash US nuclear arsenal," The Guardian, September 20, 2009, http://www.guardian.co.uk/world/2009/sep/20/barack-obama-us-nuclear-weapons.

874   "Russia general says missile plan not shelved," Reuters, September 21, 2009, http://www.reuters.com/article/idUSTRE58K12S20090921.

875   Alister Bull, "U.S. to push for new economic world order at G20," Reuters, September 21, 2009, http://www.reuters.com/article/2009/09/21/us-g-idUSTRE58G34Z20090921.

876   Gustavo Palencia and Edgar Garrido, "Ousted president Zelaya returns to Honduras," Reuters, September 21, 2009, http://www.reuters.com/article/2009/09/21/us-honduras-zelaya-idUSTRE58K3JY20090921.

877   Huma Khan, After "Inappropriate' NEA Conference Call, White House Pushes New Guidelines," ABC News, September 22, 2009, //blogs.abcnews.com/politicalpunch/2009/09/after-inappropriate-nea-conference-call-white-house-pushes-new-guidelines.html.

878   Gustavo Palencia, "Honduran forces clash with protesters at embassy," Reuters, September 22, 2009, http://www.reuters.com/article/2009/09/22/us-honduras-zelaya-idUSTRE58K3JY20090922.

879   Burton Frierson, "U.S. issues $7 trillion debt, supply to stabilize," Reuters, September 23, 2009, http://www.reuters.com/article/idUSTRE58M36920090923.

880   Patrick Wintour, "Barack Obama snubs Gordon Brown over private talks," The Guardian, September 24, 2009, http://www.guardian.co.uk/politics/2009/sep/23/barack-obama-gordon-brown-talks.

881   Anne Bayefsky, "Obama's U.N. Double Talk," National Review Online, September 25, 2009, http://www.nationalreview.com/corner/187754/obamas-u-n-double-talk/anne-bayefsky.

882   D.K. Jamal, "Ouch! French President Sarkozy slams 'naïve' Obama for living in 'virtual world' on Iran," Examiner, September 26, 2009, http://www.examiner.com/post-partisan-in-national/ouch-french-president-sarkozy-slams-naive-obama-for-living-virtual-world-on-iran.

883   "Commanders back Afghan troop hike assessment," Reuters, September 23, 2009, http://www.reuters.com/article/2009/09/23/idUSN23415447.

884   Matt Kelley, "Stimulus funds boost number of federal jobs," USA Today, September 23, 2009, http://www.usatoday.com/news/washington/2009-09-23-stimfed_N.htm.

885   Ambrose Evans-Pritchard, "HSBC bids farewell to dollar supremacy," The Telegraph, September 1, 2011, http://www.telegraph.co.uk/finance/comment/ambroseevans_pritchard/6211858/HSBC-bids-farewell-to-dollar-supremacy.html.

886   "Review Ordered of Video Showing Students Singing Praises of President Obama," Fox News, September 24, 2009, http://www.foxnews.com/politics/2009/09/24/review-ordered-video-showing-students-singing-praises-president-obama/.

887   Jason Trahan, Todd J. Gillman and Scott Goldstein, "Dallas bomb plot suspect told landlord he was moving out," Dallas Morning News, September 24, 2009, http://www.dallasnews.com/sharedcontent/dws/dn/latestnews/stories/092409dnmetbombarrest.1b177db8b.html.

888   Frances Robles, "They're torturing me, Honduras' Manuel Zelaya claims," Free Republic, September 24, 2009, http://freerepublic.com/focus/f-news/2347426/posts.

889   David Usborne and Andrew Grice, "Ahmadinejad has enough uranium to go whole way," The Independent, September 26, 2009, http://www.independent.co.uk/news/world/

middle-east/ahmadinejad-has-enough-uranium-to-go-whole-way-1793483.html.
890   Anne Bayefsky, "Obama's U.N. Double Talk," National Review Online, September 25, 2009,   http://www.nationalreview.com/corner/187754/obamas-u-n-double-talk/anne-bayefsky.
891   "Obama's News Conference at the G-20," New York Times, September 25, 2009, http://www.nytimes.com/2009/09/26/world/middleeast/26nuke.text.2.html.
892   David Jackson, "Obama: Iran's secret nuke facility 'inconsistent with a peaceful program,'" USA Today, September 25, 2009, http://content.usatoday.com/communities/theoval/post/2009/09/68499808/1.
893   Edwin Chen, "Obama Says He's Still Open to 'Meaningful Dialogue' With Iran," Georgian Daily, September 26, 2009, http://georgiandaily.com/index.php?option=com_content&task=view&id=14795&Itemid=133.
894   "Venezuela Seeking Uranium With Iran's Help," Fox News, September 26, 2009, http://www.foxnews.com/world/2009/09/26/venezuela-seeking-uranium-irans-help/.
895   D.K. Jamal, "Ouch! French President Sarkozy slams 'naïve' Obama for living in 'virtual world' on Iran," Examiner, September 26, 2009, http://www.examiner.com/post-partisan-in-national/ouch-french-president-sarkozy-slams-naive-obama-for-living-virtual-world-on-iran.
896   Michael Riley, "D.C. job alleged as attempt to deter Romanoff," Denver Post, September 27, 2009, http://www.denverpost.com/news/ci_13429758),,,no.
897   Amanda Carpenter, "U.S. commander in Afghanistan talked with Obama only once," The Washington Times, September 28, 2009, http://www.washingtontimes.com/weblogs/back-story/2009/sep/28/us-commander-of-afghanistan-only-talked-to-obama-o/.
898   Ibid.
899   William Branigin, "Iran Test-Fires Its Most Advanced Missiles, Washington Post, September 28, 2009, http://www.washingtontimes.com/weblogs/back-story/2009/sep/28/us-commander-of-afghanistan-only-talked-to-obama-o/.
900   Patrice Hill, "Dollar's days of dominance may end, Washington Times, September 29, 2009,   http://www.washingtontimes.com/news/2009/sep/29/dollars-days-of-dominance-may-end/.
901   "Empire State building turns red-yellow for China's 60th," Google, September 2009, http://www.google.com/hostednews/afp/article/ALeqM5hUZamhqvPGVrYZ-pGq_clUpC7dAUg.
902   Jennifer Morisco, "GM Shouldn't Be Making Campaign Contributions," Real Clear Politics, September 29, 2009, http://www.realclearpolitics.com/2010/09/29/gm_shouldn039t_be_making_campaign_contributions_242756.html.
903   Damian Paletta, "Lending Declines as Bank Jitters Persist," Wall Street Journal, November 25, 2009, http://online.wsj.com/article/SB125907631604662501.html?mod=WSJ_hpp_MIDDLTopStories.
904   Jake Sherman, "John Boehner blasts Barack Obama's Olympic move," Politico, September 30, 2009, http://www.politico.com/news/stories/0909/27742.html.
905   Byron York, "Michelle Obama: It's a 'sacrifice' to travel to Europe to pitch for the Olympics. But I'm doing it for the kids," Washington Examiner, September 30, 2009, http://washingtonexaminer.com/blogs/beltway-confidential/michelle-obama-it039s-039sacrifice039-travel-europe-pitch-olympics-i039m-d.
906   Jeff Mason, "Obama to take weeks to study Afghanistan strategy," Reuters, October 1,

2009, http://www.reuters.com/article/2009/10/01/us-afghanistan-obama-sb-idUS-TRE59002G20091001.

907   Susan Jones, "43 U.S. Troops Have Died in Afghanistan Since Gen. McChrystal Called for Reinforcements," CNS News, September 30, 2009, http://www.cnsnews.com/news/article/54807.

908   "Obama Shatters Spending Record for First-Year Presidents," Fox News, November 24, 2009, http://www.foxnews.com/politics/2009/11/24/obama-shatters-spending-record-year-presidents/.

909   "U.S. Budget Deficit Hit Record $1.4 Trillion in 2009," Fox News, October 7, 2009, http://www.foxnews.com/politics/2009/10/07/budget-deficit-hit-record-trillion/.

910   "2009 Federal Deficit Surges to $1.42 Trillion," ABC News, October 16, 2009, http://abcnews.go.com/Business/wireStory?id=8850681.

911   Michael James, "$160,000 Per Stimulus Job? White House Calls That 'Calculator Abuse,'" ABC News, October 30, 2009, http://abcnews.go.com/blogs/politics/2009/10/160000-per-stimulus-job-white-house-calls-that-calculator-abuse/?cid=6a00d8341c4df25 3ef0120a6a1b337970c.

912   "Unemployment Rate," Portal Seven, http://portalseven.com/employment/unem-ployment_rate.jsp.

913   Fred Lucas, "Gun-Running Timeline: How DOJ's 'Operation Fast and Furious' Unfold-ed," CNS News, July 7, 2011, http://www.cnsnews.com/news/article/gun-running-timeline-how-doj-s-operation-fast-and-furious-unfolded.

914   Andrew Greiner, "Obama Heading to Copenhagen for Olympic Pitch," NBC Chicago, September 28, 2009, http://www.nbcchicago.com/news/local-beat/Obama-Heading-to-Copenhagen-62317937.html.

915   Thomas Frank, "TSA to expand use of body scanners," USA Today, October 1, 2009, http://www.usatoday.com/tech/news/surveillance/2009-09-30-backscatter-body-scanners_N.htm.

916   Alex Spillius, "White House angry at General Stanley McChrystal speech on Afghani-stan," The Telegraph, October 5, 2009, http://www.telegraph.co.uk/news/worldnews/northamerica/usa/barackobama/6259582/White-House-angry-at-General-Stan-ley-McChrystal-speech-on-Afghanistan.html.

917   Peter Baker and Jeff Zeleny, "For Obama, an Unsuccessful Campaign," New York Times, October 2, 2009, http://www.nytimes.com/2009/10/03/sports/03obama.html.

918   "Obama Meets With McChrystal in Denmark," Fox News, October 2, 2009, http://www.foxnews.com/politics/2009/10/02/obama-meets-mcchrystal-denmark/.

919   Ed Whelan, "Stuart Taylor on Harold Koh's Threat to Free Speech," National Review Online, October 30, 2009, http://www.nationalreview.com/corner/189419/stuart-tay-lor-harold-kohs-threat-free-speech/ed-whelan.

920   James Sterngold, Linda Shen and Dakin Campbell, "Banks With 20% Unpaid Loans at 18-Year High Amid Recovery Doubt," Bloomberg, October 2, 2009, http://www.bloom-berg.com/apps/news?pid=newsarchive&sid=aXZinRhF5tlA.

921   Edmund Conway, "World Bank could 'run out of money' within 12 months," The Tele-graph, October 2, 2009, http://www.telegraph.co.uk/finance/financetopics/financial-crisis/6255816/World-Bank-could-run-out-of-money-within-12-months.html.

922   William J. Broad and David E. Sanger, "Report Says Iran has Data to make a Nuclear Bomb," New York Times, October 3, 2009, http://www.nytimes.com/2009/10/04/world/middleeast/04nuke.html?_r=1.

923 John Acher, "Only 10 days left for climate deal, U.N.'s Ban says," Reuters, October 3, 2009, http://www.reuters.com/article/idUSTRE59224920091003.

924 "10 Troops Killed In Deadliest Battle of the Year: Where is the Commander-in-Chief?," Fox Nation, October 5, 2009, http://www.thefoxnation.com/gen-stanley-mcchrystal/2009/10/05/obama-allegedly-furious-gen-mcchrystal-blunt-comments.

925 Alex Spillius, "Barack Obama cancels meeting with Dalai Lama 'to keep China happy,'" The Telegraph, October 5, 2009, http://www.telegraph.co.uk/news/worldnews/northamerica/usa/barackobama/6262938/Barack-Obama-cancels-meeting-with-Dalai-Lama-to-keep-China-happy.html.

926 Robert Fisk, "The demise of the dollar," The Independent, October 6, 2009, http://www.independent.co.uk/news/business/news/the-demise-of-the-dollar-1798175.html.

927 Arshad Mohammed, "Taliban Afghan momentum due to lack of U.S. troops," Reuters, October 5, 2009, http://www.reuters.com/article/2009/10/05/us-afghanistan-usa-gates-idUSTRE59462620091005.

928 Ben Feller, "White House: Leaving Afghanistan not an option," Breitbart, October 5, 2009, http://www.breitbart.com/article.php?id=D9B53AL82&show_article=1.

929 Alex Spillius, "Barack Obama cancels meeting with Dalai Lama 'to keep China happy,'" The Telegraph, October 5, 2009, http://www.telegraph.co.uk/news/worldnews/barackobama/6262938/Barack-Obama-cancels-meeting-with-Dalai-Lama-to-keep-China-happy.html.

930 Charles Hurt, "White House's botched 'op,'" New York Post, October 6, 2009, http://www.nypost.com/p/news/national/item_kTVWHZ3vEeRQbxCC0TNZHN.

931 Ibid.

932 "White House Escalates War of Words With Fox News," Fox News, October 12, 2009, http://www.foxnews.com/politics/2009/10/12/white-house-escalates-war-words-fox-news/.

933 "UN calls for new reserve currency," Breitbart, October 6, 2009, http://www.breitbart.com/article.php?id=CNG.e272eaa74dccc30f21c6ff7638b0f37b.461&show_article=1.

934 "UN calls for new reserve currency," Breitbart, October 6, 2009, http://www.breitbart.com/article.php?id=CNG.e272eaa74dccc30f21c6ff7638b0f37b.461&show_article=1.

935 Patricia Zengerle, "General wants 40,000 more U.S. troops for Afghan," Reuters, October 8, 2009, http://www.reuters.com/article/idUSN3024169220091008.

936 Peter Spiegel and Yochi Dreazen, "The Troop Request Exceeds 60,000," Wall Street Journal, October 9, 2009, http://online.wsj.com/article/SB125504448324674693.html.

937 Matt Spetalnick and Wojciech Moskwa, "Obama says Nobel Peace Prize is 'call to action,'" Reuters, October 9, 2009, http://www.reuters.com/article/idUSTRE5981JK20091009?sp=true.

938 Guy Chazan and Alistair MacDonald, "Nobel Committee's Decision Courts Controversy," Wall Street Journal, http://online.wsj.com/article/SB125509603349176083.html.

939 "Obama slams US Chanber of Commerce for anti-reform ad," Bear Market Issues, October 9, 2009, http://bearmarketnews.blogspot.com/2009/10/obama-slams-us-chamber-of-commerce-for.html.

940 Daniel Nasaw, "Washington strips immigration policing powers from Arizona sher-

iff," The Guardian, October 9, 2009, http://www.guardian.co.uk/world/2009/oct/09/obama-immigration-arpaio-arizona-sheriff.

941   Brian Stelter, "Fox's Volley With Obama Intensifying," New York Times, October 11, 2009, http://www.nytimes.com/2009/10/12/business/media/12fox.html.

942   "Arizona Sheriff Vows to Continue Immigration Sweeps Despite Federal Downgrade," Fox News, October 12, 2009, http://www.foxnews.com/politics/2009/10/12/arizona-sheriff-vows-continue-immigration-sweeps-despite-federal-downgrade/.

943   Jeff Mason and Michael Stott, "Clinton fails to win Russia pledge on Iran sanctions," Reuters, October 13, 2009, http://www.reuters.com/article/2009/10/13/us-russia-clinton-idUSTRE59B5JB20091013.

944   Darya Korsunskaya, "Russia's Putin warns against intimidating Iran," Reuters, October 14, 2009, http://in.reuters.com/article/idINIndia-43160620091014.

945   Charles Pope, "DeFazio leads effort to provide bonus to Social Security recipients," OregonLive, October 15, 2009, http://www.oregonlive.com/politics/index.ssf/2009/10/defazio_leads_effort_to_provid.html.

946   Ceci Connolly, "Health Insurers Emerge as Obama's Top Foe in Reform Effort," Washington Post, October 14, 2009, http://www.washingtonpost.com/wp-dyn/content/article/2009/10/13/AR2009101303472.html.

947   Charles Pope, "DeFazio leads effort to provide bonus to Social Security recipients," OregonLive, October 15, 2009, http://www.oregonlive.com/politics/index.ssf/2009/10/defazio_leads_effort_to_provid.html.

948   Karen Travers and Matthew Jaffe, "President Obama's Trip to New Orleans Draws Criticism – Before He Even Arrives," ABC News, October 15, 2009, http://abcnews.go.com/Politics/president-barack-obama-visit-orleans-survey-katrina-recovery/story?id=8830279.

949   "Reports: Russia warns US on missile defense," Breitbart, October 15, 2009, http://www.breitbart.com/article.php?id=D9BBJG402&show_article=1.

950   Aaron Klein, "Official: Obama 'disgusted' with Israel, Says president poised to press for withdrawal from strategic territory," World Net Daily, October 16, 2009, http://www.wnd.com/?pageId=112998.

951   Paul Thompson, "Meet 'Jihad Jane': The blonde American housewife accused in Islamic plot to kill Swedish cartoonist, The Daily Mail, March 11, 2010, http://www.dailymail.co.uk/news/article-1256886/US-Jihad-Jane-Colleen-Larose-accused-terror-plot-kill-Lars-Vilks.html.

952   Mark Knoller, "How Many 'Top Priority' Issues Does Obama Have?," CBS News, August 13, 2010, http://www.cbsnews.com/8301-503544_162-20013622-503544.html.

953   Allahpundit, "Revealed: Who else was at that secret Obama briefing with Olby and Maddow?," HotAir, October 21, 2009, http://hotair.com/archives/2009/10/21/revealed-who-else-was-at-that-secret-obama-briefing-with-olby-and-maddow/.

954   Christina Lamb, "76 days since request for more troops, Obama accused of stalling," TimesOnline, October 18, 2009, http://www.timesonline.co.uk/tol/news/world/us_and_americas/article6879511.ece.

955   Noel Sheppard, "Rahm Emanuel: Fox Isn't a News Organization Because it Has a Perspective," News Busters, October 18, 2009, http://newsbusters.org/blogs/noel-sheppard/2009/10/18/rahm-emanuel-fox-isnt-news-organization-because-it-has-perspective.

956   Mike Allen, "Fox 'not really news,' says Axelrod," Politico, October 18, 2009, http://

www.politico.com/news/stories/1009/28417.html.

957 Aaron Klein, "White House boasts: We 'control' news media," WorldNetDaily, October 18, 2009, http://www.wnd.com/index.php?fa=PAGE.view&pageId=113347.

958 "America Moving from Kingdom of Cash to Socialism Slowly but Surely," Pravda, October, 19, 2009, http://english.pravda.ru/world/americas/19-10-2009/109973-socialism-0/.

959 Devlin Barrett, "New Medical marijuana Policy: Obama Administration Will Not Seek Arrests For People Following state Laws," HuffingtonPost, October 18, 2009, http://www.huffingtonpost.com/2009/10/19/new-medical-marijuana-pol_n_325426.html.

960 Mark O'Malley, "Capital Culture: Obamas big on White House gigs (while Rome burns)," Free Republic, October 20, 2009, http://www.freerepublic.com/focus/f-news/2366571/posts.

961 Dave Camp, "7 Months After Stimulus 49 of 50 States Have Lost Jobs," Committee on Ways and Means, October 21, 2009, http://www.republicans.waysandmeans.house.gov/News/DocumentSingle.aspx?DocumentID=150826.

962 Deborah Solomon and Dan Fitzpatrick, "Pay Czar to Slash Compensation at Seven Firms," Wall Street Journal, October 22, 2009, http://online.wsj.com/article/SB125615172396299535.html?mod=WSJ_hpp_LEFTTopStories.

963 Manu Raju, "Dems seek cover to boost debt limit," Politico, October 22, 2009, http://www.politico.com/news/stories/1009/28586.html.

964 "Obama hits out at climate 'naysayers,'" Breitbart, October 23, 2009, http://www.breitbart.com/article.php?id=CNG.96323f483e0be9f6a793eaa215ad708a.131&show_article=1.

965 "Former Vice President Dick Cheney says Obama must do 'what it takes to win' in Afghanistan," CBS News, October, 22, 2009, http://www.cbsnews.com/stories/2009/10/21/ap/preswho/main5407819.shtml.

966 "Obama offers millions in Muslim technology fund," Breitbart, October 23, 2009, http://www.breitbart.com/article.php?id=CNG.96323f483e0be9f6a793eaa215ad708a.211&show_article=1.

967 "Fact Check: Health Insurers' Profits Not So Fat," Fox News, October, 26, 2009, http://www.foxnews.com/politics/2009/10/26/fact-check-health-insurers-profits-fat/.

968 Penny Starr, "IRS Launches New Global Program to Target 'High Wealth Individuals,'" CNS News, April 6, 2010, http://www.cnsnews.com/node/63761.

969 Kathryn Jean Lopez, "'Barack Obama is the most powerful writer since Julius Caesar,'" National Review, October 27, 2009, http://www.nationalreview.com/corner/189206/barack-obama-most-powerful-writer-julius-caesar/kathryn-jean-lopez.

970 "October deadliest month for US in Afghan war: Pentagon," Google, October 27, 2009, http://www.google.com/hostednews/afp/article/ALeqM5jxCcNmUs-AusQTjNjV-6i8DAV3G6g.

971 "Afghan strategy to focus on major population centers: report," Breitbart, October 28, 2009, http://www.breitbart.com/article.php?id=CNG.362497142655da8a176c01ec25272fb1.e1&show_article=1.

972 "Clunkers: Taxpayers paid $24,000 per car," CNNMoney, October, 29, 2009, http://money.cnn.com/2009/10/28/autos/clunkers_analysis/index.htm.

973 Brett J. Blackledge and Matt Apuzzo, "Stimulus Watch: Stimulus jobs overstated in report," Seattle Times, October 29, 2009, http://seattletimes.nwsource.com/html/businesstechnology/2010157585_apusstimulusjobs.html.

974   Mark Tapscott, "Newly disclosed emails link White House directly to NEA political-ization scandal," Washington Examiner, October 30, 2009, http://washingtonexaminer.com/blogs/beltway-confidential/newly-disclosed-emails-link-white-house-direct-ly-nea-politicalization-scan.

975   Bill Dedman, "Obama names 110 White House visitors," MSNBC, October 30, 2009, http://www.msnbc.msn.com/id/33556933/ns/politics-white_house/.

976   Al-Qaeda leadership in Pakistan: Hillary Clinton," The Daily Times, October 30, 2009,   http://www.dailytimes.com.pk/print.asp?page=2009%5C10%5C30%5Csto ry_30-10-2009_pg1_1.

977   David A. Patten, "Report: W.H. Engineered NY-23 Endorsement," Newsmax, No-vember 2, 2009, http://www.newsmax.com/InsideCover/scozzafava-obama-en-dorse/2009/11/02/id/335937.

978   Jeffrey Heller, "Palestinians accuse U.S. of killing Peace prospects," Reuters, November 1, 2009, http://www.reuters.com/article/idUSLV11497220091101.

979   "Unemployment Rate," Portal Seven, http://portalseven.com/employment/unem-ployment_rate.jsp.

980   Mike Spector, Vanessa O'Connell and Kate Haywood, "CIT Files Its Bankrupt-cy Plan," Wall Street Journal, November 3, 2009, http://online.wsj.com/article/SB125709781695721315.html?mod=rss_Today's_Most_Popular.

981   Jeffrey Heller, "Palestinians accuse U.S. of killing Peace prospects," Reuters, November 1, 2009, http://www.reuters.com/article/idUSLV11497220091101.

982   "Troubled Asset Relief Program: Continued Stewardship Needed As Treasury Devel-ops Strategies for Monitoring and Divesting Financial Interests in Chrysler and GM," U.S. Government Accountability Office, November 2, 2009, http://www.gao.gov/products/GAO-10-151.

983   www.marklevinshow.com.

984   Matthew Day, "Russia 'simulates' nuclear attack on Poland," The Telegraph, Novem-ber 1, 2009, http://www.telegraph.co.uk/news/worldnews/europe/poland/6480227/Russia-simulates-nuclear-attack-on-Poland.html.

985   "Water rationing for Venezuela's capital city," Breitbart, November 2, 2009, http://www.breitbart.com/article.php?id=CNG.ad409ca172435301fb479b62661e070f.36 1&show_article=1,,,AFP.

986   "Republicans Win Governor's Races in New Jersey, Virginia," Fox News, November 4, 2009, http://www.foxnews.com/politics/2009/11/03/democrats-republicans-pre-pare-possible-legal-battle-new-jersey-race/.

987   Susan Ferrechio, "After a flurry of stimulus spending questionable projects pile up," Washington Examiner, November 3, 2009, http://www.washingtonexaminer.com/politics/After-a-flurry-of-stimulus-spending_-questionable-projects-pile-up-8474249-68709732.html.

988   Jae-Soon Chang, "NKorea claims to expand arsenal of atomic bombs," Breitbart, No-vember 3, 2009, http://www.breitbart.com/article.php?id=D9BO6DAG1&show_ar-ticle=1.

989   Lara Setrakian, "Iran Protests Against U.S. and Regime on Hostage Anniversary," ABC News, November 4, 2009, http://abcnews.go.com/International/iran-cracks-protest-ers-hostage-anniversary/story?id=8998930.

990   Michael Muskal, "Obama calls for new relationship with Iran on anniversary of em-bassy takeover, Los Angeles Times, November 4, 2009, http://articles.latimes.com/2009/

nov/04/nation/la-naw-obama-iran5-2009nov05.

991 Emily Friedman, Richard Esposito, Ethan Nelson and Desiree Adib, "Fort Hood Gunman Who Killed 12, Wounded 30 Survived Gun Battle," ABC News, November 5, 2009, http://abcnews.go.com/WN/soldiers-killed-fort-hood-shooting/story?id=9007938.

992 Robert A. George, "Obama's Frightening Insensitivity Following Shooting," NBC Chicago, October 6, 2010, http://www.nbcchicago.com/news/politics/A-Disconnected-President.html.

993 Mark Knoller, "How Many 'Top Priority' Issues Does Obama Have?," CBS News, August 13, 2010, http://www.cbsnews.com/8301-503544_162-20013622-503544.html.

994 Julian Borger, "Iran tested advanced nuclear warhead design – secret report," The Guardian, November 5, 2009, http://www.guardian.co.uk/world/2009/nov/05/iran-tested-nuclear-warhead-design.

995 "Obama: Don't Jump to Conclusions," CBS News, November 6, 2009, http://www.cbsnews.com/stories/2009/11/06/national/main5551286.shtml.

996 Mark Knoller, "Obama Changes Tune on Paying for Unemployment Benefits Extension," CBS News, July 22, 2010, http://www.cbsnews.com/8301-503544_162-20011420-503544.html.

997 Martin Fletcher, "Foreign journalists arrested as Iran restricts reports on opposition," TimesOnline, November 6, 2009, http://www.timesonline.co.uk/tol/news/world/middle_east/article6906209.ece.

998 Al Yoon, "Freddie Mac posts $5 billion loss," Reuters, November 7, 2009, http://www.reuters.com/article/idUSTRE5A55PR20091107.

999 Lori Montgomery and Shailagh Murray, "House Democrats pass health-care bill," Washington Post, November 8, 2009, http://www.washingtonpost.com/wp-dyn/content/article/2009/11/07/AR2009110701504_pf.html.

1000 Peter Nicholas, "Democratic consultant says he got a warning from White House after appearing on Fox News," Los Angeles Times, November 8, 2009, http://articles.latimes.com/2009/nov/08/nation/na-obama-fox8.

1001 Daniel Cancel, "Chavez Says Venezuela to Prepare for War as Deterrent (Update3)," Bloomberg, November 8, 2009, http://www.bloomberg.com/apps/news?pid=newsarchive&sid=aZuAU4StKAQY.

1002 Richard Esposito, Matthew Cole and Brian Ross, "Officials: U.S. Army Told of Hasan's Contacts with al Qaeda," ABC News, November 9, 2009, http://abcnews.go.com/Blotter/fort-hood-shooter-contact-al-qaeda-terrorists-officials/story?id=9030873.

1003 David Johnston and Scott Shane, "U.S. Knew of Suspect's Tie to Radical Cleric," New York Times, November 10, 2009, http://www.nytimes.com/2009/11/10/us/10inquire.html?_r=1.

1004 Daniel Zwerdling, "Walter Reed Officials Asked: Was Hasan Psychotic?," National Public Radio, November 11, 2009, http://www.npr.org/templates/story/story.php?storyId=120313570.

1005 Brian Ross and Rhonda Schwartz, "Major Hasan's E-Mail: 'I Can't Wait to join You' in Afterlife," ABC News, November 19, 2009, http://abcnews.go.com/Blotter/major-hasans-mail-wait-join-afterlife/story?id=9130339.

1006 Sunlen Miller, "Interview with the President: Jail Time for Those without Health Care Insurance?," ABC News, November 9, 2009, http://abcnews.go.com/blogs/politics/2009/11/interview-with-the-president-jail-time-for-those-without-health-care-insurance/.

1007 Josh Gerstein, "Despite ban, holder to speak to CAIR-linked group," Politico, Novem-

THE BIG PICTURE

ber 9, 2009, http://www.politico.com/blogs/joshgerstein/1109/Despite_ban_Holder_to_speak_to_CAIRlinked_group.html.

1008 Caroline Glick, "Obama's failure, Netanyahu's opportunity," Carolineglick.com, November 13, 2009, http://www.carolineglick.com/e/2009/11/obamas-failure-netanyahus-oppo.php.

1009 David Martin, "Obama's Afghan Plan: About 40K More Troops," CBS News, November 9, 2009, http://www.cbsnews.com/stories/2009/11/09/world/main5592551.shtml.

1010 Ramin Mostafavi, "Iran charges three detained Americans with spying," Reuters, November 9, 2009, http://www.reuters.com/article/2009/11/09/us-iran-usa-charges-idUSTRE5A829G20091109.

1011 Mark Heinrich, "U.S. says can give Iran time to okay nuclear deal," Reuters, November 9, 2009, http://www.reuters.com/article/idUSTRE5A81TW20091109.

1012 Jeff Jacoby, "Obama's swelling ego," Boston Globe, November 14, 2009, http://www.boston.com/bostonglobe/editorial_opinion/oped/articles/2009/11/14/obamas_swelling_ego/.

1013 Tom Gjelten, Daniel Zwerdling, Scott Neuman and wire reports, "Answer South On Fort Hood Suspect's link To imam," National Public Radio, November 10, 2009, http://www.npr.org/templates/story/story.php?storyId=120266334.

1014 Declan McCullagh, "Justice Dept. Asked For News Site's Visitor Lists," CBS News, November 10, 2009, http://www.cbsnews.com/8301-504383_162-5595506-504383.html?tag=mncol%3btxt.

1015 Hana Levi Julian, "State Dept: US Goal to Expel Jews in 'Occupied' Post-67 Lands," Israel National News, November 11, 2009, http://www.israelnationalnews.com/News/news.aspx/134352.

1016 Jenn Abelson and Todd Wallack, "Stimulus job boost in state exaggerated, review finds," Boston Globe, November 11, 2009, http://www.boston.com/business/articles/2009/11/11/stimulus_fund_job_benefits_exaggerated_review_finds/.

1017 Louis Woodhill, "More Stimulus Equals More Unemployment," Real Clear Markets, November 11, 2009, http://www.realclearmarkets.com/articles/2009/11/11/more_stimulus_equals_more_unemployment_97503.html.

1018 Mark Tapscott, "Obama to weed out Bush political appointees who careered in; Establishes new political test for career jobs," Washington Examiner, November 12, 2009, http://washingtonexaminer.com/blogs/beltway-confidential/obama-weed-out-bush-political-appointees-who-careered-establishes-new-poli.

1019 Ben Blanchard, "China warns Obama about Dalai Lama, citing Lincoln on slavery," Reuters, November 12, 2009, http://www.reuters.com/article/idUSTRE5AB1BF20091112.

1020 John Solomon, "No guarantees at the Pension Benefit Guaranty Corporation," Iwatchnews.com, May 3, 2010, http://www.iwatchnews.org/2010/05/03/2686/no-guarantees-pension-benefit-guaranty-corporation.

1021 Michelle Malkin, "Bombshell: Obama bringing KSM of NYC for trial," MichelleMalkin.com, November 13, 2009, http://michellemalkin.com/2009/11/13/bombshell-obama-bringing-ksm-to-nyc-for-trial/.

1022 Tom Raum and Andrew Taylor, "Obama Wants Domestic Spending Cuts in Next Budget," ABC News, November 13, 2009, http://abcnews.go.com/Business/wireStory?id=9079511.

1023 Marc Ginsberg, "'Qum' Buy Ya,'" HuffingtonPost, November 13, 2009, http://www.

huffingtonpost.com/amb-marc-ginsberg/qum-buy-ya_b_357382.html.

1024 "Remarks by President Barack Obama at Suntory Hall," The White House, November 14, 2009, http://www.whitehouse.gov/the-press-office/remarks-president-barack-obama-suntory-hall.

1025 Andrew Malcolm, "How Low Will He Go? Obama Gives Japan's Emperor Akihito a wow bow," Los Angeles Times, November 14, 2009, http://latimesblogs.latimes.com/washington/2009/11/obama-emperor-akihito-japan.html.

1026 "China dissidents 'detained ahead of Obama visit,'" Breitbart, November 14, 2009, http://www.breitbart.com/article.php?id=CNG.a751493682512bdc967745cbdcd60551.771&show_article=1.

1027 Hans Nichols, "Obama Aide Dunn Renews Criticism of Fox, Hails Jon Stewart," Bloomberg, November 14, 2009, http://www.bloomberg.com/apps/news?pid=newsarchive&sid=aBRJYGPAmOoo.

1028 "Khalid Sheikh Mohammed civilian trial blasted by Giuliani," Big News Network, November 15, 2009, http://feeds.bignewsnetwork.com/?sid=565796.

1029 Cara Anna, "Chinese greet 'Oba Mao' with flaming statue, fakes," Breitbart, November 13, 2009, http://www.breitbart.com/article.php?id=D9BUP3J00&show_article=1.

1030 Mike Allen, "President Obama takes heat on Afghanistan timing," Politico, November 15, 2009, http://www.politico.com/news/stories/1109/29552.html.

1031 Geoff Dyer and Kevin Brown, "China says Fed policy threatens global recovery," Financial Times, November 15, 2009, http://www.ft.com/intl/cms/s/0/85f1fac2-d1dc-11de-a0f0-00144feabdc0.html#axzz1Y5n03Xx3.

1032 Jonathan Karl, "Jobs 'Saved or Created' in Congressional Districts That Don't Exist," ABC News, November 16, 2009, http://abcnews.go.com/Politics/jobs-saved-created-congressional-districts-exist/story?id=9097853.

1033 Ridgely Ochs, "Debate over mammograms and breat cancer nothing new," Newsday, November 22, 2009, http://www.newsday.com/long-island/debate-over-mammograms-and-breast-cancer-nothing-new-1.1616986.

1034 Jake Tapper, "No Mandarin Word for 'Town Hall'" Obama Introduces China to U.S. Political Tradition," ABC News, November 16, 2009, http://abcnews.go.com/Politics/president-obama-holds-town-hall-china-human-rights/story?id=9091246.

1035 James Pathokoukis, "China questions costs of U.S. healthcare reform," Reuters, November 16, 2009, http://blogs.reuters.com/james-pethokoukis/2009/11/16/china-questions-costs-of-us-healthcare-reform/.

1036 Flor Migues, "Obama's first year in office," January 27, 2010, Commonsensepoliticsusa.com, http://commonsensepoliticsusa.wordpress.com/2010/01/27/obamas-first-year-in-office-its-the-economy-stupid/.

1037 Caren Bohan, "Obama" Too much debt could fuel double-dip recession," Reuters, November 18, 2009, http://www.reuters.com/article/idUSN188108620091118.

1038 Charles Grassley, "Grassley, Judiciary Republicans Press for Answers from Holder After Being Snubbed in Response to Previous Letter on Justice Department Lawyers Working on Gitmo Detainee Policy," Grassley.senate.gov., February 26, 2010, http://grassley.senate.gov/news/Article.cfm?customel_dataPageID_1502=25444.

1039 "Senate bill weighs in at 2,074 pages," Politico, November 18, 2009, http://www.politico.com/livepulse/1109/Senate_bill_weighs_in_at_2074_pages.html?showall.

1040 Tom Cohen, "White House: $98 billion in bad payments," CNN, November 18, 2009, http://money.cnn.com/2009/11/18/news/improper_payments.cnnw/.

1041 Anne E. Kornblut, "Obama admits Guantanamo won't close by Jan. deadline," Washington Post, November 18, 2009, http://www.washingtonpost.com/wp-dyn/content/article/2009/11/18/AR2009111800571_pf.html.

1042 Jerry Lampen, "Clinton in first Afghan visit as top U.S. diplomat," Reuters, November 18, 2009, http://www.reuters.com/article/idUSTRE5AH2AG20091118.

1043 "O-Bow-Ma Does It Agan...Obama Bows to Chinese Premier Wen Jiabao and Even to the Burger King," Scared Monkeys, November 24, 2009, http://scaredmonkeys.com/2009/11/24/o-bow-ma-does-it-again-obama-bows-to-chinese-premier-wen-jiabao-and-even-to-the-burger-king/.

1044 Karen DeYoung and Michael Leahy, "Uninvestigated terrorism warning about Detroit suspect called not unusual," Washington Post, December 28, 2009, http://www.washingtonpost.com/wp-dyn/content/article/2009/12/27/AR2009122700279.html.

1045 Andy Sullivan, "Wall Street tax must be international: Pelosi," Reuters, November 19, 2009, http://www.reuters.com/article/idUSTRE5AI3ZV20091119?feedType=RSS&feedName=businessNews&rpc=23&sp=true.

1046 "Senate bill includes the Botox tax," Politico, November 18, 2009, http://www.politico.com/livepulse/1109/Senate_bill_includes_the_Botox_tax.html?showall.

1047 Anne E. Kornblut, "White House aides: No Afghan decision before Thanksgiving," Washington Post, November 19, 2009, http://www.washingtonpost.com/wp-dyn/content/article/2009/11/19/AR2009111900904_pf.html.

1048 Gabor Steingart, "Obama's Nice Guy Act Gets Him Nowhere on the World Stage," Spiegel, November 23, 2009, http://www.spiegel.de/international/world/0,1518,662822,00.html.

1049 James Delingpole, "Climategate: the final nail in the coffin of 'Anthropogenic Global Warming'?", The Telegraph, November 20, 2009, http://blogs.telegraph.co.uk/news/jamesdelingpole/100017393/climategate-the-final-nail-in-the-coffin-of-anthropogenic-global-warming/.

1050 Lou Scatigna, "Germany Warns US On Market Bubbles," The Financial Physician, November 21, 2009, http://www.thefinancialphysician.com/blog/?p=945.

1051 www.marklevinshow.com

1052 Parisa Hafezi, "Iran launches war games to protect nuclear sites," Reuters, November 22, 2009, http://uk.reuters.com/article/idUSTRE5AK0FZ20091122.

1053 "Obama says 'step closer' to climate deal," Breitbart, November 24, 2009, http://www.breitbart.com/article.php?id=TX-PAR-MWN76.

1054 "The Real Housewives of D.C.," Wikipedia, http://en.wikipedia.org/wiki/Michaele_Salahi#Michaele_Salahi.

1055 Charles Grassley, "Grassley, Judiciary Republicans Press for Answers from Holder After Being Snubbed in Response to Previous Letter on Justice Department Lawyers Working on Gitmo Detainee Policy," Grassley.senate.gov., February 26, 2010, http://grassley.senate.gov/news/Article.cfm?customel_dataPageID_1502=25444.

1056 Matt Drudge, "Obama leaves WH clutching GQ mag – featuring himself!, DrudgeReport, November 24, 2009, www.drudgereport.com.

1057 James Kirkup, Thomas Harding and Toby Hamden, "Bob Ainsworth criticizes Barack Obama over Afghanistan," The Telegraph, November 24, 2009, http://www.telegraph.co.uk/news/newstopics/politics/defence/6646179/Bob-Ainsworth-criticises-Barack-Obama-over-Afghanistan.html.

1058 Anne Gearan and Jennifer Loven, "Obama could lock in Afghanistan decision Monday," Breitbart, November 23, 2009, http://www.breitbart.com/article.php?id=D9C5HCDO0&show_article=1

1059 Andrew Malcolm, "Obama issues special Hajj message to world's Muslims," Los Angeles Times, November 25, 2009, http://latimesblogs.latimes.com/washington/2009/11/on-thanksgiving-eve-barack-obamas-special-message-to-muslims.html.

1060 Jake Tapper, "White House Pushes Back on Climate Change Email Controversy," ABC News, December 3, 2009, http://blogs.abcnews.com/politicalpunch/2009/12/white-house-pushes-back-on-climate-change-email-controversy.html.

1061 Ryan Smith, "Navy Seals Face Court Martial for Alleged Terrorist Bloody Lip?," CBS News, November 25, 2009, http://www.cbsnews.com/8301-504083_162-5773734-504083.html.

1062 Danial Schwammenthal, "Prosecuting American 'War Crimes,'" Wall Street Journal, November 26, 2009, http://online.wsj.com/article/SB10001424052748704013004574519253095440312.html.

1063 "Dubai default threat rattles world stocks," Breitbart, November 26, 2009, http://www.breitbart.com/article.php?id=CNG.dbd0d58212f48118340a6335d97e2c47.c1&show_article=1.

1064 Charlie Savage, "Justice Department Says Acorn Can Be Paid for Pre-Ban Contracts," New York Times, November 27, 2009, http://www.nytimes.com/2009/11/28/us/politics/28acorn.html.

1065 Craig Torres, "Bernanke Says Limiting Fed Independence Would 'Impair' Economy," Bloomberg, November 29, 2009, http://www.bloomberg.com/apps/news?pid=newsarchive&sid=aQS1SZ95x778.

1066 Tom Bonnett, "'Iran's 10 Uranium Plants' In Defiance of UN," Sky News, November 29, 2009, http://news.sky.com/home/world-news/article/15478325.

1067 Peter S. Goodman, "U.S. Loan Effort Is Seen as Adding to housing Woes," New York Times, January 2, 2010, http://www.nytimes.com/2010/01/02/business/economy/02modify.html?pagewanted=all.

1068 "Unemployment Rate," Portal Seven, http://portalseven.com/employment/unemployment_rate.jsp.

1069 Mike Allen and Jim Vandehei, "Dick Cheney slams President Obama for projecting 'weakness,'" Politico, December 1, 2009, http://www.politico.com/news/stories/1109/30024.html.

1070 Edwin Mora, "116 U.S. Troops Died in Afghanistan While Obama Pondered Reinforcements," CNS News, December 1, 2009, http://www.cnsnews.com/news/article/57832.

1071 Ewen MacAskill, "Barack Obama's war: the final push in Afghanistan," The Guardian, December 1, 2009, http://www.guardian.co.uk/world/2009/dec/01/barack-obama-speech-afghanistan-war.

1072 Eric Zimmerman, "Rumsfeld questions Obama's claim on troops," The Hill, December 2, 2009, http://thehill.com/blogs/blog-briefing-room/news/70221-rumsfeld-questions-obamas-claim-on-troops.

1073 Jake Tapper, "White House Pushes Back on Climate Change Email Controversy," ABC News, December 3, 2009, http://blogs.abcnews.com/politicalpunch/2009/12/white-house-pushes-back-on-climate-change-email-controversy.html.

1074 Sylvia Longmire, "Russia prepared to build Kalashnikov arms factory in Venezuela," The Examiner, December 2, 2009, http://www.examiner.com/south-america-policy-in-national/russia-prepared-to-build-kalashnikov-arms-factory-venezuela.

1075 Kara Rowland, "Critics not invited to White House 'jobs summit,'" Washington Times, December 2, 2009, http://www.washingtontimes.com/news/2009/dec/02/obama-policy-critics-not-invited-to-jobs-summit/?feat=home_features.

1076 Richard Wolf, "Obama puts renewed focus on job creation," USA Today, December 3, 2009, http://www.usatoday.com/money/economy/2009-12-03-obama-jobs_N.htm.

1077 Mark Knoller, "How Many 'Top Priority' Issues Does Obama Have?," CBS News, August 13, 2010, http://www.cbsnews.com/8301-503544_162-20013622-503544.html.

1078 Jim Hoft, "After Obama Tells America 'Everyone Must Sacrifice' the White House Throws 1 Party Every 3 Days in First Year," Gateway Pundit, January 13, 2010, http://www.thegatewaypundit.com/2010/01/after-first-family-tells-america-everyone-must-sacrifice-they-hold-white-house-party-every-3rd-day-in-first-year/.

1079 Stephen Dinan, "Researcher: NASA hiding climate date," Washington Times, December 3, 2009, http://www.washingtontimes.com/news/2009/dec/03/researcher-says-nasa-hiding-climate-data/.

1080 "India will not sign binding emission cuts-minister," Reuters, December 3, 2009, http://www.reuters.com/article/idUSDEB00309720091203.

1081 "Honduras votes agains Manuel Zelaya reinstatement," TimesOnline, December 3, 2009, http://www.timesonline.co.uk/tol/news/world/us_and_americas/article6942029.ece.

1082 Sheryl Gay Stolberg, "The Spotlight's Bright Glare," New York Times, December 6, 2009, http://www.nytimes.com/2009/12/06/fashion/06desiree.html.

1083 Laura Litvan, "Obama to Rally Senate Democrats on Health-Care Plan (Update1)," Bloomberg, December 6, 2009, http://www.bloomberg.com/apps/news?pid=newsarchive&sid=aoruBc3aj0PA.

1084 Ben Geman, "EPA Chief: The hacked e-mails change nothing," The Hill, December 7, 2009, http://thehill.com/blogs/e2-wire/677-e2-wire/70943-epa-chief-the-hacked-emails-dont-change-a-thing.

1085 David Wright, "EPA Determines Greenhouse Gases harmful to People and Environment," ABC News, December 7, 2009, http://abcnews.go.com/WN/epa-declares-greenhouse-gases-hazardous-peoples-health-environment/story?id=9272194.

1086 Bill Dedman, "Group sues for Obama White House visitor list," MSNBC, December 9, 2009, http://www.msnbc.msn.com/id/34347510/ns/politics-white_house/.

1087 "Reid Compares Opponents of Health Care Reform to Supporters of Slavery, Fox News, December 7, 2009, http://www.foxnews.com/politics/2009/12/07/reid-compares-health-care-reform-foes-slavery-supporters/.

1088 "Chavez: Venezuela acquires thousands of missiles," Breitbart, December 7, 2009, http://www.breitbart.com/article.php?id=D9CEQGF82&show_article=1.

1089 "Administration Warns of 'Command-and-Control' Regulation Over Emissions," Fox News, December 9, 2009, http://www.foxnews.com/politics/2009/12/09/administration-warns-command-control-regulation-emissions/.

1090 "Human role in climate change not in doubt – UN's Ban," Reuters, December 8, 2009, http://www.alertnet.org/thenews/newsdesk/N08198995.htm.

1091 "Obama Pitches Jobs Program, Points Finger at GOP for Economic Mess," Fox News, December 8, 2009, http://www.foxnews.com/politics/2009/12/08/obama-takes-joblessness/.

1092 Philip Elliott, "Obama plans: 'spend our way out' of downturn," Breitbart, December 8,

2009, http://www.breitbart.com/article.php?id=D9CF8SIO0&show_article=1.

1093 Richard Wolf, "Obama puts renewed focus on job creation," USA Today, December 3, 2009, http://www.usatoday.com/money/economy/2009-12-03-obama-jobs_N.htm.

1094 Matthew Brown, "U.K., U.S. Top Aaa Ratings Tested by Debt Burdens, Moody's Says," Bloomberg, December 8, 2009, http://www.bloomberg.com/apps/news?pid=newsarchive&sid=av16pDNNrMig.

1095 Brian Ross and Matt Hosford, "Massive TSA Security Breach As Agency Gives Away Its Secrets," ABC News, December 8, 2009, http://abcnews.go.com/Blotter/massive-tsa-security-breach-agency-secrets/story?id=9280503.

1096 Ed O'Keefe, "Federal employees earn 2% pay raise," Washington Post, December 8, 2009, http://voices.washingtonpost.com/federal-eye/2009/12/federal_employees_earn_2_pay_r.html.

1097 Jim Hoft, "Fistgate II: High School Students Given 'Fisting Kits' At Kevin Jennings' 2001 GLSEN Conference," Big Government, December 8, 2009, http://biggovernment.com/jhoft/2009/12/08/fistgate-ii-high-school-students-given-fisting-kits-at-kevin-jennings-2001-glsen-conference/.

1098 Mike Levine, "Americans Arrested in Pakistan," Fox News, December 9, 2009, http://liveshots.blogs.foxnews.com/2009/12/09/five-americans-arrested-in-pakistan/.

1099 Katarina Andersson, "Obama Snubs the King," The Daily Beast, December 9, 2009, http://www.thedailybeast.com/blogs-and-stories/2009-12-09/obamas-oslo-snub/.

1100 Gwladys Fouche and Ewen MacAskill, "Nobel peace prize: Norwegians incensed over Barack Obama's snubs," The Guardian, December 9, 2009, http://www.guardian.co.uk/world/2009/dec/09/obama-nobel-peace-prize-snub.

1101 David Rogers, "Democrats to lift debt ceiling by $1.8 trillion, fear 2010 backlash," Politico, December 9, 2009, http://www.politico.com/news/stories/1209/30417.html.

1102 David Shepardson, "Obama administration predicts $30B loss on auto bailout," Detroit News, December 8, 2009, http://www.detnews.com/article/20091208/AUTO01/912080414/Obama-administration-predicts-$30B-loss-on-auto-bailout.

1103 Alexander Bolton, "Mark Penn's two firms awarded millions from stimulus for public relations work," The Hill, December 9, 2009, http://thehill.com/homenews/administration/71353-mark-penn-got-6-million-from-stimulus.

1104 Mona Charen, "Democratic Payoffs, Er, Stimulus," National Review, January 5, 2009, http://www.nationalreview.com/articles/228899/democratic-payoffs-er-stimulus/mona-charen.

1105 Amanda Carpenter, "Coal company cuts 500 jobs, blames environmentalists," Washington Times, December 9, 2009, http://www.washingtontimes.com/weblogs/back-story/2009/dec/09/coal-company-cuts-500-jobs-blames-environmentalist/.

1106 Karen Travers, "Obama to Accept Nobel Peace Prize as War President, Address Afghanistan Troop Surge," ABC News, December 9, 2009, http://abcnews.go.com/Politics/president-obama-accept-nobel-peace-prize-oslo-norway/story?id=9284977.

1107 Dennis Cauchon, "For feds, more get 6-figure salaries, Average pay $30,000 over private sector," USA Today, December 11, 2009, http://www.usatoday.com/printedition/news/20091211/1afedpay11_st.art.htm?loc=interstitialskip.

1108 Tom Granahan, "Pay Czar Feinberg Caps More Bank Salaries," Fox News, December 11, 2009, http://m.foxbusiness.com/quickPage.html?page=19453&content=28132555&pageNum=-1.

1109 Mike Flynn, "UN Security Stops Journalist's Questions About ClimateGate," Big Government, December 11, 2009, http://biggovernment.com/mikeflynn/2009/12/11/un-security-stops-journalists-questions-about-climategate/.

1110 Chris Good, "Obama Grades Himself: 'A Good Solid B+'," The Atlantic, December 14, 2009, http://www.theatlantic.com/politics/archive/2009/12/obama-grades-himself-a-good-solid-b/31774/.

1111 Penny Starr, "Michelle Obama on Deciding What Kids Eat: 'We Can't Just Leave it Up to The Parents'," CNS News, December 13, 2009, http://www.cnsnews.com/news/article/michelle-obama-deciding-what-kids-eat-we-can-t-just-leave-it-parents.

1112 George Stephanopoulos, "Summers: Job Growth By Spring," ABC News, December 13, 2009, http://blogs.abcnews.com/george/2009/12/summers-job-growth-by-spring.html.

1113 Catherine Philp, "Secret document exposes Iran's nuclear trigger," TimesOnline, December 14, 2009, http://www.timesonline.co.uk/tol/news/world/middle_east/article6955351.ece.

1114 "US to transfer Guantanamo detainees to Illinois," Breitbart, December 15, 2009, http://www.breitbart.com/article.php?id=CNG.3b306542e31038bc3638f8b13efec9ae.7b1&show_article=1.

1115 Geoff Caldwell, "Did Obama lie? Signs $1.1 trillion spending bill porked with over 5,000 earmarks," The Examiner, December 17, 2009, http://www.examiner.com/independent-in-wichita/did-obama-lie-signs-1-1-trillion-spending-bill-porked-with-over-5-000-earmarks.

1116 Mark Knoller, "U.S. National Debt Tops Debt Limit," CBS News, December 16, 2009, http://www.cbsnews.com/8301-503544_162-5987341-503544.html.

1117 Karen Travers, "President Obama: Federal Government 'Will Go Bankrupt' if Health Care Costs Are Not Reined In," ABC News, December 16, 2009, http://blogs.abcnews.com/theworldnewser/2009/12/president-obama-federal-government-will-go-bankrupt-if-health-care-costs-are-not-reigned-in.html.

1118 Ambrose Evans-Pritchard, "Gulf petro-powers to launch currency in latest threat to dollar hegemony," The Telegraph, December 16, 2009, http://www.telegraph.co.uk/finance/economics/6819136/Gulf-petro-powers-to-launch-currency-in-latest-threat-to-dollar-hegemony.html.

1119 Soraya Roberts, "U.S. to contribute to $100B climate fund to help developing countries: Hillary Clinton," New York Daily News, December 17, 2009, http://www.nydailynews.com/news/world/2009/12/17/2009-12-17_us_will_contribute_to_100b_climate_fund_for_developing_countries_hillary_clinton.html.

1120 Suzanne Goldenberg and Allegra Stratton, "Barack Obama's speech disappoints and fuels frustration at Copenhagen," The Guardian, December 18, 2009, http://www.guardian.co.uk/environment/2009/dec/18/obama-speech-copenhagen.

1121 Chris Green, "China's delaying tactics threaten climate deal," The Independent, December 18, 2009, http://www.independent.co.uk/environment/climate-change/chinas-delaying-tactics-threaten-climate-deal-1844661.html.

1122 Zhou Xin and Jason Subler, "Harder to buy US Treasuries," Shanghai Daily, December 18, 2009, http://www.shanghaidaily.com/article/print.asp?id=423054.

1123 Shailagh Murray and Lori Montgomery, "Deal on health bill is reached," Washington Post, December 19, 2009, http://www.washingtonpost.com/wp-dyn/content/article/2009/12/19/AR2009121900797_pf.html.

1124 Andy Greenberg, "Finally, A Cyber Czar," Forbes, December 21, 2009, http://www.

forbes.com/2009/12/21/cyber-czar-named-security-business-in-the-beltway-schmidt.html
1125 Steve Eder, "Banks with political ties got bailouts, study shows," Reuters, December 21, 2009, http://www.reuters.com/article/idUSN2124009320091221?type=marketsNews.
1126 Pete Winn, "Rep. Stupak: White House Pressuring Me to Keep Quiet on Abortion Language in Senate Health Bill," CNS News, December 22, 2009, http://cnsnews.com/news/article/58921.
1127 Patricia Zengerle, "Obama may delay vacation over healthcare," Reuters, December 23, 2009, http://www.reuters.com/article/idUSTRE5BL2WE20091222?type=politicsNews?feedType=RSS&feedName=politicsNews&rpc=22&sp=true.
1128 Jonathan D. Salant, "Schumer Says Every State Got Special Treatment in Health Bill," Bloomberg, December 23, 2009, http://www.bloomberg.com/apps/news?pid=newsarchive&sid=a_et4JAdyG4g&pos=8.
1129 John Fund, "For Their Next Trick," Wall Street Journal, December 23, 2009, http://online.wsj.com/article/SB10001424052748704254604574614183270356274.html.
1130 James Rowley and Nicole Gaouette, "Budget Office Rebuts Democratic Claims on Medicare (Update1), Bloomberg, December 23, 2009, http://www.bloomberg.com/apps/news?pid=newsarchive&sid=ackCRQU57HhY&pos=9.
1131 "Geithner: Job Growth Should Resume by Springtime," ABC News, December 23, 2009, http://abcnews.go.com/Business/wireStory?id=9407661.
1132 Michelle Malkin, "Cash for Cloture: Demcare bribe list, Pt. II," michellemalkin.com, December 21, 2009, http://michellemalkin.com/2009/12/21/cash-for-cloture-demcare-bribe-list-pt-ii/.
1133 Laurie Kellman, "Congress raises debt ceiling to $12.4 trillion," Breitbart, December 24, 2009, http://www.breitbart.com/article.php?id=D9CPP3G01.
1134 Jake Tapper and John Parkinson, "Hawaii on the Horizon, President Obama Praises Senate's 'Historic Vote'," ABC News, December 24, 2009, http://abcnews.go.com/blogs/politics/2009/12/hawaii-on-the-horizon-president-obama-praises-senates-historic-vote/.
1135 Robert Spencer, "Al-Qaeda in the Arabian Peninsula claims responsibility for Flight 253 attack," Jihad Watch, December 17, 2009, http://www.jihadwatch.org/cgi-sys/cgi-wrap/br0nc0s/managed-mt/mt-search.cgi?search=flight%20253&IncludeBlogs=1&limit=20&page=3.
1136 Joe Swickard and Naomi R. Patton, "Reports: NWA passenger was trying to blow up flight into Detroit," Detroit Free Press, December 25, 2009, http://www.freep.com/article/20091225/NEWS05/91225022/1318/Reports-NWA-passenger-was-trying-to-blow-up-flight-into-Detroit.
1137 "Abdulmutallab in 50 Minutes," Wall Street Journal, January 26, 2010, http://online.wsj.com/article/SB10001424052748703808904575025231056290438.html.
1138 Michael Isikoff and Mark Hosenball, "White House Adviser Briefed in October on Underwear Bomb Technique," Newsweek, January 2, 2010, ttp://www.thedailybeast.com/newsweek/blogs/declassified/2010/01/02/white-house-adviser-briefed-in-october-on-underwear-bomb-technique.html.
1139 Richard Esposito and Brian Ross, "Investigators: Northwest Bomb Plot Planned by al Qaeda in Yemen," ABC News, December 26, 2009, http://abcnews.go.com/Blotter/al-qaeda-yemen-planned-northwest-flight-253-bomb-plot/story?id=9426085.
1140 Mark Whittington, "Will Michael Leiter Be Fired for the Underwear Bomber?," Yahoo,

January 7, 2010, http://www.associatedcontent.com/article/2565679/will_michael_leiter_be_fired_for_the.html.

1141 Michelle Malkin, "Clown alert: Janet Napolitano says the 'system worked;'" michellemalkin.com, December 27, 2009, http://michellemalkin.com/2009/12/27/clown-alert-janet-napolitano-says-the-system-worked/.

1142 Jennifer Parker, "Napolitano: System Like 'Clockwork' After Attack, Not So Sure About Before," ABC News, December 27, 2009, http://abcnews.go.com/blogs/politics/2009/12/napolitano-system-like-clockwork-after-attack-not-so-sure-about-before/.

1143 Susan Jones, "Obama Describes Nigerian As 'Isolated Extremist,' Despite Ties to Yemen," CNS News, December 29, 2009, http://www.cnsnews.com/node/59115.

1144 Kristina Wong, "Gibbs Passes On One Last Chance to Make Health Care Negotiations Transparent," ABC News, December 27, 2009, http://abcnews.go.com/blogs/politics/2009/12/gibbs-passes-on-one-last-chance-to-make-health-care-negotiations-transparent/.

1145 Peter Baker and Scott Shane, "Obama Seeks to Reassure U.S. After Bombing Attempt," New York Times, December 29, 2009, http://www.nytimes.com/2009/12/29/us/29terror.html.

1146 Karen DeYoung and Michael Leahy, "Uninvestigated terrorism warning abut Detroit suspect called not unusual," Washington Post, December 27, 2009, http://www.washingtonpost.com/wp-dyn/content/article/2009/12/27/AR2009122700279.html.

1147 John G. Winder, "Flight 253; Napolitano Says 'System Worked' No, Wait 'System Didn't Work'," The Cypress Times, December 28, 2009, http://www.thecypresstimes.com/article/News/Opinion_Editorial/FLIGHT_253_NAPOLITANO_SAYS_SYSTEM_WORKED_NO_WAIT_SYSTEM_DIDNT_WORK/26624.

1148 Armen Keteylan, "U.S. Intel Lapses Helped Abdulmutallab," CBS News, December 31, 2009, http://www.cbsnews.com/stories/2009/12/29/cbsnews_investigates/main6035647.shtml.

1149 Huma Khan, "U.S. Confirms American Detained in North Korea," ABC News, December 29, 2009, http://abcnews.go.com/blogs/politics/2009/12/.us-confirms-american-detained-in-north-korea/.

1150 Chris Frates, "Look for Republicans to wave this around," Politico, January 5, 2010, http://www.politico.com/livepulse/0110/Look_for_Republicans_to_waive_this_around.html?showall.

1151 Will Stewart, "Vladimir Putin calls for more weapons to stop America doing 'whatever it wants'," TimesOnline, December 30, 2009, http://www.timesonline.co.uk/tol/news/world/europe/article6970921.ece.

1152 Mike Allen, "Dick Cheney: Barack Obama 'trying to pretend'," Politico, December 30, 2009, http://www.politico.com/news/stories/1209/31054.html.

1153 Dave Camp, "Ten Months After Stimulus 49 of 50 States Have Lost Jobs," Committee on Ways and Means, January 22, 2010, http://republicans.waysandmeans.house.gov/News/DocumentSingle.aspx?DocumentID=167479.

1154 Betty Liu and Matthew Leising, "U.S. to Lose $400 Billion on Fannie, Freddie, Wallison Says," Bloomberg, December 31, 2009, http://www.bloomberg.com/apps/news?pid=newsarchive&sid=a2Z5GnTAPcuo.

1155 "Gov't workers feel no economic pain," Washington Times, March 11, 2010, http://www.washingtontimes.com/news/2010/mar/11/government-workers-feel-no-pain/.

1156 Martin Crutsinger and Bernard Condon, "Foreigners cut Treasury stakes; rates could rise," Yahoo, February, 16, 2009, http://finance.yahoo.com/news/Foreigners-cut-Treasury-apf-1402391707.html?x=0.

1157 Matt Gouras, "Report: States' tax collections fall again," Yahoo, February 23, 2009, http://finance.yahoo.com/news/Report-States-tax-collections-apf-969834970.html?x=0&.v=2.

1158 Mark Knoller, "Obama's First Year By The Numbers," CBS News, January 20, 2010, http://www.cbsnews.com/8301-503544_162-6119525-503544.html.

1159 "Unemployment Rate," Portal Seven, http://portalseven.com/employment/unemployment_rate.jsp.

1160 Mark Knoller, "Obama's First Year: By the Numbers," CBS News, January 20, 2010, http://www.cbsnews.com/8301-503544_162-6119525-503544.html.

2010

1   Peter S. Goodman, "U.S. Loan Effort Is Seen as Adding to Housing Woes," *New York Times*, January 1, 2010, http://www.nytimes.com/2010/01/02/business/economy/02modify.html?pagewanted=all.

2   Michael James, "President Obama Says Suspect Tied to al Qaeda," *ABC News*, January 2, 2010, http://abcnews.go.com/blogs/politics/2010/01/president-obama-says-suspect-tied-to-al-qaeda/.

3   Josh Gerstein, "Brennan: Deal 'on the table' for terror suspect," Politico, January 3, 2010, http://www.politico.com/blogs/politicolive/0110/Brenan_deal_on_the_table_for_terror_suspect.html.

4   Davie E. Sanger and Eric Schmitt, "Threats Led to Embassy Closings in Yeman, Officials Say," *New York Times*, January 4, 2010, http://www.nytimes.com/2010/01/04/world/middleeast/04yemen.html.

5   Mona Charen, "Democratic Payoffs, Er, Stimulus," *Town Hall*, January 5, 2010, http://townhall.com/columnists/MonaCharen/2010/01/05/democratic_payoffs,_er,_stimulus.

6   Ibid.

7   Ibid.

8   James Rosen, "Obama Administration Steers Lucrative No-Bid Contract for Afghan Work to Dem Donor," *Fox News*, January 25, 2010, http://townhall.com/columnists/MonaCharen/2010/01/05/democratic_payoffs,_er,_stimulus.

9   Devin Dwyer, "President Obama Names Transgender Appointee to Commerce Department," *ABC News*, January 4, 2010, http://abcnews.go.com/blogs/politics/2010/01/president-obama-names-transgender-appointee-to-commerce-department/.

10   Fred Lucas, "Gun-Running Timeline: How DOJ's 'Operation Fast and Furious' Unfolded," CNS News, July 7, 2011, http://www.cnsnews.com/news/article/gun-running-timeline-how-doj-s-operation-fast-and-furious-unfolded.

11   "'Forceful' POTUS message: He wants a final bill that includes a tax on Cadillac insurance plans and an independent Medicare commission," *Politico*, January 6, 2010, http://www.politico.com/livepulse/0110/Forceful_POTUS_message_He_wants_a_final_bill_that_includes_a_tax_on_Cadillac_insurance_plans_and_an_.html.

12   Nitya, "Obama Tells National Security Team: 'This Was a Screw Up,'" *ABC News*, January 5, 2010, http://abcnews.go.com/blogs/politics/2010/01/obama-tells-intel-team-this-was-a-screw-up/.

13   "Memos Detail TSA Officer's Cocaine Pranks," *The Smoking Gun*, November 2, 2010, http://www.thesmokinggun.com/file/tsa-agents-coke-joke?page=0.

14   Evan Perez, "Airliner-Bombing Suspect Indicted," *Wall Street Journal*, January 7, 2010, http://online.wsj.com/article/SB126280843246518401.html?mod=WSJ_hpp_MIDDLENexttoWhatsNewsSecond.

15   Kristina Wong, "President Obama: The Buck Stops With Me," *ABC News*, January 7, 2010, http://abcnews.go.com/blogs/politics/2010/01/president-obama-the-buck-stops-with-me/.

16   "Remarks by the President on Jobs and Clean Energy Investments," *White House*, January 8, 2010, http://www.whitehouse.gov/the-press-office/remarks-president-jobs-and-clean-energy-investments.

17   Yitzhak Benhorin, "Mitchell: Mideast stagnation endangers US aid," *Ynet News*, January 8, 2010, http://www.ynetnews.com/articles/0,7340,L-3831661,00.html.

18   Jake Sherman, "GOP senators to Obama: Try Abdulmutallab in military court," *Politico*, January 8, 2010, http://www.politico.com/news/stories/0110/31288.html

19   "MSNBC Christmas Day Bomber pleads 'not guilty' to all 6 charges pressed against him," *YouTube*, http://www.youtube.com/watch?v=Bnqa-0QZfhM.

20   Michael James, "Reid Repents for 'Negro' Remarks," *ABC News*, January 9, 2010, http://abcnews.go.com/blogs/politics/2010/01/reid-repents-for-negro-remarks/.

21   Bill Edelblute, "61 freed Gitmo prisoners fight for Taliban, reveal Rep. Kirk and NATO Major General," *The Examiner*, January 10, 2010, http://www.examiner.com/political-buzz-in-spokane/61-freed-gitmo-prisoners-fight-for-taliban-reveal-rep-kirk-and-nato-major-general.

22   Kendra Marr, "Labor leaders meet with POTUS," *Politico*, January 11, 2010, http://www.politico.com/politico44/perm/0110/in_the_house_4a70dac6-2305-4f9e-94dd-ea77c749dc64.html.

23   Janet Hook and Noam N. Levey, "Unions agree to compromise on 'Cadillac tax/ for healthcare," *Los Angeles Times*, January 15, 2010, http://articles.latimes.com/2010/jan/15/nation/la-na-health-congress15-2010jan15.

24   Lindsey Ellerson, "US, Russia Continue START Talks as Russia Vows to Develop Nuclear Arsenal," ABC News, January 11, 2010, http://blogs.abcnews.com/political-punch/2010/01/us-russia-continue-start-talks-as-russia-vows-to-develop-nuclear-arsenal.html.

25   "Pres. Obama Reacts to Haiti Earthquake Faster Than Christmas Bomber," *Fox News*, January 13, 2010, http://nation.foxnews.com/haiti-earthquake/2010/01/13/pres-obama-reacts-haiti-earthquake-faster-christmas-bomber.

26   Jeffrey Young and Jared Allen, "Obama seizes reins in daylong House-Senate healthcare meeting," *The Hill*, January 13, 2010, http://thehill.com/homenews/administration/75851-obama-seizes-reins-in-house-senate-healthcare-talks.

27   Mark Knoller, "Obama's First Year By The Numbers," *CBS News*, January 20, 2010, http://www.cbsnews.com/8301-503544_162-6119525-503544.html.

28   Phil Stewart, "Fort Hood shooting was terrorism, U.S. says," *Reuters*, January 15, 2010, http://www.reuters.com/article/2010/01/15/us-usa-shooting-pentagon-idUSTRE60E5TA20100115.

29   "Weekly Address: President Obama Vows to 'Collect Ever Dime' of Taxpayer Funds that Helped Big Banks," *White House*, January 16, 2010, http://www.whitehouse.gov/the-

press-office/weekly-address-president-obama-vows-collect-every-dime-taxpayer-funds-helped-big-ba.

30   Alister Bull, "Obama's top priority is to boost jobs: White House," Reuters, January 19, 2010, http://www.reuters.com/article/2010/01/19/us-usa-obama-economy-idUSTRE-60I4MV20100119.

31   "Obama To Dems; Don't Jam Through Health Care Bill," HuffingtonPost, January 20, 2010, http://www.huffingtonpost.com/2010/01/20/obama-to-dems-dont-jam-th_n_430134.html.

32   Damian Carrington, "IPCC officials admit mistake over melting Himalayan glaciers," The Guardian, January 20, 2010, http://www.guardian.co.uk/environment/2010/jan/20/ipcc-himalayan-glaciers-mistake.

33   "Weekly Address: Fighting for the Public Against Special Interests," YouTube, January 23, 2010, http://www.youtube.com/watch?v=XkUeqD7M5t0.

34   Devin Dwyer, "Obama Vows More Help for the Middle Class," ABC News, January 25, 2010, http://blogs.abcnews.com/politicalpunch/2010/01/obama-vows-more-help-for-the-middle-class.html.

35   Jonathan Blakely, "'The Big Difference' Between 2010 and 1994 'Is Me,' President Obama Says, Per Congressman," ABC News, January 25, 2010, http://blogs.abcnews.com/politicalpunch/2010/01/the-big-difference-between-2010-and-1994-is-me-president-obama-says-per-congressman.html.

36   "Obama on being One Term President, YouTube, January 25, 2010, http://www.youtube.com/watch?v=qKdDC4N--Uo.

37   Kristina Wong, "In Interview with Diane Sawyer, President Obama Calls Not Living Up to Transparency Promise 'A Mistake,'" ABC News, January 25, 2010, http://blogs.abcnews.com/politicalpunch/2010/01/in-interview-with-diane-sawyer-president-obama-calls-not-living-up-to-transparency-promise-a-mistake.html.

38   David Goldman, "Stimulus is now $75 billion more expensive," CNN, January 26, 2010, http://money.cnn.com/2010/01/26/news/economy/stimulus_cbo/index.htm?postversion=2010012614.

39   "US tightens cargo ship rules," Breitbart, January 27, 2009, http://www.breitbart.com/article.php?id=CNG.3bb1888ef1a1aa64be3cb69f704ec08b.2d1&show_article=1.

40   Jake Tapper, "Rahm Apologizes for Privately Calling Liberal Activists 'Retarded,'" ABC News, February 2, 2010, http://blogs.abcnews.com/politicalpunch/2010/02/rahm-apologizes-for-privately-calling-liberal-activists-retarded.html.

41   "Come Clean, Mr. Holder," New York Post, January 27, 2010, http://www.nypost.com/p/news/opinion/editorials/come_clean_mr_holder_qakritP0PaijqDmUny929I.

42   Kenneth R. Bazinet, Adam Lisberg and Samuel Goldsmith, "White House asks Justice Department to look for other places to hold 9/11 terror trial," New York Daily News, January 28, 2010, http://articles.nydailynews.com/2010-01-28/news/27088203_1_terror-trial-justice-officials-federal-court.

43   "Statement by the President on the Confirmation of Ben Bernanke as Chairman of the Federal Reserve," White House, January 28, 2010, http://www.whitehouse.gov/the-press-office/statement-president-confirmation-ben-bernanke-chairman-federal-reserve.

44   Helene Cooper, "Obama Sets Ambitious Export Goal," New York Times, January 28, 2010, http://www.nytimes.com/2010/01/29/business/29trade.html.

45   www.marklevinshow.com.

46   "More Rules: Obama To Take On College Football," *Education News*, January 29, 2010, http://www.educationnews.org/breaking_news/39136.html.

47   "China protests, US arms sales, warns of 'serious' impact," *Breitbart*, January 29, 2009, http://www.breitbart.com/article.php?id=CNG.eba0f1f44dc56eaae2cdf53db03b2f4e.661&show_article=1.

48   Michael Isikoff and Daniel Klaidman, "Justice Official Clears Bush Lawyers in Torture Memo Probe, *Newsweek*, January 29, 2010, http://www.newsweek.com/blogs/declassified/2010/01/29/justice-official-clears-bush-lawyers-in-torture-memo-probe.html.

49   Robert Arend, "Day 372/Jan30th/Saturday," *OpEd News*, January 30, 2010, http://www.opednews.com/articles/The-Obama-Administration--by-Robert-Arend-100203-184.html.

50   Rebecca Lefort, "UN climate change panel based claims on student dissertation and magazine article," *The Telegraph*, January 30, 2010, http://www.telegraph.co.uk/earth/environment/climatechange/7111525/UN-climate-change-panel-based-claims-on-student-dissertation-and-magazine-article.html.

51   "Weekly Radio Address," *YouTube*, January 30, 2010, http://www.youtube.com/watch?v=CJFB8Cg45tU.

52   Lucia Mutikani, "US Jan mass layoffs edge up on weak manufacturing," *Reuters*, February 23, 2010, http://www.reuters.com/article/2010/02/23/usa-economy-layoffs-idUSN239866720100223.

53   "Robert Gibbs on CNN: KSM 'Likely to be Executed'," *YouTube*, January 31, 2010, http://www.youtube.com/watch?v=coapmv4bozQ.

54   "Did President Obama Bow to the Mayor of Tampa?," *YouTube*, January 28, 2010, http://www.youtube.com/watch?v=MKeE4dFqmiE.

55   James Rosen, "State Department Admits No-Bid Contract 'Violates' Obama Campaign Pledges," *Fox News*, January 31, 2010, http://www.foxnews.com/politics/2010/01/31/state-department-admits-bid-contract-violates-obama-campaign-pledges/.

56   Chris McGreal, "US raises stakes on Iran by sending in ships and missiles," *The Guardian*, January 31, 2010, http://www.guardian.co.uk/world/2010/jan/31/iran-nuclear-us-missiles-gulf.

57   Nancy Benac and Calvin Woodward, "Obama's Terrible, Horrible, No Good, Very Bad Year," *CNS News*, December 21, 2010, http://www.cnsnews.com/news/article/obamas-terrible-horrible-no-good-very-ba.

58   "Unemployment Rate," *Portal Seven*, http://portalseven.com/employment/unemployment_rate.jsp.

59   Andy Sullivan, "White House to paint grim fiscal picture: source," *Reuters*, January 31, 2009, http://www.reuters.com/article/idUSTRE60U1PZ20100131.

60   "Obama Budget Projects $1.56T Deficit," *CBS News*, February 1, 2010, http://www.cbsnews.com/stories/2010/02/01/politics/main6162494.shtml.

61   Kara Rowland, "Obama acknowledges broken C-SPAN promise," *Washington Times*, February 2, 2010, http://www.washingtontimes.com/news/2010/feb/02/obama-acknowledges-broken-c-span-promise/.

62   Kenneth Chang, "Obama Calls for End to NASA's Moon Program," New York Times, February 1, 2010, http://www.nytimes.com/2010/02/02/science/02nasa.html.

63   Stephen Dinan, "Largest-ever federal payroll to hit 2.15 million," *Washington Times*, February 2, 2010, http://www.washingtontimes.com/news/2010/feb/02/burgeoning-

federal-payroll-signals-return-of-big-g/.

64   Mark Knoller, "How Many 'Top Priority' Issues Does Obama Have?," *CBS News*, August 13, 2010, http://www.cbsnews.com/8301-503544_162-20013622-503544.html.

65   David Adam and Fred Pearce, "No apology from IPCC chief Rajendra Pachauri for glacier fallacy," *The Guardian*, February 2, 2010, http://www.guardian.co.uk/environment/2010/feb/02/climate-change-pachauri-un-glaciers.

66   Devin Dwyer, "Drowning in Debt: What the Nation's Budget Woes Mean for You," *ABC News*, February 17, 2010, http://abcnews.go.com/Politics/national-debt-budget-deficit-scary-forecast-taxpayers/story?id=9854459.

67   Brian Montopoli, "Obama Mocked Commissions, Then Established Four," *CBS News*, June 30, 2009, http://www.cbsnews.com/8301-503544_162-20009286-503544.html.

68   "US debt to hit proposed ceiling by end-February Treasury," *Google*, February 3, 2010,   http://www.google.com/hostednews/afp/article/ALeqM5hEkfx_bpGC-zVoeKNR38gWLcjXdw.

69   Jimmy Orr, "Obama slams Las Vegas again – Reid upset again," Christian Science Monitor, February 3, 2010, http://www.csmonitor.com/USA/Politics/The-Vote/2010/0203/Obama-slams-Las-Vegas-again-Reid-upset-again.

70   Hans Nichols and Edwin Chen, "Obama Still Plans to Meet With Dalai lama, Aide Says (Update1)," *Bloomberg*, February 2, 2010, http://www.bloomberg.com/apps/news?pid=newsarchive&sid=aZUprzB2EYWQ.

71   James Quinn, "US credit rating at risk, Moody's warns," *The Telegraph*, February 4, 2010,   http://www.telegraph.co.uk/finance/economics/7153180/US-credit-rating-at-risk-Moodys-warns.html.

72   Kathleen Gilbert, "Lech Walesa: World has 'Lost Hope' of America's Moral Leadership," *Life Site News*, February 5, 2010, http://www.lifesitenews.com/news/archive/ldn/2010/feb/10020506.

73   Mark Whittington, "Obama Calls navy Corpsman 'Corpse Man'," *Yahoo*, February 5, 2010, http://www.associatedcontent.com/article/2671639/obama_calls_navy_corpsman_corpse_man.html?cat=9.

74   Lucy Hornby, "China to levy anti-dumping duties on US chicken," *Reuters*, February 5, 2010, http://www.reuters.com/article/idUSTOE61402H20100205.

75   Paul Joseph Watson and Alex Jones, "TSA Groping Out Of Control," *Lewrockwell.com*, November 10, 2010, http://www.lewrockwell.com/spl2/tsa-groping-out-of-control.html.

76   Rebecca Christie, "Geithner Says U.S. Will 'Never' Lose Aaa Debt Rating (Update1)," *Bloomberg*, February 8, 2010, http://www.bloomberg.com/apps/news?pid=newsarchive&sid=ahGwg7V3u3Gs.

77   Jim Kouri, "Terrorist trials may still be held in Manhattan, says President," *Canada Free Press*, February 9, 2010, http://www.canadafreepress.com/index.php/article/19831.

78   Penny Starr, "First Lady Links Childhood Obesity to national Security in launch of 'Let's Move' Campaign," *CNS News*, February 9, 2010, http://cnsnews.com/news/article/61157.

79   Chris Buckley, "China PLA officers urge economic punch against U.S.," *Reuters*, February 9, 2009, http://www.reuters.com/article/idUSTRE6183KG20100209.

80   Julianna Goldman and Ian Katz, "Obama doesn't 'Begrudge' Bonuses for Blankfein, Dimon (Update1)," *Bloomberg*, February 10, 2010, http://www.bloomberg.com/apps/news?pid=newsarchive&sid=aKGZkktzkAlA.

81   Bappa Majumdar, "India to test new 5000-km nuclear missile within year," *Reuters*, February 10, 2010, http://alertnet.org/thenews/newsdesk/SGE271543.htm.

82   Keith Weir and Michael Holden, "UK gov't forced to publish U.S. torture allegations," *Reuters*, February 10, 2010, http://www.reuters.com/article/idUSTRE61A00V20100211.

83   Rich Miller, "Obama 'Agnostic' on Deficit Cuts, Won't Prejudge Tax Increases," *Businessweek*, February 11, 2010, http://www.businessweek.com/news/2010-02-11/obama-agnostic-on-deficit-cuts-won-t-prejudge-tax-increases.html.

84   Declan McCullagh, "Feds push for tracking cell phones," *Cnet*, February 11, 2010, http://news.cnet.com/8301-13578_3-10451518-38.html.

85   "Iran is now a 'nuclear state' says Ahmadinejad as thousands take to the streets," *The Daily Mail*, February 11, 2010, http://www.dailymail.co.uk/news/worldnews/article-1250127/Iran-Revolution-day-protests-Islamic-Republic-nuclear-state.html.

86   Jonathan Blakely, "President Obama Signs Law Raising Public Debt Limit from $12.4 Trillion to $14.3 Trillion," ABC News, February 12, 2010, http://abcnews.go.com/blogs/politics/2010/02/president-obama-signs-law-raising-public-debt-limit-from-124-trillion-to-143-trillion/.

87   Robert Block, "NASA cancels KSC contract leading to charge 'Obama broke law'," *Orlando Sentinel*, February 12, 2010, http://blogs.orlandosentinel.com/news_space_thewritestuff/2010/02/nasa-cancels-ksc-contract-prompting-angry-response.html.

88   Rep. Tom Price, "Now Obama discovers GOP healthcare proposals?," *The Hill*, February 12, 2010, http://thehill.com/blogs/congress-blog/healthcare/80921-now-obama-discovers-gop-healthcare-proposals-rep-tom-price.

89   Patricia Zengerle, "W. House to post health bill before Feb 25 meeting," *Reuters*, February, 12, 2010, http://in.reuters.com/article/idINN1214860020100213.

90   Peter Baker, "Obama Making Plans to Use Executive Power," *New York Times*, February 13, 2010, http://www.nytimes.com/2010/02/13/us/politics/13obama.html.

91   Jake Tapper, "President Obama Signs Law Raising Public Debt Limit from $12.4 Trillion to $14.3 Trillion," *ABC News*, February 13, 2010, http://blogs.abcnews.com/politicalpunch/2010/02/president-obama-signs-law-raising-public-debt-limit-from-124-trillion-to-143-trillion.html.

92   Jonathan Petre, "Climategate U-turn as scientist at centre of row admits: There has been no global warming since 1995," *The Daily Mail*, February 14, 2010, http://www.dailymail.co.uk/news/article-1250872/Climategate-U-turn-Astonishment-scientist-centre-global-warming-email-row-admits-data-organised.html.

93   Arshad Mohammed and Regan E. Doherty, "Clinton tackles Mideast peace, Muslim ties in Gulf," *Reuters*, February 14, 2010, http://www.reuters.com/article/idUSTRE61D1EH20100214.

94   Robert Burns, "Saudi official questions new sanctions on Iran," *Dayton Daily News*, February 15, 2010, http://www.daytondailynews.com/news/nation-world-news/saudi-official-questions-new-sanctions-on-iran-549660.html.

95   "Taliban's Top Military Commander Captured," *Fox News*, February, 16, 2010, http://www.foxnews.com/world/2010/02/16/talibans-military-commander-captured/.

96   Harry Dunphy, "Head of IMF Proposes New Reserve Currency," *ABC News*, February 16, 2010, http://abcnews.go.com/Business/wireStory?id=9958995.

97   Jeff Mason, "Nuclear power aids White House climate push," *Reuters*, February 16, 2010, http://www.alertnet.org/thenews/newsdesk/N16216891.htm.

98   Steve Holland, "On anniversary, Obama defends economic stimulus," *Reuters*, Febru-

ary 17, 2010, http://www.reuters.com/article/idUSTRE61G38U20100217.

99   Sandra Fabry, "Happy Birthday, 'Stimulus'!? One Year By the Numbers," *Americans for Tax Reform*, February 17, 2010, http://www.atr.org/happy-birthday-stimulus-one-numbers-a4546.

100   Helene Cooper, "Obama Meets Dalai Lama, and China Is Quick to Protest," *New York Times*, February 19, 2010, http://www.nytimes.com/2010/02/19/world/asia/19prexy.html?hp.

101   Maggie Haberman, "Back-door Dalai's not-so-grand exit," *New York Post*, February 20, 2010,   http://www.nypost.com/p/news/national/back_door_dalai_not_so_grand_exit_MHe5umYwtJffh3pymuRIJN.

102   Jake Sherman, "Darrell Issa raises questions about Joe Sestak," *Politico*, March 10, 2010, http://www.politico.com/news/stories/0310/34221.html.

103   Larry Kane, "Sestak Surprises Me With A Bombshell Answer," *The Larry Kane Report*, February 18, 2010, http://www.larrykane.com/2010/02/18/sestak-surprises-me-with-a-bombshell-statement/.

104   Byron York, "Holder admits nine Obama Dept. of Justice officials worked for terrorist detainees, offers no details," *Washington Examiner*, February 19, 2010, http://washington-examiner.com/blogs/beltway-confidential/holder-admits-nine-obama-dept-justice-officials-worked-terrorist-detainees.

105   "Terrorists Lawyers at the DOJ," *National Review*, February 25, 2010, http://www.nationalreview.com/articles/229204/terrorists-lawyers-doj/editors.

106   Charles Grassley, "Grassley, Judiciary Republicans Press for Answers from Holder After Being Snubbed in Repsonse to Previous Letter on Justice Department Lawyers Working on Gitmo Detainee Policy," *Senate.gov*, February 26, 2010, http://grassley.senate.gov/news/Article.cfm?customel_dataPageID_1502=25444.

107   Erick Stakelbeck, "Fort Jackson: The Latest," *CBN*, February 19, 2010, http://blogs.cbn.com/stakelbeckonterror/archive/2010/02/19/fort-jackson-the-latest.aspx.

108   Jeannine Aversa, "Fed bumps up rate banks pay for emergency loans," *Yahoo*, February 18, 2009, http://finance.yahoo.com/news/Fed-bumps-up-rate-banks-pay-apf-4141548450.html?x=0&.v=3.

109   "'Stop interfering in our domestic affairs': Chinese fury at Obama's private meeting with the Dalai Lama," *The Daily Mail*, February 22, 2009, http://www.dailymail.co.uk/news/worldnews/article-1251888/Dalai-Lama-meet-Barack-Obama-U-S-defies-protests-China.html.

110   Sharon Terlep, "GM Chief to Get $1.7 Million Pay," *Wall Street Journal*, February 20, 2009, http://online.wsj.com/article/SB10001424052748703787304575075843943185642.html.

111   Caren Bohan, "Obama rejects criticism of agenda as 'socialism,'" *Reuters*, February, 24, 2010, http://www.reuters.com/article/2010/02/24/us-usa-economy-obama-speech-idUSTRE61N53820100224.

112   Phil Mattingly, "U.S. 'Problem' Banks Soar, Lending Drops, FDIC Says (Update2), *Businessweek*, February 23, 2010, http://www.businessweek.com/news/2010-02-23/u-s-problem-banks-soar-27-fund-deficit-widens-fdic-says.html.

113   Dan Farber, "Toyota Congressional Hearing Theater," *CBS News*, February 23, 2010, http://www.cbsnews.com/8301-503544_162-6235684-503544.html.

114   Giles Whittell and James Bone, "US refuses to endorse British sovereignty in Falklands oil dispute," *TimesOnline*, February 25, 2010, http://www.timesonline.co.uk/tol/news/

world/us_and_americas/article7040245.ece.

115   William J. Broad, James Glanz and David E. Sanger, "Iran Fortifies Is Arsenal With the Aid of North Korea," *New York Times*, November 28, 2010, http://www.nytimes.com/2010/11/29/world/middleeast/29missiles.html.

116   David Brody, "Tony Perkins disinvited to Military Prayer Breakfast," *CBN*, February 24, 2010, http://blogs.cbn.com/thebrodyfile/archive/2010/02/24/exclusive-tony-perkins-disinvited-to-military-prayer-breakfast.aspx.

117   Mark Knoller, "How Many 'Top Priority' Issues Does Obama Have?," *CBS News*, August 13, 2010, http://www.cbsnews.com/8301-503544_162-20013622-503544.html.

118   Natalie Weeks and Maria Petrakis, "Greek Police, Protesters Clash in Nationwide Strike (Update2)," *Bloomberg*, February 24, 2010, http://www.bloomberg.com/apps/news?pid=newsarchive&sid=auLLhrWZiKi8.

119   Joseph Curl, "At summit, Obama mostly hears Obama," *Washington Times*, February 26, 2010, http://www.washingtontimes.com/news/2010/feb/26/obama-listens-at-health-summit-but-mostly-hears-fr/.

120   Dawn Kopecki, "Obama May Prohibit Home-Loan Foreclosures Without HAMP Review," *Bloomberg*, February 25, 2009, http://www.bloomberg.com/apps/news?pid=newsarchive&sid=ahuuwBS8KYq8.

121   "Clinton compares Iran showdown to Cuban missile crisis," *Breitbart*, February 25, 2010, http://www.breitbart.com/article.php?id=CNG.9b1e36b31702683fb79da3c0020866d9.581&show_article=1.

122   Charles Grassley, "Grassley, Judiciary Republicans Press for Answers from Holder After Being Snubbed in Repsonse to Previous Letter on Justice Department Lawyers Working on Gitmo Detainee Policy," *Senate.gov*, February 26, 2010, http://grassley.senate.gov/news/Article.cfm?customel_dataPageID_1502=25444.

123   Daniel Foster, "Obama Appoints SEIU's Stern to Debt Panel," National Review, February 26, 2010, (http://www.nationalreview.com/corner/195512/obama-appoints-seius-stern-debt-panel/daniel-foster.

124   Hugh Son, "AIG Posts Loss Tied to Rescue, Reserves; Shares Fall (Update5)," *Businessweek*, February, 26, 2010, http://www.businessweek.com/news/2010-02-26/aig-quarterly-loss-narrows-on-shrinking-investment-writedowns.html.

125   Harry Dunphy, "Head of IMF Proposes New Reserve Currency," *ABC News*, February 26, 2010, http://abcnews.go.com/Business/wireStory?id=9958995.

126   "Obama Signs One-Year Extension of Patriot Act," *Fox News*, February 27, 2010, http://www.foxnews.com/politics/2010/02/27/obama-signs-year-extension-patriot-act/.

127   Dawn Kopecki, "Fannie Taps Treasury for $15.3 Billion More After a 10th Loss," *Bloomberg*, February 27, 2010, http://www.bloomberg.com/apps/news?pid=newsarchive&sid=alet_UTqF04M.

128   "Israel approves 600 new Jerusalem settlement homes," *Breitbart*, February 27, 2010, http://www.breitbart.com/article.php?id=CNG.992a78102b50d1a873d88feed419f295.5a1&show_article=1.

129   Chris Buckley, "China PLA officer urges challenging U.S. dominance," *Reuters*, February 28, 2010, http://www.reuters.com/article/idUSTRE6200P620100301.

130   Rex Nutting, "Payrolls fall by 36,000; U.S. jobless rate steady at 9.7%, *MarketWatch*, March 5, 2010, http://www.marketwatch.com/story/payrolls-fall-36000-jobless-rate-steady-at-97-2010-03-05?reflink=MW_news_stmp.

131   Richard Wolf, "Afghan war costs now outpace Iraq's," *USA Today*, May 13, 2010, http://

www.usatoday.com/news/military/2010-05-12-afghan_N.htm.

132 Jake Tapper, "President Obama to Say Democrats Will Use Reconciliation to Pass Senate Health Care Reform Fix, If Not given Up or Down Vote," *ABC News*, March 2, 2010, http://blogs.abcnews.com/politicalpunch/2010/03/obama-democrats-will-use-reconciliation-to-pass-senate-health-care-bill.html.

133 "DeMint: White House land grab," *Washington Times*, March 2, 2010, http://www.washingtontimes.com/news/2010/mar/02/white-house-land-grab/.

134 John McCormack, "Obama Now Selling Judgeships for Health Care Votes?," *Weekly Standard*, March 3, 2010, http://www.weeklystandard.com/blogs/obama-now-selling-appeals-court-judgeships-health-care-votes.

135 Declan McCullagh, "Feds weigh expansion of Internet monitoring," *Cnet*, March 4, 2010, http://news.cnet.com/8301-13578_3-10463665-38.html.

136 Erica Werner, "Stupak: 12 Dems ready to oppose health care bill," *Breitbart*, March 4, 2010, http://www.breitbart.com/article.php?id=D9E7QFL00&show_article=1.

137 Michael Evans and Giles Whittell, "Cyberwar declared as China hunts for the West's intelligence secrets," *TimesOnline*, March 8, 2010, http://technology.timesonline.co.uk/tol/news/tech_and_web/article7053254.ece.

138 www.marklevinshow.com.

139 "Obama calls 'entrepreneurship summit' with Muslims," *Breitbart*, March 5, 2010, http://www.breitbart.com/article.php?id=CNG.c429eac8e6bddb6d430d2b4d28386dd9.551&show_article=1.

140 Anne E. Kornblut and Peter Finn, "Obama advisers set to recommend military tribunals for alleged 9/11 plotters," *Washington Post*, March 4, 2010, http://www.washingtonpost.com/wp-dyn/content/article/2010/03/04/AR2010030405209.html.

141 Brian Faler, "Obama spending Plan Underestimates Deficits, Budget Office Says," *Bloomberg*, March 6, 2010, http://www.bloomberg.com/apps/news?pid=newsarchive&sid=aVDEHvI9WH_Q.

142 "Massa: Rahm Emanuel 'Would Sell His Own Mother' For Votes," *Real Clear Politics*, March 8, 2010, http://www.realclearpolitics.com/video/2010/03/08/massa_rahm_emanuel_would_sell_his_own_mother_for_votes.html.

143 Byron Wolf, "A Complicated Enemy: Obama Seeks to Vilify Health Insurers, Give Them $366 Billion Check," *ABC News*, March 8, 2010, http://blogs.abcnews.com/thenote/2010/03/a-complicated-enemy-obama-seeks-to-vilify-health-insurers-give-them-336-billion-check.html.

144 "Pelosi: we have to pass the health care bill so that you can find out what is in it," *YouTube*, March 9, 2010, http://www.youtube.com/watch?v=KoE1R-xH5To.

145 Michael Tanner, "Final reform; push: twisting arms," *New York Post*, March 10, 2010, http://www.nypost.com/p/news/opinion/opedcolumnists/final_reform_push_0pwRMzHMNshlHQZg8LWmcJ.

146 Michael A. Fletcher and Dana Hedgpeth, "Are unemployment benefits no longer temporary?," *Washington Post*, March 9, 2010, http://www.washingtonpost.com/wp-dyn/content/article/2010/03/08/AR2010030804927_pf.html.

147 David Kravets, "Obama Supports DNA Sampling Upon Arrest," *Wired*, March 10, 2010, http://www.wired.com/threatlevel/2010/03/obama-supports-dna-sampling-upon-arrest.

148 Jake Sherman, "Darrell Issa raises questions about Joe Sestak," *Politico*, March, 10, 2010, http://www.politico.com/news/stories/0310/34221.html.

149   "Obama Justice Department Shut Down Federal ACORN Investigation According to Documents Obtained by Judicial Watch," *Judicial Watch*, March 10, 2009, http://www.judicialwatch.org/news/2010/mar/obama-justice-department-shut-down-federal-acorn-investigation-according-documents-obt.

150   Sarah McIntosh, "Virginia Passes Health Freedom Bill, Setting Up Legal Challenge to Individual Mandate," *Heartlander*, March 22, 2010, http://www.heartland.org/health-policy-news.org/article/27323/Virginia_Passes_Health_Freedom_Bill_Setting_Up_Legal_Challenge_to_Individual_Mandate.html.

151   "Obama delays Asia trip to deal with health care," *MSNBC*, March 12, 2009, http://www.msnbc.msn.com/id/35834710/ns/politics-health_care_reform.

152   "Tom Hanks, Steven Spielberg, Join Obama For White House Movie Night," *HuffingtonPost*, March 11, 2012, http://www.huffingtonpost.com/2010/03/11/tom-hanks-steven-spielber_n_495145.html.

153   Jeremy Pelofsky, "Att'y general failed to give legal briefs to Senate," *Reuters*, March 12, 2010, http://www.reuters.com/article/idUSTRE62B48P20100312?type=politicsNews.

154   Vanessa O'Connell, Stephanie Simon and Evan Perez, "For the Love of Islam," *Wall Street Journal*, March 12, 2010, http://online.wsj.com/article/SB10001424052748704131404575118103199708576.html.

155   Emmanuel Jarry, Adrian Croft and Estelle Shirbon, "U.S. setting bad example on protectionism," *Reuters*, March 12, 2010, http://www.reuters.com/article/idUSLDE62B1CG20100312?type=marketsNews.

156   Chris Buckley and Ben Blanchard, "China calls U.S. a hypocrite over human rights," *Reuters*, March 12, 2010, http://www.reuters.com/article/idUSTRE62B0WQ20100312.

157   Gary Fields, "White House Yet to Settle on Venue for 9/11 Trials," *Wall Street Journal*, March 14, 2010, http://blogs.wsj.com/washwire/2010/03/14/white-house-yet-to-settle-on-venue-for-911-trials/.

158   Alex Spillius, "Barack Obama threatens to withdraw support from wavering Democrats," *The Telegraph*, March 15, 2010, http://www.telegraph.co.uk/news/worldnews/northamerica/usa/barackobama/7450237/Barack-Obama-threatens-to-withdraw-support-from-wavering-Democrats.html.

159   "US citizens shot dead by Mexican drug gangs," *Current*, March 15, 2010, http://current.com/news/92322880_us-citizens-shot-dead-by-mexican-drug-gangs.htm.

160   Matthew Brown, U.S., U.K. Move Closer to Losing Rating, Moody's Says (Update1)," *Bloomberg*, March 15, 2010, http://www.bloomberg.com/apps/news?pid=newsarchive&sid=a0a8xAghPS8I.

161   "Ties between Israel and US 'worst in 35 years', Israel's ambassador to the US has said relations between the two are at their lowest for 35 years, Israeli media say," *BBC*, March 15, 2010, http://news.bbc.co.uk/2/hi/8567706.stm.

162   Martin Crutsinger, "China trims holdings of Treasury securities," *Yahoo*, March 15, 2010, http://finance.yahoo.com/news/China-trims-holdings-of-apf-1411556921.html?x=0.

163   Mark Knoller, "National Debt Up $2 Trillion on Obama's Watch," *CBS News*, March 16, 2010, http://www.cbsnews.com/8301-503544_162-20000576-503544.html.

164   Rebecca Christie and Mike Dorning, "Obama Aides See 'Extended Period' of Unemployment," *Bloomberg*, March 16, 2010, http://www.bloomberg.com/apps/news?pid=newsarchive&sid=afaCdb656DNg.

165 Tim Gaynor, "U.S. puts brakes on 'virtual' border fence," *Reuters*, March 16, 2009, http://www.reuters.com/article/idUSTRE62F61T20100316.

166 Joanne Wojcik, "Utah Passes Health Insurance Reform Measure," *Workforce Management*, March 16, 2010, http://www.workforce.com/section/news/article/utah-passes-health-insurance-reform-measure.php.

167 Mark Knoller, "How Many 'Top Priority' Issues Does Obama Have?," *CBS News*, August 13, 2010, http://www.cbsnews.com/8301-503544_162-20013622-503544.html.

168 Jeremy Pelofsky, "U.S. air travelers complain about body scans," *Reuters*, March 16, 2010, http://www.reuters.com/article/idUSTRE62F4W020100316.

169 "US Cancels peace talks trip in Israel row," *The Independent*, March 16, 2010, http://www.independent.co.uk/news/world/middle-east/us-cancels-peace-talks-trip-in-israel-row-1922193.html.

170 "President Barack Obama Talks to Bret Baier About Health Care Reform Bill," *Fox News*, March 17, 2010, http://www.foxnews.com/story/0,2933,589589,00.html.

171 Peggy Noonan, "Now for the Slaughter, on the road to Demon Pass, our leader encounters a Baier," *Wall Street Journal*, March 20, 2010, http://online.wsj.com/article/SB10001424052748704207504575130081383279888.html.

172 Hibah Yousuf, "Economists: The stimulus didn't help," *CNN*, April 26, 2010, http://money.cnn.com/2010/04/26/news/economy/NABE_survey/.

173 "Idaho to Sue If Health Care Bill Passes," *CBS News*, March 19, 2010, http://www.cbsnews.com/stories/2010/03/17/politics/main6308772.shtml.

174 J.P. Freire, "16,500 more IRS agents needed to enforce Obamacare," *Washington Examiner*, March 18, 2010, http://washingtonexaminer.com/blogs/beltway-confidential/16500-more-irs-agents-needed-enforce-obamacare.

175 Vicki Needham, "Republicans assail IRS provision in health care bill," *The Hill*, March 18, 2010, http://thehill.com/blogs/on-the-money/domestic-taxes/87697-republicans-assail-irs-provision-in-health-care-bill-.

176 Jake Tapper, "Vice President Biden Says President Obama's Rescheduled Trip Not a Bad Sign for Health Care Bill's Prospects," *ABC News*, March 18, 2009, http://blogs.abcnews.com/politicalpunch/2010/03/exclusive-vice-president-biden-says-obamas-cancelled-trip-not-a-bad-sign-for-health-care-bills-prosp.html.

177 Stephen Dinan, "Obama backs plan to legalize illegals," *Washington Times*, March 18, 2010, http://www.washingtontimes.com/news/2010/mar/18/obama-endorses-immigration-blueprint/.

178 Steve Chapman, "Airport security: Government in our pants," *Chicago Tribune*, November 14, 2010, http://articles.chicagotribune.com/2010-11-14/business/ct-oped-1114-chapman-20101114_1_new-full-body-scanners-airport-screener-long-security-lines.

179 Arshad Mohammed and Conor Sweeney, "Clinton, Russia at odds over Iranian nuclear plant," *EuroNews*, March 18, 2010, http://www.euronews.net/newswires/190733-us-sees-good-progress-on-arms-control-with-russia.

180 "Obama surrenders gulf oil to Moscow," *Washington Times*, March 18, 2010, http://www.washingtontimes.com/news/2010/mar/18/obama-surrenders-gulf-oil-to-moscow/.

181 Lori Montgomery and Paul Kane, "House leaders announce $940 billion health-care compromise bill," *Washington Post*, March 18, 2010, http://www.washingtonpost.com/wp-dyn/content/article/2010/03/18/AR2010031801153_pf.html.

182   "Medicare fix would push health care into the red," *Yahoo*, March 19, 2010, http://finance.yahoo.com/news/Medicare-fix-would-push-apf-2700343586.html?x=0&.v=2.

183   "Caterpillar: Health care bill would cost it $100M," *Chicago Breaking Business*, March 19, 2010, http://chicagobreakingbusiness.com/2010/03/caterpillar-health-care-bill-would-cost-it-100m.html.

184   Mark Knoller, "Obama has Given 54 Speeches on Health Care," *CBS News*, March 19, 2010, http://www.cbsnews.com/8301-503544_162-20000825-503544.html.

185   Timothy P. Carney, "Student loans get the Obamacare treatment," *Washington Examiner*, March 19, 2010, http://washingtonexaminer.com/node/108151.

186   Brian Montopoli, "Obama, Calderon Slam Arizona Immigration Law, *CBS News*, March 19, 2010, http://www.cbsnews.com/8301-503544_162-20005395-503544.html.

187   Howard LaFranchi, "Hillary Clinton to AIPAC: New Israeli settlements complicate US goals on Iran," *Christian Science Monitor*, March 22, 2010, http://www.csmonitor.com/USA/Foreign-Policy/2010/0322/Hillary-Clinton-to-AIPAC-New-Israeli-settlements-complicate-US-goals-on-Iran.

188   "Administration Actuary Can't Analyze Health Bill Before Final Vote," *Republican.senate.gov*, March 20, 2010, http://republican.senate.gov/public/index.cfm?FuseAction=Blogs.View&Blog_Id=cbd6f99a-426d-4635-bde1-f28d1afbc057.

189   "Unserious About Iran," *Wall Street Journal*, April 5, 2010, http://online.wsj.com/article/SB10001424052702303382504575163804139815206.html?mod=WSJ_hpp_sections_opinion.

190   Daniel Kruger and Bryan Keogh, "Obama Pays More Than Buffett as U.S. Risks AAA Rating," Bloomberg, March 22, 2010, http://www.bloomberg.com/apps/news?pid=newsarchive&sid=aYUeBnitz7nU

191   "Flashback: Obama Promises Public 5 Days To View Bills Before He signs Them," *Real Clear Politics*, March 23, 2010, http://www.realclearpolitics.com/video/2010/03/23/flashback_obama_promises_public_5_days_to_view_bills_before_he_signs_them.html

192   Ibid.

193   Kevin Brady, "America's New Health Care system Revealed," *House.gov*, July 28, 2010, http://www.house.gov/apps/list/press/tx08_brady/pr_100728_hc_chart.html.

194   Kevin Hassett, "Obamacare Only Looks Worse Upon Further Review," *Bloomberg*, August 1, 2010, http://www.bloomberg.com/news/2010-08-02/obamacare-only-looks-worse-upon-further-review-kevin-hassett.html.

195   Pat Wechsler, "States Sue Over Overhaul That Will Bust State Budgets," *Bloomberg*, March 23, 2010, http://www.bloomberg.com/apps/news?pid=newsarchive&sid=ajwSWE6H1kHM.

196   Giles Whittell and James Hider, "Binyamin Netanyahu humiliated after Barack Obama 'dumped him for dinner,'" *TimesOnline*, March 26, 2009, http://www.timesonline.co.uk/tol/news/world/us_and_americas/article7076431.ece.

197   Jordan Fabian, "Obama will sign Stupak executive order on abortion Wednesday," *The Hill*, March 23, 2010, http://thehill.com/blogs/blog-briefing-room/news/88725-obama-will-sign-stupak-executive-order-on-abortion-wednesday.

198   Patricia Zengerle, "Obama dares Republicans to seek healthcare repeal," *Reuters*, March 25, 2010, http://www.reuters.com/article/idUSN2522952320100325.

199   Louis Jacobson, "It's official: The public option is dead," *St. Petersburg Times*, March 26, 2010,   http://www.politifact.com/truth-o-meter/promises/obameter/promise/518/create-public-option-health-plan-new-national-heal/.

200   Paul Haven, "Cuban leader applauds US health-care reform bill," *Yahoo*, March 25, 2010,   http://finance.yahoo.com/news/Cuban-leader-applauds-US-apf-124808403.html?x=0&.v=1.

201   "CBO report: Debt will rise to 90% of GDP," *Washington Times*, March 26, 2010, http://www.washingtontimes.com/news/2010/mar/26/cbos-2020-vision-debt-will-rise-to-90-of-gdp/.

202   Mary Williams Walsh, "Social Security to See Payout Exceed Pay-In This Year," *New York Times*, March 24, 2010, http://www.nytimes.com/2010/03/25/business/economy/25social.html.

203   Veronique de Rugy, "Democratic Stimulus haul is almost Double Republicans," *BigGovernment.com*, March 26, 2010, http://biggovernment.com/vderugy/2010/03/26/politics-democratic-stimulus-haul-is-almost-double-republicans/.

204   Amy Thomson and Ian King, "AT&T to Book $1 Billion Cost on Health-Care Reform (Update3)," *Businessweek*, March 26, 2010, http://www.businessweek.com/news/2010-03-26/at-t-to-take-1-billion-charge-on-health-care-reform-update1-.html.

205   Leora Broydo Vestel, "Transportation department Embraces Bikes, and Business Groups Cry Foul," *New York Times*, March 26, 2010, http://green.blogs.nytimes.com/2010/03/26/transportation-department-embraces-bikes-and-business-groups-cry-foul/.

206   Renae Merle and Dina ElBoghdady, "Obama readies steps to fight foreclosures, particularly for unemployed," *Washington Post*, March 25, 2010, http://www.washingtonpost.com/wp-dyn/content/article/2010/03/25/AR2010032502426.html.

207   "Obama, Russian Leader Sign Off on New Nuke Reduction Treaty," *Fox News*, March 26, 2010, http://www.foxnews.com/politics/2010/03/26/obama-medvedev-sign-nuclear-treaty-prague-april/.

208   Viola Gienger, "AT&T, Deere CEOs Called by Waxman to Back Up Health-Bill Costs," *Businessweek*, March 27, 2010, http://www.businessweek.com/news/2010-03-27/at-t-deere-ceos-called-by-waxman-to-back-up-health-bill-costs.html.

209   Alister Bull, "Obama makes 15 recess appointments," *Reuters*, March 28, 2010, http://www.reuters.com/article/idUSTRE62Q1QT20100328.

210   David Williams and Paul Bentley, "Korea tensions over claims that warship was sunk by torpedo," *The Daily Mail*, March 29, 2010, http://www.dailymail.co.uk/news/worldnews/article-1260975/BREAKING-NEWS-South-Korean-ship-100-board-sinking-torpedo-attack-North-Korea.html.

211   Ed Morrissey, "Is Obama Avoiding Red States?," *Keyboard Militia*, March 30, 2010, http://keyboardmilitia.com/2010/03/30/is-obama-avoiding-red-states/.

212   "Female suicide bombers blamed in Moscow subway attacks," *CNN*, March 29, 2010, http://www.cnn.com/2010/WORLD/europe/03/29/russia.subway.explosion/index.html

213   Devin Dwyer, "Health Reform Law to Spawn More Tax Men?," *ABC News*, March 30, 2010, http://abcnews.go.com/Politics/Tax/health-reform-law-expanded-irs-threat-taxpayers/story?id=10238411.

214   Bill Gertz, "CIA: Iran capable of producing nukes," *Washington Times*, March 30, 2010, http://www.washingtontimes.com/news/2010/mar/30/cia-iran-has-capability-to-produce-nuke-weapons/.

215   Jim Harper, "A Flagging Obama Transparency Effort," *Cato Institute*, April 9, 2010, http://www.cato-at-liberty.org/a-flagging-obama-transparency-effort/.

216   Jenny Marlar, "Underemployment Rises to 20.3% in March," *Gallup*, April 1, 2010, http://www.gallup.com/poll/127091/Underemployment-Rises-March.aspx.

217   Dennis Cauchon, "Private pay shrinks to historic lows as gov't payouts rise," *USA Today*, May 26, 2010, http://www.usatoday.com/money/economy/income/2010-05-24-income-shifts-from-private-sector_N.htm.

218   Philip Elliott, "Obama clears way for oil drilling off US coasts," *Breitbart*, March 31, 2009, http://www.breitbart.com/article.php?id=D9EPO6880&show_article=1.

219   Avi Yellin, "Is the US Eroding Israel's Qualitative Edge?," *Canada Free Press*, March 31, 2010, http://www.canadafreepress.com/index.php/article/21556.

220   Lucian Kim, "Putin Visits Chavez in Bid by Russia to Expand Sway in Obama's Backyard," *Bloomberg*, March 31, 2010, http://www.bloomberg.com/news/2010-03-31/putin-visits-chavez-in-bid-by-russia-to-expand-sway-in-obama-s-backyard.html.

221   Nancy Benac and Calvin Woodward, "Obama's Terrible, Horrible, No Good, Very Bad Year, *CNS News*, December 21, 2010, http://www.cnsnews.com/news/article/obamas-terrible-horrible-no-good-very-ba.

222   "Unemployment Rate," *Portal Seven*, http://portalseven.com/employment/unemployment_rate.jsp.

223   David Gardner, "Blessed is the Blackberry: How Barack Obama worships with prayers sent to his trusty phone," *The Daily Mail*, April 1, 2010, http://www.dailymail.co.uk/news/article-1262634/Blessed-Blackberry-How-Barack-Obama-worships-prayers-trusty-phone-prayers-trusty-phone.html.

224   Amy Thomson and Olga Kharif, "Verizon Joins AT&T, Caterpiller in Booking Expenses From Health-Care Law," *Bloomberg*, April 2, 2010, http://www.bloomberg.com/news/2010-04-02/verizon-joins-at-t-in-booking-health-care-costs.html.

225   Stephanie Condon, "Obama: 'I can Go to My Right, but I Prefer My Left," *CBS News*, April 1, 2010, http://www.cbsnews.com/8301-503544_162-20001596-503544.html.

226   "Karzai stands by vote fraud claims against West," *The Independent*, April 5, 2010, http://www.independent.co.uk/news/world/asia/karzai-stands-by-vote-fraud-claims-against-west-1936517.html.

227   Anne E. Kornblut, "Obama's 17-minute, 2,500-word response to woman's claim of being 'over-taxed'," *Washington Post*, April 2, 2010, http://www.google.com/search?client=safari&rls=en&q=anne+kornblut+obama+doris+17-minute+we+are+over-taxed&ie=UTF-8&oe=UTF-8.

228   Anne E. Korblut and Spencer S. Hsu, "U.S. changing the way air travelers are screened," *Washington Post*, April 2, 2010, http://www.washingtonpost.com/wp-dyn/content/article/2010/04/02/AR2010040204131_pf.html.

229   Matthew Rosenberg and Habib Zahori, "Karzai Slams the West Again," *Wall Street Journal*, April 4, 2010, http://online.wsj.com/article/SB10001424052702303917304575162012382865940.html?mod=WSJ_hpp_MIDDLENexttoWhatsNewsThird.

230   Giles Wittell, "Barack Obama aims to drive gas guzzlers off the road with greener laws," *TimesOnline*, April 3, 2010, http://www.timesonline.co.uk/tol/news/world/us_and_americas/article7086362.ece.

231   "Obamacare's secret," *Washington Times*, April 3, 2010, http://www.washingtontimes.com/news/2010/apr/3/obamacares-secret-surveillance/.

232 "Karzai stands by vote fraud claims against West, *The Independent*, April 5, 2010, http://www.independent.co.uk/news/world/asia/karzai-stands-by-vote-fraud-claims-against-west-1936517.html.

233 "Social Security, Medicare Finance Report Delayed," *CBS News*, April 5, 2010, http://www.cbsnews.com/stories/2010/04/05/politics/main6365621.shtml.

234 Kim Dixon, "IRS could tap refunds for health insurance penalties," *Reuters*, April 5, 2010, http://www.reuters.com/article/idUSN0517093120100405.

235 Mary Pilon, "Bank of Mom and Dad Shuts Amid White-Collar Struggle," *Wall Street Journal*, April 5, 2010, http://online.wsj.com/article/SB10001424052748704207504575130171387740744.html?mod=WSJ_hpp_RIGHTTopCarousel.

236 David E. Sanger and Peter Baker, "Obama Limits When U.S. Would Use Nuclear Arms," *New York Times*, April 6, 2010, http://www.nytimes.com/2010/04/06/world/06arms.html.

237 "Karzai stands by vote fraud claims against West, *The Independent*, April 5, 2010, http://www.independent.co.uk/news/world/asia/karzai-stands-by-vote-fraud-claims-against-west-1936517.html.

238 Juliet Eilperin, "U.S. exempted BP's Gulf of Mexico drilling from environmental impact study," *Washington Post*, May 4, 2010, http://www.washingtonpost.com/wp-dyn/content/article/2010/05/04/AR2010050404118.html?hpid=topnews.

239 Nick Baumann, "Obama 'Committed' To Net Neutrality Despite Court Ruling," *Mother Jones*, April 6, 2010, http://motherjones.com/mojo/2010/04/obama-committed-net-neutrality-despite-court-ruling.

240 David Martin, "Obama Limits U.S. Policy for Nuclear Weapons," *CBS News*, April 6, 2010, http://www.cbsnews.com/stories/2010/04/06/eveningnews/main6369524.shtml.

241 "Ahmadinejad: U.S. Can't Do "Damn Thing" on Nukes," CBS News, April 7, 2010, http://www.cbsnews.com/stories/2010/04/07/world/main6371169.shtml.

242 "Obama Bans Islam, Jihad From National Security Strategy Document," *Fox News*, April 7, 2010, http://www.foxnews.com/politics/2010/04/07/obama-bans-islam-jihad-national-security-strategy-document/.

243 "American sentenced to hard labor," *Washington Times*, April 7, 2010, http://www.washingtontimes.com/news/2010/apr/07/nkorea-sentences-us-man-8-years-hard-labor/.

244 "Obama skips Polish funeral, heads to golf course," *Washington Times*, April 18, 2010, http://www.washingtontimes.com/news/2010/apr/18/obama-skips-polish-funeral-heads-to-golf-course/.

245 John Kartch, "Obama floats a VAT: Admission explains attempt to alter tax pledge," *Americans for Tax Reform*, April 21, 2010, http://www.atr.org/obama-floats-vat-br-admission-explains-a4814.

246 "U.S.-Russia Nuclear Treaty Runs Into Resistance on Capitol Hill," *Fox News*, April 11, 2010, http://www.foxnews.com/politics/2010/04/11/nuclear-treaty-runs-resistance-capitol-hill/.

247 Matthew Campbell, "Whistleblowers on US 'massacre' fear CIA stalkers," *TimesOnline*, April 11, 2010, http://www.timesonline.co.uk/tol/news/world/us_and_americas/article7094234.ece.

248 Craig Schneider, "Oxendine says no to 'high-risk insurance pool for Georgia," *Atlanta Journal-Constitution*, April 12, 2010, http://www.ajc.com/news/georgia-politics-elec-

tions/oxendine-says-no-to-457331.html.

249 Jonathan Serrie, "Georgia Official to Feds: 'We Don't Have to Play Ball'," *Fox News*, April 13, 2010, http://onthescene.blogs.foxnews.com/tag/john-oxendine.

250 Christopher Neefus, "White House Science 'Czar' Tells Students; U.S. Can't Expetct to Be Number One in Science and Technology Forever," *CNS News*, April 12, 2010, http://cnsnews.com/news/article/64073.

251 Michael Evans, "Hillary Clinton fears al-Qaeda is obtaining nuclear weapons material," *TimesOnline*, April 12, 2010, http://www.timesonline.co.uk/tol/news/world/us_and_americas/article7094876.ece.

252 David E. Sanger and Mark Landler, "China Pledges to Work With U.S. on Iran Sanctions," *New York Times*, April 13, 2010, http://www.nytimes.com/2010/04/13/world/13summit.html.

253 Declan McCullagh, "Google backs Yahoo in privacy fight with DOJ, *Cnet*, April 13, 2010, http://news.cnet.com/8301-13578_3-20002423-38.html.

254 Jake Sherman, "Hoyer: Dems might not pass a budget," *Politico*, April 13, 2010, http://www.politico.com/news/stories/0410/35739.html.

255 Jeremy Pelofsky, "Texas man pleads guilty to hiding money at UBS," *Reuters*, April 13, 2010, http://www.reuters.com/article/idUSWBT01379520100413?type=marketsNews.

256 "Obama: America a Superpower 'Whether We Like It or Not'," *Fox News*, April 15, 2010, http://www.foxnews.com/politics/2010/04/15/obama-america-superpower-like/.

257 "Sarah Palin taken aback by Obama 'superpower' remark," *Boston Herald*, April 18, 2010, http://www.bostonherald.com/news/us_politics/view.bg?articleid=1248120&srvc=rss

258 Denis Dyomkin and Helen Popper, "Russia says Iran reactor on track for August launch," *Reuters*, April 14, 2010, http://www.reuters.com/article/idUSN1413223820100414.

259 Julie Mason, "Obama heralds nuke talk," *Washington Examiner*, April 14, 2010, http://washingtonexaminer.com/politics/white-house/obama-heralds-nuke-talk.

260 Miriam Jordan, "Arizona Clears Strict Immigration Bill," *Wall Street Journal*, April 14, 2010, http://online.wsj.com/article/SB100014240527023046020457518272146663 2104.html?mod=WSJ_hpp_MIDDLENexttoWhatsNewsForth.

261 Jim Miklaszewski and Mark Murray, "Army to court martial 'birther' officer," *MSNBC*, April 13, 2010, http://firstread.msnbc.msn.com/_news/2010/04/13/4429371-army-to-court-martial-birther-officer.

262 Erica Werner, "Obama makes Light of Anti-Tax Protests," *ABC News*, April 15, 2010, http://abcnews.go.com/US/wireStory?id=10388577.

263 John Kartch, "Obama floats a VAT," *Americans for Tax Reform*, April 21, 2010, http://www.atr.org/obama-floats-vat-br-admission-explains-a4814.

264 John Berlau, "Obama-Dodd Financial bill Would Further Enrich Goldman Sachs," *Open Market*, April 16, 2010, http://www.openmarket.org/2010/04/16/obama-dodd-financial-bill-would-futher-enrich-goldman-sachs/.

265 Timothy P. Carney, "Goldman rallies for Obama in Wall Street 'reform'," *Washington Examiner*, April 16, 2010, http://washingtonexaminer.com/node/98166.

266 Brendan Scott, "Dem Web war on Sachs," *New York Post*, April 20, 2010, http://www.nypost.com/p/news/national/dem_web_war_on_sachs_KFbf4AqtQR2tMo-2rYKyZTO.

267 Matt Cover, "EPA Contest Seeks Videos Promoting Government Regulations," *CNS News*, April 16, 2010, http://www.cnsnews.com/node/64297.

268   Declan McCullough, "DOJ abandons warrantless attempt to read Yahoo e-mail," *Cnet*, April 16, 2010, http://news.cnet.com/8301-13578_3-20002722-38.html.

269   "Geithner Says Economy Growing faster Than Expected," *ABC News*, April 18, 2010, http://abcnews.go.com/Business/wireStory?id=10406603.

270   "Chavez: China to Devote $20B to Venezuela Projects," *ABC News*, April 18, 2010, http://abcnews.go.com/Business/wireStory?id=10405070.

271   "Obama goes golfing instead of attending Kaczynskis' funeral," *Warsaw Busniness Journal*, April 18, 2010, http://www.wbj.pl/article-49272-obama-goes-golfing-instead-of-attending-kaczynskis-funeral.html?typ=wbj.

272   "Obama skips Polish funeral, heads to golf course," *Washington Times*, April 18, 2010, http://www.washingtontimes.com/news/2010/apr/18/obama-skips-polish-funeral-heads-to-golf-course/.

273   Jordan Fabian, "Gay rights protesters interrupt Obama speech at fundraiser," *The Hill*, April 19, 2010, http://thehill.com/blogs/blog-briefing-room/news/93193-obama-speech-interrupted-by-gay-rights-protesters.

274   Ben Smith, "Most Transparent White House Ever," *Politico*, April 20, 2010, http://www.politico.com/blogs/bensmith/0410/Most_transparent_White_House_ever.html?showall.

275   Michael Graham Richard, "BP Gulf Oil Spill Cheat Sheet: A Timeline of Unfortunate Events," *Tree Hugger*, May 5, 2010, http://www.treehugger.com/files/2010/05/bp-gulf-oil-spill-timeline.php.

276   Peter Baker, "Obama Denies Link to Timing of S.E.C. Case," *New York Times*, April 21, 2010, http://thecaucus.blogs.nytimes.com/2010/04/21/obama-denies-link-to-timing-of-s-e-c-case/?hp.

277   John Kartch, "Obama floats a VAT," *Americans for Tax Reform*, April 21, 2010, http://www.atr.org/obama-floats-vat-br-admission-explains-a4814.

278   Leo Standora, "While economy crumbled, top financial watchdogs at SEC surfed for porn on Internet: memo," *New York Daily News*, April 23, 2010, http://www.nydailynews.com/money/2010/04/23/2010-04-23_porn_among_daily_duties_of_top_sec_honchos_sez_report.html.

279   Michael Graham Richard, "BP Gulf Oil Spill Cheat Sheet: A Timeline of Unfortunate Events," *Tree Hugger*, May 5, 2010, http://www.treehugger.com/files/2010/05/bp-gulf-oil-spill-timeline.php.

280   Jake Tapper and Sunlen Miller, "President Obama Says 'Poorly-Conceived' Immigration Law Could Mean Hispanic-Americans Are Harassed," *CBS News*, April 27, 2010, http://abcnews.go.com/blogs/politics/2010/04/president-obama-says-arizonas-poorlyconceived-immigration-law-could-mean-hispanicamericans-are-haras/.

281   Randal C. Archibold, "Arizona Enacts Stringent law on Immigration, *New York Times*, April 24, 2010, http://www.nytimes.com/2010/04/24/us/politics/24immig.html.

282   Roger Runningen, "Obama Seeks Immigration Overhaul, Slams Arizona Law," *Bloomberg*, April 23, 2010, http://www.bloomberg.com/news/2010-04-23/obama-calls-for-immigration-law-overhaul-after-misguided-arizona-action.html.

283   Garance Franke-Ruta and Frank Ahrens, "Biden predicts economy will create up to 500,000 jobs a month soon," *Washington Post*, April 23, 2010, http://voices.washingtonpost.com/44/2010/04/biden-predicts-economy-will-cr.html.

284   Shikha Dalmia, "Still Government Motors," *Forbes*, April 23, 2010, http://www.forbes.com/2010/04/23/general-motors-economy-bailout-opinions-columnists-

shikha-dalmia.html.

285   Darrell Issa, "SEC Investigates Goldman," *House Oversight Committee*, April 23, 2010, http://republicans.oversight.house.gov/images/stories/Letters/20100423issalettert oseciginvestigation.pdf.

286   Jamal Washington, "Obama Administration Rejected Help with Oil Spill Cleanup," *Fort Liberty*, June 11, 2009, http://www.fortliberty.org/obama-administration-rejected-help-with-oil-spill-cleanup.html.

287   "Civil rights groups fight Ariz. Immigration law," *MSNBC*, April 24, 2010, http://www.msnbc.msn.com/id/36735281.

288   Chris Baltimore, "U.S. backs plan to stop leaking Gulf of Mexico oil well," *Reuters*, April 25, 2010, http://www.reuters.com/article/idUSTRE63O27L20100425?feedType=RSS&feedName=domesticNews.

289   Campbell Robertson and Clifford Krauss, "Robots Work to Stop Leak of Oil in Gulf," *New York Times*, April 26, 2010, http://www.nytimes.com/2010/04/27/us/27rig.html.

290   Michael Graham Richard, "BP Gulf Oil Spill Cheat Sheet: A Timeline of Unfortunate Events," *Tree Hugger*, May 5, 2010, http://www.treehugger.com/files/2010/05/bp-gulf-oil-spill-timeline.php.

291   Jake Tapper and Sunlen Miller, "President Obama Says Arizona's 'Poorly-Conceived' Immigration Law Could Mean Hispanic-Americans Are Harassed," *ABC News*, April 27, 2010,   http://blogs.abcnews.com/politicalpunch/2010/04/president-obama-says-arizonas-poorlyconceived-immigration-law-could-mean-hispanicamericans-are-haras.html.

292   Matt Drudge, "Send in the Drones: Predators to Fly Above Tex-Mex Border," *DrudgeReport*, April 28, 2010, http://www.drudgereportarchives.com/data/2010/04/28/20100428_032214_flashhs.htm.

293   Ed O'Keefe, "SEC porn scandal results in zero firings, agency says," *Washington Post*, April 27, 2010, http://voices.washingtonpost.com/federal-eye/2010/04/new_sec_porn_bust_details_rele_1.html.

294   Cecilia Kang, "Under financial overhaul, FTC could gain enforcement power over Internet," *Washington Post*, April 26, 2010, http://www.washingtonpost.com/wp-dyn/content/article/2010/04/26/AR2010042604335.html.

295   Kim Dixon, "W. House's Orszag warns of dangers of huge deficits," *Reuters*, April 27, 2010,   http://www.reuters.com/article/idUSN2725802520100427?type=marketsNews.

296   Mark Knoller, "How Many 'Top Priority' Issues Does Obama Have?," *CBS News*, August 13, 2010, http://www.cbsnews.com/8301-503544_162-20013622-503544.html.

297   Kristina Wong, "While Oil Slick Spread, Interior Department Chief of Staff Rafted with Wife on 'Work-Focused' Trip in Grand Canyon," *ABC News*, May 5, 2010, http://blogs.abcnews.com/politicalpunch/2010/05/while-oil-slick-spread-interior-department-chief-of-staff-rafted-with-wife-in-grand-canyon-.html.

298   "Obama To Wall Street: 'I Do Think At A Certain Point You've Made Enough Money," *Real Clear Politics*, April 28, 2010, http://www.realclearpolitics.com/video/2010/04/28/obama_to_wall_street_i_do_think_at_a_certain_point_youve_made_enough_money.html.

299   Mark Knoller, "How Many 'Top Priority' Issues Does Obama Have?," *CBS News*, August 13, 2010, http://www.cbsnews.com/8301-503544_162-20013622-503544.html.

300   Michael Graham Richard, "BP Gulf Oil Spill Cheat Sheet: A Timeline of Unfortunate

Events," *Tree Hugger*, May 5, 2010, http://www.treehugger.com/files/2010/05/bp-gulf-oil-spill-timeline.php.

301 Chris Baltimore, "U.S. Coast Guard sets oil slick ablaze," *Reuters*, April 28, 2010, http://www.reuters.com/article/idUSN2815957620100428.

302 Ben Raines, "Despite plan, not a single fire boom on hand on Gulf Coast at time of oil spill," *Al.com*, May 3, 2010, http://blog.al.com/live/2010/05/fire_boom_oil_spill_raines.html.

303 Mia Saini, "ECB President Favors Global Governance," *Forbes*, April 29, 2010, http://blogs.forbes.com/face-to-face/2010/04/29/ecb-president-favors-global-governance/.

304 Michael Graham Richard, "BP Gulf Oil Spill Cheat Sheet: A Timeline of Unfortunate Events," *Tree Hugger*, May 5, 2010, http://www.treehugger.com/files/2010/05/bp-gulf-oil-spill-timeline.php.

305 "Oil slick poses political peril for Obama," *Washington Times*, April 29, 2010, http://www.washingtontimes.com/news/2010/apr/29/expanding-oil-slick-poses-political-peril-obama/.

306 "Arizona immigration law rewrite 'lays to rest' worries about racial profiling, Brewer says," *St. Petersburg Times*, April 30, 2010, http://www.politifact.com/truth-o-meter/statements/2010/may/04/jan-brewer/arizona-immigration-law-rewrite-lays-rest-worries-/.

307 Frank Newport, "Federal Government Outpaces Private Sector in Job Creation," *Gallup*, May 3, 2010, http://www.gallup.com/poll/127628/Federal-Government-Outpaces-Private-Sector-Job-Creation.aspx.

308 Glenn Somerville, "U.S. posts 19th straight monthly budget deficit," *Reuters*, May 12, 2010, http://www.reuters.com/article/2010/05/12/us-usa-budget-idUSTRE64B53W20100512.

309 Marc Ambinder, "The Night Beat: Obama to Louisiana Coast?," *The Atlantic*, April 30, 2010, http://www.theatlantic.com/politics/archive/2010/04/the-night-beat-obama-to-lousiana-coast/39780/.

310 Michael Graham Richard, "BP Gulf Oil Spill Cheat Sheet: A Timeline of Unfortunate Events," *Tree Hugger*, May 5, 2010, http://www.treehugger.com/files/2010/05/bp-gulf-oil-spill-timeline.php.

311 David A. Fahrenthold and Juliet Eilperin, "Scientists watch for environmental effects of Gulf of Mexico oil spill," *Washington Post*, April 30, 2010, http://www.washingtonpost.com/wp-dyn/content/article/2010/04/30/AR2010043001788_pf.html.

312 "Florida declares state of emergency for Panhandle," *Breitbart*, April 30, 2010, http://www.breitbart.com/article.php?id=D9FDG7301.

313 "Unemployment Rate," *Portal Seven*, http://portalseven.com/employment/unemployment_rate.jsp.

314 Kathleen Sebelius, "Medicare and the New Health Care Law," Department of Health and Human Services, May 2010, http://www.medicare.gov/Publications/Pubs/pdf/11467.pdf.

315 Pete Yost and Mark S. Smith, "Obama Takes Direct Aim at Anti-Government Rhetoric," *ABC News*, May 1, 2010, http://abcnews.go.com/US/wireStory?id=10528621.

316 Al Baker and William K. Rashbaum, "Police Find Car Bomb in Times Square," *New York Times*, May 2, 2010, http://www.nytimes.com/2010/05/02/nyregion/02timessquare.html.

317   Tom Hays and Larry Neumeister, "Times Sq. bomber sentenced, warns of more attacks," *ABC News*, October 5, 2010, http://abcnews.go.com/US/wireStory?id=11800425.

318   Tony Allen-Mills and Craig Guillot," "Oil spill disaster 'out of control'," *TimesOnline*, May 2, 2010, http://www.timesonline.co.uk/tol/news/world/us_and_americas/article7114015.ece.

319   Campbell Robertson and Henry Fountain, "BP Moves to Fix a Leak as Obama Warns of Damage," *New York Times*, May 3, 2010, http://www.nytimes.com/2010/05/03/us/03spill.html?hp.

320   Paul Simao, "U.S. to keep heat on BP oil leak," *Reuters*, May 2, 2010, http://www.reuters.com/article/2010/05/02/usa-rig-salazar-idUSN0215833120100502.

321   Anne E. Kornblut, Jerry Markon and Spencer S. Hsu, "Pakistan native arrested in Times Square bomb case," *Washington Post*, May 4, 2010, http://www.washingtonpost.com/wp-dyn/content/article/2010/05/03/AR2010050300847.html?hpid=topnews.

322   Henry Blodget, "Guess Who's Paying For The Greece Bailout? That's Right – YOU," *Business Insider*, May 3, 2010, http://articles.businessinsider.com/2010-05-03/news/30032465_1_bailout-parthenon-aig-creditors.

323   "Robert Gibbs Gets Very Defensive When Pressed Why Obama has Held No Press Conferences since July," *Freedom's Lighthouse*," May 3, 2010, http://www.freedomslighthouse.com/2010/05/robert-gibbs-gets-very-defensive-when.html.

324   Ynji de Nies and Hanna Siegel, Nashville Flooding: At Least 29 Dead From Record Rains In Mid-South," *ABC News*, May 4, 2010, http://abcnews.go.com/WN/nashville-flooding-29-dead-flash-flooding-south/story?id=10555626.

325   "Pakistan Taliban leader 'killed by CIA drone' surfaces on internet to threaten U.S.," *The Daily Mail*, May 4, 2009, http://www.dailymail.co.uk/news/worldnews/article-1271225/Pakistan-Taliban-leader-alive.html.

326   Stephen Dinan, "Bank bill could help feds snoop, GOP warns," *Washington Times*, may 5, 2010, http://www.washingtontimes.com/news/2010/may/05/bank-bill-could-help-feds-snoop-gop-warns/print/.

327   Ed Carson, "Money Pit: Freddie Mac Seeks $10.6 Billion More From Treasury," *Investors.com*, May 5, 2010, http://blogs.investors.com/capitalhill/index.php/home/35-politicsinvesting/1733-money-pit-freddie-mac-seeks-106-billion-more-from-treasury.

328   Josh Rogin, "U.S. not accepting foreign help on oil spill," *Foreign Policy*, May 6, 2010, http://thecable.foreignpolicy.com/posts/2010/05/06/us_not_accepting_foreign_help_on_oil_spill.

329   Amy Schatz, "New U.S, Push to Regulate Internet Access," *Wall Street Journal*, May 5, 2010, http://online.wsj.com/article/SB10001424052748703961104575226582865344548758.html?mod=WSJ_hpp_LEFTWhatsNewsCollection.

330   Tony Romm, "Boehner slams FCC for 'takeover of Internet," *The Hill*, May 6, 2010, http://thehill.com/blogs/hillicon-valley/technology/96503-boehner-slams-fcc-for-takeover-of-internetq.

331   Damien Pearse, "Oil Starts To Wash Ashore Off Louisiana," *Sky News*, May 7, 2010, http://news.sky.com/home/world-news/article/15626665.

332   Marisa Taylor, "Since spill, feds have given 27 waivers to oil companies in gulf," *McClatchy*, May 7, 2010, http://www.mcclatchydc.com/2010/05/07/93761/despite-spill-feds-still-giving.html.

333   "Holder: Feds may sue over Arizona immigration law," *CNN*, May 9, 2010, http://www.

cnn.com/2010/POLITICS/05/09/holder.arizona.immigration/index.html?hpt=T2.

334 "Obama bemoans 'diversions' of IPod, Xbox era," *Google*, May 9, 2010, http://www.google.com/hostednews/afp/article/ALeqM5hcoyG-Ck3-VwZB7fqpUFXbffoObg.

335 Steven Erlanger, Katrin Bennhold and David Sanger, "Debt Aid Package for Europe Took Nudge From Washington," *New York Times*, May 11, 2010, http://www.nytimes.com/2010/05/11/business/global/11reconstruct.html.

336 "One million votes against Obamacare," *Washington Times*, May 12, 2010, http://www.washingtontimes.com/news/2010/may/12/one-million-votes-against-obamacare/.

337 Denis Dyomkin, "Russia says may build nuclear power plant in Syria," *Reuters*, May 11, 2010, http://in.reuters.com/article/idINIndia-48399220100511?sp=true.

338 BP, Transocean and Halliburton to Testify on Rig Disaster, *Forbes*, May 11, 2010, http://www.forbes.com/2010/05/11/bp-transocean-and-haliburton-to-testify-on-rig-disaster-marketnewsvideo.html.

339 Stephen Dinan, "Holder hasn't read Arizona law he criticized," *Washington Times*, May 13, 2010, http://www.washingtontimes.com/news/2010/may/13/holder-hasnt-read-ariz-law-he-criticized/.

340 William H. McMichael, "Hold Fire, Earn a Medal," *Navy Times*, May 11, 2010, http://www.navytimes.com/news/2010/05/military_restraint_medal_051110mar.

341 Paul Howard, "Obamacare's Hidden Costs," *City Journal*, May 13, 2010, http://www.city-journal.org/2010/eon0513ph.html.

342 Sunlen Miller, "Obama Says Republicans Cannot have the Keys Back to the Car: 'No! You Can't Drive'," *ABC News*, May 13, 2009, http://blogs.abcnews.com/politicalpunch/2010/05/obama-says-republicans-cannot-have-the-keys-back-to-the-car-no-you-cant-drive.html.

343 "Diplomats: Iran expands enrichment facility," *USA Today*, May 14, 2010, http://www.usatoday.com/news/world/2010-05-14-iran-nuclear_N.htm?csp=34.

344 Mark Guarino, "EPA scolds BP in Gulf oil spill: dispersant is too toxic, change it," *Christian Science Monitor*, May 20, 2010, http://www.csmonitor.com/USA/2010/0520/EPA-scolds-BP-in-Gulf-oil-spill-dispersant-is-too-toxic-change-it.

345 Chip Reid, "Angry Obama Seeks to Deflect Blame for Gulf Oil Spill Crisis," *CBS News*, May 14, 2010, http://www.cbsnews.com/8301-503544_162-20005039-503544.html.

346 Ibid.

347 Jon Vaala, "Obama Administration Gave Gulf Oil Rig Safety Award in '09," *Jon Vaala. Wordpress*, May 16, 2010, http://jonvaala.wordpress.com/2010/05/16/obama-administration-gave-gulf-oil-rig-safety-award-in-09/.

348 Kirit Radia, "US Cites AZ Immigration Law During Human Rights Talks with China, Conservatives Call It An Apology," *ABC News*, May 17, 2010, http://blogs.abcnews.com/politicalpunch/2010/05/arizona-immigration-law-human-rights-china-conservatives-apology.html.

349 Charles Gasparino, "Lenders Agree to Prop Up Ailing ShoreBank," *Fox News*, May 17, 2010, http://www.foxbusiness.com/story/markets/industries/finance/lenders-agree-prop-ailing-shorebank/.

350 Laurel J. Sweet and Joe Dwinell, "Court grants asylum to Obama's aunt Zeituni Onyango," *Boston Herald*, May 17, 2010, http://www.bostonherald.com/news/regional/view.bg?articleid=1255429&srvc=rss.

351 Charles Krauthammer, "The fruits of weakness," *Washington Post*, May 20, 2010, http://www.washingtonpost.com/wp-dyn/content/article/2010/05/20/

AR2010052003885.html.

352 Jared Favole and Stephen Power, "Obama to Name Panel to Probe Disaster," *Wall Street Journal*, May 18, 2010, http://online.wsj.com/article/SB1000142405274870331540457 5250022249767784.html?mod=WSJ_hpp_MIDDLENexttoWhatsNewsSecond.

353 "Napolitano Admits She Hasn't Read Arizona Immigration Law in 'Detail,'" *Fox News*, May 18, 2010, http://www.foxnews.com/politics/2010/05/18/napolitano-admits-read-arizona-immigration-law/.

354 Walter Alarkon, "Next year's budget sinking in deep red ink," *The Hill*, May 18, 2010, http://thehill.com/blogs/on-the-money/budget/98409-senate-budget-chairman-says-prospect-for-budget-resolution-fading-.

355 "Mexican President Knocks Arizona Law From White House Lawn," *Breitbart.tv*, May 19, 2010, http://www.breitbart.tv/mexican-president-knocks-arizona-law-from-white-house-lawn/.

356 "Top Official Says Feds May Not Process Illegals Referred From Arizona," *Fox News*, May 21, 2010, http://www.foxnews.com/politics/2010/05/21/official-says-feds-process-illegals-referred-arizona/.

357 Robert Wenzell, "32 States Have Borrowed from the Federal Government to Make Unemployment Payments; California Haas Borrowed $7 Billion," *Economic Policy Journal*, May 21, 2010, http://www.economicpolicyjournal.com/2010/05/32-states-have-borrowed-from-treasury.html.

358 "Calderon Gets Standing Ovation From Dems For Criticizing AZ Immigration Crackdown," *Breitbart.tv*, May 20, 2010, http://www.breitbart.tv/calderon-before-congress-az-immigration-law-carries-great-amount-of-risk/.

359 Mark Guarino, "EPA scolds BP in Gulf oil spill: dispersant is too toxic, change it," *Christian Science Monitor*, May 20, 2010, http://www.csmonitor.com/USA/2010/0520/EPA-scolds-BP-in-Gulf-oil-spill-dispersant-is-too-toxic-change-it.

360 Neil deMause, "Stealth IRS changes mean millions of new tax forms," *CNN*, May 21, 2010, http://money.cnn.com/2010/05/21/smallbusiness/1099_deluge/index.htm?source=cnn_bin&hpt=Sbin.

361 Neil deMause, "IRS starts mopping up Congress's tax-reporting mess," *CNN*, July 9, 2010, http://money.cnn.com/2010/07/09/smallbusiness/irs_1099_flood/index.htm.

362 Robert Burns, "US lifts sanctions against Russians linked to Iran," *Breitbart*, May 21, 2010, http://www.breitbart.com/article.php?id=D9FREE2G0&show_article=1.

363 Tim Dickinson, "The Spill, The Scandal and the President," *Rolling Stone*, June 8, 2010, http://www.rollingstone.com/politics/news/the-spill-the-scandal-and-the-president-20100608.

364 "Britain faces aggressive cuts in 'age of austerity': minister," *Breitbart*, May 22, 2010, http://www.breitbart.com/article.php?id=CNG.818e03363d37aed733b8e1d6484580c4.511&show_article=1.

365 David Sanger, "U.S. Implicates North Korean Leader in Attack," *New York Times*, May 23, 2010, http://www.nytimes.com/2010/05/23/world/asia/23korea.html.

366 John Bresnahan and Jake Sherman, "DoJ nixes Sestak special counsel," *Politico*, May 24, 2010, http://www.politico.com/news/stories/0510/37713.html.

367 Matt Drudge, "GOP takes House seat in Obama's Hawaiian home district," *DrudgeReport*, May 22, 2010, www.drudgereport.com.

368 Matthew Bigg, "Louisiana blasts BP, U.S. govt for slow oil response," *Reuters*, May 23, 2010, http://www.reuters.com/article/idUSN2310234520100523?type=marketsNe

ws.

369   Jake Tapper, "BP Oil Spill: Gov. Jindal Asks for Permission to Build Barrier Islands," *ABC News*, May 24, 2010, http://abcnews.go.com/WN/bp-oil-spill-louisiana-governor-bobby-jindal-asks/story?id=10731680.

370   Ibid.

371   John Bresnahan and Jake Sherman, "DoJ nixes Sestak special counsel," *Politico*, May 24, 2010, http://www.politico.com/news/stories/0510/37713.html.

372   "Obama Call for 'International Order' Raises Questions About U.S. Sovereignty," *Fox News*, May 24, 2010, http://www.foxnews.com/politics/2010/05/24/obama-international-order-raises-questions-sovereignty/.

373   Jeff Jarvis, "How *not* to save news, Bad gov't ideas for journalism," *New York Post*, June 3, 2010, http://www.nypost.com/p/news/opinion/opedcolumnists/how_not_to_save_news_2g7IgzaZNuwuZU80CVcQ7M.

374   "FTC floats Drudge tax," *Washington Times*, June 4, 2010, http://www.washingtontimes.com/news/2010/jun/4/ftc-floats-drudge-tax/.

375   "FTC dodges Drudge Tax questions," *Washington Times*, June 10, 2010, http://www.washingtontimes.com/news/2010/jun/10/ftc-dodges-drudge-tax-questions/.

376   "Feds respond, file motion to dismiss Virginia suit," *Multistatelawsuit.com*, May 24, 2010, http://multistatelawsuit.com/?p=84.

377   Mark Mazzetti, "U.S. Is Said to Expand Secret Actions in Mideast," *New York Times*, May 25, 2010, http://www.nytimes.com/2010/05/25/world/25military.html?_r=1&hp.

378   "Syria: Obama has failed in peace efforts and lost influence in Mideast," *Haaretz*, May 24, 2010, http://www.haaretz.com/news/diplomacy-defense/syria-obama-has-failed-in-peace-efforts-and-lost-influence-in-mideast-1.291963.

379   "Hu says China to hold firm on yuan policy," *Breitbart*, May 24, 2010, http://www.breitbart.com/article.php?id=CNG.0636a7bb93c2e767c0fc1df2b1bfff7e.791&show_article=1.

380   "U.S. backs South Korea in punishing North," *MSNBC*, May 24, 2010, http://www.msnbc.msn.com/id/37309788/ns/world_news-asiapacific/.

381   Jake Tapper, "BP Oil Spill: Gov. Jindal Asks for Permission to Build Barrier Islands," *ABC News*, May 24, 2010, http://abcnews.go.com/WN/bp-oil-spill-louisiana-governor-bobby-jindal-asks/story?id=10731680.

382   Karen Tumulty and Steven Mufson, "Obama administration conflicted about relying on BP to stop gulf oil spill," *Washington Post*, May 24, 2010, http://www.washingtonpost.com/wp-dyn/content/article/2010/05/24/AR2010052404071_pf.html.

383   Manu Jaju, "President Obama clashes with John McCain in Republican luncheon," *Politico*, May 25, 2010, http://www.politico.com/news/stories/0510/37746.html.

384   Jacques Billeaud, "Lawmaker: Obama to send 1,200 troops to border," *Breitbart*, May 25, 2010, http://www.breitbart.com/article.php?id=D9FU1TN05&show_article=1.

385   Mary Childs, "Debt level, Spending Pose Risk to U.S.'s Aaa Credit Rating, Moody's Says," *Bloomberg*, May 25, 2010, http://www.bloomberg.com/news/2010-05-25/debt-level-spending-pose-risk-to-u-s-s-aaa-credit-rating-moody-s-says.html.

386   Binyamin Appelbaum, "Regulators Seek Global Capital Rule," *New York Times*, May 26, 2010, http://www.nytimes.com/2010/05/26/business/global/26basel.html?dbk.

387   Eric Zimmermann, "Obama to aides: 'Plug the damn hole,'" *The Hill*, May 25, 2010, http://thehill.com/blogs/blog-briefing-room/news/99713-obama-to-aides-plug-the-damn-hole.

388   Andrew Malcolm, "Karl Rove: Joe Sestak's lying or he's protecting a felon in Barack Obama's White House," *Los Angeles Times*, May 27, 2010, http://latimesblogs.latimes.com/washington/2010/05/joe-sestak-karl-rove-chris-dodd-george-w-bush.html.

389   Liz Goodwin, "What's exactly happened with the government's Solyndra loan?," Yahoo, September 14, 2011, http://news.yahoo.com/blogs/lookout/exactly-happened-goverment-solyndra-loan-212111448.html.

390   Omar Villafranca, "Perry's request goes ignored for more than a year," *NBC Dallas-Fort Worth*, June 30, 2010, http://www.nbcdfw.com/news/politics/Troops-to-TexasMexico-Border-No-Answer.html.

391   Spencer S. Hsu, "Obama Considering Guard Troops on Texas-Mexico Border," *Washington Post*, March 12, 2009, http://voices.washingtonpost.com/44/2009/03/12/obama_considering_guard_troops.html.

392   Bridget Johnson, "Issa: Sestak scandal could be Obama's Watergate," *The Hill*, May 26, 2010, http://thehill.com/blogs/blog-briefing-room/news/100067-issa-sestak-scandal-could-be-obamas-watergate.

393   Rowan Scarborough, "Obama at odds with Petraeus doctrine on 'Islam'," *Washington Times*, July 11, 2010, http://www.washingtontimes.com/news/2010/jul/11/obama-at-odds-with-petraeus-doctrine-on-islam/.

394   "Clinton says world must respond to N. Korea," *MSNBC*, May 26, 2010, http://www.msnbc.msn.com/id/37329506/ns/world_news-asiapacific/.

395   Stephen Power, "Regulators Accepted Gifts From Oil Industry," *Wall Street Journal*, May 26, 2010, http://online.wsj.com/article/SB10001424052748704026204575266112115488640.html?mod=e2tw.

396   Jake Tapper and Huma Khan, "'Political Stupidity': Democrat James Carville Slams Obama's Response to BP Oil Spill," *ABC News*, May 26, 2010, http://abcnews.go.com/GMA/Politics/bp-oil-spill-political-headache-obama-democrats-slam/story?id=10746519&tqkw=&tqshow=GMA.

397   www.marklevinshow.com.

398   "Democrats stop bid to send 6,000 troops to border," *Breitbart*, May 27, 2010, http://www.breitbart.com/article.php?id=D9FV86NG4&show_article=1.

399   Ben Smith, "Clinton: 'The rich are not paying their fare share'," *Politico*, May 27, 2010, http://www.politico.com/blogs/bensmith/0510/Clinton_The_rich_are_not_paying_their_fair_share.htm.

400   Sunlen Miller, "The Presidential Planner," *ABC News*, May 27, 2010, http://abcnews.go.com/blogs/politics/2010/05/the-presidential-planner-17-7/.

401   Brian Montopoli, "Obama: Malia Asked 'Did you Plug The Hole Yet, Daddy?'" *CBS News*, May 27, 2010, http://www.cbsnews.com/8301-503544_162-20006183-503544.html.

402   Christi Parsons and Peter Nicholas, "Obama defends his team's handling of gulf oil spill," *Los Angeles Times*, May 27, 2010, http://articles.latimes.com/2010/may/27/nation/la-na-oil-spill-obama-20100528.

403   Tim Dickinson, "The Spill, The Scandal and the President," *Rolling Stone*, June 8, 2010, http://www.rollingstone.com/politics/news/the-spill-the-scandal-and-the-president-20100608.

404   Molly Hooper, "McCarthy: Obama hasn't returned call of lawmaker representing district affected by rig explosion," *The Hill*, May 27, 2010, http://thehill.com/blogs/blog-briefing-room/news/100279-mccarthy-obama-hasnt-returned-call-of-gulf-law-

maker.

405   Greg Sergeant, "White House asked Bill Clinton to talk to Joe Sestak about Senate run," *Washington Post*, May 27, 2010, http://voices.washingtonpost.com/plum-line/2010/05/exclusive_white_house_asked_cl_1.html.

406   Lynn Sweet, "President Obama official schedule and guidance," *Chicago Sun-Times*, May 28, 2010, http://blogs.suntimes.com/sweet/2010/05/president_obama_official_sched_323.html.

407   Nicholas Johnston and John McCormick, "Obama Heads to Gulf as Oil-Spill Crisis Shifts to White House," *Bloomberg*, June 4, 2010, http://www.bloomberg.com/news/2010-06-04/obama-heads-for-third-visit-to-gulf-as-furor-shifts-toward-white-house.html.

408   Steve Geimann and Carol Wolf, "U.S. Now Telling BP What to Do as Company Seeks to Stem Oil Spill," *Bloomberg*, May 30, 2010, http://www.bloomberg.com/news/2010-05-30/u-s-telling-bp-what-to-do-as-company-seeks-to-contain-majority-of-oil.html.

409   "Jindal slams Feds over skepticism about Louisiana plan to build sand barriers against the oil spill," *Politifact*, June 1, 2010, http://politifact.com/truth-o-meter/statements/2010/jun/01/bobby-jindal/jindal-slams-feds-over-skepticism-about-louisianas/.

410   Amos Harel, Avi Issacharoff and Anshel Pfeffer, "Israel navy commandos: Gaza flotilla activists tried to lynch us," *Haaretz*, May 31, 2010, http://www.haaretz.com/news/diplomacy-defense/israel-navy-commandos-gaza-flotilla-activists-tried-to-lynch-us-1.293089.

411   "Obama Friends Bill Ayers, Code Pink Top Activists Behind Gaza Flotilla," Fox News, June 1, 2010, http://nation.foxnews.com/gaza-flotilla-raid/2010/06/01/obama-friends-bill-ayers-code-pink-top-activists-behind-gaza-flotilla.

412   Tovah Lazaroff, "Israel faces int'l fury over flotilla," *Jerusalem Post*, June1, 2010, http://www.jpost.com/International/Article.aspx?id=177063.

413   "Israel recoils as US backs nuclear move," *Breitbart*, May 31, 2010, http://www.breitbart.com/article.php?id=CNG.5eaf6bbb255b23063c3b3635bd5f7c52.161&show_article=1.

414   Anne E. Kornblut and Ed O'Keefe, "President Obama will skip Memorial Day visit to Arlington national Cemetery," *Washington Post*, May 28, 2010, http://www.washingtonpost.com/wp-dyn/content/article/2010/05/27/AR2010052702696.html?wprss=rss_metro.

415   "Food stamp use hit record 40.8m in May," *Boston Globe*, August 5, 2010, http://www.boston.com/news/nation/washington/articles/2010/08/05/food_stamp_use_hit_record_408m_in_may/.

416   Census Worker Claims Jobs Numbers Inflated, *Fox News*, April 28, 2011, http://video.foxnews.com/v/4225776/census-worker-claims-jobs-numbers-inflated/.

417   "Obama's endless summer of spending," *Washington Times*, June 17, 2010, http://www.washingtontimes.com/news/2010/jun/17/obamas-endless-summer-of-spending/.

418   "Unemployment Rate," *Portal Seven*, http://portalseven.com/employment/unemployment_rate.jsp.

419   Matt Negrin, "Gibbs: 'I'd refer you to the memo'," *Politico*, June 1, 2010, http://www.politico.com/politico44/perm/0610/secretive_on_sestak_435a43c7-f633-414e-adf7-b50533599c78.html.

420   "Privacy fears 'should not hamper airport security'," *Breitbart*, June 1, 2010, http://www.breitbart.com/article.php?id=CNG.65f63a08624c205d2725bece35f5588b.3e

1&show_article=1.

421   Adam Entous, "China delays Gates trip in Apparent snub for Taiwan, *Reuters*, June 2, 2010, http://www.reuters.com/article/idUSTRE6511ZH20100602?type=politicsNews.

422   "Arizona Governor Gets Few Results From Meeting With Obama," *Fox News*, June 3, 2010, http://www.foxnews.com/politics/2010/06/03/arizona-governor-gets-results-meeting-obama/.

423   Michael Booth, "Romanoff confirms White House job discussions," *Denver Post*, June 3, 2010, http://www.denverpost.com/ci_15213784.

424   Ori Lewis, "Israel prepares to intercept Gaza-bound ship," *Reuters*, June 4, 2010, http://www.reuters.com/article/idUSTRE65005R20100604.

425   Steven Ertelt, "Second Document Has Kagan Defending Clinton Partial-Birth Abortion Ban Veto," *Life News*, June 4, 2010, http://www.lifenews.com/2010/06/04/nat-6397/.

426   "Kagan: Affirmative Action Good Law, Good Politics," *Newsmax*, June 4, 2010, http://www.newsmax.com/InsideCover/US-Kagan-Affirmative-Action/2010/06/04/id/361100.

427   Jim Efstathiou, Jr., "Obama's Offshore Drilling Ban May Slow U.S. Job Gains," *Bloomberg*, June 3, 2010, http://www.bloomberg.com/news/2010-06-03/jindal-says-obama-s-moratorium-on-drilling-may-cost-louisiana-20-000-jobs.html.

428   "Gulf Lawmakers Plead With Obama to Ease Drilling Ban, Warn of Economic Blow," *Fox News*, June 4, 2010, http://www.foxnews.com/politics/2010/06/04/gulf-lawmakers-plead-obama-ease-drilling-ban-warn-economic-blow/.

429   "Thousands rally in favor of Arizona immigration law," *ABC15*, June 5, 2010, http://www.abc15.com/dpp/news/region_phoenix_metro/central_phoenix/rally-to-hit-capitol-in-favor-of-arizona-immigration-law.

430   Ian Urbina, "In Gulf, It Was Unclear Who Was in Charge of Rig," *New York Times*, June 5, 2010, http://www.nytimes.com/2010/06/06/us/06rig.html?_r=1&pagewanted=1.

431   Brian Lysaght, "BP's CEO hasn't Spoken Directly With Obama About Leak (Update1)," *Bloomberg*, June 6, 2010, http://www.bloomberg.com/apps/news?pid=newsarchive&sid=asQDvBNvDFIE.

432   Peter Grier, "Soldier arrested in WikiLeaks classified Iraq video case," *Christian Science Monitor*, June 7, 2010, http://www.csmonitor.com/USA/Military/2010/0607/Soldier-arrested-in-WikiLeaks-classified-Iraq-video-case.

433   Tim Martin and Darlene Superville, "Obama to high school grads: 'Don't make excuses,'" *Breitbart*, June 7, 2010, http://www.breitbart.com/article.php?id=D9G6KTGO0&show_article=1.

434   "Protesters descent on Ground Zero for anti-mosque demonstration," *CNN*, June 6, 2010, http://www.cnn.com/2010/US/06/06/new.york.ground.zero.mosque/index.html?section=cnn_latest.

435   "Obama Seeking 'Ass To Kick' Over Oil Spill," *Real Clear Politics*, June 7, 2010, http://www.realclearpolitics.com/video/2010/06/07/obama_seeking_ass_to_kick_over_oil_spill.html.

436   Donna Smith, "U.S. debt to rise to $19.6 trillion by 2015," *Reuters*, June 8, 2009, http://www.reuters.com/article/idUSN088462520100608.

437   Thomas Nagorski, "Afghan War Now Country's Longest," *ABC News*, June 8, 2009, http://abcnews.go.com/Politics/afghan-war-now-longest-war-us-history/

story?id=10849303

438   Dmitry Solovyov, "Russia says Iran sanctions do not bar missile deal," *Reuters*, June 10, 2010, www.reuters.com/article/idUSLDE6591FC20100610.

439   Ed O'Keefe, "Obama issuing memos of all sorts," *Washington Post*, June 9, 2010, http://voices.washingtonpost.com/federal-eye/2010/06/obama_issuing_memos_of_all_sor.html.

440   Jonathan J. Cooper and Jacques Billeaud, "Clinton Comment On Immigration Law Riles Ariz. Gov," *Newsmax*, June 17, 2010, http://www.newsmax.com/InsideCover/US-Immigration-Law-Clinton/2010/06/17/id/362346.

441   Guy Chazzan and Susan Daker, "As Missteps Mount, So Does the Backlash," *Wall Street Journal*, June 10, 2010, http://online.wsj.com/article/SB10001424052748703302604575294523724355994.html?mod=WSJ_hpp_MIDDLENexttoWhatsNewsFifth.

442   "FTC dodges Drudge Tax questions," *Washington Times*, June 10, 2010, http://www.washingtontimes.com/news/2010/jun/10/ftc-dodges-drudge-tax-questions/.

443   Declan McCullagh, "Senators propose granting president emergency Internet power," *Cnet*, June 10, 2010, http://news.cnet.com/8301-13578_3-20007418-38.html.

444   William Kristol, "Obama Administration to Support Anti-Israel Resolution at UN Next Week," *Weekly Standard*, June 11, 2010, http://www.weeklystandard.com/blogs/sources-obama-administration-support-anti-israel-resolution-un-next-week.

445   Jamal Washington, "Obama Administration Rejected Help with Oil Spill Cleanup," *Fort Liberty*, June 11, 2010, http://www.fortliberty.org/obama-administration-rejected-help-with-oil-spill-cleanup.html.

446   Lori Montgomery, "Obama pleads for $50 billion in state, local aid," *Washington Post*, June 13, 2010, http://www.washingtonpost.com/wp-dyn/content/article/2010/06/12/AR2010061204152.html.

447   Lorraine Woellert and John Gittelsohn, "Fannie-Freddie Fix at $160 Billion With $1 Trillion Worst Case," *Bloomberg*, June 13, 2010, http://www.bloomberg.com/news/2010-06-13/fannie-freddie-fix-expands-to-160-billion-with-worst-case-at-1-trillion.html.

448   "Alabama governor blasts oil spill response leadership," *Breitbart*, June 13, 2009, http://www.breitbart.com/article.php?id=CNG.55afc2f458ef4cadcb6e3e32530d858a.1d1&show_article=1.

449   Jaqui Goddard, "Boldly going nowhere: Nasa ends plan to put man back on Moon," *TimesOnline*, June 14, 2010, http://www.timesonline.co.uk/tol/news/science/space/article7149543.ece.

450   Jonathan Weisman, "WH Takes Cues fro Liberal Think Tank on Spill," *Wall Street Journal*, http://blogs.wsj.com/washwire/2010/06/14/wh-takes-cues-from-liberal-think-tank-on-spill/?utm_source=feedburner&utm_medium=feed&utm_campaign=Feed%3A+wsj%2Fwashwire%2Ffeed+%28WSJ.com%3A+Washington+Wire%29.

451   David Muir, "Gov. Bobby Jindal Orders National Guard to Build Barrier Wall Off Louisiana Shore," ABC News, June 14, 2010, http://abcnews.go.com/WN/article/bp-oil-spill-gov-bobby-jindal-orders-national/story?id=10914348.

452   Ibid.

453   Tom Jensen, "Fallout from the Spill," *Public Policy Polling*, June 15, 2010, http://publicpolicypolling.blogspot.com/2010/06/fallout-from-spill.html.

454   John Boehner, "Statement on President Obama's Oval Office Address," *GOP Leader*, June 15, 2010, http://gopleader.gov/News/DocumentSingle.aspx?DocumentID=190777.

455   Michael O'Brien, "White House says it could contain 90 percent of spilling oil," *The Hill*, June 15, 2010, http://thehill.com/blogs/blog-briefing-room/news/103159-white-house-says-it-could-contain-90-percent-of-oil-spilling-per-day-by-months-en?page=2.

456   Mark Knoller, "How Many 'Top Priority' Issues Does Obama Have?," *CBS News*, August 13, 2010, http://www.cbsnews.com/8301-503544_162-20013622-503544.html.

457   John Gizzi, "Arizona Governor Blasts Eric Holder," *Human Events*, June 16, 2010, http://www.humanevents.com/article.php?id=37516.

458   Olga Kharif, "High-Speed Internet Rules Might Prove Costly," *Business Week*, June 17, 2010, http://www.businessweek.com/technology/content/jun2010/tc20100616_751009.htm.

459   David Muir and Bradley Blackburn, "BP Oil Spill: Against Gov. Jindal's Wishes, Crude-Sucking Barges Stopped by Coast Guard," *ABC News*, June 18, 2010, http://abcnews.go.com/WN/bp-oil-spill-gov-bobby-jindals-wishes-crude/story?id=10946379.

460   Carol E. Lee, Glenn Thrush, Kendra Marr, "President Obama meets BP chairman, who says company is helping the 'small people'," *Politico*, June 16, 2010, http://www.politico.com/news/stories/0610/38612.html.

461   "Obama's endless summer of spending," *Washington Times*, June 17, 2010, http://www.washingtontimes.com/news/2010/jun/17/obamas-endless-summer-of-spending/.

462   Jonathan J. Cooper and Jacques Billeaud, "Clinton Comment On Immigration Law Riles Ariz. Gov," *Newsmax*, June 17, 2010, http://www.newsmax.com/InsideCover/US-Immigration-Law-Clinton/2010/06/17/id/362346.

463   Randal C. Archibold and mark Landler, "Justice Dept. Will Fight Arizona on Immigration," *New York Times*, June 18, 2010, http://www.nytimes.com/2010/06/19/us/politics/19arizona.html.

464   "Uptick in Violence Forces Closing of Parkland Along Mexico Border to Americans," *Fox News*, June 16, 2010, http://www.foxnews.com/us/2010/06/16/closes-park-land-mexico-border-americans/.

465   Philip Klein, "Obama Admin. Argues in Court That Individual mandate Is a Tax," *American Spectator*, June 17, 2009, http://spectator.org/blog/2010/06/17/obama-admin-argues-in-court-th.

466   Stephanie Kirchgaessner, "FCC in move to regulate internet," *Financial Times*, June 18, 2010, http://www.ft.com/cms/s/2/6231b0b8-7a70-11df-9cd7-00144feabdc0.html#axzz18l7E5cDE.

467   Bill Gertz, "Inside the Ring," *Washington Times*, June 16, 2010, http://www.washingtontimes.com/news/2010/jun/16/inside-the-ring-382424672/.

468   David Muir and Bradley Blackburn, "BP Oil Spill: Against Gov. Jindal's Wishes, Crude-Sucking Barges Stopped by Coast Guard," *ABC News*, June 18, 2010, http://abcnews.go.com/WN/bp-oil-spill-gov-bobby-jindals-wishes-crude/story?id=10946379.

469   Ibid.

470   Bridget Johnson, "Obama hits golf course with Biden on another hot, humid weekend," *The Hill*, June 19, 2010, http://thehill.com/blogs/blog-briefing-room/news/104313-obama-hits-golf-course-with-biden-on-another-hot-humid-weekend.

471   Mort Zuckerman, "World Sees Obama as Incompetent and Amateur," *US News*, June 18, 2010, http://www.usnews.com/opinion/mzuckerman/articles/2010/06/18/mort-zuckerman-world-sees-obama-as-incompetent-and-amateur.

472   "Gov. Brewer: We Can't Continue to Be the Gateway for Illegal Immigration," *Fox*

News, June 16, 2010, http://drupal.foxnews.com/on-air/on-the-record/transcript/gov-brewer-we-can039t-continue-be-gateway-illegal-immigration.

473   "Napolitano: Internet Monitoring Needed to Fight Homegrown Terrorism," *Fox News*, June 18, 2010, http://www.foxnews.com/politics/2010/06/18/napolitano-internet-monitoring-needed-fight-homegrown-terrorism/?utm_source=feedburner&utm_medium=feed&utm_campaign=Feed%3A+foxnews%2Fpolitics+%28Text+-+Politics%29.

474   Ulf Laessing, "25 Saudi Guantanamo prisoners return to militancy," *Reuters*, June 19, 2010, http://www.reuters.com/article/idUSTRE65I22220100619.

475   Paul Abelsky, "Medvedev Promotes Ruble to Lessen Dollar Dominance (Update1), *Business Week*, June 19, 2010, http://www.businessweek.com/news/2010-06-19/medvedev-promotes-ruble-to-lessen-dollar-dominance-update1-.html.

476   David Muir and Bradley Blackburn, "BP Oil Spill: Against Gov. Jindal's Wishes, Crude-Sucking Barges Stopped by Coast Guard," *ABC News*, June 18, 2010, http://abcnews.go.com/WN/bp-oil-spill-gov-bobby-jindals-wishes-crude/story?id=10946379.

477   Sharyn Alfonsi, David Muir, Bradley Blackburn, "BP Oil Spill: As Pay Czar Promises Money, Workers Turned Away From BP Claims Center," *ABC News*, June 18, 2010, http://abcnews.go.com/WN/bp-oil-spill-ken-feinberg-promises-money-abc/story?id=10956385.

478   Seth Borenstein, "Gulf Oil Spill Commission Short On Technical Expertise," *HuffingtonPost*, June 21, 2010, http://www.huffingtonpost.com/2010/06/21/gulf-oil-spill-commission_n_618968.html.

479   "Obama Labor Chief: Illegals Have a Right to Fair Wages," *Fox News*, June 21, 2010, http://nation.foxnews.com/illegal-immigration/2010/06/21/obama-labor-chief-illegals-have-right-fair-wages.

480   "Kyl: Obama Won't Secure Border Until Lawmakers Move on Immigration Package," Fox News, June 21, 2010, http://www.foxnews.com/politics/2010/06/21/kyl-obama-wont-secure-border-lawmakers-immigration-package/.

481   "Survey: Individual health insurance Premiums Jump," *ABC News*, June 21, 2010, http://abcnews.go.com/Business/wireStory?id=10971283.

482   Alan Zibel, "Borrowers exit troubled Obama mortgage program," *Yahoo*, June 21, 2010, http://finance.yahoo.com/news/Borrowers-exit-troubled-Obama-apf-887634101.html?x=0&sec=topStories&pos=3&asset=&ccode.

483   Rainer Buergin, "Germany Rejects Obam's Call on Growth, Stoking G-20 Conflict," *Bloomberg*, June 21, 2010, http://www.bloomberg.com/news/2010-06-21/u-s-urgently-needs-to-reduce-deficit-economy-minister-bruederle-says.html.

484   "White House mocks BP CEO's yacht race, defends Obama golf," *Google*, June 21, 2009, http://www.google.com/hostednews/afp/article/ALeqM5hfQ62qTEIbRH__q_rUMpzykNDtkQ.

485   "White House mocks BP CEO's yacht race, defends Obama golf," *Google*, June 21, 2009, http://www.google.com/hostednews/afp/article/ALeqM5hfQ62qTEIbRH__q_rUMpzykNDtkQ.

486   Lori Montgomery, "Business leaders say Obama's economic policies stifle growth," *Washington Post*, June 23, 2010, http://www.washingtonpost.com/wp-dyn/content/article/2010/06/22/AR2010062205279.html.

487   Laurel Brubaker Calkins and Margaret Cronin Fisk, "Deepwater Drilling Ban Lifted by new Orleans Federal Judge," *Bloomberg*, June 22, 2010, http://www.bloomberg.com/

news/2010-06-22/u-s-deepwater-oil-drilling-ban-lifted-today-by-new-orleans-federal-judge.html.

488   Erica Werner, "Salazar seeks to reimpose drilling moratorium," *Breitbart*, June 22, 2010, http://www.breitbart.com/article.php?id=D9GGL7R06&show_article=1.

489   Brian Montopoli, "Poll: Most Say Obama Lacks Clear Plans on the Oil Spill, Energy or Jobs," *CBS News*, June 21, 2010, http://www.cbsnews.com/8301-503544_162-20008373-503544.html.

490   "How 1,300 prisoners got the home buyer tax credit," *The Week*, June 28, 2010, http://theweek.com/article/index/204502/how-1300-prisoners-got-the-home-buyer-tax-credit.

491   Fabiola Sanchez, "Venezuela seizes oil rigs owned by US company," *Seattle Times*, June 24, 2010, http://seattletimes.nwsource.com/html/businesstechnology/2012198337_apltvenezuelaoilrigs.htm.

492   Scott Wilson and Michael D. Shear, "Gen. McChrystal is dismissed as top U.S. commander in Afghanistan," *Washington Post*, June 23, 2010, http://www.washingtonpost.com/wp-dyn/content/article/2010/06/23/AR2010062300689_pf.html.

493   "Federal Gov't Halts Sand Berm Dredging," *WDSU.com*, June 22,2010, http://www.wdsu.com/news/23997498/detail.html.

494   Rowan Scarborough, "Obama at odds with Petraeus doctrine on 'Islam'," *Washington Times*, July 11, 2010, http://www.washingtontimes.com/news/2010/jul/11/obama-at-odds-with-petraeus-doctrine-on-islam/print/.

495   "Geithner says US can 'no longer drive global growth'," *BBC*, June 24, 2010, http://www.bbc.co.uk/news/10406463.

496   Stephanie Condon, "Biden: We Can't Recover All the Jobs Lost," *CBS News*, June 25, 2010, http://www.cbsnews.com/8301-503544_162-20008924-503544.html.

497   Adam Cassandra, "Napolitano: 'You're Never Going to Totally Seal That Border'," *CNS News*, June 25, 2010, http://cnsnews.com/news/article/68494.

498   "AZ Gov. slams Obama for posting warning signs in AZ and tells him to do his job." *YouTube*, June 25, 2010, http://www.youtube.com/watch?v=bzDlN7VLmXQ&feature=player_embedded.

499   Charlie Savage, "Closing Guantanamo Fades as a Priority," *New York Times*, June 26, 2010, http://www.nytimes.com/2010/06/26/us/politics/26gitmo.html?bl.

500   Damian Paletta, "U.S. Lawmakers Reach Accord on New Finance Rules," *Wall Street Journal*, June 25, 2010, http://online.wsj.com/article/SB10001424052748703615104575328020013164184.html?mod=WSJ_hpp_LEADNewsCollection.

501   "IRS says it wants its share of BP payments received by oil spill victims," *Al.com*, June 25, 2010, http://blog.al.com/live/2010/06/irs_says_it_wants_its_share_of.html.

502   "Milwaukee custard shop owner tells Biden to lower taxes…Biden says don't be a smart-ass," *YouTube*, June 26, 2010, http://www.youtube.com/watch?v=PQK2YchAnnM.

503   Caren Bohan, "Obama calls for bank tax as next step in reform," *Reuters*, June 26, 2010, http://www.reuters.com/article/idUSTRE65P0VP20100626.

504   Alexander Bolton, "Obama's golf game tees up image debate," *The Hill*, June 25, 2010, http://thehill.com/homenews/administration/105505-obamas-golf-game-tees-up-presidential-image-debate.

505   "Obama Calling 'Bluff' Of Those Complaining About 'Deficits And Debt'," *Real Clear Politics*, June 27, 2010, http://www.realclearpolitics.com/video/2010/06/27/obama_calling_bluff_of_those_complaining_about_debt_he_created.html.

506 Caren Bohan, "Obama says he's serious about tackling deficits," *Reuters*, June 28, 2010, http://www.reuters.com/article/idUSTRE65R0ON20100628.

507 "Medvedev: CIA warning on Iranian nukes 'troubling'," *Breitbart*, June 27, 2010, http://www.breitbart.com/article.php?id=CNG.340a18756652d27eb073ecb1cf345176.12 d1&show_article=1.

508 "Recovery means no 'undue' edge for nations: Obama," *New Media Blog*, June 27, 2010, http://www.newmediablog.com/2010/06/recovery-means-no-undue-edge-for-nations-obama/.

509 Howard Schneider and Scott Wilson, "President Obama urges G-20 nations to spend; they pledge to halve deficits," *Washington Post*, June 27, 2010, http://www.washingtonpost.com/wp-dyn/content/article/2010/06/27/AR2010062701754.html.

510 Robert Barnes and Dan Eggen, "Supreme Court affirms fundamental right t bear arms," *Washington Post*, June 28, 2010, http://www.washingtonpost.com/wp-dyn/content/article/2010/06/28/AR2010062802134_pf.html.

511 "With the Debate Over Arizona's Illegal Immigration Raging On, Why Isn't Obama Running to the Border?," *Fox News*, June 28, 2010, http://www.foxnews.com/on-air/on-the-record/transcript/debate-over-arizona039s-illegal-immigration-raging-why-isn039t-obama-running-border.

512 Ambrose Evans-Pritchard, "RBS tells clients to prepare for 'monster' money-printing by the Federal Reserve," *The Telegraph*, June 28, 2010, http://www.telegraph.co.uk/finance/comment/ambroseevans_pritchard/7857595/RBS-tells-clients-to-prepare-for-monster-money-printing-by-the-Federal-Reserve.html.

513 Timothy P. Carney, "Obama closes curtain on transparency," *Washington Examiner*, August 12, 2010, http://washingtonexaminer.com/node/468316.

514 Tom Hays and Pete Yost, "The Spy Next Door: Tri-Staters Charged as Russian Agents," *NBC New York*, June 28, 2010, http://www.nbcnewyork.com/news/local-beat/The-Spy-Next-Door-Tri-Staters-Charged-wiith-Espionage-for-Russia-97334329.html.

515 Dick Morris and Eileen McGann, "How Obama Bungled the Oil Spill: An Inside Story," Dickmorris.com, June 28, 2010, http://www.dickmorris.com/blog/how-obama-bungled-the-oil-spill-an-inside-story/.

516 Matthew Jaffe, "GOP Sen To Obama: You Can't Talk energy Bill Without Talking BP," *ABC News*, June 29, 2010, http://blogs.abcnews.com/thenote/2010/06/gop-sen-to-obama-you-cant-talk-energy-bill-without-talking-bp.html.

517 "US accepts international assistance for Gulf spill," *Yahoo*, June 29, 2010, http://finance.yahoo.com/news/US-accepts-international-apf-4104246595.html?x=0&.v=2.

518 Stephen Dinan, "U.S. marks 3rd-largest, single-day debt increase," *Washington Times*, July 7, 2010, http://www.washingtontimes.com/news/2010/jul/7/us-marks-3rd-largest-single-day-debt-boost/.

519 Ibid.

520 John Fritze, "National debt soars to highest level since WWII," *USA Today*, June 30, 2010, http://content.usatoday.com/communities/onpolitics/post/2010/06/national-debt-soars-to-highest-level-since-wwii/1.

521 "The Long-Term Budget Outlook," *Congressional Budget Office*, June 2010, http://www.cbo.gov/ftpdocs/115xx/doc11579/06-30-LTBO.pdf.

522 Ambrose Evans-Pritchard, "With the US trapped in depression, this really is starting to feel like 1932," *The Telegraph*, July 5, 2010,.

523   Lorraine Woellert, "Fannie Mae Seeks $1.5 Billion From U.S. Treasury After 12th Straight Loss," *Bloomberg*, August 5, 2010, http://www.bloomberg.com/news/2010-08-05/fannie-mae-seeks-1-5-billion-from-u-s-treasury-after-12th-straight-loss.html.

524   Jasmin Melvin, "US Postal Service loses $3.5 billion in third quarter," *Reuters*, August 5, 2010, http://www.reuters.com/article/idUSN0517225620100805.

525   Candice Zachariahs and Ron Harui, "China Favors Euro Over Dollar as Bernanke Alters Path," *Bloomberg*, August 15, 2010, http://www.bloomberg.com/news/2010-08-15/china-favors-euros-over-dollars-as-bernanke-shifts-course-on-fed-stimulus.html.

526   Nancy Benac and Calvin Woodward, "Obama's Terrible, Horrible, No Good, Very Bad Year," *CNS News*, December 21, 2010, http://www.cnsnews.com/news/article/obamas-terrible-horrible-no-good-very-ba.

527   "Unemployment Rate," *Portal Seven*, http://portalseven.com/employment/unemployment_rate.jsp.

528   Stephen Dinan, "Obama tries to put Republicans on immigration hot seat," *Washington Times*, July 1, 2010, http://www.washingtontimes.com/news/2010/jul/1/obama-tries-put-gop-immigration-hot-seat/.

529   "Obama: Being American is 'not a matter of blood or birth'," *New York Post*, July 1, 2010, http://www.nypost.com/p/news/national/obama_being_american_is_not_matter_GNtpkvIMqG8AEztZLtl0aK?CMP=OTC-rss&FEEDNAME.

530   Pia Malbran, "TSA to Block 'Controversial Opionion' on the Web," *CBS News*, July 6, 2010, http://www.cbsnews.com/8301-31727_162-20009642-10391695.html.

531   Paul Joseph Watson, "Dollar Plunges After UN Call To Ditch Greenback," *Prison Planet*, July 1, 2010, http://www.prisonplanet.com/dollar-plunges-after-un-call-to-ditch-greenback.html.

532   Julian Pecquet, "Health law risks turning away sick," *The Hill*, July 2, 2010, http://thehill.com/business-a-lobbying/106887-health-law-risks-turning-away-sick.

533   Paul H. Rubin, "Why Is the Gulf Cleanup So Slow?," *Wall Street Journal*, July 2, 2010, http://online.wsj.com/article/SB10001424052748703426004575339650877298556.html?mod=WSJ_hpp_sections_opinion.

534   David Fox, "General Petraeus in Afghanistan warns of tough mission," *Reuters*, July 3, 2010, http://www.reuters.com/article/idUSTRE6611PB20100703?feedType=RSS&feedName=worldNews&rpc=22&sp=true.

535   Tom Breen, "Giant oil skimmer being tested in Gulf of Mexico," Breitbart, July 3, 2010, http://www.breitbart.com/article.php?id=D9GNPEC00&show_article=1.

536   "US soldier linked to Iraq helicopter video leak charged," *BBC*, July 6, 2010, http://www.bbc.co.uk/news/10529110.

537   "Feds File Lawsuit Over Arizona Immigration Law," *Newsmax*, July 6, 2010, http://www.newsmax.com/InsideCover/US-Immigration-Enforcement-Lawsuit/2010/07/06/id/363883.

538   Robert Pear, "Obama to Bypass Senate to Name Health Official," *New York Times*, July 7, 2010, http://www.nytimes.com/2010/07/07/health/policy/07recess.html.

539   "Donald Berwick on Redistributing Wealth," *YouTube*, http://www.youtube.com/watch?v=r2Kevz_9lsw.

540   "Ex-Official Accuses Justice Department of Racial Bias in Black Panther Case," *Fox News*, July 6, 2010, http://www.foxnews.com/politics/2010/07/06/ex-official-accuses-justice-department-racial-bias-black-panther-case/.

541   Andrew Alexander, "Why the silence from The Post on Black Panther Party story?,"

Washington Post, July 18, 2010, http://www.washingtonpost.com/wp-dyn/content/article/2010/07/16/AR2010071604081.html.

542 Charles Levinson and Jay Solomon, "U.S., Israel to Burnish Ties," *Wall Street Journal*, July 5, 2010, http://online.wsj.com/article/SB10001424052748704535004575348353632023866.html?mod=WSJ_hpp_MIDDLENexttoWhatsNewsSecond.

543 Gena Somra and Mitra Mobasherat, "Son pleads for help as mother awaits stoning in Iran," *CNN*, July 6, 2010, http://www.cnn.com/2010/WORLD/meast/07/06/iran.stoning/index.html?section=cnn_latest.

544 Lara Setrakian, "Iran Launches Holy War on Haircuts," *ABC News*, July 6, 2010, http://abcnews.go.com/International/iran-launches-holy-war-haircuts/story?id=11095053.

545 Siobhan Gorman, "U.S. Plans Cyber Shield for Utilities, Companies," *Wall Street Journal*, July 7, 2010, http://online.wsj.com/article/SB10001424052748704545004575352983850463108.html?mod=WSJ_hpp_MIDDLETopStories.

546 Andrew C. McCarthy, "United States v. Arizona – How 'Bout United States v. Rhode Island?," National Review, July 7, 2010, http://www.nationalreview.com/corner/232909/united-states-v-arizona-how-bout-united-states-v-rhode-island-andrew-c-mccarthy.

547 *Estrada v. Rhode Island*, 594 F.3d 56 (2010), http://www.ca1.uscourts.gov/pdf.opinions/09-1149P-01A.pdf.

548 "Obama: Israelis suspicious of me because my middle name is Hussein," *Haaretz*, July 9, 2010, http://www.haaretz.com/news/diplomacy-defense/obama-israelis-suspicious-of-me-because-my-middle-name-is-hussein-1.300793.

549 Ron Claiborne, "Gulf Oil Spill" Latest Plan Lousiana Governor Bobby Jindal Supports DrawsCriticism From Federal Government and Scientists," *ABC News*, July 7, 2010, http://abcnews.go.com/WN/bp-oil-spill-louisiana-governor-bobby-jindal-plan/story?id=11111136.

550 www.marklevinshow.com.

551 "EU-US agree to share citizens bank data," *Breitbart*, July 8, 2010, http://www.breitbart.com/article.php?id=CNG.ec5c2bbd6ec1548e816faf716d5e53e6.521&show_article=1.

552 "Obama loses drilling moratorium appeal," *Breitbart*, July 8, 2010, http://www.breitbart.com/article.php?id=CNG.5812f97c10bdfbe8edaa2f9744f1bba2.41&show_article=1.

553 Dan Balz, "Obama's debt commission warns of fiscal 'cancer'," *Washington Post*, July 11, 2010, http://www.washingtonpost.com/wp-dyn/content/article/2010/07/11/AR2010071101956_pf.html.

554 Abby Goodnough, "Governors Voice Grave Concerns on Immigration," *New York Times*, July 12, 2010, http://www.nytimes.com/2010/07/12/us/politics/12governors.html.

555 Ambrose Evans-Pritchard, "Chinese rating agency strips Western nations AAA status," *The Telegraph*, July 12, 2010, http://www.telegraph.co.uk/finance/china-business/7886077/Chinese-rating-agency-strips-Western-nations-of-AAA-status.html.

556 Denis Dyomkin, "Russia says Iran close to nuclear weapons," *Reuters*, July 12, 2010, http://www.reuters.com/article/idUSWLA813120100712.

557 Jonathan Karl and Gregory Simmons, "Signs of the Stimulus," *ABC News*, July 14, 2010,

http://abcnews.go.com/Politics/signs-stimulus/story?id=11163180.

558   Gary Stoller, "Backlash grows vs. full-body scanners," *USA Today*, July 13, 2010, http://www.usatoday.com/printedition/news/20100713/1abodyscans13_st.art.htm.

559   "Obama Plans to Cut Up to 40 Percent of Nukes," *Fox News*, July 13, 2010, http://www.foxnews.com/politics/2010/07/13/obama-plans-cut-percent-nukes/.

560   Susan Jones, "Obama Administration Approves First direct Taxpayer Funding of Abortion Through New High-Risk Insurance Pools," *CNS News*, July 14, 2010, http://www.cnsnews.com/news/article/69384.

561   Michael Tenant, "ObamaCare Abortion Funding Has Begun," *The New American*, July 19, 2010, http://www.thenewamerican.com/index.php/usnews/health-care/4065-obamacare-abortion-funding-has-begun.

562   Matt Cover, "Obesity Rating for Every American Must Be Included in Stimulus-Mandated Electronic Health Records," *CNS News*, July 14, 2010, http://cnsnews.com/news/article/69436.

563   Stephen Dinan and Kara Rowland, "Justice: Sanctuary cities safe from law," *Washington Times*, July 14, 2010, http://www.washingtontimes.com/news/2010/jul/14/justice-sanctuary-cities-are-no-arizona/.

564   Patrice Hill, "Finance bill favors interests of unions, activists," *Washington Times*, July 14, 2010, http://www.washingtontimes.com/news/2010/jul/14/finance-bill-favors-interests-of-unions-activists/.

565   Luca di Deo, "Fed Gets More Power, Responsibility," *Wall Street Journal*, July 16, 2010, http://online.wsj.com/article/SB10001424052748703722804575369072934590574.html?mod=WSJ_hpp_MIDDLETopStories.

566   "Michelle Obama Visits Gulf In Beachwear," HuffingtonPost, July 13, 2010, http://www.huffingtonpost.com/2010/07/13/michelle-obama-visits-gul_n_643817.html#113354.

567   Campbell Robertson and Henry Fountain, "BP Says Oil Flow Has Stopped as Cap Is Tested," *New York Times*, July 15, 2010, http://www.nytimes.com/2010/07/16/us/16spill.html.

568   Kristi Keck, "Obama vacation brings rest, relaxation and rebuke," *CNN*, July 16, 2010, http://articles.cnn.com/2010-07-16/politics/obama.vacation_1_obama-vacation-camp-david-oil-disaster?_s=PM:POLITICS.

569   Ashish Kumar Sen and Bill Gertz, "Obama calls on China to restrain North Korea," "Clinton: Corruption isn't just Afghan problem," *MSNBC*, July 19, 2010, http://www.msnbc.msn.com/id/38304435/ns/world_news-south_and_central_asia.

570   Ewen MacAskill and Simon Tisdall, "White House shifts Afghanistan strategy towards talks with Taliban," *The Guardian*, July 19, 2010, http://www.guardian.co.uk/world/2010/jul/19/obama-afghanistan-strategy-taliban-negotiate.

571   John Hughes and Catherine Larkin, "TARP auditor criticizes Obama administration's push to close auto dealerships," *Washington Post*, July 19, 2010, http://www.washingtonpost.com/wp-dyn/content/article/2010/07/18/AR2010071802375.html.

572   Ashish Kumar Sen and Bill Gertz, "Obama calls on China to restrain North Korea," *Washington Times*, November 24, 2010, http://www.washingtontimes.com/news/2010/nov/24/us-sends-carrier-yellow-sea-exercises/.

573   "Forcing Ga. Official to Resign Over YouTube Clip was the Right Call, Agriculture Chief Says," *Fox News*, July 20, 2010, http://www.foxnews.com/politics/2010/07/20/ex-ag-official-says-video-showing-white-farmer-story-excludes-key-context/.

574 "Time to admit Obamanomics has failed," Washington Examiner, August 8, 2010, http://washingtonexaminer.com/opinion/time-admit-obamanomics-has-failed.

575 James Gattuso, "Senator Dodd's Regulation Plan: 14 Fatal Flaws," Heritage Foundation, April 22, 2010, http://www.heritage.org/research/reports/2010/04/senator-dodds-regulation-plan-14-fatal-flaws.

576 Mary Clare Jalonick, "E-mails: Vilsack hastily decided to oust Sherrod," Yahoo, July 21, 2010, http://news.yahoo.com/s/ap/us_usda_racism_resignation.

577 Rich Blake, "Gold Coin Sellers Angered by New Tax Law," ABC News, July 21, 2010, http://abcnews.go.com/Business/gold-coin-dealers-decry-tax-law/story?id=11211611.

578 Daniel Wagner, "Gov't watchdogs: mortgage program is not working," Yahoo, July 21, 2010, http://finance.yahoo.com/news/Govt-watchdogs-mortgage-apf-1527849934.html?x=0.

579 Jason Brown, "Thousands protest drilling moratorium at rally," The Advocate, July 21, 2010, http://www.2theadvocate.com/news/98937374.html.

580 Penny Starr, "White House Backs Bill to Collect Employee Pay Information fro Businesses," CNS News, July 22, 2010, http://cnsnews.com/news/article/69746.

581 Deborah Solomon, "Pay Czar to Blast Payments," Wall Street Journal, July 22, 2010, http://online.wsj.com/article/SB10001424052748704421304575383620582719174.html.

582 Mark Knoller, "Obama Changes Tune on Paying for Unemployment Benefits Extension," CBS News, July 22, 2010, http://www.cbsnews.com/8301-503544_162-20011420-503544.html.

583 "White House Predicts Record $1.47T Deficit," CBS News, July 23, 2010, http://www.cbsnews.com/stories/2010/07/23/business/main6706903.shtml.

584 "Obama Birthday Party in Chicago: $30,000 Donation To The DNC Reportedly Required For Admission," HuffingtonPost, July 23, 2010, http://www.huffingtonpost.com/2010/07/23/obama-birthday-party-in-c_n_656873.html.

585 Karen Mracek and Thomas Beaumont, "Goldman reveals where bailout cash went," USA Today, July 24, 2010, http://www.usatoday.com/money/industries/banking/2010-07-24-goldman-bailout-cash_N.htm.

586 "China may switch to currency basket for forex rate," MarketWatch, July 23, 2010, http://www.marketwatch.com/story/china-may-link-yuan-trade-to-currency-basket-2010-07-23.

587 Michael Isikoff, "WikiLeaks founder vows more leaks," MSNBC, July 30, 2010, http://www.msnbc.msn.com/id/38493475/ns/us_news-security/t/wikileaks-founder-vows-more-leaks/#.TnQ983Ps6Go.

588 Jason Allardyce and Tony Allen-Mills, "White House backed release of Lockerbie bomber Abdel Baset al-Megrahi," The Australian, July 26, 2010, http://www.theaustralian.com.au/news/world/white-house-backed-release-of-lockerbie-bomber-abdel-baset-al-megrahi/story-e6frg6so-1225896741041.

589 Doug Powers, "The Obamas Prove They Aren't Far Removed From What Most Americans are Going Through," MichelleMalkin.com, July 26, 2010, http://michellemalkin.com/2010/07/26/the-obamas-prove/.

590 "Expensive massages, top shelf vodka and five-star hotels: First Lady accused of spending $10m in public money on her vactions," The Daily Mail, August 25, 2011, http://www.dailymail.co.uk/news/article-2029615/Michelle-Obama-accused-spending-10m-public-money-vacations.html.

591   Lynn Sweet, "Obama family heading to Florida Gulf Coast, Martha's Vineyard for vacations," *Chicago Sun-Times*, July 26, 2010, http://blogs.suntimes.com/sweet/2010/07/obama_family_heading_to_florid.html.

592   Rachel Stevens, "SIGIR: Defense can't account for $8.7 billion," *Federal News Radio*, July 27, 2010, http://www.federalnewsradio.com/?sid=2012362&nid=35.

593   Aaron Mahta and John Solomon, "Haphazard Firefighting Might Have Sunk BP Oil Rig," *Center for Public Integrity*, July 28, 2010, http://www.publicintegrity.org/articles/entry/2286/

594   Dunstan Prial, "SEC Says New Financial Regulation Law Exempts it From Public Disclosure," *Fox News*, July 28, 2010, http://www.foxbusiness.com/markets/2010/07/28/sec-says-new-finreg-law-exempts-public-disclosure/?test=latestnews.

595   Nicholas Riccardi and Anna Gorman, "Federal judge blocks key parts of Arizona immigration law," *Los Angeles Times*, July 28, 2010, http://articles.latimes.com/2010/jul/28/nation/la-na-arizona-immigration-20100729.

596   Kevin Brady, "America's New Health Care System Revealed," *House of Representatives*, July 28, 2010, http://www.house.gov/apps/list/press/tx08_brady/pr_100728_hc_chart.html.

597   Stephen Dinan, "Memo outlines backdoor 'amnesty' plan," *Washington Times*, July 29, 2010, http://www.washingtontimes.com/news/2010/jul/29/memo-outlines-backdoor-amnesty-plan-for-obama/.

598   Ellen Nakashima, "White House proposal would ease FBI access to records of Internet activity," *Washington Post*, July 28, 2010, http://www.washingtonpost.com/wp-dyn/content/article/2010/07/28/AR2010072806141_pf.html.

599   Elizabeth Williamson, "Gibbs Takes on rush Limbaugh," *Wall Street Journal*, July 29, 2010, http://blogs.wsj.com/washwire/2010/07/29/gibbs-takes-on-rush-limbaugh/.

600   "Obama wants Rangel to end career with dignity," *CNN*, July 31, 2010, http://articles.cnn.com/2010-07-31/politics/obama.rangel_1_harlem-democrat-charlie-rangel-end-career?_s=PM:POLITICS.

601   Casey Stegllno, "Timing of National Guard's Deployment to Southwest Border Stirs Confusion, Anger," *Fox News*, July 31, 2010, http://www.foxnews.com/politics/2010/07/31/timing-national-guards-deployment-southwest-border-stirs-confusion-anger/.

602   Penny Starr, "Arizona Sheriff: 'Our Own Government Has Become Our Enemy,'" *CNS News*, August 1, 2010, http://www.cnsnews.com/news/article/70324.

603   Kevin Hassett, "Obamacare Only Looks Worse Upon Further Review," *Bloomberg*, August 2, 2010, http://www.bloomberg.com/news/2010-08-02/obamacare-only-looks-worse-upon-further-review-kevin-hassett.html.

604   Jacqueline Sit, "EPA to Crack Down on Farm Dust," *News 9*, August1, 2010, http://www.news9.com/Global/story.asp?S=12899662.

605   Jeff Bater and Darrell A. Hughes, "Deficit in July Totals $165.04 Billion," *Wall Street Journal*, August 11, 2010, http://online.wsj.com/article/SB10001424052748704901104575423601722830706.html.

606   Alan Bjerga, "Food Stamp Recipients at Record 41.8 Million Americans in July, U.S. Says," *Bloomberg*, October 5, 2010, http://www.bloomberg.com/news/2010-10-05/food-stamp-recipients-at-record-41-8-million-americans-in-july-u-s-says.html.

607   Nancy Benac and Calvin Woodward, "Obama's Terrible, Horrible, No Good, Very Bad Year," *CNS News*, December 21, 2010, http://www.cnsnews.com/news/article/obamas-terrible-horrible-no-good-very-ba.

608 "Unemployment Rate," *Portal Seven*, http://portalseven.com/employment/unemployment_rate.jsp.

609 Kate McCarthy and Rich McHugh, "Treasury Secretary Timothy Geithner: Unemployment Could Go Up Before It Comes Down," *ABC News*, August 3, 2010, http://abcnews.go.com/GMA/treasury-secretary-timothy-geithner-unemployment/story?id=11308157.

610 Jonathan Karl, Matthew Jaffe and Gregory Simmons, "Stimulus Slammed: Republican Senators Release Report Alleging Waste," *ABC News*, August 3, 2010, http://abcnews.go.com/GMA/summer-recovery-slammed-stimulus-waste-report-released/story?id=11309090.

611 John Irish and Daniel Flynn, "Pakistan's Zardari says war with Taliban being lost," *Reuters*, August 3, 2010, http://www.reuters.com/article/idUSTRE6721R820100803.

612 Tony Messenger, "Prop C passes overwhelmingly," *St. Louis Today*, August 3, 2009, http://www.stltoday.com/news/local/govt-and-politics/article_c847dc7c-564c-5c70-8d90-dfd25ae6de56.html.

613 Charles Hurt, "Sheriff Taylor's health pitch sparks cardiac arrest," *New York Post*, August 4, 2010, http://www.nypost.com/p/news/national/sheriff_taylor_health_pitch_sparks_IO4A3hqygAspuyCVuzzCNO.

614 Sheryl Gay Stolberg, "Obama's Playbook After Nov. 2," *New York Times*, October 24, 2010, http://www.nytimes.com/2010/10/25/us/politics/25agenda.html.

615 Declan McCullagh, "Feds admit storing checkpoint body scan images," *Cnet*, August 4, 2010, http://news.cnet.com/8301-31921_3-20012583-281.html.

616 "Me and my heavies: Michelle Obama goes walkabout in Marbella after 'racist' Spaniards gaff," *The Daily Mail*, August 5, 2010, http://www.dailymail.co.uk/news/worldnews/article-1300240/Michelle-Obama-goes-walkabout-Marbella-racist-Spaniards-gaff.html.

617 Caroline Black, "Feds Store Body Scans; US Marshals Saved 35,000 Images from Just One Courthouse," *CBS News*, August 5, 2010, http://www.cbsnews.com/8301-504083_162-20012785-504083.html.

618 T.W. Farnam, "GM donates $41,000 to lawmakers' pet projects," *Washington Post*, August 4, 2010, http://www.washingtonpost.com/wp-dyn/content/article/2010/08/04/AR2010080407086_pf.html.

619 Kirk Victor, "Romer to Leave White House," *National Journal*, August 5, 2010, http://hotlineoncall.nationaljournal.com/archives/2010/08/romer_to_leave.php.

620 "Me and my heavies: Michelle Obama goes walkabout in Marbella after 'racist' Spaniards gaff," *The Daily Mail*, August 5, 2010, http://www.dailymail.co.uk/news/worldnews/article-1300240/Michelle-Obama-goes-walkabout-Marbella-racist-Spaniards-gaff.html.

621 Andrea Tantaros, "Material girl Michelle Obama is a modern-day Marie Antoinette on a glitzy Spanish vacation," *New York Daily News*, August 4, 2010, http://www.nydailynews.com/opinions/2010/08/04/2010-08-04_material_girl_michelle_obama_is_a_modernday_marie_antoinette_on_a_glitzy_spanish.html

622 Sherry Jacobson, "Across Texas, 60,000 babies of noncitizens get U.S. birthright," *Dallas News*, August 8, 2010, http://www.dallasnews.com/sharedcontent/dws/dn/latestnews/stories/080810dnmetbabies.2be9a7e.html.

623 Peter Nicholas and Katherine Skiba, "Lavish Obama vacation in time of economic turmoil raises eyebrows," *Seattle Times*, August 7, 2010, http://seattletimes.nwsource.com/

html/nationworld/2012557439_mobama07.html.

624   Ross Colvin, "Obama attacks Bush policies in Bush's home state," *Reuters*, August 9, 2010, http://www.reuters.com/article/idUSN0910217920100809.

625   Ibid.

626   R.G. Ratcliffe, "Perry invites Obama to tour the border with him," *Houston Chronicle*, August 9, 2010, http://www.chron.com/news/houston-texas/article/Perry-invites-Obama-to-tour-the-border-with-him-1609206.php.

627   Corbett B. Daly, "Freddie Mac says needs $1.8 billion from taxpayers," *Reuters*, August 9, 2010, http://www.reuters.com/article/idUSTRE67826A20100809.

628   Scott Lanman, "Fed Looks to Spur Growth by Buying Government Debt," *Bloomberg*, August, 10, 2010, http://www.bloomberg.com/news/2010-08-10/fed-to-reinvest-principal-on-mortgage-proceeds-into-long-term-treasuries.html.

629   "Democrats, Advocacy Groups Blast Cuts to Food Stamps to Fund $26B Aid Bill," *Fox News*, August 11, 2010, http://www.foxnews.com/politics/2010/08/10/democrats-advocacy-groups-blast-cuts-food-stamps-fund-m-jobs/.

630   Martin Chulov, "Fears of al-Qaida return in Iraq as US-backed fighters defect," *The Guardian*, August 10, 2010, http://www.guardian.co.uk/world/2010/aug/10/al-qaida-sons-of-iraq.

631   Dennis Cauchon, "Federal workers earning double their private counterparts," *USA Today*, August 10, 2010, http://www.usatoday.com/money/economy/income/2010-08-10-1Afedpay10_ST_N.htm.

632   "Greg Gutfeld Wants to Build Gay Bar Next to 'Ground Zero' Mosque," *Fox News*, August 11, 2010, http://www.foxnews.com/story/0,2933,599202,00.html.

633   Luke Pachymuthu and Vladimir Soldatkin, "Russia's LUKOIL resumes gasoline supply to Iran-trade," *Reuters*, August 11, 2010, http://af.reuters.com/article/energyOilNews/idAFLDE67A17G20100811.

634   Mark Knoller, "How Many 'Top Priority' Issues Does Obama Have?," *CBS News*, August 13, 2010, http://www.cbsnews.com/8301-503544_162-20013622-503544.html.

635   Abby Phillip, "Obama defends ground zero mosque," *Politico*, August, 15, 2010, http://www.politico.com/news/stories/0810/41060.html.

636   Sheryl Gay Stolberg, "Obama Strongly Backs Islam Center Near 9/11 Site," *New York Times*, August 13, 2010, http://www.nytimes.com/2010/08/14/us/politics/14obama.html.

637   Alex Veiga, "Homes lost to foreclosure up 6 percent from last year," *KATU*, August 12, 2010, http://www.katu.com/news/business/100538829.html.

638   "Obama Declare gulf Coast 'Open for Business," *Newsmax*, August 15, 2010, http://www.newsmax.com/US/US-Obama/2010/08/15/id/367496.

639   Nick Allen and Andrew Hough, "US breast cancer drug decision 'marks start of death panels," *The Telegraph*, August 17, 2010, http://www.telegraph.co.uk/health/health-news/7948878/US-breast-cancer-drug-decision-marks-start-of-death-panels.html.

640   "Shutting Up Business," *Wall Street Journal*, October 10, 2010, http://online.wsj.com/article/SB10001424052748703735804575536370151720874.html.

641   Jonathan Stempel, "U.S. says bankruptcies reach nearly 5-year high," Reuters, August 17, 2010, ttp://www.reuters.com/article/2010/08/17/us-bankruptcies-idUS-TRE67G52420100817.

642   Bill Gertz, "China targets U.S. troops with arms buildup," *Washington Times*, August 16, 2010, http://www.washingtontimes.com/news/2010/aug/16/china-targets-us-

troops-with-arms-buildup/.

643 "Mosque Developer Rejects Moving to New Location," *NBC New York*, August 18, 2010, http://www.nbcnewyork.com/news/local-beat/Mosque-Developer-Says-No-Meeting-Scheduled-With-Gov-100967889.html.

644 Erin Einhorn, Adam Lisberg and Richard Sisk, "Ailing 9/11 responders slam President Obama," *New York Daily News*, August 18, 2010, http://www.nydailynews.com/ny_local/2010/08/18/2010-08-18_focus_on_zadroga_bill_bam_mosque_site_not_an_issue_911_heroes_fume.html.

645 Josh Rogin, "State Dept. sponsors trip for imam connected to N.Y. mosque project," *Washington Post*, August 19, 2010, http://www.washingtonpost.com/wp-dyn/content/article/2010/08/18/AR2010081805702.html.

646 Toby Harnden, "Obamas to begin sixth holiday of the year," *The Telegraph*, August 19, 2010, http://www.telegraph.co.uk/news/worldnews/northamerica/usa/barackobama/7952796/Obamas-to-begin-sixth-holiday-of-the-year.html.

647 "State Department Stands By Decision to Include Arizona in U.N. Human Rights Report," *Fox News*, August 30, 2010, http://www.foxnews.com/politics/2010/08/30/state-department-stands-decision-include-arizona-human-rights-report/.

648 Marcus Stern, "U.S. shifts approach to deporting illegal immigrants," *USA Today*, September 10, 2010, http://www.usatoday.com/news/washington/2010-09-10-immigration10_ST_N.htm.

649 Martin Crutsinger, "Nearly 50 percent leave Obama mortgage-aid program," *Breitbart*, August 20, 2010, http://www.breitbart.com/article.php?id=D9HNEND00&show_article=1.

650 James Sterngold, "ShoreBank of Chicago Said to Be Closed Today by FDIC," *Bloomberg*, August 20, 2010, http://www.bloomberg.com/news/2010-08-20/shorebank-of-chicago-said-to-be-closed-today-by-fdic.html.

651 Donna Goodison, "New Logan Searches Blasted," *Boston Herald*, August 21, 2010, http://bostonherald.com/business/general/view.bg?articleid=1276131.

652 Edith Honan and Chris Michaud, "Muslim center dispute sparks New York rallies," *Reuters*, August 22, 2010, http://www.reuters.com/article/idUSTRE67J45U20100822.

653 Thomas Catan, "Mosque Planner Says Opposition goes 'Beyond Islamophobia'," *Wall Street Journal*, August 23, 2010, http://online.wsj.com/article/SB10001424052748703589804575445671238186074.html?mod=WSJ_hpp_LEFTTopStories.

654 Jason Mattera, "Ground Zero Imam Says U.S. Worse than al-Qaeda," *Human Events*, August 23, 2010, http://www.humanevents.com/article.php?id=38673.

655 Sara Jerome, "Net-Neutrality group challenged by ties to MoveOn.Org, ACORN," *The Hill*, http://thehill.com/blogs/hillicon-valley/technology/115367-as-elections-near-net-neutrality-backers-challenged-by-moveonorg-and-acorn-ties.

656 Jake Tapper, "What Does a President Do on a Rainy Vacation Day?," *ABC News*, August 23, 2010, http://blogs.abcnews.com/politicalpunch/2010/08/what-does-a-president-do-on-a-rainy-vacation-day.html.

657 Andy Greenberg, "Full-Body Scan Technology Deployed In Street-Roving Vans," *Forbes*, August 24, 2010, http://blogs.forbes.com/andygreenberg/2010/08/24/full-body-scan-technology-deployed-in-street-roving-vans/.

658 Steve Watson, "Pre-Crime Technology To Be Used In Washington D.C.," *Prison Planet*, August 24, 2010, http://www.prisonplanet.com/pre-crime-technology-to-be-used-in-washington-d-c.html.

659   Eric Bland, "Software Predicts Criminal Behavior," *ABC News*, August 22, 2010, http://abcnews.go.com/Technology/software-predicts-criminal-behavior/story?id=11448231.

660   "U.S. Admits Human Rights Shortcomings in UN Report," *U.S. News*, August 24, 2010, http://www.usnews.com/news/articles/2010/08/24/us-admits-human-rights-shortcomings-in-un-report.html.

661   Susan Carroll, "Feds moving to dismiss some deportation cases," *Houston Chronicle*, August 24, 2010, http://www.chron.com/disp/story.mpl/special/immigration/7169978.html.

662   Mike Memoli, "Biden: 'we've seen this movie before," *Swamp Politics*, August 24, 2010, http://www.swamppolitics.com/news/politics/blog/2010/08/biden_weve_seen_this_movie_bef.html.

663   "US general: Afghan deadline 'giving enemy sustenance," *BBC*, August 24, 2010, http://www.bbc.co.uk/news/world-us-canada-11078966.

664   Peggy Venable, "Texas fights global-warming power grab," *Washington Times*, August 25, 2010, http://www.washingtontimes.com/news/2010/aug/25/texas-fights-global-warming-power-grab/?page=1.

665   Peter Finn, "Administration halts prosecution of alleged USS Cole bomber," *Washington Post*, August 26, 2010, http://www.washingtonpost.com/wp-dyn/content/article/2010/08/26/AR2010082606353.html?hpid=moreheadlines&sid=ST2010082700364.

666   Devin Dwyer, "Justice Department Gives Second Ultimatum in Sheriff Arpaio Investigation," *ABC News*, August 26, 2010, http://blogs.abcnews.com/politicalpunch/2010/08/justice-department-gives-second-ultimatum-in-sheriff-arpaio-investigation.html.

667   Mortimer B. Zuckerman, "The Most Fiscally Irresponsible Government in U.S. History," *U.S. News*, August 26, 2010, http://www.usnews.com/opinion/mzuckerman/articles/2010/08/26/the-most-fiscally-irresponsible-government-in-us-history.html.

668   "Brewer Condemns Report to UN Mentioning Ariz. Law," *Newsmax*, August 27, 2010, http://www.newsmax.com/InsideCover/US-Brewer-UN-Report/2010/08/27/id/368617.

669   "Shutting Up Business," *Wall Street Journal*, October 10, 2010, http://online.wsj.com/article/SB10001424052748703735804575536370151720874.html.

670   Joan Gralla, "Ground Zero Muslim center may get public financing," *Reuters*, August 27, 2010, http://www.reuters.com/article/idUSTRE67Q5BW20100827.

671   Steven Portnoy, "Sebelius: Time for 'Reeducation' on Obama Health Care Law," *ABC News*, August 30, 2010, http://blogs.abcnews.com/thenote/2010/08/sebelius-time-for-reeducation-on-obama-health-care-law.html.

672   Richard Wolf, "Record number in government anti-poverty programs," *USA Today*, August 30, 2010, http://www.usatoday.com/news/washington/2010-08-30-1Asafetynet30_ST_N.htm.

673   Donna Bowater, "Climate Change Likes Are Exposed," *The Daily Express*, August 31, 2010, http://www.dailyexpress.co.uk/posts/view/196642.

674   Helene Cooper and Sheryl Gay Stolberg, "Obama Declares an End to Combat Mission in Iraq," *New York Times*, August 31, 2010, http://www.nytimes.com/2010/09/01/world/01military.html.

675   Joseph Pisani, "Foreclosures Rise; Repossessions Set Record, *CNBC*, September 16, 2010, http://www.cnbc.com/id/39192246.

676 Nancy Benac and Calvin Woodward, "Obama's Terrible, Horrible, No Good, Very Bad Year," *CNS News*, December 21, 2010, http://www.cnsnews.com/news/article/obamas-terrible-horrible-no-good-very-bad-year.

677 "Unemployment Rate," *Portal Seven*, http://portalseven.com/employment/unemployment_rate.jsp.

678 Penny Starry, "Arizona Now Has 'Whopping 30' National Guard Troops and 15 Billboard Signs Warning Citizens About Drug Cartels Operating on Public Lands," *CNS News*, September 1, 2010, http://www.cnsnews.com/news/article/72068.

679 "Arpaio: Justice Dept. 'Sandbagged' Me With Lawsuit in civil Rights Probe," *Fox News*, September 2, 2010, http://www.foxnews.com/politics/2010/09/02/justice-dept-sues-arizona-sheriff-civil-rights-probe/

680 "Addicted to Stimulus: $50,000,000,000 More," *Teaparty.org*, September 6, 2010, http://www.teaparty.org/article.php?id=209.

681 Jackie Calmes, "Obama Is Against a Compromise on Bush Tax Cuts," *New York Times*, September 8, 2010, http://www.nytimes.com/2010/09/08/us/politics/08obama.html.

682 John Hughes, "Airport 'Naked Image' Scanners May Get Privacy Upgrades," *Bloomberg*, September 8, 2010, http://www.bloomberg.com/news/2010-09-08/airport-naked-image-scanners-in-u-s-may-get-avatars-to-increase-privacy.html.

683 Terence P. Jeffrey, "Obama Added More to National Debt in First 19 Months Than All Presidents from Washington Through Reagan Combined, Says Gov't Data," *CNS News*, September 8, 2010," http://cnsnews.com/news/article/72404.

684 Michael Barone, "Gangster Government Stifles Criticism of Obamacare," *Town Hall*, September 13, 2010, http://townhall.com/columnists/MichaelBarone/2010/09/13/gangster_government_stifles_criticism_of_obamacare/page/full/.

685 Ibid.

686 Huma Khan and Jake Tapper, "Obama Assails GOP on Economy, Addresses NYC Islamic Center," *ABC News*, September 10, 2010, http://abcnews.go.com/Politics/obama-tap-austan-goolsbee-chair-council-economic-advisers/story?id=11602792.

687 Joe Walker, Douglas Montero, Amber Sutherland and Kathianne Boniello, "Thousands rally for, against mosque on tragic day," *New York Post*, September 11, 2010, http://www.nypost.com/p/news/local/man_burns_koran_pages_near_ground_8s6OKcRfcnZ0Ztz9y07ZoL.

688 Thomas Frank, "Homeland Security to test iris scanners," *USA Today*, September 13, 2010, http://www.usatoday.com/tech/news/surveillance/2010-09-13-1Airis13_ST_N.htm.

689 Jake Tapper, "New Children's Book Coming from President Obama," *ABC News*, September 14, 2010, http://blogs.abcnews.com/politicalpunch/2010/09/new-childrens-book-coming-from-president-obama.html.

690 "Bank of America warns of new fees after financial reforms," *Breitbart*, September 14, 2010, http://www.breitbart.com/article.php?id=CNG.bb54d137200b27d4f18a20472252604a.10b1&show_article=1.

691 Paul Joseph Watson, "Big Sis To Get Expanded Role In Policing Internet," *InfoWars*, September 14, 2010, http://www.infowars.com/big-sis-to-get-expanded-role-in-policing-internet/.

692 Christina Wilkie, "Big party week for the Obamas," *The Hill*, September 12, 2010, http://thehill.com/capital-living/in-the-know/118269-big-party-week-for-the-obamas.

693   Carol Morello, "About 44 million in U.S. lived below poverty line in 2009, census data show," *Washington Post*, September 16, 2010, http://www.washingtonpost.com/wp-dyn/content/article/2010/09/16/AR2010091602698_pf.html.

694   "Employment generation disappointing: LA City Controller," *International Business Times*, September 17, 2010, http://www.ibtimes.com/articles/63228/20100917/american-recovery-and-reinvestment-act-arra-los-angeles-stimulus-wendy-greuel.htm.

695   "White House: Global Warming Out, 'Global Climate Disruption' In," *Fox News*, September 16, 2010, http://www.foxnews.com/politics/2010/09/16/white-house-global-warming-global-climate-disruption/.

696   Jim Forsyth, "Texas Sues to Block Bizarre "Global Warming" EPA Rules, lawsuit says science behind 'global warming' claims is junk, discredited," WOAI, September 16, 2010, http://radio.woai.com/cc-common/news/sections/newsarticle.html?feed=119078&article=7606198.

697   Christopher Weber, "Robert Gibbs Slams Forbes Magazine For Dinesh D'Souza Article on Obama," *Politics Daily*, September 16, 2010, ttp://www.politicsdaily.com/2010/09/16/robert-gibbs-slams-forbes-magazine-for-dinesh-dsouza-article-on/.

698   Ariana Eunjung Cha, "Elizabeth Warren appointed White House 'consumer czar,'" *Washington Post*, September 17, 2010, http://voices.washingtonpost.com/political-economy/2010/09/elizabeth_warren_to_be_appoint.html.

699   "Russia 'irresponsible' for selling arms to Syria: Israel," *Breitbart*, September 19, 2010, http://www.breitbart.com/article.php?id=CNG.90b888fcd24bdb525a830c3a5842ea8b.b51&show_article=1.

700   N.C. Aizenman, "Major health insurers to stop offering new child-only policies," *Washington Post*, September 20, 2010, http://www.washingtonpost.com/wp-dyn/content/article/2010/09/20/AR2010092006665.html.

701   Guy Chazan, "Well Is Sealed; Tale Isn't Over," *Wall Street Journal*, September 20, 2010, http://online.wsj.com/article/SB10001424052748704858304575497932631276978.html?mod=WSJ_hpp_LEFTTopStories.

702   Jeff Mason, "Hillary To Give U.N. $50 Bil of US Tax Dollars For Cooking Stoves," *KT Radio Network*, September 21, 2010, http://www.ktradionetwork.com/government/hillary-to-give-u-n-50-bil-of-us-tax-dollars-for-cooking-stoves/.

703   David Kravets, "Feds: Privacy Does Not Exist in 'Public Places,'" *Wired*, September 21, 2010, http://www.wired.com/threatlevel/2010/09/public-privacy/#ixzz10GwocAiu.

704   Michael Brush, "Why CEOs can't stand Obama," *Microsoft Network*, September 21, 2010, http://articles.moneycentral.msn.com/Investing/CompanyFocus/why-CEOs-cannot-stand-obama.aspx.

705   Hans Nichols, "Summers to Leave White House After Election," *Bloomberg*, September 21, 2010, http://www.bloomberg.com/news/2010-09-21/summers-may-leave-as-head-of-obama-s-national-economic-council-in-november.html.

706   Matthew Jaffe, "TARP Chief Stepping Down From Treasury Post," *ABC News*, September 22, 2010, http://blogs.abcnews.com/politicalpunch/2010/09/tarp-chief-stepping-down-from-treasury-post.html.

707   Peter Whoriskey, "GM must sell for $134 a share for U.S. to recover investment," *Washington Post*, September 22, 2010, http://www.washingtonpost.com/wp-dyn/content/article/2010/09/22/AR2010092205674.html

708   Mark S. Smith, "Obama heckled on AIDS, gay rights at fundraiser," *Seattle Times*, September 22, 2010, http://seattletimes.nwsource.com/html/nationworld/2012970132_

apusobamahecklers.html?syndication=rss.

709 "Remarks by the President to the United Nations General Assembly," *White House*, September 23, 2010, http://www.whitehouse.gov/the-press-office/2010/09/23/remarks-president-united-nations-general-assembly.

710 "US Walks out of Ahmadinejad UN Speech," *Newsmax*, September 24, 2010, http://www.newsmax.com/Newsfront/UNUNWorldSummit/2010/09/24/id/371388.

711 Avi Issacharoff, Natasha Mozgovaya, Shlomo Shamir and Barak Ravid, "Peace talks deadlocked as settlement freeze set to expire," *Haaretz*, September 26, 2010, http://www.haaretz.com/print-edition/news/peace-talks-deadlocked-as-settlement-freeze-set-to-expire-1.315697.

712 "Hundreds protest FBI raids on anti-war activists," *Fox News*, September 27, 2010, http://www.foxnews.com/us/2010/09/27/hundreds-protest-fbi-searches-anti-war-activists-minneapolis-chicago/.

713 "Russia, China celebrate completion of oil pipeline," *DrudgeReport*, September 27, 2010, www.drudgereport.com.

714 "Trade War: China imposes tariff on chicken," *DrudgeReport*, September 27, 2010, www.drudgereport.com.

715 "FBI investigates prominent labor leader Andy Stern," *DrudgeReport*, September 28, 2010, www.drudgereport.com.

716 "Shutting Up Business," *Wall Street Journal*, October 10, 2010, http://online.wsj.com/article/SB10001424052748703735804575536370151720874.html.

717 Steven Thomma, "As Muslim claim lingers, Obama talks up his faith in Jesus," *McClatchy*, September 28, 2010, http://www.mcclatchydc.com/2010/09/28/101294/obama-talks-up-his-faith-in-jesus.html.

718 David Lawder, "Government liabilities rose $2 trillion in FY 2010: Treasury," *Reuters*, December 21, 2010, http://www.reuters.com/article/idUSTRE6BK6WC20101221.

719 Sara Murray, "Food Stamp Rolls Continue to Rise," *Wall Street Journal*, December 8, 2010, http://blogs.wsj.com/economics/2010/12/08/food-stamp-rolls-continue-to-rise/.

720 Kevin Drawbaugh, "Economy still needs reinforcement: Geithner," *Reuters*, September 30, 2010, http://www.reuters.com/article/idUSTRE68T5ZZ20100930?feedType=RSS&feedName=politicsNews&rpc=22&sp=true.

721 Randy Dye, "The Couldn't even pass a budget," *Randy's Right*, September 30, 2010, http://randysright.wordpress.com/2010/09/30/they-couldnt-even-pass-a-budget-congress-punts-tough-choice-until-after-election/.

722 "Health reform to worsen doctor shortage: group," *Reuters*, September 30, 2010, http://www.reuters.com/article/idUSTRE68T67120100930.

723 "Pakistan doesn't reopen border despite US apology," *Pakistan Defence*, October 7, 2010, http://www.defence.pk/forums/pakistans-war/75647-pakistan-doesnt-reopen-border-despite-us-apology.html.

724 Nancy Benac and Calvin Woodward, "Obama's Terrible, Horrible, No Good, Very Bad Year," *CNS News*, December 21, 2010, http://www.cnsnews.com/news/article/obamas-terrible-horrible-no-good-very-bad-year.

725 "Unemployment Rate," *Portal Seven*, http://portalseven.com/employment/unemployment_rate.jsp.

726 Michael McAuliff, "Rahm Emanuel steps down as chief of staff; President Obama taps Pete Rouse to take over," *New York Daily News*, October 1, 2010, http://www.nydailynews.

com/news/politics/2010/10/01/2010-10-01_rahm_emanuel_steps_down_as_
chief_of_staff_president_obama_taps_pete_rouse_to_tak.html.

727   "Healthamburglar, McDonald's meets ObamaCare," *Wall Street Journal*, October 2, 2010, http://online.wsj.com/article/SB1000142405274870448300457552398046457
3518.html?mod=WSJ_hpp_sections_opinion.

728   Kevin Dolak, "Man Killed by Mexican Pirates on Texas Lake," *ABC News*, October 2, 2010, http://abcnews.go.com/US/mexican-pirates-shot-tourist-head/
story?id=11784598

729   Adam Entous, Julian E. Barnes and Siobhan Gorman, "CIA Escalates in Pakistan," *Wall Street Journal*, October 2, 2010, http://online.wsj.com/article/SB10001424052748704
029304575526270751096984.html?mod=WSJ_hpp_MIDDLENexttoWhatsNews-
Second.

730   "Defiant Chavez orders land takeover of British food giant," *Breitbart*, October 3, 2010, http://www.breitbart.com/article.php?id=CNG.649318c517e989a6cb277015a7fa7
2dd.12a1&show_article=1.

731   Ian James, "Chavez: Civilian militia should be armed full-time," *Washington Post*, October 3, 2010, http://www.washingtonpost.com/wp-dyn/content/article/2010/10/03/
AR2010100303313_pf.html.

732   Sebastian Abbot, "Troubled Pakistan faces ruling coalition collapse," *Yahoo*, October 3, 2010, http://news.yahoo.com/s/ap/as_pakistan.

733   "Biden Says He'll 'Strangle' Republicans," *Fox News*, October 6, 2010, http://www.foxnews.com/politics/2010/10/06/biden-says-hell-strangle-
republicans/?test=latestnews.

734   "Pelosi: Food Stamps and Unemployment Give 'Biggest Bang for Our Buck,'" *The Lonely Conservative*, October 7, 2010, http://lonelyconservative.com/2010/10/pelosi-food-
stamps-and-unemployment-give-biggest-bang-for-our-buck/.

735   Brian Bakst, "Gingrich brands Democrats 'party of food stamps,'" *Yahoo*, October 7, 2010, http://news.yahoo.com/s/ap/20101007/ap_on_el_ge/us_gingrich_food_
stamps.

736   Ed O'Keefe, "Treasury IG to review allegations against Austan Goolsbee," Washington Post, October 6, 2010, Washington Post, http://voices.washingtonpost.com/federal-
eye/2010/10/treasury_watchdog_to_probe_aus.html.

737   Gregory Korte, "$162 million in stimulus funds not disclosed," *USA Today*, October 6, 2010, http://www.usatoday.com/news/washington/2010-10-06-stimulus06_ST_N.
htm.

738   Stephen Power and Tennille Tracy, "Spill Panel Finds U.S. Was Slow to React," *Wall Street Journal*, October 7, 2010, http://online.wsj.com/article/SB100014240527487037
35804575536042567062622.html?mod=WSJ_hps_MIDDLETopStories.

739   Stephen Ohlemacher, "72,000 stimulus payments went to dead people," *Yahoo*, October 7, 2010, http://news.yahoo.com/s/ap/20101007/ap_on_go_ca_st_pe/us_stimu-
lus_checks_dead_people.

740   Drew Armstrong, "McDonald's, 29 other firms get health care coverage waivers," *USA Today*, October 7, 2010, http://www.usatoday.com/money/industries/health/2010-
10-07-healthlaw07_ST_N.htm?loc=interstitialskip.

741   "Shutting Up Business," *Wall Street Journal*, October 10, 2010, http://online.wsj.com/
article/SB10001424052748703735804575536370151720874.html.

742   Jim Geraghty, "A 'Casting Call' for Obama's MTV/BET/CMT Town Hall Meet-

ing," *National Review*, October 7, 2010, http://www.nationalreview.com/campaign-spot/249034/casting-call-obamas-mtvbetcmt-town-hall-meeting.

743   Timothy P. Carney, "Why is Obama putting a Fannie Mae/Goldman Sachs lobbyist/consultant as NSA?," *Washington Examiner*, October 14, 2010, http://washingtonexaminer.com/blogs/beltway-confidential/why-obama-putting-fannie-maegoldman-sachs-lobbyistconsultant-nsa.

744   Allison Bennett, "Dollar Falls Below 82 Yen for First Time Since 1995 After Cuts in Payrolls," *Bloomberg*, October 8, 2010, http://www.bloomberg.com/news/2010-10-08/dollar-falls-below-82-yen-for-first-time-since-1995-on-u-s-payroll-report.html.

745   Martin Crutsinger, "Geithner Urges Greater IMF Role in Currencies," *ABC News*, October 10, 2010, http://abcnews.go.com/Business/wireStory?id=11841591.

746   "Fed Undaunted by Uncertain Prospects for Money Printing," *Reuters*, October 11, 2010, http://www.foxbusiness.com/markets/2010/10/11/fed-undaunted-uncertain-prospects-money-printing/.

747   Fred Lucas, "Obama Administraton Gave General Electric – Parent Company of NBC – $24.9 Million in 'Stimulus' Grants," *CNS News*, October 12, 2010, http://cnsnews.com/news/article/obama-administration-gave-general-electr.

748   Michael D. Shear, "President Obama Looks Forward – and Back," *New York Times*, October 13, 2010, http://thecaucus.blogs.nytimes.com/2010/10/13/president-obama-looks-forward-and-back/.

749   Brian Montopoli, "Obama: 'Tribal Attitude' Surfaces in tough Times," *CBS News*, October, 14, 2010, http://www.cbsnews.com/8301-503544_162-20019673-503544.html.

750   Bassem Mroue and Lee Keath, "Ahmadinejad heads to border with Israel," *MyWay*, October 14, 2010, http://apnews.myway.com/article/20101014/D9IRD4000.html.

751   Bob Connors, "Health Care Reform Blamed for Huge Hike in Premiums," *NBC Connecticut*, October 21, 2010, http://www.nbcconnecticut.com/news/local-beat/Health-Care-Reform-Blamed-for-Huge-Hike-in-Premiums-105041674.html.

752   Stephen Ohlemacher, "Gov't: No increase for Social Security next year," *Yahoo*, October   15,   2010,   http://finance.yahoo.com/news/Govt-No-increase-for-Social-apf-2340203916.html?x=0&.v=9.

753   Kristina Cooke, "Bernanke sees case for more Federal Reserve easing," *Yahoo*, October   15,   2010,   http://finance.yahoo.com/news/Bernanke-sees-case-for-more-rb-4235164349.html?x=0.

754   Luke Harding, "Russia and Venezuela strike nuclear power station deal," *The Guardian*, October 15, 2010, http://www.guardian.co.uk/world/2010/oct/15/venezuela-nuclear-power-station-russia.

755   Doug Palmer, "U.S. backs off in currency dispute with China," *Reuters*, October 16, 2010, http://www.reuters.com/article/idUSTRE69E0OB20101016.

756   Susan Carroll, "Immigration cases being tossed by the hundreds, Docket review pulls curtain back on procedure by Homeland Security," *Houston Chronicle*, October 16, 2010, http://www.chron.com/disp/story.mpl/metropolitan/7249505.html.

757   Erica Werner, "Obama plays voters' psychatrist-in-chief on trail," *Yahoo*, October 26, 2010, http://news.yahoo.com/s/ap/20101026/ap_on_go_pr_wh/us_obama_angry_voters.

758   Karl Rove, "Obama's Incoherent Closing Argument," *Wall Street Journal*, October 21, 2010, http://online.wsj.com/article/SB10001424052702304741404575564383870852928.html?mod=WSJ_hpp_sections_opinion.

759   Mark Knoller, "National Debt Up $3 Trillion on Obama's Watch," *CBS News*, October 18, 2010, http://www.cbsnews.com/8301-503544_162-20019931-503544.html.

760   Ricardo Alonso-Zaldivar, "Citing health care law, Boeing pares employee plan," *Yahoo*, October 18, 2010, http://news.yahoo.com/s/ap/20101018/ap_on_bi_ge/us_health_costs_boeing.

761   Penny Starr, "Obama Strips the 'Creator' from Declaration of Independence – Again," *CNS News*, October 19, 2010, http://www.cnsnews.com/news/article/obama-strips-creator-declaration-independence-again.

762   "China halting key minerals to US," *Breitbart*, October 19, 2010, http://www.breitbart.com/article.php?id=CNG.6f626669dcc738e805f26ad8400c014c.51&show_article=1.

763   Christina Boyle, "Body scanners unveiled at JFK Airport; Homeland Security Sect. Janet Napolitano doesn't volunteer," *New York Daily News*, October 22, 2010, http://www.nydailynews.com/ny_local/2010/10/22/2010-10-22_body_scanners_unveiled_at_jfk_airport_homeland_security_sect_janet_napolitano_do.html.

764   Rhys Blakely, "Barack Obama may avoid Sikh temple on Asia visit over fears of being branded a Muslim," *The Australian*, October 20, 2010, http://www.theaustralian.com.au/news/world/barack-obama-may-avoid-sikh-temple-on-asia-visit-over-fears-of-being-branded-a-muslim/story-e6frg6so-1225941032704.

765   Byron York, " After news of Google tax dodges, Obama raises money with Google execs," October 21, 2010, http://washingtonexaminer.com/blogs/beltway-confidential/2010/10/after-news-google-tax-dodges-obama-raises-money-google-execs.

766   Jesse Drucker, "Google slashes overseas tax rate through 'Double Irish' and 'Dutch Sandwich' strategy," *Washington Post*, October 30, 2010, http://www.washingtonpost.com/wp-dyn/content/article/2010/10/30/AR2010103004613.html.

767   Damian Paletta and David Wessel, "Geithner's Goal: Rebalanced World Economy," *Wall Street Journal*, October 20, 2010, http://online.wsj.com/article/SB1000142405270 2304011604575564661615005500.html?mod=WSJ_hpp_LEFTWhatsNewsCollection.

768   Russell Goldman and Luis Martinez, " WikiLeaks: At Least 109,000 Killed During Iraq War," *ABC News*, October 22, 2010, http://abcnews.go.com/Politics/wikileaks-dumps-thousands-classified-military-documents/story?id=11949670.

769   Lesley Wroughton, "Analysis: IMF power shift opens way for more breakthroughs," *Reuters*, October 24, 2010, http://www.reuters.com/article/idUSTRE69N1WR20101024.

770   David Espo, "Obama assails GOP on clouded final campaign push," *Yahoo*, October 25, 2010, http://news.yahoo.com/s/ap/20101025/ap_on_el_pr/us_obama.

771   Deborah Levine and William I. Watts, "Dollar hits 15-year low vs. yen after G-20, Pledge to avoid competitive devaluation fails to halt slide," *Market Watch*, October 25, 2010, http://www.marketwatch.com/story/dollar-slips-after-g-20-disappoints-2010-10-25.

772   Alissa J. Rubin, "Karzai Rails Against America in Diatribe," *New York Times*, October 26, 2010, http://www.nytimes.com/2010/10/26/world/asia/26karzai.html.

773   "Chinese investment soars in Brazil, with eye on resources," *Breitbart*, October 25, 2010, http://www.breitbart.com/article.php?id=CNG.135bb89cab5c7dfce021f53c3 286a72b.6e1&show_article=1.

774   Nelson Acosta, "Cuba self-employed to pay taxes up to 50 percent," *Reuters*, October 25, 2010, http://www.reuters.com/article/idUSTRE69O45K20101025.

775   "Obama Admits That Midterms Are A Referendum On His Policies," *Say Anything*,

October 27, 2010, http://sayanythingblog.com/entry/obama-admits-that-midterms-are-a-referendum-on-his-policies/.

776 Ken Boehm, "FTC Drops Investigation of Google Less Than a Week After Company Exec Hosts Obama Fundraiser," *BigGovernment.com*, October 28, 2010, http://biggovernment.com/kboehm/2010/10/28/ftc-drops-investigation-of-google-less-than-a-week-after-company-execs-host-obama-fundraiser/.

777 Rick Klein, "Democrats Ask Pentagon for Info on Potential Obama Challengers," *ABC News*, October 27, 2010, http://abcnews.go.com/Politics/exclusive-democrats-pentagon-information-potential-obama-challengers/story?id=11985974.

778 Saurabh Shukla, "Obama's trip to be biggest ever," *India Today*, October 27, 2010, http://indiatoday.intoday.in/site/Story/117956/India/obamas-trip-to-be-biggest-ever.html.

779 Dan Elliott, "Napolitano: Military to Aid Civilian Cybersecurity," *ABC News*, October 28, 2010, http://abcnews.go.com/Technology/wireStory?id=11994801.

780 Barbara Surk and Lara Jakes, "Christian mourn after church siege kills 58, *Boston Globe*, November 1, 2010, http://www.boston.com/news/world/middleeast/articles/2010/11/01/baghdad_church_siege_ends_with_52_dead/.

781 Nancy Benac and Calvin Woodward, "Obama's terrible, horrible, no good, very bad year," *Real Clear Politics*, December 21, 2010, http://www.realclearpolitics.com/news/ap/politics/2010/Dec/21/obama_s_terrible__horrible__no_good__very_bad_year.html.

782 "Unemployment Rate," *Portal Seven*, http://portalseven.com/employment/unemployment_rate.jsp.

783 Steve Holland, "Obama seeks to blunt Republican attack over comment," *Reuters*, November 1, 2010, http://www.reuters.com/article/idUSTRE69929420101101.

784 Caroline Salas and Alex Tanzi, "Fed Will Probably Start $500 Billion of Bond Buys, Survey Shows," *Bloomberg*, November 1, 2010, http://www.bloomberg.com/news/2010-11-01/fed-likely-to-announce-500-billion-of-purchases-survey-shows.html.

785 "US to spend $200 mn a day on Obama's Mumbai visit," *NDTV*, November 3, 2010, http://www.ndtv.com/article/india/us-to-spend-200-mn-a-day-on-obama-s-mumbai-visit-64106.

786 Randall Smith and Sharon Terlep, "GM Could Be Free of Taxes for Years," *Wall Street Journal*, November 3, 2009, http://online.wsj.com/article/SB10001424052748704462704575590642149103202.html?mod=WSJ_hp_LEFTWhatsNewsCollection.

787 Ambrose Evans-Pritchard, "QE2 risks currency wars and the end of dollar hegemony," *The Telegraph*, November 1, 2010, http://www.telegraph.co.uk/finance/currency/8103462/QE2-risks-currency-wars-and-the-end-of-dollar-hegemony.html.

788 Jon Hilsenrath, "Fed Fires $600 Billion Stimulus Shot," *Wall Street Journal*, November 4, 2010, http://online.wsj.com/article/SB10001424052748703506904575592471354774194.html?mod=WSJ_hp_LEADNewsCollection.

789 Langi Chiang and Simon Rabinovitch, "U.S. dollar printing is huge risk – China c.bank adviser," *Reuters*, November 4, 2010, http://www.reuters.com/article/idUSTOE6A301Q20101104.

790 Steve Matthews and Timothy R. Human, ""Bernanke Defends Bond Purchases, Predicts Stronger Growth," *Bloomberg*, November 6, 2010, http://www.bloomberg.com/news/2010-11-06/bernanke-defends-fed-securities-purchases-says-growth-will-support-dollar.html.

791   Alan Beattie, Kevin Brown and Jennifer Hughes, "Backlash against Fed's $600bn easing," *Financial Times*, November 4, 2010, http://www.ft.com/intl/cms/s/0/981ca8f4-e83e-11df-8995-00144feab49a.html#axzz1YMcX2FRB.

792   Steve Matthews and Timothy R. Human, ""Bernanke Defends Bond Purchases, Predicts Stronger Growth," *Bloomberg*, November 6, 2010, http://www.bloomberg.com/news/2010-11-06/bernanke-defends-fed-securities-purchases-says-growth-will-support-dollar.html.

793   Ibid.

794   Alan Beattie, Geoff Dyer and Chris Giles, "China tees up G20 showdown with US," *Financial Times*, November 5, 2010, http://www.ft.com/cms/s/0/03567a28-e8a3-11df-a383-00144feab49a.html#axzz1AVfL3Xs4.

795   Ibid.

796   "Obama On '60 Minutes'" 'Leadership Isn't Just Legislation," *CBS New York*, November 5, 2010, http://newyork.cbslocal.com/2010/11/05/obama-acknowledges-failures-says-leadership-isnt-just-legislation/.

797   Ricardo Alonso-Zaldivar, "Citing health overhaul, AARP hikes employee costs," *Yahoo*, November 5, 2010, http://news.yahoo.com/s/ap/20101104/ap_on_bi_ge/us_aarp_health_plan.

798   "US to spend $200 mn a day on Obama's Mumbai visit," *NDTV*, November 3, 2010, http://www.ndtv.com/article/india/us-to-spend-200-mn-a-day-on-obama-s-mumbai-visit-64106.

799   "34 warships sent from US for Obama visit," *NDTV*, November 4, 2010, http://www.ndtv.com/article/india/34-warships-sent-from-us-for-obama-visit-64459.

800   Ibid.

801   "US to spend $200 mn a day on Obama's Mumbai visit," *NDTV*, November 3, 2010, http://www.ndtv.com/article/india/us-to-spend-200-mn-a-day-on-obama-s-mumbai-visit-64106.

802   Kevin Cullum, "Obama calls for compromise, won't budge on tax cuts," *The Hill*, November 6, 2010, http://thehill.com/homenews/administration/127983-obama-calls-for-compromise-wont-budge-on-tax-cuts.

803   Mort Zuckerman, "America's Love Affair With Obama Is Over," *U.S. News*, November 5, 2010, http://www.usnews.com/opinion/mzuckerman/articles/2010/11/05/mort-zuckerman-americas-love-affair-with-obama-is-over.html.

804   Jonathan Weisman, "Fed Global Backlash Grows," *Wall Street Journal*, November 7, 2010, http://online.wsj.com/article/SB10001424052748703514904575602820114533804.html?mod=WSJ_hp_LEFTTopStories.

805   Ibid.

806   John D. McKinnon, "Deficit Panel's Leaders Push Cuts," *Wall Street Journal*, November 8, 2010, http://online.wsj.com/article/SB10001424052748703805004575606643067587042.html?mod=WSJ_hp_LEFTWhatsNewsCollection.

807   "Obama to use teleprompter for Hindi speech," *Hindustan Times*, November 8, 2010, http://www.hindustantimes.com/Obama-to-use-teleprompter-for-Hindi-speech/H1-Article1-622605.aspx.

808   "Obama acknowledges decline of US dominance," *Times of India*, November 8, 2010, http://timesofindia.indiatimes.com/india/Obama-acknowledges-decline-of-US-dominance/articleshow/6885877.cms.

809   Patricia Zengerle and Krittivas Mukherjee, "Obama returns fire after China slams

Fed's move," *Reuters*, November 8, 2010, http://www.reuters.com/article/idUS-TOE6A706720101108.

810   Andrew Malcolm, "The VP meets on government transparency today. But that meeting is closed," *Los Angeles Times*, November 9, 2010, http://latimesblogs.latimes.com/washington/2010/11/joe-biden-transparency.html.

811   "Obama: Israel construction plans unhelpful," *Yahoo*, November, 9, 2010, http://news.yahoo.com/s/ap/20101109/ap_on_go_pr_wh/obama_israel.

812   Matt Phillips, "Chinese Credit Rater Downgrades U.S.," *Wall Street Journal*, November 9, 2010, http://blogs.wsj.com/marketbeat/2010/11/09/chinese-credit-rater-down-grades-us/.

813   Dennis Cauchon, "More federal workers' pay tops $150,000," *USA Today*, November 10, 2010, http://www.usatoday.com/news/nation/2010-11-10-1Afedpay10_ST_N.htm.

814   Christopher Sign, "Flight attendants union upset over new pat-down procedures," *ABC 15*, November 10, 2010, http://www.abc15.com/dpp/lifestyle/travel/flight-attendants-union-upset-over-new-pat-down-procedures.

815   Greg Stohr, "Obama Lawyers Back Military Gay Ban at Supreme Court," *Bloomberg*, November 10, 2010, http://www.bloomberg.com/news/2010-11-10/obama-lawyers-back-military-don-t-ask-don-t-tell-gay-ban-at-high-court.html.

816   Charles Hurt, "BAM AWOL on Vets Day," *New York Post*, November 11, 2010, http://www.nypost.com/p/news/national/bam_awol_on_vets_day_IxEoyioHbtjAsNjGmbZoIP#ixzz14yjr9zaE.

817   Dina Cappiello, "White House edits stain its reliance on science," *Yahoo*, November 10, 2010, http://news.yahoo.com/s/ap/20101110/ap_on_bi_ge/us_gulf_oil_spill.

818   Ibid.

819   Zhou Xin, "China lashes Fed easing as risk to global recovery," *Reuters*, November 11, 2010, http://www.reuters.com/article/idUSTOE6AA0BA20101111.

820   Carol E. Lee and John Maggs, "President Obama can't close deals at G-20 summit," *Politico*, November 11, 2010, http://www.politico.com/news/stories/1110/44989.html.

821   Paul Joseph Watson and Alex Jones, "Big Sis Forced To Respond To nationwide Revolt Against TSA," *InfoWars*, November 12, 2010, http://www.infowars.com/big-sis-forced-to-respond-to-nationwide-revolt-against-tsa/.

822   Jeremy Pelofsky, "Pilots and passengers rail at new airport patdowns," *Reuters*, November 11, 2010, http://www.reuters.com/article/idUSTRE6AA55S20101111.

823   Jonathan Martin, "Bobby Jindal hammers Barack Obama in new book," *Politico*, November 12, 2010, http://www.politico.com/news/stories/1110/45021.html.

824   Ricardo Alonso-Zaldivar, "Doctors brace for possible big Medicare pay cuts," *Yahoo*, November 13, 2010, http://news.yahoo.com/s/ap/20101113/ap_on_he_me/us_medicare_cuts.

825   "WH hands out 111 Obamacare waivers," *DrudgeReport*, November 14, 2010, www.drudgereport.com.

826   Jonathan Weisman, "Russian Arms Pact Faces New Obstacle," *Wall Street Journal*, November 16, 2010, http://online.wsj.com/article/SB100014240527487043125045756186660151287450.html?mod=WSJ_hp_MIDDLETopStories.

827   Paul Joseph Watson, "TSA Hit With Lawsuits As Revolt Explodes," *Prison Planet*, November 17, 2010, http://www.prisonplanet.com/tsa-hit-with-lawsuits-as-revolt-explodes.html.

828   "Big Sister's police state," *Washington Times*, November 16, 2010, http://www.washingtontimes.com/news/2010/nov/16/big-sisters-police-state/.

829   Eileen Sullivan, "Feds holding firm on intrusive airport security," *MyWay*, November 17, 2010, http://apnews.myway.com/article/20101117/D9JI6A0G0.html.

830   Jack Mirkinson, "Roger Ailes: Obama 'Has Different Belief System Than Most Americans'," *HuffingtonPost*, November 17, 2010, http://www.huffingtonpost.com/2010/11/17/ailes-obama-far-left-socialist_n_784670.html.

831   Ryan G. Murphy, "Sen. Rockefeller Suggests Eliminating FOX, MSNBC," *Radio Television Digital News Association*, November 18, 2010, http://www.rtdna.org/pages/posts/sen.-rockefeller-suggests-eliminating-fox-msnbc1143.php.

832   Clare Baldwin and Soyoung Kim, "GM IPO raises $20.1 billion," Reuters, November 17, 2010, http://www.reuters.com/article/2010/11/17/us-gm-ipo-idUSTRE6AB43H20101117.

833   Kim Hart, "Sources: FCC chief to move on net neutrality proposal," *Politico*, November 18, 2010, http://www.politico.com/news/stories/1110/45371.html.

834   "Critics: Obama Administration Pushed Largest Arms Deal in U.S. History While Congress In Recess," *Matzav*, November 20, 2010, http://matzav.com/critics-obama-administration-pushed-largest-arms-deal-in-us-history-while-congress-in-recess.

835   "Obama: Missile defence shield for all Nato members," *BBC*, November 19, 2010, http://www.bbc.co.uk/news/world-11711042.

836   "WTO chief warns against currency wars," *Breitbart*, November 19, 2010, http://www.breitbart.com/article.php?id=CNG.019256bfe6ccb3a315e27f0faf7bcd07.8b1&show_article=1.

837   Yuliya Chernova, "Union Drops Health Coverage for Workers' Children," *Wall Street Journal*, November 20, 2010, http://blogs.wsj.com/metropolis/2010/11/20/union-drops-health-coverage-for-workers-children/.

838   Foster Klug, "Scientist: NKorea has 'stunning' new nuke facility," *Yahoo*, November 21, 2010, http://news.yahoo.com/s/ap/20101121/ap_on_re_as/koreas_nuclear.

839   Byron York, "Obama panel probes stimulus waste – at Ritz Carlton," *Washington Examiner*, November 11, 2010, http://washingtonexaminer.com/blogs/beltway-confidential/2010/11/obama-panel-probes-stimulus-waste-ritz-carlton.

840   Angela Greiling Keane and Jeff Green, "Obama Bolsters U.S. Hybrid Automobile Sales in Waning Consumer Market," *Bloomberg*, November 22, 2010, http://www.bloomberg.com/news/2010-11-23/obama-bolsters-u-s-hybrid-auto-sales-in-waning-consumer-market.html.

841   Eileen Sullivan, "TSA: Some gov't officials to skip airport security," *MyWay*, November 23, 2010, http://apnews.myway.com/article/20101124/D9JM7I381.html.

842   P. Solomon Banda, "Full-body scanners popping up at courthouses," *Yahoo*, November 24, 2010, http://news.yahoo.com/s/ap/20101124/ap_on_re_us/us_courthouse_scanners.

843   Sam Kim, "N. Korea threatens additional attacks, accuses S. Korea of provocation," *Yonhap News*, November 23, 2010, http://english.yonhapnews.co.kr/news/2010/11/23/0200000000AEN20101123012800315.HTML.

844   Hyung-Jin Kim and Kwang-Tae Kim, "Tensions high as North, South Korea trade shelling," *Yahoo*, November 23, 2010, http://news.yahoo.com/s/ap/20101123/ap_on_re_as/as_koreas_clash.

845   Ben Smith, "IRS to Jewish group: 'Does your organization support the existence of the land of Israel?'," *Politico*, November 24, 2010, http://www.politico.com/blogs/ben-

smith/1110/IRS_to_Jewish_group_Does_your_organization_support_the_existence_of_the_land_of_Israel.html?showall.

846 Su Qiang and Li Xiaokun, "China, Russia quit dollar," *China Daily*, November 24, 2010, http://www.chinadaily.com.cn/china/2010-11/24/content_11599087.htm.

847 Ashish Kumar Sen and Bill Gertz, "Obama calls on China to restrain North Korea," *Washington Times*, November 24, 2010, http://www.washingtontimes.com/news/2010/nov/24/us-sends-carrier-yellow-sea-exercises/.

848 Nigel Duara and Tim Fought, "Defense, friends say Ore. Bomb plot suspect set up," *MyWay*, November 30, 2010, http://apnews.myway.com/article/20101130/D9JQC-MNG5.html.

849 Daniel Dombey and George Parker, "US tries to limit WikiLeaks damage," *Financial Times*, November 28, 2010, http://www.ft.com/cms/s/0/d2bc69f8-fb2c-11df-b576-00144feab49a.html#axzz1AVfL3Xs4.

850 Tom Raum, "Obama calls for 2-year freeze on federal pay," *Yahoo*, November 29, 2010, http://news.yahoo.com/s/ap/us_obama_pay_freeze.

851 Doug Powers, "UN Climate Summit Leader Prays to Mayan Moon Goddess," MichelleMalkin.com, December 3, 2010, http://michellemalkin.com/2010/12/03/un-climate-summit/.

852 "Unemployment Rate," *Portal Seven*, http://portalseven.com/employment/unemployment_rate.jsp.

853 Jeannine Aversa, "Fed ID's companies that used crisis aid programs," *Yahoo*, December 1, 2010, http://news.yahoo.com/s/ap/20101201/ap_on_bi_ge/us_fed_crisis_lending.

854 Caroline Salas and Matthew Leising, "Fed Withholds Collateral Data for $885 Billion in Financial-Crisis Loans," *Bloomberg*, December 1, 2010, http://www.bloomberg.com/news/2010-12-01/taxpayer-risk-impossible-to-know-for-some-fed-financial-crisis-programs.html.

855 Howard Portnoy, "Fed secretly bailed out GE, most commonly held stock by members of Congress," *Examiner*, December 3, 2010, http://www.examiner.com/libertarian-in-national/fed-secretly-bailed-out-ge-most-commonly-held-stock-by-members-of-congress.

856 Ed Henry, "Obama may delay Hawaiian vacation over tax fight," *CNN*, November 30, 2010, http://www.cnn.com/2010/POLITICS/11/30/obama.vacation.tax.cuts/index.html.

857 Luke Harding, "WikiLeaks cables condemn Russia as 'mafia state'," *The Guardian*, December 1, 2010, http://www.guardian.co.uk/world/2010/dec/01/wikileaks-cables-russia-mafia-kleptocracy.

858 "US Ready to Back Bigger EU Stability Fund: Official," *CNBC*, December 1, 2010, http://www.cnbc.com/id/40454469.

859 "Wave goodbye to Internet freedom," *Washington Times*, December 2, 2010, http://www.washingtontimes.com/news/2010/dec/2/wave-goodbye-to-internet-freedom/.

860 Susan Jones, "FCC Commissioner Wants to Test the 'Public Value' of Every Broadcast Station," CNS News, December 3, 2010, http://www.cnsnews.com/news/article/fcc-commissioner-wants-test-public-value.

861 Ryan Single, "Feds Warrantlessly Tracking Americans' Credit Cards in Real Time," *Wired*, December 2, 2010, http://www.wired.com/threatlevel/2010/12/realtime/.

862 "Government Reports Violations of Limits on Spying Aimed at U.S. Citizens," *Fox News*, December 4, 2010, http://nation.foxnews.com/fisa/2010/12/04/government-reports-violations-limits-spying-aimed-us-citizens.

863 Paul Joseph Watson, "CNN Reporter Put On Watch List After Criticizing TSA," *Prison Planet*, December 3, 2010, http://www.prisonplanet.com/cnn-reporter-put-on-watch-list-after-criticizing-tsa.html.

864 Damian Carrington, "WikiLeaks cables reveal how US manipulated climate accord," *The Guardian*, December 3, 2010, http://www.guardian.co.uk/environment/2010/dec/03/wikileaks-us-manipulated-climate-accord.

865 Josh Rogin, "Cat and mouse: Iranian foreign minister shakes hands with senior U.S. official...but dodges Hillary Clinton," *Foreign Policy*, December 4, 2010, http://thecable.foreignpolicy.com/posts/2010/12/04/iranian_foreign_minister_shakes_hands_with_senior_us_official_but_dodges_hillary_cl.

866 "During Surprise Trip to Afghanistan, Obama Thanks U.S. Troops for Their Service," *Fox News*, December 3, 2012, http://www.foxnews.com/politics/2010/12/03/obama-makes-surprise-visit-troops-afghanistan/.

867 Stephen Dinan, "Senate blocks Obama's tax plan," *Washington Times*, December 4, 2010, http://www.washingtontimes.com/news/2010/dec/4/senate-blocks-obamas-tax-plan/

868 Shane D'Aprile, "Gingrich: Leaks show Obama administration 'shallow,' 'amateurish'," *The Hill*, December 5, 2010, http://thehill.com/blogs/blog-briefing-room/news/132037-gingrich-blames-obama-on-wikileaks-labels-assange-a-terrorist.

869 Jonathan Weisman, John D. McKinnon and Janet Hook, "Deal Struck on Tax Package," *Wall Street Journal*, December 7, 2010, http://online.wsj.com/article/SB10001424052748704156304576003441518282986.html?mod=WSJ_hp_LEFTWhatsNewsCollection.

870 "1984 Arrives in America," *InfoWars*, December 6, 2010, http://www.infowars.com/big-sis-invades-wal-mart-if-you-see-something-say-something/.

871 Stephen Losey, "Federal pay freeze plan wouldn't stop raises," *Federal Times*, December 6, 2010, http://www.federaltimes.com/article/20101206/BENEFITS01/12060301/1001.

872 Sara A. Carter, "Catch-and-release of Taliban fighters in Afghanistan angers troops," *Washington Examiner*, December 6, 2010, http://washingtonexaminer.com/news/world/2010/12/catch-and-release-taliban-fighters-afghanistan-angers-troops.

873 "Obama calls GOP hostage takers over tax cut compromise," *Real Clear Politics*, December 7, 2010, http://www.realclearpolitics.com/video/2010/12/07/obama_calls_the_gop_hostage_takers_over_tax_cut_compromise.html.

874 Steve Holland and Patricia Zengerle, "Testy Obama fires back at Democrats over tax deal," *Reuters*, December 7, 2010, http://www.reuters.com/article/idUSTRE6B31Z020101207.

875 Jaimie Dupree, "More Health Waivers," *Atlanta Journal-Constitution*, December 7, 2010, http://blogs.ajc.com/jamie-dupree-washington-insider/2010/12/07/more-health-waivers/.

876 Thomas Joscelyn, "Gitmo Recidivism Rate Soars," *Weekly Standard*, December 7, 2010, http://www.weeklystandard.com/blogs/gitmo-recidivism-rate-soars_521965.html.

877 Stephen Dinan, "House acts to block closing of Gitmo," *Washington Times*, December 8, 2010, http://www.washingtontimes.com/news/2010/dec/8/congress-deals-death-

blow-gitmo-closure/.

878 "Obama Ditches Tax Cut Presser, Bill Clinton Takes Control," *Real Clear Politics*, December 10, 2012, http://www.realclearpolitics.com/video/2010/12/10/obama_ditches_tax_cut_presser_after_bill_clinton_takes_control.html.

879 Ben Feller, "Bill's Back: Clinton commands stage at White House," *Yahoo*, December 10, 2010, http://finance.yahoo.com/news/Bills-Back-Clinton-commands-apf-4065249916.html?x=0.

880 Kytja Weir, "Metro to start random bag searches," *Washington Examiner*, December 16, 2010, http://washingtonexaminer.com/local/dc/2010/12/metro-start-random-bag-searches.

881 Juan Forero, "Venezuela acquires 1,800 antiaircraft missiles from Russia," *Washington Post*, December 11, 2010, http://www.washingtonpost.com/wp-dyn/content/article/2010/12/11/AR2010121102586.html.

882 Tom Skchoenberg, and Margaret Cronin Fisk, "Obama's Health-Care Law Ruled Unconstitutional Over Insurance Requirement," *Bloomberg*, December 13, 2010, http://www.bloomberg.com/news/2010-12-13/u-s-health-care-law-requirement-thrown-out-by-judge.html.

883 "Moody's May Cut US Rating on Tax Package," *CNBC*, December 13, 2009, http://www.cnbc.com/id/40641123.

884 David Jackson, "Obama vows to fight Republicans – next year," *USA Today*, December 13, 2010, http://content.usatoday.com/communities/theoval/post/2010/12/obama-vows-to-fight-republicans----next-year/1.

885 Hyung-Jin Kim, "NKorea threatens SKorea with nuclear war," *MyWay*, December 13, 2010, http://apnews.myway.com/article/20101213/D9K2VUKO0.html.

886 David Rogers, "Democrats' budget bill: $1.1. trillion; 1,900 pages," *Politico*, December 14, 2010, http://www.politico.com/news/stories/1210/46383.html.

887 Fabiola Sanchez, "Chavez seeks power to rule by decree for 1 year," *Yahoo*, December 14, 2010, http://news.yahoo.com/s/ap/20101214/ap_on_re_la_am_ca/lt_venezuela_chavez.

888 Alexander Bolton, "Senate plans weekend work to ratify START, pass spending bill," *The Hill*, December 15, 2010, http://thehill.com/homenews/senate/133763-after-passing-tax-deal-senate-looks-to-take-up-start-treaty.

889 "IRS audits jump by 11 percent; wealthiest targeted," *Yahoo*, December 15, 2010, http://finance.yahoo.com/news/IRS-audits-jump-by-11-percent-apf-557157715.html?x=0&.v=4.

890 Yaakov Katz, "Stuxnet virus set back Iran's nuclear program by 2 years," *Jerusalem Post*, December 15, 2010, http://www.jpost.com/IranianThreat/News/Article.aspx?id=199475.

891 Stephen Ohlemacher, "13M get unexpected tax bill from Obama tax credit," *ABC News*, December 16, 2010, http://abcnews.go.com/Politics/wireStory?id=12413198.

892 "Big Sis Miss: Secret tests at LAX, O'Hare, Newark show TSZ screeners overlook guns, bombs," *DrudgeReport*, December 16, 2010, www.drudgereport.com.

893 "Flashback: Obama promised 5-day, public review of bills before signing; signs tax bill within hours of house vote," *DrudgeReport*, December 16, 2010, www.drudgereport.com.

894 J. Brady Howell, "Napolitano Says DHS to Begin Battling Climate Change as Homeland Security Issue," *CNS News*, December 17, 2010, http://cnsnews.com/news/article/napolitano-says-dhs-begin-battling-clima.

895　Frank Jack Daniel, "Venezuela assembly gives Chavez decree powers," *Reuters*, December 17, 2010, http://www.reuters.com/article/idUSN1729156220101217.

896　"Govt 'creating vast domestic snooping machine'," *Breitbart*, December 20, 2010, http://www.breitbart.com/article.php?id=CNG.35fe9afbf5c0253f885080ba82e978 4c.781&show_article=1.

897　Dana Priest and William M. Arkin, "Monitoring America," *Washington Post*, December 20, 2010, http://projects.washingtonpost.com/top-secret-america/articles/monitoring-america/?hpid=topnews.

898　Robert M. McDowell, "The FCC's Threat to Internet Freedom," *Wall Street Journal*, December 19, 2010, http://online.wsj.com/article/SB10001424052748703395204576 023452250748540.html.

899　"12 arrested over suspected U.K. terrorism plot," *MSNBC*, December 20, 2010, http://www.msnbc.msn.com/id/40746655/ns/world_news-europe/#.TnTU9XPs6Go.

900　Wesley Pruden, "Nothing neutral abut this unholy scheme," *Washington Times*, December 20, 2010, http://www.washingtontimes.com/news/2010/dec/20/nothing-neutral-about-this-unholy-scheme/.

901　Jasmin Melvin, "Divided US FCC adopts Internet traffic rules," *Reuters*, December 21, 2010, http://www.reuters.com/article/idUSTRE6BK5X320101221.

902　Mark Tapscott, "DeMint vows to reverse FCC's 'Internet takeover'," *Washington Examiner*, December 21, 2010, http://washingtonexaminer.com/blogs/beltway-confidential/2010/12/demint-vows-reverse-fccs-internet-takeover.

903　Jack Cloherty and Pierre Thomas, "Holder Warns of Threat Within: 'Radical' Citizens," *Prison Planet*, December 21, 2010, http://www.prisonplanet.com/holder-warns-of-threat-within-radical-citizens.html.

904　Malia Zimmerman, "32 states borrow billions from feds to cover unemployment benefits," *Mangod*, December 21, 2010, http://mangod-mangod.blogspot.com/2010/12/32-states-borrow-billions-from-feds-to.html.

905　Jake Tapper, "After Early Administration Denials, Director of National Intelligence Admits He Hadn't Been Briefed on Alleged Terrorist Arrests in London," *ABC News*, December 22, 2010, http://blogs.abcnews.com/politicalpunch/2010/12/after-early-administration-denials-director-of-national-intelligence-admits-he-hadnt-been-briefed-on.html.

906　"Obama pledges economic focus during next 2 years," *Yahoo*, December 22, 2010, http://news.yahoo.com/s/ap/20101222/ap_on_bi_ge/us_obama_economy.

907　Daniel Wagner, "More people fell out of Obama mortgage-aid program," *Breitbart*, December 22, 2010, http://www.breitbart.com/article.php?id=D9K939S01&show_article=1.

908　George Warren, "Sacramento-area pilot punished for YouTube video," *News 10*, December 22, 2010, http://www.news10.net/news/article.aspx?storyid=113529&provider=top&catid=188.

909　"Obama extends vacation until Tuesday," *Breitbart*, December 30, 2010, http://www.breitbart.com/article.php?id=CNG.894f9613dde7faf0e564d8d311b3922e.131&show_article=1.

910　Jack Kim and Sylvia Westall, "North Korea warns of 'sacred war' in standoff with South," *Yahoo*, December 23, 2010, http://news.yahoo.com/s/nm/20101223/wl_nm/us_korea_north.

911　Ben Feller, "Obama toasts 'season of progress' after big wins," *Yahoo*, December 23,

2010, http://news.yahoo.com/s/ap/20101223/ap_on_bi_ge/us_obama.

912 David Gordon Smith, "Barack Obama Was the Biggest Loser of 2010," *Spiegel*, December 23, 2010, http://www.spiegel.de/international/world/0,1518,736320,00.html.

913 "Vice Admiral: Obama was outmaneuvered by Russians on START," *U.S. Naval Institute*, December 23, 2010, http://www.usni.org/vice-admiral-obama-was-outmaneuvered-russians-start.

914 "Nuclear treaty 'goes easy on Russia," *Breitbart*, December 26, 2010, http://www.breitbart.com/article.php?id=CNG.cdc63f449543115516a6ee1f2c569704.171&show_article=1.

915 "EPA moving unilaterally to limit greenhouse gases," *Google*, December 24, 2010, http://www.google.com/hostednews/ap/article/ALeqM5gRb2CA1DnQdPvlWmI-5ADfjTz-lTw?docId=328b30b21ef54b97a51fdacdcbeb06dc.

916 "US to step up security at hotels and malls," *Breitbart*, December 26, 2010, http://www.breitbart.com/article.php?id=CNG.cdc63f449543115516a6ee1f2c569704.4f1&show_article=1.

917 Daniel Estrin, "Israeli foreign minister: peace is 'impossible," *Yahoo*, December 26, 2010, http://news.yahoo.com/s/ap/20101226/ap_on_re_mi_ea/ml_israel_palestinians.

918 Karin Tanabe, "Obama Is Glad Eagles Signed Michael Vick," *Politico*, December 27, 2010, http://www.politico.com/click/stories/1012/obama_is_glad_eagles_signed_vick.html.

919 Terence P. Jeffrey, "111th Congress Added More Debt Than First 100 Congresses Combined: $10,429 Per Person in U.S," *CNS News*, December 27, 2010, http://www.cnsnews.com/news/article/111th-congress-added-more-debt-first-100.

920 "Chris Matthews: Why Doesn't Obama Just Release The Birth Certificate?," *Real Clear Politics*, December 27, 2010, http://www.realclearpolitics.com/video/2010/12/27/chris_matthews_why_doesnt_obama_just_release_the_birth_certificate.html.

921 Kathrin Hille, "Chinese missile shifts power in Pacific," *Financial Times*, December 28, 2010, http://www.ft.com/cms/s/0/3e69c85a-1264-11e0-b4c8-00144feabdc0.html#axzz1ApkczLtp.

922 Kimberly Schwandt, "White House Plans to Push Global Warming Policy, GOP Vows Fight," *Fox News*, December 29, 2010, http://www.foxnews.com/politics/2010/12/28/white-house-plans-push-global-warming-policy-gop-vows-fight/.

923 Patrick Gavin, "Barack Obama Golfs A Lot, PGA Producer Says," *Politico*, December 29, 2010, http://www.politico.com/click/stories/1012/pga_producer_obama_golfs_a_lot.html.

924 Matthew Lee, "US, Venezuela evict ambassadors in diplomatic spat," *CNS News*, December 30, 2010, http://www.cnsnews.com/news/article/us-venezuela-evict-each-other-s-ambassadors-diplomatic-spat.

925 "Chavez, Clinton chat at Brazil inauguration," *Breitbart*, January 1, 2011, http://www.breitbart.com/article.php?id=CNG.99e856a0fb5a9fea7bf35be7ef15b71d.e61&show_article=1.

926 Peter Foster, "China preparing for armed conflict 'in every direction," *The Telegraph*, December 29, 2010, http://www.telegraph.co.uk/news/worldnews/asia/china/8229789/China-preparing-for-armed-conflict-in-every-direction.html.

927 Hilary Leila Krieger, "Republicans blast Obama for posting new Syrian envoy," *Jerusalem Post*, December 30, 2010, http://www.jpost.com/International/Article.

aspx?id=201497.

928   Daryl Huff, "TV Crew Covering President Claims Mistreatment," *KITV*, December 31, 2010, http://www.kitv.com/news/26327764/detail.html.

929   "Egypt bomb kills 21 at Alexandria Coptic church," *BBC*, January 1, 2011, http://www.bbc.co.uk/news/world-middle-east-12101748.

930   Sara Murray, "Bankruptcy Filings Leapt 9% Last Year," *Wall Street Journal*, January 4, 2011, http://online.wsj.com/article/SB100014240527487041115045760601816311440482.html?mod=WSJ_hp_LEFTWhatsNewsCollection.

931   Mark Knoller, "Obama's 2010: By the Numbers," *CBS News*, December 31, 2010, http://www.cb

2011

1   Sharyl Attkisson, "Medicare Bound to Bust as First Boomers Hit 65," *CBS News*, December 30, 2010, http://www.cbsnews.com/stories/2010/12/30/eveningnews/main7199116.shtml.

2   Aislinn Laing, "Ivory Coast president refuses phone call from Barack Obama," *The Telegraph*, December 30, 2010, http://www.telegraph.co.uk/news/worldnews/africaandindianocean/cotedivoire/8232288/Ivory-Coast-president-refuses-phone-call-from-Barack-Obama.html.

3   William McQuillen, "Goolsbee Says Failure to Raise U.S. Debt Ceiling Would Be 'Catastrophic," *Bloomberg*, January 2, 2011, http://www.bloomberg.com/news/2011-01-02/goolsbee-says-failure-to-raise-u-s-debt-ceiling-would-be-catastrophic-.html.

4   Mike Levine, "Napolitano: Israeli-Style Security Won't Work for U.S.," *Fox News*, January 4, 2011, http://www.foxnews.com/politics/2011/01/04/napolitano-israeli-style-security-wont-work/?test=latestnews.

5   "H.R. 2: Repealing the Job-Killing Health Care Law Act," *Govtrack.us*, http://www.govtrack.us/congress/bill.xpd?bill=h112-2.

6   Jasmin Melvin, "FCC challenges app makers to protect open Internet," *Reuters*, January 5, 2011, http://www.reuters.com/article/2011/01/05/fcc-internet-competition-idUSN0528374520110105.

7   Tony Capaccio, "China's Ballistic-Missile, Stealth-Fighter Advances Draw Attention of U.S.," *Bloomberg*, January 5, 2011, http://www.bloomberg.com/news/2011-01-05/china-s-ballistic-missile-stealth-fighter-advances-draw-attention-of-u-s-.html.

8   Samuel Shen and Jason Subler, "World Bank taps offshore yuan bond market for first time," *Yahoo*, January 5, 2011, http://ph.news.yahoo.com/rtrs/20110105/tbs-worldbank-yuan-bond-7318940.html.

9   "US Treasury asks Congress to lift debt ceiling," *Breitbart*, January 6, 2011, http://www.breitbart.com/article.php?id=CNG.24aed2d4393365e0c8062dcc2cd184cf.791&show_article=1.

10   "Jobless Claims Jump, Wholesale Food Costs Surge," CNBC, January 13, 2001, http://www.cnbc.com/id/41055028.

11   Craig Whitlock, "Pentagon to cut spending by $78 billion, reduce troop strength," *Washington Post*, January 7, 2011, http://www.washingtonpost.com/wp-dyn/content/article/2011/01/06/AR2011010603628.html.

12   Adam Entous and Julian E. Barnes, "U.S. Boosts Afghan Surge," *Wall Street Journal*, January 6, 2011, http://online.wsj.com/article/SB10001424052748703675904576066

4021086613148.html?mod=WSJ_hp_LEFTTopStories.

13 "'We're digging ourselves out of a hole': Obama upbeat as jobless rate falls to lowest level for 19 months," *The Daily Mail*, January 7, 2011, http://www.dailymail.co.uk/news/article-1345047/Glimmer-hope-U-S-economy-jobless-rate-falls-lowest-level-19-months.html.

14 Declan McCullagh, "Obama eyeing Internet ID for Americans," *CBS News*, January 7, 2011, http://www.cbsnews.com/8301-501465_162-20027837-501465.html.

15 "Sarkozy: Mideast Christians victims of 'cleansing'," *Middle East Online*, January 7, 2011, http://www.middle-east-online.com/english/?id=43513.

16 "China Backs Europe, Euro for Investment, Central Bank Deputy Governor Says," *Bloomberg*, January 7, 2011, http://www.bloomberg.com/news/2011-01-07/china-will-put-currency-reserves-into-europe-euro-central-bank-s-yi-says.html.

17 Byron York, "Journalists urged caution after Ft. Hood, no race to blame Palin after Arizona shootings," *Washington Examiner*, January 9, 2011, http://washingtonexaminer.com/blogs/beltway-confidential/2011/01/journalists-urged-caution-after-ft-hood-now-race-blame-palin-afte.

18 Jeffrey Heller, "U.S. criticizes Israel over Jerusalem settlement," *Reuters*, January 9, 2011, http://www.reuters.com/article/idUSTRE70834K20110109.

19 "US concerned over China's rapid development of new weapons," *The Guardian*, January 9, 2011, http://www.guardian.co.uk/world/2011/jan/09/china-us-gates-new-weapons.

20 Julie Appleby, "Feds to decide what benefits health insurers must cover," *McClatchy*, January 10, 2011, http://www.mcclatchydc.com/2011/01/10/106515/feds-to-decide-what-benefits-health.html.

21 Sarah Netter, "Arizona Sheriff Blasts Rush Limbaugh for Spewing 'Irresponsible' Vitriol," *ABC News*, January 10, 2011, http://abcnews.go.com/Politics/arizona-sheriff-blasts-rush-limbaugh-spewing-irresponsible-vitriol/story?id=12583285.

22 Bill Gertz, "China spurns strategic security talks with U.S.," *Washington Times*, January 10, 2011, http://www.washingtontimes.com/news/2011/jan/10/china-spurns-strategic-security-talks-with-us/.

23 Graham Bowley, "The Fed's QE2 Traders, Buying Bonds by the Billions," *CNBC*, January 11, 2011, http://www.cnbc.com/id/41019109.

24 Cindy Perman, "Housing Market Slips Into Depression Territory," *CNBC*, January 11, 2011, http://www.cnbc.com/id/41019790.

25 Tim Shipman, "France is our biggest ally, declares Obama: President's blow to Special Relationship with Britain," *Daily Mail*, January 11, 2011, http://www.dailymail.co.uk/news/article-1346006/Barack-Obama-declares-France-biggest-ally-blow-Special-Relationship-Britain.html.

26 Elisabeth Bumiller and David E. Sanger, "Gates Warnes of North Korea Missile Threat to U.S.," *New York Times*, January 11, 2011, http://www.nytimes.com/2011/01/12/world/asia/12military.html?_r=2&hp.

27 Jonathan Weisman and Laura Meckler, "Obama Begins Greaing Up Re-Election Bid," *Wall Street Journal*, January 12, 2011, http://online.wsj.com/article/SB1000142405274870379190457607615046970565 0.html?mod=WSJ_hp_MIDDLENexttoWhatsNewsTop.

28 "Hong Kong ranked world's freest economy: report," *The China Post*, January 13,

2011, http://www.chinapost.com.tw/business/asia/hong-kong/2011/01/13/287500/
Hong-Kong.htm.

29   Michael Birnbaum, "E.U. seeks to expand bailout fund to calm markets," *Washington Post*, January 12, 2011, http://www.washingtonpost.com/wp-dyn/content/article/2011/01/12/AR2011011205973.html.

30   "Biden arrives in Baghdad 'to celebrate,'" *Breitbart*, January 13, 2011, http://www.breitbart.com/article.php?id=CNG.4a0cfc22213226686d07c51e14f8109f.4f1&show_article=1.

31   "Baghdad violence kills three, wounds 14," *Breitbart*, January 13, 2009, http://www.breitbart.com/article.php?id=CNG.2ae8d10289d05e80ecb077f1af8fa46d.701&show_article=1.

32   Zeina Karam, "Government fall plunges Lebanon into uncertainty," *MyWay*, January 13, 2011, http://apnews.myway.com/article/20110113/D9KNEDMO0.html.

33   David D. Kirkpatrick, "Behind Tunisia Unrest, Rage Over Wealth of Ruling Family," *New York Times*, January 13, 2011, http://www.nytimes.com/2011/01/14/world/africa/14tunisia.html?_r=1&hp.

34   Mark Gongloff, Mark Brown and Nathalie Boschat, "S&P, Moody's Warn On U.S. Credit Rating," *Wall Street Journal*, January 14, 2011, http://online.wsj.com/article/SB10001424052748703583404576079311379009904.html?mod=WSJ_hp_LEFTWhatsNewsCollection.

35   Michael Cooper and Mary Williams Walsh, "U.S. Bills States $1.3 Billion in Interest Amid Tight Budgets," *New York Times*, January 14, 2011, http://www.nytimes.com/2011/01/15/us/politics/15stimulus.html?hp.

36   Adriana Gomez, "Mexican gunman fires across border toward U.S. highway workers," *El Paso Times*, January 14, 2010, http://www.elpasotimes.com/ci_17087113?source=most_viewed.

37   Steve Gutterman, "Russia declares option to withdraw from START treaty if feels threatened by West," *Prison Planet*, January 14, 2011, http://www.prisonplanet.com/russia-declares-option-to-withdraw-from-start-treaty-if-feels-threatened-by-west.html.

38   Lesley Clark, "Obama to ease travel restrictions to Cuba, allow more U.S. cash to island," *Miami Herald*, January 14, 2011, http://www.miamiherald.com/2011/01/14/2016622/obama-to-ease-travel-restrictions.html.

39   Tom Raum, "US debt passes $14 trillion, Congress weighs caps," *InlandPolitics.com*, January 15, 2011, http://inlandpolitics.com/blog/2011/01/15/yahoofinance-apus-debt-passes-14-trillion-congress-weighs-caps/.

40   Huma Khan, "Homeland Security Axes bush-Era 'Virtual Fence' Project," *ABC News*, January 14, 2011, http://blogs.abcnews.com/thenote/2011/01/homeland-security-axes-bush-era-virtual-fence-project.html.

41   "Prime minister takes over as Ben Ali flees Tunisian turmoil," *France 24*, January 15, 2011, http://www.france24.com/en/20110114-tunisia-prime-minister-assumes-power-amid-reports-president-ben-ali-has-left.

42   "Hu calls currency system 'product of the past,'" *Breitbart*, January 16, 2011, http://www.breitbart.com/article.php?id=CNG.9964072691a62252d0a98b0308fb8063.281&show_article=1.

43   "Venezuela Says Oil Reserves Surpass Saudi Arabia's," *CNBC*, January 16, 2011, http://www.cnbc.com/id/41101601.

44   Elaine Ganley and Bouazza Ben Bouazza, "More Tunisia unrest: Presidential palace gunbattle," *MyWay*, January 16, 2011, http://apnews.myway.com/article/20110116/D9KPL3I80.html.

45   Meredith Jessup, "Detroit May Close Half Of Its Schools To Pay For Union Benefits," *The Blaze*, January 17, 2011, http://www.theblaze.com/stories/detroit-may-close-half-of-its-schools-to-pay-for-union-benefits/.

46   Daniel Strauss, "Cheney: Obama has learned that Bush policies were right," *The Hill*, January 17, 2011, http://thehill.com/blogs/blog-briefing-room/news/138341-cheney-obama-has-learned-from-experience-that-bush-moves-were-necessary.

47   Nicholas Johnston and Hans Nichols, "Hu Gets Full State Honors as Visit Displays Obama's Dueling Views of China," *Bloomberg*, January 18, 2011, http://www.bloomberg.com/news/2011-01-18/hu-gets-full-state-honors-as-visit-displays-obama-s-dueling-views-of-china.html.

48   "Obama Wants to Shed Rules That Hurt Job Growth," *CNBC*, January 18, 2011, (http://www.cnbc.com/id/41131176.

49   Nicole Bullock, "States Warned of $2 Trillion Pensions Shortfall," *CNBC*, January 18, 2011, http://www.cnbc.com/id/41129099.

50   Emma Rowley, "World needs $100 trillion more credit, says World Economic Forum," *The Telegraph*, January 18, 2011, http://www.telegraph.co.uk/finance/financetopics/davos/8267768/World-needs-100-trillion-more-credit-says-World-Economic-Forum.html.

51   Jason Millman, "Number of healthcare reform law waivers climbs above 1,000," *The Hill*, March 6, 2011, http://thehill.com/blogs/healthwatch/health-reform-implementation/147715-number-of-healthcare-reform-law-waivers-climbs-above-1000.

52   "Failed Bank List," *FDIC*, http://www.fdic.gov/bank/individual/failed/banklist.html.

53   "Roll Call: HR 2 'Repealing the Job-Killing [ObamaCare] Health Care Law Act' Passes House," *Ironic Surrealism*, January 19, 2011, http://ironicsurrealism.blogivists.com/2011/01/19/roll-call-hr-2-repealing-the-job-killing-health-care-law-act-passes-house/.

54   Maggie Michael, "Arab League chief says Tunisia is dire warning," *MyWay*, January 19, 2011, http://apnews.myway.com/article/20110119/D9KRCORG1.html.

55   Matthew Pennington and Jim Kuhnhenn, "Obama, Hu spar over human rights, hail econ ties," *The China Post*, January 21, 2011, http://www.chinapost.com.tw/international/americas/2011/01/21/288460/Obama-Hu.htm.

56   Stephanie Condon, "Obama: 'We Welcome China's Rise'," *CBS News*, January 19, 2011, http://www.cbsnews.com/8301-503544_162-20028958-503544.html.

INDEX

Akihito – 11/14/09

Alabama – 3/23/10, 6/13/10

Al-Assad, Bashar – 5/24/10

Al-Awlaki, Anwar – 11/9/09, 11/10/09

Alexander, Lamar – 6/29/10

Allen, Adm. Thad – 6/19/10

Al-Megrahi, Abdelbaset (Lockerbie bomber) – 8/12/09, 8/20/09, 9/6/09, 7/26/10

Al-Nashiri, Abd al-Rahim – 8/26/10

Al Qaeda – 6/3/09, 6/22/09, 8/11/09, 11/9/09, 12/25/09, 12/26/09, 12/27/09, 1/2/10, 1/3/10, 1/7/10, 4/6/10, 4/12/10, 5/26/10, 6/24/10, 8/10/10, 8/22/10

American Exceptionalism – 4/4/09

AmeriCorps – 4/21/09, 6/10/09

Amtrak – 7/13/09

Argentina – 2/24/10

Arizona – 2/9/09, 10/10/09, 12/12/09, 3/19/10, 4/14/10, 4/23/10, 4/24/10, 4/27/10, 4/30/10, 5/9/10, 5/13/10, 5/17/10, 5/18/10, 5/19/10, 5/20/10, 5/27/10, 6/3/10, 6/5/10, 6/8/10, 6/16/10, 6/17/10, 6/19/10, 6/25/10, 7/1/10, 7/6/10, 7/11/10, 7/28/10, 7/31/10, 8/24/10, 8/27/10, 9/1/10

Army Corps of Engineers – 5/30/10, 6/5/10

Arpaio, Sheriff Joe – 10/10/09, 12/12/09, 8/26/10, 9/1/10

Axelrod, David – 4/19/09, 7/14/09, 8/15/09, 10/18/09, 3/14/10, 3/15/10, 10/17/10

Ayers, William – 5/31/10

Babeu, Sheriff Paul – 6/17/10, 7/31/10

Backdoor Amnesty – 7/29/10, 8/20/10, 8/24/10, 10/16/10

Castro, Fidel - 1/21/09, 6/2/09, 6/28/09, 3/25/10

Raul Castro – 8/1/09

Caterpillar, Inc. – 2/11/09, 2/12/09, 3/19/10

Census – 4/30/09, 9/11/09, 1/4/10, 6/1/10, 9/16/10

Center for American Progress – 6/14/10

Chafee, Lincoln – 10/25/10

Chavez, Hugo - 3/4/09, 4/18/09, 6/2/09, 6/28/09, 8/1/09, 9/5/09, 9/23/09, 11/2/09,
      11/8/09, 12/7/09, 3/31/10, 5/9/10, 10/3/10, 10/15/10, 12/14/10, 12/17/10,
      12/20/10, 12/29/10

Checci, Vincent – 1/4/10, 1/31/10

Cheney, Dick - 3/16/09, 3/22/09, 4/20/09, 5/10/09, 5/21/09, 10/22/09, 12/1/09, 12/30/09,
      1/17/11

Cheng Siwei – 9/7/09

China - 1/29/09, 2/20/09, 3/4/09, 3/11/09, 3/12/09, 3/13/09, 3/14/09, 3/15/09, 3/23/09,
      3/25/09, 3/30/09, 4/1/09, 4/6/09, 4/7/09, 4/12/09, 4/21/09, 4/26/09, 4/30/09,
      5/14/09, 5/18/09, 5/26/09, 5/27/09, 5/31/09, 6/2/09, 6/8/09, 6/16/09, 6/17/09,
      7/28/09, 9/7/09, 9/11/09, 9/12/09, 9/13/09, 9/17/09, 9/29/09, 10/5/09, 11/12/09,
      11/14/09, 11/15/09, 11/16/09, 11/19/09, 12/18/09, 1/29/10, 2/3/10, 2/5/10,
      2/9/10, 2/19/10, 2/28/10, 3/4/10, 3/12/10, 3/15/10, 3/21/10, 4/18/10, 5/14/10,
      5/17/10, 5/24/10, 6/2/10, 6/8/10, 6/19/10, 6/30/10, 7/19/10, 7/23/10, 8/11/10,
      8/17/10, 9/27/10, 10/9/10, 10/15/10, 10/19/10, 10/24/10, 10/25/10, 11/3/10,
      11/4/10, 11/8/10, 11/11/10, 11/24/10, 12/28/10, 12/30/10, 1/5/11, 1/7/11,
      1/9/11, 1/10/11, 1/16/11, 1/17/11, 1/19/11

Christmas – 12/4/09, 12/13/09, 12/24/09

Chrysler - 2/16/09, 2/17/09, 3/21/09, 3/30/09, 4/7/09, 4/10/09, 4/28/09, 4/29/09, 4/30/09,

Dunn, Anita – 6/5/09, 10/11/09, 10/15/09, 10/18/09, 11/14/09

Dupnik, Sheriff Clarence – 1/10/11

Durham, John – 8/24/09

Earth Day – 4/22/09

Edmunds – 10/29/09

Education - 3/10/09, 7/23/09, 8/27/09, 9/3/09, 9/8/09, 6/7/10

Eisen, Norm – 6/28/10

Elizabeth II, Queen – 4/1/09

Elmendorf, Doug – 7/16/09, 7/21/09

Emanuel, Rahm – 4/12/09, 4/19/09, 6/25/09, 7/22/09, 10/18/09, 1/26/10, 3/8/10, 5/28/10, 10/1/10

Emmer, Tom – 8/17/10

Environment - 2/4/09, 2/5/09, 2/18/09, 2/20/09, 3/3/09, 3/4/09, 3/23/09, 4/2/09, 4/17/09, 5/19/09, 6/23/09, 6/28/09, 7/8/09, 7/15/09, 7/20/09, 9/25/09, 10/3/09, 11/5/09, 11/20/09, 11/24/09, 11/25/09, 12/2/09, 12/3/09, 12/7/09, 12/8/09, 12/9/09, 12/17/09, 12/18/09, 1/8/10, 1/20/10, 1/30/10, 2/1/10, 2/12/10, 2/14/10, 4/3/10, 6/29/10, 8/25/10, 8/31/10, 9/16/10, 11/22/10, 11/29/10, 12/17/10, 12/24/10, 12/29/10

Environmental Protection Agency (EPA) - 2/18/09, 4/17/09, 12/7/09, 12/8/09, 4/16/10, 4/29/10, 5/13/10, 5/20/10, 7/2/10, 7/31/10, 8/25/10, 9/16/10, 12/24/10, 12/29/10

Evans, Jodie – 5/31/10

Falkland Islands – 2/24/10

Fannie Mae - 1/26/09, 3/18/09, 6/24/09, 8/6/09, 12/31/09, 2/27/10, 6/13/10, 6/30/10,

7/21/10, 12/1/10

FBI – 5/30/09, 12/25/09

FDIC – 1/30/09, 3/2/09, 2/23/10,

Federal Communications Commission (FCC) – 9/21/09, 4/6/10, 4/27/10, 5/6/10, 5/9/10, 6/16/10, 6/17/10, 11/17/10, 11/18/10, 12/2/10, 12/20/10, 12/21/10, 12/28/10, 1/5/11

Federal Reserve - 3/18/09, 3/19/09, 4/10/09, 4/29/09, 5/8/09, 5/27/09, 6/3/09, 7/15/09, 8/2/09, 8/24/09, 8/25/09, 9/7/09, 9/18/09, 9/21/09, 9/24/09, 11/20/09, 11/29/09, 1/28/10, 2/18/10, 6/28/10, 6/30/10, 7/14/10, 7/21/10, 8/10/10, 10/11/10, 10/15/10, 11/1/10, 11/3/10, 11/4/10, 11/7/10, 11/9/10, 11/11/10, 12/1/10, 1/11/11

Federal Trade Commission (FTC) – 4/27/10, 5/24/10, 6/10/10, 10/27/10

Feinberg, Kenneth – 6/10/09, 10/22/09, 12/11/09, 6/19/10, 7/22/10

Feinberg, Robert – 7/27/09

Feith, Douglas – 6/24/10

Financial Regulation and Reform – 3/24/09, 3/26/09, 4/1/09, 4/2/09, 4/3/09, 5/12/09, 6/16/09, 9/18/09, 9/19/09, 9/25/09, 4/16/10, 4/21/10, 5/5/10, 5/25/10, 6/25/10, 6/26/10, 7/8/10, 7/14/10, 7/21/10, 7/28/10, 9/14/10

Fish and Wildlife Service – 4/27/10, 6/5/10, 6/17/10

Fisher, Richard – 5/27/09

Florida – 12/24/09, 3/23/10, 4/30/10

Flynn, Gen. Michael – 1/10/10

Food and Drug Administration (FDA) – 5/12/09, 7/20/09, 4/3/10

Food Stamps – 8/6/09, 5/31/10, 7/31/10, 8/10/10, 8/30/10, 9/30/10, 10/6/10

Ford Motors – 6/23/09, 11/22/10

Ft. Hood – 11/5/09, 11/6/09, 1/15/10

Foster, Richard – 3/20/10

FOX – 4/29/09, 5/9/09, 6/16/09, 8/16/09, 9/18/09, 10/6/09, 10/11/09, 10/18/09, 11/8/09, 11/14/09, 3/17/10

France - 2/1/09, 2/2/09, 4/4/09, 6/7/09, 7/13/09, 1/11/11

Freddie Mac - 1/23/09, 3/11/09, 3/18/09, 6/24/09,11/7/09, 12/31/09, 5/5/10, 6/13/10, 7/21/10, 8/9/10, 12/1/10

Fukino, Dr. Chiyome – 7/27/09

G20 - 3/11/09, 3/13/09, 3/15/09, 3/29/09, 4/1/09, 4/2/09, 4/3/09, 4/14/09, 9/21/09, 9/24/09, 9/25/09, 6/24/10, 6/27/10, 10/15/10, 10/21/10, 10/24/10, 11/7/10, 11/11/10

Gaspard, Patrick – 10/31/09

Gates, Henry Louis – 7/22/09, 7/30/09

Gates, Robert – 3/2/09, 3/29,09, 8/30/09, 10/5/09, 4/6/10, 6/2/10, 1/6/11, 1/9/11, 1/10/11, 1/11/11

Gaza Flotilla – 5/31/10, 6/11/10, 7/6/10

Gbagbo, Laurent – 1/1/11

Geithner, Timothy - 1/21/09, 1/30/09, 2/10/09, 2/23/09, 3/3/09, 3/4/09, 3/13/09, 3/14/09, 3/18/09, 3/25/09, 3/26/09, 3/29/09, 4/1/09, 4/6/09, 4/22/09, 4/23/09, 5/31/09, 6/2/09, 7/28/09, 8/2/09, 9/21/09, 12/23/09, 2/7/10, 3/16/10, 4/18/10, 6/24/10, 8/2/10, 9/30/10, 10/9/10, 10/21/10, 10/24/10, 10/25/10, 11/7/10, 1/6/11

Genachowski, Julius – 9/21/09, 11/18/10, 12/2/10

General Electric – 9/17/09, 11/24/09, 5/17/10, 8/20/10, 10/12/10

LaHood, Ray – 5/21/09, 8/19/09, 3/26/10

Lakin, Lt. Col. Terry, 4/14/10

Lamy, Pascal – 11/19/10

Landesman, Rocco – 10/28/09

Land Grab – 3/1/10

Landrieu, Mary – 6/4/10

Landry, Rear Adm. Mary – 4/28/10

LaRose, Colleen – 10/16/09

Lauria, Thomas – 5/2/09

Lebanon – 1/13/11

LeBaron, Richard – 8/12/09, 7/26/10

Leibowitz, Jon – 5/24/10, 6/10/10

Leiter, Michael – 12/26/09

Lieberman, Joe – 6/11/09

Limbaugh, Rush - 1/23/09, 3/16/09, 4/1/10, 7/29/10, 1/10/11

Liu Mingfu, Col. – 2/28/10

Liu Mingkang – 11/15/09

Lloyd, Mark – 8/1/09, 5/9/10

Lockerbie Bomber – 8/12/09, 8/20/09, 9/6/09, 7/26/10

Lofgren, Zoe – 8/20/09

Loughner, Jared Lee – 1/8/11

Louisiana – 12/24/09, 3/23/10, 4/20/10, 4/28/10, 4/30/10, 5/23/10, 5/24/10, 5/28/10, 5/30/10, 6/4/10, 6/5/10, 6/14/10, 6/16/10, 6/19/10, 6/23/10, 6/25/10, 7/21/10,

11/12/10

Louisiana Purchase – 12/24/09

Luxembourg – 11/7/10

Mao Tse Tung – 6/5/09, 9/8/09, 10/15/09, 11/15/09, 12/25/10

Maddow, Rachel – 10/17/09

Manning, Pvt. Bradley – 6/7/10, 7/5/10

Marijuana - 2/5/09, 2/27/09, 3/18/09, 10/19/09

Martha's Vineyard – 7/27/09, 8/20/09, 8/25/09, 8/19/10, 8/27/10

Massa, Eric – 3/8/10

Massachusetts – 12/24/09, 1/19/10

Matheson, Jim – 3/2/10

Matthews, Chris – 12/28/10

McAleer, Phelim – 12/11/09

McCain, John – 6/11/09, 2/3/10, 2/25/10, 4/14/10, 5/18/10, 5/27/10, 8/2/10

McChesney, Robert, 8/9/09, 8/23/10

McChrystal, Gen. Stanley – 5/11/09, 8/30/09, 8/31/09, 9/23/09, 9/28/09, 9/30/09, 10/1/09, 10/2/09, 10/8/09, 10/28/09, 12/1/09, 6/22/10, 6/23/10

McClarty, Mack – 5/26/09

McConnell, Mitch – 8/4/10

McKiernan, Gen. David – 5/11/09

Medicaid/Medicare – 7/17/09, 7/20/09, 9/21/09, 12/23/09, 12/24/09, 3/19/10, 3/23/10, 4/5/10, 5/1/10, 7/6/10, 11/8/10, 11/13/10, 1/1/11

Medvedev, Dmitry – 4/1/09, 7/5/09, 7/6/09, 7/7/09, 7/10/09, 3/26/10, 6/19/10, 6/27/10, 7/12/10, 11/14/10

Merkel, Angela – 5/9/10

Meshal, Khaled – 5/9/09

Messina, Jim – 8/6/09, 9/11/09, 6/3/10

Michigan – 3/23/10, 5/19/10

Michigan, University of – 5/1/10

Middle Class Task Force - 1/30/09, 1/25/10

Minerals Management Service (MMS) – 4/6/10, 5/26/10

Missile Defense Shield - 1/28/09, 3/2/09, 6/10/09, 7/5/09, 7/10/09, 8/27/09, 9/17/09, 9/18/09, 9/21/09, 10/15/09, 12/30/09

Mississippi – 5/4/10

Missouri – 5/11/10, 8/4/10

Mitchell, George - 1/22/09, 4/19/09

Modi, Kalpen – 10/30/09

Mohammed, Khalid Sheikh – 11/13/09, 11/15/09, 12/1/09, 1/28/10, 1/31/10, 2/9/10, 3/5/10, 3/14/10

Mollohan, Alan – 9/9/10

Montana – 12/24/09

Moody's – 1/1/10

Morales, Evo – 6/28/09

Morgan Stanley – 4/30/09

Morris, Dick – 4/3/09

Mortgage Programs - 2/18/09, 3/2/09, 7/13/09, 7/15/09, 11/20/09, 1/1/10, 2/25/10, 3/26/10, 6/21/10, 6/23/10, 7/21/10, 8/20/10

Morton, John – 5/19/10, 8/20/10

"Race To The Top" – 6/7/10

Ramanathan, Karthik – 9/23/09

Rangel, Charles – 7/30/10

Rattner, Steve – 3/21/09, 3/30/09, 4/29/09, 5/26/09, 7/13/09

Rauf, Imam Feisal Abdul – 8/19/10, 8/22/10

Recovery Summer – 6/17/10 through 9/23/10

Reid, Harry – 8/6/09, 12/7/09, 1/9/10

Resale Roundup – 8/31/09

Reserve Currency - 1/29/09, 3/17/09, 3/18/09, 3/25/09, 3/26/09, 4/1/09, 4/6/09, 5/18/09,
      6/8/09, 6/10/09, 6/16/09, 7/10/09, 9/8/09, 9/24/09, 9/28/09, 10/5/09, 10/6/09,
      12/16/09, 2/15/10, 6/19/10, 7/1/10, 7/23/10, 11/24/10, 1/5/11, 1/16/11

Rhode Island – 7/7/10

Riley, Gov. Bob – 6/13/10

Roberts, Pat – 5/25/10

Rockefeller, Jay – 11/17/10

Rodgers, T.J. – 9/21/10

Rogers, Desiree – 12/4/09

Romanoff, Andrew – 9/11/09, 9/27/09, 6/3/10

Romer, Christina – 3/16/10, 8/5/10, 10/11/10

Romney, Mitt – 10/27/10

Rotenberg, Marc – 9/16/09

Roubini, Nouriel – 3/5/09

Rouse, Pete – 10/1/10

Scozzafava, DeDe – 10/31/09

Sebelius, Kathleen - 3/2/09, 3/31/09, 4/12/10, 7/14/10, 7/31/10, 8/30/10, 9/9/10, 10/2/10

Securities Exchange Commission (SEC) – 4/16/10, 4/21/10, 4/22/10, 4/23/10, 4/27/10, 5/13/10, 7/28/10

SEIU – 1/11/10, 2/26/10, 3/27/10, 8/23/10, 11/20/10

Seidenberg, Ivan – 6/22/10, 9/21/10

Sergant, Yosi – 8/10/09, 9/22/09

Sestak, Joe – 8/15/09, 2/18/10, 3/10/10, 5/22/10, 5/24/10, 5/26/10, 5/28/10, 6/1/10, 6/3/10

Sessions, Jeff – 5/19/10

Shahzad, Faisal – 5/1/10, 5/3/10

Sharpton, Rev. Al – 10/17/10

Shaw, Bryan – 8/25/10

Sherrod, Shirley – 7/20/10, 7/21/10

ShoreBank – 5/17/10, 8/20/10

Shulman, Doug – 10/26/09, 3/29/10, 4/5/10, 5/21/10, 9/28/10

Simpson, Amanda – 1/4/10

Social Security – 7/16/09, 3/25/10, 4/5/10, 10/15/10, 11/8/10

Solis, Hilda – 6/21/10

Solyndra – 9/3/09, 5/26/10

Somali Pirates – 4/8/09, 4/12/09

Soros, George - 3/14/09, 6/14/10

Sotomayor, Sonia – 5/26/09, 8/6/09, 8/8/09

Uigher Prisoners – 6/15/09

United Auto Workers – 4/27/09, 4/28/09, 5/28/09, 6/2/09

United Nations - 3/18/09, 3/26/09, 4/8/09, 4/11/09, 4/20/09, 9/8/09, 9/23/09, 10/2/09, 10/3/09, 10/6/09, 11/29/09, 12/8/09, 12/11/09, 1/20/10, 1/30/10, 2/1/10, 3/21/10, 5/21/10, 5/24/10, 6/8/10, 6/11/10, 7/1/10, 8/11/10, 8/24/10, 8/31/10, 9/16/10, 9/21/10, 9/23/10, 9/24/10, 11/29/10, 9/16/10

U.S. Chamber of Commerce – 10/10/09, 12/3/09, 7/14/10

U.S. Maritime Administration – 6/11/10

U.S. Naval Academy – 5/22/09

Utah – 10/8/09, 3/16/10, 3/23/10

Venezuela - 1/26/09, 3/4/09, 3/14/09, 5/31/09, 6/23/09, 7/30/09, 8/1/09, 8/6/09, 8/15/09, 8/29/09, 9/5/09, 9/13/09, 9/26/09, 11/2/09, 12/2/09, 12/7/09, 3/31/10, 4/18/10, 5/9/10, 6/23/10, 10/3/10, 10/15/10, 12/12/10, 12/14/10, 12/17/10, 12/20/10, 12/29/10, 1/16/11

Vermont – 12/24/09

Veterans – 3/16/09, 4/7/09, 4/9/09

Vilsack, Tom – 7/20/10, 7/21/10

Virginia – 11/3/09, 3/11/10, 3/23/10, 5/24/10

Volcker, Paul – 3/25/09

Walesa, Lech – 10/10/09, 2/5/10

Wallace, Chris – 9/18/09

Wallis, Jim – 8/20/09

Walpin, Gerald – 6/10/09, 6/16/09, 6/17/0

Warren, Elizabeth – 4/7/09, 9/17/10

Washington (state) – 3/23/10

Waxman, Henry – 3/27/10, 4/27/10

Wen Jiabao – 3/13/09, 11/24/09

West Point – 5/24/10

White, Maureen – 5/26/09

White House Visitors List – 9/4/09, 10/30/09, 12/7/09

Wikileaks – 4/11/10, 7/5/10, 7/25/10, 8/21/10, 8/30/10, 10/22/10, 11/28/10, 12/1/10, 12/5/10, 1/10/11

Wilson, Joe – 9/9/09

Winfrey, Oprah – 10/1/09, 12/13/09

Wolf, Robert – 8/23/10

World Bank – 4/2/09, 9/28/09, 10/2/09, 1/5/11

Wright, Rev. Jeremiah – 6/10/09

Wyoming – 12/24/09

Xia Bin – 11/4/10

Yemen – 12/25/09, 12/27/09

Z Backscatter Vans (ZBVs) – 8/24/10

Zardari, Asif Ali – 8/2/10

Zelaya, Manuel – 6/26/09, 6/28/09, 7/7/09, 7/10/09, 7/21/09, 7/23/09, 7/28/09, 8/27/09, 9/21/09, 9/22/09, 9/24/09, 12/3/09

Zhu Chenghu, Gen. – 7/19/10

Zhu Guangyao – 7/28/09

Zhu Min – 12/18/09

CPSIA information can be obtained at www.ICGtesting.com
Printed in the USA
LVOW040346020812

292606LV00001B/111/P